# BORDER AND TERRITORIAL DISPUTES

# BORDER AND TERRITORIAL DISPUTES

A Keesing's Reference Publication

Edited by Alan J. Day

Contributors: Judith Bell, Henry W. Degenhardt, Roger East,
Gillian Goodhind, Charles Hobday, Michael Wilson

**Gale Research Company**
**Detroit**

[1982]

BORDER AND TERRITORIAL DISPUTES

Published by Longman Group Limited, Longman House,
Burnt Mill, Harlow, Essex CM20 2JE, United Kingdom

Distributed exclusively in the United States and possessions,
Canada and Mexico by Gale Research Company,
Book Tower, Detroit, Michigan 48226, USA

ISBN 0 582 90251 7 (Longman)
      0 8103 2030 4 (Gale)

**Library of Congress Catalog Card Number: 82-12666**

First published 1982

**British Library Cataloguing in Publication Data**
Day, A. J.
    Border and territorial disputes. — (Keesing's reference publications).
    1. Territories, National — History
    2. Boundaries — History
    I. Title
    341.4'09    JX411

    ISBN 0 582 90251 7


**Library of Congress Cataloging in Publication Data**
Day. A. J.
    Border and territorial disputes.
      (A Keesing's reference publication).
      Bibliography: p.
      Includes index.
    1. World politics — 1945-    — Addresses, essays, lectures. 2. Boundaries —
    History — 20th century — Addresses, essays, lectures. 3. Territory, National —
    History — 20th century — Addresses, essays, lectures. I. Day, Alan J. (Alan John).
    II. Bell, Judith. III. Series.
    D843.R624 1982    341.4'09    82-12666

    ISBN 0 582 90251 7
        0 8103 2030 4 (Gale Research Co.)

Printed and bound in Great Britain by
William Clowes (Beccles) Limited, Beccles and London

# Contents

# List of Maps

# INTRODUCTION

At the beginning of June 1982 three major wars were in progress in different parts of the globe, each demonstrating in its particular way the fundamental importance of territorial dispute as a cause of conflict between states. In the South Atlantic British forces were repossessing the Falkland Islands from a country, Argentina, which two months previously had asserted its claim to sovereignty over the islands by force of arms. On the Arabian Gulf Iran appeared to have gained the upper hand against the Iraqi forces which some 20 months previously had crossed the recognized border between the two countries in active prosecution of longstanding territorial claims. Elsewhere in the Middle East a further round of the century-long Arab-Jewish struggle for supremacy in the land of Palestine was being fought out, this time with Lebanon as the battle-ground. Each of these conflicts has its own special ingredients and its own particular historical and geographical characteristics; but all three have the common theme of being essentially disputes over territory. In this sense they are three of the most critical instances of a problem which continues to generate strains in relations between states in all parts of the world, notwithstanding the considerable efforts made in the post-war era to create international or regional channels for the peaceful resolution of border and territorial disputes.

The aim of the present volume is to present concise accounts of currently unresolved border and territorial issues between states around the world, arranged alphabetically in five sections covering broad geographical areas. Each account seeks to explain the historical background of the particular dispute and to pinpoint the territorial elements involved, as well as to cover more recent exchanges and negotiations between the interested parties insofar as they relate to the dispute. The 70-plus situations dealt with in the following pages are those deemed to be of territorial and/or political significance and do not, for example, include simple boundary demarcation problems (i.e. those which do not involve important territorial claims by one state against another). Nor does the book cover the growing number of disputes between states specifically over maritime boundaries and jurisdictions —an increasingly complex question which would require a separate volume of its own.

A particular word should be said about the problem of defining what constitutes an unresolved or current territorial dispute. In the introduction to his masterly work on African boundaries[1], Prof. Brownlie takes certain earlier writers to task for including in their lists of current African disputes several which had already been settled or which have never existed under a proper

---

[1]Ian Brownlie, *African Boundaries—A Legal and Diplomatic Encyclopaedia* (G. Hurst & Company, London; University of California Press, Berkeley & Los Angeles; for the Royal Institute of International Affairs, London, 1979).

legal definition of the concept of a "dispute" between states. The present volume is doubtless not immune from similar criticism, to the extent that a number of the situations described do not currently involve the active prosecution of claims at inter-state level and others have been declared to be resolved by the governments concerned. However, in defence of some of the judgments made in the following pages it should be noted that if a book on current border and territorial disputes had gone to press in early September 1980 it would not, under strictly legal criteria, have included a section on the Iran-Iraq territorial issue, since this had ostensibly been settled by the governments concerned five years previously; yet by the end of September the two countries were at war over territorial issues. It should also be noted that territorial claims which appear to be dead or dormant are notoriously liable to acquire unexpected new life, especially where regional political alignments are unstable or where internal political conditions are susceptible to rapid change.

On these grounds the present volume contains accounts not only of existing official disputes between states but also of a number of situations where no dispute exists at government level but where other factors suggest that aspirations to territorial change cannot be regarded as having completely disappeared. In some of the latter cases the degree of currency hinges on whether existing agreements will prove to be durable; in others it is related to the extent to which actual populations may be dissatisfied with territorial arrangements made by governments, and the potential which such dissatisfaction may have for affecting the attitudes of governments in the future. In other words, the book has been compiled not from a legalistic perspective but as a contribution to greater political understanding of the strains in relations between states arising from territorial factors of several different types.

The authors of the various chapters are all present or former members of the writing staff of *Keesing's Contemporary Archives* and every effort has been made to achieve KCA-style objectivity in the presentation of conflicting claims of the governments concerned in a particular dispute. In addition to the resources of the KCA editorial office, extensive use has been made of official documentation received from government departments, as well of the International Boundary Study series published by the Geographers of the US State Department. As listed in the selected bibliography at the end of the book, published works dealing with border and territorial questions in particular regions have also been drawn upon for historical background, in which context especial acknowledgement is due not only to Prof. Brownlie's book on African boundaries but also to Husain M. Al-Baharna's *The Arabian Gulf States: Their Legal and Political Status and Their International Problems* (2nd revised edition, Beirut, 1975), *The Changing Map of Asia* edited by W. G. East and others (5th edition, London, 1971) and Gordon Ireland's *Boundaries, Possessions and Conflicts in South America* (Cambridge, Mass., 1938). Thanks are also due to the KCA indexer, Richard German, for the index to the present work and to Alan Lamb of Longman for the maps.

June 1982                                                                    A.J.D.

# 1. EUROPE

## Introduction

In the course of history the continent of Europe has been the scene of countless territorial disputes between dynasties and states, with the result that until very recent times the political map of Europe has been subject to a continual process of change. However, nearly four decades have now passed since the last major territorial adjustments were made at the end of World War II, and Europe today probably has the lowest incidence of inter-governmental dispute over territory of any continent in the world. In this context, it should be noted that the general acceptance by European governments of the post-war status quo was officially enshrined in the Final Act of the Conference on Security and Co-operation in Europe (CSCE) signed in Helsinki on Aug. 1, 1975, by all European sovereign states except Albania and also by the United States and Canada. In Article III of a "Declaration on principles guiding relations between participating states" contained in Basket One, the Final Act specified that the signatories "regard as inviolable all one another's frontiers as well as the frontiers of all states in Europe" and therefore "will refrain now and in the future from assaulting these frontiers"; accordingly, the signatories undertook to "refrain from any demand for, or act of, seizure and usurpation of part or all of the territory of any participating state".

Nevertheless, there remain among the 34 sovereign states of Europe a number of unresolved issues which can be defined as having a territorial element notwithstanding the signature of the Helsinki Final Act by 33 of them. The Northern Ireland question has as one of its central ingredients the Irish Republic's aspiration to the unity of Ireland, while the United Kingdom is also in dispute with Spain over the latter's claim to Gibraltar. There are also issues, such as the Trentino-Alto Adige (South Tyrol) question, which are not fully resolved to the satisfaction of all interested parties notwithstanding the dropping of actual territorial claims. And in southeastern Europe traditional territorial rivalries between Greeks and Turks underlie the current dispute between Greece and Turkey in the Aegean Sea and also the unresolved question of Cyprus.

As regards the post-war territorial changes in Eastern Europe, many of them cannot be regarded as involving any current inter-state dispute. For example, the Soviet Union's absorption of the formerly independent Baltic republics of Estonia, Latvia and Lithuania, although not formally recognized by a number of countries, is not a direct issue between sovereign governments; and Finland's cession of territory to the Soviet Union is regarded as final by both sides. On the other hand, the post-war territorial changes involving Germany, Poland and the Soviet Union—under which the Soviet Union acquired large tracts of former Polish and German

1

territory, while Poland's western border was moved to the Oder-Neisse line in former German territory—remains contentious in West Germany notwithstanding the Bonn Government's signature of bilateral and multilateral agreements recognizing current frontiers. Moreover, the demographic dimensions of some 20th-century territorial transfers in central and south-eastern communist Europe, notably in the Balkans, continue to involve the governments concerned in strains which reflect historical territorial antagonisms. It remains an open question, therefore, whether a transformation of existing power relationships in Eastern Europe would leave post-war territorial arrangements unchallenged.

# Albania-Greece

A dispute between Greece and Albania over the southern part of Albania inhabited by ethnic Greeks has been referred to in Greece as "the Northern Epirus question", implying that the disputed area should be regarded as part of the Greek region of Epirus on both historical and ethnic grounds. Although the question is officially regarded as settled by the Governments of the two countries, it has remained a factor in relations between the states of the region.

## History of the Dispute

An independent state of Albania was first proclaimed on Nov. 12, 1912, during the First Balkan War which resulted in the loss, by the Ottoman Empire, of all its territory in Europe except an area around Constantinople (Istanbul). The Albanian state was recognized by a peace conference of European powers held in London in December 1912, when the delimitation of its frontiers was reserved for a future decision of the Great Powers. Agreement in principle on Albania's borders was subsequently reached at an ambassadors' conference in London in the summer of 1913.

**Map 1   Present-day territorial relationship between Albania, Greece and Yugoslavia, showing Epirus and Kosovo.**

During World War I Greece occupied southern Albania in October 1914 (while the northern and central parts were occupied by Austro-Hungarian troops in 1915). In the secret treaty of London of 1915, designed to bring Italy into the war at the side of the Allies, Italy was promised a protectorate over the greater part of Albania, with the north going to Serbia and the south to Greece. This was rejected by the Albanians, who declared their own independent state in 1920. After armed Albanians had attacked an Italian-held port Italy withdrew from Albania in August 1920 and recognized Albania's independence and territorial integrity. Following Albania's admission to the League of Nations in 1920, a boundary commission composed of Britain, France and Italy delimited Albania's frontiers and completed its work in 1926. A final demarcation act was signed by the above powers and also Greece and Yugoslavia in Paris on July 30, 1926.

After the advent of the Fascist regime in Italy and the conclusion of a treaty of friendship and security between Italy and Albania in November 1926, Italian influence increased greatly in Albania, culminating in the occupation of the latter by Italian forces as from April 17, 1939. From Albanian soil Italian forces attacked Greece in October 1940, but they were defeated by the Greeks who subsequently took over about half of Albania. However, in April 1941 Hitler's forces overran both Greece and Yugoslavia, and Italy again obtained control over all of Albania.

During the period of resistance by the Albanians against the Italian (and later German) occupation forces, there emerged a National Front formed by Albanian Communists and nationalists. The Provisional Government set up by the Front under the leadership of Col. Enver Hoxha was recognized by the Allies towards the end of 1945, but the Greek Government protested against the Allies' recognition on Nov. 10, 1945, and at the demand of all Greek political parties except the Communists declared its claim "for the union of North Epirus with the Greek motherland".

This Greek claim was supported by the US Senate which in July 1946 passed the "Pepper resolution" in favour of ceding "Northern Epirus" to Greece. However, when the Greek claim was raised at a Paris meeting of Allied Foreign Ministers in August-September 1946, it was removed from the agenda by James Byrne (the US Secretary of State) after Col. Enver Hoxha, representing Albania, had declared that "neither the Paris conference nor the conference of the Big Four nor any other gathering can review the frontiers of my country, which has no foreign territory of any kind under its jurisdiction". The Allies thus de facto reaffirmed Albania's 1913 frontiers.

### Rapprochement between Albania and Greece

No mention of the Greek claim was made when the Foreign Ministers of Greece, Turkey and Yugoslavia (then members of a tripartite grouping which became the Balkan Pact) met in Athens on July 7-11, 1953, and agreed that "the independence of Albania constitutes an important element of peace and stability in the Balkans".

On July 2, 1958, the Albanian Government expressed its desire to establish "normal and good-neighbourly relations" with Greece, but at the same time it rejected a Greek statement to the effect that there was still a state of war between the two countries resulting from Albanian participation in Italy's attack on Greece in 1940. The Greek response to Albania's proposal was said to have included a reiteration of Greece's claim to "Northern Epirus" but also an offer to seek a settlement of this problem through normal channels. The Albanian side rejected the Greek reply on Aug. 14, 1958, denying again that there was "a state of war" between the two countries and rebutting the Greek territorial claim on the ground that "the question of Northern Epirus does not exist, as this is Albanian territory".

On Jan. 9, 1962, the Albanian Government again expressed its readiness to establish diplomatic relations with Greece, provided the Greek Government abandoned its "baseless" claim to part of southern Albania. A first trade agreement between the two countries at non-governmental level was concluded on June 2, 1970. It was followed by the establishment of diplomatic relations and the conclusion of a peace treaty on May 6, 1971, this step being understood to imply Greek recognition of Albania's existing borders. Further trade agreements or protocols were signed in later years, and on March 28, 1978, a direct airlink was set up between the two countries' capitals.

### The Situation of the Greek Minority in Albania

Enver Hoxha, the First Secretary of the Party of Labour of Albania, stated in a speech addressed to the Greek minority in Albania on March 23, 1978, that no harm would come to Greece from Albania and that the Greek minority in Albania should speak and study the Greek language and maintain its Greek culture.

This minority had before World War II been estimated (by Greek consular authorities) at 300,000 (or about 20 per cent of Albania's total population). However, during and immediately after the war many Greeks left Albania for Greece, and in 1981 the minority was estimated at 200,000. According to Greek sources, 62 of Albania's 250 members of Parliament were of Greek origin or Greek-speaking (including three Cabinet ministers, two under-secretaries and one Deputy Speaker of Parliament). There was a Greek newspaper published twice a week (as the only paper published by any minority in Albania); the functioning of Greek schools and the publication of books in Greek for the use of the Greek minority were allowed in two strictly defined areas; there was also a teaching academy for the training of teachers for the Greek schools; and there were exchanges of visits by artistic and folklore groups.

Among Greek nationalists, however, the claim for "Northern Epirus" has continued to be made. In particular, the Northern Epirus Society, led by Xenophon Kountouris, and the Pan-Epirus Federation of America and Canada, led by Menelaos Tzelios, have campaigned for the cause of the Greeks in Albania, alleging that they were suffering repression, with 20,000 of them being held in prisons and concentration camps; that they were prevented from having free access to their relatives in Greece; and that the suppression of all religion in Albania (since 1967) had prevented the Greek Orthodox Church from operating in Albania. In July 1981 Greek nationalists were reported to have introduced in the Greek Parliament a motion calling on the Government to "reaffirm in all directions Greece's persistent national rights in Northern Epirus".

### Alleged Albanian Aspirations to "Greater Albania"

The question of Greek-Albanian relations was again raised when a map was published in Yugoslavia in May 1981, purporting to show that the Communist Government of Albania had claims to a "Greater Albania" incorporating territories currently parts of Yugoslavia and of Greece; it was found, however, that this map had been produced by Albanian exiles in the West in 1971.

George Rallis, then Greek Prime Minister, stated in mid-1981 that the Greek Government was opposed to "any attempt to disturb the status quo in the area", while in an eight-page document issued by the Albanian embassy in Athens it was emphasized that Albania desired the continuation of good relations between the two countries, to which was added: "The healthy sections of Greek public opinion know that the so-called Northern Epirus issue is long dead and has no future."

**H.W.D.**

# Albania-Yugoslavia (Kosovo)

Since the end of World War II relations between Albania and Yugoslavia have been periodically strained by questions surrounding the predominantly Albanian population of Kosovo, a province currently forming part of the Yugoslavian Federation. Particularly since 1968 a resurgence of Albanian nationalism has been in evidence in the province, leading to the expression of demands for the establishment of Kosovo as a full republic within the Yugoslavian Federation, but also on occasions to direct demands for secession from Yugoslavia and union with Albania. Whereas until 1981 Yugoslavia refrained from direct accusations against Albania (alleging generally that "Stalinist" and "Cominformist" elements from abroad were involved in the Kosovo unrest), in that year relations deteriorated to the point where direct Yugoslavian allegations were made of Albanian involvement, both financially and organizationally, in the Kosovo disturbances. Albania for its part has consistently denied any role in the Kosovo unrest, which it sees as a spontaneous rebellion against the allegedly oppressive rule of the Serbs in the province, and has countered the Yugoslavian arguments with claims that during the post-war years Yugoslavia itself entertained the idea of annexing Albania. (For map of Balkans showing Kosovo, see page 3.)

The relationship between Albania and Yugoslavia has been particularly complicated in the post-war period by the series of fundamental changes of policy and alignment which both countries have undergone since 1945. Whereas up to 1948 both countries owed their principal allegiance to the Soviet-dominated Cominform, in that year Yugoslavia was expelled from the Cominform and adopted an independent and non-aligned policy which has frequently involved ideological and political conflict both with the Soviet Union and with Albania. Albania, for its part, broke its links with Moscow in the early 1960s to adopt a Maoist line and intensified its political and economic contacts with China; this policy was in turn abandoned in the late-1970s amid strong Albanian criticism of China's post-Mao policies and against a background of improved Chinese-Yugoslav relations. Although Albania and Yugoslavia resumed full diplomatic relations in 1971 after their breach in 1948, and although after 1976 they greatly intensified their economic contacts, a strongly nationalist and anti-Yugoslavian propaganda campaign remained evident in Albania. Thus as recently as November 1978 Enver Hoxha, the leader of the Albanian Party of Labour (ALP), published a book in which he alleged the continuing oppression and even genocide of Albanians in Kosovo and called for the overthrow of the Yugoslavian Government.

The Albanians in Kosovo have maintained a distinctive culture and in many cases have retained their Albanian dialects. The strains in their relations with the Serbs of Kosovo originate partly from specific circumstances arising from the wartime occupation of Albania and Kosovo by the Italians, but more particularly from the alleged imposition of pan-Serbian principles on the Albanian population of Kosovo. This situation changed dramatically in the 1960s, however, with the denunciation and removal of Alexander Rankovic, a strongly pan-Serbian Vice-President of the Republic, organizational secretary of the League of Communists of Yugoslavia and former chief of the security police; since the promulgation of the 1963 Yugoslavian Constitution (under which Kosovo achieved the status of an autonomous province with appropriate powers), Albanian influence in the local administrative and Communist party apparatus has grown to an extent which has even been described as oppressive by the Serbian and other non-Albanian elements in the province.

## Geographical and Demographic Aspects of the Kosovo Issue

Kosovo, or Kosovo-Metohija (Kosmet) as it was known until 1968, is generally regarded as the most economically backward part of the Yugoslavian Federation. The country is partly mountainous (although agriculture is dominant in the Metohija lowlands) and copper, coal and chromite are mined. It has received a considerable proportion of the regional development assistance given by the central Government in Belgrade since World War II, but remains chronically underdeveloped in relation to other areas of Yugoslavia, a fact which has repeatedly given rise to bitter complaints from its predominantly Albanian population that it has been neglected by Belgrade. This sentiment became particularly apparent in 1968-69, when large-scale riots broke out in Pristina, the provincial capital, and again in the late 1970s, when the economic pressures affecting the national economy as a whole coincided with a wave of Albanian irredentism to provoke an increasing number of anti-Yugoslavian and anti-Tito activities in the region. These culminated in 1981 in further riots in the course of which a state of emergency was declared. Paradoxically, much of the unrest centred on the University of Pristina, the fourth largest in Yugoslavia, which was set up by the central Government with the aim of raising the general level of culture in the area (it being reported in 1963 that only about 30 per cent of schoolchildren were completing the official minimum of eight years' schooling).

Kosovo has the highest population density in the Yugoslavian Federation, with 140 persons per square kilometre (1977 figures), compared with the national average of 86. About 75 per cent of its 1,486,000 inhabitants (1977) were then Albanian, this proportion having risen steadily since the late 1960s due partly to the extensive emigration of Serbs to other parts of Yugoslavia but also to the unusually high annual birth rate, particularly among Albanians as compared with Serbs and Magyars. The results of the 1981 census showed that, whereas Yugoslavia's population as a whole had increased in size by 9.3 per cent since 1971, the country's Albanian population had grown by about 30 per cent over the same period.

## Development of the Dispute since 1944

The Constitution promulgated on Jan. 31, 1946, by the Federal People's Republic of Yugoslavia incorporated the region of Kosovo-Metohija within the republic of Serbia, giving it the status of an autonomous region, or oblast, with a number of administrative organs and competences of its own. The region had in fact belonged to Yugoslavia since before World War II but from 1941, the year of the German/Italian occupation of Yugoslavia, until the liberation in 1944 it had been integrated into the administrative structure of Albania (which had itself been in effect controlled by Italian economic interests since 1926 and which had in 1939 been occupied by Italy).

The period 1944-48 was marked by extensive co-operation, both economic and administrative, between the new Communist regimes of Albania and Yugoslavia, which in 1946 briefly formed a customs union; in consequence, the question of Kosovo was effectively dormant. On the expulsion of Yugoslavia from the Cominform in 1948, however, the Albanian Government adopted a hostile attitude to Yugoslavia: Yugoslavian advisers, politicians and military staff were pressurized to leave or actually expelled from Albania, and in 1949-50 a series of shooting incidents took place along the Albanian border with Macedonia and Kosovo, leading in November 1950 to the closure of the Yugoslavian legation in Tirana, the

Albanian capital. In December 1953, as the attacks along the border continued, it was agreed by the two countries to mark their communal border with demarcation posts, and relations were to some extent normalized.

The nationality issue in Kosovo was re-opened in August and September 1958, however, by the news of the death of an Albanian who was attempting to escape from a Yugoslavian detention camp. Like many others of his countrymen, the Albanian in question had collaborated during the war with the Italian Fascists and German Nazis and had spent the period since the war in refuge in West Germany, but had been arrested in Belgrade in May 1958 while returning to Albania. In this connexion the Albanian press also made allegations that up to 36,000 Albanians in Yugoslavia had been massacred by the Titoist forces directly after the liberation in 1944, and that severe repression by the Serbs still continued in Kosmet. Yugoslavia responded with a series of trials of alleged Albanian spies, claiming in a White Paper circulated to members of the United Nations on April 7, 1961, that between 1948 and 1960 Albania had sent 657 agents, mostly armed, into Yugoslavia, of whom 115 had been caught and convicted, and also that 649 frontier incidents involving 12 deaths had occurred.

In the Federal Constitution promulgated in Yugoslavia in 1963 Kosmet was elevated to the status of an autonomous province, and in 1968 the designation Metohija was dropped from its name so that it became simply Kosovo. By this time there was growing evidence of nationalist and secessionist unrest in the province which had been heightened by the removal in 1966 of Vice-President Rankovic for the propagation of pan-Serbian ideals and for the violent repression of Albanians in Kosovo through the UDBA (State Security Administration), which he had controlled. The troubles, further exacerbated by economic difficulties which followed the reforms introduced throughout Yugoslavia in 1965, led on Nov. 29, 1968, to the first major wave of rioting in Kosovo, when students at the University of Pristina led well-co-ordinated but often violent demonstrations calling inter alia for the designation of Kosovo as an autonomous Yugoslavian republic in which Albanians would have a dominant role. The demonstrations coincided with others in Macedonia and also with Albania's national day (Nov. 27). Certain Serbian members of the Kosovo League of Communists who protested at what they saw as Albanian irredentism were in turn subjected to criticism for alleged Serbian nationalism.

In addition to Rankovic, many of his associates were also removed from power, including Vojin Lukic, the Serbian Minister of the Interior, who was in 1973 imprisoned for pan-Serbianism and for describing the Albanians of Kosovo as "an unsafe element"; moreover, a major purge of the Serbian League of Communists was instituted, involving some 2,000 dismissals. Nevertheless, the tensions in the province persisted and were regarded as particularly serious in view of a general re-awakening of nationalism in various Yugoslavian republics, notably in Serbia and Croatia. In February 1973 greatly increased penalties, including the death penalty, were introduced for crimes such as terrorism and "hostile propaganda", while trials of both Albanian separatists and Serbian nationalists continued.

The third Federal Constitution since World War II was promulgated on Feb. 21, 1974, and provided inter alia that each socio-political community (the autonomous provinces, the republics and the Federation) would have an assembly enjoying a considerable degree of autonomy within the context of its respective community; it also specified that 20 delegates from Kosovo were to form part of the Federal Chamber, which was to have the power to decide inter alia on any alterations to Yugoslavia's boundaries. The number of members of the collective presidency (created in 1971 in order primarily to minimize inter-republican quarrelling on President Tito's death or retirement) was reduced from 23 to nine, in which the

Kosovo representative had equal status with those of the six full republics and with the other autonomous province of Vojvodina. The ninth member was the president of the League of Communists, then President Tito, who was appointed President for an unlimited term.

In a significant development on Sept. 20, 1974, the Federal Public Prosecutor issued a statement on the recent trials of 27 persons on Kosovo and of five in Montenegro (north of Albania and directly north-west of Kosovo) who had been charged with "conspiring against the people and the state", and who had received prison sentences of up to 14 years. The statement referred to "pro-Cominform emigrés who are engaged in hostile activities abroad against our country", and who had distributed "propaganda and other material of a seditious nature". President Tito had himself described the "Cominformists" on Sept. 12 as undertaking "an attempt . . . to create a new communist party which disputes all our actions and all our successes" and which was "evidently some kind of Stalinist party". (It was known at this time that, apart from the still tense relationship with the Soviet Union, fears were being expressed in Yugoslavia that post-Maoist Albania might revert to the Soviet model of communism.)

In December 1974 over 100 demonstrators at Pristina were reported to have been detained for promoting the concept of a "Greater Albania" including Kosovo, and for directly accusing President Tito and the Government of persecuting Yugoslavian Albanians; five persons were subsequently imprisoned in January 1975 for "attempting to overthrow the constitutional order and attacking the territorial integrity of Yugoslavia". Further incidents continued to be reported in the Yugoslav and foreign press, although as relations between Yugoslavia and Albania improved in the latter's post-Maoist period the disturbances evidently became increasingly embarrassing to Yugoslavia and led in early 1980 to a highly confused situation surrounding the apparent arrest of some 50 Yugoslavian Albanians in connexion with demonstrations in December 1979.

The weekly Yugoslavian journal *Politika* reported in March 1980 that the nationalists had been charged with "crimes against the state and against public security", the trials being held, as was usual, in camera. The president of the Kosovo League of Communists, Mahmut Bakali, reacted angrily on April 4 to the *Politika* report, which he described as false and unfounded, while it was claimed elsewhere that only relatively few persons had been charged. Eight of the accused were on June 9, 1980, sentenced to prison terms of up to eight years for distributing "anti-state propaganda with conspiratorial intent".

The Albanian embassy in Belgrade, while issuing its usual denial of involvement in the disturbances, described the timing of the incident as unfortunate. In early July 1980 Nedin Hoxha, the Albanian Minister of Commerce, undertook an official tour of the Yugoslavian republics (the first such ministerial visit since 1948), including a visit to the province of Kosovo, while on July 14 the two countries signed a five-year trade agreement which provided for a significant increase in their bilateral trade.

Relations between Albania and Yugoslavia were, however, again strained in mid-1981 following a particularly severe wave of rioting which occurred in Kosovo during March and early April, and again in mid-May of that year. During the disturbances, which again centred on the University of Pristina, at least nine persons were killed, over 250 injured and over 500 arrested. A state of emergency was declared in the province (the first use of such a measure since World War II), and the area sealed off for several months to foreign reporters; information concerning Yugoslavia's measures against the insurgents has therefore been scarce, but a series of trials of those accused of involvement in the disturbances is known to have been conducted during the second half of 1981. Enver Hoxha, speaking at the eighth congress of the Albanian Party of Labour on Nov. 1, 1981, accused Yugoslavia of conducting a reign of terror over the Kosovo Albanians, including a process of "differentiation" (referring to police investigations into the loyalties of such persons).

The Yugoslavian embassy in Tirana was damaged by two small bombs on May 24, 1981 (the Yugoslavian "Youth Day", marking the late President Tito's official birthday). Yugoslavia delivered a sharp diplomatic protest to Albania over the incident, but the latter denied all responsibility, accusing Yugoslavia in turn of provocation.

Meanwhile Mahmut Bakali, having on April 20 admitted to being "surprised" at the rapid development of the Kosovo unrest, was forced to resign from office, as were also Dzavid Nimani, the president of the province, Bahri Oruci, the provincial premier, and Dusan Ristic, the president of the provincial parliament, along with most of the local Communist Party leadership and several other provincial ministers.

**M.W.**

# Austria-Italy (South Tyrol)

Since the end of World War I relations between Italy and Austria have been affected by the problem of the large contingent of native German speakers living in the northern part of the Italian region of South Tyrol (i.e. in the province of Bolzano, formerly known as Oberetsch and now part of the autonomous region of Trentino-Alto Adige). The territory was ceded to Italy by Austria in 1919 following Italy's intervention on the side of the Allies in the recent hostilities. Although Austria has raised no territorial claims as such on the province since 1946, it has gained the acknowledged right to oversee the treatment of the German speakers in the region and on many occasions has expressed deep concern at what was felt to be a serious threat to the German-speaking community and its language in the form of prejudicial treatment by successive Italian governments.

Austria has campaigned both in bilateral negotiations and within the United Nations for the establishment of a separate statute of autonomy for Bolzano province, in accordance with its interpretation of an agreement signed by the two countries in 1946. Italy for its part has maintained that the autonomy guaranteed by the agreement has in fact been fulfilled by the creation in 1948 of the

Map 2   The autonomous region of Trentino-Alto Adige.

autonomous region of Trentino-Alto Adige, which comprises the predominantly German-speaking province of Bolzano (334,000 inhabitants in 1948 and 432,073 in 1980) and the almost entirely (98 per cent) Italian-speaking province of Trento (394,000 inhabitants in 1948 and 444,176 in 1980). The latter lies directly to the south of Bolzano and was also ceded to Italy by Austria in 1919.

Austria has always maintained that the linguistic balance resulting from the 1948 fusion of the two provinces was inappropriate to the preservation of German culture (also guaranteed by the 1946 agreements), particularly in view of the relatively limited powers hitherto exercised by the Bolzano provincial government. However, intensified bilateral negotiations have since 1964 resulted in an extensive convergence of views on the issues relating to the non-Italian population of Bolzano province. Within the framework of a package of measures and definitions backed up by an 18-point "calendar of operations" (sequence of reforms), extensive progress has been made towards the achievement of equal opportunity and equal rights for German and Ladin speakers in the Trentino-Alto Adige region.

### Regional and Demographic Characteristics

The province of Bolzano (740 sq km) is delineated in the north by the Italian Alpine border with Austria (including the Brenner Pass), in the south-east by the Dolomites and in the south-west by the Adige river valley; its southernmost point is near Salurn. The province is predominantly agricultural in character, though industry and commerce are developing rapidly in Bolzano and Merano. Trento province (621 sq km), apart from a strip running north-east along the southern edge of the Dolomites, centres on the middle reaches of the Adige, to the south of Bolzano province.

An official census carried out in 1971 revealed that only about 33.3 per cent of the population of Bolzano province gave Italian as their mother tongue, while speakers of German and Ladin (a Rhaeto-Romanic dialect spoken mainly in the valleys to the south-east of Bolzano province) between them accounted for 66.7 per cent of the population. The proportion of German speakers has grown in recent years, due partly to an unusually high birth rate.

The 1971 census also showed strong regional discrepancies in the distribution of linguistic groups; whereas Italian speakers represented only 5 per cent of the agricultural workforce, they occupied 72 per cent of all posts in public administration, partly because of their generally higher standard of education but also because of the general pattern of employment in the public sector; consequently the great majority live in the urban centres, more than two-thirds in Merano and Bolzano alone.

### The South Tyrol Question to 1946

Although most of the possessions of the Habsburg empire in northern Italy were incorporated into the unified Italian state established by 1870, the predominantly Italian-speaking region of Trento remained under Austrian control as part of the Tyrol, in which Habsburg rule dated back to the 14th century. Italian "irredentist" aspirations towards Trento (which had come under Austrian rule as recently as 1803) were clearly expressed by many Italians towards the end of the 19th century, supported by numerous nationalist groups in Trento itself.

At the outbreak of World War I Italy declared itself neutral and negotiated briefly with Austria for the acquisition of the *terre irredente* in recognition of its neutrality; however, in a secret treaty signed in London on April 26, 1915, Italy agreed to enter the war on the side of the Allies, in return for which Great Britain, France and Russia offered the cession to Italy not only of Trento but also of the whole of southern Tyrol as far north as the Brenner Pass (as well as Trieste,

Gorizia and Istria and part of Dalmatia). Consequently, on May 23, 1915, Italy declared war on Austria-Hungary and the following year also opened hostilities against Germany. An armistice was signed with Austria on Nov. 3, 1918, and in February 1919 the Italian Government submitted to the Paris peace conference a memorandum claiming substantially the same territories which had been agreed under the Treaty of London; subsequently, in Article 27 of the Treaty of St-Germain-en-Laye, signed on Sept. 10, 1919, Italy received, among other territories, the South Tyrol as far north as the Brenner Pass.

Austria protested strongly at the loss of South Tyrol, but immediately after its annexation by Italy in 1919, both the Italian monarchy and the commander of the army occupying the region gave assurances that the customs and language, the local institutions and the self-determination of the South Tyrol would be respected. Nonetheless, the province of Bolzano was immediately united with Trento to form the Italian province of Venezia Tridentina, and although the new province was in 1927 re-divided into the provinces of Bolzano and of Trento, the latter retained numerous lowland areas previously administered from Bolzano.

Particularly decisive in the development of the South Tyrol region was the advent to power of the Italian Fascists under Mussolini in 1922. Mussolini embarked upon an intensive policy of "Italianization" of the South Tyrol in the course of which the Italian population of Bolzano province (which according to the 1921 census comprised only 20,000 of the total population of 243,000) grew steadily in numbers and in significance. The German-speaking communal administrative offices in Bolzano province were dissolved and were replaced by mayors brought in from other parts of Italy; German-speaking schools were abolished and even private German tuition banned; German ceased to be recognized as a legitimate medium for legal transactions; virtually all place names were changed and many families were obliged to "Italianize" their surnames; and the active policy of appointing Italians to public service posts was accompanied by an influx of Italian labour brought about by the expansion of industries in the province.

A major resettlement of German-speaking South Tyroleans occurred at the beginning of World War II as a result of the pact signed by Hitler and Mussolini in May 1939. An agreement was published by the two powers on Oct. 21, 1939, relating to the "return of Germans of the Reich and emigration of ethnic Germans from the Alto Adige" and in effect obliging the Germans and Ladines of the South Tyrol to choose either German nationality (meaning compulsory resettlement in Germany or in Austria) or acceptance of Italian nationality (which in itself offered no effective guarantee of the right to remain in the province). Some 212,000 persons accepted the first option (although in fact only about 75,000 were moved due to the disturbances produced by the war) and about 34,000 opted for Italy; of the Ladine population, about 45 per cent opted for Italy. Although after the war Italy offered the right of return to the resettled persons, only a relatively small proportion were thought to have accepted.

German troops occupied the South Tyrol in late 1943, receiving the general support of much of the population, many of whom collaborated in the handing over of fugitive Italian soldiers to the Nazi authorities. Germany made no attempt to annex the South Tyrol, however.

## The Paris Agreement of 1946

Pressure for the return of the South Tyrol to Austria mounted again at the end of World War II. The Austrian Chancellor, Leopold Figl, was on April 22, 1946, presented with a petition bearing the signatures of 159,628 South Tyrolean citizens and calling for its return to Austria, and three days later the Austrian Government submitted a memorandum to the member states of the United Nations reiterating

Austria's claims to the South Tyrol. However, on April 30 a conference of Allied Foreign Ministers in Paris decided to make no major changes to the Italian-Austrian border—although it stated that applications for minor adjustments would be considered. An Austrian application was made on May 30 for the return of a border area, but a subsequent Foreign Ministers' conference in Paris rejected this request on June 24, 1946.

Austria's response to the failure of its applications to the Paris conference was to seek a bilateral agreement with Italy whereby it could argue on behalf of the South Tyrol for the achievement of autonomy for the region and for the protection of the German-speaking community. Consequently the Austrian Foreign Minister, Dr Karl Gruber, and the Italian Prime Minister, Alcide de Gasperi, signed an agreement in Paris on Sept. 5, 1946, relating to the province of Bolzano and to the lowland territories lost to Trento in 1927. The first two articles of the agreement read as follows:

"(1) German-speaking inhabitants of the Bolzano province and of the neighbouring bilingual townships of the Trento province will be assured a complete equality of rights with the Italian-speaking inhabitants within the framework of special provisions to safeguard the ethnical character and the cultural and economic development of the German-speaking element.

"In accordance with legislation already enacted or awaiting enactment the said German-speaking citizens will be granted in particular: (a) elementary and secondary teaching in the mother tongue; (b) parification of the German and Italian languages in public offices and official documents as well as in bilingual topographic naming; (c) the right to re-establish German family names which were Italianized in recent years; [and] (d) equality of rights as regards the entering upon public offices with a view to reaching a more appropriate proportion of employment between the two ethnical groups.

"(2) The population of the above-mentioned zones will be granted the exercise of autonomous legislative and executive regional power. The frame within which the said provisions of autonomy will apply will be drafted in consultation also with local representative German-speaking elements."

Article 3 of the agreement contained a pledge by the Italian Government to consult with the Austrian Government within one year on the revision of the 1939 citizenship options, on the mutual recognition of academic qualifications, and on the facilitation of goods and passenger transit between the two countries.

The Gruber-de Gasperi agreement became Annex IV of the overall peace treaty signed between the Allies and Italy in Paris on Feb. 10, 1947, and was thus, in accordance with the stipulation of Article 85, to be considered an integral part of the treaty.

### Autonomy Statute for Trentino-Alto Adige

On June 27, 1947, the Italian Legislative Assembly decided on the amalgamation of the provinces of Bolzano and Trento in order to create a single region. The autonomy statute for the new region of Trentino-Alto Adige was accordingly approved by the Assembly on Jan. 29, 1948, and came into effect on March 14, 1948. Under the new statute Bolzano province retrieved the lowland and border territories lost to Trento in 1927, but lost much of its legislative and executive authority to the newly-created joint Regional Council for Trentino-Alto Adige. Under the new arrangements the Regional Council, which was to be returned by general election, would elect the Regional Government (Regional Committee) and would be presided over alternately by German and Italian speakers. The Regional Council deputies from Bolzano province would also comprise the Bolzano provincial assembly and would elect the Bolzano provincial government (a parallel arrangement being established in Trento province); the president of the Bolzano provincial assembly was to be elected for a term of two years and was to be alternately an Italian and a German speaker.

Over the following years the Austrian and Italian Governments exchanged a series of memorandums relating to the new provisions in terms of the fulfilment of the Paris agreement. Austrian complaints centred on (i) the claim that the overall five-to-two predominance of Italian speakers in the new region as a whole precluded the administrative autonomy which had been promised in Article 2 of the Paris agreement; (ii) the allegation that the effective equality of the German and Italian languages in public life, as provided in Articles 1 (*b*) and 1 (*d*), had not been adequately implemented in practice; and (iii) the fact that the Italian Government had effective rights of veto over the decisions of the Bolzano provincial assembly and that it had imposed certain budgetary measures without consultation. The Italian Government, while admitting to certain delays in implementation, maintained that the essential provisions relating to the autonomy of Bolzano province had been fulfilled by the new arrangements.

Particular resentment arose among the German speakers of Bolzano province over the decision of the Italian Council of Ministers, taken on Jan. 16, 1959, to implement a People's Housing Project in Bolzano. The project, which was expected to provide housing for some 20,000 people, was regarded with suspicion in Bolzano, where it was seen primarily as promoting the influx of Italian speakers. Following representations from the South Tyrol People's Party (which enjoyed widespread support in the province), the Austrian Government issued a statement which claimed that according to the provisions of the autonomy statute the decision on the project should have been left to the province of Bolzano.

Meanwhile, a series of explosions and other violent attacks perpetrated by right-wing extremists in South Tyrol caused repeated tensions between the Austrian and Italian Governments. The attacks first occurred in late 1956 but continued throughout the 1960s and (to a lesser degree) also through the 1970s, being directed not merely at such material targets as electricity pylons but also at Italian soldiers, border guards and other personnel. In the first Milan trial of persons accused of such attacks, 46 of the 94 defendants were on July 17, 1964, sentenced to prison terms of up to 25½ years (the heaviest sentences being passed against Austrians tried in absentia); in the second and third Milan trials held in 1966 and 1969 respectively, and in a Bologna trial held in 1969, some 80 other defendants were tried, many also in absentia, receiving prison sentences of up to 30 years.

In Austria, however, a court in Graz raised strong Italian protests by its acquittal in October 1965 of 27 Austrians and West Germans accused of attacks in Italy (to which several had freely confessed). The Italian Government repeatedly accused the Austrian authorities of aiding and protecting the extremists, and on July 11, 1961, following a particularly sharp exchange of notes, Italy introduced a visa requirement on all Austrians visiting Italy in view of Austria's alleged failure to stop the passage of explosives across the border. The requirement, which gave rise to strong protests from Austria, was lifted on Sept. 14, 1962.

### Negotiations leading to 1969 Agreement on South Tyrol

In the period 1959-61 Austria made repeated representations to the United Nations concerning the alleged non-realization of the 1946 Paris agreement, and on Oct. 27, 1960, the UN General Assembly unanimously passed a resolution calling on Italy and Austria to seek a solution bilaterally or, failing this, to seek recourse to any peaceful means of their choice. (Italy had until this point maintained that the International Court of Justice was the only appropriate arbitrator in the dispute.)

In September 1961 the Italian Government appointed a mixed "Commission of 19", comprising experts and politicians—some of whom were South Tyrol People's Party (SVP) deputies in the Italian Parliament—to study the problem of the South Tyrol. By 1963 its investigations had reached such a point that Austria and Italy decided to resume bilateral negotiations, and in May 1964, following the final report, the two countries set up a joint committee of experts. The package offered by Italy in December 1964, including extended powers for Bolzano and the creation of a special referee commission (later retracted), was rejected by Austria, however. Following prolonged negotiations a new package of legislation, backed up by a "calendar of operations", or fixed sequence of agreements and reforms, was devised and was published in the autumn of 1969. Although they did not fully satisfy the party's demands for full regional autonomy for Bolzano, these measures went sufficiently far to receive the SVP's approval at a party conference held on Nov. 22-23, 1969.

The new package of reforms provided essentially that, although Bolzano was to remain a province within the Trentino-Alto Adige region, it was to receive extensive additional powers including a number of capabilities previously exercised by the region or by the Italian state.

Economic powers guaranteed by the new package related to responsibilities in agriculture, trade, transport and the promotion of industry. The province was to receive a large degree of self-determination in cultural and educational matters, including a separate director of education to be nominated by the provincial government, and in German-language broadcasting. Detailed clauses also concerned the achievement of linguistic equality, and special provisions were made for the preservation of the rights of Ladins as well as Germans. The package also provided that the right to contest laws at the Italian Constitutional Court, previously held only by regions, should be extended to Bolzano, and that a special permanent commission was to be set up by the presidium of the Italian Council of Ministers to examine any further problems which might arise in the province.

The calendar of operations, which specified no fixed time-span but only a fixed sequence, was designed to offer all parties the maximum security in the realization of the package. Its main stages were as follows: (i) agreement on amendments to Article 27 of the European convention on the peaceful settlement of international conflicts and recognition of the rights of jurisdiction of the International Court of Justice in the dispute; (ii) alteration of the Italian Regolamento to permit inter alia changes in the use of the German and Italian languages; (iii) and (iv) government statements in Austria and Italy; (v) the establishment of an Italian commission to propose formulations for legislative and constitutional amendments; (vi) statements by both countries to the UN General Assembly; (vii)-(ix) the signature of agreement (i) above and its approval, together with constitutional amendments, by the Italian Parliament; (x) development by Italy of individual executive laws; (xi) declaration of the executive laws; (xii) publication of a decree on the transfer of powers to Bolzano; (xiii) concluding declaration by Austria within 50 days of the publication of the last executive law and an exchange of documents ratifying (i) above; (xiv)-(xvii) Italian acknowledgement of (xiii) and notifications of the end of the dispute to the United Nations, the International Court of Justice and the Council of Europe; and (xviii) signature of an Austrian-Italian treaty of co-operation.

By the end of 1969 the sequence had reached stage (v) of the above schedule; the agreement mentioned as (i) above was signed by Austria and Italy on July 17, 1971, and the Italian constitutional reforms came into effect on Oct. 27, 1971. The lengthy and complex process of stage (x) above was still in progress at the end of 1981, though by this date most of the envisaged laws had been agreed. Particular problems still outstanding were those relating to the equality of the German and Italian languages in courts of law and to certain administrative capacities of the proposed autonomous province. Following representations from the leader of the SVP and head of the provincial government of Bolzano, Dr Silvius Magnago, the Italian Government formed on Oct. 19, 1980, by Arnaldo Forlani undertook in its policy statement on Oct. 22 to expedite the negotiations.

However, tensions continued to grow within the province during 1980 and on March 11, 1981, the Austrian ambassador in Rome delivered to the Italian Foreign Ministry an aide-mémoire pressing for the rapid realization of the autonomy statutes for the province; this was the first diplomatic action to be taken over the issue by Austria since 1969. Meanwhile, terrorist attacks continued in the province, and in late 1981 a right-wing pressure group developed within the SVP, demanding a provincial referendum to decide the future of the Alto Adige.

A census conducted in Bolzano province in October 1981 showed that the number of Italian speakers had fallen since 1971 by 3.9 per cent, while German speakers had increased by 3.4 per cent. Ladin speakers were found in the census to represent 4.2 per cent of the population, compared with 3.6 per cent in 1971.

M.W.

# The Cyprus Question

Cyprus, the third largest island in the Mediterranean after Sardinia and Sicily, is situated in the eastern Mediterranean about 80 miles (130 km) west of Syria, 50 miles (80 km) south of the Turkish coast and some 550 miles (885 km) south-east of the Greek mainland. Having been a Greek island in terms of population and culture since ancient times, Cyprus was taken by the Ottoman Turks in the 1570s and remained under Turkish dominion for more than three centuries, during which it acquired a significant Moslem Turkish population. In the modern era the existence of the two distinct communities in the island, the one gravitating towards Greece and the other towards Turkey, has effectively precluded the establishment of agreed political and constitutional arrangements for Cyprus, which in consequence has proved a major source of strain in relations between the Athens and Ankara Governments. Although Cyprus became an independent republic in 1960 after 82 years of British rule, intractable differences between the two communities have led in recent years to the effective division of the island into Greek and Turkish areas—a process consolidated by the intervention of Turkish military forces in 1974 and the proclamation the following year of a Turkish Cypriot Federated State in the northern part of the island. Since then inter-communal talks have been pursued periodically under United Nations auspices; however, although both sides support the principle of preserving Cyprus as an independent state, no resolution has yet been achieved of the complex political, constitutional, territorial and security issues which divide the two communities. In the broader context, the Cyprus question represents a major current issue deriving from historical conflict between Greeks and Turks in the eastern Mediterranean region (other aspects of which are dealt with on pages 46-51).

The Cyprus question, which has become increasingly contentious since the late 1950s, revolves around a political conflict between the two major ethnic groups in the Island, the Greek majority and the Turkish Moslem contingent (which at the time of the last reliable census in 1961 comprised 18 per cent of the population). Turkey has always rejected the term "minority" in respect of this group, claiming rather that it constitutes one of the two dominant and distinct communities on the island, and has assumed the role of protector of the Turkish Cypriots against what it regards as a danger of their being overridden by the Greek Cypriot majority; in particular, Turkey consistently opposed the concept of *enosis* (political union with Greece) traditionally espoused by many Greeks, on the grounds that its fulfilment would be to the serious disadvantage of the Turkish Cypriots.

The 1960 Constitution, which came into effect upon the independence of the Republic of Cyprus, made various fundamental allowances for the preservation of the separate cultural and political identities of the two groups, and was initially felt to protect the interests of the Turkish community within the framework of a number of international guarantees and alliances. However, the predominantly Greek Cypriot Government under Archbishop Makarios, the first President of Cyprus, soon expressed the view that the maintenance of certain of these distinctions was economically and administratively cumbersome, and adopted a number of steps for their removal. Fierce and often violent confrontations ensued between

**Map 3   The de facto partition of Cyprus.**

Greek and Turkish Cypriots, leading to the decision of the United Nations Security Council in 1964 to establish a peace-keeping force in Cyprus. The UN has since then played a central role in encouraging and organizing inter-communal debate between the two groups.

In July 1974 the Government of President Makarios was overthrown by Greek officers of the Cyprus National Guard, and a strongly pro-*enosis* Government was installed under President Nicos Sampson. Within five days Turkish troops had invaded Cyprus, whereupon a period of bitter fighting ensued at the end of which Turkish forces controlled a substantial area in the north of the island. A Turkish Cypriot Federated State was proclaimed in February 1975 and has since then administered the northern occupied area, although it is recognized neither by the official Government of Cyprus nor by any other state except Turkey.

President Sampson resigned on July 23, 1974 (the day of the overthrow of the military regime in Greece), and Glafcos Clerides became acting President until Makarios resumed his presidential functions in December of that year; Makarios died in August 1977 and was succeeded as President by Spyros Kyprianou. Meaningful bilateral negotiations between the two communities were resumed in 1977 after the Greek Cypriots accepted in principle the Turkish Cypriot proposal that a bi-communal, federated state of Cyprus should be created rather than the unitary state provided for under the 1960 Constitution.

### Early Background to the Cyprus Issue

The historical existence of the two distinct communities in Cyprus derived in part from the economic importance of the island, its fertility and its location on Eastern Mediterranean trading routes, but more significantly from its strategic importance as a base for military operations in the Middle East region. These factors explain why Cyprus has been ruled by a succession of foreign powers throughout much of recorded history, which in turn has exposed the island to a continuous series of cultural influences from outside.

The Greek language is believed to have been brought to Cyprus between 1500 and 1200 BC, when first Mycenean and then Achean merchants began to establish themselves. In the fourth century BC Cyprus became part of the empire of Alexander the Great, on whose death it passed to the dominion of the Ptomelaic kings of Egypt. In the first century BC the island was annexed by the Romans, and by the fourth century AD it had become part of the Eastern Roman (Byzantine) empire. Richard I (Coeur de Lion) of England conquered Cyprus during the Crusades in 1191 and used it as a Mediterranean strategic base; it then passed to the dispossessed King of Jerusalem, who ran it as a feudal monarchy. In the early 14th century Cyprus formed an alliance with the Papacy against the Turks, and by the 15th century first the Genoese and then the Venetians had enjoyed periods of possession. The Ottoman Turks conquered Cyprus in 1570-71, however, and the island then remained under Turkish rule for more than three centuries.

The Moslem Turks were at first relatively generous to the Christians, giving them a wide degree of autonomy and restoring the Greek Orthodox archbishopric. However, as the Ottoman empire declined in the 18th and 19th centuries its rule became increasingly oppressive, and a series of revolts took place among the Greek-speaking population, the most important being that of 1821. At the 1878 Congress of Berlin it was agreed that Britain should take over the administration of Cyprus under continued Turkish sovereignty, in return for a British pledge of support for Turkey against any aggression from Russia. By this time *enosis* was a recurrent theme among the Greek Cypriots, who comprised some 80 per cent of the total population.

Britain annexed Cyprus at the outbreak of World War I when Turkey declared war on the Allied powers, and under the 1923 Treaty of Lausanne Turkey recognized British sovereignty as having commenced in 1914 and renounced its claims to the island. Cyprus became a British Crown Colony in 1925, but a rising tide of anti-British feeling among the supporters of *enosis* led in 1931 to serious rioting in the course of which the British Government suspended the constitution, abolished the legislative council and transferred all powers to the British governor. After World War II British efforts to restore democratic rule in Cyprus under continued British sovereignty met with constant opposition from the Greek Government (who demanded *enosis*) and from the Greek Orthodox Church in Cyprus, led by Archbishop Makarios; consequently attempts to devise an acceptable constitution made little headway until the late 1950s. Meanwhile, anti-British violence mounted both in Greece and in Cyprus, the latter being instigated largely by the pro-*enosis* EOKA (*Ethniki Organosis Kypriakon Agonos*—National Organization of Cypriot Struggle) guerrillas led by Gen. George Grivas.

At a tripartite meeting called in London in late August 1955 and attended by representatives from Greece, Turkey and the United Kingdom (as well as members of the Greek and Turkish Cypriot communities), Archbishop Makarios repeated his calls for *enosis*. However, the Turkish Cypriot representative, Dr Fazil Kütchük, adopted the standpoint that Cyprus was historically Turkish and geographically an extension of the Anatolian peninsula, and that the "so-called Cyprus question" had been invented by Greeks who, he contended, had no right to be consulted. The talks were broken off in early September and two months later, amid mounting anti-British violence and inter-communal strife, the Governor of Cyprus declared a state of emergency (which was not revoked until December 1959). In March 1956 Archbishop Makarios was deported to the Seychelles for "seditious activities" including alleged involvement with EOKA; although allowed to return to Greece in April 1957 (following the declaration of a ceasefire by EOKA the previous month), the Archbishop remained barred from Cyprus until March 1959.

In June 1956 Dr Kütchük presented his own proposals for a self-governing Cyprus within the British Commonwealth. These envisaged a bicameral system whose lower house would comprise one elected member for every 10,000 of the electorate (giving Greek Cypriots an effective 4-1 majority over Turkish Cypriots) and whose upper house, with powers of veto over lower house decisions, would comprise eight Greek Cypriot and eight Turkish Cypriot members. By mid-1957, however, he had adopted the view of the Turkish Government that partition of the island between Greece and Turkey (*taksim*) was the only viable solution to the problem. In June 1958, as Turkish Cypriot riots broke out in Nicosia and Larnaca, some 200,000 people demonstrated in Istanbul for *taksim*. Meanwhile, EOKA had resumed its attacks in the autumn of 1957, these provoking the formation of a Turkish Cypriot resistance movement called TMT.

## Formulation of the 1960 Constitution

As the hostilities in Cyprus mounted the United Nations adopted a resolution on Dec. 5, 1958, expressing its confidence that all involved parties would reach "a peaceful, democratic and just solution in accordance with the UN Charter". After Greece and Turkey had on Feb. 11, 1959, concluded the "Zurich agreement" on the structure of an independent Cyprus, a trilateral conference in London later in the month (also attended by Greek and Turkish Cypriot representatives) resulted in the initialling on Feb. 19, 1959, of an agreement which formed the basis of the Cypriot Constitution of 1960. However, this outcome produced a bitter dispute, never completely resolved, between Archbishop Makarios and Gen. Grivas, the latter accusing the former of making unnecessary and secret verbal concessions to the other parties at the London meeting. The London agreement was ratified on

Feb. 28, 1959, by the Greek Parliament and on March 4 by the Turkish Parliament.

The Constitution subsequently drafted came into effect on Aug. 16, 1960—the day on which Cyprus became independent. It stipulated that the Republic of Cyprus would be presided over by a Greek Cypriot President and a Turkish Cypriot Vice-President, each of whom would have certain rights of veto over various laws. The President would nominate a fixed contingent of seven Greek Cypriot Ministers to the Council of Ministers (the chief executive organ) and the Vice-President three Turkish Cypriot Ministers. In general elections the Greek and Turkish Cypriot communities were to vote separately in divided municipalities, the former electing 35 deputies to the House of Representatives and the latter 15. Any modification of the electoral law, or the adoption of any law pertaining to the separate electoral municipalities or to certain areas of financial legislation, would require the approval of simple majorities of both the Greek and the Turkish Cypriot contingents of the House. The Supreme Constitutional Court and the High Court of Justice were to be presided over by a neutral president, the Constitution providing that Turkish Cypriot judges should try cases involving only Turkish Cypriots, that Greek Cypriots should try Greek Cypriot cases and that mixed courts should try cases involving both communities. Although the Turkish Cypriot community at this time constituted only 18 per cent of the population it was guaranteed 30 per cent of all civil service posts and 40 per cent of army and police force positions.

Under a Treaty of Guarantee initialled in London by Cyprus, Turkey, Greece and the United Kingdom in February 1959, any or all of the three latter parties retained certain rights of political intervention for the purpose of restoring the conditions specified by the London agreement, if they were deemed to be endangered. A Treaty of Alliance, also initialled in London in February 1959 and signed in 1960 by Greece, Turkey and Cyprus, provided for the maintenance of limited contingents of Turkish and Greek troops in Cyprus. The United Kingdom also negotiated its retention of sovereignty—which it still maintains—over two military bases totalling 99 square miles (256 sq km) at Akrotiri (south-western coast) and Dhekelia (south-eastern coast).

On Dec. 13, 1959, Archbishop Makarios was elected as the first President of Cyprus and Dr Kütchük as Vice-President. Cyprus joined the United Nations on Aug. 24, 1960, and became a member of the British Commonwealth on Sept. 20, 1960. The Maronite, Roman Catholic and Armenian communities of Cyprus, who between them comprised some 5 per cent of the population, voted on Nov. 13, 1960, in favour of association with the Greek majority for constitutional purposes.

## Constitutional Crises and the Turkish Involvement of 1964

Despite the specific recommendations made by the 1960 Constitution in relation to the respective rights of the Greek and Turkish Cypriot populations, a series of differences arose during 1961 and 1962 over their interpretation, leading to a constitutional crisis and to fullscale inter-communal hostilities in which, it was claimed, the Turkish armed forces were involved. The situation was eventually contained by the installation in March 1964 of a United Nations peace-keeping force in Cyprus (UNFICYP).

The first dispute arose in March 1961 over a Greek Cypriot bill which the Turkish Cypriots feared would erode certain community rights embodied in the tax system; the Turkish Cypriot deputies in the House of Representatives used their veto to block the passage of the bill, and for two years the tax situation remained very uncertain. The second and more significant dispute arose over the maintenance of separate Greek and Turkish Cypriot communities. The Government proposed, despite the strong opposition of its Turkish Cypriot members, (i) to replace the segregated National Guard units with mixed ones under a Greek Cypriot commander, (ii) to remove the provision guaranteeing Turkish Cypriots 30 per cent of administrative positions in local government, and (iii) to dissolve the divided municipalities in the five largest towns (Nicosia, Limassol, Larnaca, Famagusta and Paphos), replacing them with "improvement boards" appointed directly by the Government under a 1950 law passed under British rule.

In opposition to this third and most controversial proposal, the Turkish Communal Chamber on Dec. 29, 1962, approved a bill to preserve the five divided municipalities and to create one more, whereupon President Makarios rejected the decision as "legally non-existent" and issued a decree abolishing the municipalities as from Jan. 1, 1963. The House of Representatives (the Turkish members being absent) approved on Jan. 2, 1963, a bill installing the "improvement boards", and although the Supreme Constitutional Court subsequently rejected this move it caused deep resentment among Turkish Cypriots. On Nov. 30, 1963, President Makarios made 13 proposals for constitutional reform aimed especially at the removal of communal distinctions, but the Turkish Cypriots, supported by the Turkish Government, rejected them as endangering the preservation of their rights. From December 1963 the Turkish Cypriot Ministers and parliamentary deputies boycotted sessions of their respective bodies, to which they have never returned.

Serious inter-communal fighting broke out in late 1963, and despite the efforts of all sides to establish a permanent ceasefire it continued periodically throughout most of 1964. Turkish naval units were reported to have left Istanbul during December 1963 for the eastern Mediterranean, giving rise to complaints from Greek Cypriots that a Turkish invasion was imminent. Meanwhile, part of the Turkish Army contingent in Cyprus took up a position outside Nicosia, so as to command the strategically important road linking Nicosia with Kyrenia, the only major port on the north coast of Cyprus. After the Greek and Cypriot Governments had rejected a UK-US proposal that a NATO peace-keeping force should be installed on the island, on March 4, 1964, the United Nations Security Council decided to establish a UN force (UNFICYP) in Cyprus. Initially introduced for a three-month period, its mandate was thereafter repeatedly renewed, and at the end of 1981 it was still present on the island. On April 27, 1964, the then UN Secretary-General, Dr U Thant, also appointed a special representative for Cyprus to oversee and report on the situation.

On the arrival of the UN force in late March 1964, President Makarios asked the Turkish Government to withdraw its troops from the Nicosia-Kyrenia road; Turkey replied that its troops were overseeing the restoration of order, whereupon Cyprus unilaterally terminated the 1959 Treaty of Alliance (a step which Turkey refused to recognize). Despite the presence of the UN force the inter-communal fighting continued, and on Aug. 9 the Turkish Air Force bombed Greek Cypriot targets in north-western Cyprus. A ceasefire was declared the next day in accordance with a resolution passed by the UN Security Council, to which Turkey protested concerning the alleged reduction of Turkish Cypriots to "ghetto" conditions by the Greek Cypriot imposition of economic sanctions. The sanctions had been applied particularly to the Turkish Cypriot-controlled villages of Kokkina and Mansoura in north-western Cyprus following Greek Cypriot allegations that they were being used for clandestine landings of Turkish troops and equipment, and had led to acute shortages of food in the area. The blockade was eased on Aug. 18, however, following the intervention of UNFICYP and the International Red Cross.

Turkey at this time claimed that Greece was maintaining some 10,000 troops in Cyprus compared with the 950 specified by the Zurich and London agreements, but was itself believed to have marginally exceeded its own quota of 650. A further confrontation arose in this connexion during August 1964, when Cyprus refused to allow the regular rotation of one-third of the Turkish contingent of troops on the island, claiming that it had the right to do so in view of its unilateral abrogation of the Treaty of Alliance. The issue was eventually settled, however, and control of the Nicosia-Kyrenia road was handed over to UNFICYP.

Meanwhile Dean Acheson, Secretary of State in the Truman Administration, had proposed in Geneva in July 1964 an arrangement whereby Cyprus was to be allowed union with Greece in return for concessions including (i) the creation of rented areas in north-eastern Cyprus which were to be used for Turkish military bases and refugee areas; (ii) the cession to Turkey of the small Greek island of Castellorizo, close to the Anatolian coast; (iii) the placing of certain areas of Cyprus under Turkish Cypriot administration; and (iv) the creation of a central body under an international commissioner to protect Turkish rights. The Turkish Government approved of these measures despite its demand for ownership, not merely tenancy, of the military areas, whereas the Greek Cypriots rejected them as "a betrayal of the whole of Hellenism". Turkey responded to the Greek and Greek Cypriot positions with an escalation of anti-Greek and anti-British feeling, and during 1964 many thousands of ethnic Greeks were expelled from Turkey (particularly from Istanbul and Izmir) under the pretext of alleged espionage or other subversive activities.

### Establishment of Turkish Cypriot Autonomous Administration

Despite the stabilization of the internal security situation in late 1964, no real progress was achieved over the next six years in bilateral communal talks which were embarked upon by the two communities. In June 1965 the Cypriot House of Representatives (still without its 15 Turkish Cypriot deputies) unanimously passed bills (i) extending for one year the five-year term of President Makarios in view of the alleged impossibility of conducting proper elections (this exercise being repeated annually until 1968); and (ii) abolishing the separate electoral registration of Greek and Turkish Cypriot voters. It was also announced that Dr Kütchük's post as Vice-President was regarded as having lapsed in view of his continued absence, and that the three Turkish Cypriot Ministers (also absent) had been replaced by Greek Cypriots. Turkish and British protests at these moves were rejected by Cyprus, which told the UN Security Council on Aug. 3-10 that they represented an interference in its internal affairs.

Initiatives adopted by the United States and the UN led in December 1967 to an undertaking by the Greek and Turkish Governments to withdraw from Cyprus all troops in excess of the contingents permitted in the 1959 agreements. This withdrawal was said to have been completed by mid-January 1968, but towards the end of that year the deadlock intensified when Turkish Cypriot leaders announced on Dec. 29 the setting up of a "Turkish Cypriot Autonomous Administration" to run Turkish Cypriot affairs "until such time as the provisions of the 1960 Constitution have been fully implemented". A set of 19 "basic laws" on executive, judicial and legislative matters received the support of the Turkish Government, and Dr Kütchük was appointed President of the Autonomous Administration and Rauf Denktash as its Vice-President. (Denktash, a former president of the Turkish Communal Chamber, had returned to Cyprus in April 1968 following two periods of exile in Turkey dating back to 1964.) The new Administration also set up a Legislative Assembly comprising the Turkish deputies of the House of Representatives and the members of the Turkish Communal Chamber, and established a nine-member Executive Council (i.e. Cabinet). President Makarios described the new Turkish Cypriot Administration as "totally illegal", and warned foreign diplomats against attempting to contact it (though this ban was lifted on Dec. 31, 1968). U Thant expressed his misgivings that it could harm relations in Cyprus, but Dr Kütchük claimed that it was non-political, purely administrative and fully constitutional.

Elections for the 35 Greek Cypriot seats to the House of Representatives were held on July 5, 1970 (for the first time since 1960), and passed off quietly; on the same day the Turkish community held elections for its 15 House of Representatives mandates and its 15 Communal Chamber seats. Following the unopposed return of President Makarios as President of the Republic on Feb. 8, 1973, Rauf Denktash was on Feb. 16 declared elected by the Turkish Cypriots as Vice-President in succession to Dr Kütchük. The two leaders were separately inaugurated on Feb. 28, Denktash at an unofficial ceremony held in the Turkish quarter of Nicosia.

## Overthrow of President Makarios and Turkish Invasion of 1974

On July 15, 1974, President Makarios was overthrown by a military coup led by officers of the Cypriot National Guard; he fled to Malta, subsequently arriving in the United Kingdom and the United States. For some years the President had faced growing opposition among Greek Cypriots, not only from Gen. Grivas (until his death in January 1974) also but from the National Guard (accused by him of involvement with the EOKA-B movement). He had, moreover, come into conflict with the three Greek Orthodox bishops of Paphos, Kyrenia and Kitium, who objected to his simultaneous functions as Archbishop and President and who had tried to vote him out of his religious office, only to be defrocked at his instigation in July 1973. The President had apparently also survived a number of assassination attempts by extreme supporters of *enosis* since 1960.

Nicos Sampson, the leader of the Progressive Party and a former EOKA leader, was sworn in on July 15 as the new President of the Republic, and the following day formed a Government of *enosis* supporters. He immediately announced that the new Government would honour all international agreements, continue to strive for an inter-communal solution to the problems of Cyprus and pursue the goal of independence, adding that there was thus no justification for Turkish intervention. Meanwhile, however, a conference was held in London on July 16 at which the then Turkish Prime Minister, Bülent Ecevit, claimed that the Greek Government had landed troops on Cyprus—an action which, he said, was tantamount to an invasion by Greece—and announced that "we cannot tolerate a Government which has no legal basis".

At an emergency session of the UN Security Council on July 16, Zenon Rossides (the Cyprus permanent representative to the UN) urged "appropriate measures to protect the independence, sovereignty and territorial integrity of Cyprus", while the Greek permanent representative, Emmanuel Megolokonomos, described the matter as purely internal and denied that his Government was involved. On the other hand, Osman Olcay (Turkey) claimed that what he called the Greek intervention violated the agreements guaranteeing the independence of Cyprus, and stressed Turkey's obligations to protect the interests of the Turkish Cypriot contingent. President Makarios told the Security Council on July 19 that there had been "an invasion which violated the independence and sovereignty of the Republic", and urged the Security Council to "call on the military regime of Greece to withdraw from Cyprus the Greek officers serving in the National Guard and to put an end to the invasion".

An armed invasion force of Turkish troops landed near Kyrenia at dawn on July 20, 1974, and engaged immediately in heavy fighting with the Greek Cypriot National Guard for control of the port of Kyrenia. By July 22, when the first ceasefire was declared on the recommendation of the UN Security Council, Turkey had gained control of the entire region surrounding the Kyrenia-Nicosia road as well as a large part of Nicosia itself, which had been taken by paratroopers dropped into the Turkish Cypriot quarter of the city. Altogether some 30,000 Turkish troops were thought to have been involved in the invasion.

The UN Security Council again held an emergency session on July 20, this time to discuss the Turkish invasion, and adopted on the same day a resolution calling on all states to respect the sovereignty, independence and territorial integrity of Cyprus and also urging (i) the declaration of a ceasefire by all parties, (ii) the immediate cessation of foreign military intervention in the Republic and (iii) the withdrawal of all invasion forces, as well as of 650 Greek officers of the Cypriot National Guard (whom President Makarios had accused of plotting his overthrow). Greece, Turkey and the United Kingdom were urged to begin negotiations for the restoration of peace in the area, and a ceasefire was agreed for July 22.

The peace talks were opened in Geneva on July 25, 1974, under the chairmanship of James Callaghan, then British Foreign and Commonwealth Secretary. By July 30 a ceasefire line was agreed, a security zone proclaimed, an exchange of prisoners provided for, the evacuation of Greek Cypriot or Greek forces from Turkish Cypriot enclaves agreed and the convening of a second round of talks initiated. By Aug. 9, when the ceasefire line agreement was signed, the Turks had extended their area of control to the east and west of the Nicosia-Kyrenia road and had more than doubled the extent of the Turkish-controlled coastline.

Meanwhile, following the fall of the military regime in Greece on July 23, Nicos Sampson resigned on that day as President of Cyprus and, in the absence of President Makarios, was replaced by Glafcos Clerides, the moderate Speaker of the Cypriot House of Representatives who had conducted the inter-communal talks with the Turkish Cypriots. On Aug. 8 President Clerides appointed a new Cabinet of moderates and liberals.

The second phase of the Geneva talks opened on Aug. 8, but broke down on Aug. 14 following disagreements between Greece, Turkey and Cyprus over the question of self-determination for Turkish Cypriots. It was understood that Denktash had rejected a proposal for a federal system giving a large degree of autonomy to Turkish Cypriots and had proposed instead the creation of an autonomous Turkish Cypriot region in the north of the island, occupying about 34 per cent of the total area of Cyprus. Turkey had proposed a compromise plan which gave the Turkish Cypriots half of the northern part of the island as well as pockets of autonomous territory in other parts of the island, but rejected the requests of Greek and Greek Cypriot representatives for time to discuss the proposals with their respective Governments. Two hours after the breakdown of the talks a new Turkish offensive was launched, and by Aug. 16, when a new ceasefire was declared, Turkey controlled about one-third of the territory of Cyprus, including most of the northern and eastern coastline. The UN Security Council, which had repeatedly deplored the resumption of hostilities, adopted a resolution on Aug. 16 calling on both sides to resume the Geneva peace talks without delay.

### Economic, Demographic and Human Consequences of Island's Division

In 1975 the (Greek Cypriot) Government of Cyprus published material claiming that the geographical area controlled by the Turks accounted for 65 per cent of the country's tourist accommodation capacity and 87 per cent of hotel beds then under construction, 83 per cent of the general cargo handling capacity (i.e. mainly the port of Famagusta), 56 per cent of the mining and quarrying output, 41 per cent of the livestock production, 48 per cent of agricultural exports and 46 per cent of the total plant production. On the basis of such statistics, Turkey was claimed to be in control of some 70 per cent of the overall gross output of Cyprus.

Since 1974 the Cypriot Government has repeatedly claimed that quite apart from refugee migration the demographic pattern of northern Cyprus is being changed by a deliberate Turkish policy of colonization, involving the immigration of large numbers of Turkish families from the Turkish mainland, their registration on arrival as Cypriots and offers of financial assistance. Figures published by the Public Information Office in Nicosia in December 1979 suggested that some 27,000 such Turkish settlers had arrived by late January 1976 and that since mid-1976 the number had remained stable at about 50,000. Fears were expressed in the document, however, that as many as 100,000 settlers might eventually arrive, and that the Turkish Cypriots could lose their Cypriot identity and come to regard themselves as Turks. Figures published by the UN on Aug. 29, 1974, showed that 225,600 of the approximately 650,000 inhabitants of Cyprus were at that time classified as displaced, having lost their homes either through military attack or through forced flight to other zones of Cyprus.

### Proclamation of the Turkish Cypriot Federated State and Subsequent Developments

The transitional Turkish Cypriot Autonomous Administration announced on Feb. 13, 1975, that it supported the formation of a "Federal Republic of Cyprus", which was to be a "bi-regional federation" of the two Cypriot communities; it added that, in order to pursue such a federation, it had restructured itself into "a secular and federated state" in the north of the island, to be known as the Turkish Cypriot Federated State. Rauf Denktash was appointed President of the new state, being confirmed in this office in elections held on June 20, 1975, in which his National Unity Party won 30 of the 40 seats in the newly-formed Constituent Assembly. On Feb. 13 the Greek side was sent the new Administration's proposals for a bi-communal and bi-regional federated state in which the state itself would be vested "only with the powers necessary for the establishment of the federation, so as to enable the state to function effectively". The proposals also maintained that the 1959 international treaties of guarantee should remain in force after the formation of the new state.

Archbishop Makarios (who had returned to Cyprus on Dec. 7, 1974, to resume his presidential functions) met Denktash on Jan. 27, 1977, when it was agreed to continue the inter-communal talks. The two subsequently announced on Feb. 13 their agreement on a set of guidelines envisaging the formation of an independent, bi-communal, non-aligned federal republic in which the central government would hold only such powers as required to safeguard the unity of the state. UN Secretary-General Kurt Waldheim, who attended the February talks, applauded the guidelines as a first sign of a willingness to discuss substantive issues such as the size of the areas to be administered by the respective regional bodies.

The Greek Cypriots subsequently published proposals on April 2, 1977, which accepted the principle of the bi-communal state, and published a map offering 20 per cent of the total area of Cyprus to the Turkish Cypriots. However, the talks broke down over the issue of Varosha, a largely Greek Cypriot area of Famagusta whose original population (which had largely fled) should, Turkish Cypriots argued, be subject to the administration of the Turkish Cypriot Federated State on their return. A deadlock ensued over this point, but on May 18-19, 1979, President Spyros Kyprianou (who had succeeded President Makarios on the latter's death in August 1977) met Denktash and the two reached agreement on a 10-point programme for the resumption of negotiations which were to give priority to the resettlement of Varosha under UN auspices and to the intensive consideration of a permanent settlement on this area. The programme also defined as its basis the Makarios-Denktash guidelines of February 1977, and envisaged the demilitarization of Cyprus. Talks were resumed on June 15-22, 1979, and have continued at intervals since then, although so far without result on any of the substantive issues.

A new element was the introduction in August 1980 of the word "bi-zonal" in an address given by Dr Waldheim at the inauguration of a preliminary round of bi-communal talks. The Greek Cypriots have expressed strong reservations about the use of this term by the Turks and Turkish Cypriots, seeing in it a suggestion that internal borders might be set up when the new federated state is created. Moreover, concern was voiced by Greek Cypriots following the removal on Sept. 12, 1980, of the Turkish Government in Ankara by a military coup, particularly when the new military administration under Gen. Kenan Evren sent the Turkish Cypriot leaders a message in which it pledged its support for "the daughter of the motherland as an integral part of Turkey".

On the basis of the August 1980 preliminary meeting, substantive inter-communal talks between Greek and Turkish Cypriot representatives (led respectively by George Ioannides and Umit Onan) opened on Sept. 16, 1980. Four main areas of discussion had been set out by the UN Secretary-General's special representative in Cyprus (Hugo Gobbi), namely (i) agreement on the resettlement of Varosha, (ii) "initial practical measures to promote goodwill, mutual confidence and the return to normal conditions", (iii) constitutional aspects and (iv) territorial aspects. The talks, which were held initially on a weekly basis but latterly rather less frequently, continued into late 1981.

During this time little progress was noted, but on Aug. 5, 1981, firm proposals were submitted by the Turkish Cypriot side which—although not made public— were understood to relate principally to constitutional matters, Varosha, the buffer zone between the two parts of Cyprus and security arrangements. The Greek Cypriot side—which maintained that these represented no advance on proposals already submitted by the Turkish Cypriots in January 1981—put forward its initial response on Aug. 26, and on Sept. 9 submitted further proposals elaborating its previous constitutional and territorial proposals on the establishment of a new federal state.

**M.W.**

# Finland-Sweden (Aaland Islands)

Situated at the entrance to the Gulf of Bothnia (between Finland and Sweden), the Aaland Islands (with a Swedish-speaking population of some 23,000) were part of Sweden until 1809 and have been part of Finland since then. Although the islands have not been a cause of dispute between the Governments of Finland and Sweden since a 1921 League of Nations decision maintained their status quo as part of Finland, there has been continued dissatisfaction with this decision among the inhabitants of the islands, of whom a majority decided, both during World War I and at the end of World War II, to ask for the islands' return to Sweden. However, their 1945 request was not supported by the Swedish Government and has not been met. The issue is of special significance because of the League of Nations decision in favour of the maintenance of the frontiers of an existing state against the expressed wishes of a minority in part of that state. The Finnish name of the islands is Ahvenanmaa.

## Historical Background

The Aaland Islands were part of Sweden until 1809, when they were seized by Russia and joined with Finland (which had also been Swedish territory); Finland then became a partially autonomous Grand-Duchy within the Russian Empire, with its own Diet responsible for internal matters, but not for foreign affairs. In 1854 British and French fleets destroyed the islands' fortifications at Bomarsund, and under the 1856 Treaty of Paris, which ended the Crimean War (between the Western powers and Russia), the islands were demilitarized and neutralized, but remained with Finland under Russian suzerainty.

During World War I the Finnish Diet assumed, on Nov. 15, 1917 (i.e. after the October Revolution in Russia), supreme powers and constituted a Republic with a national Government, which was recognized by Russia in January 1918 and later also by other states. The communes of the Aaland Islands, however, had, in August 1917, informed the King of Sweden that they had, at a meeting at Finström, adopted a resolution expressing their desire to be reunited with Sweden, and in two plebicites held subsequently an overwhelming majority of the islanders voted in favour of reunion with Sweden. The King of Sweden supported their move and in February 1920 a Swedish military expedition was sent to the islands in order to secure the withdrawal of all Finnish forces, i.e. of the White and Red Guards who were then at war with each other.

The Aalanders had earlier set up a central representative body, which the Finnish Senate refused to recognize but which nevertheless sent a delegation to the peace conference in Versailles in 1919. A law passed in Finland granting the Aalanders considerable autonomy within the Finnish state was not accepted by them, and in 1920 their representative body appealed to the Council of the League of Nations for a decision on their status. As the matter was considered to be a potential cause for war between Finland and Sweden, the British Government also called on the League of Nations Council to deal with the issue.

## The League of Nations Decision

In June 1920 both Finland and Sweden put their cases to the League of Nations Council. As against the islanders' call for self-determination, the Finnish Government pointed out that the islands had been part of Finland for over 100 years, and that they were also recognized as part of the independent Finland constituted in 1917, with the result that the destiny of the islands was a purely domestic matter in which the League had no authority to intervene.

The Council appointed a commission of jurists to decide whether or not the Council had a right to intervene, and this commission concluded that the issue involved "a situation of doubt and ambiguity concerned with the break-up of nations" and was therefore "a problem of great concern to the international community and of great importance for the growth of international law", and that the League of Nations Council was competent to adjudicate in the matter. The commission also stated that the principle of self-determination had to be balanced against other principles and that a compromise along the lines of minority guarantees might be the best solution.

**Map 4   The Aaland Islands.**

The Council thereupon sent a commission of rapporteurs to the area and charged it with making specific recommendations. The commission, in its opinion given in April 1921, concluded that "to detach the islands from Finland would be . . . an alteration of its status, depriving this country of a part of that which belongs to it". Regarding the principle of self-determination, the commission stated that it was "not, properly speaking, a rule of international law but a general principle expressed in a vague formula", and that it would certainly not apply to "fractions of states" (like the Aaland Islands) in the same way as it applied to "a people with a defined national life" (like the Finns). The commission stated explicitly: "To concede to minorities, either of race or of religion, or to any fractions of a population, the right to withdraw from the community to which they belong, because it is their good will or their good pleasure, would be to destroy order and stability within states and to inaugurate anarchy in international life; it would be to uphold a theory incompatible with the very idea of the state as a territorial and political unity."

The commission also recommended, however, that Finland should be obliged to give a number of guarantees to the Aalanders to preserve their national culture and identity, namely the right of pre-emption of land in the Aalands; five years' minimum residence as a qualification for the franchise; the exclusion of Finnish from the schools in favour of Swedish; the assurance that governors would not be appointed against the wish of the people; and the right of recourse to the League of Nations Council. The commission's report was endorsed by the Council in June 1921, and both Finland (which undertook to give the required guarantees) and Sweden subsequently accepted this decision.

The decision was embodied in a London Convention of Oct. 20, 1921, providing for the islands' regional autonomy within the Finnish Republic and their demilitarization and neutralization, with their inhabitants being exempt from Finnish military service. This convention was signed not only by Finland and Sweden but also by Britain, Denmark, Estonia, France, Germany, Italy, Latvia and Poland (but not by the Soviet Union) and it has remained in force for all the signatories except Estonia and Latvia (which became part of the Soviet Union in 1940).

### Temporary Remilitarization of the Islands in 1939-40

When the outbreak of war between Germany and the Soviet Union was considered possible, Finland and Sweden agreed on Jan. 8, 1939, on a plan for limited remilitarization of the islands, including fortification in the south and military service for the inhabitants. The two governments explained their decision in a note addressed to the signatories of the 1921 convention, stating that in case of imminent war in the Baltic Sweden reserved the right to collaborate, at the request of Finland, in applying measures to safeguard the neutrality of the islands, and that both parties would decline any offer by a belligerent power to "protect" the islands. During April-May 1939 the plan was approved by all the signatories of the convention except Germany. However, the islanders themselves, in a petition bearing 10,800 signatures, protested to the League of Nations Council against the proposed remilitarization.

On a request by Finland and Sweden the League of Nations Council considered the remilitarization plan on May 22-29, 1939, but reached no agreement because the Soviet Union did not consider itself to be in possession of all the information necessary for defining its attitude, although Finland and Sweden claimed that they had supplied the USSR with the same information as had been furnished to all the other powers.

On May 31, 1939, the Soviet Union proposed an effective pact of mutual assistance against aggression to be concluded by Britain, France and the Soviet Union, with the possibility of guarantees against aggression being given to the Baltic states.

Sweden thereupon withdrew from the remilitarization plan on June 3, whereas the Finnish Minister of Defence stated on June 5 that his Government would proceed with the fortification of some of the Aaland Islands. With regard to the guarantees proposed by the Soviet Union, the Finnish Foreign Minister stated on June 6 that Finland could not accept them but would have to treat as an aggressor every state which, on the basis of such an unasked-for guarantee, intended to give its so-called assistance whenever it considered that the "guaranteed" state required help.

Following the outbreak of war between Finland and the Soviet Union on Nov. 30, 1939, the Finnish Government informed the League of Nations on Dec. 4 that it had decided to fortify the Aaland Islands. However, after the conclusion of the Finnish-Soviet peace treaty (ratified by the Finnish Parliament on March 15, 1940), the Finnish Government announced on July 18, 1940, that it had begun to demilitarize the islands, and on Oct. 12 of that year Finland and the Soviet Union ratified an agreement under which Finland undertook to demilitarize the islands and not to place them at the disposal of other states.

### The Aaland Islanders' Renewed Request for Reunion with Sweden (1945)

At the end of World War II the *Landsting* (Legislative Assembly) of the Aaland Islands unanimously demanded, on Sept. 12, 1945, the islands' reunion with Sweden and the dissolution of the existing union with Finland, and requested an opportunity of putting their case to the Allies in their peace negotiations with Finland. In the *Landsting* resolution it was recorded that the islands had been compulsorily separated from Sweden under the 1809 peace treaty of Frederikshamn but that their inhabitants had never given up hope of a reunion; it was also claimed that the 1921 convention no longer conformed to the existing situation. In Sweden, however, the Foreign Ministry officially denied on Sept. 13 any Swedish initiative in the islanders' demand for a revision of their islands' status.

In the event, the peace treaty concluded between the Allied powers (including the Soviet Union) and Finland—which was signed on Feb. 10, 1947, ratified by Finland on April 18 and effective from Sept. 16, 1947—laid down (in Article 5) that the Aaland Islands would remain demilitarized as part of Finland. Their status as it had obtained between 1921 and 1939 was thus restored.

**H.W.D.**

# Federal Republic of Germany-German Democratic Republic-Poland

At intergovernmental level the existing frontiers between the Federal Republic of Germany (FRG), the German Democratic Republic (GDR) and Poland have been agreed (i) as determined first at the end of World War II in Europe, notably under the Potsdam agreement of Aug. 2, 1945; and (ii) as subsequently confirmed in treaties concluded between the GDR and Poland (on July 6, 1950), the FRG and the Soviet Union (on Aug. 12, 1970), the FRG and Poland (on Nov. 20, 1970) and the FRG and the GDR (on Dec. 21, 1972). The frontiers were, moreover, reaffirmed as being inviolable in the

1975 Helsinki Final Act of the Conference on Security and Co-operation in Europe.

However, the 1970 treaties were ratified by the FRG only with the proviso that its policy was aimed at "the peaceful restoration of national unity" and that the treaties did not affect earlier agreements concluded between the Western powers (Britain, France and the United States) with the Soviet Union, in particular on the status of Berlin. It has therefore been argued that in concluding these treaties the Government of the FRG was not acting as a fully sovereign government. Moreover, the treaties were ratified by the West German Parliament only with the abstention of the majority of the (Christian Democratic) opposition, who continued to insist that in terms of the Potsdam agreement the western frontiers of Poland could be finally determined only under a peace treaty formally ending the war between the Allies and Germany (which has never been concluded).

Notwithstanding the 1970 treaties the Government of the FRG continued to refuse to recognize the GDR as a "foreign" country, and it also insisted on recognizing only one German citizenship (i.e. it has treated citizens of the GDR as citizens of the FRG). The contradictions in the development of the relationship between the FRG on the one hand and the GDR and Poland on the other have had their origin in the FRG's need of security, which it has sought to achieve by fostering international détente (albeit as a member of the North Atlantic Treaty Organization). This in turn involved the normalization of relations with the Eastern-bloc countries at the cost of postponing the pursuit of the long-term aim of all West German governments of the reunification of all Germans in one state (on the nature of which there has been no unanimity).

### Origins of the Present-Day Eastern Frontiers of Germany

Proposals for the frontiers of Germany after World War II were first agreed upon by a European Advisory Council (constituted by Britain, the Soviet Union and the United States) as laid down in two protocols signed in London on Sept. 12 and Nov. 14, 1944. These proposals were finally agreed to by Britain in December 1944, by the United States on Feb. 1, 1945, and by the Soviet Union on Feb. 6 of that year. The protocol of Sept. 12 provided for the division of Germany (within its frontiers as at Dec. 31, 1937, i.e. before Hitler's annexations) into three occupation zones (British, US and Soviet), with Greater Berlin (as defined by a German law of April 27, 1920) to be occupied in separate sectors by the three Allied powers and to be administered by a joint *Kommandatura*. The protocol of Nov. 14 specified the limits of the western zones and laid down (in 11 articles) details of the administration by the three military commanders who would form a Control Council.

At the Yalta conference, held on Feb. 4-10, 1945, the leaders of the three Allied powers (Churchill, Roosevelt and Stalin) agreed that France should be invited to occupy a zone of Germany (including a zone of Berlin) and to co-operate in the Control Council as a fourth member.

On the question of Poland's frontiers it was stated in the Yalta agreement: "The three heads of government consider that the eastern frontier of Poland should follow the Curzon line (Poland's eastern border in 1919) with digressions from it in some regions of five to eight kilometres in favour of Poland. It is recognized that Poland must receive substantial accessions of territory in the north and west. They feel that the opinion of the new Polish Provisional Government of National Unity should be sought in due course on the extent of these accessions and that the final delimitation of the western frontier of Poland should thereafter await the peace conference.''

In accordance with the London protocols, US troops who had advanced to the Elbe river by the end of the war in Europe, withdrew on July 1, 1945, from Saxony and Thuringia, which had been allocated to the Soviet occupation zone. British troops similarly withdrew from parts of Mecklenburg, while British and US units entered sections of Berlin which had been taken by the Soviet Army. In a message to the German people Marshal Stalin declared on May 9 inter alia: ''The USSR celebrates victory but it has no intention of dismembering or destroying Germany.''

However, the Soviet Union had on April 21, 1945, in an agreement with the Polish Provisional Government, specified that former German territories to the east of the Oder and the western Neisse should be placed under Polish administration. This agreement did not become known to the Western powers until at least two months later. The British Government protested against it, and the US State Department declared on June 29 that the transfer of the territories to Polish control was ''an infringement of the Crimea [Yalta] decision and of the general tripartite understanding regarding the disposal of occupied German territory''.

President Truman, speaking on behalf of the three Western powers, stated in a message to the Polish Provisional Government on Aug. 1, 1945: ''The territorial

**Map 5  Territorial changes in Eastern Europe following World War II. The territory of the Free City of Danzig, now part of Poland, had been occupied by the Germans in 1939.**

boundaries have been established. The actual agreement of the three heads of government [of Britain, the Soviet Union and the United States], however, was that the final delimitation of the western frontier of Poland should await the peace settlement and that, pending the final determination of the frontier, Stettin and the area east of the Oder-Neisse line should be under the administration of the Polish state.''

In the final communiqué of the Potsdam conference, held by the heads of government of Britain, the Soviet Union and the United States between July 17 and Aug. 2, 1945, it was stated with regard to Poland's western boundaries that their ''final delimitation . . . should await the peace settlement'' but that ''pending the final determination of Poland's western frontier the former German territories east of a line running from the Baltic Sea immediately west of Swinemünde, and thence along the Oder river to the confluence of the western Neisse river, and along the western Neisse to the Czechoslovak frontier, including that portion of East Prussia not placed under the administration of the USSR, and including the area of the former Free City of Danzig, shall be under the administration of the Polish state, and for such purposes shall not be considered as part of the Soviet zone of occupation in Germany''. In a previous section of the communiqué it was stated that the conference had ''agreed in principle to the proposal of the Soviet Government concerning the ultimate transfer to the Soviet Union of the city of Königsberg and the area adjacent to it . . .'' and that the President of the United States and the British Prime Minister would ''support the proposal of the conference at the forthcoming peace settlement''. Among the Western Allies, France, which was not represented at Potsdam, had earlier tacitly accepted the Oder-western Neisse line as Poland's western frontier.

Between 1945 and 1947 the British and US Governments repeatedly stated that they had only reluctantly agreed to the frontier changes insisted upon by the Soviet Union and that they were not committed to supporting the ''provisional'' arrangements concerning Poland's western borders at a peace conference. The Soviet Union, however, appeared to depart from the position which it had taken at the Potsdam conference (when it had agreed that the transfer of former German territories to Poland was made ''pending final determination''). On Sept. 17, 1946, the Soviet Foreign Minister (V. M. Molotov) declared that the Potsdam ''decision to shift the western Polish frontier to the Oder and western Neisse'' had been taken after prolonged discussion, including also the Polish Provisional Government, and that the three Allied powers ''never envisaged any revision of this decision in the future''; at the same time, he admitted that it was correct that the conference had ''believed it necessary to postpone a final definition of the Polish western frontier until the peace conference''.

The Polish Government has always regarded the Potsdam decision on Poland's western frontiers as quite unambiguous on the following grounds: (i) that it refers, in an introductory section, to ''the western frontier of Poland'' and not to any provisional line of demarcation; (ii) that it uses the term ''former German territories'', thereby indicating that they are no longer regarded as belonging to Germany; (iii) that, as these territories were ''not part of the Soviet zone of occupation'', they were not part of Germany (the whole of which was placed under Allied occupation), and the ''administration'' referred to in the agreement had nothing in common with the Allied occupation but meant that the parties to the agreement consented to Polish administration in these territories; and (iv) that the transfer of the German population from the territories confirmed that the words ''final delimitation'' meant only the formal tracing of the border on the ground, which was also, in the Polish view, confirmed by the statement that the ''final delimitation'' would await a ''peaceful settlement''—not a peace treaty.

The US State Department announced on Dec. 7, 1945, that within eight months 6,550,000 Germans had been moved from neighbouring countries to Germany (including 3,500,000 from Poland). According to a West German census of Sept. 13, 1950, almost 8,000,000 German "refugees and expellees" had reached the Federal Republic of Germany so far, and it was said that the majority of them had been integrated and assimilated in an expanding economy. Some of the Germans who entered the FRG from the east organized themselves in *Landsmannschaften* (regional expellees' organizations), which were encouraged by some FRG politicians in their hope of returning one day to their region of origin, perhaps simultaneously with the restoration of a German Reich. Although a Charter of German Expellees, adopted on Aug. 5, 1950, expressed the wish of the *Landsmannschaften* to refrain from any act of revenge or the use of force, there existed in the FRG extremist anti-Polish groups which, among other activities, distributed maps showing Germany's frontiers as being those of 1914.

The Polish Government has also regarded the former German territories as part of Poland on historical grounds going back to the existence of a Polish state embracing these areas 1,000 years ago. In January 1949 the *Sejm* (Polish Parliament) passed a law placing the newly-acquired territories under the Ministry of the Interior. Under the Treaty of Zgorzelec (Görlitz), signed on July 6, 1950, the Oder-Neisse line was declared to be the "frontier of peace and friendship" between the GDR and Poland. An agreement on the final delimitation of this frontier was signed on Jan. 27, 1951.

From 1946 onwards developments in the Soviet occupation zone on the one hand and in the Western occupation zones on the other diverged increasingly with the establishment of a communist regime in the East and the gradual integration of the Western zones in the alliance of Western states—first in the Western European Union and later in the North Atlantic Treaty Organization. Owing to these developments the border between the Eastern and Western occupation zones eventually became a border between states, and the city of Greater Berlin was also divided into two separately administered parts.

## Development of the GDR

In the Soviet zone the military commander began in 1945 to hand over power to the German Communists, of whom a group led by Walter Ulbricht had arrived in Berlin from Moscow in April 1945. On April 22, 1946, the Communists together with leaders of the "official" Social Democratic Party (SPD) formed the Socialist Unity Party of Germany (SED)—while a reorganized SPD, opposed to the formation of the SED, had been formed in the US sector of Berlin on April 7 (and held its first conference in Hanover on May 9-11, 1946). Both the SED and the SPD were recognized by the Allied Control Council on May 28, 1946.

A new Constitution, approved by a "German People's Congress" in East Berlin on May 30, 1949, declared inter alia: "Germany is an indivisible democratic republic built upon the *Länder*. . . . There is only one German citizenship." A new state, the German Democratic Republic (GDR), was proclaimed on Oct. 7, 1949. It was immediately recognized by the Soviet Union whereas the Western powers and the FRG declared it to be "without legal basis" as its Government had not been freely elected. On March 25, 1954, the Soviet Union recognized the GDR as a sovereign independent state, in which the functions of the Soviet High Commission would be limited to security questions and to liaison with the Western Allies on all-German questions, with Soviet troops remaining in the GDR under the existing four-power agreements.

The *Bundestag* (Lower House of Parliament of the FRG), however, in a resolution adopted unanimously on April 7, 1954, refused to recognize the Soviet Union's right "to create an East German state" and reiterated the previously expressed West German view that the Federal Government had the sole right to represent the German people. The three Western High Commissioners declared on April 8 that their governments would continue to regard the Soviet Union as the power responsible for the Soviet zone and would not recognize the Government of the GDR but would regard the Federal Government as "the only freely-elected and legally-constituted Government of Germany".

The GDR became a member of the Warsaw Treaty Organization at the latter's establishment on May 13, 1955. A treaty concluded between the USSR and the GDR on Sept. 20, 1955, stated in its preamble that both sides would respect the obligations undertaken by them under "international agreements relating to Germany as a whole" (and thus recognized by implication the four-power status of Berlin). In Article 1 it was stated that the GDR was henceforth "free to decide questions concerning its internal and foreign policy, including its relations with the FRG as well as its relations with other states". In Article 4 it was stated: "The Soviet forces at present stationed in the GDR under international agreements will continue to be stationed there temporarily with the approval of the Government of the GDR and on conditions to be settled by an additional agreement between the two governments." In Article 5 the two sides stated that they would "make the necessary efforts towards a settlement by a peace treaty and towards the restoration of the unity of Germany on a peaceful and democratic basis".

In documents published at the same time it was confirmed that the GDR would have control of traffic (other than military traffic) across its territory from the FRG to Berlin and also of the frontiers of the GDR; that all laws and orders issued by the Soviet control organs in 1945-48 were rescinded; and that the Soviet High Commission in the GDR would be replaced by a Soviet embassy.

A new Constitution approved by the *Volkskammer* (the Parliament of the GDR) on Jan. 31, 1968, and in a referendum on April 6 (by 94.5 per cent of the voters) and in force from April 9, 1968, stated (in Article 1, first paragraph) that the GDR "is a socialist state of the German nation and the political organization of the working people in town and country who are jointly implementing socialism under the leadership of the working class and its Marxist-Leninist party". Article 8 stated: "The GDR and its citizens . . . strive to overcome the division of Germany imposed upon the German nation by imperialism and support the step-by-step rapprochement between the two German states until the time of their unification on the basis of democracy and socialism."

However, among numerous amendments to this Constitution which were approved by the *Volkskammer* on Sept. 27, 1974, and which entered into force on Oct. 7 of that year, the words "of the German nation" were deleted from Article 1, and the whole of Article 8 was also deleted. In Article 6 of the amended Constitution it was stated inter alia: "The GDR is linked irrevocably and for ever with the Soviet Union. . . . The GDR is an inseparable part of the socialist community of states."

On Oct. 16, 1972, the *Volkskammer* passed a bill on citizenship, under which GDR citizens who had illegally left the GDR before Jan. 1, 1972, and had not since resumed residence in the GDR would lose their GDR citizenship; their descendants, if they were resident outside the GDR without the latter's authorization, would also lose their GDR citizenship; but no criminal proceedings would be instituted against these persons for having left the GDR without permission.

### Evolution of the Western Occupation Zones into the FRG

The British and US occupation zones were, with effect from Jan. 1, 1947, merged in a single economic zone under an agreement signed on Dec. 2, 1946, and a German Economic Council was set up for this new bi-zone on June 25, 1947 (under an agreement of May 29, 1947). A conference of six Western powers held in London from April 20 to June 1, 1948, decided inter alia that it was necessary to "enable the German people to achieve, on the basis of a free and democratic form of government, the eventual restoration of German unity which does not exist at present" and to prepare the adoption of a Constitution.

The Soviet Union denounced all these developments as contravening the Potsdam decisions and as a first step towards the establishment of a West German state. The Soviet representative left the Allied Control Council (set up under the Potsdam agreement) on March 20, 1948, and the Council did not meet again thereafter.

The Basic Law (Constitution) of the FRG, finally approved by a Parliamentary Council on May 8, 1949, and in force from May 24 of that year, was (under its Article 23) to apply, in the first instance, not only in the *Länder* of the Western occupation zones but also in Greater Berlin. In a preamble to the law it was stated that its authors had "acted also on behalf of those Germans to whom participation was denied" and that "the entire German people is called upon to accomplish by free self-determination the unity and freedom of Germany". The Foreign Ministers of the three Western powers had made it clear, on April 22, 1949, that Berlin should not, at that stage, be included in the FRG as a *Land*. The Chief Burgomaster of West Berlin, however, signed the Basic Law on May 23. The FRG was inaugurated on Sept. 7, 1949, when its Parliament elected the first Federal President, and on Sept. 14 the *Bundestag* elected the first Federal Chancellor (Dr Konrad Adenauer).

Allied military government in the western occupation zones was ended on Sept. 21, 1949, with the entry into force of an occupation statute (issued on April 10, 1949), which was "designed to encourage and facilitate the closest integration . . . of the German people under a democratic federal state within the framework of the European association". The statute laid down inter alia that any amendment of the Basic Law of the federal state would require the express approval of the occupation authorities before becoming effective.

The Foreign Ministers of the three Western powers, meeting in New York on Sept. 12-14, 1950, declared that their governments "consider the Government of the FRG as the only German Government freely and legitimately constituted and therefore entitled to speak for Germany as the representative of the German people in international affairs". In a convention on the relations between the three Western powers and the FRG, signed on May 26, 1952, it was laid down (in Article 2) that, in view of the international situation which had until then prevented the reunification of Germany and the conclusion of a peace treaty the three powers retained the rights and responsibilities which they exercised or held in respect of Berlin and of Germany as a whole, including the reunification of Germany and a settlement through a peace treaty.

The FRG became a full and equal member of the Brussels Treaty Organization (later the Western European Union) and the North Atlantic Treaty Organization (NATO), as laid down in declarations embodied in the Final Act of a nine-power conference which ended in London on Oct. 3, 1954, and in agreements signed in Paris on Oct. 23 of that year. All of these texts subsequently entered into force on May 5, 1955.

Following the establishment of diplomatic relations between the FRG and the Soviet Union during a visit to Moscow by the Federal Chancellor (Dr Adenauer) on Sept. 9-14, 1955, the Soviet Government stated on Sept. 15: "The Soviet Government regards the FRG as a part of Germany. The other part of Germany is the GDR. . . . The question of the frontiers of Germany was solved by the Potsdam agreement. . . . The FRG is carrying out its jurisdiction on the territory under its sovereignty." Dr Adenauer, however, had stated at a press conference in Moscow on Sept. 14 that in the GDR's opinion a final settlement of Germany's frontiers must await the conclusion of a peace treaty and the Government of the FRG was "the only legitimate government of all Germany".

In a note sent by the Government of the FRG on March 25, 1966, to all governments with which it had diplomatic relations, and also to East European and Arab states, and containing proposals for peace and disarmament, it was asserted that under the 1945 Potsdam agreements the settlement of Germany's frontiers had been "postponed until the conclusion of a peace treaty with the whole of Germany" and that under international law Germany continued to "exist within its frontiers of Dec. 31, 1937, until such time as a freely elected all-German Government recognizes other frontiers". In response to this note the Soviet Union declared on May 17, 1966, that the Oder-Neisse frontier was "final and unalterable"; it accused the FRG of trying "to restore the German Reich with all its pretensions"; and it pointed out that not a single European state had territorial claims against the FRG.

However, following the election to the federal chancellorship in October 1969 of Willy Brandt (former SPD Chief Burgomaster of West Berlin and Vice-Chancellor and Foreign Minister in the "grand coalition" Government of 1967-69), the Government of the FRG embarked on a new "*Ostpolitik*" designed, as the new Chancellor stated on Oct. 28, to "arrive at a modus vivendi [with the GDR] and from there to proceed to co-operation" on the basis of the existing "two states of Germany" which "are not foreign countries to each other". Over the next three years the FRG proceeded to conclude treaties with the Soviet Union, Poland and the GDR respectively and these treaties incorporated various passages relating to the existing German borders.

Article 3 of the treaty of Aug. 12, 1970, with the Soviet Union states: "The USSR and the FRG share the realization that peace in Europe can only be maintained if no one disturbs the present frontiers. They undertake to respect the territorial integrity of all states in Europe within their existing frontiers; they declare that they have no territorial claims whatsoever against anybody, and will not assert such claims in the future; they regard as inviolable now and in the future the frontiers of all states in Europe as they are on the date of the signing of this treaty, including the Oder-Neisse line, which forms the western frontier of the Polish People's Republic, and the frontier between the FRG and the GDR." In Article 4 it is stated: "The present treaty between the USSR and the FRG does not affect any bilateral or multilateral treaties and agreements previously concluded by them."

In the treaty with Poland, published on Nov. 20, 1970, Article 1 states: "The FRG and the People's Republic of Poland state in mutual agreement that the existing boundary line, the course of which is laid down in Chapter IX of the decisions of the Potsdam conference of Aug. 2, 1945, as running from the Baltic Sea immediately west of Swinemünde, and thence along the Oder river to the confluence of the western Neisse river and along the western Neisse to the Czechoslovak frontier, shall constitute the western state frontier of the People's Republic of Poland. They reaffirm the inviolability of their existing frontiers now and in the future and undertake to respect each other's territorial integrity without restriction. They declare that they have no territorial claims whatsoever against each other and that they will not assert such claims in the future." Article IV of this treaty states: "The present treaty shall not affect any bilateral or multilateral international arrangements previously concluded by either contracting party or concerning them."

In a separate letter the FRG expressly stated: "This treaty does not conflict with the political objective of the FRG to work for a state of peace in Europe in which the German nation will recover its unity in free self-determination."

Article 3 of the Basic Treaty of Dec. 21, 1972, between the FRG and the GDR states: "[The FRG and the GDR] affirm the inviolability, now and in the future, of the border existing between them, and pledge themselves to unrestricted respect for each other's territorial integrity.'' The treaty also states, in Article 6: "The FRG and the GDR proceed from the principle that the sovereign power of each of the two states is confined to its [own] state territory. They respect the independence and sovereignty of each of the two states in its internal and external affairs.'' Under Article 9 the two sides also "agreed that bilateral and multilateral international treaties and agreements previously concluded by or concerning them are not affected by this treaty''. Under a supplementary protocol the two sides agreed to set up a commission to "examine and, so far as is necessary, renew or supplement the demarcation of the border between the two states'' and to "compile the necessary documentation on the line of the border''.

The treaties with the Soviet Union and Poland entered into force on June 3, 1972, having not been ratified by the *Bundestag* (the Lower House of the FRG Parliament) until May 17, 1972, and then only with the abstention of the opposition Christian Democratic and Christian Social Unions and after the adoption (with only five abstentions and no opposition) of a joint resolution intended to clarify the FRG's position. In this resolution it was stated inter alia that "the treaties proceed from the frontiers as existing today, the unilateral alteration of which they exclude''; that "the treaties do not anticipate a peace settlement for Germany by treaty and do not create any legal basis for the frontiers existing today''; that "the policy of the FRG, which aims at a peaceful restoration of national unity within the European framework, is not inconsistent with the treaties, which do not prejudice the solution of the German question''; that "the rights and responsibilities of the four powers with regard to Germany as a whole and to Berlin are not affected by the treaties''; and that the *Bundestag*, "in view of the fact that the final settlement of the German question as a whole is still outstanding, considers as essential the continuance of these rights and responsibilities''.

The Basic Treaty between the FRG and the GDR was approved by the *Bundestag* on May 11, 1973, and by the *Volkskammer* on June 13, and it entered into force on June 21, 1973. The *Bundestag* approved the relevant bill at its second reading by 268 votes to 217 (of the Christian Democratic and Christian Social Unions). An application by the Christian Social *Land* Government of Bavaria to the Federal Constitutional Court for a ruling as to whether the treaty was in conflict with the Basic Law (the Constitution of the FRG) resulted in a court ruling, given on July 31, 1973, to the effect that the treaty did not conflict with the Basic Law. In this ruling the Court reaffirmed the continued existence in law of the German Reich (a thesis which, in the Court's view, had formed the basis of the 1949 Basic Law, or Constitution, of the FRG) and took the view that the FRG was "a state identical with the state of the German Reich''. The Court also declared reunification as being "constitutionally imperative'' and explicitly referred in its decision to "the borders of the German Reich as at Dec. 31, 1937'' as one of several legal possibilities.

The Final Act of the Conference on Security and Co-operation in Europe, signed in Helsinki on Aug. 1, 1975, by 35 countries (including all those of Europe except Albania), reaffirmed the inviolability of frontiers and the territorial integrity of states. The relevant passages—in Basket One, (A) I and IV—read as follows: "The participating states regard as inviolable all one another's frontiers as well as the frontiers of all states in Europe and therefore they will refrain from now on and in the future from assaulting these frontiers. Accordingly they will also refrain from any demand for, or act of, seizure and usurpation of part or all of the territory of any participating state. . . . The participating states will respect the territorial integrity of any of the participating states.''

Under a protocol agreed to at the conclusion of the Helsinki Final Act on Aug. 1, 1975, between 120,000 and 125,000 ethnic Germans were allowed to leave Poland

and settle in the FRG during the following four years, with further emigration applications being permitted after the expiry of that period. The protocol was signed on Oct. 9, 1975, and was finally approved on March 15, 1976. In the FRG it was stated that between early 1950 and September 1975 a total of 471,760 ethnic Germans had been allowed to emigrate from Poland to the FRG.

In a treaty signed in Prague on Dec. 11, 1973, by the FRG and Czechoslovakia it was laid down (in Article 1) that the Munich agreement of Sept. 29, 1938 (after which Hitler had annexed the Sudeten areas of Czechoslovakia), was "null and void" because it had been "imposed on the Czechoslovak Republic by the National Socialist regime under the threat of force". Article 4 stated that the two sides "have no territorial claims of any kind against each other and likewise in the future will not raise any such claims".

### Continued East-West Disagreement over Berlin

The division of Berlin into an Eastern (Soviet) sector and a Western sector (under the commandants of the three Western powers) was intensified following the introduction of a currency reform by the Western powers in their respective occupation zones on June 18, 1948. The Soviet Government in turn announced, on June 23, a currency reform which was to apply to the Soviet zone of Germany as well as to Greater Berlin, and on June 23-24 the Eastern authorities stopped the supply of electric current, coal, food and other goods to Berlin's Western sectors. A slightly

**Map 6  Present-day Poland and its neighbours. The Oder and Neisse rivers forming Poland's western border have the Polish names Odra and Nysa Luzycka respectively.**

modified form of Western mark was introduced by the Western commandants on June 24.

On June 28, 1948, the US Government announced the creation of an airlift designed to break the Soviet blockade of West Berlin, and on July 1 all co-operation between the members of the four-power *Kommandatura* (the Allied authority in Greater Berlin) was ended. In an announcement the Soviet chief of staff at the Berlin *Kommandatura* stated that Soviet representatives would no longer attend meetings of any organization of the *Kommandatura*, on the ground, inter alia, of the introduction of the new Western currency into Berlin which, he said, was "part of the economic system of the Soviet zone". The Western powers did not accept this view and explained their position in notes handed to the Soviet side on July 8, stating that Berlin was "not part of the Soviet zone but an international zone of occupation". The notes also made it clear that the Western powers now shared "the responsibility . . . for the physical well-being of 2,400,000 persons in the western sectors of Berlin" and demanded that the lines of communication between the western zones of Germany and West Berlin should be fully restored.

The Soviet Union rejected this reply of the Western powers on July 14 and accused them of having violated the Yalta and Potsdam agreements, in particular by the introduction of the currency reform and by taking separatist action in West Germany (especially through the London agreement), which had "destroyed the system of quadripartite administration of Germany", with the effect that the Allied Control Council had ceased to function, and had thereby "undermined the legal basis on which rested the right to participate in the administration of Berlin". The Soviet note continued: "Berlin is the centre of the Soviet zone and is part of that zone." It added: "The entire mass of currency notes invalidated in the western zone threatened to pour into Berlin and into the Soviet zone. The Soviet Command was therefore compelled to adopt urgent measures to safeguard the interests of the German population as well as of the economy of the Soviet zone and of Greater Berlin." If necessary, the note declared, the Soviet Government would "not object to ensuring sufficient supplies for the whole of Greater Berlin by its own means".

Under a Soviet decree of July 23, 1948, an Eastern Deutsche Mark was introduced for the Soviet zone and Greater Berlin. The three Western powers accepted this currency for West Berlin until March 20, 1949, when they announced that only the Western Deutsche Mark would be used as legal tender in West Berlin.

The city of Berlin was effectively divided into two separately administered sectors as from Nov. 30, 1948. On that date the 26 SED members of the City Assembly declared the City *Magistrat* to be deposed, set up a new *Magistrat* and elected a new provisional chief burgomaster, and on Dec. 1 this new *Magistrat* took over what had been the municipal headquarters for the whole city (situated in the Soviet sector). It claimed to represent the whole of Berlin as "the capital of a unified democratic German republic". However, the legally elected City Assembly repudiated the SED-controlled *Magistrat* and set up its own headquarters in the western sector. Elections to a new City Assembly were held on Dec. 5, when the SED abstained from voting. In the event, about 13.8 per cent of the electorate of West Berlin took no part in these elections. (In elections to the City Assembly of Greater Berlin, held on Oct. 20, 1946, the SED had gained 19.8 per cent of the vote and 26 out of the 130 seats.) Under the 1949 Basic Law of the FRG the West Berlin City Assembly (and later the House of Representatives) has appointed 22 delegates to sit as members of the *Bundestag*, although without a vote (except on procedural matters).

The airlift, carried out jointly by the United States and Britain, kept West Berlin supplied with basic needs in food and fuel until the Soviet military government lifted the blockade on May 12, 1949, under an agreement reached on May 4 and laying down that the problem should be discussed at a meeting of the Allied Council of Ministers. However, such a meeting, held between May 23 and June 20, 1949, reached no agreement on the future of Berlin other than that the blockade should not be reimposed.

On May 14, 1949, the three Western commandants in Berlin signed a new charter granting wide powers to the Western City Assembly, with the *Kommandatura* retaining only specified powers in regard to disarmament, demilitarization, reparations, currency and credit policy, banking and foreign trade, protection and security of the Allied forces, relations with authorities abroad and supervision of the police. It was also announced that the power of veto hitherto held by each member of the *Kommandatura* was abolished and that this body would in future take decisions by majority vote.

On Sept. 30, 1949, the *Bundestag* adopted a resolution (opposed only by the 15 Communist members of the House) declaring "solemnly that it is the wish of the German people that Greater Berlin should form an integral part of the FRG and should become its capital". The resolution also appealed to the Allied occupying powers to revise their "negative attitude" towards the integration of Berlin as the twelfth *Land* of the FRG. On Oct. 8 the *Magistrat* of West Berlin formally applied to the Western powers to agree to the integration of Berlin as the twelfth *Land* of the FRG.

On Oct. 21, 1949, however, the Federal Chancellor (Dr Konrad Adenauer) stated in the *Bundestag* that Berlin could not, for the present, become the twelfth *Land* of the FRG and that it was "in the interests of Berlin itself" that Article 23 of the Basic Law (relating to the inclusion of Greater Berlin in the territories in which the Basic Law was to apply) should not be invoked, but that the Federal Government welcomed the city's intention of bringing its laws into conformity with those of the FRG and thereby achieving its de facto membership of the FRG. He also said that the Government regarded Berlin as a "distressed area" and were "determined not to abandon Berlin but to do everything to revitalize the city's economy and finances".

A proposal made on April 10, 1950, by the Assembly of West Berlin for the holding of city-wide elections on the basis of the 1948 Constitution was not rejected by the Soviet commandant of the eastern zone but was (on May 8) made subject to Soviet conditions—including the withdrawal of all occupation forces from Berlin and the abolition of its division into sectors—most of which were unacceptable to the western City Assembly, which feared that acceptance of these conditions would eventually lead to Soviet occupation of the whole city. The Soviet conditions were also rejected by the Western military commandants who laid down, on June 10, four general principles which, they stated, guided their "approach to the reunification of Berlin": (i) a freely elected city government operating under a constitution drafted by representatives of the people; (ii) city-wide freedom for all democratic political parties before, during and after the elections; (iii) individual freedom of movement, freedom from arbitrary arrest and detention, freedom of association, assembly, speech, press and radio throughout the city; and (iv) the resumption of quadripartite work by the *Kommandatura*, but without the right of veto of any one member.

The West Berlin Constitution of Sept. 1, 1950, stated in Article 3 that "(i) Berlin is a German *Land* and at the same time one city; (ii) Berlin is a *Land* of the FRG; (iii) the Basic Law and laws of the FRG are binding for Berlin". In Article 7 it was stated (without any mention of the division of the city into two sectors) that the Berlin House of Representatives (which replaced the City Assembly) was entitled to decide, during a transitional period, that a law of the FRG would be applied without modification in Berlin.

An anti-communist rising by workers in East Berlin and other East German cities was crushed in June 1953 with the help of Soviet occupation troops, casualties being officially stated to include 25 persons killed and 378 injured, whereas the Government of the FRG believed that 62 persons had been sentenced to death and 25,000 imprisoned. The number of refugees from East Berlin and the GDR was, in 1956, given as 122,000 in 1952, over 300,000 in 1953, over 184,000 in 1954 and over 252,000 in 1955, with the grand total since 1950 exceeding 1,500,000.

In the joint declaration issued by the Western powers at the end of the London nine-power conference which was held on Sept. 28-Oct. 3, 1954, and which led to the admission of the FRG to the Brussels Treaty Organization (later the Western European Union) and to the North Atlantic Treaty Organization (NATO), it was stated with reference to Berlin: "The security and welfare of Berlin and the maintenance of the position of the three powers there are regarded by the three powers as essential elements of the peace of the free world in the present international situation. Accordingly they will maintain armed forces within the territory of Berlin as long as their responsibilities require it. They therefore reaffirm that they will treat any attack against Berlin from any quarter as an attack upon their forces and themselves."

### Developments leading to Construction of Berlin Wall

A new crisis arose over Berlin in 1958 out of what the West regarded as a Soviet attempt to incorporate the whole of Berlin in the GDR. Walter Ulbricht (the First Secretary of the SED) declared on Oct. 27, 1958: "The whole of Berlin lies within the territory of the GDR. The whole of Berlin belongs to the area under the sovereignty of the GDR. The authority of the Western occupying powers no longer has any legal basis in Berlin." Nikita Khrushchev (then USSR Prime Minister) stated in a speech on Nov. 10, 1958, inter alia: "The German question—if this means unification of the two German states now in existence—can be solved only by the German people themselves through the rapprochement of those states. The conclusion of a peace treaty with Germany is another matter." Accusing the Western powers of having violated the Potsdam agreement, he stated that virtually all that remained of that agreement was the "so-called four-power status of Berlin", to which, he said, the Western powers were clinging because it was beneficial to them. He continued: "The time has evidently come for the powers which signed the Potsdam agreement to abandon the remnants of the occupation regime in Berlin and thus make it possible to create a normal atmosphere in the capital of the GDR. The Soviet Union, for its part, will hand over to the sovereign GDR those functions in Berlin which are still wielded by the Soviet organs."

In a note of Nov. 27, 1958, the Soviet Government notified the United States that it regarded as "null and void" the protocol of Sept. 12, 1944, on the occupation zones of Germany and the administration of Greater Berlin and also the associated supplementary agreements, including a quadripartite agreement of May 1, 1945, on the control mechanism in Germany; it added that, if no agreement was reached within six months on examining a Soviet proposal to make West Berlin an independent political entity as a Free City, then the Soviet Government would carry out its own arrangements with the GDR.

Khrushchev said at a mass rally in East Berlin on March 9, 1959, that the implementation of the proposed inclusion of West Berlin in the GDR would only terminate the occupation status but would not change West Berlin's social system and mode of social life, as Berlin would be a free city, the independence of which would be guaranteed by the great powers. On March 19 he acknowledged that the United States, Britain and France had "lawful rights for their stay in West Berlin".

The Soviet proposals for Berlin were reiterated in a memorandum presented to President John F. Kennedy of the United States and published on June 11, 1961.

41

President Kennedy, however, declared on July 6 that since March 1958 the Soviets had conducted "a new campaign to force the Western Allies out of Berlin" and that the "obvious purpose" of this campaign was "to make permanent the partition of Germany". In a note presented to the Soviet Union on July 17, 1961, the US Government stated that it was the USSR which had "blocked all progress towards a peace settlement" in Germany; that the United States supported "the clearly expressed wish of the West Berliners that no change be made in the status of their city which would expose them . . . to the domination of the regime which at present controls the surrounding areas". The note also rejected as "entirely without foundation" Soviet references to Berlin being "situated in the territory of the so-called GDR" and emphasized that since the protocol of Sept. 12, 1944 (which had been approved by the USSR on Feb. 6, 1945), there had been "no legal alteration in the special status of Berlin".

On July 25, 1961, President Kennedy announced in a broadcast that he was taking a number of defence measures "based on our need to meet a world-wide threat on a basis which stretches far beyond the Berlin crisis". The measures involved an increase in the strength of the US armed forces and a call-up of reservists "if necessary". Khrushchev in turn announced on Aug. 7 that the USSR would have to call up reservists and move forces to the Western borders in response to the measures taken by the United States. At the same time he called on the Western powers to "sit down sincerely at the conference table" and to "clear the atmosphere".

However, upon a decision by the Political Advisory Council of the Warsaw Treaty Organization, the GDR, on Aug. 13, 1961, closed the border between East and West Berlin (except for 13 official crossing points) and from Aug. 17 onwards it erected a wall along this border. On Aug. 22 the number of crossing points was reduced to six, and a no man's land of 100 metres' width was established on both sides of the border. The official grounds for taking these measures were "to put an end to the hostile activities of the revanchist and militarist forces" in West Germany and West Berlin, especially those of "espionage organizations" which were "systematically luring GDR citizens and carrying out a regular slave traffic".

On Aug. 17 the three Western powers delivered strong protest notes to the Soviet Union, stating that the border restrictions were "a flagrant and particularly serious violation of the quadripartite status of Berlin", as reaffirmed by the four-power agreements of May 4, 1949, and the Paris decision of June 20, 1949. These protests were rejected by the Soviet Union on Aug. 19, when the West was specifically accused of spying, of damaging the population and national economy of the GDR by arbitrarily introducing "a speculative rate of exchange of Western marks into GDR currency" and "buying up valuable goods and foodstuffs in the GDR", and of directing "a whole army of recruiters . . . to impel part of the GDR population to move to West Germany". (Figures published by the FRG's Ministry of Refugees showed that between 1949 and June 30, 1961, over 2,600,000 refugees had left the GDR, over 300,000 of them during the last 18 months of that period.)

The military forces in the GDR were at that time stated to consist of at least 400,000 Soviet troops equipped with tactical nuclear weapons; the GDR National People's Army of about 65,000 men; and 75,000 armed members of two police forces. On the other hand there were about 11,000 Allied troops in West Berlin (4,000 British, 5,000 US and 2,000 French); 24,000 armed policemen in West Berlin; and NATO forces in the FRG consisting of about 50,000 British, 180,000 US, 30,000 French and 150,000 FRG troops, as well as one Canadian brigade group. There were no Western troops in an 18-mile wide strip along the FRG's border with the GDR—which the GDR subsequently provided with strong fences supervised from watchtowers.

There followed further military preparations of both the NATO and the Warsaw Pact sides, as well as exchanges of notes between East and West. Walter Ulbricht stated on Aug. 25 that the Allied air traffic to West Berlin would remain subject to Soviet—and not GDR—control until a peace treaty was signed. On Sept. 7 he said that after the signing of a peace treaty with the Soviet Union the GDR would have the right to control air entry into Berlin and that visas would be needed to travel between the FRG and the GDR. Khrushchev, speaking before the Central Committee of the Communist Party of the Soviet Union on Oct. 17, 1961, said that if the Western powers showed readiness to settle the German problem he would not insist on the signing of a peace treaty before Dec. 31, 1961 (as previously envisaged by him).

President Kennedy, visiting Western Europe between June 23 and July 2, 1963, inspected the Berlin wall and declared in a speech in West Berlin on June 26: "Today, in the world of freedom, the proudest boast is *'Ich bin ein Berliner'*." Of the ultimate reunification of Germany he said: "In 18 years of peace and of good faith this generation of Germans has earned the right to be free, including the right to unite their family and nation in lasting peace with the goodwill of all people."

However, towards the end of 1963 there were signs that the tension over the status of Berlin was abating. On Dec. 17, 1963, agreement was reached between the West Berlin authorities and the GDR on one-day visits to East Berlin by West Berliners between Dec. 20, 1963, and Jan. 5, 1964 (for the first time since the building of the Berlin wall in August 1961). On Sept. 24, 1964, a "technical" agreement was signed between the West Berlin Senate (which under the 1950 Constitution had succeeded the *Magistrat*) and the GDR Government to enable West Berliners to visit their relatives in East Berlin. On the Western side it was emphasized that both these agreements, which had been approved by the FRG, did not imply any recognition of the GDR. Further travel concessions were made by the GDR on March 10, 1964, to enable West Berliners to meet relatives in certain GDR towns, and on Sept. 24, 1964, to allow elderly East Germans to visit relatives in West Berlin and the FRG.

Dr Ludwig Erhard, then Federal Chancellor of the FRG, could declare with satisfaction in a policy statement on Nov. 10, 1965, that the Soviet Union's intention of separating Berlin from West Germany had not been carried out because of "the firm stand of our Allies, our own firm will and above all the gallant attitude of the Berliners". He stated that the future of the city rested on four principles and demands—(i) "the presence of the three Allies in Berlin"; (ii) "unrestricted free access to Berlin"; (iii) Berlin's forming part of free Germany; and (iv) respect for "the unequivocal will of the Berliners" as the basis of any agreement on Berlin.

In a note to the three Western ambassadors in Bonn the Soviet ambassador to the GDR alleged on Feb. 14, 1968, that the FRG had "systematically extended" its "illegal activity" in West Berlin—by holding "regular parliamentary weeks", convening meetings of the FRG Cabinet and of *Bundestag* committees, establishing ministries and other government offices, planning to build an official residence for the Federal President and claiming to exercise state power in West Berlin (whose Chief Burgomaster had been elected President of the *Bundesrat*, the Upper House of the FRG's Parliament). In their reply of March 3 the three Western ambassadors pointed out that the special status of Berlin laid down in the four-power agreements was not limited to West Berlin but covered the whole city, and that in the view of their governments the FRG's concern for "the welfare and validity" of Berlin did not conflict with that status.

On April 13, 1968, the GDR issued an order forbidding FRG ministers and senior officials from travelling through the GDR to Berlin. The Western ambassadors, however, reminded the Soviet Government on April 19 that the GDR authorities were "not competent to modify the four-power agreements" on access to Berlin. In further decrees issued on June 11, 1968, the GDR imposed new restrictions on West German and West Berlin citizens and goods, involving the carrying of passports or identity cards, the requirement of visas and payment of taxes. The official GDR motivation for these measures was the 17th amendment to the Basic Law (Constitution) of the FRG, granting the Government far-reaching powers to deal with any emergency (which had been approved by the *Bundestag* on May 30, 1968, and had thereafter been condemned as "anti-democratic and militaristic" by the GDR and the Soviet Government).

### Signature of 1971 Quadripartite Agreement on Berlin

As a result of protracted negotiations by the four occupation powers a new quadripartite agreement on Berlin was signed on Sept. 3, 1971. In this agreement it was decided that all disputes should be "settled solely by peaceful means" and that the situation in the area (of Greater Berlin) should "not be changed unilaterally". The agreement provided that transit traffic through the territory of the GDR between the western sectors of Berlin and the FRG should be unimpeded, and that "the ties between the western sectors of Berlin and the FRG will be maintained and developed, taking into account that these sectors continue not to be a constituent part of the FRG and not to be governed by it".

In an annex on the status of West Berlin, Britain, France and the United States agreed that "the provisions of the Basic Law of the FRG and of the Constitution operative in the western sectors of Berlin which contradict the above have been suspended and continue not to be in effect", and also that no constitutional or official acts would be performed in the western sectors of Berlin by state bodies of the FRG.

The conclusion of this agreement was followed by further agreements, in particular (i) an agreement between the FRG and the GDR on transit traffic between the FRG and West Berlin, signed on Dec. 17, 1971, and (ii) agreements between the West Berlin Senate and the GDR on the facilitation of visits by West Berliners to East Berlin and the GDR, and another one on an exchange of territory designed to provide West Berlin with access to what had hitherto been an enclave in East Berlin territory—both these agreements being signed on Dec. 20, 1971. All three agreements came into force on June 3, 1972, together with the quadripartite agreement.

A new transit agreement replacing one of Dec. 19, 1975 (providing for annual tolls to be paid by the FRG to the GDR), was signed on Nov. 16, 1978, between the FRG and the GDR involving inter alia the construction of a motorway link between Hamburg and West Berlin at the expense of the FRG. (According to a statement made on March 4, 1979, by the FRG Minister of Inter-German Affairs, about 100,000,000 visitors to West Berlin had used the road and rail transit routes since the entry into force of the four-power agreement on Berlin in 1972.)

After 1975 it became apparent that there were differing interpretations of the 1971 quadripartite agreement on Berlin in East and West. The Soviet ambassador to the GDR declared on Sept. 3, 1976, that the agreement's conditions applied to West Berlin only, and that West Berlin should not be drawn into the process of West European integration (and in particular not be represented in the European Parliament of the European Communities).

Under a GDR passport law (published on Dec. 30, 1976, in the *Legal Gazette for Greater Berlin* and entering into force on Jan. 1, 1977), all persons (i.e. also non-Germans) entering East Berlin or the GDR would require a visa valid until midnight on the day of entry. A GDR government spokesman claimed that this law did not infringe the four-power agreement, to which in his view East Berlin was not subject. The GDR at the same time withdrew control points between East Berlin and the GDR. The Governments of Britain, France and the United States protested against this action on Jan. 6, 1977, emphasizing that the 1971 agreement applied to the whole of Berlin and calling on the Soviet Union to carry out its obligations under the agreement.

However, on Jan. 11 Moscow radio claimed that the four-power status of the whole of Berlin had been destroyed by the unilateral action of the Western Allies in 1948 (at the six-power London conference). Moreover, a spokesman for the Government of the FRG said on Jan. 18 that the GDR was not a signatory to the four-power agreement and therefore had no authority regarding West Berlin.

The Western attitude to the 1971 quadripartite agreement on Berlin was strongly reaffirmed by the Presidents of France and the United States, the UK Prime Minister and the Federal Chancellor of the FRG in a statement issued on May 8, 1977, confirming inter alia that the status of the special area of Berlin could not be modified unilaterally, and that the ties between West Berlin and the FRG should be maintained and developed. The statement was subsequently rejected by the Soviet Union, and in *Pravda* (the organ of the Central Committee of the Communist Party of the Soviet Union) it was claimed on May 15, 1977, that it was "well known that for a long time there has been neither a Germany nor a Berlin; there is the FRG, there is the GDR and there is West Berlin with its occupation regime"; and that the four-power status of Berlin had not existed since 1948, following the London six-power conference and the division of the Berlin *Magistrat*.

Incidents arose on a number of occasions during 1977-78 from GDR refusals to admit FRG political representatives to the GDR or to East Berlin, or even to the West Berlin transit routes. For their part, the Western powers repeatedly protested against the presence (and in particular traditional parades) of units of the GDR's National People's Army, which the West considered to be "illegal" and in contravention of the four-power agreements under which Berlin was to be a demilitarized zone.

The de facto incorporation of East Berlin in the GDR was further confirmed on June 28, 1979, when the *Volkskammer* unanimously decided to extend full status and voting rights to the 66 representatives of East Berlin in the House (who had hitherto been appointed to the *Volkskammer* by the East Berlin Municipal Assembly) and to amend the 1967 electoral law so as to enable them to be directly elected like all other members of the *Volkskammer*. This decision led to protests by the Western powers, the Government of the FRG and the *Bundestag*, the Western powers stating in particular that this "unilateral action" was altering the special status of Berlin in contravention of the four-power agreement of Sept. 3, 1971.

**H.W.D.**

45

# Greece-Turkey

Disputes between Greece and Turkey over the Aegean Sea, which lies between the Greek and Turkish mainlands, have for some years been a source of tension between the two countries and have on several occasions given rise not merely to diplomatic measures but also to states of military alert in either or both states. In the present day the only major islands in the Aegean under Turkish sovereignty are Gökçeada (Imbroz) and Bozcaada (Tenedos) in the northern Aegean close to the mouth of the Dardanelles. Greek sovereignty over most of the others was confirmed in the dismemberment of the non-Turkish parts of the Ottoman empire which followed World War I, while the Dodecanese (Sporades) in the south-eastern Aegean were ceded to Greece by Italy at the end of World War II. Although neither side is officially seeking to challenge the respective sovereignties resulting from these earlier territorial adjustments, an unresolved dispute over the delimitation of the Aegean continental shelf to some extent reflects historical animosities between Greeks and Turks and a continuing feeling among sections of both populations that existing territorial arrangements are unsatisfactory.

The establishment of Greece's sovereignty over most of the Aegean islands in the 20th century has stemmed from its aspiration to bring within the national territory all those areas traditionally inhabited by Greeks which had previously been excluded for various reasons: moreover, the eastern Aegean islands have major strategic importance for Greece in that they command most of the eastern coastline of Turkish Anatolia. Since 1970, however, attention has been increasingly focused on the mineral potential of the continental shelf in the Aegean itself, and consequently questions of maritime, strategic, economic and purely territorial advantage have become intermixed. The arguments surrounding the sovereignty of the continental shelf between the eastern Aegean islands and the Greek mainland remain problematic, insofar as there is as yet no complete or definitive set of international rulings on the law of the sea, but only a complex and often contradictory body of individual rulings and conventions, parts of which can be and frequently are quoted to the advantage of either party.

The Aegean dispute, although currently centring on an issue of undefined maritime law, is nonetheless relevant to a consideration of the territorial relationships between Greece and Turkey insofar as it has often been the theatre in which other disputes were enacted. It has been particularly important, for example, at various stages of the Cyprus dispute [see pages 16-26], whether in terms of military strategy or of actual

**Map 7   The Aegean Sea.**

territorial bargaining; moreover, the resentment still felt by many Turks at the Greek possession of the islands can be seen as a significant factor in the general and continuing tension between the two countries. Although Turkey has at present no formal claims for their return, the issue remains politically alive in Turkey and has frequently been exploited as a source of electoral support, particularly by extremist nationalist forces. For example, following the entry of the extreme right-wing National Action Party (NAP) into a four-party coalition government in March 1975, the NAP leader and Deputy Prime Minister, Col. Alparslan Türkes, made a series of controversial statements on the alleged Turkish character of the Greek Aegean islands, notably a demand in March 1976 that all islands within 50 kilometres of the Anatolian coast (including Lesbos and the Dodecanese) should be returned to Turkey.

As far as Greek opinion is concerned, its perception of Turkish intentions remains historically coloured by the disastrous defeat suffered by Greek forces in the 1921-22 war with Turkey, initiated by Greece in an attempt to secure the Ottoman territories which it had been awarded under the 1920 Treaty of Sèvres —i.e. most of Thrace west of Constantinople (Istanbul), the islands of Imbros and Tenedos and the Dodecanese (except Rhodes), as well as mandated authority over the Anatolian port of Smyrna (Izmir) and its hinterland, then with a predominantly Greek population. Lacking any support from the European powers, the Greek forces were driven out of Anatolia by Kemal Atatürk in 1922 and under the 1923 Treaty of Lausanne Greece recognized Turkish sovereignty over the disputed territories, except that the Dodecanese were ceded to Italy (which had backed the Turks in the recent war). Although the 1922 disaster effectively marked the end of "Greater Greece" aspirations, in many Greek minds the episode is still seen as an avoidable defeat for "Christian Europe" at the hands of the Moslem East.

In the post-World War II era the exigencies of the international balance of power brought both Greece and Turkey into the North Atlantic Treaty Organization (NATO) and the two countries have also come together under the umbrella of the Council of Europe. Nevertheless, their relations have continued to be adversely affected by underlying historical strains and in particular by Greek suspicions concerning Turkey's military intentions in the area. These strains have from time to time escalated into open diplomatic conflict, notably in connexion with the occupation of northern Cyprus by Turkish troops in July 1974—in protest against which Greece withdrew its armed forces from NATO. Although Greece resumed its participation in NATO's military activities in October 1980, the question was reopened with the election in October 1981 of a Socialist Government in Greece and by the assertion by the new Prime Minister, Dr Andreas Papandreou, that there was "no meaning in our belonging to the military wing of an alliance which does not guarantee our eastern frontiers against any possible threat and which at the same time, as a result of the unlimited supply of military matériel to Turkey, upsets the balance of power in the Aegean".

## Basic Greek and Turkish Positions on the Continental Shelf Issue

The argument adduced by Greece as regards the current Aegean Sea dispute is fundamentally based on the theses (i) that every island is entitled to a full continental shelf and 12-mile territorial water limit of its own, and (ii) that the area between such an island and the country of which it forms part should, in the interests of "the indivisibility of sovereignty, political unity and national territory, be it continental or insular", be considered also part of that sovereign area. Accordingly, because of the proximity of many Greek Aegean islands to the Turkish coastline, Greece claims by far the greater part of the Aegean seabed, extending to points east of its easternmost islands. Greece has quoted parts of a number of judgments and conventions in support of this argument, and claims that some of them have become international customary law, binding even on non-signatory states.

The first-mentioned argument concerning the continental shelf of islands is based primarily on a convention adopted by certain nations (including Greece but not Turkey) at the first United Nations Conference on the Law of the Sea, which took place on Feb. 24-April 28, 1958, in Geneva. The convention, which was the first of its type to attempt a definition of a continental shelf, defined the shelf in Article 1 as "(a) the seabed and subsoil of the territorial areas adjacent to the coast, but outside the area of the territorial sea, up to a depth of 200 metres or, beyond that limit, to where the depth of the superjacent waters admits of the exploitation of the natural resources of the said areas; (b) the seabed and subsoil of similar submarine areas adjacent to the coasts of islands". Articles 2 and 3 provide inter alia that the coastal state exercises exclusive rights to the exploitation of mineral resources in the shelf, although these rights "do not affect the legal status of the superjacent waters as high seas, or that of the airspace above those waters" (implying that international shipping, etc., would normally enjoy free passage over the continental shelf).

Greece asserts that the 1958 Geneva convention on the continental shelf has passed into international customary law, and claims in support of this argument that the International Court of Justice, in its February 1969 judgment on the North Sea continental shelf (involving disputes between West Germany, Denmark and the Netherlands), included in Paragraph 63 the observation that Articles 1-3 of the Geneva convention were regarded at least as "reflecting or crystallizing received or emergent rules of customary international law relative to the continental shelf".

The 1958 convention also provided that, in cases where a continental shelf bordered on two or more countries (as, for example, the Aegean borders on Greece and Turkey), the boundary of the shelf was to be determined by mutual agreement; failing that, and unless unusual circumstances justified a different solution, it would, according to Article 6, follow the median line "every part of which is equidistant from the nearest points of the baselines from which the breadth of the territorial sea of each state is measured" (i.e. a line half-way between what could reasonably be described as the broad coastal outlines of the two countries). Failing bilateral agreement, disputes were to be settled by the compulsory jurisdiction of the International Court of Justice (a principle rejected by Turkey as a non-signatory of the convention), or by an independent arbitral tribunal.

The Turkish argument is based on the claim that the Aegean is a special case. While not at present seriously disputing Greek sovereignty over the Greek Aegean islands, Turkey maintains that in geological terms they represent an extension of the Anatolian peninsula and that they thus fall within the scope of a statement made by the International Court of Justice during the 1969 North Sea continental shelf case, to the effect that the rights of the coastal state extend over "the areas of the continental shelf which constitutes a natural prolongation of its land territory". Proceeding on this basis, Turkey has claimed what amounts to half of the Aegean, defining the rightful delineation of the continental shelf as that which follows the north-south median line between the Greek and Turkish mainlands. On Nov. 1, 1973, the Turkish *Official Gazette* published a map based on this principle and showing a line which starts from the mouth of the River Evros (Meric) on the Greek/Turkish mainland border and passes to the west of Samothrace, Lemnos, Aghios Efstratios, Lesbos, Psara and Chios. Turkey allows each of the Greek islands a six-mile territorial waters limit but rejects the Greek view that a 12-mile limit should become the international standard; it has repeatedly expressed the view that a 12-mile limit, coupled with Greek sovereignty over the continental shelf, would effectively turn the Aegean into a "Greek lake".

Greece responds to this argument with the claim that Turkish shipping would enjoy the right to innocent passage both through Greek territorial waters and over the Greek continental shelf, although military shipping would be subject to certain restrictions including a ban on manoeuvres.

## Oil Prospecting in the Aegean

Although the prospects of finding significant oil deposits in the Aegean appear modest at present (only one minor oilfield having been tapped so far), the question of Greek and Turkish prospecting rights in the Aegean has prompted the most open manifestations of Greek and Turkish claims in respect of the continental shelf, and has at times led to military tensions and confrontations in the area. Greek prospecting in the Aegean has to date been conducted solely by an international consortium, the North Aegean Petroleum Company led by the Denison Mines Company of Canada—although it is planned to open up the area to other companies such as the Romanian state-owned company Rompetrol, which has already conducted extensive explorations on the Greek mainland. The only productive well so far drilled in the Aegean is that located in 1973 near Thasos in the northern Aegean; early estimates of a potential production of 50,000-70,000 barrels per day (bpd) have proved optimistic, and the well is currently expected to produce an average of 25,000 bpd during its first 10 years of production.

Turkish prospecting was until early 1980 restricted to the state-owned Turkish Petroleum Company (TPAO), which received exclusive exploration rights in November 1973 (from the Turkish Government) covering the continental shelf and territorial waters claimed by Turkey. Exploration was first carried out in June 1973 by the Turkish naval vessel *Candarli*, but since then has been conducted under licence by Norwegian, Canadian, American and Turkish vessels, notably the Turkish *Sismik I* [see below]. A new regulation passed by the Turkish Parliament on Jan. 24, 1980, allowed other foreign companies to prospect for oil in the disputed waters, although it was stipulated that 65 per cent of all oil thus obtained should be sold on the Turkish market.

Turkey has on the whole treated its regular seismic exploration of the Aegean as part of the process of registering its claim to the sovereignty of the eastern Aegean continental shelf; Greece on the other hand describes this kind of practice as an attempt to resolve the dispute by fait accompli, and rejects the legitimacy of the Turkish explorations, although it accepts the right of the Turkish seismic vessels to innocent passage when they are not actually prospecting.

## Confrontations arising from the Dispute

Following the November 1973 publication of the Turkish map claiming half of the continental shelf, the Turkish Government offered on Feb. 27, 1974, to negotiate with Greece on the question of jurisdiction over the Aegean outside the two countries' territorial waters. No Greek reply being forthcoming, work was started in April-May 1974 on the seismic exploration by Turkey of 27 sites in the Aegean. Greece offered on May 25 to negotiate with Turkey on the basis of the 1958 Geneva convention, but repeatedly asserted its claim to any oil found under the continental shelf; however, Turkey rejected the Geneva convention as a basis for discussion, and a deadlock ensued which repeated bilateral discussions at ministerial level failed to resolve.

Hostilities between the Turkish Government and what was then the Greek military regime worsened steadily during the following months, but deteriorated markedly on July 20, 1974, when Turkish troops launched an invasion of northern

Cyprus. On that day Turkey issued a Notice to Airmen (Notam 714) in which it declared the air space over the eastern Aegean to be a dangerous zone for international aviation; on Aug. 6, moreover, it unilaterally extended its flight information region to the north-south median line which it claimed to be the just delineation of the continental shelf. Greece, which had under IATA regulations hitherto administered the flight control region over the entire Aegean, was thus obliged to close all Aegean air corridors. This situation prevailed until Feb. 22, 1980, when Turkey withdrew the 1974 instruction, the Aegean air space being re-opened on Feb. 23 to international air traffic.

Turkey resumed its plans to explore the Aegean seabed in January 1975 following the end of the airlift of Turkish Cypriot refugees to Turkey. However, on Jan. 30 the Norwegian vessel *Longva*, which had contracted to undertake the mission, refused to prospect in disputed waters, so that the project was cancelled, causing bitter controversy in Turkish political circles. Seismic research vessels of various nationalities continued the research on behalf of Turkey for the next year, but the most serious military confrontation to arise over the prospecting rights issue involved the Turkish vessel *Sismik I* (a converted ship formerly known as the *Hora*), which began in late July 1976 an exploration of the disputed waters between Lemnos and Lesbos despite calls from several countries, including the United States, for a postponement of its activities. Turkey had already on July 15 threatened that any Greek interference with the mission would be met by force, but when the *Sismik I* sailed on July 23 it was shadowed by the Greek oceanographic research vessel *Naftilos* and by several Greek warships. Greece protested to Turkey on Aug. 7 at the alleged violation of its continental shelf, although Turkey replied that there was neither a Greek nor a Turkish continental shelf while the issue was in dispute.

On Aug. 9, 1976, the Greek Government called for an emergency meeting of the United Nations Security Council in view of what appeared to be a threat of war. The Security Council met on Aug. 12 and passed a resolution on Aug. 25 recommending that the two countries should take the dispute to the International Court of Justice (which the following day refused a Greek application for an injunction preventing the Turkish explorations, with the result that the Turkish seismic research continued). A wide range of issues were raised by the two sides in presenting their cases to the UN Security Council. Turkey referred to the "unwarranted harassment" of the *Sismik I*, accused Greece of attempting to annex Cyprus by the overthrow of Archbishop Makarios on July 15, and complained particularly of what it described as the illegal Greek militarization of the eastern Aegean islands (i.e. in contravention of the 1947 Paris peace treaty between the Allies and Italy, under which the Dodecanese had been ceded to Greece).

Particularly after the 1964 Turkish intervention in Cyprus, Greece had engaged in the military development of certain of the eastern Dodecanese in view of what was regarded as a direct military threat from Turkey. Turkey had responded in July 1975 by creating a new "Aegean Army", comprising all ground and naval units on the Aegean coast, with its headquarters in Izmir. Both Greek and Turkish armed forces were placed on alert during the 1976 crisis, and troops of both countries were also understood to have massed along the Greek/Turkish border in Thrace. Although the state of military tension receded after 1976, both countries accused each other periodically of breaches of their alleged maritime or aerial sovereignty by both military and civilian craft.

## Moves towards a Settlement

Greece proposed to Turkey on Jan. 27, 1975, that the Aegean dispute should be placed before the International Court of Justice, to which suggestion Turkey immediately agreed. It rapidly became clear, however, that opinions within Turkey were divided on the advisability of this course, and Turkey began later that year to insist that the International Court of Justice should be invited to rule only on matters which could not be decided by bilateral negotiation. Greece, while agreeing to conduct such bilateral discussions, nevertheless continued to propose jurisdiction by the Court, and on July 18, 1977, following the 1976 confrontation and a similar period of tension in March 1977 over Turkish drillings and military manoeuvres in the Aegean, it submitted a memorial to the Court stating its arguments. Turkey, however, refused to recognize the authority of the Court to rule on what it described as a domestic dispute, and consequently refused to attend or to submit memorials to the Court. The Court began an examination of the case in late 1977 but concluded in a decision of Dec. 19, 1978, that it was incompetent to make a ruling on what it described as a matter of "domestic jurisdiction" between the two countries.

Meanwhile, in accordance with Turkey's wishes, the two countries engaged from September 1976 onwards in bilateral discussions with the aim of determining a technical basis for the delineation of Aegean seabed rights. The first such discussions took place in New York in September 1976 between the Greek and Turkish Foreign Ministers, Dimitrios Bitsios and Ihsan Sabri Caglayangil respectively, and have continued at ministerial and technical level since then. Although the talks were broken off in 1977 during a period of particular tension over naval manoeuvres in the Aegean, they resumed in March 1978, when it was agreed by both countries to refrain from publishing details of the discussions in order to avoid disturbance by domestic factors on either side.

M.W.

# Hungary-Romania

Under the territorial changes made in Eastern Europe after World War II Hungary ceded Northern Transylvania to Romania, which had acquired the whole of Transylvania in the post-World War I break-up of the Austro-Hungarian empire but had been forced to cede the northern part to Hungary in 1940. To the extent that the post-1945 territorial adjustments made in the Soviet sphere of influence in Europe were accepted by all governments concerned as final, no formal dispute exists between Hungary and Romania over the sovereignty of Transylvania (the majority of whose inhabitants are Romanians). Nevertheless, there have been periodic manifestations of official Hungarian concern at the Romanian Government's treatment of the Hungarian inhabitants of the region (who constitute the largest national minority group in Europe), suggesting that territorial issues cannot be regarded as completely closed between two countries.

### Historical Background

The province of Transylvania, a naturally well-endowed plateau of some 24,000 square miles (62,000 sq km) separated from the rest of Romania by the Carpathian mountains and the Transylvanian Alps, has been the subject of contending national aspirations for a thousand years. Magyar-speaking settlers (*Szeklers*) began to move into Transylvania in the 10th century and the province was eventually conquered by King Stephen of Hungary in 1003. After a substantial admixture of Germans had arrived in the 12th and 13th centuries, the so-called "three nations" of the province (i.e. Romanians, Magyars and Germans) enjoyed self-government under Hungarian and later (from 1526) Ottoman Turkish suzerainty. At the end of the 17th century Transylvania came under the dominion of the Austrian Habsburgs and later became an important factor in Hungarian efforts to throw off Austrian rule, notably as the scene of much strife during the Hungarian revolt of 1848-49.

Regarded by the Hungarians as part of their historic national territory, Transylvania was incorporated into the Hungarian part of the Austro-Hungarian empire born in 1867. But the new independent state of Romania which emerged at this time aspired to incorporate the province into its territory, on the grounds that a majority of its inhabitants were Romanians. Having entered World War I on the side of the Allies in 1916 with this end in view, Romania initially suffered humiliation at the hands of the Central Powers, but on the eventual defeat of the latter Transylvania was one of its territorial rewards. After 20 years of Romanian rule, however, the northern half of Transylvania was transferred to Hungary by the August 1940 "Vienna award", under which Romania also lost Bessarabia and

**Map 8    Present borders of Hungary, Romania and the Soviet Union, showing Transylvania and Bessarabia.**

Northern Bukovina to the Soviet Union and Southern Dobruja to Bulgaria. The arbitrators on this occasion were Nazi Germany and Italy, to which Axis Hungary was then allied, and their findings were widely believed to reflect secret agreements reached between Hitler and Stalin in the context of their short-lived non-aggression pact of August 1939.

The following year Romania joined Germany in its invasion of the Soviet Union and succeeded in recovering Bessarabia and Northern Bukovina (as well as annexing a large adjacent area of Soviet territory), although Northern Transylvania remained under the sovereignty of Hungary. The eventual victory of the Red Army transformed the situation yet again, Romania being obliged to restore Bessarabia and Northern Bukovina to Soviet sovereignty (notwithstanding the former's substantial Romanian majority) and Hungary being constrained to restore Northern Transylvania to Romania. (For a full account of the Bessarabian question, see pages 81-86.) These dispositions were enshrined in the 1947 Paris peace treaties signed by the Allies with Hungary and Romania (treaties which also confirmed Bulgarian sovereignty over Southern Dobruja, the reversion of Eastern Slovakia from Hungary to Czechoslovakia and the transfer of Ruthenia from Czechoslovakia to the Soviet Union).

### Post-War Dissension over Minorities Question

In the first post-war decade the Hungarian and German minorities in Transylvania were afforded the protection of the occupying Soviet authorities against attempts to suppress their national identities made by the Romanian Government. However, after the departure of Soviet troops in 1956 a number of measures were taken by the Romanian authorities which were regarded by the Hungarian minority as inimical to its interests and which in consequence generated strains in relations between the allied governments of Hungary and Romania. During the 1960s the grievances of the Hungarian minority in Romania included—according to *The Times* of London dated Aug. 12, 1971—"restrictions on instruction in their mother tongue, the forcible merging of universities with Romanian ones, job discrimination, inadequate representation in the higher party and state organs, and isolation from the mainstream of Hungarian cultural life".

The same report continued, however, that President Ceausescu (who had assumed the leadership of the Romanian Communist Party in 1965 and the presidency in 1967) had taken steps to correct "the grosser injustices of his Stalinist predecessor's nationalist policies" and to ease "the suspicions of the minorities"; accelerated in the wake of the 1968 Soviet-led intervention in Czechoslovakia (in which Romania did not participate), such measures were intended "to improve the position of the Transylvanian Hungarians and Germans and cement national unity". The report also made the following observation: "The restiveness of the Germans and the fear that Russia might exploit the grievances of the Hungarians in Transylvania have added fresh impetus to efforts to improve their lot. In the past few months their cultural and educational rights have been strengthened, and the radio, television and mass media generally have provided more material in minority languages. The frequent visits of Soviet representatives in Romania to the Hungarian-speaking regions of Transylvania, giving an impression of Soviet support for Hungary, are not helping matters. . . ."

During this period recriminations between Hungary and Romania over the latter's increasingly forceful assertion of independence from Moscow-line communist orthodoxy were given a special flavour by the Transylvania question. Thus in August 1971 a member of the Hungarian Politburo, Zoltan Komocsin, said that Hungarian Communists were "fundamentally interested that the people of both our countries—including the Hungarians living in Romania—should come to understand that the fate and destiny of our peoples are inseparable from socialism". This remark brought a retort from a Romanian Politburo member, Paul Nicolescu-Mizil, that "no-one can set himself up as an arbiter or judge of the progress of socialism in one country or another", especially not those who in 1956 were "unable to cope with the task of governing their own party and people and registered lamentable political failures".

Such exchanges did not prevent Hungary and Romania from renewing (on Feb. 24, 1972) their 1948 treaty of friendship, co-operation and assistance for a further 20 years. Moreover, in mid-1977 President Ceausescu had talks with the Hungarian party leader, János Kádár, in Debrecen (Hungary) on June 15 and in Oradea (Romanian Transylvania) on June 16, during which it was agreed that the minorities question was a "domestic affair" of each individual host country and that the existence of Hungarians in Romania and of Romanians in Hungary was "the result of the development of history and several centuries of neighbourhood". (Romanian statistics gave the number of Hungarians in Romania as 1,700,000, whereas Hungary put the total at 2,000,000; the number of Romanians living within Hungary's borders was estimated at 20,000.) Nevertheless, such attempts to defuse the Transylvania question at inter-governmental level were accompanied by further indications of unrest among the Hungarian minority in Romania and by the appearance in various Hungarian and Romanian publications of polemical articles on the issue.

Allegations of government repression of the Hungarian minority in Romania were made in an open letter sent in December 1977 to the leadership of the Romanian Communist Party (RCP) by Carol Kiraly, a former high-ranking party official of Hungarian extraction, who maintained in particular that Hungarians living in Romania were subject to discrimination in employment and education. The Romanian Government responded by branding Kiraly a traitor, threatening to expel him from the party and denying all allegations that minorities were being repressed—this last contention being quickly endorsed by meetings in Bucharest of both the Hungarian and the German National Councils of Romania. Nevertheless, it was reported on April 24, 1978, that three prominent members of the Hungarian community who held leading positions in the RCP—namely Janos Fazekas (a Deputy Premier), Prof. Lajos Takacs (a former chancellor of the University of Cluj in Transylvania) and Andreas Suto (a well-known writer)—had sent separate appeals to the Romanian leadership protesting against the Government's alleged discriminatory policies towards its minority groups and demanding a number of improvements.

Although the Hungarian Government made no official comment on these developments, its continuing interest in the Transylvania question was indicated by the appearance during this period of a number of articles by individuals expressing dissatisfaction with Romania's treatment of its Hungarian minority. Moreover, in December 1977 the Budapest newspaper *Magyar Hirlap* published comments by a Hungarian historian who called into question official Romanian theories on the origins of the Romanian people and their continued presence in Transylvania. The Romanian authorities responded with their own articles denying allegations of anti-minority discrimination and criticizing Hungary for permitting the publication of material "hostile" to Romania. At the same time (i.e. early May 1978) the official Romanian news agency Agerpres republished in full an article by the Romanian historian Dr Ion Spalatelu dealing in depth with the atrocities perpetrated by Hungary under Admiral Horthy during its occupation of Northern Transylvania in 1940-44. This article concluded with the assertion that, although the overwhelming majority of Hungarian nationals lived in complete harmony and shared equal rights with Romanian citizens, they still had to fight against "fascist and Horthyist elements in various parts of the world" who were attempting "to revive the chauvinistic, irredentist policy which caused so much suffering to broad masses of citizens".

In the light of such exchanges and other factors, it is the view of many observers that the Transylvania question remains a "live" issue within the context of East European power politics. As stated above, there is no territorial dispute as such between the present Governments of Hungary and Romania, each of which remains committed to the territorial adjustments made in the wake of the Red Army's victory in 1945. At the same time, the Soviet guarantee of Romania's existing borders is seen as an important factor in relations between Bucharest and Moscow in that it provides the latter with the option of reopening the Transylvania question should Romania's pursuance of an independent line within the communist fold come to be regarded as unacceptable by the Soviet Union.

**A.J.D.**

# The Northern Ireland Question

The partition of Ireland in 1922 into an independent and overwhelmingly Catholic state on the one hand and a northern Protestant-majority province which remained part of the United Kingdom on the other has been the source of serious dispute and conflict ever since. In what was to become the Irish Republic the partition of Ireland has always been regarded as artificial and successive Governments have remained committed to re-unification as a basic objective, while recognizing that this should be achieved with the consent of the majority of the people in the North. Within Northern Ireland itself the overwhelming majority of the Protestant community have consistently opposed union with the Republic, while successive UK Governments have upheld the principle that no change should be made in Northern Ireland's status without the consent of a majority of its population. In recent years this fundamental political deadlock has been accompanied by a serious escalation of violence in the form both of armed struggle between militant pro-unification movements and the security forces on both sides of the border and of sectarian conflict between the Protestant and Catholic communities in Northern Ireland itself.

The existing boundary between the Republic of Ireland and Northern Ireland (a province of the United Kingdom of Great Britain and Northern Ireland) was laid down in 1925, following the establishment of the Irish Free State as a self-governing dominion under an Anglo-Irish treaty which was signed on Dec. 6, 1921, and which came into force in 1922. Under this treaty the Irish Free State became a coequal member of the Commonwealth with the rights of an independent country, but its ambassadors were accredited by the British monarch, who was represented in the Irish Free State by a governor-general; moreover, members of the Irish Parliament were required to swear an oath of allegiance to the British Crown.

The conclusion of the treaty was preceded by the passage in Britain of the Government of Ireland Act, which became law on Dec. 23, 1920, and came into operation in June 1921. This Act effectively enabled the Protestant Unionists in the north to retain control of six counties of the Irish province of Ulster—i.e. of Antrim, Armagh, Down, Fermanagh, Londonderry and Tyrone, but not of Cavan, Donegal and Monaghan—and reflected their belief (as stated in a report to a cabinet committee) that the inclusion of the latter counties in a separate political entity in the north would "provide such an access of strength to the Roman Catholic party that the supremacy of the Unionists would be seriously threatened". Under the 1921 treaty the Unionists were given the option of retaining the six counties' status under the 1920 Act, and they exercised this option immediately, so that the partition of Ireland became a fact in 1922, with Cavan, Donegal and Monaghan becoming part of a 26-county Irish Free State.

The 1920 Act also gave Northern Ireland its own Government and Parliament (for which a new building was completed at Stormont, Belfast, in 1932). Moreover, the Act created a Council of Ireland to encourage co-operation between the two parts of Ireland, but after the settlement of the boundary in 1925 this Council was formally dissolved in 1926. Those parts of the Act referring to the Irish Free State were repealed by the British Parliament in 1927. In 1936 the Irish Free State, by its External Relations Act, removed all mention of the Crown from its Constitution, and a new Constitution adopted in 1937 removed any distinction between the Free State and Northern Ireland. Articles 2 and 3 of the 1937 text claimed de jure jurisdiction for the Dublin Government over the whole island (which was referred to as Eire), although it was acknowledged that temporarily the clauses of the Constitution would not be enforceable in the six northern counties.

Under a 1948 Act Eire formally became the Republic of Ireland on Easter Sunday 1949, on which day it left the Commonwealth. The British Government thereupon passed the Ireland Act 1949, which guaranteed Northern Ireland's constitutional position, stating in particular: "It is hereby declared that Northern Ireland remains part of His Majesty's dominions and of the United Kingdom, and it is hereby affirmed that in no event will Northern Ireland or any part thereof cease to be part of His Majesty's dominions and of the United Kingdom without the consent of the Parliament of Northern Ireland."

The conflict over the boundary of the six counties with the rest of Ireland has run parallel with the conflict within the six counties themselves, where boundaries have become established (from village to village, or between parts of villages and between one street and another in towns and cities) between Protestants and Roman Catholics. On either side of these boundaries the two communities have for generations lived

**Map 9   Ireland.**

Boundaries of four historic Irish provinces
The six counties of Northern Ireland
1 = Antrim
2 = Armagh
3 = Down
4 = Fermanagh
5 = Londonderry
6 = Tyrone
0     km     100

largely in their own world of beliefs and practices and in ignorance of those followed on the other side, as a result of which the two sides have been referred to as "the two nations" of Northern Ireland.

Northern Ireland has a land area of 5,452 square miles (14,121 sq km) and its total population was, as at June 30, 1978, estimated at 1,536,000. The 1971 census showed the population as being 1,519,640, who were, according to their religion, divided as follows: Protestants 811,270 (i.e. Presbyterians 405,717, Church of Ireland members 334,318, and Methodists 71,235), Roman Catholics 477,921, other denominations 87,938, not stated 142,511. The Irish Republic extends to some 26,600 square miles (68,900 sq km) and according to a census of April 1, 1979, its total population was 3,368,217, of whom almost 95 per cent were Roman Catholics. The total length of the border between Northern Ireland and the Republic is 280 miles (450 km).

## Early Historical Background

After the collapse of the Roman empire the inhabitants of Ireland had a common Gaelic language and culture and a common (Brehon) law but no political unity. At the end of the eighth century Norsemen founded settlements which later became the towns of Ireland. From England Anglo-Normans entered the country about 1170, and by 1172 the various kings of Ireland were forced to acknowledge the overlordship of King Henry II, who had planned the English conquest of Ireland and who brought the Irish Church, until then independent, into complete union with the Church of Rome. In the following two centuries the Anglo-Normans were more or less absorbed into the Irish population but in 1366 the English forbade intermarriage between English and Irish (in the Statutes of Kilkenny). The Irish were subsequently regarded as enemies by the English, whose overlordship was secure only in a limited area around Dublin known as "The Pale". In the 15th century there was a degree of home rule in Ireland, but this was ended when King Henry VII in 1494 sent Sir Edward Poynings who (under Poynings' Law) enforced that no Irish parliament should initiate legislation without prior consent of the King and Council in England.

The power of the Norman feudal lords was broken by King Henry VIII, who in 1541 adopted the title of King of Ireland. However, his doctrine of ecclesiastical superiority received little support in Ireland, and the "reformation", although carried out with much bloodshed, was largely ineffective as regards the Irish people, who conformed only outwardly with the reformed doctrines. Under Queen Elizabeth I Roman Catholics in Ireland were persecuted, and Irish nationalism and Catholic religion combined to resist English rule. During the counter-reformation insurrections took place (including the Geraldine rebellion of 1579-83 supported by the Spanish and the Italians, and the O'Neill, Earl of Tyrone, rebellion of 1595) but were crushed by the English. Under King James I Irish lands were apportioned to English and Scottish settlers (the latter mainly Presbyterians). After 1649 the recalcitrant Irish were crushed by the troops of Cromwell and Ireton, and land was distributed among Cromwellian soldiers and London merchants; the Catholic religion was suppressed until the Restoration in 1660, when it was given a degree of toleration. However, newly imposed trade restrictions again alienated the Irish people.

The Catholic Irish supported King James II in his fight against William of Orange but were defeated both in the north (at the Battle of the Boyne in 1690) and in the south, where the fighting was concluded by the Treaty of Limerick (1691), which allowed the remnants of the Irish fighting force to go into exile. A new penal code denied the Catholics any rights of citizenship or ownership of property, and the government of Ireland passed into the hands of a Protestant oligarchy, with the Irish peasantry being treated with the utmost cruelty. Thousands of Irish people emigrated and many served in the armies of England's enemies.

The American War of Independence caused the British Government to make some concessions to the Irish, the principal results being the granting of an independent parliament and the repeal (in 1782) of Poynings' Law. The outbreak of the French revolution brought about the establishment in 1791 of the Society of United Irishmen by Wolfe Tone (a Protestant) as a revolutionary organization (which later became separatist). A planned invasion by a French revolutionary force in support of the United Irishmen failed in 1796, and a subsequent rebellion, aimed at achieving Catholic emancipation, parliamentary reform and the separation from Great Britain, was crushed.

A political solution applied by the British Prime Minister, William Pitt the Younger, was the Act of Union (passed in 1800 and in force from 1801), under which the Irish were to be represented in the British Parliament by 28 peers and four bishops (elected to the House of Lords for life by the Irish peerage) and by 100 members in the House of Commons. Pitt had intended the Act to be accompanied by a measure of Catholic emancipation but King George II opposed this and Pitt resigned in 1801. Roman Catholics were unable to sit in the House of Commons until 1829, when the Roman Catholic Emancipation Act allowed them to do so.

During the middle of the 19th century the Irish nation suffered the greatest human and economic setback in its history. Failure of the potato crop in 1846, United States competition in the grain market and Britain's adoption of free trade (whereby Ireland lost protection for its wheat) brought about famine, a state of general misery and mass emigration, mainly to the Americas. Of Ireland's then total estimated population of 8,000,000, over 1,000,000 died as a direct consequence of the famine and 1,250,000 left the country (250,000 of them for Britain). Between 1864 and 1914 Ireland changed from being a land of tillage to being one of pasturage.

Following the failure of British Liberal governments to secure adoption of Irish Home Rule bills in 1986 and 1893, another Home Rule bill received the royal assent in 1914 but its implementation was suspended owing to the outbreak of World War I.

## The Protestant Domination of Northern Ireland

The evolution, in parts of Ulster, of a society different in certain fundamental respects from that in the rest of Ireland received its greatest impetus from what has been called "the plantation of Ulster", i.e. the settlement in northern Ireland, begun in 1607, of some 170,000 people from Britain—150,000 of them Presbyterians from the lowlands of Scotland. This settlement followed the flight of the last of the Irish earls who had been defeated by the English. The plantation was resisted by the original inhabitants who in 1641 murdered thousands of Protestants and expelled others from their lands, but were themselves ultimately put down, in particular by Cromwell's troops. The success of the plantation was finally secured by the Battle of the Boyne in 1690, when Protestant forces of William of Orange defeated Catholics led by James II. (The anniversary of this battle, July 12, is celebrated by Northern Ireland's Protestants to this day.)

By 1703 the remaining Catholics in Ulster owned less than 14 per cent of the land. The Presbyterians were responsible for rapid capital accumulation and the development of industry in Ulster in the 19th century, and this further distinguished Ulster from the rest of Ireland.

Nevertheless the Catholic and Protestant communities in Northern Ireland were not always in opposite camps. Some Ulster Protestants were hostile to the British Government even in the 17th century, and a number of them emigrated to America at the time of the American War of Independence and fought against the Crown's forces. Both Protestants and Catholics had to pay tithes to the Established (Episcopalian) Church and were deprived of effective participation in political life in Britain. There was a temporary alliance between them in the United Irishmen formed in Belfast in 1791 (largely by Protestants) with the object of uniting "the whole people of Ireland" and "to abolish the memory of all past dissensions and to substitute the common cause of Irishmen in place of the denominations of Protestant, Catholic and dissenter". They both contributed to the passing of the 1793 Catholic Relief Act which gave parliamentary franchise to Catholics on equal terms with Protestants (but without allowing them to sit in Parliament). This alliance was ended in 1798, however, when an Irish rebellion received virtually no support from either community in the north.

By the end of the 19th century, the basis of Belfast's prosperity was (in the estimation of a late 19th century Unionist, Thomas Sinclair) its "economic link with Britain", for which reason it was "not prepared to come under the rule of a Dublin parliament dominated by impoverished small farmers from Munster and Connaught". Both employers and workers among the Protestants feared that Home Rule for all Ireland (as proposed by the British Government) might sever the commercial ties which bound them to Britain; the Protestant tenant farmers had not suffered from extortionate landlords as had the farmers in the south; and they all feared Catholic domination and perhaps oppression.

These arguments were taken up by the Conservatives of Britain, among whom Lord Randolph Churchill in 1886 expressed the view that the British Parliament should not leave the Protestants of Ireland in the lurch and that, if necessary, Ulster should "resort to the supreme arbitrament of force", adding: "Ulster will fight [against Home Rule or separation], Ulster will be right."

In 1912 Sir Edward Carson (later Lord Carson), a Protestant Dublin lawyer who stood for the maintenance of the Union of 1800, read out in Belfast what became known as the Ulster Covenant, which was said to have been signed by 471,414 people who undertook to use "all means which may be found necessary to defeat the present conspiracy to set up a Home Rule Parliament in Ireland" and, if it were set up, to "refuse to recognize its authority". Also in 1912 an Ulster Volunteer Force was recruited from among Protestants and was armed with rifles and ammunition smuggled in from the continent of Europe. Its formation was backed by the Ulster Unionist Council (founded in 1905) which regarded itself as a provisional government and was led by Carson. The formation of the Volunteer Force was also encouraged by the Conservatives in Britain, whose leader (Bonar Law) was the son of an Ulster Presbyterian minister and believed that a Parliament in Dublin would mean the destruction of the Protestant north. When early in 1914 the authorities took precautionary steps to protect military supplies from possible Volunteer Force raids, some of the officers responsible for such protection were prepared to resign rather than carry out orders. This "Curragh Mutiny" was supported by Sir Henry Wilson, head of military operations at the War Office, with the result that it became clear that the Army could not be relied upon to enforce Home Rule.

For most of the 20th century the political mouthpiece of the Protestant community in Northern Ireland has been the Unionist Party, founded in 1898 and the predominant force in the province's politics until the 1970s, since when it has been challenged by other formations and has itself split into different groupings. The Unionist Party has been permeated by the spirit of the Orange Order, which was founded in 1795 as an Episcopalian peasant self-defence group and did not officially admit Presbyterians until 1834, since when it has served to weaken confessional antagonisms within the Protestant community. In the 19th century one of the

Order's leaders defined as its enemy "popery . . . a religio-political system for the enslavement of the body and soul of man [which] cannot be met by any mere religious system or by any mere political system" and must be opposed "by such a combination as the Orange Society, based upon religion and carrying over religion into the politics of the day". Every Prime Minister of Northern Ireland and 95 per cent of all elected Unionist representatives in the Westminster Parliament were (in 1973) said to have been Orangemen.

Northern Ireland's major Protestant denominations were united in the Irish Council of Churches (which first met in 1923), all of them being united in their aim to maintain the existing border and to resist "Rome rule". An Ancient Order of Hibernians, which had adopted this title in 1938 and formed a Roman Catholic counterpart to the Orange Order, stood for loyalty to the Pope, the principle of a united Ireland, support for the Irish language, and anti-communism. However, it never attracted more than a small percentage of Northern Ireland's Catholic population into membership.

### The Rise of Militant Irish Republican Movements

The famine of 1846 entailed the rise of an Irish nationalist movement, first of all of a Young Ireland movement whose leaders were sentenced to transportation to a penal colony before they could carry out a rebellion planned for 1848. It was followed by the Fenians (named after a legendary band of Irish warriors), the core of whom was constituted by the Irish Republican Brotherhood (IRB), founded in 1858 as a conspiratorial revolutionary organization responsible for many acts of violence both inside and outside Ireland. It carried its "war of independence" to England in 1867 by bombing Clerkenwell prison in London and shooting a police officer in Manchester in attempts to rescue Fenian prisoners. Members of the "Invincibles", an offshoot of the IRB, murdered the (Liberal) Chief Secretary for Ireland (Sir Frederick Cavendish) in Dublin's Phoenix Park in 1882, whereupon the British Government introduced a drastic Coercive Act.

The effect of this Act was that at the 1885 general elections the Irish nationalists, standing for Home Rule and led by Charles Stewart Parnell, won every seat in the three provinces of Connaught, Leinster and Munster and even a small majority in Ulster, thus gaining the balance of power between Liberals and Conservatives in the House of Commons. However, an attempt by the Liberal Prime Minister (Gladstone) to give Ireland Home Rule was defeated by the defection of a number of Liberals led by Joseph Chamberlain, and in a fresh election in 1886 the Conservatives and Chamberlain's Liberal Unionists obtained a majority large enough to make any Home Rule legislation impossible at that stage.

In response to the formation of the (Protestant) Ulster Volunteer Force, a National Volunteer Force was recruited in the south in 1913 (at the suggestion of Eoin MacNeill) and was soon infiltrated by the IRB. However, when this latter force was, in 1914, called upon (by the Irish Home Rule party) to fight on the side of the Allies in World War I in order to prove Ireland's right to full nationhood, it became divided. A minority, which regarded the proposal as a betrayal of Irish nationalism, was supported by the IRB, *Sinn Fein* (a group founded as a political party in 1905 by Arthur Griffith as a purely nationalist movement) and the infant Irish labour movement. This determined and well-disciplined minority formed, with a Labour Citizen Army, the group which carried out the 1916 Easter Rising in Dublin, which had been prepared by the IRB. The original plans for this rising were not fully implemented, and in the event it was only a relatively small force of 1,500 men who occupied the General Post Office in Dublin, where their leader, Padraic Pearse, proclaimed the Irish Republic. Within less than a week the rising was crushed and some 1,000 people had lost their lives; several of the rebel leaders were executed over a period of days, while others, including Eamonn de Valera, were given life sentences (but were released under a general amnesty in 1917).

The effect of the executions was to strengthen the nationalist movement and in particular *Sinn Fein* which, although most of its leaders were under arrest, gained 73 of the 105 Irish seats in the House of Commons in the 1918 general elections, standing on an outright Republican programme. *Sinn Fein* thereupon decided to withdraw all elected Irish members from the British Parliament and to set up a Constituent Assembly (*Dail Eireann*) in Dublin. However, when this Assembly met in January 1919, only 28 members attended, the Ulster Unionists staying away and half the *Sinn Fein* members being in prison.

Under the leadership of Michael Collins *Sinn Fein* embarked on guerrilla warfare against the British Government, which decided to reinforce the country's constabulary by an additional security force which became known as the Black and Tans. This force became immensely unpopular because of its indiscriminate raids, which included attacks even on the houses of Unionist families. *Sinn Fein*, however, obtained control of much of the machinery of government, and in 1921 the British Prime Minister (Lloyd George) began negotiations with Eamonn de Valera, the president of *Sinn Fein*, which led to the conclusion of the Anglo-Irish treaty in December of that year.

The 1921 treaty, however, divided *Sinn Fein*. One section led by Arthur Griffith (who died in August 1922) and Michael Collins (who was assassinated, also in August 1922) regarded the 1920 Government of Ireland Act and the treaty as a first step towards independence, but another section led by Eamonn de Valera rejected the settlement because it abandoned the principle of an all-Ireland Republic. The settlement was endorsed by a small majority of the Irish Parliament and by a decisive majority at the ensuing general election. The extremist wing of *Sinn Fein* began a civil war which lasted until 1923, and in 1927 de Valera formed the Republican Party (*Fianna Fail*) and brought his followers into the *Dail*, agreeing to take the oath of allegiance (by disregarding it as "an empty formula").

During the civil war the Volunteer Force adopted the name of Irish Republican Army (IRA), which at a meeting in Dublin in July 1923 broke with the IRB. It later decided, in April 1924, to support the *Sinn Fein* party, but its influence subsequently declined. In 1936 the Dublin Government declared it an illegal organization and its leaders were imprisoned. During World War II some of its members were pro-German and were responsible for bomb explosions in England in 1940. In 1956-62 the IRA emerged in Northern Ireland with a bombing campaign, which the authorities were able to confine to the border areas.

## Provisional IRA Campaign in Northern Ireland since 1969

The political scene in Northern Ireland changed with the establishment in Belfast in February 1967 of the Northern Ireland Civil Rights Association by non-political liberals who wished to co-ordinate the activities of local associations aiming at improving the status of Catholics. In the late 1960s the Association was infiltrated by members of People's Democracy, a group founded in 1968 by (Trotskyite) International Socialists at Queen's University, Belfast, but after People's Democracy had broken away from the Association in 1970 its leadership was gradually taken over by the Official IRA. The latter was the rump of the IRA, from which the Provisional IRA had broken away in 1969 as a direct-action organization intent upon launching a guerrilla campaign with the aim of making Northern Ireland ungovernable and forcing the British to withdraw their armed forces from the province and to relinquish all responsibility for it.

While both the Official and the Provisional IRA have been declared illegal, their respective political wings have remained legal organizations—(i) the official

(Marxist) *Sinn Fein*—which later became *Sinn Fein* the Workers' Party, with the aim of uniting the working class and rejecting sectarianism because it "killed workers", and which is known as the Republican Clubs in Northern Ireland, and (ii) the Provisional *Sinn Fein*.

An Irish Republican Socialist Party broke away from the Official IRA in December 1974 and became a legal party in the Republic, with the aim of "ending British rule in Ireland" and establishing "a united democratic socialist republic". The military wing of this party, the Irish National Liberation Army (INLA), emerged in 1975 with the object of conducting armed warfare to bring about a British military withdrawal from Northern Ireland, which was to be united with the Republic on the basis of "socialist" principles. The INLA was proscribed in Northern Ireland and in Britain in July 1979.

The sectarian conflict in Northern Ireland took on a violent complexion after the Civil Rights Association had, in a march on Oct. 5, 1968, defied a police ban designed to keep it out of a traditionally Unionist area in Londonderry, and had thus clashed with the police. William Craig, then Northern Ireland Minister of Home Affairs, said afterwards that the Association was "definitely a Republican front" and "clearly unacceptable to the loyalist community". Further marches and clashes took place in the ensuing months, and early in 1969 the British Government agreed to make troops available to protect key installations against attacks, especially by militant Protestants. Disturbances nevertheless spread and reached a climax in Belfast in August 1969, when troops moved in to prevent Protestants from invading the Catholic Falls Road area and to create a "peace line".

In October 1969 the Provisional IRA began its campaign of sniping at soldiers and bombing property; by September 1971 the IRA was using rocket launchers, and in April 1973 letter bombs appeared, to be followed by parcel bombs sent to senior civil servants. In August 1971 the authorities introduced internment without trial of suspects, which remained in force for four years despite a civil disobedience campaign called by the Catholic opposition parties in Northern Ireland. Action by British troops against the Provisional IRA led to the death of 13 persons in Londonderry from army gunfire on Jan. 30, 1972, and in a reprisal action for this so-called "bloody Sunday" the British embassy in Dublin was attacked. The front was now clearly drawn between, on the one hand, the Provisional IRA and, on the other, the British Army, the Ulster Defence Regiment (UDR) and the Royal Ulster Constabulary (the Northern Ireland police), while members of paramilitary Protestant organizations such as the Ulster Defence Association were held responsible for numerous deaths (not all of them of Catholics).

The Provisional IRA also made use of its international contacts to obtain arms supplies from Europe (some Soviet-bloc weapons being intercepted) and from the Middle East. The INLA was held responsible for the killing of the British ambassador in The Hague in March 1979 and of Airey Neave, Conservative spokesman on Northern Ireland, in London the same month. By the late 1970s, however, the military membership of the Provisional IRA was thought to have fallen from a peak of 1,000 men in 1972-73.

According to figures supplied on June 24, 1981, by the British Secretary of State for Northern Ireland (then Humphrey Atkins) the total number of deaths caused by terrorist or sectarian violence, rioting or security forces operations between August 1969 and June 1981 was 2,117, consisting of 1,213 civilians (not believed to have been members of paramilitary organizations), 456 members of the Army (including the UDR) and 297 suspected members of paramilitary organizations. By the end of 1981 there were still 11,000 British troops in Northern Ireland. The material and spiritual damage caused to the social fabric of Northern Ireland in these 12 years has not been assessed even approximately.

Public support for the Provisional IRA among Irish Catholics has been reflected not only at public gatherings, in particular at funerals of IRA members, but also in election results both in the Republic and in Northern Ireland. In general elections to the Irish Parliament held in June 1981 two Provisional IRA members, both of them prisoners then on hunger strike at the Maze prison in Belfast in support of demands for political status to be given to IRA prisoners, were elected (one of them dying on Aug. 2). In a by-election held in the Fermanagh-South Tyrone constituency of the British House of Commons in April 1981 Robert (Bobby) Sands, another IRA hunger striker at the Maze prison, was also elected, and after his death Owen Carron, a member of the Provisional *Sinn Fein*, was elected with an increased majority in August of that year.

## The Search for a Political Solution

Northern Ireland's relations with the South were in a state of "cold war" during the rule of Eamonn de Valera, who regarded the ending of partition as the overriding goal of the Irish Government. The division between North and South was further exacerbated by provisions of the 1937 Constitution of the Republic, which not only (as stated above) asserted de jure jurisdiction over the whole of Ireland but also included certain other provisions in sharp conflict with traditions and practices in the Protestant North. In particular, the Constitution made the Irish language the country's first official language, forbade divorce, recognized the family as "a moral institution possessing inalienable and imprescriptible rights antecedent and superior to all positive law", gave the Roman Catholic Church a "special position" (which was, however, abandoned in 1972), and embodied Catholic social doctrine.

The situation changed with the advent of Sean Lemass as Prime Minister of the Republic in 1959, when a period of state-aided industrialization began and the Dublin Government started to play a role in international affairs (e.g. at the United Nations). In 1965 Lemass went to Belfast to meet the Northern Ireland Prime Minister (Capt. Terence O'Neill), this being the first meeting of the heads of the two Irish Governments for 40 years, and a return visit took place a few weeks later. These meetings, however, led to the downfall of Capt. O'Neill, not only owing to loyalist agitation against him led by the Rev. Dr Ian Paisley but also because of opposition from within the Unionist Party led by Brian Faulkner. O'Neill was replaced as Prime Minister on May 1, 1969, by Maj. James Chichester-Clark, who was himself replaced by Faulkner in March 1971.

In the wake of the January 1972 "bloody Sunday" incident, the Northern Ireland Catholics withdrew all co-operation with the Northern Ireland Government, and talks between that Government and the British Government broke down on March 23, 1972, over the question of which of the two was to control security. The British Government thereupon invoked powers granted under the 1920 Act to enact legislation (on March 30, 1972) which prorogued the Northern Ireland Parliament and provided for the assumption of direct rule over the province by the UK Parliament and Government for an initial period of one year (which was extended for another year in March 1973). In conjunction with this step a new UK office of Secretary of State for Northern Ireland was created and William Whitelaw appointed as its first incumbent.

A year after the imposition of direct rule, a referendum was held in Northern Ireland on March 8, 1973, to ascertain the views of the population on any possible change in the province's status. However, this so-called "border poll" was boycotted by the Catholic community with the result that only 58.6 per cent of the eligible electorate went to the polls. The results showed that 591,820 people (57.4 per cent of the total electorate of 1,030,084) had voted in favour of Northern

Ireland remaining part of the United Kingdom and 6,463 (0.63 per cent) for Northern Ireland to be joined with the Irish Republic outside the United Kingdom, while 5,973 (0.58 per cent) spoiled their ballot papers.

The British Government thereupon enacted the Northern Ireland Constitution Act, which confirmed the status of Northern Ireland as part of the United Kingdom for as long as a majority wished it to be so, but abolished the Northern Ireland Parliament and put in its place (i) a Northern Ireland Assembly, to be elected by the single transferable vote method of proportional representation (as used in the Republic of Ireland but not in Britain), this system also to be used for electing the 12 members of the British House of Commons, and (ii) an Executive based on the principle of power-sharing between the Protestant and Catholic communities.

This Act, however, led to disagreement within the Unionist movement, where it was opposed by the Orange Order, Dr Paisley's Democratic Unionist Party and the Vanguard Unionist Party (VUP) newly founded in March 1973 by William Craig (who in 1972 had formed the paramilitary Ulster Vanguard Movement to resist any change in Unionist rule). In the Assembly elected under the Act in June 1973, the 78 seats were distributed as follows: Unionist followers of Brian Faulkner in favour of power-sharing 22, Official Unionists opposed to power-sharing 13, Paisley supporters 8, Craig supporters 7, Social and Democratic Labour Party (SDLP, founded in 1970 as a mainly Roman Catholic party standing for reconciliation and partnership between Catholics and Protestants in Northern Ireland with a view to achieving Irish unity by peaceful means) 19, the Alliance Party (AP, also formed in 1970 "to cross the sectarian divide in Northern Ireland") 8, Northern Ireland Labour Party (NILP) 1.

The principle of power-sharing was endorsed at a conference held in December 1973 at Sunningdale (Berkshire) between members of the British Government (led by Edward Heath), of the Irish Cabinet (led by Liam Cosgrave) and of the Northern Ireland Executive-designate (set up by Faulkner with SDLP and AP participation); at the same time agreement was reached on the formation of a Council of Ireland consisting of representatives of Northern Ireland and the Republic to develop North-South relations. At the conference the Irish Government "fully accepted and solemnly declared" that there could be no change in Northern Ireland's status until a majority in the province so wished, while the UK Government reaffirmed that its policy remained to support the wishes of the majority of the people of Northern Ireland and that if in the future such a majority "should indicate a wish to become part of a united Ireland the British Government would support that wish".

Direct rule was ended under a Northern Ireland Constitution (Devolution) Order which (effective Jan. 1, 1974) implemented an amendment to the Northern Ireland Constitution Act by allowing for the appointment of an 11-member Executive and a 15-member Administration in Belfast. However, on Jan. 4, 1974, the Ulster Unionist Council, the policy-making body of Faulkner's party, rejected the Sunningdale proposals by 427 votes to 374, and the first meeting of the Assembly on Jan. 22 had to be suspended when Faulkner's opponents prevented members of the Executive from taking their seats; on the following day the Official Unionists led by Harry West and also the Paisley and Craig parties withdrew from the Assembly. In elections to the British House of Commons on Feb. 28, 1974 (held under the traditional first-past-the-post system), the 12 Northern Ireland constituencies returned 11 candidates opposed to the Sunningdale agreement.

The anti-Faulkner Unionists were supported by two paramilitary organizations, namely (i) the Ulster Volunteer Force (UVF), originally formed in 1912 and reconstituted in 1966, and (ii) the Ulster Defence Association (UDA), formed in 1972 to defend Protestant areas from IRA incursions and estimated to have recruited

50,000 members within three months. These groups in turn supported a general strike called in May 1974 and widely endorsed in the Protestant community. The British (Labour) Government declared a state of emergency in the province on May 19 and sent in troops. The Executive resigned on May 28, the Assembly was prorogued on May 29 and the British Government again assumed direct authority in Northern Ireland.

On May 1, 1975, elections were held to a Constitutional Convention which was to report on the establishment of a future government of Northern Ireland commanding the support of the whole community. The result of these elections was not very different from that of the elections for the Assembly of June 1973, seats being gained as follows: the anti-power-sharing United Ulster Unionist Council (UUUC) 46, Unionist Party of Northern Ireland (UPNI, supporting Faulkner) 5, SDLP 17, AP 8, NILP 1, Independent Loyalist 1. The UUUC was divided into 19 Official Unionists (led by West), 14 VUP members, 12 Paisley supporters and an independent with UUUC support. However, all UUUC members of the Convention except Craig stated during September 1975 that they were opposed to any coalition with the SDLP, and the Convention ceased to meet on Nov. 7 of that year and was formally dissolved on March 5, 1976, having failed to agree on a government system based on partnership between Protestants and Catholics. The British Government admitted in February 1976 that there was "no instant solution to the problems of Northern Ireland". Since then no further attempts have been made to convene an elected representative body for the whole of Northern Ireland.

Also on March 5, 1976, the British and Irish Prime Ministers (respectively Harold Wilson and Liam Cosgrave) met and agreed that "an acceptable form of government for Northern Ireland could be established only by both communities agreeing on a system of government providing for partnership and participation" and that, pending such an agreement, a period of direct rule (by Britain) and stability was necessary.

There had earlier been some changes in local government in Northern Ireland, as under proportional representation a Catholic mayor had been elected in Londonderry (for the first time in 50 years) in 1973, when the SDLP won 82 and the AP 63 local council seats throughout the province out of a total of 526. In May 1977 power-sharing was achieved in all except three out of Northern Ireland's 26 local councils.

A call for a general strike made in May 1977 by a United Unionist Action Council, which included the Paisley formation and the UDA, with the aim of forcing the British Government to carry out the Unionist demand for a virtual return to the 1920 Act, was called off on May 13 for lack of support. It led, however, to the foundation in October 1977 of two new parties—the Irish Independence Party and the Ulster Independence Party—to promote the idea of an ultimate declaration of independence by Northern Ireland from the United Kingdom. (William Craig's VUP was dissolved in February 1978, when he joined the Official Unionist Party.)

In the Republic the Prime Minister (then Jack Lynch, the *Fianna Fail* leader) on Jan. 8, 1978, called for a British declaration of intent to withdraw from Northern Ireland and stated in particular that he would like to see a start in "bringing Irish people together", that the British Government should indicate "in a general way" that they did "not wish to continue subsidizing a small corner of Ireland to the extent that they have been doing over the past 50 years", and that the British people themselves had "no stomach for that kind of subsidization which involves taxation on them". He added that "the people of Northern Ireland would be realistic enough to know that there should be, and ought to be, accommodation found between the [Catholic] minority and themselves in the first instance, and between them and us in the long term".

Lynch's successor, Charles Haughey, called, on Feb. 16, 1980, for a joint initiative on Northern Ireland by the United Kingdom and Irish Governments. He found the picture in Northern Ireland "a depressing one" as its agriculture and industry were producing less than in the early 1970s and the population had remained static. While emphasizing that in the Republic the rule of law would be firmly upheld and democracy defended, he said that for over 60 years the situation in Northern Ireland had been a source of instability because "the very entity [of Northern Ireland] itself is artificial and has been artificially sustained". The reality, he claimed, was that Northern Ireland as a political entity had failed and that a new beginning was needed. He added that it would be his concern to ensure that the place of Protestants in the Ireland of the future would be secure and that their traditions were honoured and respected. He looked forward to "some free and open arrangement in which Irish men and women on their own without a British presence but with active British goodwill will manage the affairs of the whole of Ireland in a constructive partnership with the European Community".

A constitutional conference held in Belfast from Jan. 7 to March 24, 1980, but not attended by the Official Unionist Party, was adjourned after it had failed to reach agreement by the parties represented on the role of the Roman Catholic minority in a devolved government of the province. After the publication in July 1980 of further British proposals on Northern Ireland, Humphrey Atkins, the British Secretary of State for Northern Ireland, announced in the House of Commons on Nov. 27, 1980, that there was not sufficient agreement among the parties to justify bringing forward proposals for setting up a devolved administration at that stage, and that new ways would have to be explored. As a means of promoting this exploration the Secretary of State announced on July 2, 1981, that the Government intended to set up a new Northern Ireland "advisory council" composed of some 50 people already elected to other representative bodies. The purpose of this council would be to advise the Government on Northern Ireland affairs and to consider how agreed executive powers might be exercised in the province in the future. However, all the major political parties in Northern Ireland, including the SDLP, gave the proposal a cool reception.

On the other hand Charles Haughey and Margaret Thatcher (the British Prime Minister), meeting in London on May 21, 1980, stated that they agreed that "they wished to develop a new and closer political co-operation between the two Governments" and to hold regular meetings. At a further meeting (held in Dublin on Dec. 8, 1980) the two Prime Ministers agreed inter alia that the economic, social and political interests of their peoples were "inextricably linked" but that the full development of these links had been "put under strain by division and dissent in Northern Ireland" and that peace, reconciliation and stability must be achieved there.

The Anglo-Irish meetings at Prime Ministers' level were particularly strongly opposed by Dr Paisley, who on Feb. 19, 1981, signed in Belfast, with other members of his party, a covenant similar to that of 1912 in which the signatories pledged themselves to use all means necessary "to defeat the present conspiracy . . . to edge Northern Ireland out of the United Kingdom and to establish an ongoing process of all-Ireland integration".

## The Present Situation

Taking all factors into consideration, most observers have concluded that for the foreseeable future no solution is in sight to the Northern Ireland question, which has now bedevilled UK-Irish relations for more than 60 years. At the most basic level the essence of the problem remains what it has always been: that the Government and people of the Irish Republic together with the Catholic population of Northern Ireland aspire to the unity of Ireland (albeit with varying degrees of intensity), while the Protestant majority in the North remains opposed to any move in that direction. In such a situation of fundamental divergence of aspiration extremists on both sides have inevitably continued to find a hearing and the trend towards political polarization within Northern Ireland has gathered pace.

As regards opinion on the British mainland, the failure of successive Governments to find a political solution to the Northern Ireland question has generated increasing support for more drastic options, ranging from withdrawal of British troops in the short term (and their possible replacement by a UN or other international peace-keeping force) to complete severance of the British connexion with the province in the longer term. As British soldiers have continued to be killed in Northern Ireland and as the cost to the British Exchequer of maintaining the economic viability of the province has escalated, advocacy of such steps has inevitably met with a growing response. However, successive British Governments (and those in Dublin) have taken the view that a withdrawal of troops would provoke open civil war between the two communities in Northern Ireland and that any question of changing the status of the province comes back to the matter of obtaining the support of a majority of its inhabitants. Moreover, the view advocated in some quarters that the so-called "Protestant guarantee" should be unilaterally withdrawn by Britain raises the difficult question as to whether the UK Parliament could or would legislate to give up or transfer sovereignty over part of the present national territory.

As indicated in the foregoing, the British Government approach to the Northern Ireland question since it became critical a decade or so ago has been largely bipartisan, with successive Labour and Conservative administrations seeking a solution on the basis of the same underlying principles and being supported by the opposition of the day. It should be noted, however, that at its 1981 conference the opposition Labour Party adopted a Northern Ireland policy document incorporating a major shift from the previous bipartisan approach, notably by asserting that a future Labour government would declare as a basic policy objective the establishment of unity between the two parts of Ireland. To the extent that the document asserts that Irish unity must be "based on agreement and consent" and achieved "by a process of negotiations between the Governments of the United Kingdom and the Republic of Ireland, with the support of the people in both the North and the South of Ireland", the Labour Party continues to uphold the Protestant guarantee; nevertheless, the explicit assertion that the reunification of Ireland is the only viable long-term solution to the Northern Ireland question represents a significant departure for the previous bipartisan formula, which (as expressed at the 1973 Sunningdale conference) provided that the British Government would not favour Irish unity until and unless a majority of the population of Northern Ireland expressed a wish for it.

For its part, the Conservative Government which came to power in Britain in May 1979 has given priority in its Northern Ireland policy to the development of closer relations with the Dublin Government, in the belief that greater integration and co-operation at UK-Republic level will promote reconciliation between the two communities in the North, especially since both countries are members of the European Community. As regards the political logjam in Northern Ireland, the eventual achievement of a power-sharing administration is seen as the only practical alternative to the continuation of direct rule from Westminster. It remains to be seen, however, whether the degree of Protestant support for power-sharing which existed in the early 1970s still survives in the early 1980s. What is certainly clear is that strategies of long-term reconciliation and power-sharing will not placate the various militant Republican organizations seeking to remove the border by violent means.

**A.J.D.**

# Italy-Yugoslavia (Trieste)

The dispute over Trieste and its surroundings—which had been part of Italy between 1919 and 1945—arose out of a Yugoslav claim to this area made in 1945, the principal grounds why it should not continue to be part of Italy being (i) that the latter had been one of the defeated Axis powers and had been guilty of aggression against Yugoslavia; (ii) that as part of Italy the port of Trieste would be cut off from its natural hinterland; and (iii) that the area was partly inhabited by Slovenes and Croats. Although a final settlement of the dispute was achieved by the two Governments under the 1975 Treaty of Osimo, certain aspects of this agreement have continued to be opposed by a substantial minority of the Trieste population.

### Trieste between World Wars I and II

Trieste, which had with its hinterland been under Austrian control during most of the period since the 14th century, was at the outbreak of World War I in 1914 the principal port of the Austro-Hungarian Empire. Of its population at that time about two-thirds were Italian (of either Italian or Austrian nationality), while most of the remainder were Slovenes or Croats. In a then secret Treaty of London, concluded on April 26, 1915, by Britain, France and Russia with Italy, the latter was promised, in return for joining the war on the side of the Allies and against Germany and Austria-Hungary, control of specified territories which were then part of the Austro-Hungarian Empire but had been claimed as Italian by an Italian irredentist movement. These territories included Trieste, the counties of Gorizia and Gradisca and all Istria (as well as certain islands in the Adriatic and the province of Dalmatia).

After President Wilson of the United States had insisted on a revision of these promises, the final frontiers of Italy in this region at the end of World

**Map 10   The position of Trieste.**

68

War I were fixed under the Treaty of Rapallo concluded between Italy and Yugoslavia in 1920. Under this treaty most of the coast of Dalmatia (except the Zara enclave and the island of Lagosta) was given to Yugoslavia; Fiume (Rijeka), east of Istria, became a Free City until Jan. 27, 1924, when under a new Italo-Yugoslav treaty it was annexed to Italy after it had already been seized by an Italian force led by Gabriele d'Annunzio. For Trieste its transfer to Italy after World War I meant that it was cut off from its natural hinterland (now part of Yugoslavia), and its port activities declined considerably.

## The 1945 Attempt by Yugoslavia to seize Trieste

Towards the end of World War II Marshal Tito of Yugoslavia (who had on April 11, 1945, signed a treaty of friendship, mutual assistance and post-war collaboration with the Soviet Union) officially claimed, on April 15, 1945, Trieste and the Istrian peninsula (Venezia Giulia) for Yugoslavia, and his claim was immediately strongly opposed by all political parties in Italy except the Communists (then led by Palmiro Togliatti). On April 30 Marshal Tito announced that his armed forces had entered the area, in particular Rijeka (Fiume), Pilj (Pula) and Trst (Trieste), and on May 1 he added that these forces had occupied Trzic (Monfalcone) and Goriza (Gorizia). On May 3, 1945, however, it was announced that a New Zealand division had occupied Trieste and received the surrender of its German garrison. In an official statement by the Allied authorities it was affirmed that all Italo-Yugoslav frontier questions could be settled at a peace conference but that in terms of the armistice concluded between the Allies and Marshal Badoglio (for Italy) the disputed territory was to be entrusted to an Allied military administration.

On May 14 the US Government expressed its opposition to "the unilateral action" taken by Marshal Tito in the Trieste area and asserted that the Marshal had himself, in negotiations with Field Marshal Alexander of Britain in February 1945, agreed to Allied military control in Istria and Trieste. In identical British and US notes presented in Belgrade on May 15 it was reported to have been stated (i) that military occupation in the wake of the enemy's surrender could not be allowed to prejudge final decisions; and (ii) that the disposal of disputed territories must form part of the general peace settlement.

In Yugoslavia the territories concerned were on May 14 described as "our own sovereign land snatched from Yugoslavia in the past". The Italian Government, on the other hand, insisted on the same day on a neutral administration of Trieste for the time being by the powers with which Italy had concluded the armistice, although it also declared its readiness to have the pre-war frontiers revised in "a pacific fair compromise carried out in the proper manner at the proper time". At the same time Palmiro Togliatti (the Italian Communist Party leader) stated that Trieste was Italian and its fate should not be compromised by unilateral actions and declarations.

The Yugoslav position was made clear in a reply to the Allied notes (of May 15), issued on May 19, 1945, as follows: "The Yugoslav Army, as one of the Allied armies, has equal rights to remain in the territory it has liberated in the struggle against the common enemy. . . . The fact that the population of these regions has for two years taken part in the war of liberation, that in its overwhelming majority it is Yugoslav, and that it has borne enormous sacrifices in the struggle against Italian and German Fascism, cannot be an obstacle to our demand to entrust our army with the organization of military administration and to entrust the People's Committee of Liberation, chosen from the people, with the organization of civil administration. The needs of our Allies concerning ports and communications have been completely safeguarded in the spirit of the talks between Marshal Tito and Field-Marshal Alexander. The honour of our country demands the presence of the

Yugoslav Army in Istria, Trieste, and on the Slovene coastline. The decisions of the peace conference, which will be final as regards the apportioning of the regions concerned, are in no way prejudiced. Yugoslavia is opposed to all unilateral declarations.''

In Trieste itself the Anglo-American forces which had entered the city did not interfere with the Yugoslav civil authority constituted by an Italo-Slovene Executive Committee with an Italian chairman and one Italian and one Slovene vice-chairman. This committee was, however, opposed by a Trieste National Committee of Liberation, which had sought refuge in Rome.

### Establishment of the Free Territory of Trieste

Subsequent negotiations between the Allied and Yugoslav authorities led to the conclusion of an agreement officially announced on June 9, 1945. This agreement on a temporary military administration of the area laid down (i) that part of Istria, including Trieste, the railways and roads from Trieste towards Gorizia, Caporetto and Tarvisio, as well as Pula and anchorages along the coast, should be under the control of the Supreme Allied Commander; (ii) that Yugoslav troops not exceeding 2,000 could occupy, in this area, a district to be selected by the Supreme Allied Commander but not have access to other areas; (iii) that the Supreme Commander would govern these areas through an Allied Military Government, while a small Yugoslav military mission might be attached to the Eighth Army headquarters as observers; (iv) that Yugoslav forces would be withdrawn from this area by June 12; (v) that the Yugoslav Government would return residents of the area whom it had deported or arrested (except persons possessing Yugoslav nationality in 1939) and make restitution for property confiscated or removed; and (vi) that the agreement was not to prejudice the ultimate disposal of the two zones thus created—Zone A (northern Istria, including the city of Trieste) under Allied Military Government and Zone B (southern Istria) under Yugoslav administration.

The agreement was implemented accordingly; Yugoslav forces were withdrawn from the Western zone within the time-limit set, and an agreement on the demarcation of the boundaries between the two zones was signed in Trieste on June 20, 1945. However, a four-power commission of experts (from Britain, France, the Soviet Union and the United States) appointed in March 1946 to make a final boundary delimitation failed to reach unanimous conclusions in a report published the following month. The Allied Council of Foreign Ministers, after considering the commission's report, approved (on July 12, 1946) an agreement on the constitution of a Free Territory of Trieste, with boundaries (based on a French recommendation) running from north of Duino to south of the port of Cittanuova (Novigrad), and with all territory east of the Free Territory and east of a northward extension of the latter's boundary to a point east of Tarvisio to be ceded to Yugoslavia (but with Monfalcone and Gorizia remaining Italian). Under this agreement the Free Territory was to have a permanent statute subject to the UN Security Council, which was to appoint a Governor after consultation with Italy and Yugoslavia, and legislative and executive authorities were to be established in the Free Territory on democratic lines and on the basis of universal suffrage. The agreement was, however, rejected as unacceptable by both Italy and Yugoslavia.

Nevertheless, the UN Security Council took over the administration of the Free Territory on Jan. 10, 1947. In the peace treaty signed in Paris on Feb. 10, 1947, by the Allied powers and Italy, the Free Territory of Trieste was declared demilitarized and neutral, and all its inhabitants were guaranteed equal rights and fundamental freedoms, with Italians resident in it becoming citizens of the Territory unless they opted for Italian citizenship, in which case they could be required to leave the Territory. However, no agreement was subsequently reached on the appointment of a Governor, as all candidates, although drawn mainly from neutral powers, proved unacceptable to either the Western powers or the Soviet Union. The treaty also provided for the cession of the Zara (Zadar) enclave, Lagosta (Lastovo) and other Dalmatian coast islands to Yugoslavia.

On March 20, 1948, the British, French and US Governments proposed to the Soviet Union and Italy that Trieste should be placed under Italian sovereignty on the grounds that the statute which it had been given under the UN Security Council had proved unworkable, and there had been frequent incidents between Italians and the Slovenes. In the latter context, the British head of the Allied administration reported to the Security Council that the Italians tended "to look to the democratic ideals of the West" while the Slovenes rallied "round the standard of communist totalitarianism". The Western powers' proposal was immediately rejected by Yugoslavia.

On June 25, 1948, the Anglo-American military authorities in Trieste issued a decree on reforms in Zone A of the Free Territory designed to bring its administration into line with Italian practices, and on July 3 they appointed an Italian as Trieste's first Mayor (*Sindaco*). As no agreement had been reached on the appointment of a Governor for the Free Territory between the Western powers and the Soviet Union, the UN Security Council shelved the question sine die on Feb. 21, 1949.

The first free elections in Trieste since 1922 were held in Zone A in June 1949. (i) In elections held on June 12 to the 60-member Trieste Municipal Council, 40 seats were gained by the Italian parties—25 of them by Christian Democrats; of the remaining 20 seats, 13 went to the "Cominform" wing of the Trieste Communist Party and only one to the "Tito" wing (which had been expelled from the party in August 1948, following the break between Tito and the Cominform); a Christian Democrat was thereupon elected Mayor of Trieste. (ii) In elections held on June 19 in five communes in Zone A the "Cominform" Communists polled 51 per cent of the vote, the combined Italian parties 30 per cent, the (anti-communist) Slovene Democrats about 6 per cent and the "Tito" Communists about 4 per cent.

On March 18, 1950, the Yugoslav Military Government of Zone B announced that the zone had been completely integrated in the Yugoslav economy, with all customs barriers having been abolished and the Yugoslav dinar having replaced the Italian lira as legal currency in July 1949. Elections held on April 16, 1950, for the Zonal Administrative Council of Zone B resulted (according to the State Electoral Commission in Belgrade) in the Italo-Slovene Popular Front (supporting the Yugoslav Government) gaining almost 89 per cent of the valid votes cast (with Socialists gaining 1.7 per cent and Christian Socials 1.1 per cent).

### Separate Developments in Zones A and B of the Free Territory

Meanwhile Count Carlo Sforza, the Italian Foreign Minister, had on April 8, 1950, offered to enter into direct negotiations with Yugoslavia, but had made this conditional on "substantial acceptance" by Yugoslavia that the whole of the Free Territory would have to be returned to Italy. The Soviet Government, on the other hand, on April 20 called for the withdrawal of Anglo-American troops from Trieste and the appointment of a Governor of the Free Territory, alleging in particular that the Western powers had unlawfully violated the Italian Peace Treaty as a Governor should have been appointed for the Territory by Sept. 15, 1947, and the troops withdrawn a few months later, and that the United States and Britain had converted Trieste into "an unlawful Anglo-American naval base" which constituted "a threat to the peace and security of Europe". The Soviet demand and allegations were rejected by the three Western powers on June 16.

An indication that Yugoslavia might adopt a compromise solution of the Trieste problem was first given on Sept. 21, 1951, when Edvard Kardelj, the Yugoslav Federal Secretary for Foreign Affairs, said in the National Assembly in Belgrade that, although Yugoslavia could not agree to the tripartite proposal for the reversal of Trieste to Italy, the question could not be solved by the incorporation of the Free Territory in Yugoslavia and that a third solution should therefore be sought. In February 1952 the Yugoslav Government submitted its proposals for a direct settlement of the Trieste question between Italy and Yugoslavia to the Italian Government. These proposals involved inter alia the integration of Zones A and B in one Free Territory to be placed under a Governor to be nominated alternately for three years by the Italian and Yugoslav Governments. These proposals were, however, rejected by the Italian Government on Feb. 25.

Anti-British and anti-Yugoslav demonstrations, accompanied by disturbances, took place in Trieste on March 20-27, 1952, when Italians, including the mayor of Trieste, called for the return to Italy not only of Trieste but of the whole of Istria. Talks were thereupon held in London between the British Foreign Secretary and the Italian ambassador on Italian proposals for the virtual transfer of Zone A to Italy, with Italian forces joining in its occupation within the framework of the North Atlantic Treaty Organization (NATO).

Under a memorandum of understanding signed in London on May 9, 1952, Italy was more fully associated with the administration of Zone A "in preparation for a final settlement", but the Yugoslav Government declared on May 13 that these changes should not have been made without Yugoslav consent and were "an unlawful and unilateral violation" of the international status of the zone. On May 15 the Yugoslav Military Government of Zone B announced a series of measures designed to link the zone more closely with Yugoslavia (providing inter alia for travel of Zone B residents to and from Yugoslavia without identity documents and for their travelling abroad on Yugoslav passports).

Further municipal elections held in Trieste and five smaller towns in Zone A took place on May 25, 1952, and had the following results:

|  | Whole of Zone A | Trieste City |
|---|---|---|
| Italian parties .. .. .. .. | 116,258 | 112,616 |
| Yugoslav parties .. .. .. | 12,116 | 8,483 |
| Independent Autonomy parties* .. | 27,094 | 26,907 |
| Cominform Communists and Nenni Socialists .. .. .. .. | 38,348 | 33,759 |
| Total of valid votes .. .. .. | 193,816 | 181,765 |

* Standing for the continued status of Trieste as an independent Free Territory.

In the Trieste City Council seats were thereupon distributed as follows: Christian Democrats 28, Socialist Party 5, Republicans 4, (right-wing) Italian Social Movement (MSI) 4, Liberals 3, Communists 6, Independence Party 5, others 5.

Administrative elections held in Zone B on Dec. 7, 1952, resulted, according to the Yugoslav Military Government, in 97 per cent of the 42,000 registered voters casting their votes for candidates of the Popular Front, except for 1.2 per cent of the votes declared invalid.

Following further conflicting statements made by Italian and Yugoslav leaders on the future of Trieste and a deterioration in relations between the two countries, the British and US Governments announced on Oct. 8, 1953, that they were "no longer prepared to maintain responsibility for the administration of Zone A" and that they had "therefore decided to terminate Allied Military Government, to withdraw their troops and, having in mind the predominantly Italian character of Zone A, to relinquish the administration of that zone to the Italian Government''. The Yugo-slav Government officially protested against the decision on Oct. 9, calling it (i) ''a unilateral violation of the Italian Peace Treaty of 1947 for the benefit of a power which committed aggression against Yugoslavia and waged war on the side of the Axis powers'' and (ii) ''unjust'' because it included the cession of territory inhabited by Slovenes and cut off Trieste from its natural hinterland.

The Anglo-US decision was also followed by anti-British, anti-American and anti-Italian speeches and demonstrations in Yugoslavia. After the (British) Allied Zone Commander had forbidden the hoisting of the Italian flags on official build-ings in Trieste, anti-Allied riots took place in the city, and also anti-British demonstra-tions in Italy, during November 1953. However, Italian and Yugoslav troops which had been deployed on both sides of the Italian-Yugoslav border since the end of August 1953 were, under an agreement reached on Dec. 5 of that year, withdrawn by Dec. 21.

## Four-Party Agreement reached in 1954

Following negotiations between Italy and Yugoslavia (partly sponsored by John Foster Dulles, US Secretary of State under President Eisenhower), a memorandum of understanding between the Italian, Yugoslav, British and US Governments was initialled in London on Oct. 5, 1954. Under this memorandum Italy was given con-trol of Zone A of the Free Territory of Trieste—except for a strip of about five square miles (13 sq km) inhabited mainly by Slovenes—while the whole of Zone B and the above strip were entrusted to Yugoslav control; the Italian Government undertook to maintain the free port at Trieste (as laid down in the Italian Peace Treaty); no residents of the Territory would be penalized for past political activities connected with the solution of the Trieste problem; arrangements for border traffic were to be negotiated; provision was made for the protection of persons wishing to move out of or into the area, and for that of their property; and a special statute regulated the rights of the population of the areas to be transferred, including the right to use their own language and the use of bilingual street names and other public inscriptions in districts where the ethnic minority constituted at least one-quarter of the local population.

The memorandum was subject to formal approval of all the signatories of the Italian Peace Treaty, including the Soviet Union, which officially took cognizance of it in a letter to the President of the UN Security Council on Oct. 14, 1954. Because of Soviet objections, the Security Council had the previous year, during sessions held between Oct. 20 and Dec. 15, failed to reach agreement on the Trieste problem and had postponed any further session after the United States had proposed that the Western powers should be given more time to reach an amicable solution.

The memorandum was implemented on Oct. 26, 1954, when the Allied Military Government in Zone A was terminated and an Italian Military Governor entered the zone. Three days later he was replaced by a Commissioner-General directly responsible to the Italian Prime Minister. On Oct. 14 the Italian Government had approved a comprehensive programme of economic aid and development for Trieste (and in 1963 Trieste became the capital of the newly-created special-statute region of Friuli-Venezia Giulia).

## Final Settlement of the Dispute under the 1975 Treaty of Osimo

The London memorandum of 1954 was a de facto settlement of the problem but not a de jure solution, as was emphasized by the Italian Government in February 1974, when in protest against Yugoslavia's erection of border markers between the two zones (indicating an international frontier) it pointed out that neither the peace treaty nor the 1954 London memorandum had extended Yugoslav territory ''to the

Italian territory designated as Zone B''. However, on Oct. 1, 1975, the Italian Government announced that it had established "the basis for agreement" with Yugoslavia, which would accept the status quo as permanent, with slight alterations to the frontier in favour of Italy near Gorizia, where an area of about 1¼ square miles (3.2 sq km) was ceded to Italy. The total area going to Italy of about 90 square miles (233 sq km) had a population of over 302,000 (275,000 of them in Trieste) and that going to Yugoslavia (about 200 square miles) a population of about 73,500. This settlement was formalized in the Treaty of Osimo, which was signed on Nov. 10, 1975, at Osimo (Ancona), together with 10 annexes and an agreement on the development of economic relations between the two countries (with four annexes).

The treaty laid down the new frontiers (in Art. 1) and specified (in Art. 3) that "the nationality of persons who were on June 10, 1940, Italian nationals and permanent residents in the territory . . . and that of their descendants born after June 10, 1940," would be regulated by the law of one or the other of the parties to the treaty in accordance with the place of residence of these persons at the moment of the entry into force of the treaty, but that such persons (constituting respectively the Italian or the Yugoslav minority) had the right to move to Yugoslav or Italian territory and would then be regarded as possessing the nationality relating to their new place of residence. The treaty also provided for the conclusion of an agreement on compensation payable to those whose property had been nationalized, expropriated or otherwise subjected to restrictive measures by the Yugoslav military, civil or local authorities since Yugoslav armed forces had entered the territory (Art. 4).

The economic co-operation agreement provided for the creation of an industrial zone, in the region of Sezana-Fernetti, partly on the Italian and partly on the Yugoslav side of the newly-agreed frontier, which covered about 20 square kilometres and would be an extension of the regime for commodities under the free port facilities of Trieste, with imports being duty- and tax-free and labour from both countries being employed. The details for the arrangements concerning this zone were laid down in a protocol valid for 30 years and tacitly renewable for five-year periods. The establishment of the zone had been approved by the European Commission and all the members of the European Communities.

The treaty and the agreement were approved by the two Houses of the Italian Parliament on Oct. 3 and 9, 1975, with only members of the (extreme right-wing) Italian Social Movement (MSI) and a few other parliamentarians from the border areas voting against approval.

In Trieste parts of the settlement were opposed by an autonomist *Per Trieste* movement, whose members objected in particular to the proposed industrial zone and which, in municipal elections held in Trieste in June 1978, gained about one-quarter of the votes and subsequently obtained the post of mayor. However, in an official communiqué issued on Oct. 12, 1979 (at the end of a visit to Belgrade by the Italian President), it was stated that since the conclusion of the Treaty of Osimo there no longer existed any difficulties between the two countries.

**H.W.D.**

# The Macedonian Question

The period since World War II has seen the revival of arguments, which first surfaced in the late 19th century, relating to the sovereignty and the ethnic character of Macedonia, an area lying in the central southern Balkans and centring on southern Yugoslavia and the Greek/Yugoslavian/Bulgarian borders. The Yugoslavian Federation at present includes a federated republic of Macedonia which incorporates part of what was until 1913 the territory of Macedonia; other parts of what was until then Macedonian land have been distributed between Greece and Bulgaria. At present none of these countries maintains any formal claim to the Macedonian territory of any other, but the underlying tensions over the sovereignty of the area have repeatedly come to light in the form of claims regarding the cultural and ethnic unity of the area; moreover, Yugoslavia sees in Bulgaria's historical attitudes elements of a territorial claim.

Yugoslavia maintains that Macedonians in all three countries have a common cultural and historical identity separate from that of the predominant populations of any of the surrounding republics, and formally recognizes Macedonians as comprising one of its federal nationalities. Bulgaria, however, refuses to recognize the existence of a Macedonian minority within its own borders and regards the Macedonian language as a Bulgarian dialect, giving rise to Yugoslavian complaints that it is suppressing the Macedonian culture. Greece for its part similarly refuses to accept the existence of a true Macedonian minority within its territory, claiming rather that its Slav-speaking minority living in former Macedonian areas is in fact

**Map 11 Present territorial relationship of Yugoslavia, Albania, Greece and Bulgaria with reference to the Macedonian question. The borders of the Yugoslav republic of Macedonia are shown in map 1 on page 3.**

composed of ethnic Greeks who were forced by centuries of Slavic domination to relinquish their original Greek language. Greece, Yugoslavia and Bulgaria all base their cases to some extent on the findings of archaeologists and of art and architectural historians who have, however, to date arrived at no consensus as to the cultural unity of the Macedonian people as propounded by Yugoslavia.

The main developments in the post-war debate on the Macedonian issue have centred on Yugoslavia and Bulgaria, with Greece regarding itself as only peripherally involved. The Yugoslavian/Bulgarian debate has often been highlighted by the continuous and periodically intensifying differences between Yugoslavia and the countries of the Warsaw Pact, to which Bulgaria belongs. It also received a new impetus in the late 1960s when Bulgarian historians began to present Macedonian historical figures as Bulgarians, and to celebrate the short-lived 1878 Treaty of San Stefano (which had created a "Greater Bulgaria" including Macedonia and part of Albania, but which had in the same year been drastically altered at the Congress of Berlin to reduce the area of Bulgarian territory). Yugoslavia sees in this "chauvinist" Bulgarian attitude an implicit territorial claim by Bulgaria to the whole of Macedonia, and the resulting escalation of polemics over the issue has since then been a serious obstacle to international co-operation in the Balkans.

### The Treaty of San Stefano and the Congress of Berlin

Macedonia was inhabited from the seventh century BC onwards by Greek, Thracian and Illyrian peoples, achieving its peak under Philip and Alexander of Macedon before its incorporation in the second century BC into the Roman Empire. The influx of Turkish, Bulgarian and Slavic peoples began in the sixth century AD, and in the ninth and 10th centuries Macedonia belonged to the Bulgarian empire, although in 1018 it returned to the Byzantine empire. In 1230 the second Bulgarian empire recaptured its southern part (except Salonika); it then passed to the Serbians, but by 1371 the whole of Macedonia had fallen to the Ottoman Turks (who controlled it until 1912). The rest of the Bulgarian empire fell to the Turks in 1396 and for almost 500 years thereafter Bulgaria had no independent political existence.

Bulgarian aspirations to the restoration of the Bulgarian state re-emerged during the early 19th century with the decline of the Ottoman empire; a revolt against the Turkish rulers in May 1876 was put down with much brutality against the Bulgarian population. In the same year (amid general signs of unrest in Macedonia, Serbia and Albania) Serbia and Montenegro, supported by Bulgarian volunteers, declared war on Turkey, as did Imperial Russia in 1877. The combined Russian and Slav forces achieved notable victories against the Turks,[1] leading on March 3, 1878, to the signature of the Treaty of San Stefano, which created inter alia the principality of Bulgaria. The new principality, which continued under the suzerainty of the Turkish Porte, was to comprise some three-fifths of the Balkan peninsula and was to include parts of Serbia, almost all of Macedonia with its extensive Aegean coastal territories except for Salonika and Khalkidiki, as well as part of the present Albanian state.

The European powers expressed strong concern that the new greater Bulgarian state, with its population of some 4,000,000, would prove to be dangerously dependent on Russia, and pressed at the Congress of Berlin for a reduction of its size. Consequently the final treaty signed at the congress on July 13, 1878, returned Macedonia to Turkey, limiting Bulgaria to most of the territory between the Danube and the Balkan mountains; the area between the Balkan mountains and the Rhodope mountains became the autonomous province of Eastern Rumelia,

---

[1] See also section on Romania-Soviet Union, pages 81-86.

subject to the Turks but under a Christian governor-general. Bulgaria annexed Eastern Rumelia in 1885, and in 1909 the powers recognized the independent kingdom of Bulgaria including Eastern Rumelia, which territory currently forms the southern half of Bulgaria.

## The Division of Macedonia

The return of Macedonia to Turkey at the Congress of Berlin caused great resentment in the Balkans and resulted in widespread unrest in Macedonia which contributed considerably to the eventual overthrow of Turkish rule during the First Balkan War of 1912. Resistance to the Turks was conducted by a wide range of groups pursuing widely varying aims. The first was pro-Bulgarian "Internal Macedonian Revolutionary Organization (IMRO)" which was formed in 1893 and which campaigned under the slogan "Macedonia for the Macedonians". Two years later the Bulgarians formed a "Supreme Committee for Macedonia and Adrianopolis" (the latter being the present-day Turkish border town of Edirne); known as the "Komitajis", this movement campaigned for the restoration of the Treaty of San Stefano and attempted to persuade Macedonians to declare themselves Bulgarians. Also in the 1890s Serbia sent its "Chety" to Macedonia to instigate pro-Serbian unrest, while the Greeks created a "National Society" whose guerrillas were largely responsible for the outbreak of the Greek-Turkish war in 1897. In 1903 the "Komitajis" instigated an uprising in all parts of Macedonia.

In March 1912 Serbia and Bulgaria reached basic agreement, under Russian auspices, on the eventual division of Macedonia, and thereupon, joined by Greece, formed an alliance which later that year declared war on Turkey. They achieved considerable victories in the First Balkan War, liberating inter alia Serbia, Macedonia and Northern Greece and driving the Turks back almost as far as Constantinople (Istanbul), but disagreed almost immediately over the actual division of Macedonia. In June 1913 Bulgaria therefore attacked Greece and Serbia, precipitating the Second Balkan War, but was rapidly defeated; the originally agreed division of Macedonia was restored, although Bulgaria ceded additional territory to Romania (which, seeing Bulgaria's weakness, had simultaneously attacked from the north).

The peace treaty signed in Bucharest on Aug. 10, 1913, established basically the present Macedonian borders of Greece and Bulgaria, while Serbian Macedonia was later to become the Yugoslavian republic of Macedonia. Under the treaty Greece received Aegean Macedonia, amounting to 34,602 square kilometres and including all of the Aegean coastal area, while Serbia received Vardar Macedonia (northern and central Macedonia, amounting to 25,744 square kilometres) and Bulgaria received Pirin Macedonia, the eastern region amounting to 6,789 square kilometres. (N.B. Greece does not recognize the designations "Aegean", "Vardar" or "Pirin" Macedonia, since it regards the political use of the term "Macedonia" as a Yugoslavian/Bulgarian usurpation of a Greek concept, and as suggesting what it claims is a non-existent historical unity; it therefore accepts, as exclusively geographical concepts, the terms "Greek Macedonia", "Yugoslavian Macedonia" and "Bulgarian Macedonia".)

Bulgaria, thus thwarted in its aspirations to direct access to the Aegean, sought redress by joining the Central Powers in World War I, and indeed occupied Aegean Macedonia from 1915 to 1918. However, the Paris Peace Conference of 1919 decided broadly in favour of the 1913 division of Macedonia and thus confirmed what are essentially the present-day borders in the region, while the treaties of Neuilly and Lausanne provided for exchanges of populations between the relevant Balkan states. This exchange resulted in what Greece now describes as a highly homogeneous population in Aegean (Greek) Macedonia, in support of which claim it has quoted figures compiled by the League of Nations showing that between 1912 and 1926 the proportion of Greeks in the area rose from 42.6 per cent to 88.8 per cent; the same figures show that the proportion of Moslems fell from 39.4 per cent to 0.1 per cent, Bulgarians from 9.9 per cent to 5.1 per cent, and miscellaneous others from 8.1 per cent to 6.0 per cent. A Greek census of 1928 is reported to have found that of a national population of 6,032,761 only 81,984 (1.36 per cent) were Slavophones.

## World War II and the Balkan Federation

Although Bulgarian-inspired unrest in non-Bulgarian Macedonia continued throughout the 1920s, the Macedonian issue remained largely dormant in the years before the outbreak of World War II. In 1941 Bulgaria joined the Axis Powers in the tripartite Pact and permitted German forces to use its territory as a base for attacks on Yugoslavia, receiving in return permission to annex Greek Thrace and Yugoslavian Macedonia. On Sept. 5, 1944, however, the Soviet Union declared war on Bulgaria, whereupon it abruptly changed sides and declared war the next day on Germany. Accounts of the ensuing period have varied considerably. The Bulgarians claim that their forces made a major and decisive contribution to the liberation of Macedonia and Serbia from the Nazis; on the other hand, some relatively recent Yugoslavian sources have described this account as a falsification and have even suggested that Yugoslavian partisans were opposed by pro-fascist troops from Bulgaria until the end of the war.

After Georgi Dimitrov became the Communist Prime Minister of Bulgaria in October 1946, a period of rapprochement with Yugoslavia began. In 1947 Dimitrov visited Marshal Tito, his Yugoslavian counterpart and personal friend, and the two discussed plans for the creation of a Balkan Federation including Bulgaria, a reunited Macedonia, Greek Thrace and all the Yugoslavian republics. The plan was strongly opposed by the Soviet Union, however, and in 1948 Yugoslavia was expelled from the Soviet-dominated Cominform, which thereupon commenced a prolonged anti-Yugoslavian campaign (although Dimitrov himself, who died in 1949, did not participate in it). Greece had meanwhile also opposed the planned Balkan Federation, and protested throughout the period 1944-47 that Yugoslavia, Bulgaria and Albania were harbouring communist guerrillas in the Greek border regions and thereby furthering the communist cause in the Greek civil war (a charge which was supported in 1947 by a United Nations commission of inquiry).

## Development of Balkan Relations, 1949-66

Although in August 1947 Bulgaria and Yugoslavia had signed a treaty of mutual assistance, this was revoked on Oct. 3, 1949, by Bulgaria following the denunciation of Yugoslavia by all of the other Cominform countries. Yugoslavia responded by accusing Bulgaria of sabotaging the proposed Balkan Federation by demanding an excessively large say in it, and of expansionism and provoking border incidents. Bulgaria in 1949-50 tried and executed Traicho Kostov, a former Deputy Prime Minister and secretary of the Bulgarian Communist Party (BCP), for allegedly plotting to overthrow the Bulgarian Government with Yugoslavian assistance, to murder Dimitrov and to sabotage Bulgaria's trade links with other Cominform countries, as well as promoting "the absorption of Bulgaria by Yugoslavia". Yugoslavia replied to this and other political trials with similar trials, and although Kostov was subsequently rehabilitated by the BCP in 1956 lasting damage was done to relations between the two countries.

During the next 10 years, however, relations in the Balkans showed signs of relaxation. Greece re-opened full diplomatic relations with Yugoslavia in 1952 and with Bulgaria in 1954, and a Treaty of Alliance (Balkan Pact) was signed in August

1954 by Yugoslavia, Greece and Turkey (although it had collapsed by 1960 because differences between Greece and Turkey over Cyprus had effectively paralysed its Council of Ministers and its Secretariat). Bulgaria agreed with Greece in 1953, 1955 and 1958 on the avoidance and settlement of frontier incidents, although Greek suspicion of its neighbours was reflected in its continued opposition to the holding of various proposed Balkan ministerial conferences.

Bulgaria began a new anti-Yugoslavia campaign in September 1958, when Dimitri Ganev, a leading member of the Bulgarian Politburo, accused the Belgrade Government of "denying the national individuality of the Macedonian people" by refusing to accept their alleged communality with the Bulgarians and of forcing upon its own Macedonians an "artificial language" bearing more resemblance to Serbian than to their native tongue. Soviet concern at this deterioration in relations was expressed in May 1962 during a visit to Sofia by Nikita Khrushchev, the Soviet party leader and Prime Minister. Consequently Bulgaria and Yugoslavia adopted more conciliatory paths, signing on June 28, 1964, 12 agreements on war reparations, joint developments and other matters, while Bulgaria also agreed in 1963 with Greece on an arrangement giving it direct access to the Mediterranean via the free port area of Salonika harbour. Yugoslavia received a similar facility at Salonika in 1975.

### Deterioration of Bulgarian-Yugoslavian Relations over Macedonian Issue

In December 1967 the BCP approved a speech by Todor Zhivkov, the Bulgarian Prime Minister and First Secretary of the BCP, in which he called for the intensification of "patriotic education" concentrating inter alia "on the golden centuries of Bulgarian national history, their kings and emperors", adding the observation that "we Bulgarians are the descendents of the Thracian culture". During the following months Bulgarian publishers began to produce a number of books referring to allegedly Bulgarian characters who were normally regarded by Yugoslavia as Macedonians. Although Yugoslavia immediately expressed its reservations at this practice, on March 2 and 3, 1968, demonstrations were held in the Bulgarian capital to celebrate the 90th anniversary of the Treaty of San Stefano; in May, moreover, the Bulgarian *Narodna Kultura* was alleged to have carried an article describing the Yugoslavian Macedonians as slaves to the Serbs. Yugoslavian press sources regarded these actions as open provocations and reacted angrily, countering the Bulgarian argument that there were no Macedonians in Bulgaria with the claim that a 1946 census had shown that about 70 per cent of Pirin residents had described themselves as Macedonians. (In the 1956 Bulgarian census only 179,000 or about 10 per cent fewer than in 1946 had so described themselves; the 1965 census had shown only 8,750 Macedonians, while none at all were recorded in 1975. This fall in numbers was attributed to the wording of the census forms and to a general loss of Macedonian identity in Bulgaria, rather than to any major demographic development.)

A visit to Yugoslavia in December 1969 by the Bulgarian Foreign Minister, Ivan Bashev, for discussions on the Macedonian question led to such heated debate that the discussions were broken off without a concluding communiqué being issued. Zhivkov proposed further talks in July 1970, but a proposed discussion with President Tito did not take place because of the Bulgarian insistence during preliminary rounds that Yugoslavian Macedonians were in fact Bulgarians. President Tito, speaking at Skopje (the Macedonian capital) on Nov. 10, 1972, referred to the Bulgarian attitudes as "illusions which are founded on a distant past" and indicated that they still represented a major obstacle to satisfactory relations.

Further bilateral discussions took place in Bulgaria in February 1973 and in Belgrade in November 1975, but led to no progress on the issue. Stane Dolanc, then a secretary of the Yugoslavian League of Communist Youth, referred in a speech on Oct. 1, 1976, to the policies of "countries where not even the fundamental rights of nationalities are respected", adding: "There are countries—unfortunately even among our own neighbours—in which the policy of denationalization of our minorities is even today pursued more or less openly and brutally." Although each side continued to stress that it was making no territorial claims against the other, Yugoslavia was by this time regularly publishing allegations that the Bulgarian Government, by intimidation, resettlement and indoctrination, was attempting to eradicate the notion of a Macedonian nationality. A further round of talks in Bulgaria on Sept. 22-28, 1976, had again produced no significant progress on the issue.

Bulgaria took a new initiative on June 15, 1978, when Zhivkov offered in a speech at Blagoevgrad (the administrative capital of Pirin Macedonia) to sign with Yugoslavia a bilateral treaty on the final recognition of the Bulgarian/Yugoslavian border. Furthermore, on July 24 (the day before the opening of a conference of the non-aligned countries in Belgrade) he presented a lengthy memorandum to the Yugoslavian Government containing an undertaking to respect the borders and autonomous character of Yugoslavian Macedonia. At the same time, however, he added that Bulgaria could not accept "the formulation of the Macedonian nation on an anti-Bulgarian basis involving the distortion of well-known historical facts", and asserted that the problem of the alleged Macedonian minority in Bulgaria had been solved by the only people with the right to do so, namely the Bulgarians.

President Tito indicated in a speech on Nov. 26, 1978, his intention to avoid further escalation of the dispute, but Bulgarian/Yugoslavian relations suffered another setback in January 1979 with the publication of (i) a 900-page Bulgarian documentation on the "indissoluble links" between the Macedonians and the Bulgarians from 681 AD onwards, and (ii) the memoirs of Mrs Tsola Dragoicheva, a member of the Politburo of the BCP, who claimed that Macedonia had been "snatched" from Bulgaria at the 1878 Congress of Berlin and again in 1945. Later in the year, in response to strong Yugoslavian protests, Mrs Dragoicheva added that Yugoslavia, in the guise of concern for Pirin Macedonians, was encroaching on the territorial and ethnic integrity of Bulgaria.

Konstantinos Karamanlis, then Prime Minister (and later President) of Greece, held talks with Todor Zhivkov in Athens on April 29-30, 1979, during which the former was understood to have expressed concern at the escalation of tensions over the Macedonian issue and to have appealed for the multilateral solution of problems in the Balkans. Bulgaria and Yugoslavia subsequently resumed discussions in Belgrade during June 1979, but failed to reach any resolution of the Macedonian question. On Aug. 2 of that year Bulgaria protested in strong terms at Yugoslavia's decision to celebrate Nicholas Vapsarov as a prominent Macedonian poet, claiming that this writer was in fact Bulgarian.

The two sides have continued to be sharply at odds over their respective historical approaches to the Macedonian question in particular and Bulgarian-Yugoslavian relations in general. Thus on Feb. 11, 1981, the official Yugoslavian news agency Tanjug issued a strong criticism of an extensive article published in the latest issue of *Vekove* (the journal of the Society of Bulgarian Historians) under the title "Yugoslav historiography on Bulgarian-Yugoslavian relations, 1941-44". According to Tanjug, the author of the article claimed that the Yugoslavian press and publishers were continuing "a rabid anti-Bulgarian campaign to falsify the historic past and to appropriate the history and the cultural heritage of the Bulgarian people" with the aim of imposing on Bulgaria the Yugoslavian nationalistic and hegemonistic line on the Macedonian question.

**M.W.**

# Romania-Soviet Union

The territorial settlement established between Romania and the Soviet Union after World War II was intended to be a definitive and final solution of longstanding Romanian-Russian conflict over the eastern part of Moldavia (Bessarabia) and certain other territories which had been under Romanian sovereignty in the inter-war period but which were now incorporated into the Soviet Union. In the post-war period the Communist Government of Romania has consistently stressed that it has no territorial dispute with its fellow Warsaw Pact member, but the "Bessarabian question" has nevertheless remained an important underlying factor in Romanian-Soviet relations. Within what is now the Moldavian Soviet Socialist Republic the predominantly Romanian population has not only resisted Russification but has also shown increasing support for Romanian nationalist and irredentist ideas. Since the late 1960s, moreover, the Romanian Government has steadily distanced itself from Soviet authority and a number of Romanian publications have emphasized the historical unity of the Romanian-speaking peoples. (For position of Bessarabia, see map on page 52.)

The present-day Bessarabian question is essentially a continuation of disagreements which arose as far back as the early 18th century, when Tsarist Russia first began to threaten what were then the Turkish-dominated principalities of Moldavia and Walachia. Since 1812 Russia, and subsequently the Soviet Union, have held almost continuous sovereignty over most of Bessarabia—the exceptions being the periods 1918-1940 and 1941-1944, when it was held by Romania. However, the long years of Russian rule have made little impact on the essentially Romanian character of the people, almost two-thirds of whom still speak a Romanian dialect. The result has been prolonged dissension over this densely populated and fertile piece of land, in the course of which some parts have changed hands up to seven times since 1812 as a result of successive conquests, agreements and ultimatums.

Up to 1812 Moldavia was a Turkish-dominated principality reaching westwards from the right bank of the Dnestr (Dniester) river across the Prut river as far as the Carpathians; in that year, however, Russia annexed the area between the Dnestr and the Prut (i.e. Bessarabia), the rest of Moldavia remaining under Turkish suzerainty until it became part of the independent state of Romania which received international recognition in 1878. Some 40 years later Bessarabia was among the territories acquired by Romania at the end of World War I and was thereupon reintegrated into Romanian Moldavia. The Soviet Union refused to recognize the transfer and was ceded Bessarabia (as well as Northern Bukovina) in mid-1940 after presenting an ultimatum to the Romanian Government. Although Romania reconquered Bessarabia and Northern Bukovina in 1941 as Germany's ally in the war against the Soviet Union (and also annexed a large additional tract of Soviet territory), the eventual Soviet victory in Eastern Europe again forced Romania to relinquish the disputed territories and to accept the incorporation of Bessarabia into the Moldavian Soviet Socialist Republic (SSR)—the post-war status quo being formally recognized by Romania in 1947. Thus the term Moldavia, as used in the context of Romania, nowadays means the area immediately to the west of the Prut.

### Geographical and Demographic Aspects of the Region
The Moldavian SSR (essentially Bessarabia) covers an area of some 33,700 square

kilometres to the east of the River Prut. It is bounded in the east by the Dnestr river valley, although its territory does not, as formerly, follow the Dnestr down to the Black Sea but turns south-west before reaching Odessa and joins the Prut at Galati. The area is of particular importance in agricultural terms, producing important tobacco, grape and rose-oil crops, as well as sunflower seeds, maize and wheat, and is also a major producer of wines and of preserved foods.

The January 1979 census showed a population of 3,948,000, of whom the great majority live on the land. Clear cultural, economic and political distinctions must be drawn, however, between the Romanian-speaking Moldavians (who according to a 1970 survey made up 64.6 per cent of the population of the republic), the Ukrainians (14.2 per cent in 1970), the Russians (11.6 per cent in 1970, but rapidly increasing in numbers), the Turkish-speaking Gagauzi (3.5 per cent in 1970), the Jews (2.7 per cent in 1970) and the Bulgarians (2.1 per cent in 1970).

The Moldavian SSR has a very high birth rate (more than 20 live births per thousand of the population each year) and a low death rate, and the consequent increase in the population has been accentuated since the 1950s by the development of urban centres, in which the great majority of the Russians have come to live. Thus, although Russians accounted for only 11.6 per cent of the population in 1970, 77 per cent of them lived in urban areas (compared with 67 per cent in 1959). On the other hand, only 18 per cent of Moldavians lived in the towns in 1970, compared with 10 per cent in 1959. The growth in the proportion of Russians living in the towns appears to be a continuing development, and has been accompanied inter alia by the appointment of Russians to many, or indeed most, of the key positions in local administration. This latter process has applied particularly to the Moldavian Communist Party, of which 7.3 per cent of all Russians in the Moldavian SSR were members in 1970, compared with 3.8 per cent of all Ukrainians and only 1.3 per cent of the Moldavian majority.

It has been claimed in some Romanian quarters that the growing influence of Russian speakers in the Moldavian SSR has a political character. Whatever the truth of such allegations, it is clear that an attempt has been made to establish a new national culture within the Moldavian SSR which largely overlooks the ever-present Romanian influence in the traditional Bessarabian culture. For example, the Romanian dialect still spoken by much of the population has been renamed "Moldavian" and is listed by the Soviet Union among its national languages; "Moldavian" differs from Romanian only in that it is nowadays written in the Cyrillic alphabet instead of the Roman letters previously used, and Moldavians have no difficulty in understanding Romanian radio or television broadcasts. These factors apart, however, Moldavian links with Romania have been largely suppressed since the Soviet annexation of Bessarabia.

A consequence of this policy has been what some Romanians have described as the cultural isolation of the Soviet Moldavians. More than 55 per cent of the news-papers and periodicals on sale are in Russian, a language which in 1970 only a very small proportion of Moldavians living in the Moldavian SSR gave as their first language and only 33.9 per cent as a fluent second language. In the same census 97.7 per cent of Moldavians living in the Moldavian SSR gave "Moldavian" as their first language, but although illiteracy (formerly widespread) has been virtually eliminated since 1946, the absence of important writers or other artists using the "Moldavian" language has been noticeable.

### Historical Background to the Bessarabian Question

Bessarabia was until 1812 part of the autonomous principality of Moldavia under Ottoman suzerainty; in that year it was formally ceded by the Peace of Bucharest to the Russian empire (whose troops had in fact invaded it many times since the early 18th century and which had occupied almost all of Moldavia and Walachia since defeating the Turks in 1806). War broke out again between Russia and Turkey in 1828, whereupon Russian troops again occupied all of Moldavia and Walachia, and remained in a protective capacity until 1834, by which time the Turkish Porte had approved the promulgation of constitutions for the two principalities (the Moldavian territory extending only as far east as the Prut and thus excluding Bessarabia). The Russians returned in 1848 to put down a peasants' rebellion and stayed this time until 1851.

Throughout this period the Russians had retained the sovereignty of Bessarabia itself; however, under the 1856 Treaty of Paris which ended the Crimean War they returned a strip of southern Bessarabia to Moldavia (then still under Turkish suzerainty), and Moldavia and Walachia were placed under a form of international guarantee. The Turkish divans were dissolved in 1858, and in 1859 the state of Romania was created from the two provinces; however, when Romanian independence was formally recognized at the Congress of Berlin in 1878 the whole of Bessarabia was declared Russian territory. Romania protested at this decision, since it had expected to be awarded the Bessarabian territory in return for having joined the recent war against Turkey and for having signed in 1877 a secret pact allowing Russian troops free passage against the Turks. Although Romania received instead the northern Dobruja (whose Romanian population was small) its dissatisfaction with the 1878 settlement gave rise to an irredentist campaign for the return of Bessarabia.

Since 1812 Russia had pursued a policy of Russification of Bessarabia, largely through resettlement; however, by 1917 at least two-thirds of the population were still Romanian, and in December 1917, shortly after the October Revolution, the dominant and anti-Bolshevik political forces in Bessarabia set up a Council whose main purpose was to facilitate the eventual return of Bessarabia to Romania. In November 1918 it voted for unconditional union with Romania, and in December 1918 Romania therefore annexed Bessarabia. The fusion, which was formalized in the Treaty of St Germain, has never been recognized by the Soviet Union, which in October 1924 demonstrated its position by setting aside a narrow strip of Ukrainian land to the east of the Dnestr for the establishment of the "Autonomous Moldavian Soviet Socialist Republic".

The new republic, whose constitution was approved in April 1925, was clearly intended eventually to incorporate Bessarabia and indeed subsequently formed the basis of the Soviet annexation in 1940. This followed the presentation on June 26, 1940, of a direct Soviet ultimatum to King Carol of Romania and his Government demanding the cession of Bessarabia and Northern Bukovina and claiming that in 1918 "Romania took advantage of the military weakness of Russia and robbed the USSR by force of part of her territory—namely Bessarabia—and thus broke the century-old unity of Bessarabia". The demand for the cession of Northern Bukovina was based on the Soviet claim that "the predominant majority is connected with the Soviet Ukraine by common historical destinies" and that the two areas were similar in their language and national composition. (Bukovina as a whole had been a Moldavian province until 1777, when the Ottoman empire had ceded it to the Austrians, and had thereafter been administered by the Austro-Hungarian empire until its transfer to Romania in November 1919; Northern Bukovina had a mixed population consisting of Romanian, Jewish, Ukrainian and Russian elements.)

Faced with the June 26 ultimatum Romania was obliged to cede Bessarabia and Northern Bukovina to the Soviet Union, whose troops occupied them within seven days. Most of Bessarabia was thereupon joined to the former Autonomous Moldavian SSR and became the Moldavian SSR, although one southern area of about

1,900 square miles (5,000 sq km) on the Black Sea coast was incorporated into the Ukraine. Romanian nationalists have since claimed that the Soviet annexations of 1940 were carried out in accordance with secret provisions of the non-aggression pact signed in August 1939 between Germany and the Soviet Union. At about the same time Romania was forced to cede Northern Transylvania to Hungary and part of the Dobruja to Bulgaria, losing altogether about one-third of its territory and over 6,000,000 subjects.

The period immediately preceding World War II had been characterized in Romania by considerable political confusion. A succession of short-lived governments, many of them anti-semitic and extreme right-wing in character, culminated on July 4, 1940 (i.e. directly after the cession of Bessarabia and Northern Bukovina), in the formation of a fascist Government under Ion Gigurtu, who intensified Romania's links with Nazi Germany. Gigurtu was in turn replaced on Sept. 5, 1940, by Gen. Ion Antonescu (whose similarly fascist Government was to remain in power until 1944), whereupon King Carol abdicated and was succeeded by King Michael.

Romania quickly declared its support for Germany and in June 1941 declared war on the Soviet Union. A joint Romanian/German advance swiftly captured Bessarabia and made rapid progress deep into Soviet territory, enabling the Romanians to set up the province of Transdnistria in the land between the Dnestr and the Bug (nowadays mostly in the Ukraine). By 1944, however, the Red Army was advancing into Romania, and on Aug. 23, 1944, the Antonescu Government was overthrown. In September 1944, following negotiations with the Allies, Romania signed an armistice with the Soviet Union in which it recognized the legality of the 1940 Soviet annexation of Bessarabia and Northern Bukovina, and the acknowledgement was further confirmed in the Soviet-Romanian peace treaty of 1947. The consolidation of effective power in the hands of the Soviet-backed Romanian Communists culminated in the abdication of King Michael in December 1947 and the declaration in early 1948 of the Romanian People's (later Socialist) Republic within its present borders.

### Post-war Developments and the Resurgence of Moldavian Nationalism

A Treaty of Alliance was signed between Romania and the Soviet Union on Feb. 4, 1948, in which each country undertook to adhere to the principles of mutual respect for the independence and sovereignty of the other, and to refrain from interference in the other's internal affairs. The Treaty was valid for 20 years, and on its expiry in 1968 was replaced by a similar 20-year agreement. In 1955 Romania joined Albania, Bulgaria, Czechoslovakia, the German Democratic Republic, Hungary, Poland and the Soviet Union in the inauguration of the Warsaw Pact.

From 1956 onwards, however, Romania began to distance itself from the Soviet conception of the internationalist character of communism, and on numerous occasions expressed clearly nationalistic attitudes. At the time of the Hungarian uprising in October 1956 the Romanian Workers' Party (as the Communist Party was then called) expressed its belief in "differing forms and methods for the construction of socialism", and in December 1964 Romania caused considerable offence to the Soviet Union by its publication of one of the works of Marx, his *Notes on the Romanians*, in which he had strongly condemned Tsarist Russia's annexation of Bessarabia in 1812 and had argued for the indivisibility of the Romanian people. Although the work was not openly circulated in the Moldavian SSR, its content became known there, leading the first secretary of the Moldavian Communist Party, Ivan Bodyul, to make a speech at a 1965 party congress in which he strongly denounced the book as well as all Moldavians who accepted its implicit endorsement of the Romanian claim to Bessarabia. In 1966, moreover, documents were published by the Soviet Union indicating that in 1940 the Romanian Communists had welcomed the Soviet annexation.

By late 1966, however, Soviet concern had clearly increased, and on Dec. 15-17 a "Scientific Conference on Problems of the Development and Reconciliation of Soviet Nations and Peoples" was held at Tiraspol in the Moldavian SSR. In February 1967 Ivan Bodyul toured the republic with Alexander Shelepin, a member of the Politburo of the Soviet Communist Party (CPSU), and subsequently called for "an elucidation in depth of the real history of the Moldavian people" since, he said, "our children and future generations must know that their fathers did not conceive of a life for themselves outside Russia". In an ensuing intensification of historical argument the Soviet Communist side frequently took issue with Romanian portrayals of Moldavian history.

Meanwhile, the Romanian position had become more openly nationalistic with the election of Nicolae Ceausescu as First Secretary of the Romanian Communist Party (as it now became) at the July 1965 party congress. Ceausescu promoted the ideas of increased economic independence, protested at the numbers of Soviet-appointed officials in his administration, and at one point in 1966 proposed that, in view of the reduced danger of international conflict, both the Warsaw Pact and the North Atlantic Treaty Organization should be simultaneously dissolved. At the 1965 party congress he quoted a text of Engels which implied that Romanian communism had already arisen by 1888 and that it had thus preceded Russian communism. The revised Romanian Constitution of 1965 referred to the "inalienable and indivisible" territory of the Republic and dropped the specific pledge of alliance with the Soviet Union which had featured in the 1952 Constitution. Moreover, in 1968 Romania joined with Yugoslavia in strongly denouncing the intervention of Warsaw Pact troops in Czechoslovakia, while Soviet-Romanian relations were further strained as a result of Ceausescu's visit to China.

Following the virtual abolition in March 1974 of preliminary censorship in the Romanian press, a book was published in April 1976 which was widely interpreted as re-opening the Bessarabian question. The book, entitled *Political Life in Romania between 1918 and 1921*, pointed out that a Tsarist census carried out in 1817 had found that 87 per cent of the Bessarabian population were Romanian. Meanwhile, there were continued unofficial reports of nationalist unrest in the Moldavian SSR, where Ivan Bodyul had informed the 24th local party congress (in April 1971) that "harmful phenomena" had recently occurred, instigated by countries promoting "so-called special roads to socialism" (regarded as a clear reference to Romania). *Pravda* had also attacked those who presented what it termed a distorted view of socialist reality through their adherence to outmoded traditions.

On June 4, 1976, Ceausescu asserted that Romania had "no territorial or other problem with the Soviet Union or with the other neighbouring socialist countries", and in a further apparent attempt to pacify the Soviet Union he visited the Moldavian SSR on Aug. 2 before passing on to the Crimea on an official visit. On the Soviet side, Brezhnev himself stated during a visit to Bucharest on Nov. 22-24, 1976, that there were "no important unsolved problems between our two countries", and on Nov. 24 he signed with Ceausescu a "statement on the further development of co-operation and on fraternal friendship between the Communist Party of the Soviet Union and the Romanian Communist Party, and between the Soviet Union and Romania". Ivan Bodyul also visited Romania in December 1976 and said that the two sides would expand their contacts in all fields.

Nevertheless, notwithstanding the absence of government-level conflict on territorial issues, evidence continued to surface concerning underlying Romanian attitudes to the post-war settlement of boundaries. In mid-1979 two Romanian historians, Stefan Lache and Gheorghe Tsutsiu, published a controversial book entitled *Romania and the Paris Peace Conference of 1946* in which they sharply attacked the manner in which the Soviet Union had negotiated and carried out the annexation of Bessarabia and Northern Bukovina in 1940. Alleging the "spoliation" of Romania's territory, the book claimed that, in view of the Aug. 23, 1944, overthrow of the Antonescu Government, the advancing Soviet troops should have treated Romania as a country which had "freely decided to put an end to the war", instead of which they had treated it as a "conquered country". (Ceausescu himself had also dwelt on this theme as early as 1965.)

Against a background of continued unofficial reports through the 1970s of sporadic unrest in the Moldavian SSR and other Soviet republics, new constitutions were promulgated on April 12-21, 1978, for each of the union republics, it being claimed that the main theme of the new texts was the extension of the rights of national minorities in the Soviet Union. Like those of several other republics, the Constitution for the Moldavian SSR, which was promulgated on April 15, included a provision (Article 103), according to which the laws of the republic, decrees and other notices issued by the Supreme Soviet (Parliament) of the Republic, were to be published in both the Russian and (in this case) the "Moldavian" languages.

M.W.

# Spain-United Kingdom (Gibraltar)

British sovereignty over Gibraltar—a strategic naval base on the tip of southern Spain acquired by Britain in 1713—has in the last 30 years been persistently disputed by Spain, which claims it as part of its national territory. In 1969 the land frontier between Spain and Gibraltar was closed and all other communications cut by Gen. Franco in pursuance of the Spanish claim, to which the UK Government has consistently responded by upholding the self-proclaimed desire of the Gibraltarian people to retain their British status. Although the basic dispute over Gibraltar remains unresolved, the death of Franco in 1975 and the subsequent decision of the new democratic Government in Madrid to seek membership of the European Community and the North Atlantic Treaty Organization brought about an improvement in Spanish-UK relations. This in turn led to the conclusion of an agreement in Lisbon in April 1980 that the Gibraltar border would be reopened and substantive negotiations on the Gibraltar issue initiated. Although it was subsequently agreed that these provisions would be put into effect on April 20, 1982, implementation was postponed because of the development of an Argentinian-UK crisis over the Falkland Islands in early April 1982.

Gibraltar covers an area of only 2¼ square miles (5.8 sq km) and has a population of some 30,000. It faces the coast of north Africa, from which it is about 14 miles (22 km) distant. The area around Gibraltar is known as the Campo de

Gibraltar and includes the towns of La Linea and San Roque (whose economies were badly affected by the 1969 border closures) as well as Algeciras.

Gibraltar was held by the Moors for many centuries until the Spanish captured it in the 15th century. During the War of the Spanish Succession it was taken by a combined British and Dutch force in 1704, and British possession was confirmed in 1713 under the Treaty of Utrecht. Spanish efforts to regain the Rock included an unsuccessful 3½-year siege from 1779 to 1783 by a combined French and Spanish force, but British proposals in the 18th century to exchange Gibraltar for other pieces of territory were turned down by Spain.

Gibraltar was declared a Crown Colony in 1830. It was granted a greater measure of internal self-government in 1964, and in 1967 a referendum was held in which it voted overwhelmingly to retain links with Britain. In 1969 it received a new Constitution giving it a House of Assembly, executive authority being vested in a Governor who represents the Queen. Gibraltar has been part of the European Community since 1973 by virtue of its association with Britain.

## British and Spanish Positions on Gibraltar

Britain bases its claim to continued sovereignty over Gibraltar on the Treaty of Utrecht, which specified (in Article 10) that the "Catholic Sovereign by this treaty cedes to the Crown of Great Britain for itself as well as for its heirs full and entire ownership of the city and castle of Gibraltar with its port, fortifications and forts . . . without any territorial jurisdiction over, and without any open communication by land with, the surrounding regions''. The same article stated that Gibraltar was to be "held and enjoyed absolutely [by Britain] with all manner of right for ever, without any exception or impediment whatsoever'', while another article provided that if Britain wished to dispossess itself of Gibraltar, Spain should have preferential rights to it. The British title to Gibraltar was reaffirmed in the Treaties of Paris (1763) and of Versailles (1783).

Spain, however, has described the provisions of the Treaty of Utrecht as anachronistic and has accused Britain of consistently violating them. A contentious visit to Gibraltar in May 1964 by Queen Elizabeth gave rise to protests by Spanish students, the closure of the Spanish consulate in Gibraltar and the tighten-

**Map 12   Southern Spain and North Africa, showing Gibraltar and the Spanish enclaves on the north Moroccan coast.**

ing of border controls by the Spanish authorities on Spanish workers crossing into Gibraltar. Since then the question of the cession of Gibraltar had been brought up at intervals by Spain.

After the introduction in August 1964 of a new Constitution granting Gibraltar a greater measure of internal self-government, the Spanish Government in October of that year began to enforce restrictions on the transit of people, traffic and goods from Spain into Gibraltar in support of its claim to Gibraltar. The Gibraltar issue had also been considered by the UN Decolonization Committee at the request of Spain in September 1963 (for the first time) and in September-October 1964. On April 5, 1965, the British Government published a White Paper dealing with these and other aspects of the Gibraltar issue and reiterating Britain's full support for Gibraltar's wish to remain British. The White Paper made the following points:

*Historical Background.* The paper noted that "when the British captured Gibraltar in 1704 almost the entire Spanish population left the town and settled in the neighbouring countryside" and that the present population began to establish itself in Gibraltar from 1727 onwards, consisting of "time-expired British soldiers" and "Genoese and other foreign elements". By the time the Napoleonic wars had ended, the population also comprised British, Maltese, Moroccan and Portuguese elements, and "this community has now existed in Gibraltar for over 250 years and, since 1830 when a Charter of Justice was proclaimed, has had legal recognition".

*Constitutional Position.* The paper said that the institutions of Gibraltar and the arrangements in force corresponded with the wishes of the Gibraltarian people and were "in accordance with modern democratic ideals and the principles of the UN Charter". The Gibraltarian people wished Gibraltar to remain in close association with Britain.

*Consideration of Gibraltar at the UN.* The White Paper described the proceedings in the UN Decolonization Committee in September-October 1964 during which the three parties concerned had put forward their positions [namely, the Spanish claim that Gibraltar formed part of Spanish territory notwithstanding the views of its inhabitants; the Gibraltarian wish to remain closely associated with Britain without becoming independent and their opposition to being handed over to Spain; and the British assertion that the grant of Gibraltar to Britain in the Treaty of Utrecht was absolute and that Spain had no right to be consulted on any change in its status or relations with Britain]. The paper noted the UN Committee's conclusion of Oct. 16, 1964, that there was a dispute between Britain and Spain over the status and situation of Gibraltar, its invitation to Britain and Spain to seek a negotiated solution, and its statement that the UN declaration on the granting of independence to colonial countries and peoples was fully applicable to Gibraltar. It also noted that Britain had not accepted that there was a dispute over status, nor a conflict between the Treaty of Utrecht's provisions and the application of the principle of self-determination to the Gibraltarians.

*The Situation at the Frontier.* Describing the situation at the frontier since the Spanish authorities at La Linea began enforcing procedures and regulations more strictly on Oct. 17, 1964, the White Paper said that cars and visitors had been delayed and most exports into Gibraltar stopped. Traffic, including tourist traffic, was almost at a standstill, restrictions were affecting Spanish workers commuting daily to Gibraltar, and the customs were refusing to accept as valid any British passports issued or renewed in Gibraltar, or those issued or renewed "on behalf of the Government of Gibraltar".

*Conclusion.* The White Paper pointed out that the civilian population, who were not Spanish, had "been established there for longer than many immigrant communities in the New World" and concluded: "Great Britain has at no time renounced her title to Gibraltar or failed to defend her position there, and she will not do so now. She has no desire to quarrel with Spain but she will stand by the people of Gibraltar in their present difficulties and take whatever measures may be necessary to defend and sustain them.''

In December 1965 the Spanish Government in response published a Red Book on the Gibraltar issue, incorporating many maps. This said that the "sole legal basis" for the British presence in Gibraltar was Article 10 of the Treaty of Utrecht and that legally the cession of Gibraltar to Great Britain was therefore "subject to a series of limitations". In practice, these had been consistently ignored by Britain, it went on, notably in that since 1713 Britain had advanced its sphere of control steadily northwards "in quest of more space for the [Gibraltar] fortress over and above that stipulated at Utrecht". By the end of the 19th century Britain had advanced her frontier half a mile across the neutral zone north of Gibraltar, and as evidence of this "encroachment" the Red Book cited the construction in 1938 (i.e. during the Spanish Civil War) "of a military/civilian aerodrome, in the heart of the neutral zone, that is to say on Spanish sovereign territory". Britain had also erected a wall "which, after the Berlin manner, physically separates from Spain by walls, wire and railings a territory which is Spanish and which the British had been gradually engulfing in their advance through the so-called neutral zone".

The Red Book accused Britain of "passivity or even benevolence" towards smuggling by land and sea from the Rock in contravention of the treaty provision prohibiting land communications and trade; it described the economic bases of the life of Gibraltar as "artificial" and added that the population of the Rock was also "artificially planned" to the prejudice of the original population, which had been driven out. After referring to the border measures taken by Spain in 1964 as normal police and customs measures, the Red Book said that in strict compliance with the Treaty of Utrecht Spain would be justified in (i) requesting the removal of the wall and fence at Gibraltar 800 metres further south "to evacuate a piece of Spanish sovereign territory which . . . was unjustifiably annexed by Britain on the isthmus of Gibraltar and in which the present aerodrome of Gibraltar is situated"; (ii) exercising the right to cut off land communications with Gibraltar, leaving only sea communications open; (iii) abolishing trade with Gibraltar; and (iv) refusing to recognize the political institutions created in Gibraltar since 1950.

### Commencement of Anglo-Spanish Talks on Gibraltar

Following the adoption by the UN General Assembly at its 20th session on Dec. 16, 1965, of a resolution (2070) inviting Spain and Britain to enter into negotiations on the Gibraltar issue without delay (both Spain and Britain voting in favour of the resolution), the two countries met for an initial round of talks in London in May 1966. In the course of the talks Spain made a formal claim to sovereignty over Gibraltar in a four-point plan. It proposed (i) that an Anglo-Spanish convention should be signed cancelling Article 10 of the Treaty of Utrecht and providing for "the restoration of the national unity and territorial integrity of Spain through the reversion of Gibraltar"; (ii) that Spain would accept a British military base at Gibraltar "whose structure, legal situation and co-ordination with the defence organization of Spain or the free world would be the subject of a special agreement" attached to the proposed convention; (iii) that a legal regime protecting the interests of the present citizens of Gibraltar should be the subject of an additional Anglo-Spanish agreement which would be negotiated with the UN and that it should contain, in addition to the appropriate economic and administrative formulae, a personal statute by which fundamental rights including the British nationality of the inhabitants of Gibraltar would be respected and their right of residence guaranteed, as well as the free exercise of their lawful acts and a guarantee of permanence in their place of work; and (iv) that such a convention would take effect after the additional agreements provided for under (ii) and (iii) had been regulated with the United Nations.

At the second round of talks in July 1966 Britain made counter-proposals which inter alia envisaged the exercise of internal self-government by the municipal authorities instead of by Legislative and Executive Councils. However, no progress was made on either set of proposals at this or the next round of talks in September (which was preceded by the introduction in August 1966 of a Spanish ban on British military aircraft overflying Spanish territory).

On Oct. 5, 1966—just before a fourth round was due to commence—the Spanish Government issued a decree closing the frontier with Gibraltar to all but pedestrian traffic, with the result that several thousand Spaniards who entered Gibraltar every day to work had to travel on foot. The measure took effect on Oct. 24, and in November the Spanish frontier authorities at La Linea also began to refuse to accept Gibraltarian passports issued by the Governor, thus effectively placing a ban on Gibraltarians entering Spain.

The British delegation proposed at the October 1966 round of talks that the legal issues involved in the Gibraltar dispute should be referred to the International Court of Justice. However, this was rejected by Spain in a note of Dec. 14 on the grounds that it would contradict a UN Decolonization Committee resolution adopted on Nov. 17 which (i) recommended that Britain should "expedite, without any hindrance and in consultation with the Government of Spain, the decolonization of Gibraltar", (ii) regretted "the delay in the process of decolonization" and (iii) called on Britain and Spain to "continue their negotiations taking into account the interests of the people of the territory". A similar resolution (2231)—which did not, however, contain the latter reference to the interests of the Gibraltarian people—was adopted by the UN General Assembly on Dec. 20, 1966, with both Spain and Britain voting in favour.

## The 1967 Referendum in Gibraltar

On June 14, 1967, the British Government announced that a referendum would be held in Gibraltar to allow the people to decide whether to "pass under Spanish sovereignty" in accordance with the terms proposed by the Spanish Government on May 18, 1966, or "voluntarily to retain their link with Britain with democratic local institutions and with Britain retaining its present responsibilities". If the majority voted in favour of the first option, Britain would, it stated, enter into further negotiations with Spain, but if the majority voted for the second option Britain would regard this choice as constituting "a free and voluntary relationship of the people of Gibraltar with Britain" and would "thereafter discuss with representatives of Gibraltar appropriate constitutional changes which may be desired".

The decision to hold a referendum was regarded by Spain as unilateral and in violation of UN resolutions and the Treaty of Utrecht, and in a note of July 3, 1967, it declined Britain's invitation to send an observer on the grounds that this would imply approval of the measure. After a Spanish complaint to the United Nations was filed on Aug. 18, 1967, the Decolonization Committee on Sept. 1 adopted a resolution stating that the holding of the referendum would "contradict" previous UN resolutions. Britain denounced this resolution as "wholly partisan", and said that the referendum would go ahead in accordance with the UN Charter, which laid down that the interests of the inhabitants of a non-self-governing state were paramount. A similar point was made by Gibraltar's Chief Minister, Sir Joshua Hassan, who said that the resolution appeared to "disregard the interests of a colonial people and would seem to deny them the elementary human right of stating their interests through a referendum".

The referendum took place in Gibraltar on Sept. 10, 1967, and resulted in an overwhelmingly pro-British vote. Out of 12,762 registered voters (all of them normally resident in Gibraltar), 12,138 voted for continued association with Britain and 44 voted for Spanish sovereignty. A Commonwealth observer team which had been present in Gibraltar during the referendum said that it had been conducted in a fair and proper manner with adequate facilities for the free expression of views.

The UN General Assembly on Dec. 19, 1967, adopted a further resolution (2353) which had already been adopted by the Trusteeship Committee on Dec. 16 and which (i) described the holding of the referendum as a "contravention" of Resolution 2231 and of the Decolonization Committee's resolution of Sept. 1, 1967; (ii) regretted the interruption of negotiations; and (iii) urged the resumption of negotiations without delay in order to put an end to the "colonial situation" in Gibraltar and to safeguard the interests of the population "upon the termination of that situation". The Spanish Government meanwhile on Dec. 11, 1967, published a second Red Book reiterating its repudiation of the referendum and recapitulating the state of negotiations with Britain since May 1966.

Anglo-Spanish talks resumed on March 18, 1968, but broke down again on March 20. With effect from May 5 of that year Spain began what it described as a progressive implementation of the Treaty of Utrecht by closing the land frontier to all traffic including pedestrians with the exception of those Spaniards holding work permits for Gibraltar and permanent residents of Gibraltar; the others were obliged to use the ferry from Algeciras.

### 1969 Constitutional Changes leading to Closure of the Border and Severance of Communications

In July 1968 Britain and Gibraltar held talks on proposed constitutional changes at the instigation of Gibraltar, which sought a new political status under the continued, permanent and exclusive sovereignty of Britain. It was agreed that such changes would give Gibraltarians maximum control over their domestic affairs but should not conflict with the Treaty of Utrecht or worsen Anglo-Spanish relations.

At the conclusion of these talks a joint communiqué was issued, which revealed that the British Government believed that it could best respond to the wishes of the Gibraltarian people by inserting in the revised Gibraltar Constitution a declaration to the effect that Gibraltar was "a part of Her Majesty's Dominions and will remain so unless an Act of Parliament otherwise provides, and furthermore that HM Government has made it clear that it will never hand over the people of Gibraltar to another state against their freely and democratically expressed wishes". Other constitutional changes agreed at the talks covered the replacement of the Legislative and City Councils of Gibraltar by a House of Assembly and the installation of an Executive headed by a Governor, a Gibraltar Council and a Council of Ministers. The new Constitution for Gibraltar (which was henceforth to be known as the City of Gibraltar) entered into force on May 30, 1969.

In strongly attacking the Constitution, the Spanish Government accused Britain of disregarding a recent UN General Assembly resolution, adopted on Dec. 18, 1968, which declared that the "colonial situation in Gibraltar" was "incompatible with the UN Charter" and which called upon Britain to "terminate the colonial situation in Gibraltar" not later than Oct. 1, 1969. As a reprisal the Spanish Government on June 8, 1969, closed the border and customs post at La Linea "to defend Spanish interests in Gibraltar", with the result that some 5,000 Spanish workers (about one-third of Gibraltar's normal labour force) were prevented from going to their jobs. On June 27 Spain suspended the ferry service from Algeciras to Gibraltar, and on July 4 it announced that Spanish nationality would be offered to all residents of Gibraltar or those born there. Finally, only hours after the expiry of the Oct. 1 deadline contained in the December 1968 UN resolution, Spain on Oct. 1 cut telephone links between the Spanish mainland and Gibraltar. Against a background of the deployment of large Spanish and British naval forces off Gibraltar, the Gibraltar Government was obliged to put into effect contingency plans to deal with its new situation in the face of the Spanish restrictions.

Despite the tension which the Spanish measures caused, relations between Britain and Spain had already begun to improve by the end of 1969 and continued on a cordial basis with informal contacts taking place throughout 1970-72, although the Spanish restrictions remained in force. Finally, formal talks resumed on May 30-31, 1974.

Later in 1974 Spanish proposals for a new regime in Gibraltar were published for the first time in Britain, although they had been handed to Sir Joshua Hassan in February 1973 (and he had described them as "utterly unacceptable" in the light of the result of the 1967 referendum). The proposals foresaw (i) that as soon as Spanish sovereignty was recognized over Gibraltar, the Gibraltar area [i.e. the Campo] would become a special territory with legislative, judicial, administrative and financial autonomy; (ii) that Gibraltarians would take Spanish nationality but need not renounce their British nationality; (iii) that the Spanish legal system "as developed by the special legislation of Gibraltar" would apply after the 1969 Constitution had been suitably amended, and that Spanish penal and police laws would apply in all areas concerning Spain's internal and external security; (iv) that the senior authority in Gibraltar would be a civil governor appointed by the Spanish head of state; (v) that the most senior members of the executive would be Spaniards or Gibraltarians of Spanish nationality; and (vi) that Spanish would be the official language of Gibraltar, although a wide use of English would be safeguarded.

## Developments since Death of Franco

Following the death of Gen. Franco on Nov. 20, 1975, King Juan Carlos stated on ascending the Spanish throne two days later that Spain's efforts to regain sovereignty over Gibraltar would continue. The following month, however, he restored telephone links between Spain and Gibraltar over the Christmas-New Year period and subsequently in April 1976 for the Easter period, setting a pattern for subsequent years. In July 1977—following Spain's first general elections since 1936 —the democratically-elected Government headed by Adolfo Suárez González as Prime Minister stated that it would insist on resuming negotiations with Britain "with the aim of restoring Spain's territorial integrity"; and in September 1977 Dr David Owen became the first UK Foreign and Commonwealth Secretary to visit Spain since 1961. During this visit (when Dr Owen met King Juan Carlos, Suárez and the new Spanish Foreign Minister, Marcelino Oreja Aguirre) and in the course of a subsequent brief visit to London in October by Suárez in connexion with Spain's recently-filed application to join the European Community, talks were held on the Gibraltar issue.

Dr Owen told a press conference on Sept. 7 after the visit that Britain had requested Spain to lift the restrictions on Gibraltar. He also said that Britain's support for Spain's application to join the European Community would not be dependent on the settlement of the Gibraltar issue and that the attitude of the Spanish Government contained "a degree of sensitivity and understanding which did not exist before", and which he felt was the best ingredient for a settlement.

The Spanish Prime Minister for his part told a press conference in London on Oct. 19 (after talks with Dr Owen and James Callaghan, the Prime Minister) that he believed that Spain's political evolution and restructuring on a regional basis could permit a negotiated solution of the Gibraltar issue which would respect the "identity, culture and special characteristics of the Gibraltarian people and eventually can bring about the reintegration of Gibraltar into Spanish territory in conformity with UN resolutions". However, he ruled out the removal of restrictions, which, according to a British communiqué issued after the London talks, would have to be lifted if there was to be progress on the Gibraltar issue.

After routine talks in Madrid in November 1977 between Spanish and British representatives, later that month a meeting took place in Strasbourg between Dr Owen, his Spanish counterpart, Sir Joshua Hassan and Maurice Xibberas (for the Gibraltar opposition). At a subsequent meeting of these four representatives in Paris in March 1978 it was agreed to set up Anglo-Spanish working groups to deal with matters including telephone communications and maritime links, and the working groups held two meetings in 1978, in July and December (a Gibraltarian delegation attending the latter).

## Lisbon and London Agreements on Reopening Border

After the Conservative election victory in Britain in May 1979 the new Government was reported to have indicated to Spain—contrary to Dr Owen's assurance of Sept. 7, 1977—that British support for Spain's entry into the European Community would not be forthcoming as long as restrictions on Gibraltar remained in force. With fresh moves afoot in Spain itself to reopen the frontier and negotiate over Gibraltar, Lord Carrington (the new UK Foreign and Commonwealth Secretary) and Marcelino Oreja Aguirre met in Lisbon on April 9-10, 1980, and agreed in principle to reopen the land frontier and to "suspend" the other restrictions imposed in 1969. A joint communiqué issued on April 10 stated that "the British and Spanish Governments, desiring to strengthen their bilateral relations and thus to contribute to Western solidarity, intend, in accordance with the relevant UN resolutions, to resolve in a spirit of friendship the Gibraltar problem", and that they had thus agreed to start negotiations. Agreement had been reached, it continued, on the re-establishment of direct communications in the region; future co-operation should be on the basis of "reciprocity and full equality of rights"; and in seeking to re-establish its territorial integrity Spain intended that "in the outcome of the negotiations the interests of the Gibraltarians should be fully safeguarded". For its part Britain reaffirmed its commitment to "honour the freely and democratically expressed wishes of the people of Gibraltar".

The communiqué concluded by stating that British and Spanish experts would meet to work out by June 1, 1980, a timetable for reopening the border and formally restoring postal communications—telephone links having remained informally in operation since their restoration for the Christmas period in December 1977. Lord Carrington told the House of Lords on April 14 that after the completion of these practical preparations by June 1 at the latest the agreement could be speedily implemented.

By the end of 1980, however, the border was still closed and Anglo-Spanish contacts appeared deadlocked, it being reported that Spain was stipulating fresh conditions, among them that Spaniards working in Gibraltar should be granted equal status to Gibraltarians as soon as the border reopened. Gibraltar's response was that the local labour market was too complex and fragile for Spain to be given immediate access to it, and also that there were now several thousand Moroccan workers to be protected. The Gibraltar House of Assembly on Dec. 30, 1980, adopted a resolution urging that Spanish nationals should not enjoy equal rights to nationals of other EEC countries until Spain itself became a full member of the Community.

In mid-1981 further aggravation in Spanish-UK relations over the Gibraltar issue arose when King Juan Carlos and Queen Sofia of Spain declined an invitation to attend the wedding of Prince Charles and Lady Diana Spencer on July 29 in view of an earlier announcement that the latter couple would embark on the royal yacht *Britannia* at Gibraltar to begin their honeymoon. Relations between the two sides subsequently improved, however, and on Jan. 8, 1982, talks in London between the UK and Spanish Prime Ministers (Margaret Thatcher and Leopoldo Calvo Sotelo) resulted in an agreement that the Gibraltar border would be reopened on April 20, 1982, and that negotiations would begin on that day to resolve the Gibraltar issue in terms of the April 1980 Lisbon agreement. However, in view of the development of a serious crisis between Argentina and Britain in early April 1982 over the Falkland Islands, it was agreed between the UK and Spanish Governments that implementation of the Lisbon agreement would be further postponed.

**J.B.**

# 2. AFRICA

## Introduction

With regard to the boundaries between African states, the political map of Africa today is not very different from the political map of 1914, as Prof. Brownlie noted in the introduction to his book *African Boundaries*,[1] although of course there have been dramatic changes in the *colour* of the map, brought about by the post-1945 decolonization process. "The generalization which certainly holds up under scrutiny", Brownlie comments, "is the statement that African boundaries are those of the colonial period, providing allowance is made for the fact that many of the boundaries are the former *intra*-colonial boundaries of the units of French West Africa and French Equatorial Africa."

Many nationalist leaders, it is true, initially expressed a commitment to pan-Africanism—even to the extent of a fullscale political union of Africa in the post-colonial era. However, as Brownlie describes, this commitment gave way to an acceptance that for the foreseeable future African self-determination and nation-building should be pursued within the framework of numerous independent states defined for the most part by the former colonial boundaries; thus the Charter of the Organization of African Unity (OAU) set up in 1963 reflects "the least dynamic common denominator of pan-African thinking" and places emphasis on "the equality and the sovereignty and territorial integrity of member-states".

Moreover, a resolution adopted by the OAU Assembly of Heads of State and Government held in Cairo in July 1964 recorded that "all member states pledge themselves to respect the borders existing on their achievement of national independence", on the grounds inter alia that "border problems constitute a grave and permanent factor of dissension" and that "the borders of African states, on the day of their independence, constitute a tangible reality". The reasoning behind this decision "is clear enough", wrote Brownlie: "If the colonial alignments were discarded, alternative alignments would have to be agreed upon. Such a process of redefinition would create confusion and threats to peace. Even if the principles on which revision was to be based were agreed upon, there would be considerable difficulty in applying the principles to the ethnic and tribal complexities of African states."

The 1964 Cairo resolution has had considerable effect in discouraging the development of territorial disputes between OAU member states, and those which have arisen have often been resolved by negotiation (e.g. the Algerian-Moroccan border dispute, settled in 1972). Nevertheless, as described in the following pages, there do exist between various OAU member

---

[1] Ian Brownlie, *African Boundaries—A Legal and Diplomatic Encyclopaedia.* The following section draws heavily on this comprehensive work.

states a number of outstanding issues with a territorial dimension of one sort or another, even though it may not be appropriate to describe some of them as intergovernmental disputes in the international legal sense.

Certain African border disputes, such as those between Chad and Libya and between Malawi and Tanzania, involve specific territorial claims (mainly centring on uncertain boundaries drawn in the colonial period). And notwithstanding the 1964 OAU resolution, ethnic or tribal divisions created by colonial boundary-drawing continue to surface in tensions and rivalries between certain African states, for example in the Horn of Africa.

In addition, there are a number of outstanding territorial issues between ex-colonial powers and their former African dependencies, mostly involving Indian Ocean islands which have remained under the sovereignty of the former but which are claimed by the latter. The position of the one remaining European state which continues to exercise territorial sovereignty on the African continent itself—namely Spain in its enclaves on the north Moroccan coast—is under challenge from Morocco. Moreover, Morocco is currently involved in an assertion of sovereignty over the territory of the former Spanish Sahara—an issue which has recently taken on the character of a national liberation struggle but which was originally a territorial issue.

The remaining category of disputes dealt with in this section involves South Africa, the only internationally-recognized independent state in Africa which is not a member of the OAU. Territorial claims against South Africa are made by Lesotho, as well as by the "independent" Black homelands created by the Pretoria Government (and not internationally recognized). In addition, South Africa is in dispute with the international community over the status of Walvis Bay on the Atlantic coast of Namibia (South African control over Namibia itself being regarded as illegal by the United Nations).

# Cameroon-Nigeria

Relations between Nigeria and Cameroon were temporarily strained in May-July 1981 by what was in Nigeria officially described as a border dispute, centring on the frontier between the adjoining coastal regions of the two states. (A map of the region is published on page 125.)

## Background to Dispute

On the question of the two countries' common border President Ahmadou Ahidjo of Cameroon had stated in an interview (published in *Le Monde* on July 18-19, 1976) that, although Cameroon had strongly challenged the correctness of a plebiscite held in 1961 and resulting in the transfer of Northern Cameroon to Nigeria and had unsuccessfully tried to appeal to the United Nations and the International Court of Justice, his Government had bowed to the facts and preferred to refrain from making any territorial claims. He added that where Cameroon's boundaries with any of its six neighbours (Nigeria and Chad to the north, the Central African Republic to the east and Congo, Gabon and Equatorial Guinea in the south) were imprecisely delimited the problem would be solved amicably.

It was, however, widely acknowledged that in parts of Western Cameroon (i.e. near the border with Nigeria) there remained a minority of people who were opposed to the incorporation of their area in Cameroon as a result of a plebiscite also held in 1961, when almost 30 per cent of the valid votes were cast against such incorporation. In particular, the Bakassi peninsula, situated on the Cameroon side of the border and to the west of the Rio del Rey river, was largely inhabited by Nigerians who had settled there before this part of the former British Cameroon was united with the former French Cameroon in 1961. Many of these Nigerians were fishermen and some were engaged in smuggling, and they tended to seek protection from the authorities of the Nigerian Cross River State.

A maritime border agreement signed at the northern Cameroon town of Maroua on May 31, 1975, by Gen. Yakubu Gowon (then Nigeria's head of state) and President Ahidjo had left the access channel to the port of Calabar in Nigerian territorial waters and had also provided that the lawful activities of Nigerian fishermen in a two-kilometre-wide strip should not affect the territorial waters issue. However, Gen. Gowon was deposed in July 1975 and the agreement was never ratified by Nigeria on the grounds that it was "defective in parts".

## Escalation of Tension in 1981

On May 18, 1981, Prof. Ishaya Audu, the Nigerian Minister of External Affairs, announced that, although the Nigerian President had recently visited Cameroon as "part of the exercise of defusing the tension along this border and generally trying to settle issues by peaceful means", the situation had taken "a different turn". He maintained that "at a Nigerian village in Cross River State, well within Nigerian territory and separated from the Cameroon border by the Akpa Yafi river [also referred to as the Ate Akate or Agpa Yafé river] . . . on May 15, 1981, "a platoon of Nigerian soldiers and five support boats were fired upon by a Cameroonian support boat" and five Nigerian soldiers had been killed and three others seriously wounded, while the Cameroonians had fled. The Minister added that his Government had sent the Cameroonian Government "a very stern note of protest"; that it reserved the right to take any appropriate action to protect the lives and property of Nigerians; and that it would report the matter to the Organization of African Unity (OAU).

Prof. Audu later contended that there had been "regular harassment" of Nigerians living in the border area and also incursions by Cameroonians into Nigerian villages. The Cameroonians, on the other hand, alleged that the incident of May 15 had taken place on the Rio del Rey river, i.e. in Cameroonian territorial waters 20 miles to the east of the boundary. On May 22 President Ahidjo was reported to have ordered an inquiry into an earlier exchange of artillery fire on the Rio del Rey river.

However, in a message delivered in Lagos on May 24 by a delegation led by Paul Dontsop (Cameroon's Foreign Minister) President Ahidjo expressed his regrets at the incident of May 15 and made proposals for working out a peaceful solution to the border problem, but the National Security Council of Nigeria found that these proposals did not cover all the issues referred to in Nigeria's protest note.

There followed strong expressions of hostility to Cameroon in the Nigerian press, where it was claimed that Cameroon was massing forces for a military confrontation and was prospecting for oil in Nigerian waters. Alhaji Akanbi Oniyangi (the Minister of Defence) refused to rule out the possibility of war, and demonstrating university students called for war and caused damage to Cameroon's embassy in Lagos. A presidential spokesman admitted in a statement issued on June 2 that President Shehu Shagari was restraining calls for war (which had also been made by the Speaker of the Federal House of Representatives).

Ayissi Mvodo, Cameroonian Minister of State for Territorial Administration, said in an interview published on June 3 that many other incidents had occurred in the past and had been settled peacefully by the authorities of both countries, and that the position of the Cameroonian Government was always to seek such a settlement without recourse to force, in particular because the two "brotherly and neighbouring countries" harboured "huge numbers of each other's citizens".

With regard to Nigeria's appeal to the OAU, the Secretariat of the OAU declined to place the matter on the agenda of the OAU Assembly of Heads of State and Government held in Nairobi on June 24-28, 1981, and President Shagari thereupon refused to attend the Assembly session. However, Edem Kodjo, the OAU Secretary-General, and Dr Robert Ouko, the Foreign Minister of Kenya (whose President was currently President of the OAU), visited Lagos and Yaoundé (the capital of Cameroon) for discussion of the issue during the second week of July 1981.

Lagos radio stated on July 15 that, while Nigeria wished the OAU Secretary-General success in his "mediation efforts in the Nigeria-Cameroon border dispute", it was necessary to ask why the issue was not placed on the OAU Assembly's agenda; whether the OAU Secretariat was "inadvertently inciting Nigeria into embarking on a military adventure against Cameroon"; or whether "Edem Kodjo and his men" felt that the matter was "not serious enough".

After it had been disclosed that mediation efforts had also been made by Presidents Houphouët-Boigny of the Ivory Coast, Seyni Kountché of Niger and Gnassingbe Eyadema of Togo, it was reported on July 15 that an OAU ministerial committee was to be set up to look into the situation. President Ahidjo had earlier (on July 7) been reported to have emphasized that calm had been restored to the area; that Cameroon would not be the origin of any eventual conflict with its neighbours; and that it was ready to take part in any mediation efforts.

In Lagos it was announced on July 20, 1981, that President Ahidjo had promised that his country would pay compensation to the families of the five Nigerian soldiers killed on May 15, and that he had tendered an unreserved apology. President Shagari, in accepting this offer (as reported on July 24), suggested the establishment of "an arbitration tribunal comprising countries acceptable to both nations to look into the entire boundary question with a view to forestalling further unrest''. The details of this plan were to be worked out during a proposed visit to Nigeria by President Ahidjo at the invitation of President Shagari, tendered on July 22.

On Aug. 6 it was reported from Lagos that the Director of Immigration had told a parliamentary committee that a border fence was to be erected along Nigeria's boundaries with Benin, Cameroon, Chad and Niger, but that this fence would not initially affect the Nigeria-Cameroon border, the main purpose of the fence being to keep out illegal immigrants.

In a joint communiqué issued on Jan. 13, 1982, at the end of President Ahidjo's visit to Lagos, it was stated inter alia that the two countries' Presidents had expressed their regret at the border clash of May 1981, had resolved not to allow the incident to affect co-operation between them, and had decided to reactivate a Nigeria-Cameroon joint commission to strengthen co-operation in all fields.

**H.W.D.**

# Chad-Libya

In 1973 the Libyan Government of Col. Moamer al Kadhafi annexed an area south of the existing border between Libya and Chad known as the Aozou strip. Whereas the Libyan action met with no opposition from the then Government of Chad led by President Ngarta (François) Tombalbaye nor from other states in the area, objections to the annexation were first raised by Gen. Félix Malloum, who had become President of Chad after the overthrow of President Tombalbaye in April 1975. In 1980, by which time Chad had been devastated by civil war, Libyan forces, invited into the country by a provisional Government ''of national unity'' formed in November 1979 under the presidency of Goukouni Oueddei, temporarily occupied the greater part of Chad. President Oueddei accepted the Libyan annexation of the Aozou strip as ''an accomplished fact'', whereas rebel groups, especially that led by Hissène Habré, continued to dispute Libya's right to the strip.

### History of Chad's Northern Boundary

The boundary between Libya and Chad was first laid down under a convention signed in Paris by France and the United Kingdom on June 14, 1898 (with ratifications being exchanged in Paris on June 13, 1899), with the object of delimiting the spheres of influence of France and the United Kingdom east of the Niger river. Under an Anglo-French declaration of March 21, 1899, the French zone was delimited to the north-east and east by a line starting ''from the point of intersection of the Tropic of Cancer with the 16th degree of longitude east of Greenwich'' and running ''thence to the north until it meets the 24th degree of longitude east of Greenwich''. Italy concurred with the above line in an exchange of notes with France on Nov. 1, 1902. Under a convention of Sept. 8, 1919, France and the United Kingdom determined the line's point of intersection with the 24th meridian (which had not been specified in the 1899 declaration) at 19°30′N.

Whereas the territory to the north of this line had been under Turkish suzereignty as part of the Ottoman Empire, Italy occupied the region of Tripoli in September 1911, and in the Treaty of Ouchy of Oct. 18, 1912, the Ottoman Empire recognized Italian sovereignty over the territory which became officially known as Libya after 1934. Following Libya's declaration of independence on Dec. 24, 1951, the boundary between Libya and French Equatorial Africa was recognized in a French-Libyan treaty of Aug. 10, 1955, as fixed under the above-mentioned agreements. Chad, which had been part of French Equatorial Africa, became independent on Aug. 11, 1960.

### Libya's Annexation of the Aozou Strip

In June 1973 the Libyan Government of Col. Kadhafi annexed the Aozou strip, basing its action on the provisions of a Franco-Italian protocol signed in Rome on Jan. 7, 1935. This protocol, dealing with the delimitation of "the frontier between Libya and the French colonies" (and also "between Eritrea and the French coast of Somaliland", i.e. Djibouti), defined the proposed southern frontier of Libya (as described in an official communiqué of Jan. 8, 1935) as follows: "The frontier separating Libya from French West Africa and French Equatorial Africa is determined by the line which runs from Tummo, the terminating point of the line traced in the Italo-French agreement of Sept. 12, 1919, meeting the western frontier of the Anglo-Egyptian Sudan at 24°E, 18°45′N. This line leaves (in Italian territory) Aozou and Guezendi, and in French territory Bardai and Tecro. The size of the territories thus recognized as belonging to Italian Libya is approximately 114,000 square kilometres (43,000 square miles)."

This protocol was agreed to "in application of Article 13 of the Treaty of London"—which had been concluded by France, Italy, Russia and the United Kingdom in 1915 with the object of inducing Italy to join the Allies in World War I. The article in question read as follows: "In the event of France and Great Britain increasing their colonial territories in Africa at the expense of Germany, those two powers agree in principle that Italy may claim some equitable compensation, particularly as regards the settlement in her favour of the questions relative to the frontiers of the Italian colonies of Eritrea, Somaliland and Libya and the neighbouring colonies belonging to France and Great Britain." However, France never ratified the protocol (which was said to have been interpreted by Mussolini as giving him, as far as France was concerned, a free hand in his invasion of Abyssinia in October 1935).

The timing of Libya's annexation of the Aozou strip was widely regarded as being connected with the existence of uranium deposits in the strip (in the same geological formation which included uranium deposits in Gabon). Although consisting (according to the European Nuclear Energy Agency) of low-grade, high-cost ores, the deposits were considered adequate to complete

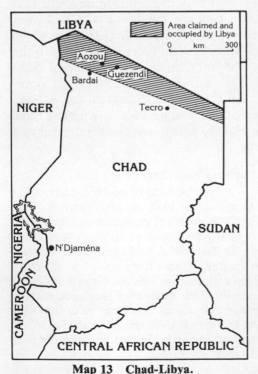

**Map 13   Chad-Libya.**

the required basis for the nuclear independence of Libya, which had concluded an agreement with the Soviet Union for the supply of a 10-megawatt nuclear reactor and associated technology to Libya.

The annexation of the Aozou strip was not officially announced in Libya until early September 1975 (in the Tripoli newspaper *Al Fateh*).

### Reactions in Chad

At the time of the annexation of the Aozou strip Chad had close relations with Libya. Following a visit to Tripoli by President Tombalbaye, the Libyan Government had, on Dec. 23, 1972, undertaken to "contribute to the strengthening of unity" in Chad, to grant Chad development credits and (reportedly) also to hand over to the Government of Chad any members of the rebel *Front de libération nationale (Frolinat)* who might be in Libya. During a visit to Chad by Col. Kadhafi on March 5-6, 1974, the Aozou strip was not officially referred to. However, on April 26, 1976, President Malloum, who accused both Libya and Algeria of supporting the *Frolinat* rebels, denounced Libya for having illegally occupied the Aozou strip. On Oct. 16 of that year Chad closed its border with Libya, and a few days later President Malloum notified Col. Kadhafi that there could be no talk of co-operation between the two countries until Libya had withdrawn from the Aozou strip.

At a meeting of the Council of Ministers of the Organization of African Unity (OAU) in Libreville (Gabon) in June 1977, the Foreign Minister of Chad accused Libya of arming and aiding rebels in northern Chad, and he asked the OAU to use all its authority "to restore Chad's rights in the Aozou strip". The Libyan representative at the meeting asserted in turn that the strip was in fact "not northern Chad" but "southern Libya". The OAU Assembly of Heads of State and Government, meeting also in Libreville early in July 1977, thereupon set up a commission to deal with the dispute. On Feb. 6, 1978, the Government of President Malloum suspended its diplomatic relations with Libya.

At an OAU Assembly of Heads of State and Government, meeting in Khartoum, President Malloum on July 20, 1978, denounced Libya's "expansionist desires" and called on the OAU to demand Libya's withdrawal from Chad and to set up a mission to be sent to northern Libya to ascertain that it had been invaded by Libyan forces. The OAU subsequently established a committee of five African Presidents to investigate Chad's allegations and also Libyan accusations to the effect that Chad had been relying on French "colonial forces" to suppress a popular uprising in Chad by "genocidal methods". Subsequent OAU efforts were directed mainly at the prevention of further escalation of the civil war in Chad and had no bearing on the status of the Aozou strip which remained firmly under Libyan control.

President Malloum resigned on March 23, 1979, and after lengthy negotiations a provisional Government "of national unity" was established under the presidency of Goukouni Oueddei on Nov. 10, 1979. On June 15, 1980, this Government signed a treaty of friendship with Libya, under which both sides undertook "to mutually defend each other in the event of one of the two parties being threatened by direct or indirect aggression". On Jan. 6, 1981, the two Governments announced, at the end of a visit to Tripoli by President Goukouni Oueddei, their intention to work towards "full unity" between the two countries, with Libya sending military personnel to Chad to help preserve security and maintain peace. After it had become apparent that there was widespread opposition to any eventual merger between Libya and Chad (not only outside but also inside Chad), it was stated in Libya and in Chad that no such merger was intended. The Vice-President of Chad, in particular, said in a broadcast on Jan. 11, 1981, that the Tripoli announcement did not represent a treaty with Libya but concerned only "complete unity of the two peoples in historical, ethnical and ideological terms'' and not a merger of the two countries.

President Goukouni Oueddei had stated on Dec. 26, 1980, that the Libyan occupation of the Aozou strip had placed him before an ''accomplished fact'' inherited from the Tombalbaye regime, and he added: ''Nobody will be able to intervene to disunite Chad and Libya.''

**H.W.D.**

# Comoros-France (Mayotte)

The dispute between the Governments of the Comoros and France over the island of Mayotte in the Indian Ocean arose when the people of Mayotte opted by a large majority in favour of remaining a French dependency rather than joining the other Comoro islands in their assertion of independence in 1975. Since Mayotte had previously been part of the French overseas territory of the Comoro Islands, the Comoro Government has consistently asserted that the island is part of its national territory, whereas the French Government has upheld the right of its people to determine their own future status.

The Comoro Islands, situated in the Indian Ocean some 300-500 kilometres (200-320 miles) north-west of Madagascar, consist of four main islands—Njazidja, Nzwani, Mwali (until 1980 known respectively as Grand Comoro, Anjouan and Mohéli) and Mayotte (or Mahoré)—as well as numerous smaller islands, covering 2,236 square kilometres (or 833 square miles) and having a population of about 340,000 (while an almost equal number of Comoro islanders have settled in Tanzania and Madagascar).

The islands were an Arab sultanate until the 1840s, when they became a French protectorate, with Mayotte being declared a French colony in 1843, and the three other islands on July 21, 1912. Between 1914 and 1946 the Comoros were attached to the French government-general of Madagascar but on May 9, 1946, they were granted administrative autonomy. Under a French loi-cadre of June 26, 1956, the Comoros were given the status of a French overseas territory with its own Council of Government and with wider powers for its Territorial Assembly. Under a French law promulgated on Dec. 29, 1961, the Comoros were granted full internal autonomy, with the existing Territorial Assembly becoming a Chamber of Deputies, which elected the President of the territorial Council of Government, and with France retaining responsibility for foreign affairs, defence, currency and external economic relations—these arrangements coming into effect in April 1962. In January 1968 the islands were given a new Statute, extending the powers of the Chamber of Deputies vis-à-vis the Government and the local councils, and also in regard to courts administering both Islamic and territorial law, and giving the Prime Minister sole responsibility for internal security.

### The Character of Mayotte

The population of Mayotte (which covers about 375 square kilometres or 145 square miles) has had a tradition of independence vis-à-vis the other islands of the archipelago. In 1590 the people of Mayotte refused to recognize the authority of the successor of Sultan Mohamed ben Haissa of Anjouan, who had died, and there followed a four-year war between the two islands. Their differences with the other islanders are enhanced by the fact that they are mainly Christians, whereas Islam predominates elsewhere in the archipelago. Living on a subsistence basis and trading by barter until the 1970s, they have enjoyed better basic living standards than the other islanders, although most are illiterate (in 1978 only 45 per cent of children between the ages of six and 11 went to school). The island's total population numbers about 40,000, of whom only 10 per cent speak French, the main language being Swahili.

Politically the people of Mayotte, in their majority, follow the *Mouvement populaire mahorais* (MPM), which was founded in 1958 and which has normally been linked with the centrist current in French metropolitan politics, most recently with the *Union pour la démocratie française* (UDF). The party is well organized, with cells in every village, usually led by women; the fact that its leaders hold not only many key political posts but also the economic power in the island has made it difficult for opposition parties to gain ground. Among such opposition parties is the *Parti pour le rassemblement démocratique des Mahorais* (PRDM), which is led by Ali Said as its secretary-general and which held its first meeting on Jan. 21, 1979. It favours the return of Mayotte to the Comoros, i.e. independence for Mayotte within the framework of the Comoro state, and it holds the view that French departmental status for Mayotte would destroy the island's indigenous

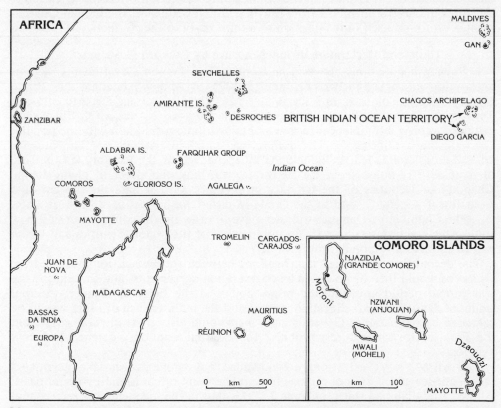

**Map 14  The Indian Ocean islands off the eastern coast of Africa, illustrating the residual territorial claims of the Comoros, Madagascar and Mauritius against France and the Mauritius-UK dispute over Diego Garcia.**

culture. Apart from the MPM and the PRDM, the French (neo-Gaullist) *Rassemblement pour la république* (RPR) is represented in Mayotte by the *Rassemblement mahorais pour la république* (RMPR), which was launched in January 1979 by Frédéric Gabriel, a former RPR deputy of St Pierre and Miquelon (the French overseas department off Newfoundland). About the same time the *Union démocratique des Mahorais* (UDM) was founded by young people who had left Madagascar (from which about 16,000 Comoro islanders were repatriated early in 1977 after serious rioting in which over 100 others had lost their lives).

In 1961 the MPM strongly opposed the Comoro Government for moving the islands' capital from Dzaoudzi (Mayotte) to Moroni (Grand Comoro), and from then onwards the movement campaigned for complete integration with France. It held four of 31 seats in the Comoros' Chamber of Deputies until 1972, and five seats in the 39-member Chamber elected thereafter. An MPM leader, Senator Marcel Henry, was quoted in *Le Monde* in June 1975 as saying: "We do not want independence, but even the status quo does not satisfy us at all. Indeed, we have always shown our opposition to the status of internal autonomy because we wish to be administered directly by Paris and reject any form of Comoro administration." As a result of this attitude the MPM was often in conflict with the French-appointed Prefect of Mayotte.

The conflict between the Government of the Comoros and the majority of the inhabitants of Mayotte came into the open in 1972, when the majority parties in the Chamber of Deputies joined forces, on Sept. 10, 1972, in order to promote independence for the islands "in friendship and co-operation with France", against the votes of the five members from Mayotte. In consequence, the French Government soon found itself in the position of a third party to the conflict.

## Unilateral Declaration of Independence by Comoro Government

Following negotiations between the Comoro and French Governments, a joint declaration was signed in Paris on June 15, 1973, by Ahmed Abdallah, then Prime Minister of the Comoros, and the French Minister of Overseas Departments and Territories, providing for independence for the Comoro Islands within five years, provided approval of independence was obtained "in consultation with the populations of the archipelago". The declaration stated in particular: "The popular consultation summoned to endorse the independence of the territory, in the case of a positive response from the electorate, will have the effect of giving to the Chamber of Deputies of the territory in existence at that date the powers of a Constituent Assembly, and to the Prime Minister the powers of a head of state. . . . The Chamber of Deputies will then have to draw up the constitution of a new state, which will preserve the rights and interests of the regional entities and which will be submitted to popular ratification."

The declaration also stated that relations between the French Republic and the Comoros would then be governed by co-operation agreements, and that during the transitional period governmental responsibility in the fields of finance, external trade, utilization of aid, education, justice and the maintenance of order was to be exercised by the Comoro Government, which would also gradually take over from the French Government responsibility for external relations, defence and civil aviation.

The MPM, however, strongly condemned any moves towards a negotiated independence which did not provide for a referendum on an island-by-island basis. Ahmed Abdallah had stated on June 7, 1973, that in the independence referendum the four islands would be consulted collectively, since according to the terms of the law they constituted a single territorial entity. The referendum itself was held on Dec. 22, 1974, when a total of 154,184 votes (or 95.96 per cent of the valid votes) were cast in favour of independence, compared with only 8,854 votes against it. On Mayotte, however, 63 per cent of those who went to the polls were understood to have come out against and about 25 per cent of the 16,000 registered electors did not vote.

After a visit to the Comoros by a French parliamentary mission in March 1975 and the submission of its report, the French National Assembly adopted, on June 26, 1975 (by 291 votes to 184, the latter including the Socialists and Communists), a Comoro Islands Independence Bill. This bill provided for independence for the islands and for the creation, within six months from the promulgation of the act, of a constitutional committee (consisting of representatives of all political groups which had been allowed to take part in the December 1974 referendum campaign, the territory's representatives in the French National Assembly and Senate and the members of the Comoro Chamber of Deputies) to draw up a constitution guaranteeing the democratic freedom of citizens and the political and administrative individuality of the islands comprising the future state. This draft constitution was to be approved "island by island" by a majority of votes cast in a referendum; if one or several of the islands rejected the draft, the committee would have to submit a new text within three months, and if the new draft was not approved by all the islands it would apply only to those islands which had adopted it.

The bill was, on June 27, 1975, rejected as "unacceptable and inapplicable" by Ahmed Abdallah, then President of the Comoro Council of Government, and subsequently also by ministers of his Government and by his *Oudzima* (Unity) party, but it was nevertheless approved by the French Senate and enacted on June 30, 1975. A week later the Comoro Chamber of Deputies (on July 6) voted by 33 votes to none (with one member being absent and the five MPM members taking no part in the vote) in favour of immediate independence; the President of the Chamber thereupon announced the islands' independence on the same day, while Ahmed Abdallah subsequently declared "the independence of the Comoros within their colonial frontiers". On July 7 the Chamber elected Ahmed Abdallah as head of state by 32 votes to one (with the MPM members again taking no part in the vote), and it also constituted itself as the new state's National Assembly and decided to set up a constitutional committee composed of representatives of all parties and charged with drafting a new constitution, which would have to be approved by the electorate as a whole and not "island by island".

Meanwhile, the five MPM deputies telegraphed the French President, placing their island "under the protection of the French Republic" and declaring that the population of Mayotte would refuse to recognize Ahmed Abdallah's Government. In a statement issued on July 9, the French Government took note of the declaration of independence of deputies from Grand Comoro, Anjouan and Mohéli, expressed readiness to engage in talks on the transfer of power, but added that the French Government would have to take account of the desire of Mayotte to follow the procedure approved by the French National Assembly involving approval of the accession to independence "island by island".

President Abdallah declared on the same day that France had "shattered the unity" of the new state and that he would call on the International Court of Justice to arbitrate; he also claimed that France wished to retain control of Mayotte in order to establish a military base on it, and he called for the earliest possible withdrawal of French armed forces from the Comoro Islands. In response, the French Secretary of State for Overseas Departments and Territories (Olivier Stirn) stated on July 10 that it was the unilateral declaration of independence by the other three islands which had created the "secession" of Mayotte; that France could grant independence but not unity; and that French law continued to apply on Mayotte.

On July 22, 1975, the French Government announced that it had decided to withdraw from Grand Comoro the last remaining military detachment of 26 men. However, some 200 soldiers of the French Foreign Legion remained stationed on Mayotte, to which the French Government had appointed a representative on July 14. On Aug. 1 pro-French demonstrators entered the French administration offices on Mayotte, asked officials of the newly-established independence Government to leave and installed members of the local council in these offices and also appointed Younoussa Bamana (one of the MPM leaders) as prefect.

### Developments following Deposition of President Abdallah

On Aug. 3, 1975, the Government of President Abdallah was overthrown by armed supporters of the *Front uni national,* which combined four (pro-independence) opposition parties under the leadership of Ali Soilih. The latter declared on Aug. 3 that he wished to preserve the territorial integrity of the archipelago and to "maintain the ties of friendship and co-operation with France which have been broken by President Abdallah", whom he also accused of having "provoked" the break-up of the Comoros. On Aug. 10 the Revolutionary Council formed by Ali Soilih handed its powers over to a 12-member National Executive Council which included two members from Mayotte, one being a member of the MPM.

On Oct. 27, 1975, the National Executive Council claimed that 2,000 people, who had many years earlier moved from Anjouan to Mayotte, had been expelled from the latter island by the MPM. According to reports from Mayotte itself, at least 200 people had been forcibly expelled by the MPM which had threatened to use the French troops stationed on the island against them. The French authorities declared on Oct. 28 that no ships leaving Mayotte would be allowed to carry passengers and that earlier deportations would be the subject of an inquiry.

The following month, on Nov. 21, a total of 160 men led by Ali Soilih flew from Grand Comoro to Mayotte in an attempt to persuade the inhabitants of Mayotte to end their "secession", but they were met by a hostile crowd and withdrew from Mayotte after a few hours. At the same time, the National Executive Council decided to launch a "general mobilization for the cause of national liberation", and on Nov. 26 the Council declared that all property of the French administration on the Comoro Islands was the property of the new state (including a radio station and civil aviation equipment). Two days later, the Comoro authorities announced that all French nationals would be repatriated; accordingly, the teachers at the 1,000-pupil lycée in Moroni left and the school was closed on Dec. 2, and as the last of some 400 French nationals the French Delegate-General (Henri Beaux) left on Dec. 14.

A bill approved by the French Government on Oct. 29, 1975, recognized the independence of Grand Comoro, Anjouan and Mohéli and provided for a referendum to be held on Mayotte within two months from the promulgation of the act in order to determine that island's future. If the decision was in favour of its remaining part of the French Republic, a second referendum to be held within another two months was to decide whether Mayotte was to be a French overseas department or an overseas territory. The bill was approved by the National Assembly (in amended form) on Dec. 10, 1975, by 300 votes to 179, and by the Senate on Dec. 31 by 198 votes to 78, and it was enacted on Dec. 31, 1975, when the three islands ceased to be part of the French Republic. During the proceedings, the then left-wing opposition claimed that the bill did not conform to the French Constitution and violated the UN Charter, and pointed out that the new state "of four islands" had been admitted to the United Nations [see below].

### Comoro-French Relations following Ahmed Abdallah's Return to Power

The Ali Soilih regime, which had attempted to introduce a radical socialist system on the Chinese model, involving the suppression of traditional Islamic practices, on the three islands of the independent Comoro state, was overthrown on May 12-13, 1978, in a coup organized with the help of Col. Robert Denard, a French mercenary. A new Government of the state, henceforth to be known as the Federal and Islamic Republic of the Comoros, was set up by May 24 with the participation of ex-President Ahmed Abdallah as one of two co-presidents of a Political-Military Directory. Later that year, on Oct. 22, Ahmed Abdallah was, as the sole candidate, elected head of state with 99.95 per cent of the votes cast.

In a referendum held on the three islands on Oct. 1, 1978, a new Constitution was approved by 99.31 per cent of the 187,124 voters. With regard to the situation of Mayotte, the Constitution stated (in Article 44) that "where the regular functioning of the constitutional institutions is interrupted by force the present Constitution's provisions relating to these institutions are suspended and the island [concerned] will provisionally exercise on its territory all powers previously held by the Federal Republic". In an order of Sept. 16 it had been stated that the Constitution, when approved in the referendum, would be applied to Mayotte "as soon as the administration of Mayotte returns to the Comoro community".

Between the new Government and France a treaty of friendship and co-operation and four co-operation agreements, including a military one, were signed on Nov. 10, 1978. Under the military agreement France was to supply aid in the event of external aggression against the Federal and Islamic Republic of the Comoros and to provide technical assistance in the training of the Comoros' Army.

### The French Government's Position in the Dispute

The French Government's attitude to the MPM's demand for continued close links between Mayotte and France was, generally speaking, that France was not opposed to such links but did not consider the granting of the status of a French department to Mayotte as appropriate. Pierre Messmer, then French Minister of State for Overseas Departments and Territories, declared during a visit to Mayotte in January 1972: "Mayotte, which has been French for 130 years, can remain French for as many years as it wishes. The population will be consulted to this end, and on that occasion a referendum will be held island by island."

In the event, however, the proposals approved by the Government on Oct. 2, 1974, were for a global referendum on all four islands as one entity, although the Government accepted amendments to its proposals, moved in the National Assembly and the Senate in November 1974, to the effect, inter alia, that parliamentary ratification of independence should not be sought until Mayotte had received a measure of regional autonomy as proposed by the Comoro Chamber of Deputies in January 1974.

President Giscard d'Estaing made a strong case for the unity of the Comoros at a press conference on Oct. 24, 1974, as follows: "The population of the Comoros is homogeneous, with a virtually non-existent or very limited element of French descent. Was it reasonable, confronted with the request for independence presented by the Government of the islands, to imagine part of the archipelago becoming independent and one island, however much one may sympathize with its inhabitants, retaining a different status? I think we have to accept contemporary realities. The Comoros are and always have been an entity, and it is natural for them to share a common destiny, even though some of them might have wanted a different solution, a fact that naturally touches us although we were not to act in consequence. It is not for us, on the occasion of a territory's independence, to propose to break up the unity of what has always been one Comoro archipelago."

During a visit to all four islands of the Comoros on Feb. 24-26, 1975, Olivier Stirn, then French Secretary of State for Overseas Departments and Territories, described the question of Mayotte as "an internal problem of the Comoros" which could be "settled within the framework of an agreement between the different parties on a draft constitution" which would embody "the maximum respect for a very broad autonomy of the islands". Subsequently, during the debate on the 1975 bill, Olivier Stirn denied that there was any link between the Government's position and the maintenance of a naval base on Mayotte. (The island's large lagoon offered exceptionally good shelter to ships and, situated at the northern entrance to the Mozambique Channel, it serves as base for a French fast patrol boat and as a staging post for French naval units in the Indian Ocean.)

The French Government's objectives in Mayotte were redefined during a visit to the island on Sept. 10-11, 1980, by Paul Dijoud, who had been appointed Secretary of State for Overseas Departments and Territories on April 6, 1978. He said at public meetings and also before the island's mayors and members of its *conseil-général* (who were all members of the MPM) that the inhabitants of Mayotte should not be afraid of talking about their future; that public debates should be organized with all representatives of political life; and that all political parties should be enabled to express their views on the radio. He also said that Mayotte should make progress "within reason"; that the "irreversible" status of a department was not suitable for the conditions of the island; and that it ought to improve its relations with the rest of the archipelago. Before the elected representatives of the island he declared that France wished to raise the standard of living of the whole population, and not just that of a few to a great extent. (Since August 1975 Mayotte's development under French administration had been concentrated on the provision of roads, water and schools; electricity was first introduced in 1977, and the number of motor vehicles rose from 30 in 1971 to 800 in 1979.)

### French Legislation and Administrative Measures concerning Mayotte

On Mayotte the first referendum provided for under the French act of Dec. 31, 1975, was held on Feb. 8, 1976, and, according to official results published on March 13, 18,061 voters or 83.3 per cent of the registered electorate of 21,671 had taken part in it; 17,949 had cast valid votes; and 17,845 (or 99.4 per cent of the votes cast) had been for remaining with France and only 104 for union with the other Comoro Islands.

In a second referendum held on April 11, 1976, Mayotte's voters were asked whether they wished the island "to retain its status as an overseas territory" or to abandon that status. As the voters were not expressly asked whether they favoured the status of an overseas department for Mayotte, the MPM had a third ballot paper printed (in addition to the two official ones, one for each alternative) containing the demand for overseas departmental status. The MPM realized that these additional ballot papers would be declared invalid, and it therefore instructed voters in certain areas to use the official ballot paper rejecting territorial status (to ensure the defeat of those who favoured maintenance of the existing territorial status), while massive casting of the unofficial ballot paper would make it clear that there was a majority in favour of departmental status.

In the event the official result, announced on April 2, showed that of 21,659 registered voters 17,384 had taken part in the poll; 13,837 papers (or 79.59 per cent) had been blank or invalid; 3,547 (or 20.4 per cent) had been valid; and of these 3,457 (or 97.46 per cent of the valid votes) had been in favour of abandoning the overseas territory status and only 90 (or 2.53 per cent) in favour of maintaining it. Olivier Stirn commented afterwards that the result had shown that Mayotte wished to be given departmental status "now".

Following the introduction of the French franc as legal tender in Mayotte in February 1976, under a bill approved by the French Government on Dec. 1, 1976, and passed, with amendments, by the National Assembly on Dec. 14 and by the

Senate on Dec. 18, Mayotte was given a special status as a *"collectivité territoriale"*. According to this new status Mayotte was administered by a 17-member *conseil-général* elected by direct universal suffrage; a representative of the French Government with the rank of prefect was in charge of national interests (including defence), administrative control and respect for the law; and laws which had applied in the Comoros before their independence remained valid on Mayotte. After at least three years from the date of the bill's promulgation the people of Mayotte would, if the *conseil-général* demanded it by a two-thirds majority, be consulted on the statute which they wished to adopt. Under another bill passed at the same time a senator from Mayotte was to be elected to the French Senate in 1977.

After the opposition PRDM had, on the French administration's insistence, been allowed to broadcast its views, the MPM temporarily boycotted all prefectural activities and also instructed its followers to vote against the centrist UDF list in the elections to the European Parliament held on June 10, 1979. The result was that out of a total of 15,249 valid votes 13,826 were cast for the list headed by Jacques Chirac, i.e. the *Défense des intérêts de la France en Europe* (DIFE), opposed to the "Giscardian" UDF, with which the MPM had traditionally been associated.

### Hostile Attitude of United Nations and Organization of African Unity to French Status of Mayotte

The continued adherence of Mayotte to the French Republic was strongly opposed by a majority of the member states of the United Nations and by the Organization of African Unity (OAU). Thus the UN General Assembly unanimously decided on Nov. 12, 1974, with France not taking part in the vote, to approve a recommendation by the UN Security Council to accept the Comoros as a whole as a member of the United Nations. The French permanent representative at the United Nations explained that France did not wish to oppose the Comoros' admission but had to reconcile the need to facilitate the creation of the new state with the procedure required by the French Constitution.

Upon an urgent call by Ali Soilih (then head of state of the Comoros) the UN Security Council met on Feb. 4-6, 1976, and eventually formulated a draft resolution declaring the proposed referendum on Mayotte to constitute interference in the Comoros' internal affairs, and calling on France to abandon the referendum and to hold immediate talks with the Comoro Government on safeguarding that country's unity and territorial integrity. However, the draft resolution was vetoed by France, which had argued that the principle of self-determination would override that of territorial integrity, while Italy, the United Kingdom and the United States abstained from voting on the resolution.

A commission of inquiry sent to the Comoros in June 1976 by the UN General Assembly reported that the "French occupation" of Mayotte involved "atrocities", including the enforced marriage of women to French soldiers ("to make the island White") and the expulsion of Comoro citizens opposed to Mayotte's "illegal occupation", and that there existed a French military base on the island. The French Ministry of Defence stated, however, that it had no intention of establishing such a base on Mayotte.

On Oct. 21, 1976, the UN General Assembly called, by 102 votes to one (France) with 28 abstentions, on France to withdraw from Mayotte. The resolution condemned the Mayotte referendums as "null and void" and asked France to negotiate with the Comoro Government on the integration of Mayotte in the independent Republic of the Comoros. The French permanent representative at the United Nations, however, declared that Mayotte was an integral part of France, that its inhabitants had freely chosen to remain so, and that France had no strategic ambitions on Mayotte, did not wish to recolonize it and would give it an "evolutionary" status.

On Dec. 6, 1979, the UN General Assembly adopted, by 112 votes to one (France) with 23 abstentions, a further resolution reaffirming the sovereignty of the Comoro Islands over Mayotte and calling on the French Government to enter into early negotiations with the Comoro Government in order to comply with UN resolutions in this matter, but the French permanent representative rejected the resolution as "impermissible interference in the internal affairs" of his country. On Nov. 28, 1980, the UN General Assembly reaffirmed "the sovereignty of the Islamic Federal Republic of the Comoros over the island of Mayotte" in a resolution adopted by 100 votes to one (France) with 26 abstentions.

After the Comoros had, early in July 1975, been admitted as a member of the OAU, the latter also repeatedly condemned France for its continued "occupation" of Mayotte. On Dec. 15, 1976, the OAU rejected the bill passed by the French National Assembly on Dec. 14, granting Mayotte a special status within the French Republic. On July 8, 1978, however, the OAU Council of Ministers excluded the new Comoro Government from current OAU sessions on the grounds that it had been installed with the help of a White mercenary. Nevertheless the subsequent Assembly of Heads of State and Government of the OAU, held on July 18-22, 1978, again condemned the continuing presence of France on Mayotte.

At its session held in Freetown (Sierra Leone) on July 1-4, 1980, the OAU Assembly of Heads of State and Government decided to send to Moroni a committee of seven members to discuss with the Comorian Government "appropriate means likely to speed up the settlement of the question".

### December 1979 French Law on Status of Mayotte

In a further law, approved by the French Senate and the National Assembly and promulgated on Dec. 22, 1979, it was laid down that the island of Mayotte was "part of the French Republic and cannot cease to belong to it without the consent of its population"; and that within five years the people of Mayotte would be consulted, following the opinion of their *conseil-général,* as to whether the statute defined in the law of Dec. 26, 1976, should be maintained, or Mayotte should be made a department, or possibly a different statute should be adopted; meanwhile the Government was authorized to extend by order, before Sept. 30, 1982, existing laws on internal affairs with amendments as deemed necessary. While the then left-wing opposition in the National Assembly abstained from voting on the legislation, the then deputy for Mayotte (Younoussa Bamana) voted against it and again called for departmental status for Mayotte.

Before the Assembly's law commission Paul Dijoud, Secretary of State for Overseas Departments and Territories, had earlier stated that the obstacles to giving departmental status to an island of whose population only 10 per cent spoke French were the lack of sanitary, social, economic and cultural structures, illiteracy, the specific character of its Moslem culture and customs, and underdevelopment.

H.W.D.

# Djibouti-Somalia

A dispute existed between Somalia and France arising from Somali claims to the territory of French Somaliland (now independent Djibouti, with a population estimated at 250,000 in 1977 and an area of some 22,000 sq km) on the grounds that its major population group formed part of the historic Somali nation. Although in recent years the Somali Government has not actively prosecuted the claim, it remains committed under its 1979 Constitution to encouraging "the unity of the Somali people through their own free will". (For Somalia's related disputes with Ethiopia and Kenya, see pages 114-19 and 131-37 respectively.)

Prior to independence in 1977 Djibouti was a French-administered territory, established as the protectorate of French Somaliland in 1884-88; the name was changed to the French Territory of the Afars and Issas in 1967. Ethnic Somalis

**Map 15   Present territorial relationship of Somalia with Djibouti, Ethiopia and Kenya.**

111

comprised the largest group in the population, the Issa being the principal local Somali clan, and Somalis regarded them as one of the five elements of the historic Somali nation. From 1960, when the Republic of Somalia became independent, successive Somali governments espoused the goal of unification of the Somali nation, of which the Republic embraced only two of five elements, namely the former British Somaliland Protectorate and Italian-administered Somalia (which had latterly been a United Nations trust territory). Somali irredentism was expressed as a demand for the right of self-determination for Somali-speaking peoples under foreign administration not only in Djibouti but also in Ethiopia and Kenya.

The eastern border between the territory and Somalia had been defined in an Exchange of Notes in February 1888 between France and the United Kingdom, the then relevant colonial authorities, while the border between the territory and Ethiopia was defined in general terms in a Convention of March 20, 1897, between France and Ethiopia (elaborated by exchange of notes on June 3, 1947, Aug. 28, 1948 and Oct. 29, 1949, and by Protocols of Jan. 16, 1954, and Nov. 2, 1954). However, the issue raised by Somalia was not explicitly couched as a territorial claim but as a matter of decolonization, with the added contention that nationalist leaders in the territory desired union with Somalia.

The Liberation Committee of the Organization of African Unity responded to Somali requests that it consider this issue by appointing a sub-committee in January 1965 to report on the situation in the territory, but the sub-committee was refused permission to enter French Somaliland itself. With its investigation thus restricted to interviewing nationalist leaders from the territory in Somalia (where it was claimed that the population desired union with Somalia) and in Ethiopia (where it was claimed that the population desired union with Ethiopia), the sub-committee concluded that the future of the territory would have to be decided by the population itself. The United Nations Committee of 24 (on colonialism), considering the matter in 1966, heard similar conflicting assertions.

Following an announcement by the French administration in August 1966 that a referendum would be held on the future of the territory, Somalia called for international supervision of the voting, and unsuccessfully proposed that the OAU at its meeting in Addis Ababa (Ethiopia) in November 1966 should call on the population to vote for independence. The UN General Assembly adopted on Dec. 21, 1966, a resolution calling for international supervision, but this was ignored by the French authorities; the referendum was held as scheduled on March 19, 1967, and recorded a vote of 22,523 for continued association with France and 14,734 against.

Somalia rejected the result of the referendum and called for an international investigation into its conduct. Ethiopia, however, accepted the result, having reportedly received French assurances at meetings in the latter part of 1966 that a continuing French administration in the territory would respect Ethiopian interests (notably regarding the railway linking the Ethiopian hinterland with the port of Djibouti).

Although in the wake of the controversy over the referendum Somalia continued to advocate independence for the territory, later in 1967 the new Prime Minister of Somalia, Mohammed Ibrahim Egal, visited Paris on Sept. 20-21 for talks with President De Gaulle, and a joint communiqué issued after this meeting expressed the commitment of both parties to the right of all peoples to self-determination, and to the principle of non-interference by states in the internal affairs of others.

In the succeeding years the French authorities reiterated on a number of occasions their intention of continuing to administer the territory, which following the referendum had been renamed the French Territory of the Afars and Issas. Increasing nationalist agitation, however, which received support from Somali Government spokesmen in international forums, resulted in 1975 in the reversal of this policy and the announcement by the French Government at the end of the year (on Dec. 31) that independence would shortly be granted. Whereas in this context the relationships between ethnic Somali and non-Somali (principally Afar) groups remained a matter of primary political significance, it was notable that leaders of both groups worked towards the goal of independence without articulating any objective of subsequent unification with Somalia or per contra with Ethiopia. Assurances were sought from these two countries that there would be no interference in the internal affairs of the proposed new independent state. The Somali delegate at the UN stated on Nov. 10, 1976, that Somalia would be "the first to recognize the new state's sovereignty and territorial integrity", and the UN General Assembly on Dec. 1 welcomed solemn declarations made by Ethiopia and Somalia that they would "recognize, respect and honour the independence and sovereignty" of Djibouti "and its territorial integrity after its accession to independence". Somalia reaffirmed this in a joint communiqué issued on Jan. 6, 1977, following a visit to Mogadishu by Pierre-Christian Taittinger, then French Secretary of State for Foreign Affairs.

Following a referendum on May 8, 1977, in which a majority of 81,847 to 199 (with 784 ballot papers declared invalid) voted in favour of independence in a 77.2 per cent poll, the Republic of Djibouti became independent on June 26, 1977; its governing coalition (in which ethnic Somalis were in the majority alongside Afar representatives) officially adopted a policy of rapid detribalization and the strengthening of national unity.

The independence of Djibouti, within its existing borders, would appear to have met the Somali demand that the territory be allowed self-determination. Somalia (and Ethiopia) recognized the Republic of Djibouti, supporting its admission to the OAU and other international organizations, and establishing diplomatic relations at ambassadorial level.

The Ethiopian and Kenyan Governments, in calling for the explicit renunciation by Somalia of all territorial claims against its neighbours, have continued to refer to the existence of a Somali territorial claim on Djibouti, although Somalia has in effect not pursued any such claim. Emphasis on promoting the unity of the Somali nation, as expressed in Somalia's original (1960) Constitution, was amended in the 1979 Constitution approved by referendum on Aug. 25, which states in Article 16 that "the Somali Democratic Republic, adopting peaceful and legal means, shall support the liberation of Somali territories under colonial occupation and shall encourage the unity of the Somali people through their own free will".

**R.E.**

# Ethiopia-Somalia

The status of the Ogaden area, regarded by the Ethiopian Government as belonging to the country's eastern provinces of Hararghe, Bale and Sidamo, has been called into dispute by the successive governments of Somalia since that country's independence in 1960. The Somalis refer to the area as Western Somalia, and regard it as a Somali-inhabited region under foreign (Ethiopian) domination, for which they assert that the principle of self-determination should be applied. (For Somalia's related disputes with Djibouti and Kenya, see pages 111-13 and 131-37; a map of the region appears on page 111.)

Properly speaking, the name "Ogaden" refers to a geographical area defined by its physical characteristics as the Ogaden desert rather than by clearly demarcated political boundaries. A sub-area known as the Haud or Reserve, lying on the southern side of the border of former British Somaliland, is generally also included when reference is made to the "Ogaden dispute". Insofar as the disputed area can be defined precisely, it is that area inhabited by nomadic pastoral peoples belonging ethnically to the Somali nation, their numbers being variously estimated at between one and three million. Somali irredentist claims have also a historical dimension, in that the Somali tribes of the Horn of Africa constituted one political system prior to the colonial divisions of territory in the late 19th century. In modern history, Ethiopian sovereignty prior to 1886 extended no further eastward than the line of the Awash river, i.e. excluding the towns of Diredawa, Harar and Jijiga and the whole of the now-disputed area. It was only in the last part of the 19th century, as the European powers were establishing their authority over what became British and Italian Somaliland, that the Ethiopian Empire extended its control eastwards, to the limits set in subsequent agreements with the British and Italians [see below].

A brief summary is given below of historical developments affecting the disputed area up to the establishment of an independent Somali Republic in former British and Italian Somaliland in 1960. This is followed by an account of the nature of the conflicting arguments put forward by the parties to the dispute, and an indication of the extent to which such arguments have found international acceptance. The chapter concludes with a review of the manner in which the dispute has been pursued since 1960.

## Historical Developments up to 1960

The British protectorate on the northern Somali coast, which was to become British Somaliland, was established in a series of treaties concluded with local tribes in 1884-86. Its extent was to be limited both by competing Italian ambitions (resulting in the establishment of Italian Somaliland) and by the westward expansion in 1886-92 of the Ethiopian Empire under Emperor Menelek II.

This Ethiopian expansion included the capture in 1887 of the independent Moslem citadel of Harar and the installation of Ras Makunan (father of the late Emperor Haile Selassie of Ethiopia) as Governor of Harar and its dependencies. The Ethiopian Emperor, in his circular letter to the European powers in 1891, declared that Ethiopia "has been for centuries a Christian island in a sea of pagans". The letter went on to state that "if powers at a distance come forward to partition Africa between them, I do not intend to be an independent spectator". In a military campaign culminating in the Battle of Adowa in 1896 the Ethiopian Empire successfully defended its independence vis-à-vis Italian imperialist aspirations. The borders between Ethiopia and the British and Italian protectorates in Somaliland were the subject of treaties in the ensuing period which left the Somali-inhabited Ogaden area under Ethiopian jurisdiction.

The treaty between Ethiopia and Britain, signed on May 14, 1897, established a boundary between Ethiopia and British Somaliland which was subsequently demarcated by an Anglo-Ethiopian boundary commission in 1932-35 (an agreed report being signed in Addis Ababa on March 28, 1935). This boundary was that existing at the time of the independence of Somalia in 1960. Its alignment explicitly accepted that certain Somali tribespeople would come under Ethiopian jurisdiction; thus in Annex I to the 1897 treaty the British envoy required and obtained of the Ethiopian emperor an assurance that "in the event of a possible occupation by Ethiopia of territories inhabited by tribes who have formerly accepted and enjoyed British protection in the districts excluded from the British protectorate . . . it will be your special care that these tribes receive equitable treatment and are thus no losers by this transfer of suzerainty". In Annex 3, agreed on June 4, 1897, the representatives of both sides agreed that "the tribes occupying either side of the line shall have the right to use the grazing grounds on the other side, but during their migrations it is understood that they shall be subject to the jurisdiction of the territorial authority". These treaty-based grazing rights were in existence until Somalia's independence in 1960, at which time the Ethiopian Government took the position that they would cease to exist.

The boundary between Ethiopia and Italian Somaliland was rather more complex. The 1896 peace treaty signed on Oct. 26 stated that the frontier should be settled within one year, but this was not done until 1908, when a further treaty was concluded (on May 16). The fact that the two sides gave different interpretations to this agreement, as to the line of the frontier, made it impossible for a joint boundary commission to complete its work of delimitation and demarcation, and the precise alignment intended by the 1908 treaty was still in dispute at the time of Somali independence in 1960. Essentially, the Ethiopians maintained that a frontier line agreed in negotiations in 1897 between Emperor Menelek and the Italian representative, Maj. Nerazzini, ran more or less parallel with the coast and 140 miles (225 km) from it, to a tripoint with British Somaliland. The Ethiopian contention was that the southern part of this frontier (from Dolo to the Uebi Scebeli river) was then pushed northward in favour of Italy in return for the payment of 3,000,000 lire, as stipulated in an Additional Act to the 1908 treaty. The Italian interpretation was that the Menelek-Nerazzini agreement in 1897 (to which the 1908 treaty refers only as "the line accepted by the Italian Government in 1897") covered only the frontier north of the Uebi Scebeli river and that this frontier ran at a distance of some 180 miles (290 km) from the coast.

It should be pointed out that this dispute between Ethiopia and Italy did not strictly relate to the Ogaden itself; the 1908 treaty stated clearly that "all the territory of Ogaden and all that of the tribes towards the Ogaden shall remain dependent on Abyssinia".

In the period from 1935, Ethiopia was first conquered by the Italians, and then reconquered during World War II by the British, who by 1941 had taken control of the whole of the Horn of Africa. The British restored Emperor Haile Selassie to his throne in Ethiopia, but retained temporary responsibility for the administration of the Reserved Area and the Ogaden, under the terms of an Anglo-Ethiopian Treaty concluded in December 1944.

In the immediate post-war period, therefore, the British were administering British Somaliland (as a colony), Italian Somaliland (under military arrangements following their conquest of the former Italian colony) and the Somali-inhabited Ogaden area (under the temporary arrangements described above). The then British Foreign Secretary, Ernest Bevin, suggested in 1948 the creation in these territories of a unified Somali nation, as a UN trust territory under British administration. As he described it at the UN, this would allow the nomadic people of the area to "lead their frugal life with the least possible hindrance, and there might be a real chance of a decent economic life in that territory". However, the idea failed to win international support and was strongly opposed by Ethiopia; the British Government consequently dropped the idea and made provision for the return of the Reserved Area and the Ogaden to Ethiopia. This was agreed on Nov. 29, 1954, with the Imperial Ethiopian Government reassuming jurisdiction and administration of, in and over the territories with effect from Feb. 28, 1955.

British military administration over the former Italian Somaliland was withdrawn in 1950 when Italy took over the administration of what had become the UN Trust Territory of Somaliland. There being still no agreement on where the border should run between this territory and Ethiopia, a provisional line was defined by the British prior to their withdrawal. This provisional line was described in detail in a British letter on March 1, 1950, to the UN Trusteeship Council, when it was justified as apparently representing "the maximum degree of administrative convenience to both parties". It was, however, only a provisional line "pending the demarcation of the frontier" and "without prejudice to the final settlement of this question". Notwithstanding these sentiments, the provisional line represented the de facto border at the time of the independence of Somalia in 1960.

## The Ethiopian and Somali Cases

Ethiopia takes the position that the Ogaden area is an integral part of its territory, and consequently regards Somali challenges as acts of aggression against Ethiopia's integrity. The Ethiopians insist that Somalia must accept its boundaries as they existed at the time of independence, i.e. in 1960. They consider that the northern sector of the boundary was defined beyond any possibility of subsequent argument by the Anglo-Ethiopian treaty of 1897, substantiated by the demarcation of the boundary in 1932-35. (However, the Ethiopian Government took the position in 1960 that trans-border grazing rights as provided by their agreements with the British would cease to apply after Somalia became independent.) With regard to the southern sector of the boundary, the Ethiopians base their position on the existence of the 1908 treaty between Ethiopia and Italy. Their contention is that a dispute with Somalia could only properly exist within the framework of the known Ethiopian-Italian disagreement over interpretation of that 1908 treaty. Such a dispute, it is argued, would be susceptible to resolution by careful inquiry into the treaty, and possibly by arbitration over its meaning.

The Somali argument is that the Ogaden area, to which they refer as Western Somalia, is inhabited by ethnic Somalis and belonged to the historic Somali nation, before undergoing foreign conquest during the colonial period. According to the Somali position, the area should be viewed as a case for decolonization; the fact that the colonial conquest was not by a European power but by an African one (the "Black Abyssinian imperialists", as the Ethiopians are frequently termed in Somali propaganda) should not affect this principle, in the Somali view. The Government of Somalia accordingly presents itself in the role of supporter of an indigenous liberation struggle for the right to self-determination of the people of so-called Western Somalia.

The objective of Somali nationalism and irredentism has been to secure the independence of each of the five parts into which the Somali nation was divided in the colonial period. It was assumed that a unified Somali state would then be formed by the voluntary merger of these five parts. Independent Somalia as established in 1960 consisted of two of these units (former British and Italian Somaliland); the new country's constitution included a commitment to furthering the process, and the ideal of unity is symbolized by the five-pointed star on Somalia's flag. "Western Somalia", with its estimated one to three million inhabitants, is the most populous of the three Somali-inhabited areas remaining outside the Somali state (the other two being what is now Djibouti and the north-eastern part of Kenya).

The Organization of African Unity (OAU), when it was set up in 1963, was immediately faced with the existence of this dispute between two of its member countries. The Somali Government sought to involve the OAU in the matter by calling for a plebiscite to establish the wishes of the inhabitants of the Ogaden. The Ethiopians meanwhile condemned as an act of aggression the support given by Somalia to ethnic Somali guerrilla forces in the area. Somalia referred to Article III of the OAU Charter, setting out the organization's principles including the inalienable right of each state to independent existence, and (in 1964 and 1965 respectively) called for an OAU fact-finding mission and for direct discussions to be held with Ethiopian leaders in Khartoum. These proposals came to nothing, in the face of (i) Ethiopia's insistence that its territorial integrity was not open to any discussion, and (ii) the great reluctance of African leaders in general to encourage any variation in the African state boundaries inherited from the colonial period. A resolution was adopted by the OAU Assembly of Heads of State and Government in Cairo in July 1964, solemnly declaring "that all member states pledge themselves to respect the borders existing on their achievement of national independence", although this resolution was not accepted by Somalia.

### Recent Conflict in the Disputed Area

Relations between Ethiopia and Somalia deteriorated as far as a brief direct military conflict in 1964 over the question of Somali Government support for guerrillas in the Ogaden. Somali irredentist feeling was held more strictly in check after 1967 by the Government of Mohammed Ibrahim Egal, who favoured a policy of dialogue with Somalia's neighbours. According to a communiqué published simultaneously in Addis Ababa and Mogadishu on Sept. 22, 1967, Ethiopia and Somalia agreed to "eliminate all forms of tension" between themselves, to establish a joint military commission to examine complaints by either side, and to "perfect co-operation" by means of quarterly meetings of their administrative authorities.

After the military takeover in Somalia in 1969 and the military overthrow of the Ethiopian Emperor in 1974, the Somali Government led by Gen. Siyad Barreh sought to re-open the Ogaden question in a diplomatic initiative towards Ethiopia. However, the new Ethiopian regime showed itself no less intent than its imperial predecessor on retaining possession of the Ogaden. Under these circumstances, the Government of Somalia in 1977 ceased its attempt to restrain the militant irredentism of Ogaden Somali groups, principal of which was the Western Somalia Liberation Front (WSLF), together with the Somali Abo Liberation Front (SALF).

Guerrilla violence in the Ogaden escalated in mid-1977 to the point of full-scale direct warfare, with heavy casualties on both sides. An initial phase of the war was characterized by Somali successes, including notably the capture of the town of Jijiga in September 1977 and an advance as far as Harar by November. A successful Ethiopian counter-offensive was launched in January 1978 with the backing of Soviet and Cuban forces (the Soviet Union having in 1977 reversed its former policy of providing military aid to the Somali Government). Ethiopian forces recaptured Jijiga in early March 1978 and regained control of strategic points in the region. However, despite the maintenance of Ethiopian garrisons in a network of towns and villages in the Ogaden, Somali-backed guerrilla forces remained active in the countryside and continued to broadcast (by radio from Mogadishu) claims of heavy casualties inflicted against Ethiopian and Cuban troops.

It was not until Feb. 21, 1978, that the Somali Government had acknowledged the presence of its troops in the Ogaden area alongside WSLF forces. Prior to this acknowledgement, the Somali Government had alleged that the Ethiopians were not fighting only in the Ogaden as they claimed, but that they were also launching air attacks on towns over the border in Somalia. A general mobilization was declared in Somalia on Feb. 9, 1978, and on the following day Cyrus Vance, the US Secretary of State, declared that the US would supply arms to Somalia in the event of Ethiopian aggression. Responding to a ceasefire proposal made by the US, the Somali Government announced on March 8 that all Somali regular troops would be withdrawn from the Ogaden area. The following day a further announcement appealed to the great powers to ensure "the withdrawal of all foreign forces present in the Horn of Africa", called for "recognition by the interested parties of the right to self-determination" of the Ogaden people, and looked for the initiation of a process which would lead to "a negotiated, peaceful, just and durable settlement". The Ethiopian Government responded on March 11, 1978, and has subsequently repeatedly reiterated, that one requirement for a just and durable peace would be unconditional abandonment by Somalia of all claims to territory in Ethiopia, Kenya and Djibouti, and the abrogation of all juridical bases for such claims.

The Ogaden dispute has continued, since the 1977-78 war, with guerrilla warfare and heavy casualties, and the Somali Government giving its backing to the guerrillas while denying Ethiopian allegations that its regular troops were involved. Somalia has also made repeated complaints of Ethiopian air raids on its territory, while in human terms the conflict has led to many hundreds of thousands of displaced persons pouring into refugee camps in both Somalia and Ethiopia, with a resultant heavy burden being placed on both the Ethiopian and Somali economies and on international relief organizations.

There was an apparent increase in tension between Ethiopia and Somalia in 1980, with reciprocal allegations of attempted invasions. A restatement of the Ethiopian position was contained in a joint Ethiopian-Kenyan communiqué issued in Nairobi on Dec. 4, 1980, following a visit there by Lt.-Col. Mengistu Haile Mariam, the Ethiopian head of state. The communiqué emphasized co-operation against what was described as Somali expansionism and called on Somalia to "renounce publicly and unconditionally all claims to the territories of Ethiopia, Kenya and Djibouti". Referring to international principles of the inviolability of frontiers and non-interference in internal affairs, it called on Somalia to withdraw its reservation (entered on July 23, 1964) whereby Somalia had refused to be bound by the 1964 OAU resolution on the acceptance of frontiers existing at independence. The communiqué referred to the intention of the Kenyan and Ethiopian Governments of eliminating "the root cause of tension and insecurity in the region" and called on all countries to cease military assistance to Somalia. In the latter context, the United States and Somalia had negotiated an agreement in August 1980 allowing US use of Somali base facilities. The implementation of this agreement, which provided for US military assistance to Somalia for the purchase of large quantities of "defensive weapons and equipment", was delayed until January 1981, the US Congress having insisted that the State Department should first provide "verified assurances" that there were no Somali troops in the Ogaden area.

The Somali Government responded to the Ethiopian-Kenyan communiqué, which it described as provocative and threatening, by urging "the Somali people whereever they are" to be ready to defend their national sovereignty and their motherland. A statement issued by the Somali Government on Dec. 7, 1980, commented inter alia that the Kenyan Government had been ensnared in an Ethiopian trap, and called on both countries to withdraw their communiqué, which it described as tantamount to a declaration of war.

The apparently intractable nature of this dispute has meant that there has been little prospect of successful mediation during the period of over 20 years since Somalia attained independence. An eight-member OAU "good offices" committee was set up in 1973, at a time when the dispute was in a less acute phase, and the OAU committee held a meeting in Lagos on Aug. 18-20, 1980, which ended with the reaffirmation of the OAU's principles for the resolution of disputes. Although both Ethiopia and Somalia claimed this to be a vindication of their own position, it has generally been seen as underlining, by one more instance, the failure of Somalia to win support for changing the status of the Ogaden area. Meanwhile, it must be noted that the ethnic composition of the Ogaden population is being affected by the displacement of people caused by the conflict, and by an Ethiopian policy to promote new settlement in the area.

R.E.

# France-Madagascar

There exists a dispute between the Governments of France and of Madagascar concerning sovereignty over a number of small islands, originally uninhabited, off the coast of Madagascar, and having a total area of 28 square kilometres (about 11 square miles). These islands are the Glorioso Islands (Iles Glorieuses) to the north of Madagascar, as well as Juan de Nova, Bassas da India and Europa, situated in the Mozambique Channel. (For map illustrating this dispute, see page 103.)

The islands in question have been under French sovereignty since 1896 and are administered by the prefect of the French overseas department of Réunion (east of Madagascar and south-west of Mauritius) through the intermediary of Réunion's Director of Meteorological Services, who has stationed personnel on them for weather observation (except on Bassas da India, which is almost totally submerged at high tide). Since December 1973 the French Government has had small "symbolic" contingents drawn from a parachute regiment (itself stationed on Réunion) on each of these islands (again except Bassas da India), and an airstrip on Juan de Nova has been enlarged so as to enable Transall transport aircraft to use it. The Government of Madagascar, however, has forbidden such aircraft to overfly Malagasy territory, and all supplies flown in from Réunion to the islands in the Mozambique Channel are therefore flown round the northern end of Madagascar.

The Government of Madagascar has persisted in claiming sovereignty over the islands. During negotiations conducted on new co-operation agreements between France and Madagascar, President Didier Ratsiraka of Madagascar stated on May 22, 1973, that the problem of these islands had been raised by his Government in the talks; that the French Government had, however, replied that the question would be settled later between the two Governments; that no agreement or consensus had been reached on the question and that it had therefore not been dealt with within the framework of the co-operation agreements; and that the dispute might eventually be placed before the International Court of Justice.

119

In September 1973 the Government of Madagascar announced that it had extended its territorial waters limit to 90 kilometres (56 miles) and that of its continental shelf to 180 kilometres (112 miles) from its coasts so as to include the above-mentioned islands, and it accordingly informed the United Nations in 1976. In an interview given in June 1976 President Ratsiraka said: "We are not giving up hope that one day these islands will revert to us. I do not see why France should not surrender them seeing that it has granted independence to all its former colonies in Asia and Africa." The French Government, on the other hand, under a decree of Feb. 3, 1978, declared exclusive 200-mile (320-km) economic zones around its dependencies in the Indian Ocean, expressly including the above-mentioned islands.

On March 21 of that year the Government of Madagascar officially protested against the French decision to include the islands in France's exclusive economic zone and affirmed that the Iles Glorieuses, Juan de Nova, Bassas da India and Europa were "an integral part of Madagascar's territory". In this protest no mention was made of the island of Tromelin, about 560 kilometres, or 350 miles, north of Réunion, also included in the French Government decree of Feb. 3, 1978; the Government of Madagascar had in fact ceded its claim for this island to Mauritius, which had claimed it for itself [see pages 122-24].

Madagascar's claim was, however, not raised by President Ratsiraka when he visited Paris on Sept. 24-27, 1978, and had discussions with President Giscard d'Estaing, with the result of which he afterwards declared himself to be "fairly satisfied". A statement made in May 1979 by Rear-Admiral Jean-Paul Orosco, then commander of French naval forces in the Indian Ocean, reiterated that the disputed islands formed part of the French dependencies in the Indian Ocean, the defence of which would have to be conducted from the French base in Djibouti.

### Endorsement of Madagascar's Claim by the UN General Assembly

At the request of Madagascar the United Nations General Assembly took up the question of the sovereignty over these islands in 1979 and 1980. The UN General Assembly, in a resolution (34/91) adopted on Dec. 12, 1979, noted Madagascar's claim for the reintegration in its territory of the Iles Glorieuses, Juan de Nova, Bassas da India and Europa; requested the Government of France to repeal measures which "infringe the sovereignty and territorial integrity of Madagascar"; and called on the French Government to initiate negotiations with Madagascar on the reintegration of these islands in Madagascar. The resolution was approved by 93 votes to seven (Belgium, France, Italy, Luxembourg, Senegal, the United Kingdom and the United States) with 36 abstentions (including other Western countries).

The Special Political Committee of the UN General Assembly (which has the same composition as the Assembly) adopted, on Nov. 25, 1980, a resolution demanding that the islands, which, the Committee claimed, had been "arbitrarily separated" from Madagascar, should be returned to that country. The resolution was passed by 83 votes to 13 (Belgium, France, the Federal Republic of Germany, Greece, Guatemala, Honduras, Italy, Luxembourg, Morocco, the Netherlands, Senegal, the United Kingdom and the United States) with 32 abstentions.

In a further resolution (35/123), adopted on Dec. 11, 1980, by 81 votes to 13 with 37 abstentions, the UN General Assembly expressed regret that the negotiations envisaged in its previous resolution had not been initiated; took note of a report of the UN Secretary-General on the subject; and again invited France urgently to initiate negotiations with Madagascar in order to settle the question "in accordance with the purposes and principles of the United Nations". Those voting against this resolution included the member states of the European Community except Denmark and Ireland (which both abstained) and also the United States.

## Madagascar's Appeals to the OAU and the Non-Aligned Movement

In an explanatory statement deposited with the Organization of African Unity (OAU) the Government of the Democratic Republic of Madagascar declared inter alia that on April·1, 1960 (on the eve of Madagascar's achievement of independence), France had presented Madagascar with a fait accompli by the arbitrary detachment of the islands from Madagascar and their transfer to the direct control of the French Ministry of Overseas Departments and Territories; that under a decree of Sept. 19, 1960 (confirmed on March 11, 1972, and April 17, 1973) the French Government had entrusted the administration of the islands to the Prefect of Réunion; but that until 1960 France had consistently confirmed the "organic unity" of Madagascar and the islands; that under international law a state had "a natural right of sovereignty" over nearby small islands; that the Government of Madagascar therefore intended to denounce all measures taken by France in relation to the disputed islands, to ask for the opening of significant negotiations on the subject, and to inform regional and national organizations accordingly.

The Government of Madagascar also stated that it had denounced the progressive militarization of the islands and their inclusion in a strategy which was incompatible with the demands of national and regional security and with the creation of a zone of peace in the Indian Ocean; had protested against the French declaration of 200-mile economic zones round the islands; had taken part in the work of a joint Franco-Malagasy commission from March to June 1979, without result; had placed the question before the OAU in July 1979 and before the non-aligned movement in September 1979, with the result that (i) the 16th OAU Assembly of Heads of State and Government (in Monrovia on July 12-17, 1979) had approved a resolution stating that the islands were an integral part of the territory of the Democratic Republic of Madagascar and inviting the French Government to restore them to Madagascar, and (ii) the sixth conference of heads of state and government of non-aligned countries (in Havana on Sept. 3-9, 1979) had similarly demanded the restoration of the islands to Madagascar.

## French Rejection of UN Resolutions

In a statement made in reply to claims made by the permanent representative of Madagascar at the UN General Assembly, Jacques Leprette, the French permanent representative at the United Nations, said before the vote of Dec. 11, 1980, inter alia: "The territories concerned have been part of the French Republic since the last century. These small islands, with a total area of about 11 square miles, were 'vacant lands without owner' and without any population. They were taken possession of under international law within the legal forms required and without any protest from the international community. These territories were [on April 1, 1960] placed under the authority of the [French] Minister of Overseas Departments and Territories. The Government of Madagascar took note of this situation on April 2, 1960, when the first series of co-operation agreements with France was concluded. On the legal level . . . French sovereignty, which had been uncontested until recent years, has never been interrupted since its inception. It has been expressed by the effective and continued exercise of state functions."

Stating that Madagascar's claim to the islands was in conflict with Art. 2, Paragraph 7, of the UN Charter (laying down that "nothing in the Charter shall authorize the United Nations to intervene in matters which are essentially within the domestic jurisdiction of any state"), the French representative also rejected the argument of "contiguity" (advanced by the representative of Madagascar) as not recognized in international law and as inapplicable to territories at a distance of 150 to 380 kilometres (about 90 to 240 miles). He also dismissed the argument that the new 200-mile sea limit would ipso facto give Madagascar territorial and maritime control over most of the Mozambique Channel and over vast ocean areas towards Mauritius and Réunion as being in total conflict with the work of the Third Conference on the Law of the Sea. The delimitation of such territories, he said, must be effected in agreement between neighbouring states, and he continued: "If any coastal state were able to claim all the islands situated at less than 200 miles off its coasts the world's political map would be overturned and world peace would be threatened."

The French representative also rejected the Madagascan argument that the islands were part of the continental shelf of Madagascar, stating that in fact they were separated from Madagascar by ocean depths of more than 3,000 metres. In this context he referred to a decision by the International Court of Justice laying down that parts of the continental shelf situated at about 100 miles (160 km) from a coast, or separated from these coasts by a trench, could not be regarded as lying adjacent to the coast.

On the constitutional aspect he said that the decision of Oct. 15, 1958 (when Madagascar became an autonomous republic within the French Community), which rendered void the law on the annexation of Madagascar, contained no mention of the islands in question; that they had not been annexed at the same time as Madagascar but had been the object of a direct occupation; and that they could therefore not be regarded as dependencies of Madagascar. He also emphasized that the question was not one of decolonization, as these islands lacked all resources, even drinking water, and had never been able to sustain any living soul.

Following Madagascar's achievement of full independence on June 26, 1960, the property records of the Iles Glorieuses and of Juan de Nova (there being none for Bassas da India, Europa or Tromelin), which had been held by the French authorities in Madagascar, were transferred to the French ambassador to Madagascar; the French Government regarded this fact as implying recognition of French sovereignty over the islands by Madagascar.

**H.W.D.**

# France-Mauritius (Tromelin Island)

The Government of Mauritius formally claimed sovereignty, with retroactive effect from 1814, over the island of Tromelin in a document presented to the French ambassador to Mauritius by the latter's Prime Minister on April 2, 1976, and the French Government officially rejected this claim on Dec. 17, 1976. (For map illustrating this dispute, see page 103.)

The island of Tromelin, situated about 450 kilometres (280 miles) east of Madagascar and 550 kilometres (340 miles) north of Mauritius and the island of Réunion (a French overseas department), consists of a volcano which is crowned by a coral plateau and the ocean floor around which is about 4,000 metres deep. Its total area is only about one square kilometre, and its highest point rises to only seven metres above sea-level. The island has no economic importance (except for the export of turtles), there is no fresh water and no agriculture is possible. It is difficult of access by sea but has a landing strip suitable for light aircraft only.

Tromelin was discovered by French seafarers in 1722 and was named after a Frenchman who landed there in 1776. There is no evidence that the French Government ever announced its occupation or notified foreign powers of such occupation, but the island's status was not in dispute until the middle of the 20th century.

At the first session of the regional association of the World Meteorological Organization (WMO) held in Tananarive (Madagascar) in January 1953 France was asked to examine the possibility of setting up a weather observation station on Tromelin. According to some sources the British Government acceded to a request by the French meteorological services in Tananarive to be allowed to set up such a station on Tromelin. A permanent observation station was eventually set up on the island by France on May 7, 1954, which thus constituted a date of effective French occupation of Tromelin. At a further WMO congress held in 1959, however, Mauritius declared that it considered Tromelin to be part of its territory. The French delegation stated in reply that France had always considered the island to be French and that the French title to it dated back to the island's discovery by a Frenchman in 1722. Since 1961 the weather station on Tromelin had been attached to the French meteorological service in Saint Denis (Réunion), although it has functioned in liaison with Madagascar's service, which has, however, made no financial contribution to the cost of its operation.

Until 1960 Tromelin had been administered from Madagascar, which after its achievement of independence had also laid claim to the island, but after 1976 this claim was waived in favour of Mauritius, as confirmed by President Didier Ratsiraka during a visit to Madagascar by Paul Bérenger, a leader of the left-wing Mauritian Militant Movement, which had emerged as the strongest political party in general elections held in Mauritius in 1976.

The Government of Mauritius—since its achievement of independence on March 12, 1968, the legal successor of Britain in matters concerning Mauritius—based its claim to Tromelin on its own interpretation of the first Treaty of Paris of May 30, 1814, under which Britain restored to France certain Indian Ocean islands which it had taken in 1810, "except the Isle of France (i.e. Mauritius) and its dependencies, especially Rodrigues and the Seychelles" (over which France ceded sovereignty to Britain). In its claim of April 2, 1976, the Mauritian Government interpreted the word "especially" as meaning "in particular, among others or notably" and asserted that in addition to Rodrigues and the Seychelles the exception included also "minor dependencies" (among them Tromelin) such as the Chagos Archipelago, Agalega and the Cargados-Carajos (St Brandon) islands, which have in fact, with French acquiescence, remained under British sovereignty. The Mauritian Government also referred to certain administrative acts carried out by the Port Louis authorities after 1814, in particular to leases issued between 1901 and 1956 to Mauritian nationals for the exploitation of guano. According to French sources, however, there was no guano on Tromelin and the leases had never been taken up.

The French Government's interpretation of the 1814 Treaty of Paris is based on the treaty's French text which it considers as authentic (French having then been the accepted language of diplomacy) and in which the word "especially" is rendered as "nommément" (i.e. namely). In the French view Tromelin, which had never been occupied by Britain, therefore again became a French territory in 1814; this had never been contested by any of the signatories to the treaty; and the question of Tromelin's status had not been affected by juridical or political changes in the south-western Indian Ocean area. In addition, the British Foreign and Commonwealth Office had stated on April 2, 1973, that there had never been, and was not, any Franco-British dispute over Tromelin.

The Government of Mauritius reiterated its claim during an international conference on radio diffusion by satellite in Geneva in February 1977, when it called for individual receiving installations to be erected on Tromelin. The French delegation at the conference insisted on the inclusion in the final protocol of the conference of an express restatement of the French position in regard to continued sovereignty over the island. The Mauritian Government's claim was also reaffirmed on June 20, 1980, when it was announced that the Constitution of Mauritius would be amended so as to include Tromelin in a list of dependencies. The Mauritian claim to Tromelin is supported by all political parties of Mauritius except the (pro-Western) Mauritian Social-Democratic Party (*Parti mauritien social-démocrate*).

H.W.D.

# Ghana-Togo

Relations between the neighbouring West African Republics of Ghana and Togo have been impaired, especially between 1957 and 1962 and again in 1974-78, by a dispute which has its origins in the colonial era. The dispute has centred on (i) the division of the former German colony of Togoland under a 1920 League of Nations mandate into French-administered and British-administered territories, the former eventually becoming present-day Togo and the latter being now part of Ghana, and (ii) the separation of the Ewe tribe between the two countries, about four-fifths of this tribe forming the majority of the population of Togo and the remainder living in Ghana (although not all in the area which was once part of German Togoland). Although not much publicized since 1978, the dispute has remained unresolved, especially in the view of some Ewes living on both sides of the border. The Government of Ghana has, however, made it clear on many occasions that it will not agree to any request for the surrender to Togo of the former British-administered Togoland, while the Togolese Government has for its part consistently rejected Ghanaian aspirations towards the integration of Togo with Ghana to achieve Ewe reunification.

### Origins of the Dispute

At the beginning of World War I Togo, which had been a German colony since 1884 (formally since Dec. 24, 1885), was occupied by both British and French forces, and on July 10, 1919, Britain and France divided the territory between them, with France obtaining two-thirds of it, including the entire coast line and the railways, and with Britain obtaining the remainder which was contiguous with the (British) Gold Coast Colony. This division was confirmed in 1920, when the League of Nations granted Britain and France mandates for the administration of their respective parts of Togo. Greatly affected by the division was the Ewe tribe, which had first been divided between British and German colonial territories (in 1884) and of which the section previously resident in Togo was now divided further between British and French administration.

According to J. R. V. Prescott[1], the Ewe tribe had, before European intervention,

---

[1] *The Geography of Frontiers and Boundaries*, London, 1965.

124

been divided politically into about 120 sub-tribes, lying between the centralized military kingdoms of Abomey and Ashanti; during periods of war the Ewe groups had formed temporary alliances, but these had been dissolved in times of peace, and no complaints had been recorded from the various Ewe groups when they were first divided in 1884. Opposition to the division after World War I among some Ewes in the Lomé area was unsuccessful. The Ewes in French Togoland were encouraged to assume French culture, were conscripted (for local defence) and were ruled by a centralized Government. In British Togoland, however, and later in Ghana, the Ewes were taught in their own language, were encouraged to maintain their Ewe traditions, were not conscripted and had representatives in government councils at all levels.

At the end of World War II the two Togoland territories became UN trust territories and remained respectively under French and British administration, with unchanged boundaries. At this stage, a revived pan-Ewe movement made new demands for Ewe reunification but did not agree on the methods of union. A UN

**Map 16** **The above map of part of West and Central Africa illustrates the disputes between Cameroon and Nigeria and between Mali and Upper Volta as well as that between Ghana and Togo.**

Commission stated in 1950 inter alia: "The problem has attained the force and dimensions of a nationalistic movement and a solution should be sought with urgency in the interests of peace and stability in that part of the world." In 1952 the Ewe area in the British-administered Togoland was constituted into a Trans-Volta-Togoland region, so that the western section of the Ewes was administered as a single group.

The British Government announced in 1955 that British Togoland would cease to be a UN trust territory when the Gold Coast attained independence, which was then being prepared for. Upon a recommendation made by a United Nations mission which had visited Togoland and submitted its report on Oct. 30, 1955, a plebiscite was held in British Togoland on May 9, 1956, on the question whether the territory should be integrated with the Gold Coast on the latter's achievement of independence or whether it should remain a UN trust territory under British administration. The plebiscite resulted in 93,365 votes being cast for integration with the Gold Coast and 67,422 for continued British administration (with 161,687 voters having cast valid votes out of a total of 194,613 electors). However, of the territory's six districts only four showed majorities for integration, whereas in the other two districts—Ho and Kpandu (inhabited by Ewes of whom many wished for eventual unification of their territory with the French-administered Togoland)—there was a majority of 35,940 votes in favour of continued British trusteeship (as against only 16,068 votes for integration with the Gold Coast).

The United Nations General Assembly, in a resolution approved on Dec. 13, 1956, noted the result of the plebiscite and also the proposed granting of independence to the Gold Coast by Britain with effect from March 6, 1957, and declared that as from that date the UN trusteeship over British Togoland would cease and the territory would be united with the Gold Coast (which upon independence would become Ghana).

In the French-administered Togoland, on the other hand, the Territorial Assembly approved, on Aug. 14, 1956, a new statute published by the French Government early in August and conferring self-government on the territory within the French Union. This new statute and the consequent abolition of the territory's trusteeship status were approved in a referendum held on Oct. 28, 1956, by a total of 313,458 of the territory's 438,175 registered voters (this majority varying from about 62 per cent in the south to 80 per cent in the north), with the principal opposition to the new statute coming from those Ewes who favoured union of both British- and French-administered Togoland. The UN General Assembly, however, declined to recognize the referendum and to comply with a French request for the ending of the trusteeship over the territory and instead appointed, on Dec. 13, 1956, a commission to examine the situation. As a result of this commission's report the Assembly decided in December 1957 that elections should be held in (French) Togoland in 1958 to enable its inhabitants to decide on their future. Such elections were held under UN supervision in April 1958 and resulted in a majority voting for the termination of UN trusteeship and for the independence of the territory, which became the independent Republic of Togo (outside the French Community) on April 27, 1960, after the UN General Assembly had agreed to its independence on Nov. 14, 1958, and to the date of independence on Dec. 5, 1959.

### Secessionist Activities among the Ewe Minority in Ghana, 1957-63

Inside Ghana the integration of the former British Togoland with Ghana continued to be opposed by a minority of Ewes organized in a Togoland Congress (although many Ewes within Ghana live in the south-east and outside the former British-administered area—a reunification of which with Togo would, incidentally, divide the Dagomba people of north-east Ghana). Riots with fatal results occurred in the Ho and Kpandu districts in March 1957, and two military training camps with ammunition and explosives were earlier said to have been discovered by the police. Four leaders of the Togoland Congress (which was by then defunct) were on March 11, 1958, sentenced to six years' hard labour for conspiring to show that the integration of British Togoland with Ghana had been a failure and to persuade the United Nations to intervene; three other defendants were given three-year prison sentences at the same time.

Dr Kwame Nkrumah, then Prime Minister of Ghana, said at Ho on Oct. 28, 1959, that, speaking "for our kinsmen on the other side of the border" (meaning the 700,000 Ewes out of Togo's total population of then 1,100,000, as against some 200,000 Ewes living in Ghana), he would enter into discussions with Togolese leaders on the integration of the two countries after the achievement of independence by Togo. He renewed his appeal at the end of January 1960 when he said that integration should be achieved by peaceful means based on the wishes of the people involved. The suggestion was, however, rejected as "an insult" by Sylvanus Olympio, then Prime Minister of Togoland, who said on Feb. 4, 1960, that his Government would never accept a unitary state with Ghana, and that he himself had always opposed the union of British Togoland with Ghana and had sought the formation of a single Togolese state. His attitude was supported by Nicolas Grunitzky, a former Prime Minister and then leader of the principal opposition party in Togoland.

On March 15, 1960, the Ghanaian Foreign Ministry published the text of a note sent to the French Government alleging that "a draft constitution" circulated in French Togoland defined a considerable area of Ghana as part of Togo, and that "certain steps" were being taken in Togoland "with a view to creating disturbances in Ghana". In the note the Ghanaian Government requested France to take steps to prevent the territory from being used as "a base for an armed attack on Ghana". These allegations were rejected in toto by the Togoland Government on March 16, and the French Government categorically denied on March 25 that there existed any Togolese "draft constitution". While 14 persons were detained in Ghana in connexion with charges that they were "planning violence in conjunction with persons in French Togoland", it was announced in Lomé (the capital of French Togoland) on March 19 that 12 persons who had fled from Ghana had been granted political asylum. By 1961 several thousand refugees were said to have fled from Ghana to Togo for fear of being detained (under Ghana's Preventive Detention Act) because of their membership of the (opposition) United Party or of being opposed to the incorporation of the former British Togoland in Ghana.

The attitude of the Government of the Republic of Ghana—of which Dr Nkrumah had become President upon its proclamation on July 1, 1960—towards the Republic of Togo was set out in a White Paper published on Dec. 11, 1961. In this White Paper it was stated that the partition of the former German colony of Togo after World War I had produced "a continuing source of trouble", leading inter alia to an unsuccessful "revolt" in the Ghanaian part of Togoland on the eve of Ghana's independence in 1957. It was alleged that a current "plot" consisted in part of "an attempt to repeat what was unsuccessfully tried in 1957, this time with the support of the Republic of Togo", which was described as "one of the countries on the African continent where neocolonialism has its strongest hold". The White Paper implicitly reiterated Ghanaian territorial claims to the Republic of Togo and stated that a plebiscite on the issue of union with Ghana was desirable in Togo. The White Paper also accused Dr Kofi A. Busia, the leader of Ghana's United Party, then in exile, of planning to set up a government-in-exile in Lomé.

During 1962 the Ghanaian Government made further accusations against Togo, alleging in particular that Togo had given asylum to persons responsible for attempts to assassinate President Nkrumah, and that it tolerated the existence of a "subversive organization" among Ghanaian refugees in Togo. The Togolese Government, however, stated on Dec. 19, 1962, that Ghanaian exiles were allowed to remain in Togo only on condition of taking no part in political activities.

On Jan. 6, 1963, the Government of Ghana demanded the extradition by Togo of Dr Busia and of other Ghanaian exiles. On Jan. 13, however, President Olympio (an Ewe) was killed in a military coup, and upon a request by the newly-appointed President Grunitzky the Ghanaian Government recognized the new regime in Togo on Jan. 21 and reopened the border between the two countries which had been virtually closed to road traffic for about a year. The frontier was, however, subsequently closed again by Togo and was not officially reopened until April 23, 1966 (i.e. after the overthrow of President Nkrumah on Feb. 24 of that year).

### Ghanaian Measures against Pro-Togolese Secessionists, 1973-76

No further political activities in favour of secession of the former British Togoland from Ghana were officially reported from that country until 1973, by which time the country was under a military regime with Col. Ignatius Kutu Acheampong as head of state. In July 1973 the Government of Ghana disclosed that there had been a secessionist conspiracy among chiefs of the Ewe tribe and that all those concerned had been temporarily arrested.

On Feb. 21, 1975, a delegation of chiefs from the Volta region of Ghana and former nationals of British Togoland, who had become Ghana nationals in 1957, reported to Col. Acheampong that a resolution had been adopted by chiefs in the region on Dec. 28, 1974, calling for negotiations between the Government of Ghana and the National Liberation Movement of Western Togoland (NLMWT or Tolimo), a clandestine organization said to be active on both sides of the border and agitating for the secession from Ghana of the former British Togoland. Early in 1975 the Government offered an amnesty to all NLMWT members who ended their secessionist activities by Dec. 1, 1975, stating that they would not be punished and that those in voluntary exile could return to Ghana and live there as law-abiding citizens. On Dec. 23, 1975, Col. Acheampong declared before a delegation of chiefs from the Volta region that the deadline of the amnesty had been extended to the end of January 1976; he also stated that the authorities had recently uncovered a plot to overthrow the Government and that the persons involved, whom he described as "a small group of political agitators in the Volta Region" who wished part of that region to be joined to the neighbouring Togo, would be prosecuted.

While many NLMWT members were reported to have taken advantage of the amnesty, some 22 leading members of the movement (some of them being employees of the Togolese Government) remained in Togo. The NLMWT had responded to the amnesty in an open letter to Col. Acheampong, asking for negotiations "directly or through the Organization of African Unity in order that permanent peace should exist in the territory, if necessary by handing over this problem, which cannot be done away with by the mere granting of an amnesty, to an arbitration which shall find a means by which it can be solved permanently". On Jan. 13, 1976, it was reported that the Ewe people of Ghana had "reacted strongly" to a government reorganization which had reduced their representation in the Cabinet and thus ended "the ethnic neutrality of the regime".

The Government of Togo, in a statement published as an advertisement in *The Times* (of London) on Jan. 13, 1976, called upon Col. Acheampong to "show his statesmanship and restore Togo as she was before the Europeans got to work" and asserted that "no one could call the 'plebiscite' of 1956 fair or a thoughtful reflexion of the aspirations of the local inhabitants". The Ghanaian authorities, however, officially terminated the amnesty on March 3, 1976, under a decree (amended on March 18) which banned "any organization whose objects include advocating and promoting the secession from Ghana of the former British-mandated territory of Togoland or any part of it, or the integration of this territory with any foreign territory", and specifically the NLMWT, "variously known as the Togoland Liberation Movement and Tolimo", under pain of a fine of up to 5,000 cedis (£2,000) or imprisonment for up to five years, or both, for any activities on behalf of the movement.

During a treason trial held in Accra between May 19 and July 28, 1976, the chief accused, Capt. (retd.) Kojo Tsikata, was reported to have said that the Acheampong Government had "a psychosis of an Ewe plot against it" which, he claimed, was being played out at this trial. The eight defendants in the trial, all members of the Ewe tribe, pleaded not guilty, but seven of them were sentenced (five to death and two to 20 and 15 years' imprisonment respectively).

### Official Togolese Statement of January 1977 and Renewed Ghanaian Accusations against Togo

The Government of Togo took up the border issue once again by issuing a statement, published as an advertisement in *The Times* of Jan. 28, 1977, by the Togolese Ministry of Information. In this statement it was claimed that the plebiscite of "May 9, 1957" (which in fact took place a year earlier and, as stated above, showed a majority in favour of integration of the British-administered Togoland with the Gold Coast, later Ghana), had "not completely resolved" the problem and that "the question of reunification" had "never ceased to affect relations between Ghana and independent Togo", although "this thorny problem" was "rarely mentioned elsewhere". While Togo did not wish to quarrel with her neighbours, the statement said: "One thing is certain: sooner or later a peaceful solution will be found to this problem."

The January 1977 Togolese statement continued: "Border problems are common in Africa, of course. Throughout the world, except in a few privileged nations, there are no natural frontiers to separate nations, large or small. Borders have always been created by men. It is hardly surprising, but in Togo men have flouted principles which have been defended at such high cost elsewhere. . . . The Togo drama in fact began with World War I. In 1884 colonization by the Germans was a matter of negotiation between the traditional leaders and representatives of the people and the German authorities. From August 1914, however, the allied forces set about breaking up the inherent unity of Togo (political, economic, social and cultural), sharing the occupation of the colony between themselves. Following the Franco-British agreement of July 10, 1919, confirming this act of demolition, a senior official on the spot in Togo declared: 'As it is traced today, the Franco-British border has many political drawbacks and places us at such economic disadvantage that it would be impossible not to grasp any opportunity of abolishing it, especially as the two parties will suffer from it one day. Whole peoples have been split by the new frontier: the Kondombas, the Adeles, the Akpossos, the Ewes. It should be borne in mind that the divided region is particularly fertile and that cocoa is a crop that is widely grown in it.'

"Many arguments are advanced in favour of maintaining the status quo, both in the Organization of African Unity and at the international level. The principle that the frontiers inherited from colonialism are sacrosanct undoubtedly prevents Africa from tearing itself apart, but general principles have never ruled out consideration of individual cases. Togo existed as an entity before and during colonization. In view of the reunification of British and French Cameroons, the Togolese wonder why there should be one law for one nation and another for the other. They are inclined to place the responsibility for dismemberment upon the British, who were confident of the results of the 1957 [*sic*] plebiscite in advance. The Gold Coast of the time—now Ghana—never formulated territorial claims against its neighbour; it was merely caught up in the manoeuvres of the European nations.

"It is not hard to understand why the peoples concerned were not able to express themselves freely at the time of the plebiscite. A period should have been allowed during which they would have been able to free themselves of the pressure in fact exerted by Great Britain and Ghana. Peoples who are administered by a foreign power and who are economically linked with that power cannot be said to have a free choice. The United Nations Organization was not wrong in applying the universal principle of self-determination, but it should first have created the conditions in which a full and free decision could have been reached.

"In the capital of Togo it is generally emphasized that Ghana has never been looked on as an enemy, despite the expansionist goals nurtured by the former President, Nkrumah, against Togo. Notwithstanding statements by the current Ghana Minister of Foreign Affairs, Togolese officials point out that a hostile climate cannot exist while the two countries are brought together by objective ties. The Ghana-Togo Grand Commission meets twice a year, meetings are arranged fairly frequently between the two Presidents, and Togo uses power supplied by the Akomsombe dam in Ghana; finally both countries are members of the ODEAC [which should presumably read CEDEAO, as referring to the *Communauté Économique des États de l'Afrique de l'Ouest* or Economic Community of West African States, ECOWAS].

"Nevertheless, the 1957 [*sic*] plebiscite has not really solved the problem of unification of the Togolese people. . . . Many of them believe that the day will come when all its people will be united in peace, stability and progress, and can direct all its efforts to the objective of development."

This statement was followed by further accusations against Togo made by the Ghanaian Government during 1977. Ghana's head of state (the former Col. Acheampong, promoted general on March 7, 1976) said on Aug. 27, 1977, that Ghana had "no territorial ambitions on any country" but would "never permit an inch of its territory to be encroached upon by any country".

The Ghanaian Chief of Defence Staff alleged in September of that year that Togo was harbouring certain subversive elements and in complicity with another member state of the Organization of African Unity was giving military training to those elements in order to subvert Ghana. Moreover, on Oct. 10, 1977, the commander of Ghana's border guard (Maj.-Gen. Emmanuel K. Utuka) said that since the formation of the NLMWT in 1972 there had been "ample evidence of the complicity of the Togolese authorities" in its activities, and that an unnamed North African country was reliably known to have voted a considerable amount of money in support of secessionist movements operating against the Volta region. It was generally assumed that the unnamed North African country referred to by Maj.-Gen. Utuka was Col. Moamer al Kadhafi's Libya.

In November 1977 Gen. Acheampong issued a further warning against the activities of secessionists in the border region and stated that his country was "prepared to shed blood to the last drop to defend the territorial integrity of the nation". In February 1978 he declared that his Government would "foster closer relations with Togo" once that country stopped "supporting the so-called reunification of parts of Ghana with Togo". However, on July 5, 1978, Gen. Acheampong was removed from office, and since then the issue of the border with Togo has not been officially raised again. On May 18, 1979, the commander of the Ghanaian border guard said that relations between the two countries were "very cordial" and that there was nothing that the two countries could not agree on.

As a result of the military coup in Ghana on Dec. 31, 1981, all Ghana's borders with neighbouring countries, including Togo, were temporarily closed; although Ghana reopened its borders on Jan. 8, 1982, the Togolese Government closed its side of the Ghana-Togo border the following day without official explanation.

H.W.D.

# Kenya-Somalia

The boundaries of the former British colony of Kenya at independence on Dec. 12, 1963, encompassed an area of approximately 50,000 square miles or 130,000 sq km (defined as the country's North-Eastern Province) whose population was predominantly Somali-speaking (the number of ethnic Somalis being estimated at approximately 200,000). Somalis have regarded this population as one of the five elements of the historic Somali nation, and from 1960, when the Republic of Somalia became independent, its successive governments espoused the goal of unification of the Somali nation, of which the Republic comprises only two of the five elements, namely the former British Somaliland Protectorate and Italian-administered Somalia (which had latterly been a United Nations trust territory). Somali irredentism was expressed as a demand for the right of self-determination for Somali-speaking peoples under foreign administration not only in Kenya but also in Djibouti and Ethiopia. (For Somalia's related disputes with these countries, see pages 111-13 and 114-19 respectively; a map of the region appears on page 111.)

The demand for self-determination for Somalis within Kenya, as expressed by leaders of the local population and supported by the Government of Somalia, was addressed in the first instance to Britain as the colonial authority prior to Kenyan independence, and was subsequently pursued in the form of a dispute between Somalia and Kenya. The position adopted by the Government of Somalia has been that this does not constitute a territorial dispute as such since Somalia did not desire to annex the territory in question, although if the population should desire union with Somalia, having once achieved self-determination, such a union would be encouraged by Somalia.

### Historical Background

The situation in Kenya prior to independence was that ethnic Somalis formed approximately half the population of the Northern Frontier District (NFD), an area of 150,000 square miles (388,000 sq km) which in fact comprised six administrative districts, the eastern three of which (Garissa, Wajir and Mandera) were inhabited almost entirely by Somali-speaking people. The border demarcation between Kenya (specifically the NFD) and Somalia was not recognized by the latter, its alignment having been determined by a commission in 1930 on the basis of a treaty of July 15, 1924, between Britain and Italy whereby the territory known as Jubaland was detached from the British Kenya Colony and incorporated within Italian Somaliland. The NFD was administered by the British as a "closed district", entry from and exit to the rest of Kenya being subject to permit, and Somali

131

nationalist aspirations as expressed notably by the Somali Youth League (SYL—formed in 1943) were affected by a ban on all political activity in the NFD from 1948 to 1960.

Harold Macmillan, speaking as British Prime Minister, said in the House of Commons on April 11, 1960, that "Her Majesty's Government does not and will not encourage or support any claim affecting the territorial integrity of French Somaliland, Kenya or Ethiopia; this is a matter which could only be considered if that were the wishes of the governments and peoples concerned". This was apparently interpreted by Somali leaders to mean that a claim for self-determination for the NFD would indeed be considered if that were the wish of the British Government (then responsible for governing Kenya) and the Somali people.

Local Somali chiefs made clear their demand for secession from Kenya at a meeting on November 1961 with Reginald Maudling, the then British Colonial Secretary, and further representations to the same effect were made by an NFD delegation to the Kenya Constitutional Conference held in London in February-April 1962. This delegation met with a special representative group of the conference, its direct participation having been strongly opposed by Kenyan nationalist leaders.

Without acceding to Somali demands for a referendum on the NFD, the British Government proposed instead the establishment of an independent fact-finding commission, which was subsequently set up in September-October 1962 with the brief that it should ascertain and report on public opinion in the NFD "regarding arrangements to be made for the future of the area". The Commission visited the NFD in October-November 1962 and reported in December that the population was divided but vigorous and determined in its opinions, with the largest areas (in both population and size) seeking secession when Kenya became independent, and ultimate union with the Republic of Somalia.

Duncan Sandys, Reginald Maudling's successor as the British Colonial Secretary, issued a statement on March 8, 1963, at a session of the Kenyan Council of Ministers in Nairobi, containing the British Government's decision on the NFD. While the Somali-populated areas would not be allowed to secede, he said, they were to be formed into a separate, seventh (North-Eastern) province of Kenya; this decision was incorporated into the Kenyan Constitution, which was laid before Parliament in London in the form of an Order in Council on April 18, 1963. Although the decision was represented by the British Government as an interim rather than a final one, there seemed little prospect in the foreseeable future of a Kenyan government allowing the Somali-speaking area to secede. Kenyan leaders had already made clear their opposition to any such secession, during visits which they made to Somalia in the latter part of 1962, and Jomo Kenyatta (subsequently the first Prime Minister and later President of Kenya) reiterated on March 14, 1963, that Kenya would not entertain "any secession or handing over of one inch of our territory" to Somalia or to any other country. Talks between Kenyan and Somali Government representatives, held in Rome on Aug. 25-28, 1963, did nothing to alter this position. Britain made it known during this meeting that it would not take responsibility for a final decision, although legally Britain remained the responsible authority until Kenyan independence.

Meanwhile the Republic of Somalia had on March 12, 1963, broken off diplomatic relations with Britain in view of what it described as the British failure "to recognize the wishes expressed by the overwhelming majority of the peoples inhabiting the NFD of Kenya". This marked the end of Somali attempts to obtain from Britain the satisfaction of their demands for the self-determination of the NFD. The issue thereafter became one between Somalia and Kenya, in the context of relations between independent African states in the post-colonial period.

The definition of the precise area in dispute was complicated by the Kenyan regional administrative reorganization implemented during the transition to independence. The NFD, to which Somalia continued to refer, officially ceased to exist, being subdivided in such a way that ethnic Somali peoples within Kenya were for the most part incorporated within the new North-Eastern Province.

In the period immediately following the independence of Kenya, the Kenyan Government held the Somali Government responsible for rebel activity in the North-Eastern Province, as a consequence of which activity a state of emergency was declared in the region on Dec. 25, 1963. In the same month a defence pact was ratified between Kenya and Ethiopia, the pact having been concluded in July 1963 with a view to safeguarding the integrity of the existing borders between the two countries and Somalia. Kenyan-Somali border hostilities continued sporadically until 1967, when (in September of that year) a degree of reconciliation was achieved following prolonged attempts at mediation by other African states.

## Kenya-Somali Dispute and the OAU

From its foundation in 1963, and indeed from its antecedents in the Pan-African movement, the Organization of African Unity has generally been associated with the doctrine that independent African states should adhere to the boundaries existing at the time of their independence. The principle of mutual respect for the territorial integrity of African states was expressly reaffirmed by a resolution adopted in Cairo on July 21, 1964, at the first ordinary session of the OAU Assembly of Heads of State or Government. The resolution included a solemn declaration that all member states pledged themselves "to respect the borders existing on their achievement of national independence". The representative of Somalia had been absent for the vote on this resolution, however, and he made it clear in a statement on July 23 that his Government did not consider itself bound by its terms. Moreover, he said, Somalia opposed the perpetuation in independent Africa of what he described as "the uncorrected mistakes which still existed" with regard to state borders inherited from the colonial era.

The substantive issue of Kenya-Somali border hostilities was removed from the agenda of the OAU's 1964 Cairo summit meeting and referred to bilateral talks. Such attempts as were made at mediation (notably talks arranged in Tanzania in December 1965) failed to resolve the matter, and violent border incidents continued, accompanied by a further deterioration in relations between the two countries and the imposition of restrictions on trade between them in July 1966. Kenyan Government sources in late 1966 estimated that 1,650 ethnic Somali "shifta" (bandits) had been killed in the border area in clashes over a three-year period, during which time it was said that 69 Kenyan forces personnel, police and administrators had also died along with over 500 Kenyan civilians.

A list of "prerequisites for normalizing relations", which the Kenyans put forward in December 1965 and subsequently reiterated, stipulated in particular that Somalia should recognize the former NFD area as an integral part of Kenya and cease all material and propaganda support for ethnic Somali "shifta" insurgents in the area. Rather to the contrary, however, a new Somali Government established in July 1967 issued an explicit statement of its position in the form of a speech by Mohammed Ibrahim Egal, the new Prime Minister and Minister of Foreign Affairs. While stating that "we in the Somali Republic make no claims on the territory of any of our neighbours", the new Prime Minister went on to say that "what we are after is simply independence through the proper process of self-determination for our brothers" and that "we do intend to champion the cause of Somali territories under foreign domination, in order that they may attain sovereign independent status through the process of self-determination". After such independence it was envisaged that unions would be arranged "out of discussion and mutual agreement between independent Somali states".

Notwithstanding these divergent positions, however, on Sept. 13, 1967 (i.e. only two months after the change of government in Somalia), the Kenyan and Somali Governments issued a joint declaration at the OAU Assembly in Kinshasa, undertaking to end the violent clashes and expressing the desire to respect each other's sovereignty and territorial integrity and to resolve their outstanding differences.

The following month a further Memorandum of Agreement was signed by President Kenyatta of Kenya and Prime Minister Egal of Somalia. Known as the Arusha Agreement, this was concluded at a meeting held in Arusha (Tanzania) on Oct. 8 under OAU auspices with the mediation of President Kaunda of Zambia. It called for the ending of clashes, the resumption of normal relations, the gradual suspension of emergency measures on both sides, the ending of hostile propaganda, and the formation of a joint committee (with Zambian mediation) to supervise the implementation of these processes and to seek solutions to outstanding differences. The agreement formed the basis for the establishment of diplomatic relations between Somalia and Kenya in January 1968, when trade restrictions were also lifted. In the same month Somalia re-established diplomatic relations with Britain, broken off over the NFD issue at the time of Kenyan independence. Continuing Kenyan-Somali bilateral contacts led to the lifting by Kenya on March 15, 1969, of the state of emergency in the North-Eastern province, and it was also agreed that restrictions on the movement of livestock across the border (i.e. by nomadic herdsmen) would be relaxed.

The essence of the Kenyan-Somali accommodation was not that their disagreement had moved towards being resolved, but rather that it had been allowed to become dormant under the mutually convenient ambiguity of the Arusha formula. The Somalis could interpret the call for a working committee "to examine ways and means of bringing about a satisfactory solution to major and minor differences between Kenya and Somalia" as an acceptance that what they continued to call "the NFD question" remained on the agenda to be settled in future negotiations. The Kenyans, meanwhile, interpreted the commitment at Arusha to respect each other's territorial integrity "in the spirit of paragraph 3 of Article III of the OAU Charter" to mean that Kenya's borders at independence, encompassing the North-Eastern province with its majority ethnic Somali population, would no longer be called into question. There was thus no further need, according to this interpretation, for Kenya to insist as a precondition for any negotiation that Somalia explicitly declare its recognition of the North-Eastern province as an integral and de jure part of the Kenya Republic.

## Course of Kenyan-Somali Relations, 1967-80

The Somali Government's acceptance of the Arusha formula had not passed entirely without domestic criticism; indeed, hostile demonstrations had met Prime Minister Egal on his return to Mogadishu, and former Prime Minister Abdirizak Hadji Hussein had denounced the agreements. The Government had responded by closing down the Mogadishu branch of the Somali Youth League, of which Abdirizak Hussein was the secretary-general, and Egal (although the SYL central committee voted to expel him from the party) had won the support of Parliament in a vote on Nov. 23, 1967, endorsing his efforts to settle outstanding differences between Somalia and her neighbours.

This policy approach continued essentially unchanged under the military government of Gen. Siyad Barreh, installed after a coup in Somalia in October 1969. Although a Revolutionary Charter, promulgated following the suspension of the 1960 Constitution, reaffirmed a commitment to "the fight for the unity of the

Somali nation'', assurances were given to Kenya that the new regime would continue its predecessor's policy of seeking co-operation to solve outstanding differences.

Reports of incidents in the area in 1977 and early 1978 were accompanied by renewed Kenyan pressure for the Somali Government to make a formal renunciation of any territorial claims against its neighbours. The first of the new series of incidents occurred on June 27, 1977, when (according to the Kenyan Government announcement) Somali troops believed to be passing through on their way into Ethiopia were involved in clashes at the Ramu border post in northern Kenya in which six Kenyan police and seven Somalis were reportedly killed. Kenyan complaints over this incident at the OAU ministerial meeting in Gabon on June 30 were met by Somali denials; the Somalis insisted that Somalia had no intention of attacking Kenya and that there had been no clashes in the area since the 1967 agreement. A Somali assertion, that the attack had in fact come from Ethiopia, was in turn denied by the Ethiopians.

A meeting was held on July 19, 1977, between Daniel arap Moi, then Kenyan Vice-President, and his Somali counterpart, Hussein Kulmia Afrah, following which a joint communiqué was issued stating that both sides had pledged to maintain the peace and to set up a border commission to ''normalize and restore tranquillity'' in the region. However, according to President Kenyatta of Kenya in a speech in Nairobi on Oct. 20, 1977, official Somali maps ''still lay false claim on Kenyan territory'', and it was reported at this time that the Kenyan Government had conveyed to the Somalis by way of the Egyptian Government as intermediary a renewed demand for the public renunciation of any Somali territorial claims against Kenya. It was further reported that the Governments of the United Kingdom and the United States were unwilling to provide military assistance sought by Somalia, unless and until Somalia formally declared that it had no territorial claims against Ethiopia, Kenya and Djibouti.

Meanwhile, Vice-President Moi of Kenya had announced on Oct. 15, 1977, his Government's intention of carrying out a census to establish the number of Kenyans of Somali origin, any of whom regarded as ''favourable to Somalia'' would be expelled from Kenyan territory. On the same day the Somali ambassador to Kenya replied to allegations that Somali travel documents had been furnished to Kenyans of Somali origin, and that the recipients of such documents had then gone abroad for military training. The issue of travel documents, he said, had occurred only for humanitarian reasons when individuals without Kenyan papers had wanted to travel abroad, and he stated that this would not happen again. In an announcement on Dec. 12, 1978, on the occasion of the release of 26 political detainees by the new Kenyan Government (now under President Moi following President Kenyatta's death), it was stated that the majority of those released were ethnic Somalis arrested in the border area for alleged subversive activities.

On Sept. 10, 1979, the first ever meeting between a Kenyan and a Somali head of state (Presidents Moi and Barreh) was arranged in the Saudi Arabian city of Taif. At this meeting the Kenyans reportedly unsuccessfully pressed their demand for a public Somali renunciation of support for the self-determination of ethnic Somalis in Kenya. Shortly after returning from this meeting, President Barreh gave on Sept. 23 his assent to the new Somali Constitution, as drawn up by the ruling Somali Revolutionary Socialist Party in January 1979, and approved in a national referendum on Aug. 25. Article 15 stated that ''the Somali Democratic Republic shall firmly uphold the principle of self-determination of peoples and fully support the national liberation movements and all peoples fighting for their freedom and independence'', while Article 16 stipulated that the Republic ''adopting peaceful and legal means shall support the liberation of Somali territories under colonial occupation and shall encourage the unity of the Somali people through their own free will''.

In November 1980 further violent incidents were reported near the Kenyan-Somali border, and the Provincial Commissioner of the North-Eastern province of Kenya announced on Nov. 10 that a curfew would be imposed throughout the province and all Kenyan citizens of Somali origin would be confined in security villages. The following day the Somali Government denied any involvement in the disturbances (in which six Kenyan officials were reportedly killed). On Nov. 13, according to Kenyan radio, President Moi sent a message to President Barreh welcoming ''assurances given yesterday by the Somali ambassador to Kenya that Somalia had no territorial claim in Kenya whatever'', and President Barreh said on Nov. 30 in a speech in Mogadishu (as reported on Somali radio) that Somalia was not seeking any Kenyan territory and that it would be to the mutual benefit of both countries if Kenya understood Somalia's desire for a peaceful relationship. He stated that Kenya was responsible for the future and the rights of the people of Kenya's North-Eastern province, but that Somalia in turn ''would not tolerate the killing and the denial to these people of their rights''. He repeated also the Somali claim that it was the Ethiopians who were responsible for creating disturbances in the area, with the intention of marring relations between Kenya and Somalia.

The Kenyan-Somali dispute, being one facet of the wider issue of Somali nationalist aspirations, was intimately connected with the most salient issue for irredentist Somali policy, namely the territorial dispute with Ethiopia over the Ogaden region (see pages 114-19). Since January 1979 Ethiopia and Kenya had had a 10-year treaty of friendship and co-operation (concluded on Jan. 31 during an official visit to Addis Ababa by President Moi) which included a pledge to maintain the inviolability of their frontiers and to mutual defence to resist ''the expansionist policies of any country or group of countries''. Kenyan-Ethiopian relations had included a ministerial meeting in Mombasa on March 24, 1980, at which border security was discussed, and on Dec. 14, 1980, Lt.-Col. Mengistu Haile Mariam, the Ethiopian head of state, made an official visit to Nairobi during which (on Dec. 1) he described Somalia's policies as ''a thorn in the flesh of both Ethiopia and Kenya''. An Ethiopian-Kenyan joint communiqué issued on Dec. 4 called on Somalia ''to renounce publicly and unconditionally all claim to the territories of Ethiopia, Kenya and Djibouti''. According to Addis Ababa radio the communiqué set out a series of conditions which Somalia must fulfil, including (besides the payment of reparations for war damages to Ethiopia) the renunciation of territorial claims, the acceptance of the inviolability of existing state frontiers and the withdrawal of Somalia's reservation entered when this principle had been reiterated at the OAU in 1964. The two leaders reportedly agreed that ''non-acceptance of these conditions by Somalia would mean the perpetuation of the existing tension and insecurity in the area'', and that active Kenyan-Ethiopian collaboration should be intensified, and they called for an end to all international military aid to Somalia.

The Somali Government responded vehemently to this communiqué, calling an emergency joint meeting on Dec. 7 of the Supreme Revolutionary Council, the SRSP Central Committee, the People's Assembly and the Council of Ministers. This meeting condemned the communiqué as provocative and threatening and tantamount to a declaration of war, and urged ''the Somali people wherever they are to be ready to defend their motherland and national sovereignty''. The President's Office issued a statement on Dec. 8 (which was substantially reiterated in a speech by President Barreh the next day) warning that the Abyssinians (i.e. Ethiopians) planned a systematic liquidation of Somalis under their rule. With Kenyan collaboration, it was alleged, Ethiopia intended to declare war on Somalia.

The statement distinguished between "Abyssinian colonialism" and the Somali-Kenya issue which it described as "a colonial legacy needing a just and responsible solution, in accordance with the OAU Charter". With regard to former colonial boundaries, Somalia "continued to uphold its 1964 principle" and to oppose "the uncorrected mistakes which still existed".

R.E.

# Lesotho-South Africa

The Kingdom of Lesotho, an enclave of territory completely surrounded by the territory of the Republic of South Africa (the length of the border being in all some 565 miles or 900 km), attained independence on Oct. 4, 1966. The validity of the country's existing borders, as inherited from the colonial era, has been called into question by the country's rulers on the grounds that these borders perpetuate an unjust arrangement imposed on the Basuto or South Sotho people in the 19th century. The following article gives an account of the historical background to Lesotho's territorial claims, which relate to substantial if imprecisely-defined areas generally described as "the conquered territories". (For map illustrating this dispute see page 171.)

### Lesotho's Existing Boundaries

Lesotho's boundaries today are essentially as defined in the Second Convention of Aliwal North, which was concluded on Feb. 12, 1869, and which brought to an end a series of wars between the Basuto and neighbouring Boer settlers. This treaty, although it was signed by the Basuto ruler King Moshoeshoe, had actually been negotiated between the British Governor of the Cape of Good Hope (to whom Moshoeshoe had successfully appealed for protection) and the (Boer) authorities of the Orange Free State. The new boundary was adjusted the following year to include in Basutoland a parcel of territory (Chief Molapo's territory) in the north-west around Butha Buthe. The revised border ran from the confluence of the Caledon and Putisani (or Phuthiatsana) rivers eastwards to the Drakensberg following the centre of the Caledon river rather than the centre of the more southerly Putisani.

The British High Commissioner's Notice of May 13, 1870, as amended by Government Notice No. 74 of Nov. 6, 1871, defines the borders of Basutoland (now Lesotho) as follows: "From the junction of the Cornetspruit [Makhaleng] with the Orange river, along the centre of the former to the point nearest to Olifantsbeen; from that point, by Olifantsbeen, to the southern point of Langeberg to its north-western extremity; from thence to the eastern point of Jammerberg; along the top of Jammerberg to its north-western extremity; from thence by a prolongation of the same, to the Caledon river; along the centre of the Caledon river to the heads of the Orange river at the Mount aux Sources; thence westward [in fact first south-eastward and then south-westward—ed.] along the Drakensberg, between the watersheds of the Orange river and the St John's river [Umzimvubu] to the

137

source of the Tees [Telle]; down the centre of the river to its junction with the Orange river, and down the centre of the latter river to its junction with the Cornet-spruit.''

## Extent of Earlier Basuto Settlement and Authority

Moshoeshoe I had succeeded, in the period to 1835, in establishing his authority as king over the Basuto people, whose area of settlement extended into areas to the north and west of the Caledon river as well as to the south-west of Lesotho's modern boundaries. Other tribes migrating into the northern part of the Basuto-dominated area were brought into a vassal relationship as tributaries of King Moshoeshoe. (See below, however, for dispute over the status of the Barolong tribe in the Thaba Nchu area.)

From the late 1830s the position of the Basuto was affected by the migration into this area of Afrikaner or Boer farmers from the south, notably in the so-called Boer treks which began on a large scale in 1836. By these treks the Boers aimed to remove themselves from British colonial rule (the colony of the Cape of Good Hope having been ceded by the Netherlands to Britain in 1814) and to establish themselves anew in what are now the South African territories of the Orange Free State, Transvaal and parts of Natal.

King Moshoeshoe signed a treaty with the British Governor of Cape Colony on Oct. 5, 1843, in which the extent of Moshoeshoe's territory was described in Article III. According to this description (known as the Napier Line) the territory extended westward to the junction of the Caledon and Orange rivers, south to the Orange river, east to the Drakensberg and north to "a line extending from about 25 to 30 miles north of the Caledon river, excepting near its source and at its junction with the Gariep [Orange]''. However, neither this description, nor a series of disputed attempts to give greater precision to the boundary definition (including the so-called Maitland, Southey and Warden lines), prevented continual cross-border conflict, cattle raiding and similar disturbances between Basuto and Boers.

## First, Second and Third Basuto Wars with Orange Free State

Soon after the formal establishment of the independent Boer republic of the Orange Free State (the British having proclaimed their sovereignty over the new Boer settlements in 1848 but established a separate administration for the Orange River Territory in 1851 and allowed independence on Feb. 23, 1854), a conflict known as the First Basuto War or Senekal's War began in 1856 between Basutoland and the Orange Free State. This war was officially concluded by the First Treaty (or Convention) of Aliwal North on Sept. 29, 1858.

As shown on the map on page 171, the territorial limits of Basutoland as defined in this treaty were based on the Warden line proposals of 1849. Although the territory thus defined does not include the full extent of all areas of Basuto settlement (and notably omits an area in the south-west which had been described as part of King Moshoeshoe's territory in his 1843 treaty with the Cape Colony—see above), it is to this territory, substantially larger than modern Lesotho, that the claims expressed by Lesotho's leaders generally relate.

A subsequent Second Basuto War (Sequiti War) from 1865 to 1866 ended with the Basuto becoming subject to the Orange Free State as well as ceding part of their territory. The terms of the peace were accepted by Moshoeshoe's son Molapo in the Imperani Treaty, which was confirmed a month later by the Treaty of Thaba Bosiu, concluded between King Moshoeshoe and the Orange Free State authorities on April 3, 1866.

The Basuto, who had already sought British protection against the Boers in

1861 but without success, renewed their appeal after the outbreak of the Third Basuto War in 1867. As a result of a petition from King Moshoeshoe in January 1868, the British Governor of the Cape on March 12, 1868, proclaimed the Basuto to be British subjects and their land to be British territory. The Governor subsequently concluded a treaty with the Orange Free State (the Second Treaty or Convention of Aliwal North of Feb. 12, 1869), by which a new boundary was delimited (the agreement also being accepted by King Moshoeshoe on behalf of his people—see above).

### Complexities affecting Lesotho's Territorial Claims

Although, as already indicated, the principal basis for Lesotho's territorial claims is that the Basuto lands were unjustly taken from them by force, a more general claim to lands south and east of the Drakensberg has also been expressed. The areas in question, currently lying within Griqualand East and Transkei, in particular the districts of North and South Maluti, were settled by 19th-century Basuto migrants, with the support of the British authorities in the 1880s.

A different complication affects the Thaba Nchu area in the north-west, where an enclave within the Orange Free State has been apportioned by South Africa as part of the so-called Bophuthatswana "independent" homeland. The area was inhabited by the Barolong tribe migrating southward in 1833, and it has been disputed whether the tribal chief did or did not become a vassal of King Moshoeshoe at this time, as did other tribal chiefs. The claim that he did not do so would affect Lesotho's historical claim to that particular enclave, which falls geographically within the area regarded by Lesotho as "the conquered territories".

### Lesotho's Claims following Achievement of Independence

Basutoland, transferred to be part of the Cape Colony from 1871 to 1884 and thereafter administered as a British High Commission Territory, attained independence as Lesotho on Oct. 4, 1966, as already noted above. Prior to independence, certain members of the Legislative Assembly had demanded (on Nov. 2, 1965) that the British should secure the return to Basutoland of areas of South Africa in Orange Free State, Natal and eastern Cape Province, this demand reportedly being generally supported by all political parties in the country.

Although reference to seeking the return of the "conquered territories" was included in the programme of the ruling Basuto National Party (BNP) as well as the opposition Basuto Congress Party, the BNP adopted an attitude of restraint on the issue, at least until 1973. In June of that year the Lesotho Government requested United Nations legal advice to prepare for negotiations which it was seeking with South Africa, and in January 1975 Chief Jonathan, the Prime Minister, declared that he would press his country's claims at the UN and, if necessary, at the International Court of Justice. The then Foreign Minister, Kebby Kotsokoane, said at the UN in November 1975 that there could soon be a confrontation with South Africa over the border issue, and his successor, Charles Molapo, told the UN General Assembly in October 1976 that the South African Government should open talks on the return of land which he said had been "illegally ceded" during the colonial era.

From late 1976 the position was complicated by a dispute which arose from the Lesotho Government's refusal to recognize the sovereignty or the existence of the so-called tribal homeland of the Transkei, bordering on southern Lesotho and including areas claimed by Lesotho. In a move which received no international recognition, South Africa on Oct. 26, 1976, granted "independence" to the Transkei, which consisted of territory formerly administered as a tribal homeland within South Africa (see pages 172-75). Transkei authorities thereupon assumed jurisdiction over the territory's borders and border crossing points, which included three crossing points into Lesotho.

The Lesotho Government refused to comply with Transkeian border formalities, since this might imply recognition of Transkeian sovereignty (Lesotho allegedly being the target of South African pressure to this end). Lesotho successfully appealed at the United Nations for international assistance to compensate for what was described as the effective closure of the border crossings in question. A total of 33 other border crossings between Lesotho and South Africa, lying along the remaining sections of the border between the two countries, were apparently not affected directly.

In the wake of the dispute over the Transkei issue and its border implications for Lesotho, Chief Jonathan in February 1977 asserted his country's territorial claims in very broad terms, apparently encompassing much of the Orange Free State and other lands "fraudulently taken during the wars". It was reported in *The Times* on June 2, 1977, that Chief Jonathan had again reiterated his country's claims and expressed once again his intention of bringing the matter before the International Court of Justice.

R.E.

# Malawi-Tanzania

In 1967 the Government of Tanzania formally stated that in its view Tanzania's border with Malawi lay not along the eastern shore of Lake Nyasa (or Lake Malawi), as shown on current maps, but along the median line of the lake. This assertion implied the right of Tanzanians to enjoy access to the waters of the lake and the use of its resources.

### Origins of the Dispute over the Lake Nyasa Border

In Article I of an agreement concluded in 1890 between Britain and Germany the alignment of the western border of what had, in 1885, become German East Africa was described as running along the (eastern) shore of Lake Nyasa and to be subject to modification by agreement and demarcation (as provided for in Article VI of the 1890 agreement). In 1891 the British Government proclaimed a protectorate over the Nyasaland region (later known as the British Central African Protectorate and renamed, in 1907, the Nyasaland Protectorate). A second Anglo-German agreement (of 1901) merely gave formal approval to the conclusions of a joint boundary commission which had been surveying the frontiers of the two territories for the purpose of demarcation.

In practice, however, German sovereignty extended to the median line of Lake Nyasa until 1922, when most of German East Africa became the Mandated Territory of Tanganyika administered by Britain under the League of Nations. Official British sources for the period 1916-34 showed the western border of the territory as being the median line through Lake Nyasa (e.g. in a map attached to Britain's report for 1923 to the Council of the League of Nations, and in subsequent reports for 1924 to 1939, which referred to the western extent of the Tanganyika Territory as "the centre line of Lake Nyasa to a point due west of the Rovuma river", which constitutes the border between Tanzania and Mozambique).

After World War II Tanganyika was declared a United Nations trust territory, with the British Government being answerable for its administration to the UN Trusteeship Council, and with Britain being responsible for bringing the territory intact to independence. However, British reports issued between 1947 and 1961 for Tanganyika and Nyasaland generally abandoned the median-line alignment and showed the boundary between the two territories as being the eastern shore of Lake Nyasa in accordance with the 1890 Anglo-German agreement. This change was apparently reaffirmed with the proclamation of the Central African Federation of Rhodesia and Nyasaland in 1953.

The Government of Tanzania—since 1961 the successor to British authority in what is now mainland Tanzania—has rejected this change on the ground that no arbitrary change of boundaries by the administering authority of a UN trust territory could have any legal justification in view of the territory's UN trust status. In addition it has declared itself bound by the July 1964 resolution of the Assembly of Heads of State and Government of the Organization of African Unity which stated that the borders of African states, as on the day of their independence, constituted "a tangible reality" and that all member states pledged themselves "to respect the borders existing on their achievement of independence".

### The Tanzanian Initiative of January 1967

The Tanzanian Government raised the question of this border in a note to the Government of Malawi in January 1967, stating inter alia: "The Government of Tanzania has noted that maps produced in recent years give the impression that the international boundary between Malawi and Tanzania follows the eastern and

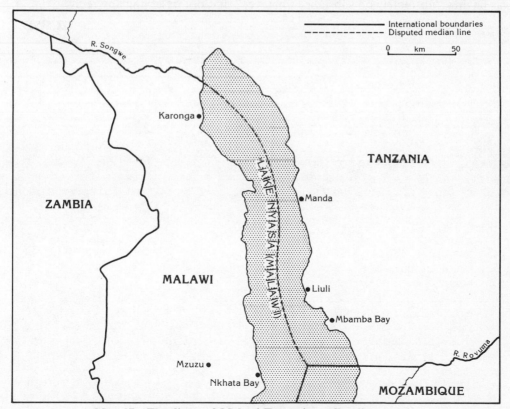

**Map 17   The disputed Malawi-Tanzania median line.**

141

northern shore of Lake Nyasa. It has also noted that certain actions of the Malawi Government appear to give [support to this impression]. The Government of Tanzania does not want an international issue to arise between countries sharing the waters of Lake Nyasa. Accordingly it wishes to inform the Government of Malawi that Tanzania has no claim over the waters of Lake Nyasa beyond a median line running through the lake and that it is this line alone which is recognized by the Government of Tanzania as both the legal and the just delineation between Malawi and Tanzania.''

The Malawi Government, in replying to this note, stated that the matter would receive consideration, but no further exchanges have taken place on this question. The dispute must therefore be considered to be dormant and as yet unsettled.

## President Banda's Territorial Claims of 1968

At a Malawi Congress Party meeting in September 1968 President Banda of Malawi declared in regard to what he considered to be Malawi's territory: "The real boundaries [of Malawi] are 100 miles (160 km) north of the Songwe River [in south-west Tanzania]. To the south it is the Zambezi River [in Mozambique]. To the west it is the Luangwa River [in Zambia], and to the east it is the Indian Ocean." He based these claims on the ancient Maravi empire shown on early Portuguese maps. In his speech he also stated that Lake Nyasa had always belonged to Malawi and that he had every right to change its name to Lake Malawi.

At a meeting at Mbeya (Tanzania) on Sept. 27, 1968, Presidents Nyerere of Tanzania and Kaunda of Zambia discussed inter alia a common stand against President Banda's claims. The Government of Tanzania subsequently dismissed them as having "absolutely no substance whatever" and not deserving any reply.

H.W.D.

# Mali-Upper Volta

An area extending along the border between the Republics of Mali and Upper Volta for about 90 miles (145 km) and of a width of between nine and 12 miles has been in dispute between the two states since their achievement of independence in April and July 1960 respectively. The area contains a chain of pools in the Dori district (*cercle*), through which flows the Béli river, the only source of fresh water in the region. It includes pasture and agricultural land and has therefore attracted settlers as well as nomads who have seasonally migrated to the area with their livestock. (A map illustrating this dispute appears on page 125.)

### Historical Background of the Dispute

The colony of Upper Volta was first created by the French Republic under a decree of March 1, 1919, which laid down that seven districts (including that of Dori) which had until then been part of Upper Senegal-Niger (renamed the French Sudan on Dec. 4, 1920) would constitute the new colony. Its creation was officially motivated by the "particularly homogeneous ethnic and linguistic character of the region", which was said to be inhabited by "Mossis, Bobos and other related ethnic groups". However, under a further French decree of Sept. 5, 1932, the Governor-General of French West Africa dissolved the colony of Upper Volta and distributed its territory among the French colonies of Niger, the French Sudan and the Ivory Coast, with the Dori district falling to Niger (except for one canton which went to the French Sudan).

This 1932 decree was in turn revoked under a French law of Sept. 4, 1947, which restored Upper Volta, laying down that its frontiers should be those which had existed on Sept. 5, 1932, but that adjustments to these frontiers could be made later by consultation among the local assemblies concerned. The frontiers created by France were in principle accepted by both Mali (the former French Sudan) and Upper Volta in their 1960 declarations of independence.

### Inconclusive Discussion of the Border Problem, 1961-74

The border problem was first discussed at a bilateral meeting at San (Mali) on Nov. 18-19, 1961, when it was agreed to have the frontier demarcated by a mixed commission of heads of border districts of the two states. This mixed commission agreed on Dec. 7, 1961, at Ansongo (Mali) that the frontier was as shown on a 1925 colonial map (of a 1:500,000 scale), and the Ansongo commander accepted that on all maps the Béli region was shown as being in Upper Volta. The San decision was, however, superseded by the creation of a new bipartisan commission set up in Bamako (the capital of Mali) on Feb. 24, 1964, and charged with proposing the demarcation of the frontier on the basis of the work done by the district heads.

The problem was again discussed at a meeting at Bobo-Diolassou (Upper Volta) in 1966 and at a meeting of the two heads of state at Orodara (Upper Volta) in May 1968, when two bodies were created—a permanent bipartisan commission to study the problems of co-operation between the two states and a mixed technical commission to explore the frontier on the basis of pre-independence documents held by the two states. On Sept. 29-30 it was agreed in Bamako that, if no texts could be found to support the frontier demarcation, then reference should be made to maps to solve the problem. The mixed technical commission was later instructed to explore the situation on the ground in certain areas, but in 1974 Mali declared that the commission had failed to carry out all its instructions fully, and it also rejected a 1926 atlas submitted by Upper Volta as a means of settling the question. All discussion was thereupon broken off.

## The Cases of the Two Governments

**Mali.** As set out in a memorandum of Dec. 11, 1972, the thesis of the Malian Government has been that the Béli region had geographically and historically always been part of the French Sudan and hence of Mali, in particular as part of the subdivision of Ansongo. In particular, Mali asserted in its memorandum that the delineation of a frontier on a map must be based on legal documents; that the maps available are often in conflict with existing legal documents and among each other; and that the people who inhabited the disputed area were of Malian origin and had contributed significantly to the development of the area during the colonial era.

The Mali government newspaper *L'Essor* declared at that time that, as the area was inhabited by Malians, the desire to keep the Béli region was "not a territorial claim" but was "simply an historically and geographically incontrovertible fact" and that "the claims of a state can be founded only on those of its population [who] have possessed and inhabited the zone". Radio Mali reiterated the claim to the region of Béli as Malian territory on Dec. 20, 1974, when it declared that Malian people had been settled there for centuries, had been born and had grown up there and had "possessed and inhabited the zone". It also stated that an additional strip extending for 140 kilometres between Coro and Bouanza was similarly in dispute.

**Upper Volta.** Upper Volta has based its claim on the following principal considerations: (i) the provisions of the French law of Sept. 5, 1947, restoring Upper Volta with its frontiers as at Sept. 5, 1932; (ii) the principles of the Charter of the Organization of African Unity (OAU), which include "respect for the sovereignty and territorial integrity of each member state and for its inalienable right to independent existence" (Art. III, Par. 3 of the Charter) and "unreserved condemnation . . . of subversive activities on the part of neighbouring states" (Art. II, Par. 5); and (iii) the provisions of a resolution adopted by the OAU Assembly of Heads of State and Government in July 1964, declaring that all member states undertook to respect the frontiers existing at the moment of their achievement of independence. In this context Upper Volta quoted a speech made at the inaugural OAU Assembly in 1963 by the then President of Mali, endorsing the maintenance of existing frontiers and calling for a multilateral non-aggression pact guaranteed by all states represented at the Assembly.

The Upper Volta point of view was set out in detail in a 58-page memorandum submitted to an OAU mediation commission appointed in December 1974. In this memorandum Upper Volta adduced historical, geographical and demographic arguments in support of its thesis that the disputed area had never been part of Mali (or of the earlier French Sudan). With regard to earlier frontiers, Upper Volta, while not excluding legal texts, considered maps to be the only objective documents because they were drawn on the basis of legal texts and by an official organ (the cartographic service of French West Africa). At the same time Upper Volta rejected a 1925 map showing part of the Béli pools to be in the French Sudan, on the ground that this map was only provisional and was replaced by later maps showing all Béli pools to be inside Upper Volta.

In connexion with migration, Upper Volta pointed out that, according to official documents, migrants had moved mainly from the north to the south, the majority of these migrants being Tuaregs and Bellahs (population groups also represented in Algeria, Mauritania and Niger); that under conventions concluded between the French Sudan (or Mali) and Upper Volta, also after their achievement of independence, to facilitate migration into the Béli region, the latter was recognized as part of Upper Volta and as not having always been inhabited by Malians; and that Mali had no right to use the presence of people of Malian origin as a basis for territorial claims as "to change the frontiers so as to embrace homogeneous groups would inevitably upset the present configuration of all African states". Upper Volta therefore considered the Malian thesis to be indefensible in law, even if it was conceivable on the strictly human level, and also to be dangerous because other states might claim sovereignty over Malian villages inhabited by Tuaregs. It also rejected Mali's claim based on the achievements of Malians in the region, pointing out that Upper Volta was not making any claims in respect of regions in neighbouring countries where people from Upper Volta had worked.

### Border Incidents and Mediation Efforts, 1974-76

Armed clashes which broke out on Nov. 25, 1974, and continued into December of that year were the subject of talks held at the frontier village of Faramana on Dec. 4 by Presidents Moussa Traore of Mali and Lamizana of Upper Volta. These talks did not lead to peace, however, and on Dec. 17, 1974, it was claimed in Bamako that Upper Volta had launched a general offensive against Mali, whereas it was announced in Ouagadougou (the capital of Upper Volta) on Dec. 18 that Malian forces had taken up positions in Upper Volta territory along the whole length of the disputed frontier. Mali claimed at the same time that it was merely taking possession of territory which was legally its own.

Following mediation efforts by Presidents Senghor of Senegal and Eyadema of Togo, a meeting was held on Dec. 26, 1974, in Lomé (the capital of Togo), at which a joint communiqué (issued on the following day) was signed by the Presidents of Mali, Niger, Togo and Upper Volta. In this communiqué it was agreed that a mediation commission was to be set up, with Guinea, Niger, Senegal and Togo as members, to guarantee the safety of the two countries' nationals on each other's territories, as well as their property; to supervise the effective withdrawal of troops from the border zone; and to seek a solution to the dispute. At the same time the Presidents of Mali and Upper Volta agreed to cease their propaganda campaigns against each other.

The mediation commission subsequently carried out this work, under the auspices of the OAU, in two sub-committees—a juridical one examining the arguments on the two sides and a military one which visited the disputed area but was not admitted to Mali. The commission eventually recommended the independent demarcation of the border by a neutral technical commission which would determine sovereignty over certain villages in the disputed area, but as a result of Mali's refusal to admit the OAU's military committee such a commission was never set up.

Fresh border incidents were reported early in June 1975, when Mali alleged that Upper Volta forces had raided two villages and killed two persons on June 3. The Government of Guinea appealed to both sides on June 5 to halt hostilities and to evacuate their troops from the contested zone pending a settlement agreement. At a further meeting held in Lomé on June 18 and attended also by the Presidents of Guinea, Niger, Senegal and Togo, the Presidents of Mali and of Upper Volta undertook to "end their dispute on the basis of recommendations of the mediation commission", which was to appoint a neutral committee (including a cartographer and an ethnologist) to determine the position of several villages, while the Government of Mali agreed to "restore to Upper Volta the equipment belonging to it and seized during the events of December 1974" and also to release two Upper Volta prisoners held in Mali. This undertaking was honoured on June 24, and on July 5 President Lamizana of Upper Volta announced that he had set free 33 detained Malians.

On July 11, 1975, the two Presidents signed, jointly with President Sekou Touré of Guinea, an agreement in which they undertook "definitely to renounce the use of force" in any dispute between them. The following year, at a meeting of ministers from the two countries held in Upper Volta on March 9, it was agreed that the two Presidents should instruct the joint commission to resume its work with the aim of achieving a final settlement of the problem of the border area between specified villages, and that the administrative officers in the border districts should meet frequently to educate the population.

### Agreed Recommendations of 1979

At a meeting between the Upper Volta and Malian Interior Ministers held in Ségou (Mali) on Nov. 21-22, 1979, the two sides agreed on recommendations for continued meetings of the administrative and local authorities in order to settle any border incidents promptly; on empowering a technical joint commission to set up a programme of action and to define its working procedures; and on the adoption of a policy of consultation to find adequate solutions to the problem. The Malian minister was quoted as saying that there was "no point of divergence between Upper Volta and Mali" and that "we could and must settle our problems without any foreign intervention".

H.W.D.

# Mauritius-United Kingdom (Diego Garcia)

A dispute concerning the island of Diego Garcia—the principal island of the Chagos Archipelago, situated in the Indian Ocean some 1,200 miles (1,900 km) to the north-east of Mauritius and forming part of the British Indian Ocean Territory—came into the open in 1980 when the Government of Mauritius demanded that the island should revert to Mauritius, of which it had been a dependency until 1965 (when Mauritius was still a British crown colony). The grounds for the claim were that, in the view of the Government of Mauritius, the British Government had violated an undertaking allegedly given in 1967 to the effect that the island of Diego Garcia would not be used as a base for military purposes. However, the UK Government has repeatedly denied having given such an undertaking. (A map illustrating this dispute appears on page 103.)

### Anglo-US Co-operation in the Development of a Communications Centre on Diego Garcia, 1965-76

The British Indian Ocean Territory (BIOT) was set up under an Order in Council of Nov. 8, 1965, as consisting of (i) the Chagos Archipelago (until then administered by the crown colony of Mauritius) and (ii) the islands of Aldabra, Farquhar and Des Roches (with a population of only a few hundred people and until then administered by the Seychelles, then also a British colony). When this decision was announced in the UK House of Commons on Nov. 10, 1965, it was explained that the arrangement had been made in agreement with the Mauritian and Seychelles Governments; that the BIOT would be "available for the construction of defence facilities by the British and US Governments''; and that ''appropriate compensation'' would be paid to the Mauritian and Seychelles Governments, the amount involved being mentioned as £3,000,000, partly for the resettlement of some 1,000 people from the Chagos Archipelago in Mauritius. (The islands of Aldabra, Farquhar and Des Roches were returned to Seychelles on the latter's achievement of independence on June 29, 1976.)

In Mauritius the transfer of the islands to Britain was opposed by the *Parti mauricien social-démocrate*, then the second largest political party, which withdrew from the existing government coalition and whose leader, Gaëtan Duval, said on Nov. 7, 1965, that the party would not accept an Anglo-American base on Diego Garcia or the other islands unless Britain and the United States agreed ''to buy all our sugar at a preferential price and to accept Mauritian immigrants''.

An agreement concluded between the United Kingdom and the United States on Dec. 30, 1966, provided that the BIOT should remain under British sovereignty but be available to meet the defence needs of both countries. On Dec. 15, 1970, it was jointly announced in London and Washington that work planned under the 1966 agreement would begin in March 1971 on the construction of an Anglo-US naval communications facility consisting of ''communications and minimum necessary support facilities, including an airstrip'', on Diego Garcia.

On March 23, 1971, the United States opened a military communications station on Diego Garcia for the purpose of controlling the movements of US submarines, surface vessels and aircraft in the area, and on Jan. 21, 1974, US Defence Department officials were reported to have confirmed plans for the expansion of the naval station into a base for the support of naval operations, as the reopening of the Suez Canal was expected to lead to increased Soviet naval activity in the Indian Ocean. The UK Foreign and Commonwealth Office disclosed on Feb. 5, 1974, that ''in response to a US proposal and in accordance with the 1966 Anglo-American agreement'' the UK Government had agreed in principle to the expansion of the facilities on Diego Garcia (which would accommodate aircraft carriers and also KC-135 tanker planes used to refuel B-52 strategic bombers). This agreement was formalized in an exchange of notes on June 22 and 25, 1976, which amended the 1966 agreement.

The High Commissioner of Mauritius in New Delhi (India) stated on April 7, 1974, that if the United States were allowed a base on Diego Garcia, Britain would be violating an undertaking given in 1967. The British Government, however, denied having given any such undertaking. In a statement made on Dec. 3, 1974, by the UK (Labour) Government's Secretary of State for Defence it was confirmed that the British Government had agreed to US proposals ''for a relatively modest expansion of the facilities on the island of Diego Garcia'', but it was added that the US use of the facilities other than for routine purposes would be a matter for joint decision of the two Governments. The proposed expansion of the US naval facilities on the island was finally approved by the US Congress on July 28, 1975, and as a result the US Navy was enabled to proceed with the construction on Diego Garcia of a 12,000-foot runway and refuelling facilities for a carrier task force, involving an increase in US military personnel from 430 to about 600 men.

The matter was apparently not raised in talks which Sir Seewoosagur Ramgoolam, the Prime Minister of Mauritius, had in London with the UK Minister of State for Foreign and Commonwealth Affairs on Sept. 24, 1975, when a Mauritian request for British assistance towards an acceptable resettlement scheme was discussed. It emerged that the British Government had paid £650,000 to Mauritius for the purpose of resettling 434 families consisting of 1,151 people (according to Mauritian Government records) who had been transferred from the entire Chagos Archipelago between 1965 and 1973, including 359 taken from Diego Garcia when the copra plantations on that island were closed down in 1971. It was later reported that the money had not been paid to these people until 1978, and that most of them were living in destitution in Mauritius. In that year the British Government offered a further £500,000 but this offer was rejected by a representative committee of the islanders. In mid-1979 a new British offer was made, amounting to £1,250,000 or about £1,000 per person payable on condition that the islanders undertook that neither they nor their children would ever return to the Chagos Archipelago. By January 1980 it appeared that this offer had been widely accepted by the evacuees.

On Oct. 13, 1975, the UK Secretary of State for Defence confirmed that under the 1966 agreement with the United States the latter had agreed to contribute half the total cost of setting up the BIOT (up to a limit of £5,000,000) by an offset arrangement against surcharges arising out of the British purchase of the US Polaris missile system.

### Establishment of US Naval Base on Diego Garcia

It was announced in Washington on Jan. 4, 1980, that as a result of the crises in Afghanistan and Iran the US Government had decided to maintain a permanent US naval presence on Diego Garcia, and on Jan. 12 the US Government accordingly informed the British Government of its intention to reinforce its military facilities on the island. In a summary of the US military position at the end of March 1980, submitted to the House of Representatives foreign affairs committee on April 2, 1980, the US Under-Secretary of Defence for Policy stated inter alia: "The network which we have developed for the region (of the Arabian Sea) is centred around Diego Garcia, where we expect to expand our facilities greatly in consultation with the United Kingdom."

The British Foreign and Commonwealth Office stated on May 29, 1980, that six or seven US cargo ships would be sent to Diego Garcia, and the UK Foreign and Commonwealth Secretary said on June 16 that the United States had a long-term programme for strengthening its military capability in the Indian Ocean. He said in particular: "This programme includes the pre-positioning of equipment to be available for use by forces deployed rapidly to the region in an emergency. At Diego Garcia such equipment will be held in converted merchant ships which will periodically be rotated within the Indian Ocean area. They do not constitute a naval task force. HM Government were fully consulted over the proposal to send these ships to Diego Garcia in accordance with the provisions of the 1976 exchange of notes." It had been reported on May 11 that, as soon as adequate facilities were built, up to 4,500 US and other military personnel would be permanently established on Diego Garcia.

### Opposition to the Militarization of Diego Garcia

Opposition to the establishment of US military facilities in the Indian Ocean area was registered by many of the states bordering the Indian Ocean (and also by the Soviet Union) and was expressed in repeated international calls for declaring the Indian Ocean a zone of peace.

On a proposal by Sri Lanka (then Ceylon) the General Assembly of the United Nations adopted, on Dec. 16, 1971 (in Resolution 2832/XXVI), a Declaration of the Indian Ocean as a Zone of Peace—the voting being 61 in favour to none against with 55 abstentions (which included those of all major powers except China and Japan, which voted in favour). In this resolution it was solemnly declared that "the Indian Ocean, within limits to be determined, together with the airspace above and all the ocean floor subjacent thereto, is hereby designated for all time as a zone of peace"; the great powers were called upon "to enter into immediate consultations with the littoral states of the Indian Ocean with a view to (a) halting the further escalation and expansion of their military presence in the Indian Ocean [and] (b) eliminating from the Indian Ocean all bases, military installations, logistical supply facilities, the disposition of nuclear weapons and weapons of mass destruction and any manifestation of great power military presence in the Indian Ocean conceived in the context of great power rivalry''.

The declaration also called on the littoral and hinterland states of the Indian Ocean, the permanent members of the UN Security Council and other maritime users of the Indian Ocean to enter into consultations with a view to implementing the declaration. They were asked specifically to ensure that warships and military aircraft should not use the Indian Ocean for any threat or use of force against the sovereignty, territorial integrity and independence of any littoral or hinterland state; that the right to free and unimpeded use of the zone by vessels of all nations was unaffected; and that arrangements should be made to give effect to any international agreement which might ultimately be reached for the maintenance of the Indian Ocean as a zone of peace.

The Declaration of the Indian Ocean as a Zone of Peace subsequently was the subject of supporting resolutions adopted at every regular session of the UN General Assembly, and also at its 10th special session (on disarmament) held from May 23 to July 1, 1978. However, various initiatives to achieve the implementation of its provisions have made no substantive progress to date.

### The Mauritian Claim to Diego Garcia

In Mauritius the claim to sovereignty over Diego Garcia was officially made with greater emphasis during 1980. Thus Sir Satcam Boolell, the Mauritian Minister of Agriculture, Natural Resources and the Environment, said in January 1980 that the US plans to improve the naval base on Diego Garcia might ''increase tension in this part of the world and constitute a potential danger to Indian Ocean countries and to Mauritius in particular''.

By early June 1980 the return of Diego Garcia to Mauritius was called for by leaders of all political parties of Mauritius. Sir Seewoosagur Ramgoolam (the Prime Minister and leader of the Labour Party) was quoted on June 17 as saying that he had originally been forced to cede Diego Garcia because Britain ''would have been able to take it anyway''; that he had understood that Britain would use the island as a communications centre; that he had not been told of plans to let it be used by the United States; and that, as Britain was not using the island for the purpose for which it was ceded, he had let it be known that Mauritius wanted it to be returned.

Paul Bérenger, the founder of the (leftist) Mauritian Militant Movement (the largest party in Parliament since the 1976 general elections) said at the same time that his party's fight was ''political and diplomatic'' for the return of Diego Garcia, which he called ''part and parcel of Mauritian territory''.

The British Foreign and Commonwealth Office, however, stated on June 24 that Mauritius had ''at no stage'' demanded the return of the island and that the matter had not been raised during a recent visit to Mauritius by the UK Minister of State at the Foreign and Commonwealth Office (Richard Luce).

On June 26 a bipartisan majority (of 48 out of the 70 members) of the Mauritian Parliament formally urged the Government to demand the return of Diego Garcia to Mauritius, and Sir Seewoosagur stated on the following day that he would make the claim in London in 10 days' time; at the same time he did not rule out the possibility of taking the matter to the International Court of Justice in The Hague. The Mauritian Parliament subsequently passed an all-party motion calling for the return of Diego Garcia, and Sir Seewoosagur formally lodged the claim in talks which he had with the British Prime Minister in London on July 7.

Following his return to Mauritius, he said on July 16 that he had pointed out to the British Prime Minister that it had been agreed that Diego Garcia would be returned to Mauritius without compensation when it was no longer needed; he denied that he had received "a polite refusal"; and he added that he would rally world opinion around Mauritius's claim.

Earlier, the Assembly of Heads of State and Government of the Organization of African Unity had on July 4, 1980, called for the demilitarization of Diego Garcia and for its unconditional return to Mauritius.

H.W.D.

# Morocco-Spain

Since achieving independence in 1956 Morocco has actively pursued a claim to four small enclaves of land and three small islands on the north Moroccan coast, all under Spanish sovereignty and comprising the only remaining Spanish possessions on the African continent. The enclaves, over which Spanish rule dates from the 15th and 16th centuries, are the towns of Ceuta and Melilla and the Peñones (Rocks) of Alhucemas and Vélez de la Gomera; the islands, which were acquired by Spain in the 19th century, are the nearby Chafarinas. Of Spain's former colonial possessions in north-west Africa, the enclave of Ifni on the south-west Moroccan coast was returned to Morocco in 1969 and Spanish (Western) Sahara was effectively ceded to Morocco and Mauritania in 1979. The Moroccan Government has demanded that this decolonization process should be completed by the cession of the northern coast enclaves, but Spain has continued to insist that for historical and demographic reasons they are part of Spanish territory rather than colonial possessions. (For map showing the enclaves see page 87.)

Ceuta, situated near Tangier and opposite Gibraltar, has a land area of 19 square kilometres, 20 kilometres of sea coast and eight kilometres of land boundaries; it has a predominantly Spanish population of about 67,000. Melilla, situated to the east of Ceuta, close to the town of Nador, has a land area of 12 square kilometres, 3.9 kilometres of sea coast and 10 kilometres of land boundaries; its population, also predominantly Spanish, numbers 65,000. There are currently some 19,000 Spanish troops stationed in Ceuta and Melilla.

The Peñones de Alhucemas are made up of three small islands facing Alhucemas (near Ajdir) and, like Peñon de Vélez de la Gomera, are situated between Ceuta and Melilla. The Chafarinas Islands, 27 sea miles east of Melilla, face Kebdana cape. The Peñones have a civilian-military population of less than 100 each, and the Chafarinas of about 200.

Of the five territories, only Ceuta and Melilla are of any economic importance, Ceuta being mainly a port for petroleum products and passenger traffic and Melilla a port for the export of iron ore as well as a fishing port. Ceuta, Melilla and the Chafarinas became free port areas in 1863, while the Peñones achieved this status in 1872. Their economic progress proved harmful to traditional Moroccan ports such as Tetouan, particularly when the Rif tribes abandoned the latter in favour of contraband trade with the free ports.

Spain bases its claim to continued possession of the enclaves (known as the Presidios, or penal colonies, because of their use as such up to the early 20th century) on its conquest of them in the past, on its lengthy occupation of the areas over several centuries, on bilateral treaties concluded with the sultans of Morocco, and on their largely Spanish population. It also points out that the enclaves were acquired before Morocco became an independent nation. The new Spanish Constitution which entered into force on Dec. 29, 1978, described Ceuta and Melilla as Spanish cities and provided for them to be represented in the Spanish *Cortes* by one deputy and two senators each.

Morocco, on the other hand, has consistently claimed the territories as being within the "natural boundaries" of its kingdom, together with the former Spanish Sahara. It adds that, because it has no access to Ceuta and Melilla, it has had to equip ports such as Nador and Tangier for passenger traffic and trade; that the territorial waters around the enclaves interfere with fishing rights; and that Spain has used the same arguments in favour of retaining the enclaves as Britain has used in defence of its possession of Gibraltar against Spain's wishes.

## Historical Background to the Dispute

Ceuta was conquered by the Portuguese in 1415 and became an important town with a military and economic role. When Portugal became attached to Spain in 1580 after the death of King Sebastian of Portugal without an heir, all Portuguese settlements on the north Moroccan coast—Ceuta, Tangier and Mazagan—became Spanish possessions. The union of Spain and Portugal ended in 1640 (when Lisbon rose against Philip IV), and Portugal claimed back its territories; however, Ceuta proclaimed its allegiance to Spain and was later definitively reincorporated into the kingdom of Castille in 1668.

Of the other enclaves, Melilla was taken by the Spanish in 1497; Peñon de Vélez de la Gomera was occupied in 1508, Spanish sovereignty being confirmed in 1509 by the Treaty of Sintra (although the Spanish lost control of the Peñon from 1522 to 1564); and the Peñones de Alhucemas were occupied in 1673 and then ceded to Charles II by the Sultan of Morocco on condition that Spain prevented the Turks from seizing strongholds on the Mediterranean coast. The Chafarinas Islands were occupied by Spain in 1848, allegedly to forestall a French occupation of the area; Spain named them Congress, Isabella II and King's Island, although a French study team had previously named them Buckland, Busch and Brongniart.

In the 17th and 18th centuries there were repeated Moroccan attempts to oust the Spanish from the enclaves. Ceuta in particular came under persistent siege from 1694 to 1720, in 1727-28, in 1732 and again in 1790-91 for a 14-month period. Melilla was besieged in 1694-96 and for 100 days in 1774-75. The Peñon de Vélez de la Gomera was besieged in 1687 and its fort was razed to the ground in 1702, although the Peñon itself remained in Spanish hands and was besieged again in 1774 at the same time as Melilla. However, although such attacks (mounted largely by undisciplined tribesmen) continued into the 19th century, the sultans of Morocco meanwhile entered into a series of treaties recognizing the sovereignty of Spain over the Presidios and also dealing with their borders.

In May 1767 a peace and trade treaty was concluded between Charles III and Sidi Mohamed ben Abdallah (Mohammed III) guaranteeing the safety of any "Christian or renegade" who took refuge in the Presidios and rejecting any request by Spain for an extension of the limits of the Presidios. It stated that "ever since these places have been occupied by Spain, their Imperial Majesties have set their limits according to the opinion of their tolbas and ulemas and have promised not to change anything".

In March 1799, following a siege of Melilla by the same Sidi Mohamed ben

151

Abdallah, a treaty on peace, friendship, navigation, trade and fishing was signed between Charles IV and Moulay Slimane. It renewed the 1767 treaty, confirmed a 1782 agreement on "the boundaries of the camp of Ceuta", and gave Spain the authority to use heavy guns against the Moors of Melilla, Alhucemas and Peñon de Vélez if they continued to cause trouble. This treaty was confirmed by the May 1845 Larache Convention (signed after further tribal incidents) which dealt with the boundaries of Ceuta. Melilla's boundaries were laid down in an August 1859 agreement and were confirmed in an 1862 boundary convention.

In August 1859 the Convention of Tetouan was signed between representatives of Isabella II and Moulay Abderrahman, allowing an extension of Melilla's borders to facilitate its defence. The convention agreed to "cede to her Catholic Majesty the possession and full jurisdiction over territory near the Spanish place known as Melilla as far as necessary for the defence and tranquillity of this Presidio". The limits of the Presidio were to be established as being equivalent to "the range of an old-model 24 cannon shot", and the demarcation took place later the same year when a cannon ball was fired from the top of Melilla's fortress and landed on a southern beach of the town 2,900 metres away, the boundary being then traced in detail from that point. An act delimiting the territory of Melilla was signed in Tangier in June 1862.

Under the Convention of Tetouan the Sultan also promised to place troops at Melilla's frontier to suppress any unrest among the Rif tribesmen which might compromise good relations, and troops were also to be placed in the vicinity of the Peñones "to enforce respect for Spain's rights and effectively to ensure free entry into these towns of the necessary foodstuffs and supplies for its garrisons". A neutral area was designated between Spanish and Moroccan territory.

In the meantime hostilities took place between Spain and Morocco in 1859-60 (over reparations for damage caused when tribesmen laid siege to Ceuta). A peace and friendship treaty signed in April 1860 (also in Tetouan) ended the war and prescribed the extent of Ceuta's territory "as far as necessary for the safety and complete defence of the garrison"; it also set out full details of reference points necessary to define a zone "ceded in full possession and sovereignty" to Spain in conformity with the results of a study which had been agreed in detail by Spanish and Moroccan commissioners in April 1860. A neutral area was declared around Ceuta as in the case of Melilla. Other agreements specifying the status of the Presidios were signed up to 1911, all of which confirmed the existing frontiers as well as dealing with the day-to-day aspects of life in the enclaves. The only Spanish "jurisdictional territory" in North Africa which did not have a status decreed by convention between Spain and Morocco was the Chafarinas Islands.

Agreements among the great powers of the day recognizing Spain's presence in the Presidios were also signed in the early 20th century, although the major content of the treaties dealt with the delimitation of the borders of Spanish Sahara (for the dispute over which, see pages 160-70). Among these, the Franco-British Declaration of April 1904 affirmed Britain's freedom of action in Egypt in return for a British guarantee of France's freedom of action in Morocco, while at the same time it took into consideration "the interests of [Spain] by reason of its possessions on the Moroccan coast of the Mediterranean". Moreover, the Franco-Spanish Convention of October 1904, which was designed to secure Spanish co-operation regarding the April 1904 agreement, recognized the "extent of Spain's rights to guarantee its interests . . . as the result of having these possessions on the Moroccan coast".

The Franco-Moroccan Treaty of Fez of March 1912 established the French Protectorate in Morocco but specified also that the French Government should "come to agreement with the Spanish Government with respect to the interest that the latter has as a result of its geographical position and its territorial possessions on the Moroccan coast". The Franco-Spanish Agreement of November 1912 was drawn up "to clarify the respective situations of the two countries with respect to the cherifien empire" and was largely concerned with Spanish Sahara and Ifni.

After Spain had extended its presence around Melilla in 1908, hostilities broke out in July 1909 when Rif tribesmen hostile to the idea of Spanish mineral prospecting in the region attacked the site of a proposed railway connecting the mines with Melilla. Violent battles that month marked the beginning of years of hostilities between Spain and the Rifs, and by 1920 Spain retained only its enclaves, Larache and Tetouan on the north African coast. The last major battle of the war was at Alhucemas in 1925, which was decisive for the Spaniards and put an end to all but isolated skirmishes.

## Moroccan Claims to Enclaves since Independence

Since its independence in 1956 Morocco has strongly reaffirmed its claims to the Presidios before international organizations and in non-aligned and Arab forums. In 1961 Morocco called on the UN General Assembly to recognize its rights over the enclaves and began a diplomatic offensive, whereupon Spain reinforced the borders of the enclaves and Morocco imposed transit restrictions. On June 29, 1962, Morocco reasserted its claim to Ceuta and Melilla and on the following day extended its territorial waters from six to 12 miles; this affected the operations of Spanish fishing boats in the waters off the enclaves and resulted in Spain sending warships to escort its fishing vessels in the area, and also in the reinforcement of the military garrisons in the enclaves. Over the next few years, however, the attention of Spain and Morocco was diverted to other questions such as the status of Gibraltar, Spanish Sahara and Ifni. A meeting in July 1963 between Gen. Franco and King Hassan at Madrid airport marked the beginning of a rapprochement between the two countries, and King Hassan visited Spain in 1965.

In the mid-1970s, as trouble blew up over the question of Spanish Sahara, Morocco again began to press its claims to the enclaves. On Jan. 27, 1975, it formally requested the UN Decolonization Committee to place on its agenda the question of the remaining Spanish enclaves on or close to the Moroccan coast and alluded to UN Resolution 1514/XV of Dec. 14, 1960, condemning colonialism. Spain, however, condemned the Moroccan move as a "threat to Spain's national unity and territorial integrity" and warned that it would use all necessary legitimate means to defend the enclaves, communicating these views to the United Nations on Feb. 12, 1975. The Spanish Government maintained that although the Presidios were "geographically separate" from Spain they were not "ethnically or culturally distinct" since their "true indigenous population was of Spanish origin, nationality and language as are their feelings, customs and culture"; it added that this was what differentiated them from Gibraltar, whose population had been driven out when the British entered. Spain also claimed that since the enclaves were "sovereignty territories", and not "non-autonomous territories", they did not come within the competence of the Decolonization Committee.

Later the same year three people were killed in bomb explosions in Ceuta and Melilla in June, and about 400 Moroccans were subsequently reported to have been arrested in Ceuta. Spanish and Moroccan troops later confronted each other on the borders of Melilla. These incidents led Morocco to protest in a letter to the UN Secretary-General on June 30, 1975, at the "violations of human rights committed by the Spanish authorities" in Ceuta and to warn that, "if such practices continue, the Moroccan Government will be constrained to take the measures necessary to protect the rights and interests of its nationals".

Attention was diverted from the question of the enclaves to the Spanish Sahara with the signature of the Madrid agreement in November 1975 under which Spain withdrew from the latter territory; since then an equilibrium of sorts has existed between Morocco and Spain. However, after King Juan Carlos ascended the Spanish throne on the death of Gen. Franco in November 1975 and reaffirmed Spain's aim of re-establishing sovereignty over Gibraltar, King Hassan asserted at a press conference the same month that if Spain came into possession of Gibraltar, Morocco would retrieve Ceuta and Melilla because "no power can permit Spain to possess both keys to the same straits".

An organization known as the Moroccan Patriotic Front carried out several bomb attacks in Ceuta and Melilla in late 1978 and early 1979 in which several people were injured.

**J.B.**

# Namibia-South Africa

The southern border between Namibia (which as South West Africa has been administered by South Africa since 1920) and South Africa itself runs for a continuous length of 600 miles (965 km). The border itself has not been the subject of dispute, the alignment having been agreed in 1890 by the then relevant colonial authorities, Britain and Germany. Questions that have been disputed, however, concern the proper status of the port of Walvis Bay, which constitutes an enclave within the territory of Namibia and which since 1977 has been administered by South Africa as an integral part of its territory. A number of small islands off the Namibian coast, known collectively as the Penguin Islands, are also regarded by South Africa as forming an integral part of its own territory.

The South African position is that Walvis Bay and the Penguin Islands became British possessions during the colonial period in the latter half of the 19th century, and were annexed by Britain to the British Cape Colony. The whole of Cape Colony became part of the Union of South Africa, established in 1910. What is now Namibia, on the other hand, had come under German colonial rule in 1884 with the establishment of the German protectorate of South West Africa. The historical details are set out below.

The South African view has in practice prevailed hitherto, since the South Africans have controlled not only the areas in question, but the whole territory of Namibia. This situation arose after the former German colony became a League of Nations mandated territory and was entrusted by the League to South African administration in 1920. After the League was dissolved, the United Nations as its post-war successor organization took over responsibility for the mandated territories (redesignating them as UN trust territories), but the South Africans refused to conclude a UN trusteeship agreement and continued to administer the territory, even framing their own abortive constitutional and independence initiative in the mid-1970s. Meanwhile, the UN General Assembly in 1966 declared the South African mandate terminated and in 1967 set up a UN Council to administer the territory, which it resolved in 1968 should be known as Namibia. The illegality of the South African presence in Namibia was confirmed by the UN Security Council in 1969 and in an advisory opinion of the International Court of Justice in 1971.

Since 1978, protracted negotiations have been under way to arrange for a transition to independence in Namibia, in a form which would be accepted by the people of the territory as well as by the UN and South Africa. The nationalist South West Africa People's Organization (SWAPO) has been recognized by the UN General Assembly since 1973 as the authentic representative, and since 1976 as the sole and authentic representative, of the Namibian people.

It is in the context of moves towards a future independent Namibia that the territorial status of Walvis Bay has become an active dispute. Having found it convenient from 1920 to 1977 to administer Walvis Bay as if it were part of the territory of South West Africa under their administration, the South Africans in 1977 announced that Walvis Bay would henceforth be administered as an integral part of Cape Province, to which it had technically belonged all the time. This was declared by SWAPO to be an act of illegal annexation, the contention that Walvis Bay is an integral part of Namibia being endorsed by the UN General Assembly and the UN Council for Namibia. The details of the recent emergence of this dispute are also set out below.

Walvis Bay is the only deep-water port along the Namibian coast, and the enclave has a total area of some 350 square miles (900 sq km). The port handles cargo including uranium from the Rio Tinto-Zinc mine at Rössing (about 40 miles inland) and has a significant fishing, canning and fishmeal industry. South Africa ranks Walvis Bay as its fifth largest port.

### Territorial Divisions by the Colonial Powers

*British annexation of the Penguin Islands.* The Penguin Islands are situated a few miles off the Namibian coast in a line running from Hollandsbird or Hallamsbird island (about 100 miles south of Walvis Bay) southward over a distance of some 250 miles (400 km), the most southerly being Roastbeef Island. The group includes the islands called Mercury, Ichaboe, Seal, Penguin, Halifax, Long, Possession, Albatross Rock, Panama and Plumpudding.

A short-lived Dutch occupation of Halifax Island in 1793 was followed by the visit of a British ship in 1795 to a number of bays which were declared British possessions. However, it was not until the 1860s that clear action was taken by the British with regard to the islands, which had become valuable as sources of guano (the guano deposits having been declared by the British Governor of Cape Colony in 1845 to be the property of Her Majesty). In 1861 the British took formal possession of Ichaboe Island, and on August 12 of that year the Governor of Cape Colony declared British sovereignty over all 12 islands and rocks. This proclamation was disallowed in 1864 but restored in 1866, when on May 5 the captain of a British ship took possession of Penguin Island and declared British sovereignty

**Map 18   Namibia-South Africa.**

155

and dominion over the others. On July 16, 1866, the Governor of Cape Colony proclaimed the islands annexed to and part of the colony, this action being authorized in the Royal Letters Patent of February 1867.

The British claim to the islands was recognized by the German colonial authorities in 1886 and 1890 (i.e. after the establishment of the German mainland protectorate), and the islands continued to be regarded as part of the Cape Colony, passing as such from British rule in 1910 and coming thereafter under the administration of the Union (later the Republic) of South Africa.

*British annexation of Walvis Bay.* Walvis Bay, where a small whaling settlement was established in the 18th century, was one of the bays claimed first by the Dutch in 1793 and then by the British two years later. However, it was not until the 1870s that the British took formal steps towards the annexation of Walvis Bay, after perceiving a possible threat to their interests in south-west Africa if Boer trekkers were to establish themselves north of the Orange River.

The Government of the British Cape Colony appointed in March 1876 a Commissioner Extraordinary for Namaland and Damaraland (the Nama and Damara being tribes indigenous to what is now Namibia), whose report in 1877 recommended the annexation of Walvis Bay (then known as Walfish Bay) and surrounding territory. The captain of a British ship accordingly landed at Walvis Bay and marked out an area which was annexed as British territory on March 12, 1878. His proclamation was ratified by Letters Patent of Dec. 14, 1878, in which it was provided that Walvis Bay and adjacent territory could be annexed to the Cape Colony if the Cape Government were to enact legislation to that effect. This was done on July 25, 1884, in the Walfish Bay and St John's River Territories Annexation Act, and the annexation was formalized by the Cape Governor's Proclamation published on Aug. 8, 1884. The proclamation set out what were the limits of "the port or settlement of Walfish Bay and certain territory surrounding the same" which with effect from Aug. 7, 1884 "shall under the name, designation and title of Walfish Bay become and be part of the Colony of the Cape of Good Hope, and subject to the laws in force therein".

*German annexation of South West Africa.* The establishment of the German protectorate followed purchases of land along the coast by a German merchant, F. Luederitz, beginning on May 1, 1883, with the bay of Angra Pequena (renamed Luederitzbucht). British and German naval vessels were sent to the area to protect their respective trading interests, and on April 24, 1884, the German consul at the Cape informed the British that Luederitz's possessions along the coast would henceforward come under German protection. A formal declaration of the German protectorate was proclaimed on Aug. 16, 1884, covering the area north of the Orange River as far as the 26th parallel, and extending some 20 miles inland. On Sept. 8, 1884, the German protectorate was extended northward to Cape Fria with the exception of Walvis Bay.

The protectorate's expansion westward was accomplished in the succeeding years by land acquisitions from the tribes of the interior, while its northern border with Portuguese possessions was settled in 1886. The British recognized South West Africa as a German sphere of influence in an agreement of July 1, 1890, in which the Germans also recognized the British title to Walvis Bay subject to the delimitation of the enclave's southern boundary, which was then in some dispute.

## Early Dispute over Boundaries of Walvis Bay

The Walvis Bay territory as annexed to the Cape Colony in 1884 was defined in the original description of 1878 as bounded "on the south by a line from a point on the coast 15 miles [24 km] south of Pelican Point to Scheppmansdorf; on the east by a line from Scheppmansdorf to the Rooibank, including the plateau, and thence to 10 miles inland from the mouth of the Swakop river; on the north by the last 10 miles of the course of the said Swakop river". However, when this definition was considered by an Anglo-German joint commission in 1885 it was found to contain certain ambiguities with regard to the southern sector, and a degree of vagueness as to what was the "plateau" and whether the distance southward from Pelican Point should be measured in statute or nautical miles.

A unilateral survey by a surveyor from Cape Town, Philip Wrey, was conducted for the Cape Government in 1885, in which the southern limit of Walvis Bay was taken as running from 15 nautical miles south of Pelican Point, and the eastern boundary was extended past Scheppmansdorf to Ururas, taking in an area regarded by Wrey as corresponding to the "plateau" of the 1878 description. Wrey's demarcation was disputed by the Germans (with respect only to the southern sector), a second joint commission failing to resolve the dispute in 1888. Under a provision for the matter to be taken to arbitration, set out in Article III of the 1890 Anglo-German agreement, the King of Spain was asked to appoint an arbitrator in 1909, after a third Anglo-German joint commission in 1904 had been unable to reach agreement. The Spanish arbitrator studied the issue and reported in May 1911, his award following Wrey's demarcation. This settled in international law the boundaries of Walvis Bay as an enclave territory.

## Contemporary Dispute over Status of Walvis Bay and Penguin Islands

The contemporary dispute turns on the contention that, if Namibia is to attain and retain independence, its aspiration for territorial integrity requires the inclusion in Namibia of Walvis Bay and the Penguin Islands. The historical developments as set out above are not themselves disputed, but rather their relevance is contested. Two factors have contributed to the recent emergence of an active dispute over Walvis Bay: the prospect of Namibian independence in the foreseeable future, and the South African decision in 1977 to resume direct administration of the enclave as part of Cape Province.

The second factor was clearly related to the first. In 1922, South Africa had found it convenient for obvious geographical reasons to commence administering Walvis Bay as if it were part of the Mandated Territory of South West Africa. The South African Government made applicable to Walvis Bay as well as to the mandated territory the terms of its South West Africa Affairs Act of 1922, validated by Proclamation No. 145 of the Governor-General, dated Sept. 11, 1922. Section 1 of the Act provided that acts of the South African Parliament or proclamations by the Governor-General relating to South West Africa would also apply to Walvis Bay unless otherwise stipulated, and that the port and settlement would be regarded as part of South West Africa for judicial purposes. However, the proclamation by the Administrator of Walvis Bay (No. 30 of Oct. 1, 1922) confirming this measure referred explicitly to "the port and settlement of Walvis Bay, which forms part of the Province of the Cape of Good Hope" being henceforth administered "as if it were" part of the mandated territory.

The convenience of this arrangement, from the South African point of view, ceased to apply when administrative provision in Namibia had to take into account the prospect of the territory's eventual transition to independent status. Unless Walvis Bay were to be part of an independent Namibia, there was little alternative but to resume administering it as part of Cape Province, and it was this latter course that the South African Government decided to pursue. The then Prime Minister, J. B. Vorster, declared in the House of Assembly in Cape Town on April 23, 1976, that there should be no misunderstanding about the status of the port of Walvis Bay, which formed part of the Republic of South Africa. In August 1977 (two months after the passing of the South West Africa Constitution Amendment Act), two separate South African Government proclamations were issued, providing respectively for the administration of South West Africa (Namibia) and Walvis Bay. The Walvis Bay Administrative Proclamation (No. R202 of Aug. 31, 1977, taking effect from Sept. 1) stated that "Walvis Bay shall cease to be administered as if it were part of the territory [Namibia] and as if inhabitants thereof were inhabitants of the territory and shall again be administered as part of the (Cape) province". In terms of Section 5 of the Proclamation, Walvis Bay ceased to be part of the electoral division of Omaruru (a division of Namibia) and later became part of the electoral division of Green Point, Cape Province. South African Defence Headquarters announced on Oct. 27 that the "dormant naval command and control facilities which already exist at Walvis Bay" would be reactivated as from Nov. 1, 1977.

Reactions from the five Western nations party to the Namibia independence negotiations (the United States, Canada, Britain, France and West Germany) reflected the perception that this development was likely to make the negotiations more difficult. A UN spokesman speaking on Sept. 1, on behalf of Dr Kurt Waldheim, then UN Secretary-General, also described the move as "unfortunate" and as a "unilateral act" at a time when concerted efforts were being made "to find a peaceful solution to the whole problem of Namibia". Although the question of Walvis Bay had not hitherto been prominent, the possibility that South Africa would press its territorial claim had already resulted in explicit references by Namibian nationalists to the territorial integrity of Namibia *including* Walvis Bay. SWAPO's draft constitutional proposals for the territory, published in 1976, had emphasized this point, and in May 1977, at the International Conference in Support of the Peoples of Zimbabwe and Namibia, held in Maputo, Mozambique, the conference declaration referred to Walvis Bay as an integral part of Namibia and the conference programme of action called upon governments to reject all attempts by South Africa to dismember the territory of Namibia and especially its design to annex Walvis Bay.

It was in similar terms that SWAPO spokesmen, and the UN Council for Namibia, denounced what they described as South Africa's annexation of Walvis Bay in statements issued in September 1977. Daniel Tjongarero, the SWAPO deputy chairman, said on Sept. 1 that Namibians could not be bound by colonial treaties of the 1880s and that South Africa's claim to Walvis Bay was "an expansionist venture and it could be used for possible aggression against Namibia" in the future. Moses Garoeb, the SWAPO administrative secretary, said in Lusaka on Sept. 8 that South Africa's claims to Walvis Bay were wild and baseless, and that he was not aware of any "colonial arrangements" which would give South Africa title over the port, which he described as "part of our country". Peter Katjavivi, the SWAPO information secretary, said in London that South Africa's historical claim to Walvis Bay was legally invalid and that "Walvis Bay is an integral part of Namibia and as our only port it will be of crucial importance to an independent Namibia". South African moves to hold on to the port were described by Katjavivi as an attempt to sabotage the economic future of Namibia. SWAPO later announced (on Oct. 15) that it would not accept any settlement plan for Namibia which did not include the retention of Walvis Bay as part of its territory.

Dirk Mudge, who was then the chairman of the Turnhalle Constitution Committee (and who was emerging as the most prominent politician working within the framework of the South African administration in Namibia), did not challenge South Africa's claim to Walvis Bay in legal terms, but he did express the hope on Sept. 9 that South Africa might at some later date feel in a position to hand Walvis Bay over to an independent Namibia.

A statement issued on Sept. 7, 1977, by the UN Council for Namibia, condemned "in the strongest possible terms this unilateral attempt by South Africa to destroy the territorial integrity and unity of Namibia". The Council stated that Walvis Bay had always been an integral part of Namibia and that South Africa had no right to change its status, and described as illegal the South African appropriation of the port as part of its territory. Walvis Bay, the statement said, was "inextricably linked by geographical, historical, cultural, and ethnic bonds" to Namibia, and without the port the independence of Namibia could not be complete. The Council called on the UN Security Council to take measures to maintain the status of Walvis Bay as part of the international territory of Namibia. The UN General Assembly, in its Resolution 32/9D of Nov. 4, 1977, also condemned South Africa's decision to annex Walvis Bay as illegal, null and void and an act of colonial expansion in violation of the Charter of the UN and of the UN Declaration on Decolonization.

The UN Council for Namibia reaffirmed its position in the Lusaka Declaration adopted on March 23, 1978, in which it was stated that "Walvis Bay is not a question of territorial claims; it is an inviolable and non-negotiable part of Namibia". The UN General Assembly has also reiterated on a number of occasions that Walvis Bay is an integral part of Namibia and that South African annexation was illegal, null and void.

Without explicitly endorsing the General Assembly's assertion that South Africa has no legal claim to Walvis Bay, the UN Security Council has nevertheless accepted the contention that Namibia's integrity, unity and economic validity requires that Walvis Bay be part of its territory. In its resolution No. 432 of 1978, adopted unanimously, the UN Security Council declared that Namibia's territorial integrity and unity must be assured by the reintegration of Walvis Bay within its territory and that, pending attainment of this objective, South Africa must not use Walvis Bay in any manner prejudicial to the independence of Namibia or the viability of its economy. It decided to lend its full support to the initiation of steps necessary to ensure early reintegration of Walvis Bay into Namibia.

In the Algiers Declaration and Programme of Action on Namibia, adopted by the UN Council for Namibia on June 1, 1980, there was a recognition of the uncertainty involved in deferring the question of Walvis Bay for settlement only after Namibian independence. The Council declared that Namibia should accede to independence with its territorial integrity intact and that Walvis Bay was an integral part of Namibia, and added that "any further steps which South Africa may take in the future to undermine the unity and integrity of Namibia are illegal, null and void". The Algiers Programme of Action calls upon the UN Security Council to declare categorically that Walvis Bay is an integral part of Namibia and that the question should not be left as a matter for negotiation between an independent Namibia and South Africa. The UN Council for Namibia also decided to take "all necessary action to ensure that South Africa's false claims with respect to the Penguin and other islands along the coast of Namibia are declared illegal, null and void by the relevant organs of the United Nations".

The continuing negotiations over Namibian independence have, however, left open the question of the future of Walvis Bay. South African policy has remained that the status of the enclave cannot be discussed in the context of Namibian independence talks, and the idea that the question should be left for separate negotiations after Namibia's independence is not acceptable to SWAPO; nor is it in line with the resolutions passed on the subject by the UN General Assembly.

In the latter part of 1981 a new diplomatic initiative was undertaken by the US Government with a view to resolving the apparent deadlock in the Namibia peace talks, and this US initiative included inter alia a proposal for the parties to hold separate negotiations on Walvis Bay after Namibia had attained independence.

R.E.

# Western Sahara

Since Morocco became independent in 1956 it has strongly pressed a claim to sovereignty over the large expanse of desert to its south known as Western Sahara. Controlled by Spain since the 19th century, Western Sahara was divided up between Morocco and Mauritania under a tripartite agreement of November 1975 when Spain decided to withdraw from the territory. However, the occupation of Western Sahara by Morocco and Mauritania was opposed by the region's main guerrilla organization, the Algerian-backed Polisario Front, which in 1976 proclaimed an independent Saharan Arab Democratic Republic (SADR) and intensified hostilities against both countries. This led to a large-scale military conflict which placed a heavy burden on the Moroccan and Mauritanian economies; in 1979 Mauritania concluded a peace agreement with Polisario, declared its neutrality in the conflict and withdrew from the southern sector. Morocco immediately occupied the area and has since been harassed on a broad front in Western Sahara and also inside Morocco proper.

The Western Sahara covers an area of 125,000 square miles (325,000 sq km) within boundaries defined by the colonial powers. Since the colonial era its northern section had been named after the Seguia el Hamra river and its southern section after the Rio de Oro; however, on occupation by Mauritania Rio de Oro was renamed Tiris el Gharbia and later, under Morocco, Oued Eddahab (the Arabic for Rio de Oro).

The Sahrawis of Western Sahara are nomadic livestock-herding Moors (*beidan*) of Berber stock whose migratory area extended from the Oued Draa in southern Morocco to the Senegal river valley in southern Mauritania. They became arabicized after invasions by the (Bedouin) Maqil from the 13th century onwards and came to speak the Hassaniya Arab dialect instead of Berber. They remained largely autonomous within the Western Sahara area and ruled themselves by councils known as *yemaâ*. The major Sahrawi tribes are the Reguibat (the largest), Izarguien, Oulad Delim, Ait Lahsen, Oulad Tidrarin and Arosien.

The Polisario Front (Popular Front for the Liberation of Seguia el Hamra and Rio de Oro) is believed to have drawn many of its recruits from the Sahrawi population outside Western Sahara—in Morocco, Mauritania and Algeria—where their numbers are estimated to be as great as the numbers in Western Sahara itself; many Sahrawis fled to Morocco in 1958 after a joint Franco-Spanish operation crushed the Army of Liberation which fought against Spanish rule in the region and others were forced into exile in neighbouring countries after the Movement for the Liberation of Seguia el Hamra and Oued Eddahab

**Map 19  Western Sahara.**

160

(MLS)—Polisario's forerunner in Western Sahara—was crushed in 1970. In addition, many Sahrawis have in recent years become sedentary, due to factors such as the rural exodus and droughts which have reduced herds, and have settled all over the region. These factors are thought to be the basis for Polisario's consistent claim that the population of Western Sahara is far greater than the 74,000 accounted for in the Spanish census of 1974.

## History of the Dispute

Morocco's ties with the region south of the Oued Draa (including Western Sahara) and also to other areas in north-west Africa including present-day Mauritania (to whose territory Morocco harboured claims as part of a proposed "Greater Morocco" until 1969) date back centuries. However, the pattern of nomadic life in the desert regions meant that Moroccan rulers in the north enjoyed only limited political control over the tribes whose leaders swore allegiance to them, since the area occupied by specific tribes was constantly changing. For this reason also no reliable maps showing the territorial limits of Morocco's old empire existed prior to the 19th century.

Spain, which claimed "historic rights" in southern Morocco because of its early presence north of Cape Yubi (in what later became the Spanish enclave of Ifni) from 1476 to 1524, was drawn to the Western Sahara region by a trading centre at Cape Yubi and established claims to areas south of the Cape, opposite the (Spanish) Canary Islands. It concluded treaties of protection with tribal leaders south of the Cape, and in 1884 it took possession of Rio de Oro—the area of Western Sahara between Cape Bojador and Cape Blanc, then arbitrarily considered to stretch 150 miles (240 km) inland—as the "Spanish Protectorate of the African Coast". It confirmed its rights to Rio de Oro in 1886 under the Treaty of Idjil, concluded with the Emir of Adrar, and the territory was attached to the General Office of the Captain of the Canary Islands by a Royal Decree of April 1887; Sultan Moulay Hassan, however, refused to confirm Spanish rights there.

By the late 19th century, with Spain in control of Rio de Oro, Morocco in the eyes of the colonial powers was exercising control only as far south as the Draa region, along the coastal strip as far as Cape Yubi and, inland, around Tindouf (now in Algeria). Moulay Hassan, however, regarded his empire as extending to the Senegal river and, inland, up to Timbuktu (Mali) and southern Algeria. Morocco later consolidated its influence over tribes south of the Oued Draa (in what became Seguia el Hamra), and in 1895 Moroccan rights to the area between the Oued Draa and Cape Bojador, including Seguia el Hamra and Cape Yubi, were established under an Anglo-Moroccan agreement. However, Seguia el Hamra was subsequently allocated to Spain under a Franco-Spanish convention of 1904, title to the territory being confirmed in an agreement of November 1912. Spain was at the same time granted a protectorate in the Tarfaya region from the northern border of Seguia el Hamra to the Oued Draa, and this zone (Spanish Southern Morocco) was not transferred back to Morocco until 1958.

At the beginning of the 20th century France defined in conjunction with Spain (but without the collaboration of Morocco) the borders of its influence in north-west Africa and the respective zones of influence of the two countries in Morocco. In June 1900 an "agreement on the delimitation of French and Spanish possessions on the coast of the Sahara and on the coast of the Gulf of Guinea" was signed in Paris, establishing the southern and eastern (but not the northern) borders of the Spanish Sahara [see map]. The agreement specified that France should be allocated the salt mines of the Idjil region (this accounting for the curve along part of Rio de Oro's eastern border) and demarcated the frontier on Cape Blanc "in such a way that the western portion of the peninsula including the western bay be given

161

to Spain, and Cape Blanc proper plus the eastern portion of the same peninsula remain in France's possession''.

The main purpose of the Franco-Spanish Convention of October 1904 was to secure Spanish co-operation regarding the April 1904 Franco-British declaration (affirming British and French freedom of action in Egypt and Morocco respectively —see page 152) in return for recognition of a Spanish zone of influence in northern Morocco. At the same time, the convention completed the delimitation of the French and Spanish zones of influence, taking the eastern border of Western Sahara up as far as the Oued Draa. Article 6 of the agreement stated that Spain had "complete freedom of action over the region (i.e. Seguia el Hamra) included between 26° and 27°40′ latitude north and the meridian 11°, which is outside Moroccan territory", but recognized as Moroccan territory everything north of the present-day border between Seguia el Hamra and Morocco.

Consequent upon the Franco-Moroccan agreement of March 1912 setting up a French protectorate of Morocco, an "agreement drawn up to clarify the respective situations of the two countries with respect to the cherifien empire" was signed in Madrid in November 1912. This agreement reduced Spain's control in the north of Morocco but stated that south of parallel 27°40′ the above provisions of the 1904 agreement remained applicable.

## Impact of Decolonization Process on Western Sahara Issue

Spain assumed full possession of its Saharan territories and Ifni only in the 1930s. In 1946 it established Spanish West Africa, in which Spanish Sahara and Ifni were distinct entities, and in January 1958 the province of Spanish Sahara was created by the merger of Rio de Oro and Seguia el Hamra, ruled by a governor-general and returning deputies to the *Cortes*. In May 1967 a *Yemaâ* was installed by Spain to govern the province in line with the "traditional institutions of the Sahrawi people".

With Morocco a French protectorate and with France controlling also south-west Algeria, the central Sahara and Mauritania, the territorial issue remained dormant until after Morocco's independence in 1956. After Algeria's subsequent independence in 1962 a Moroccan claim to Algerian territory south of the Oued Draa (containing the Gara Djebilet iron ore deposits) erupted into a brief armed conflict in 1963, and relations between these two countries were not finally regulated until the Treaty of Ifrane was signed in 1969, followed by agreements in 1972 whereby Morocco renounced claims to the Algerian Sahara and Tindouf and recognized the Oued Draa as the frontier. In return, Algeria agreed to give diplomatic support to Morocco's claim to Spanish Sahara. Also in 1969 Morocco acquired de jure sovereignty over Ifni from Spain.

Against a background of unrest in Spanish Sahara and the emergence of liberation movements committed to ending Spanish rule in north-west Africa, representatives of Morocco, Mauritania and Algeria agreed at a meeting in Nouadhibou (Mauritania) in September 1970 to collaborate closely on the Spanish Sahara issue and to act in conformity with United Nations resolutions (which since 1965 had called for the holding of a referendum in the territory under UN auspices with a view to granting Spanish Sahara self-determination). The three countries themselves also in 1970 sponsored a UN resolution inviting Spain to organize a referendum among the Sahrawis to determine the territory's future. However, relations subsequently deteriorated between Morocco and Algeria, and in July 1974 King Hassan of Morocco began a diplomatic campaign to assert the Moroccan claim to the Sahara.

In line with a number of UN resolutions—including 2983/XXVII of Dec. 14, 1972, which called for the independence of Spanish Sahara and urged the Spanish

Government to consult with the Moroccan and Mauritanian Governments to organize a referendum in the territory to this end—Spain finally announced on Aug. 21, 1974, that a referendum was to be held in Spanish Sahara in the first half of 1975 to determine the future status of the territory. This followed (i) the announcement by Gen. Franco in September 1973 of a programme of "progressive participation" by the Sahrawis in preparation for their eventual self-determination; and (ii) his announcement in July 1974 that Spanish Sahara would soon be granted internal autonomy (this being opposed by King Hassan, who warned Franco against unilateral action regarding Spanish Sahara).

The announcement of the proposed referendum was also followed by a deterioration in relations between Mauritania and Morocco, the latter accusing the former of making trouble by maintaining its own claim to Spanish Sahara (in support of which Mauritania mounted its own diplomatic campaign in August 1974).

### Submission of Dispute to ICJ for Advisory Ruling

The UN General Assembly on Dec. 13, 1974, approved a resolution (3292/XXIX) sponsored by Morocco and Mauritania urging that an advisory opinion should be sought from the International Court of Justice on two questions, namely (i) whether the Spanish Sahara was a territory belonging to no one (*res nullius*) at the time of its colonization by Spain, and (ii) if it was not, what "legal ties" existed between the territory and the Kingdom of Morocco and the "Mauritanian entity". The UN transmitted the request to the ICJ on Dec. 21, and the proposed referendum in Spanish Sahara was postponed while the ICJ considered the issue.

In the ensuing period, before the ICJ published its ruling on Oct. 16, 1975, there were a series of major developments concerning the Spanish Sahara. Against a background of diplomatic and military tension as Morocco pressed its claim to Spain's African possessions, violent guerrilla activity and disturbances erupted both in Spanish Sahara and the enclaves, and amid UN efforts to find a solution to the Spanish Sahara problem Spain announced on May 23, 1975, that it was ready to grant independence to the territory "in the shortest period possible" and made moves to open negotiations with Morocco, Mauritania and Algeria as well as with Polisario, which had by now emerged as the main guerrilla front.

Before the emergence in 1975 of Polisario as the main formation opposing the Spanish presence in the territory, several other liberation movements had also been prominent. They included the Moroccan-backed Liberation and Unity Front (FLU); the Sahrawi National Union Party (PUNS), a moderate indigenous autonomist movement sponsored by Spain in order to secure an orderly transfer of sovereignty in which its own interests would be protected; and Morehob (the *Mouvement de résistance des hommes bleus*—referring to the Reguibat or "blue people" of Spanish Sahara), which, however, had little influence.

The Polisario Front itself emerged from among Sahrawi students at Rabat University in Morocco. Its original aim was to reorganize the opposition to Spanish rule and drive the Spaniards out of Western Sahara; it adopted the aim of independence for the territory only later after it had failed to receive practical assistance from Morocco. Polisario at first based itself in Mauritania but subsequently moved to Algeria, where it received support from the Algerian Government.

At the time of the violent upsurge of guerrilla activity, a fact-finding mission of the UN Decolonization Committee visited Spanish Sahara in May 1975 and also held talks with Spain, Morocco and Mauritania. It found evidence of widespread support for Polisario among the people but little following for the Spanish-backed PUNS, and stated that almost all the people it had met in the territory were "categorically for independence and against the territorial claims of Morocco and Mauritania". In its report, published on Oct. 14, 1975, it recommended that the people of Spanish Sahara should be enabled to determine their own future "in complete freedom and in an atmosphere of peace and security".

## Spanish Decision to grant Independence

After a meeting of the Spanish Council of Ministers presided over by Franco on May 23, 1975, the Government announced that due to the "progressive deterioration" of the situation and the clear desire for independence in the territory, it was ready to "transfer the sovereignty of the Spanish Sahara in the shortest period possible" after the ICJ had delivered its opinion and the United Nations had taken an appropriate decision. It subsequently announced that it would seek to convene a quadripartite conference with Morocco, Mauritania and Algeria to discuss the future of the territory.

Morocco strongly opposed the Spanish decision, accusing Spain of creating an "equivocal situation and a climate of confusion". Mauritania for its part expressed satisfaction at the Spanish intention and recorded its wish that the decolonization should take place within a UN framework; however, at the same time President Ould Daddah of Mauritania said in an interview that Mauritania would take "all appropriate measures to preserve its legitimate rights over the Sahara, which it considers as forming part of its territory".

It became known at this stage (in mid-1975) that Morocco and Mauritania had reached a secret agreement at the end of the previous year on a plan to partition Spanish Sahara between them after the withdrawal of Spain, whereby Morocco would obtain the northern Seguia el Hamra sector and Mauritania the southern Rio de Oro sector, while the phosphate deposits at Bou Craa would be jointly exploited.

## Publication of ICJ Advisory Opinion

On Oct. 16, 1975, the ICJ published the advisory opinion that while certain "legal ties of allegiance" existed between Western Sahara and both the Kingdom of Morocco and the "Mauritanian entity" at the time of colonization by Spain in 1884, these did not in either case support a claim of territorial sovereignty, nor did they affect the application of the principle of "self-determination through the free and genuine expression of the will of the peoples of the territory", as enunciated in the 1960 UN declaration on the granting of independence to colonial countries and peoples.

It went on: "The materials and information presented to the court show the existence at the time of Spanish colonization of legal ties of allegiance between the Sultan of Morocco and some of the tribes living in the territory of Western Sahara. They equally show the existence of rights, including some rights relating to the land, which constituted legal ties between the Mauritanian entity . . . and the territory of Western Sahara. On the other hand, the court's conclusion is that the materials and information presented to it do not establish any tie of territorial sovereignty between the territory of Western Sahara and the Kingdom of Morocco or the Mauritanian entity. . . ."

*The First Question.* The court ruled that, according to state practice at the time of Spain's colonization of Western Sahara in 1884, territories inhabited by tribes or peoples having a social and political organization were not regarded as *terrae nullius*; in their case, sovereignty was not generally considered as effected through simple occupation but through agreements concluded with local rulers. Information furnished to the court showed that at the time of colonization Western Sahara was inhabited by peoples which, although nomadic, were socially and politically organized in tribes and under chiefs competent to represent them. Furthermore, it showed that Spain did not proceed upon the basis that it was establishing its sovereignty over *terrae nullius* (the King of Spain having proclaimed in his royal decree of 1884 that he was taking Rio de Oro under his protection on the basis of agreements entered into with the chiefs of local tribes).

*Legal Ties.* The court ruled that "legal ties" must be understood as referring to such legal ties as might affect the policy to be followed in the decolonization of Western Sahara and rejected the view that the ties in question could be limited to ties established directly with the territory and without reference to the people in it. The court found that at the time of its colonization the territory had a sparse population consisting for the most part of nomadic tribes of the Islamic faith, whose members traversed the desert on more or less regular routes, sometimes reaching as far as southern Morocco or regions of present-day Mauritania, Algeria or other states.

*Moroccan Claims.* Morocco had claimed "ties of sovereignty" over Western Sahara on the grounds of "alleged immemorial possession" of the territory. It had cited in support of its claim (i) the special historical structure of the Moroccan state, namely that it was founded on the common religious bond of Islam and on the allegiance of various tribes to the Sultan through their caids or sheikhs rather than on the notion of territory; (ii) evidence said to show the allegiance of Saharan caids to the Sultan; and (iii) certain treaties dating from the 18th to the early 20th century said to constitute recognition by other states of Moroccan sovereignty over the whole or part of Western Sahara.

The court found that none of the internal or international acts relied upon by Morocco indicated the existence at the relevant period of either the existence or the international recognition of legal ties of territorial sovereignty between the Western Sahara and the Moroccan state. They did, however, provide indications that a legal tie of allegiance existed between the Sultan and some of the nomadic peoples of the territory and that the Sultan was recognized by other states to possess some authority or influence with respect to these tribes.

*Claims of "Mauritanian Entity".* The court noted that the term "Mauritanian entity" had been used to denote the cultural, geographical and social entity within which the Islamic Republic of Mauritania was later to be created. According to Mauritania, at the relevant period that entity—the Bilad Shinguitti or Shinguitti country—was a distinct human unit, characterized by a common language, way of life, religion and system of laws, with political authority emanating from emirates and tribal groups. While recognizing that the latter did not constitute a state, Mauritania had suggested that the concepts of "nation" and "people" would be most appropriate to explain the position of the Shinguitti people at the time of colonization. At that period, Mauritania said, the Mauritanian entity extended from the Senegal river to the Oued Seguia el Hamra, so that the territory at present under Spanish administration and the Islamic Republic of Mauritania together constituted indissoluble parts of a single entity and had legal ties with one another.

The court found, however, that while these various links existed, the emirates and many of the tribes in the entity were independent in relation to one another and had no common institution or organs; the entity therefore did not have the character of a personality or corporate entity distinct from the several emirates or tribes which comprised it. On the other hand, the nomadic peoples of the Shinguitti possessed rights, including rights to the lands through which they migrated; these rights constituted legal ties between Western Sahara and the Mauritanian entity which knew no frontier between the territories and were vital to the maintenance of life in the region.

*Overlapping Moroccan and Mauritanian Claims.* The court noted (i) that Morocco and Mauritania had both laid stress on the overlapping character of the respective legal ties which they claimed Western Sahara had had with them at the time of

165

colonization; and (ii) that, although their views appeared to have evolved considerably in that respect, they both asserted at the end of the proceedings that there was a north appertaining to Morocco and a south appertaining to Mauritania without any geographical void in between, but with some overlapping as the result of the intersection of nomadic routes.

On this aspect the court confined itself to noting that this geographical overlapping indicated the difficulty of disentangling the various relationships existing in the Western Sahara at the time of colonization.

### Moroccan Green March and November 1975 Tripartite Agreement

Immediately upon the delivery of the ICJ ruling King Hassan on Oct. 16, 1975, declared his intention to stage a "green [i.e. peaceful] march" of 350,000 unarmed Moroccans into Spanish Sahara to claim the territory symbolically for Morocco. Despite Spanish and Algerian warnings to Morocco and the convening of the UN Security Council by Spain (which itself was experiencing a political crisis with Franco in the last stages of a fatal illness), the march went ahead on Nov. 6. The marchers penetrated about six miles (10 km) into the north of Western Sahara, kneeling to pray as they crossed the border for the return of "the land of our forefathers, after 90 years of separation". All Spanish troops in Western Sahara had withdrawn behind a mined "dissuasion line" about seven miles inside the Western Sahara frontier on the Tarfaya-El Aaiún road, and the area in between this line and the frontier formed a no-man's-land into which the marchers were allowed to penetrate without reprisals; however, Spanish destroyers, aircraft and troops waited on the alert in the Canary Islands, and Moroccan and Algerian troops were reported to be facing each other within striking distance near their borders. Finally, at the instigation of the United Nations, King Hassan ordered the marchers on Nov. 9 to withdraw to Tarfaya.

Shortly after the march ended it was announced from Madrid on Nov. 14, 1975, that Spain, Morocco and Mauritania had reached an agreement satisfactory to all three parties on the withdrawal of Spain from Western Sahara following talks in November. After the publication in Spain of a decolonization bill, the terms of the agreement were revealed on Nov. 21. They provided for the immediate establishment by Spain of a provisional administration in the territory "with the participation of Morocco and Mauritania and with the co-operation of the *Yemaâ* [the Spanish Sahara General Assembly]" and for Spain to hand over to it "the responsibilities and powers which it has discharged in the territory in its capacity as administering power". Two assistant governors would be appointed respectively by Morocco and Mauritania to assist the Governor-General of the territory in his duties, and the Spanish presence would come to an end in Spanish Sahara on Feb. 28, 1976.

The agreement was strongly opposed by Algeria and by Polisario, which said that the implementation of the tripartite agreement would open the way for "a bloody war with disastrous consequences for the entire region".

### Moroccan and Mauritanian Occupation of Western Sahara

Although according to the agreement a Spanish presence was to be maintained in Western Sahara until Feb. 28, Morocco rapidly asserted its influence over the territory and during December 1975 and January 1976 occupied the main towns of northern Spanish Sahara, including the capital, El Aaiún. In the meantime the UN General Assembly on Dec. 10, 1975, adopted two contrasting resolutions on the future of Western Sahara. The first (3458A/XXX), known as the "Algerian resolution", made no mention of the tripartite agreement, requested Spain to take immediate steps to enable "all Saharans originating in the territory" to exercise their "inalienable right to self-determination" under UN supervision, and appealed to all parties to refrain from unilateral or other action. The second (3458B/XXX), known as the "Moroccan resolution", noted the tripartite agreement and requested the interim administration to take all necessary steps to ensure that "all the Saharan populations originating in the territory" were able to exercise their "inalienable right to self-determination" through free consultations organized with the help of a UN representative.

The last Spanish troops left Western Sahara on Jan. 12, 1976, and the Spanish presence in the territory terminated on Feb. 26, two days before the date laid down in the agreement. On the same day the *Yemaâ* (meeting in El Aaiún with only two-thirds of its full contingent) unanimously voted to ratify the Madrid agreement. The Polisario Front thereupon on Feb. 27-28 proclaimed the Western Sahara as a free, independent and sovereign state known as the Saharan Arab Democratic Republic (SADR), and formed a government which was recognized by Algeria (causing Morocco and Mauritania to break off diplomatic relations with the latter).

Under a convention signed in Rabat on April 14, 1976, Morocco and Mauritania agreed on the delimitation of their border in Western Sahara. This was to run eastwards from a point on the Atlantic coast, north of Dakhla (formerly Villa Cisneros), leaving Bir Enzaran in the Moroccan sector as a border post, and then south-east in the direction of Zouerate (Mauritania). Mauritania received less than one-third of the territory, which became known as Tiris el Gharbia. The Moroccan sector was divided into the administrative provinces of El Aaiún, Smara and Bojador, and the Bou Craâ phosphate mines remained in this sector, a majority share in the Spanish Sahara phosphate company, Fosbucraâ, being in February 1976 transferred to Morocco.

## Mauritanian Withdrawal from Conflict

Over the ensuing years the Polisario Front intensified its hostilities in Western Sahara against both Morocco and Mauritania. Mauritania's involvement in the conflict resulted in over 9,000 Moroccan troops being stationed in the country itself, particularly after Polisario attacks on Nouakchott (the capital) in 1976 and 1977, and Mauritania was forced to expand its own Army to 12,000 men and to devote 60 per cent of its budget to defence, with disastrous effects on the economy and on development projects.

In July 1978, however, the Government of President Ould Daddah was overthrown by the armed forces, which said that they had seized power because the country was on the verge of bankruptcy and which vowed to co-operate with Morocco in seeking a solution to the war. The Polisario Front immediately ordered a ceasefire in Mauritania and the Mauritanian Government began diplomatic initiatives to bring about peace in Western Sahara, and later in 1978 commenced negotiations with Polisario, which in September extended its ceasefire indefinitely and concentrated its hostilities against the Moroccan sector of Western Sahara. Mauritania also sought closer relations with Algeria following the death in December 1978 of President Houari Boumedienne of Algeria.

In May 1979 there were further changes of orientation in the Mauritanian leadership, the outcome being the recognition by Mauritania on July 17, 1979, of the right to self-determination of the Tiris el Gharbia sector; the conclusion by Mauritania and Polisario of a peace agreement on Aug. 5, 1979; and the withdrawal of Mauritania from Tiris el Gharbia during that month.

The first section of the August 1979 agreement stated that "considering the urgent need to find a definitive global solution to the conflict between the two parties which will guarantee the Sahrawi people their full national rights, and the region peace and stability", Mauritania relinquished all present and future claims to Western Sahara and resolved to "extricate itself definitively from the unjust war over Western Sahara''; Polisario declared that ''it neither has nor will make any territorial claims on Mauritania'' and resolved, in the name of the Sahrawi people, to sign a definitive peace agreement with Mauritania. A second section of the agreement, apparently referring to the application of ''agreed principles'', remained secret.

The Mauritanian Prime Minister, Lt.-Col. Kaydalla, visited Morocco for talks on Aug. 10 and, before leaving later that day, he read out a statement to the press which said (i) that Mauritania had ''renounced all claims to Tiris el Gharbia and considers itself definitively disengaged from this conflict'', (ii) that Morocco, ''noting this new situation, intends to ensure the defence of its rights, its territorial integrity, its security and the stability of the region'', and (iii) that Morocco and Mauritania had undertaken not to do ''anything which might damage the reciprocal security of the two countries''.

Morocco immediately afterwards took control of the Mauritanian sector of Western Sahara, renamed it Oued Eddahab and allocated seats in the Moroccan Parliament to the new ''province''. Lt.-Col. Kaydalla described the occupation as an aggression against Mauritania, but he received no response to his demand for the withdrawal of Morocco's troops. Mauritania and Algeria on Aug. 13 re-established diplomatic relations, and later in August, after the withdrawal of its own troops, Mauritania declared its ''total neutrality'' in the Western Sahara conflict.

## Recent Developments

During the remainder of 1979 and throughout 1980 the Polisario Front concentrated its hostilities in southern Morocco proper as well as continuing to attack positions mainly in the north of Western Sahara. The Front became increasingly better armed and organized, and proved a strong adversary for the Moroccan Army, which now had a land border with Algeria and Mauritania of some 2,000 miles (3,200 km) to defend and which was obliged to spend one quarter of its annual budget on the war.

Over this period a ''committee of wise men'', which had been established at the 1978 OAU summit to mediate in the conflict and which comprised a number of African heads of state, held meetings and the OAU itself passed a number of resolutions on the Western Sahara issue. At the organization's Council of Ministers' meeting in Freetown (Sierra Leone) in June 1980 the SADR submitted an application for OAU membership. In the event 26 of the 50 OAU members favoured the admission of the SADR, but Morocco (supported by a number of other states) claimed that the SADR was not a sovereign state, maintained that according to some interpretations the OAU Charter required a two-thirds majority for the admission of new members, and threatened to leave the OAU if the SADR was admitted.

The matter of admittance was put in abeyance and a compromise was eventually reached whereby the committee of wise men was charged with organizing a meeting of all interested parties within three months. This accordingly took place in Freetown in September 1980, attended by the Presidents of Guinea, Mali and Nigeria; representatives of Sudan and Tanzania; and, as ''interested parties'', the Presidents of Algeria and Mauritania and delegations from Morocco, Polisario and other guerrilla organizations such as the FLS, the FLU, PUNS and Morehob. The meeting formulated a six-point plan for a UN-supervised ceasefire and an OAU-organized referendum, which it said should be implemented from December 1980. The plan was reportedly welcomed by Mauritania and Polisario but was described by Morocco as ''nothing new''.

In the first half of 1981 Morocco consolidated its position in Western Sahara with the help of a line of fortifications which it had constructed across the desert to protect important towns and installations and which became a major target of Polisario attacks. During this period Morocco continued to receive moral and material support from the conservative Arab states and also, following the inauguration of President Reagan in January 1981, from the United States. The SADR, on the other hand, had by mid-1981 been recognized by at least 50 states, in eight of which it had ambassadors and three of which (Mexico, Cuba and Nicaragua) had in March 1981 become the first countries to accredit ambassadors to the SADR.

In a speech on March 3, 1981, on the 20th anniversary of his accession to the throne, King Hassan called on Algeria to hold a summit meeting to "end the spilling of blood in the region"; at the same time he asserted that any agreement to end the conflict should not be "detrimental to an integral part of our national territory". Amid a renewed Moroccan diplomatic offensive in May 1981 directed in particular against Libya for its support of Polisario, the latter accused Morocco of using Libya as a scapegoat for its own failure to end the war and of refusing to submit to the decisions of international bodies.

However, when the Western Sahara issue was discussed at the 18th annual summit of the OAU held in Nairobi on June 24-28, 1981, proceedings were dominated by a rapprochement between Morocco and Libya and by a proposal by King Hassan that a referendum should be held in the territory. Addressing the assembled heads of state and government, King Hassan said that to avoid the OAU being "torn apart" on the Western Sahara issue, Morocco envisaged a procedure for a "controlled referendum" which would "simultaneously respect" the objectives of the latest recommendations of the committee of wise men and "the conviction which Morocco has of its legitimate rights". Earlier, at a press conference in Rabat on June 1, 1981, King Hassan had asserted that the OAU Charter was clear and free of ambiguity in stating that "only countries legally and internationally recognized within recognized frontiers established on the human and geophysical foundation necessary for entering into a regional grouping" could be members of the OAU. He had also warned that Morocco and other states would leave the OAU if the SADR were admitted to membership.

A resolution adopted by the Nairobi OAU summit recorded its decision to set up an implementation committee in respect of the Moroccan referendum proposal, it being specified that the committee would have full powers and would consist of Guinea, Kenya, Mali, Nigeria, Sierra Leone, Sudan and Tanzania. The same resolution (i) invited the parties to the conflict to observe an immediate ceasefire; (ii) requested the implementation committee to meet before the end of August 1981 to work out, in collaboration with the parties to the conflict, the modalities and all the details relating to the establishment of a ceasefire as well as to the organization and the holding of a referendum; (iii) requested the United Nations to furnish, in collaboration with the OAU, a peacekeeping force to be stationed in Western Sahara to maintain peace and security during the referendum and subsequent elections; and (iv) instructed the implementation committee to take, with the participation of the United Nations, all necessary measures to guarantee the holding of a general and regular referendum on self-determination for the people of Western Sahara.

The resolution contained no reference to the Polisario Front or to its demand for the withdrawal of Moroccan forces and administration from the territory, even though such a concession had been urged on Morocco by a number of OAU member states and was included in a series of conditions laid down in July by Polisario for the holding of a referendum. The other major conditions were (i) that direct negotiations should be held between Morocco and Polisario to agree on steps to bring about a ceasefire and create favourable conditions for the referendum; (ii) that a provisional international administration of the United Nations and the OAU should be established in co-ordination with the SADR to ensure the necessary conditions and security; and (iii) that all Sahrawis should return to their towns and villages.

By the end of 1981 little progress had been made towards holding a referendum in Western Sahara, the major problem facing the OAU implementation committee being the refusal of Morocco to engage in direct negotiations with the Polisario Front. Moreover, the military conflict acquired a new dimension in late 1981 when Polisario began to deploy sophisticated new weaponry, including tanks and anti-aircraft missiles, in its operations against Moroccan forces. Within the OAU, a deep rift developed after the SADR was given an OAU seat for the first time at the 38th regular session of the Council of Ministers held in Addis Ababa on Feb. 22-28, 1982. In protest against this step—which was taken at the instigation of the OAU Secretary-General, Edem Kodjo, on the grounds that 26 of the 50 member states had recognized the SADR—the representatives of a third of OAU members walked out of the conference. Subsequently, another OAU conference (of Information Ministers) was indefinitely adjourned in Dakar (Senegal) on March 15 after 14 of the 27 participating countries withdrew in protest against Senegal's refusal to admit SADR delegates.

**J.B.**

# South Africa-Black Homelands

The emergence in South Africa of Black homelands—either as territories with varying degrees of internal autonomy or as "independent" states (without their independence being recognized by the international community)—has created what are now territorial disputes, which have arisen out of the division of land between Blacks and Whites during the 19th and the early part of the 20th century.

### Historical Background

The clash between Blacks (successively referred to as Natives, Bantu or Africans) on the one hand and Whites on the other over the right to land has at its roots two entirely different concepts: (i) the Black tribal concept based on occupation rights, which might refer to land of three different types—communal grazing areas, residential sites and small areas for the growing of crops—all based on occupation but not ownership of land; and (ii) the White concept of private ownership of land, which could involve the possible renting, sale, subdivision or other disposal, even for speculative purposes.

During more than 100 years tribally-owned land in southern Africa gradually passed into White ownership until a first effort to halt this process was made by the (South African) Bantu Land Act, No. 27 of 1913, which fixed the boundaries of the tribally-occupied land, or "Native reserves".

Until 1913 Africans had been legally entitled to acquire land from Whites in parts of the country which were outside the Native reserves (which later became the homelands), but the 1913 Act prohibited such purchases unless they were in areas which various commissions had recommended for "release" to Africans. Gen.

J. B. M. Hertzog, then Minister of Native Affairs, said at the introduction of the 1913 bill that in their own areas the Natives were free to live as they liked and added that if possible they should govern themselves, perhaps "in an autonomous way".

No further action was taken until the Bantu Trust and Land Act, No. 18 of 1936, which tried to reverse the process of further reduction and fragmentation of the tribally-occupied land by encouraging the "release" from White ownership of certain lands which were to be added to and consolidated with the reserves. Whereas the courts had found that the 1913 prohibition of land purchases from Whites by Blacks unless the land had been recommended for release could not be applied in the Cape Province, the 1936 Act extended the prohibition to the whole country,

Map 20   The South African Black homelands, also showing the disputed Lesotho-South Africa border.

while it upheld the right of Africans to purchase land in "released" areas. The 1936 Act also enabled the Government to eliminate so-called "black spots", i.e. tribal land wholly surrounded by White-owned land. The Act provided that a quota of 6,209,857 hectares (over 7,250,000 morgen) should gradually be added to the scheduled reserves. However, the total land area to be assigned to Africans, who constituted 70 per cent of the country's population, was only 13 per cent of South Africa's total area.

The Government subsequently proceeded with its policy of apartheid, later called "separate development" or "plural democracy", establishing, from 1957 onwards, Bantu Territorial Authorities under a Bantu Authorities Act and "Bantu national units" or Bantu homelands under the Promotion of Bantu Self-Government Act of 1959, with the object (as explained in a White Paper in the same year) of, inter alia, uniting "the members of each Bantu national group in one national unit concentrated in one coherent homeland where possible".

Consolidation of the homelands was continued in the following years, and on Sept. 13, 1977, Dr F. Hartzenberg, then South African Deputy Minister of Bantu Development, stated that since the 1950s the homelands had been consolidated from 264 separate areas to 24, but that total consolidation was neither possible nor necessary for economic development.

P. W. Botha, the South African Prime Minister, conceded at a Transvaal National Party congress on Sept. 1, 1980, that the homelands could not be consolidated sufficiently to meet their economic and material aspirations, as in most homelands less than 20 per cent of their people's income was generated in their own geographical area and "of course we cannot give away the whole of South Africa merely to create economically viable states". The Government was therefore, he said, as part of its "constellation of southern African states programme", to launch an offensive to promote regional economic co-operation, to which he added: "In developing such co-operation projects we must be willing to transcend the boundaries of the traditional areas in South Africa and to extend a hand of co-operation over the borders of states."

In new guidelines for the consolidation of Black homelands—now referred to as Black national states—agreed upon by the South African Cabinet on Oct. 28, 1980, it was proposed eventually to transfer land to these states to "satisfy their most important development requirements and to end South Africa's responsibility for land through negotiation with the national states individually but with Parliament having to give its final approval to any decisions".

Land demands made by the various homelands leaders from time to time included calls for the general enlargement of their territories and also demands for specific areas to be transferred to them. In a joint statement on constitutional changes in South Africa, issued on Feb. 18, 1980, by the leaders of seven (not yet "independent") Black homelands it was demanded as a "non-negotiable prerequisite for Blacks" that "the allocation of land cannot be based on the 1913 and 1936 Land Acts but should be done on a more equitable basis".

## Territorial Demands made by Transkei

Among the demands for additional land those made by Paramount Chief Kaiser Matanzima of Transkei, both before and after the latter's achievement of "independence" on Oct. 26, 1976, were particularly persistent and far-reaching. In 1968 Chief Matanzima, then Chief Minister of Transkei, asked for the incorporation in his territory of Port St Johns, the White districts of Elliot and Maclear (eastern Cape Province) as well as Mount Currie (Kokstad) and the adjoining White parts of the districts of Matatiele and Umzimkulu (the three last-named districts being known as East Griqualand). The South African Government rejected this request in 1969, but Port St Johns was eventually incorporated in Transkei in 1976. On June 4, 1968, the Transkei Legislative Assembly passed a motion giving the Transkei Government a mandate to ask the South African Government for the amalgamation of Transkei and Ciskei into one Xhosa state under a united government.

On April 13, 1971, Chief Matanzima described the land question as "the most important aspect of the policy of separate development" and declared: "Most White South Africans are ashamed that seven-eighths of South African land is occupied by them. Unless the land question is settled fairly early there can be no really good relations between the two racial groups. We shall negotiate with the Republican Government until they accede to all our requests."

M. C. Botha, then South African Minister of Bantu Administration and Development, replied to the Chief on April 16, saying that there was "no land dispute between the South African Government and the Bantu"; that the areas claimed by the Chief had become part of the Republic "by tradition, convention and legislation and not as a result of war"; that Transkei was not overcrowded but parts of it were not properly occupied; and that according to the late Dr Verwoerd (who as Minister of Native Affairs and later Prime Minister had been the chief architect of separate development) Transkei would, with proper planning, be able to carry 50,000,000 people.

J. B. Vorster, then South Africa's Prime Minister, referring to the Transkei's requests in the House of Assembly on April 21, admitted that of the 53,400,000 acres (21,600,000 hectares) of land to be transferred to the Bantu under the 1936 Act a balance still remained to be transferred—64,682 hectares in the Cape Province and 67,372 hectares in Natal.

On Aug. 14, 1971, Chief Matanzima said that, if Africans from South Africa were resettled in the homelands (as was the policy of the South African Government), "we must be given more land". The following year, on April 11, he declared with reference to the land question: "The refusal of the South African Government to release that part of Transkei which was unilaterally expropriated after the Union of South Africa Act was passed has now put the Transkei people politically, in their relations with White South Africa, back to the pre-1963 days" (i.e. before Transkei was given internal self-government).

Vorster in turn stated in the House of Assembly on April 19, 1972, that his Government would fulfil its obligations under the 1936 Act but would reject any demand for land beyond that envisaged in the Act. However, Chief Matanzima again emphasized on May 10 that the land claim would not have arisen if it were not for the migratory labour policy of South Africa under which thousands of Africans were "repatriated" to their "homelands" every year.

On Aug. 7, 1972, the Chief stated that he envisaged a Black-controlled multi-racial Xhosaland consisting of Transkei, Ciskei, East Griqualand and White-owned land between the Fish and Kei Rivers and in which Blacks and Whites would have equal rights. In reply A. J. Raubenheimer, then South African Deputy Minister of Bantu Development, said on Aug. 9 that the South African Government would not oppose a union of Transkei and Ciskei but that it could not be a wholly contiguous territory incorporating White-owned land.

After Transkei had been granted "independence" Chief Matanzima said at a press conference on Oct. 27, 1976, that the South African Government had "no right to give the Ciskei self-government" (as had been done in 1972) and that he would "just take this land", as it belonged "to the Xhosa nation". However, a secretary in his department said on Oct. 29 that the Prime Minister had merely said that areas of the Ciskei where the people themselves wished to be governed by Transkei should be allowed to become part of Transkei.

On March 8, 1977, Chief Matanzima again named the South African districts of

Elliot and Maclear and added farms in Cedarville, Matatiele, Mount Currie, Harding and part of Port Shepstone west of the Umzimkulu River (forming part of the Transkei border with Natal) as being areas which should be "added as soon as possible to our small state under Section 1 of our Constitution Act". M. C. Botha retorted on March 9, however, that the South African Government did not agree that the Chief had "historical claims to all the areas mentioned", and emphasized that any land still to be acquired by Transkei had been scheduled in a 1976 agreement.

On March 30 Chief Matanzima claimed that East Griqualand (situated between Transkei and the Province of Natal as well as the Transkeian district of Umzimkulu physically separated from the main part of Transkei) was historically part of Transkei. This claim was, however, rejected by a committee of inquiry appointed by the Administrators of Natal and the Cape Province, which found that East Griqualand had never been a Black tribal territory but had for 115 years been an area of Griqua, Coloured (mixed-race) and White settlement.

Under a bill passed on March 9, 1978, the South African Government transferred, with effect from April 1, 1978, control of East Griqualand from the Cape Province, with which it had had no common border since Transkei's achievement of "independence", to the Province of Natal. The Transkei Government thereupon decided on April 10 to sever its diplomatic relations with South Africa.

Chief Matanzima stated on the same day that before the formation of the Union of South Africa (in 1910) the British Government had declared the East Griqualand area to be "part of Kaffraria proper, belonging to the aborigines of Transkei", and that the (White) South African Parliament of 1913 had had no right to annex the area. He claimed that Britain was "under an obligation to render all the necessary assistance to us, their former colony and subjects", but added: "Knowing the strength of the Republic of South Africa militarily, Transkei will bide its time before taking up arms to recover the land that has been cynically raped from it."

On Feb. 13, 1979, the Transkei Government made further representations to the South African Government regarding East Griqualand, and it was stated in the South African House of Assembly on Feb. 23 that the documents concerned would be studied without prejudice. On Oct. 27, 1979, Chief George Matanzima, who had earlier become Prime Minister of Transkei, was quoted as having emphasized that Kokstad and other areas in East Griqualand should be "returned" to Transkei, and that the land question was crucial to a resumption of diplomatic relations between South Africa and Transkei.

Under a Borders of Particular States Extension Bill, which passed its second reading in the South African House of Assembly on Feb. 11, 1980, with the support of the Opposition, provision was made for the transfer of land, most of which had already been set aside under the 1936 Act, to the "independent" Black states (then Transkei, Bophuthatswana and Venda). The bill in particular enabled the South African State President to transfer land or portions from the districts of Mount Currie, Maclear, Elliot, Indwe and Queenstown to Transkei. In reference to this bill, Chief George Matanzima was on Feb. 7 reported to have said: "We claim all the land that historically belonged to us." He also disclosed that negotiations were being carried out between land commissions of both the Transkei and the South African Governments. In these circumstances diplomatic relations between the two sides were resumed on March 30, 1980.

After P. W. Botha had announced on Feb. 20, 1981, that Ciskei would become fully "independent" on Dec. 4, 1981, the National Assembly of Transkei passed, on April 8, a motion resolving that political delegates from South Africa, Transkei and Ciskei should have discussions on the proposed splitting of the Xhosa nation through the granting of independence to Ciskei. In July 1981 it was reported that the Transkei Government was financing a legal action to prevent Ciskei from becoming South Africa's fourth independent homeland—but the action was not successful.

## Claims made by Other Homelands Leaders

General or specific claims for more land were also made by leaders of other homelands from time to time.

**Bophuthatswana.** Chief Lucas Mangope, the Chief Councillor of Bophuthatswana (which was then not yet "independent"), proposed on Jan. 23, 1973, that all areas predominantly occupied by Tswanas should be handed over to his Government, with Whites owning property in these areas being free to remain there. Consolidation proposals made by the South African Government on April 9, 1973, were unanimously rejected by the Territory's Legislative Assembly, which produced its own plan designed to double the size of the homeland and to take in the White towns of Kuruman, Taung, Warrenton, Vryburg, Delareyville, Lichtenburg, Mafeking, Koster, Zeerust, Rustenburg, Brits and Swartruggens.

The South African Government's plan was thereupon revised so as to give Bophuthatswana 605,000 hectares of previously White-owned land while excising from the Territory 352,000 hectares. None of the above-mentioned towns were to be handed over to Bophuthatswana except Taung and later Mafeking (which was ceded on Sept. 19. 1980, when it reverted to its original African name of Mafikeng).

When Bophuthatswana was granted "independence" on Dec. 6, 1977, it consisted of six separate areas. Under a Bophuthatswana Border Extension Bill, which passed all its stages in the South African Parliament on Feb. 22, 1978, parts of five districts of the Transvaal and northern Cape Province were transferred to the "independent" Bophuthatswana, and it was officially stated at the same time that further consolidation could follow if both parties agreed to it. On Sept. 6, 1978, it was announced that 25,000 hectares of Bophuthatswana's territory would be exchanged against 25,000 hectares of White territory adjoining Thaba Nchu.

**Venda.** Chief Patrick Mphephu, the President of the Republic of Venda (which had become "independent" on Sept. 13, 1979), announced on Sept. 13, 1980, that his Government had asked South Africa to incorporate into Venda the Northern Transvaal towns of Louis Trichardt, Messina, Soekmekaar, Tshipise and Levumbu, as they would be "growth points acting as springboards for the economic development of Venda". He added that Whites who wished to keep their land and property should be allowed to do so, as was the case in Swaziland and Botswana.

**Ciskei.** Chief Justice Mabandla, who was then Chief Minister of Ciskei, said on Aug. 2, 1972, that all White-owned land between the Kei and Fish Rivers and north from the coast to the Orange River—which would include the port of East London —should form part of Ciskei.

Chief Lennox Sebe, having become Chief Minister of Ciskei, stated on May 21, 1973, that his Government would work within the framework of South Africa's separate development policy provided that the entire Ciskei was consolidated into a single territory stretching from the Kei River in the east to the Fish River in the west and from the Indian Ocean to the Stormberg Mountains in the north, and incorporating all White-owned land in this region, probably even the towns of East London, Queenstown and King William's Town. This claim thus included what became known as the "White corridor" between Transkei and Ciskei.

After the Ciskei Government, Legislative Assembly and other leaders had on Sept. 30, 1980, accepted "independence" for Ciskei "in principle", Chief Sebe disclosed on Oct. 5 that details for the independence plan to be worked out included Ciskei's demands for more land, and on Feb. 20, 1981, he stated that negotiations over the land question would continue after "independence" (which was subsequently achieved on Dec. 4, 1981).

The South African Government, however, did not approve all of the recommendations made by its own consolidation commission for the transfer of certain towns to Ciskei. This applied in particular to King William's Town, where the White voters overwhelmingly rejected the proposed transfer in January 1981, whereupon the Government declared in April that the town would not become part of Ciskei.

**Gazankulu.** Prof. Hudson W. S. Ntsanwisi, the Chief Councillor of the Machangana Territorial Authority (which changed its name to Gazankulu as from April 1, 1972) declared on July 28, 1971, that more land would be needed if the 736,000 Shangaan people then in South Africa were to be resettled in the territory. On May 30, 1973, the Gazankulu Legislative Assembly rejected the South African Government's consolidation proposals and demanded the incorporation in its territory of the White Transvaal towns of Tzaneen, Phalaborwa, Mica, Hoedspruit, Komatipoort and White River, as well as large tracts of White-owned agricultural land and parts of the neighbouring homelands of Venda and Lebowa.

**KwaZulu.** Chief Gatsha Buthelezi, the Chief Executive Officer of the newly established Zululand Territorial Authority, said at the inauguration of the new Authority on June 11, 1970, that he expected the South African Government, if they meant what they were saying, "to provide us with more land and to consolidate it", as this was "the only way in which a meaningful state can be created".

After J. B. Vorster, then South Africa's Prime Minister, had in April 1972 stated that he was not prepared to make more land available to homelands than had been promised under the 1936 Act, Chief Buthelezi retorted that the Zulus were "not so naive as to participate in a scheme to defraud us by asking for so-called independence before land consolidation and without the purchase of foreign territories within our boundaries". He also urged that Richards Bay (then a new port being built on the Natal coast) should be developed as a seaport for KwaZulu (Zululand's new name as from April 1, 1972) instead of as an overflow port for Durban, but the South African Government made it clear, on April 27, 1972, that the new port of Richards Bay would be controlled by White South Africa. On the other hand KwaZulu gained control, as from April 1, 1977, of the Black township of KwaMashu (of some 150,000 inhabitants), previously controlled by the Durban City Council.

The (Zulu) *Inkatha* movement (officially described as a cultural movement), which had gained all 55 elective seats in the KwaZulu Legislative Assembly in elections completed on Feb. 24, 1978, had rejected early independence for KwaZulu on the grounds that the Zulus, as the largest ethnic group in South Africa, would not accept "independence of separate pieces of inadequate territory" without any share in the South African economy which they had helped to develop.

**Lebowa.** Chief M. Matlala, then Chief Councillor of the Lebowa Territorial Authority, called, in April and again in June 1971, for more land to be transferred to his territory to accommodate former squatters and tenants evicted from White-owned farms.

**KwaNdebele.** Mr Simon Skhosana, the Chief Minister of the KwaNdebele homeland, was in May 1981 reported to have stated that he had asked the South African Government for more land and to have added: "When they give it to you, you say 'thank you' and ask again."

## Conclusion

The South African Government does not appear to regard the process of consolidation of the Black homelands as having been completed and seems ready to transfer to them certain areas of agricultural land of limited extent. However, it is fair to conclude that, despite the exceptional case of the transfer of Mafeking to Bophuthatswana, the Government does not wish to alienate White voters by ceding further White towns to Black homelands.

H.W.D.

# Zambia's Border Disputes

Recent official statements in Zambia have referred to the existence of border disputes with Malawi to the east and with Zaïre to the north, although neither appears to have placed any serious strain on relations between the parties concerned.

In a statement to the Zambian Parliament on Aug. 11, 1981, Minister of State Fitzpatrick Chuula said that Zambia and Malawi had declared a dispute over an area on Zambia's Eastern province border with Malawi, to which the latter country had laid claim, but added that discussions were continuing between the two sides with a view to resolving the issue. Subsequently, a spokesman for the Zambian Foreign Ministry confirmed on Jan. 11, 1982, that 10 Zambian nationals were being held by the Malawian authorities for allegedly straying into Malawi and that a protest had been lodged with the Malawi high commissioner in an effort to secure their release. Nevertheless, in February 1982 President Kaunda of Zambia paid his first official visit to Malawi since the two former British colonies became independent in 1964 and received a warm welcome from his hosts.

In June 1981 the Zambian Prime Minister, Nalumino Mundia, announced that a dispute with Zaïre over a border area in the Kaputa district of Zambian's Northern province might be referred to the Organization of African Unity (OAU) by his Government. Official confidence was expressed that the OAU would find in Zambia's favour on the basis of the organization's 1964 declaration that the boundaries drawn up by the former colonial powers should be respected. Subsequently, a meeting of the Zambia-Zaïre permanent regional joint commission in April 1982 agreed on a reciprocal release of prisoners (involving 55 Zaïreans held by Zambia and 25 Zambians held by Zaïre) and announced that "no clouds or misunderstandings" existed between the two countries.

A.J.D.

# 3. THE MIDDLE EAST

## Introduction

Most of the present-day borders between states of the Middle East region have their origins in the territorial arrangements arising from the dismemberment of the Ottoman Turkish empire at the end of World War I. At that time the emergence of the Arab peoples from centuries of Ottoman over-lordship was accompanied by aspirations to Arab unity among their leaders, many of whom subscribed to the aim of creating a single Arab independent state, or at least a federation of states. Such aspirations were not fulfilled, however, partly because large areas of the Middle East came under the direct or indirect control of Britain and France, whose influence served to strengthen traditional rivalries between the different centres of Arab power. Although the concept of Arab unity remained a potent force, the result was that the eventual independence of the peoples of the region came about largely on the basis of the post-1918 territorial dispositions of the European powers. However, because borders across much of the vast desert tracts of the Arabian peninsula and western Asia had never been clearly demarcated, the inevitable consequence has been a substantial degree of border and terri-torial dispute between the successor states.

Since its creation in 1945 the Arab League has, as the major organ of inter-Arab co-operation, sought to act as a channel for the peaceful resolu-tion of border and territorial disputes between its member states. It has achieved some successes in this respect, notably in that few such inter-Arab disputes have been allowed to escalate into open hostilities and others have in fact been brought to a negotiated settlement under Arab League auspices. However, as detailed in the following section, there exist a number of instances where territorial uncertainties involving conflicting claims between Arab states have not been finally resolved. Even though in some cases the governments concerned have preferred to allow their claims to remain dormant in recent years, such situations may possibly become active disputes given the relative political instability of the Middle East region.

It should also be noted that the territorial relationships between the longer-established major Arab states and several of the newer and smaller states on the littoral of the Arabian sub-continent constitute a particular category of existing or potential disputes. Given that most of the littoral states came to independence relatively recently after being actual or effective British protectorates, claims have been made that they are artificial creations of the former colonial power in territories which historically owed allegiance to other centres of Arab power. Thus Iraq has in recent years laid claim to the whole of Kuwait, while Saudi Arabia's relations with its southern and eastern neighbours are coloured by the suspicions of the latter concerning Saudi territorial aspirations.

The Middle East region is also affected by territorial disputes between Arab and non-Arab states, in which the added ingredient of racial or religious difference has tended to make such antagonisms considerably more violent and protracted than those between Arab countries. Iran's longstanding dispute with Iraq over the Shatt al-Arab waterway and over Iraqi claims to Arab-populated areas of western Iran has recently escalated into a major war. And in the Arab-Israeli conflict the Middle East region has the dubious distinction of containing the world's most bitter and apparently irreconcilable territorial dispute, which the two sides have failed to resolve despite four major wars (six if the 1978 and 1982 Israeli incursions into Lebanon are counted) in the space of less than four decades.

# The Arab-Israeli Conflict

The longstanding and still unresolved conflict between Israel and the Arab world has two main territorial dimensions. At a fundamental level, many Arabs do not accept the existence of a Jewish state within any borders and assert that the Palestinian Arabs are the rightful heirs to predominant political authority in the former British mandated territory of Palestine. On another level, the Israeli conquest in 1967 of large tracts of Arab territory beyond the de facto borders resulting from the 1948-49 Arab-Israeli war brought Israel into direct territorial dispute with Egypt, Jordan and Syria, each of which demanded the return of their Israeli-occupied territories as well as a settlement of the basic Palestinian question. In March 1979 an historic breakthrough was achieved with the signature of an Egyptian-Israeli peace treaty under which the whole of Sinai (but not the formerly Egyptian-controlled Gaza Strip) was restored to Egyptian rule over the following three years. But Israel remains in total deadlock with Jordan over its continued occupation of the West Bank and with Syria over its retention of the Golan Heights, while post-1979 negotiations on the establishment of some form of Palestinian "autonomy" in the West Bank and Gaza Strip have made little progress. Moreover, the Government in power in Israel since 1977 has not only officially asserted what it regards as Israel's historic right of sovereignty over the "Land of Israel" (i.e. including the West Bank, Gaza and Jerusalem) but has also taken important steps, tantamount to formal annexation, to consolidate Israeli rule over the Golan Heights.

## Historical Background

The Zionist[1] case for the creation of a modern Jewish state in Palestine was based pre-eminently on the historical connexion between the Jewish people and the region in question; but the extent to which Palestine can be regarded as the historic homeland of the Jewish people is a subject of considerable dispute in which both sides have their distinguished supporters. Zionist historians contend that throughout most of the last 1,200 years of the pre-Christian era Jews constituted the main settled population of what in Roman times became known as Palestine and enjoyed long periods of independence and statehood. In contrast, Arab historians maintain that the Jews were only one of many Semitic tribes which penetrated the region in ancient times and that Jewish states were relatively short-lived and never at any time extended to the coastal plains (which were inhabited by Philistines, from whom the name "Palestine" is itself derived). What is not in dispute is that Palestine came under effective Roman control in the first century BC; that in 70 AD the (Roman puppet) Jewish state of Judaea was overthrown by the Roman Emperor Titus, who captured Jerusalem, destroyed the Jewish Temple and took many Jews as captives to Rome; and that after repeated rebellions by the Jews against their Roman overlords Jerusalem was finally razed to the ground in 135 AD and most of the surviving Jewish inhabitants of Palestine were expelled. This was the beginning of the diaspora (dispersion) of the Jewish people, who in the succeeding centuries became scattered throughout Europe and eventually the world in a complex sequence of large and small migrations from one country to another.

---

[1] Zionism, the movement promoting Jewish settlement of Palestine, takes its name from the hill in Jerusalem on which the ancient palace of King David, and later the Temple, were built.

In the Arab view, the dispersion of the Jews in the second century AD marked the final termination of the Jewish connexion with Palestine just as finally as the Italian connexion with Britain ended three centuries later with the Roman withdrawal. Moreover, according to this viewpoint, the conquest of Jerusalem by Moslem Arabs in 636 AD and the subsequent conversion and Arabization of the Semitic inhabitants of Palestine irreversibly established the identity of the region as part of the Arab world. Against this, Zionists point out that the dispersed Jewish people never abandoned the hope—however metaphysically expressed through the centuries—of returning to the land from which their forbears had been expelled. They also cite historical evidence indicating that Jews continued to live in Palestine after 135 AD—although the continuity and extent of this presence in the first millenium AD is again a matter of dispute. Certainly in the crusading era of the 11th, 12th and 13th centuries there were significant Jewish communities in several cities of the "Holy Land" and Jews are known to have fought alongside Arabs against the warriors of the cross in full awareness that in victory the Christian crusaders made no distinction in their treatment of Moslem and Jew.

Historians are also agreed that the Moslem reconquest of Palestine in 1291 and the relative tolerance shown thereafter to Jews stimulated a degree of Jewish migration to Palestine from European countries where anti-Jewish persecution was becoming endemic. The expulsion of the Jews from Spain in 1492 accentuated this migratory trend, which continued following the establishment of Ottoman Turkish rule over Palestine from 1517. In the early 16th century there were, for example, an estimated 10,000 Jews living in the region of Safed (north-west of the Sea of Galilee and one of the four "holy cities" of Judaism together with Jerusalem, Hebron and Tiberias) and the importance of Safed as a centre of Jewish learning is indicated by the fact that a Hebrew printing press set up there in 1563 was the first press of any language to be installed in the Asian continent. Nevertheless, as a proportion of the total population, the Jews of Palestine remained a tiny minority and formed only one non-Moslem community among the several which enjoyed a relatively tranquil existence under Turkish rule.

In 1880 there were still only 25,000 Jews in Palestine as against 470,000 Arabs; but over the next three decades there occurred a dramatic upsurge of Jewish immigration. Between 1880 and the outbreak of World War I in 1914 Jewish settlement of Palestine almost quadrupled to some 90,000, as over 60,000 Jews entered the country, mainly from Russia and Poland. And these new arrivals were of a different type and with a different motivation than previous Jewish migrants. Inspired by the Zionist ideals of Theodor Herzl (1860-1904), the new wave of Jews came as farmers and artisans, seeking to build a new Jewish society based on the land and thus to recreate a national identity for the dispersed Jewish people. As propounded by Herzl in his celebrated pamphlet *Der Judenstaat* published in 1896 and by the first Zionist congress in 1897, Zionism called for the preservation of the Jewish race by national reunion, which was to be achieved by "establishing for the Jewish people a publicly and legally assured home in Palestine". Such ideas became particularly influential in the ghettos and Jewish villages of Eastern Europe, where millions of Jews were living in poverty and facing a mounting threat from the growth of virulent anti-semitism in the host societies.

Although efforts by Zionist leaders to secure the agreement of the Turkish Sultan to the establishment of a Jewish homeland in Palestine proved inconclusive, the piecemeal purchase of land for Jewish settlers proceeded apace, the finance being provided by wealthy Jews of Western Europe (and later the United States). Such purchases were made mainly from Arab landlords (although land owned by Europeans and Turks was also sold to Jews) and often at inflated prices, considering that the tracts acquired were usually desert wasteland or malarial marsh, which were then drained, irrigated and farmed by Jewish settlers. In 1909 the first entirely Jewish town in modern Palestine was founded on the sandhills north of the Arab Mediterranean port of Jaffa and given the name Tel Aviv.

But the new wave of Jewish immigration into Palestine met with an immediate hostile response from the Arab population. As early as 1882 the Turkish authorities responded to Arab disquiet at Zionist plans by seeking to prevent the entry of Jews through the Mediterranean ports and the first Arab attacks on Jewish agricultural settlements took place in the mid-1880s. In 1891 leaders of the Arab community in Jerusalem sent a petition to Constantinople demanding the prohibition of Jewish immigration and land purchase, and in the early years of the 20th century anti-Zionist newspapers and societies were founded by Arabs in several cities of Palestine and also further afield. The scene was thus set for the fundamental confrontation of national aspirations which is still with us today. In the words of the Arab writer Neguib Azoury set down in 1905: "These two movements [i.e. Zionism and Arab nationalism] are destined to fight each other continually, until one of them triumphs over the other."[1]

## The Balfour Declaration, Arab-British Undertakings and the Sykes-Picot Agreement

Having failed to make any real progress with the Ottoman authorities, Zionist leaders concentrated their efforts on persuading European governments of the validity and desirability of establishing a Jewish homeland in Palestine. An important consideration in this respect was the realization that the days of the Ottoman empire were numbered. Ultimately, the decision of Turkey to ally itself with the central powers in World War I created a constellation of forces in which this aim became a practical proposition, given that Britain and France saw themselves as the joint post-Ottoman powers in the Middle East. In what was widely construed as a move to ensure international Jewish support for the allied war effort, the then British Foreign Secretary, Arthur Balfour, sent a letter to Lord Rothschild (a prominent British Jewish Zionist) dated Nov. 2, 1917, and worded as follows:

"I have much pleasure in conveying to you, on behalf of His Majesty's Government, the following declaration of sympathy with Jewish Zionist aspirations which has been submitted to, and approved by, the Cabinet. His Majesty's Government view with favour the establishment in Palestine of a national home for the Jewish people, and will use their best endeavours to facilitate the achievement of this object, it being clearly understood that nothing shall be done which may prejudice the civil and religious rights of existing non-Jewish communities in Palestine, or the rights and political status enjoyed by Jews in any other country. I should be grateful if you would bring this declaration to the knowledge of the Zionist Federation."

The Balfour declaration, which was approved by the French Government and published immediately, is seen by Jews as a cornerstone of the legitimacy of the eventual establishment of a Jewish state in Palestine. But it was rejected then and subsequently by the Palestinian Arabs as a colonialist instrument which contravened the fundamental principle on which the allied powers claimed to be fighting the 1914-18 war, namely the right of self-determination of peoples. It is also claimed by the Arab side that the Balfour declaration ran counter to undertakings given by Britain to its wartime Arab allies that Britain would support the independence of the Arabs once the Turks had been defeated. In the latter respect the crucial documents are the correspondence in 1915-16 between Sir Henry McMahon (the British

---

[1] Quoted by Martin Gilbert in *The Arab-Israeli Conflict—Its History in Maps* (London, 1974), p. 6, from *Le Reveil de la Nation Arabe* (Paris, 1905).

high commissioner in Cairo) and Sharif Hussain of Mecca (head of the Hashemite dynasty of Hejaz and the father of the subsequent King of Iraq, Faisal) and also the agreement between Sir Mark Sykes of Britain and Georges Picot of France concluded in May 1916. Over both these sets of undertakings considerable controversy still flourishes.

In his first note to Sir Henry McMahon (dated July 14, 1915), Sharif Hussain requested that Britain should recognize "the independence of the Arab countries" bounded (i) in the north by a line drawn from Mersin (on the northern Mediterranean coast of Turkey) running north-east through Adana to the 37°N parallel and thence eastward to the Persian frontier, (ii) on the east by the Persian frontier down to the Persian Gulf, (iii) on the south by the Indian Ocean (with the exception of Aden) and (iv) on the west "by the Red Sea and the Mediterranean Sea back to Mersin". In his reply (dated Oct. 24, 1915), Sir Henry declared on behalf of the British Government that "the districts of Mersin and Alexandretta [the present Turkish port of Iskenderun], and portions of Syria lying to the west of the districts of Damascus, Homs, Hama and Aleppo, cannot be said to be purely Arab, and must on that account be excepted from the proposed delimitation"; subject to that modification and to the proviso that nothing should be done to the detriment of the interests of France, Great Britain was "prepared to recognize and uphold the independence of the Arabs in all the regions lying within the frontiers proposed by the Sharif of Mecca". Subsequent exchanges between the two correspondents achieved no clear reconciliation of these contrasting delimitations of the future independent Arab state or states, although Britain achieved its object of securing active Arab assistance in the war against Turkey.

At no point in the Hussain-McMahon correspondence was mention made of Palestine or of the Ottoman administrative unit centred on Jerusalem. Since this area was not one of potential French interest the Arabs took the view that it had been promised as part of the territory of Arab independence, whereas the British Government consistently maintained that McMahon's reservations were intended to exclude the whole of the eastern Mediterranean littoral from Turkey down to Sinai. At the centre of this particular controversy is the meaning in the correspondence of the term "district", for which both men used the Arabic word *wilaya*, and whether the term was intended to refer precisely or at all to the *vilayet*, the largest unit of Ottoman local administration. In support of the British interpretation, it is pointed out that the Ottoman *vilayet* containing the city of Damascus stretched right down to the Gulf of Aqaba in the south, on the strength of which it is argued that all the territory to the west of this *vilayet* was excluded in the undertakings given to the Arabs. On the other hand, Arab analysts have pointed out that the "districts" referred to in the correspondence did not correspond with Ottoman *vilayets* (either in intention or in fact) and signified only geographical areas relating to the cities mentioned. On this basis, they contend that the littoral excluded from future Arab rule was that to the north of the approximate level of the city of Damascus, and also note that even this exclusion was contested by Sharif Hussain in the course of the correspondence.

The uncertainties arising from the Hussain-McMahon correspondence will probably never be resolved to universal satisfaction. There is, however, general agreement that Britain's promises to the Arabs in 1915-16 were in conflict in certain important respects with the terms of the almost concurrent Sykes-Picot agreement under which Britain and France (with Russian concurrence) drew up a plan for the post-war dismemberment of the Ottoman empire in the Middle East. This secret agreement (which was eventually disclosed to the Arabs by the Russian Bolsheviks) divided the region into French and British spheres of influence to the north and south respectively of a line roughly corresponding with the present-day

Syrian border with Jordan and Iraq (except in the east, where the Mosul region was included in the French sphere). It further specified that in these spheres the two powers would recognize and uphold "an independent Arab state or a confederation of Arab states . . . under the suzerainty of an Arab chief". But it also stipulated (i) that France and Britain would be allowed to establish "direct or indirect administration or control" in certain designated areas, France being allocated the eastern Mediterranean littoral north of a line just south of Safed, and Britain the Tigris-Euphrates basin (Mesopotamia); (ii) that Palestine from just south of Safed down to a line just south of Gaza (and bounded in the east by the Dead Sea and the Jordan river) would be under "an international administration, the form of which is to be decided upon after consultation with Russia, and subsequently in consultation with the other allies and the representatives of the Sharif of Mecca"; and (iii) that within this international zone Britain would be "accorded" the ports of Haifa and Acre and a surrounding enclave of territory.

### Establishment of British Palestine Mandate

In the event, the post-1918 disposition of former Ottoman territories showed significant variations from both the Hussain-McMahon undertakings (such as they were) and the Sykes-Picot agreement, although it was closer to the latter than to the former. After protracted and complex negotiations accompanied by confrontations and some actual military conflict between various of the interested parties, the shape of the post-war map of the Near East was not finally determined until the signature of the Treaty of Lausanne on July 24, 1923. But already, at the San Remo conference of April 1920, Britain and France had reached agreement on the establishment of British and French mandates (as opposed to spheres of influence) over territories which extended well into the area previously designated as part of an independent Arab entity.

As eventually agreed by the new League of Nations (established in January 1920), France obtained a mandate over an area almost corresponding with the present territory of Lebanon and Syria—i.e. extending substantially to the east of the littoral designated for "direct or indirect" French rule by Sykes-Picot. Moreover, the two British mandates encompassed not only Palestine (defined as including Transjordan and the Negev desert down to the port of Eilat on the Gulf of Aqaba) but also the whole of present-day Iraq. As for the rest of the Arabian peninsula to the south, this area was recognized as independent Arab territory, but through a system of protectorates, treaties and financial subsidies it became effectively a British sphere of influence.

The mandatory instrument for Palestine differed significantly from the others in that it committed Britain to securing the establishment of a Jewish national home in the mandated territory (and also in that it contained no specific provision for the constitutional development of the inhabitants towards eventual independence). As approved by the Council of the League of Nations in 1922, the instrument said in its preamble that the principal allied powers had agreed "that the mandatory should be responsible for putting into effect the declaration originally made on Nov. 2, 1917, by the Government of His Britannic Majesty, and adopted by the said powers, in favour of the establishment in Palestine of a national home for the Jewish people, it being clearly understood that nothing should be done which might prejudice the civil and religious rights of existing non-Jewish communities in Palestine, or the rights and political status enjoyed by Jews in any other country". The preamble then recorded that "recognition has thereby been given to the historical connexion of the Jewish people with Palestine and to the grounds for reconstituting their national home in that country".

In its detailed provisions the instrument specified inter alia that the mandatory "shall be responsible for placing the country under such political, administrative and economic conditions as will secure the establishment of the Jewish national home . . . and the development of self-governing institutions, and also for safe-guarding the civil and religious rights of all the inhabitants of Palestine, irrespective of race and religion" (Art. 2); that "an appropriate Jewish Agency shall be recognized as a public body for the purpose of advising and co-operating with the Administration of Palestine in such economic, social and other matters as may affect the establishment of the Jewish national home and the interests of the Jewish population in Palestine, and, subject always to the control of the Administration, to assist and take part in the development of the country" (Art. 4); that "the Administration of Palestine, while ensuring that the rights and position of other sections of the population are not prejudiced, shall facilitate Jewish immigration under suitable conditions and shall encourage, in co-operation with the Jewish Agency referred to in Article 4, close settlement by Jews on the land, including state lands and waste lands not required for public purposes" (Art. 6); and that a nationality law would be framed for Palestine "so as to facilitate the acquisition of Palestinian citizenship by Jews who take up their permanent residence in Palestine" (Art. 7). (The Jewish Agency referred to in Article 4 was eventually set up in 1929 and recognized by Britain for the purposes of the mandatory instrument.)

The importance of the mandate's terms from a Zionist point of view was that for the first time the commitment to a Jewish national home in Palestine was enshrined within an internationally recognized instrument which superseded the ambiguous and conflicting undertakings entered into previously. For the Arabs, however, the system of British and French mandates represented a betrayal of war-time promises of independence, the Palestine mandate in particular being regarded as a device to facilitate the settlement of Arab territory by an alien people, i.e. the Jews. The regime imposed was therefore seen not only as a denial of the right of self-determination proclaimed by the allies during the war but also as a direct contravention of Article 22 of the Covenant of the League of Nations, which in its rationale of the mandatory system specifically excluded "certain communities formerly belonging to the Turkish empire" from those former colonies and territories defined as "inhabited by peoples not yet able to stand by themselves under the strenuous conditions of the modern world" and therefore as appropriate for the mandatory system.

Then and subsequently Zionists pointed out that the area allotted for the establishment of a Jewish national home amounted to only a tiny fraction of the Middle East territories taken from the Turks; mandated Palestine, it was noted, covered less than 11,000 square miles (28,500 sq km), whereas the total area of Arab lands (including mandated territories) stretched to nearly 1,200,000 square miles (3,000,000 sq km). But this argument was not appreciated by Palestinian Arabs in the actual circumstances of the Palestine mandate, where a post-war new wave of Jewish immigration, mainly from Russia, was seen as a direct threat to their way of life and political future. In the latter context, the Arabs laid particular stress on the "European" character of the Jewish immigrants who were arriving under the impulse of Zionism, maintaining that the Ashkenazic Jews of Europe were not Semitic like the Sephardic Jews of the Arab world and had no historical connexion with Palestine because they were descended from the Khazar tribes of south-east Russia who embraced Judaism in the eighth century and later spread through eastern and central Europe.

Attacks by Arabs on Jewish settlements in Palestine began again in early 1920, and after one such incident at Kinneret on the Sea of Galilee the Jews decided (in June 1920) to set up their own defence force, the *Haganah*. Later in the year the first Arab riots under British rule led to a decision by the British authorities in

September (but later rescinded) that Jewish immigration to Palestine should not exceed 16,500 people a year; moreover, from 1921 the area east of the River Jordan was entirely closed to Jewish settlement (whereas Zionist plans of the period envisaged a Jewish national home stretching well across the Jordan, and also into southern Lebanon and south-west Syria). The latter measure was taken in the context of the separation of Transjordan from the rest of the mandate and its establishment as an autonomous state under Emir Abdullah, this process leading to semi-independence in 1928. The other British mandated territory became the fully independent state of Iraq in 1932 under King Faisal, whereas Lebanon and Syria remained under French mandate until being declared independent by the Free French during World War II, at the end of which they both became founder members of the United Nations. From 1923 mandated Syria included the Golan Heights, which were ceded by Britain in that year after originally forming part of the Palestine mandate.

### Development of Arab-Jewish Conflict under British Mandate

The disturbances of 1920 set the pattern of the history of the British mandate west of the Jordan, where opposing Arab and Jewish national aims not only precluded any agreement on the constitutional future of Palestine but also generated increasingly violent inter-communal conflict. As early as May 1921 the British authorities reacted to Arab rioting by placing a temporary ban on all Jewish immigration, and although this was quickly lifted the official British position became that immigration should not exceed "the economic capacity of Palestine to absorb new immigrants". In September 1921 Britain promulgated a constitution for Palestine, but it was never implemented because the Arabs were unwilling to accept its provisions relating to the Jewish national home. Thereafter, all attempts to secure Arab-Jewish political co-operation foundered against the rocks of diametrically opposed and increasingly entrenched Jewish and Arab positions.

By 1928 the Jewish population of Palestine had reached 150,000 (and the Arab population 600,000), and increasing Arab disquiet resulted in the first large-scale Arab-Jewish clashes in 1928-29. Further serious violence occurred in 1933, when Hitler's advent to power in Germany heralded a sharp increase in Jewish immigration from Europe, taking the Jewish population of Palestine to 400,000 by 1936 and close to 30 per cent of the total. In that year the Palestinian Arabs set up an Arab High Committee to organize opposition to Jewish settlement and the situation quickly deteriorated into one of widespread inter-communal violence accompanied by an Arab general strike. With increasing numbers of British soldiers being killed (almost all at this stage in clashes with armed Arab bands), the British Government responded (in April 1936) by setting up a Royal Commission under Lord Peel charged with recommending means of implementing the Palestine mandate in such a manner as to lessen Jewish-Arab friction. In its report, published on July 7, 1937, and accepted by the British Government, the Peel Commission found that "the hope of harmony between the races has proved untenable" and recommended the partition of Palestine into separate Arab and Jewish states, with Britain retaining a permanent mandate over two enclaves containing Jerusalem, Bethlehem and Nazareth. Particular features of the Peel proposals were that the Arab state would consist of Transjordan (still legally part of the mandate) united with that part of Palestine allotted to the Arabs and that there should be treaty provision for the exchange of land holdings and population between the two new states.

The Peel Commission report summarized the advantages of partition to the Arabs as follows: "(i) They obtain their national independence and can co-operate on an equal footing with the Arabs of the neighbouring countries in the cause of

Arab unity and progress. (ii) They are finally delivered from the fear of being 'swamped' by the Jews and from the possibility of ultimate subjection to Jewish rule. (iii) In particular, the final limitation of the Jewish national home within a fixed frontier and the enactment of a new mandate for the protection of the Holy Places, solemnly guaranteed by the League of Nations, removes all anxiety lest the Holy Places should ever come under Jewish control. (iv) As a set-off to the loss of territory the Arabs regard as theirs the Arab state will receive a subvention from the Jewish state [and] also, in view of the backwardness of Transjordan, obtain a grant of £2,000,000 from the British Treasury [as well as a further grant for the conversion of uncultivable land in the Arab state into productive use]."

As regards the Jews the advantages of the Peel proposals were also summarized: "(i) Partition secures the establishment of the Jewish national home and relieves it from the possibility of its being subjected in the future to Arab rule. (ii) Partition enables the Jews in the fullest sense to call their national home their own: for it converts it into a Jewish state. Its citizens will be able to admit as many Jews into it as they themselves believe can be absorbed. They will attain the primary objective of Zionism—a Jewish nation, planted in Palestine, giving its nationals the same status in the world as other nations give theirs. They will cease at last to live a 'minority life'."

The concept of partition was reluctantly accepted by the Jews as the best solution that could be hoped for in the circumstances; but it was totally rejected by the Arabs, who in 1937 launched a general revolt not only against the Zionists but also against the British authorities endeavouring to keep the peace between the two sides. A feature of the escalating violence from 1937 was the increasing incidence of Jewish retaliation against Arab attacks, despite reiterations by the Jewish National Council (the representative body of Jews in mandated Palestine) of the need for continued restraint in the face of Arab provocation. Various alternative partition plans were put forward over the next two years—notably those of the Woodhead Commission of 1938—but none overcame the fundamental opposition of the Arabs to any legitimization of a Jewish entity in the territory of Palestine.

As organized guerrilla warfare by both communities developed during 1938, the British Government abandoned partition as a possible solution and in May 1939 published a White Paper asserting that it was not British policy that Palestine should become either a Jewish state or an Arab state; that an independent Palestinian state should be set up within 10 years; that meanwhile Jews and Arabs should be asked to take an increasing share in the country's administration; and that Jewish immigration into Palestine should be limited to 75,000 people over the next five years (after which such entry would require Arab consent). In pursuance of this new policy, the British Government on Feb. 28, 1940, published regulations banning further land purchases by Jews in about two-thirds of the territory of Palestine, restricting such purchases in most of the remaining third and leaving only the narrow coastal plain from Haifa southward to beyond Tel Aviv as a free zone for further acquisitions.

Like earlier blueprints for the future, the 1939 White Paper failed to obtain any positive response from either community. The Arabs rejected it as failing to meet their longstanding demand for the termination of the mandate and the creation of an independent Palestinian state based on majority rule. For the Jews it represented a betrayal by Britain of its commitment under the mandate to promote the establishment of a Jewish national home in Palestine. And throughout the late 1930s the increasingly perilous position of Jewish communities in Europe gave particular urgency to the Zionist demand that Palestine should be open to unrestricted Jewish immigration (especially since most countries of the world were either wholly or partially closed to Jewish refugees). By 1939 the Jewish population

**Map 21   The UN partition plan, 1947.**

Legend:
- Proposed Jewish state
- Proposed Arab state
- International zone

0   km   50

**Map 22   Armistice boundaries, 1949.**

Legend:
- - - - The frontiers of Israel under 1949 armistice agreements
- Territory beyond UN line conquered by Israel, 1948-49

0   km   50

**Map 23   1967 Arab-Israeli War.**

Legend:
- Israeli territory 1949-June 1967
- Israeli conquests, June 1967

0   km   100

**Map 24   Arab-Israeli boundaries, 1975-82.**

Legend:
- - - - Israeli line under 1975 disengagement agreement with Egypt
- Returned to Egypt 1979-82
- Israeli-occupied territory designated for Palestinian autonomy
- Israeli-occupied (Syrian) territory

0   km   100

**Maps 21-24   Israel, Palestine and the Arabs, 1947-82**

188

of Palestine had risen to 445,000 (about 30 per cent of the total), but whereas over 30,000 Jews entered the country in 1939 the British authorities allowed in only 10,000 in 1940, 4,500 in 1941 and 4,200 in 1942. In this situation the Zionists sought to step up illegal immigration, but the war conditions prevailing from 1939 combined with British counter-measures seriously hampered such activities, at the very time when millions of Jews in Europe were being liquidated by the Nazis.

### Termination of the British Mandate, Establishment of the State of Israel and the 1948-49 Arab-Israeli War

The constitutional position of Palestine was frozen by the British Government for the duration of World War II, during which civil strife between Arab and Jew remained largely in abeyance. But the end of the war in 1945 signalled a resurgence of the political and inter-communal struggle in Palestine in even greater intensity than before, particularly since the cause of the Palestinian Arabs now took on concrete pan-Arab dimensions. In March 1945 the independent Arab states formed the Arab League, proclaiming their intention to give active support to Palestinian Arab aspirations and asserting that, while the League "sympathizes as deeply as anyone with the Jews for the horrors and sufferings they have endured in Europe", it nevertheless believed that "nothing would be more arbitrary or unjust than to wish to resolve the question of the Jews of Europe by another injustice of which the Arabs of Palestine . . . would be the victims". On the Jewish side, the traumatic experience of Nazi persecution massively reinforced the Zionists' determination to secure a Jewish political entity in Palestine, to which end they obtained the active support of the United States.

Despite pressure from the US Government for a relaxation of immigration restrictions, the British authorities maintained the 1939 White Paper policy, at a time when settlement in Palestine was the goal of tens of thousands of survivors of the European holocaust. The Jews responded by organizing large-scale illegal immigration and also by bringing in arms supplies (notably from the Soviet-bloc countries) for use in the increasingly ferocious struggle with the Arabs, whose armed groups were now often supplemented by units from the surrounding Arab countries. British soldiers and policemen attempting to control the rapidly deteriorating situation were frequently the target of extremists of both sides. Eventually, after various new partition-type proposals had again failed to move the Arabs from their demand for a unitary Palestinian state based on majority rule, the British Government decided in February 1947 to refer the Palestine question to the United Nations (as the successor to the League of Nations for the purposes of the mandate).

Following the British referral, a Special Committee on Palestine (UNSCOP) was established by the UN General Assembly in May 1947 and this committee quickly submitted a majority recommendation that Palestine should be partitioned into Arab and Jewish states (three of the 11 members favouring a federal state and one abstaining). With some frontier adjustments, the UNSCOP recommendation was eventually adopted by the UN General Assembly in an historic vote on Nov. 29, 1947, in which the required two-thirds majority was surpassed with 33 states voting in favour, 13 against, 10 abstaining and one absent. Those in favour of partition (and thus in favour of the creation of a Jewish state) included the Soviet Union and its satellites as well as most Western and Latin American nations; those against were Afghanistan, Cuba, Egypt, Greece, India, Iraq, Lebanon, Pakistan, Persia (Iran), Saudi Arabia, Syria, Turkey and Yemen; those abstaining were Argentina, Chile, China, Colombia, El Salvador, Ethiopia, Great Britain, Honduras, Mexico and Yugoslavia; and the absent country was Siam (Thailand).

The UN partition plan (the territorial aspects of which are shown in map 21 on page 188) provided for (i) the creation of a Jewish state in three linking segments, made up of eastern Galilee in the north, the coastal plain from Haifa south to the Rehovoth area (except Jaffa) and most of the Negev desert in the south; (ii) the creation of an Arab state in three linking areas of western Galilee, central Palestine and the southern littoral extending inland along the Egyptian border into the western Negev, with Jaffa as a coastal Arab enclave; (iii) the establishment of Jerusalem and Bethlehem as an international zone to be administered by the United Nations; and (iv) the creation of an economic union between all three parts. The General Assembly resolution specified inter alia that the British mandate should be terminated (and the withdrawal of British forces completed) as soon as possible and not later than Aug. 1, 1948; that the independent Arab and Jewish states and the special international regime for Jerusalem should come into existence two months after the British evacuation and not later than Oct. 1, 1948; and that "the period between the adoption by the General Assembly of its recommendation on the question of Palestine and the establishment of the independence of the Arab and Jewish states shall be a transitional period". The General Assembly also appointed a five-nation UN commission (Bolivia, Czechoslovakia, Denmark, Panama and the Philippines) which was to proceed to Palestine under the aegis of the UN Security Council to take over the country's administration when the British withdrew and then to transfer power to Arab and Jewish provisional governments.

The General Assembly's decision was rejected by the Arab states and the Palestinian Arabs as contrary to the principles of the UN Charter and to the terms of the original League of Nations mandate, on which grounds the six Arab governments voting against partition declared that they did not consider themselves bound by the decision and reserved full liberty of action. In contrast, although it gave them less than half of the Palestinian territory, the partition plan was immediately accepted by the Jews as the means of achieving internationally-recognized statehood. After the British Government had announced in December 1947 that it would relinquish the Palestine mandate on May 15, 1948, it was announced from Jerusalem on Jan. 12, 1948, that the Jewish Agency and the Jewish National Council had completed plans for a provisional government of the proposed Jewish state after the termination of the mandate. As Jewish units moved to secure control of the area designated for the Jews and organized warfare with Arab forces developed, President Truman of the United States proposed on March 25, 1948, that since it had "become clear that partition cannot be carried out at this time by peaceful means" the partition plan should be shelved in favour of a temporary UN trusteeship of the whole territory. This suggestion was categorically rejected by the Jews, however, and on May 14, a few hours before the termination of the British mandate at midnight, the establishment of the state of Israel was officially proclaimed in Tel Aviv by the Jewish National Council.

After recalling the origins and aims of Zionism in its preamble, the proclamation declared that the state of Israel "will be open to the immigration of Jews from all countries of their dispersion; . . . will uphold the full social and political equality of all its citizens, without distinction of religion, conscience, education and culture; will safeguard the Holy Places of all religions; and will loyally uphold the principles of the United Nations Charter". It would also be "ready to co-operate with the organs and representatives of the United Nations in the implementation of the resolution of the Assembly on Nov. 29, 1947, and will take steps to bring about the economic union over the whole of Palestine". It concluded: "In the midst of wanton aggression, we yet call upon the Arab inhabitants of the state of Israel to preserve the ways of peace and play their part in the development of the state, on the basis of full and equal citizenship and due representation in all its bodies and institutions—provisional and permanent. We extend our hand in peace and neighbourliness to all the neighbouring states and their people, and invite them to co-operate with the independent Jewish nation for the common good of all. The state of Israel is prepared to make its contribution to the progress of the Middle East as a whole. Our call goes out to the Jewish people all over the world to rally to our side in the task of immigration and development and to stand by us in the great struggle for the fulfilment of the dream of generations for the redemption of Israel.''

Simultaneously with the birth of the state of Israel at midnight on May 14-15, 1948, Palestine was invaded by the unco-ordinated forces of Egypt from the south, Transjordan and Iraq (backed by Saudi Arabian units) from the east and Syria and Lebanon from the north. The aims of these Arab armies, as proclaimed in a statement issued by the Arab League countries on May 15, was to establish the independence of Palestine for its lawful inhabitants on the basis of majority rule, which clearly implied the destruction of the new Jewish state. The same statement, after a forceful recapitulation of the alleged infringement of Arabs' rights and interests during the mandate and a reiteration of the Arabs' rejection of the UN partition plan, concluded as follows: ''The Governments of the Arab states recognize that the independence of Palestine, which has so far been suppressed by the British mandate, has become an accomplished fact for the lawful inhabitants of Palestine. They alone, by virtue of their absolute sovereignty, have the right to provide their country with laws and governmental institutions. They alone should exercise the attributes of their independence, through their own means and without any kind of foreign interference, immediately after peace, security and the rule of law have been restored to the country. At that time the intervention of the Arab states will cease, and the independent state of Palestine will co-operate with the states of the Arab League in order to bring peace, security and prosperity to this part of the world. The Governments of the Arab states emphasize . . . that the only just solution of the Palestine problem is the establishment of a unitary Palestine state, in accordance with democratic principles, whereby its inhabitants will enjoy complete equality before the law, [and whereby] minorities will be assured of all the guarantees recognized in democratic constitutional countries, and [whereby] the Holy Places will be preserved and the right of access thereto guaranteed. The Arab states most emphatically declare that [their] intervention in Palestine is due only to these considerations and objectives and that they aim at nothing more than to put an end to the prevailing conditions in [Palestine]. For this reason they have great confidence that their action will have the support of the United Nations [and that it will be] considered as an action aiming at the realization of its aims and at promoting its principles, as provided for in its Charter.''

In the first Arab-Israeli war initial Arab advances were quickly stemmed by Israeli forces, who subsequently mounted a successful counter-attack and not only secured virtually all of the territory allotted to the Jews under the UN partition plan but also took control of substantial additional areas (see map 22 on page 188). When the fighting finally ended in early 1949 on the basis of a UN-sponsored ceasefire declared on Dec. 29, 1948, the territory controlled by Israel extended to the whole of Galilee in the north and to the whole of the Negev in the south, where only a narrow coastal strip around Gaza remained in Arab hands; the proposed Arab enclave of Jaffa was also taken by the Jews. Moreover, although the Jordanian Arab Legion held much of the area of central Palestine designated for the Arabs (and also expelled the Jews from the Old City of Jerusalem), Israeli forces succeeded in establishing control over a wedge of territory connecting the coastal plain with Jerusalem. Armistices were signed by Israel with Egypt on Feb. 24, 1949, with Lebanon on March 23, with Transjordan on April 3 and with Syria on July 20 (but not with Iraq), under which Israel surrendered areas of captured territory in southern Lebanon, northern Sinai and the Gaza Strip but was left in control of over two-thirds of the territory of Palestine. Over the next decade these boundaries were to gain widespread international acceptance (outside the Arab world) as the frontiers of the state of Israel. Official Israeli figures showed that during the fighting from November 1947 to January 1949 over 4,000 Jewish soldiers and some 2,000 Jewish civilians were killed; no official Arab casualty figures were released.

An important aspect of the 1948-49 war was the massive displacement of Arab Palestinians from their homes and land, although the circumstances of this displacement and the numbers involved are both matters of considerable dispute. Arab accounts insist that the Arab Palestinians were driven out by Israelis seeking to acquire their land and to ensure that the new state had a Jewish majority; but the Israelis have always maintained that most Arab refugees simply fled to escape the fighting and were in some cases ordered to leave by Arab leaders confident of a speedy return following the destruction of the Jewish state. As regards numbers, by June 1950 the total number of refugees registered with the newly-established UN Relief and Works Agency for Palestine Refugees (UNRWA) was 960,021, the two biggest concentrations being located in the West Bank and the Gaza Strip. Only some 150,000 Arabs remained within the new borders of the Jewish state (concentrated in Galilee in the north), the Jewish population of which at the end of the war was about 660,000.

### Unsuccessful Efforts to achieve Peace leading to the 1956 Arab-Israeli War

In the immediate aftermath of the 1948-49 Arab-Israeli war UN-sponsored attempts to bring about a peace settlement between the two sides made some initial progress, the two central issues being the refugee question and the position of the borders between Israel and the neighbouring Arab states. As early as Dec. 11, 1948, the UN General Assembly established a Palestine Conciliation Commission charged with assisting the governments and authorities concerned to achieve a final settlement of all outstanding questions; the relevant resolution asserted inter alia that "refugees wishing to return to their homes and live in peace with their neighbours should be permitted to do so at the earliest practicable moment and that compensation should be paid for the property of those choosing not to return and for loss of or damage to property".

Under the auspices of the commission, representatives of Israel, Egypt, Transjordan, Lebanon and Syria began indirect negotiations in Lausanne in April 1949 and the following month signed a protocol under which they agreed that "a basis for discussions" on the refugee and border issues should be the November 1947 UN partition plan. It has since been claimed by the Arab side that Israel's signature of this protocol amounted to acceptance of the UN partition borders, whereas Israel has pointed out that the latter were to be "a" basis for discussions rather than "the" basis. In any event, the initial progress represented by the protocol quickly encountered the fundamental difficulty that Israel insisted that the Arab refugee problem should be dealt with in the context of a general peace settlement, whereas the Arab states demanded that the refugee problem should be dealt with prior to any general settlement. Under pressure from the US Government the Israeli side eventually made certain proposals on the refugee question—firstly the "Gaza plan" under which 500,000 Arab refugees would be resettled in the Gaza Strip provided that Egypt transferred this area to Israel, and then a proposal that 100,000 refugees should be repatriated to Israeli territory. However, these were rejected by the Arab side, which demanded in the first instance the immediate return of all refugees originating from areas designated for the Arabs under the UN partition plan and the establishment of an Arab state. It has subsequently been surmised by some historians that if Israel had been prepared to agree that the proposed return of 100,000 refugees applied exclusively to refugees originating in areas allocated to the Jews under the UN partition plan (and had thus moved towards acceptance of the UN plan) the Arabs would have been able to accept the Israeli proposal, thereby opening the way to substantive talks on a definitive settlement. At the time, however, neither side was prepared to make the requisite concessions and the Lausanne talks ended in deadlock.

Notwithstanding continuous efforts by the United Nations to salvage its partition plan, the attitudes of the two sides on both the refugee question and the border issue quickly hardened into diametrically opposed positions. All of the Arab states which had signed armistice agreements with Israel maintained that they nevertheless remained in a state of war with the Jewish state and refused to integrate refugees under their jurisdiction on the grounds that their rightful homes were in Palestinian territory now held by the Jews. When on April 24, 1950, the Jordanian Parliament adopted a resolution formally incorporating into the Hashemite Kingdom of Jordan (as Transjordan had been renamed in June 1949) those areas of Arab Palestine held by the Arab Legion at the armistice (i.e. the West Bank and the Old City of Jerusalem), this step was strongly opposed by the other Arab League states as undermining the objective of creating an independent Palestinian state. Earlier in the year the Israeli *Knesset* (Parliament) had, despite UN protests, adopted (on Jan. 23, 1950) a government resolution declaring that Jerusalem had resumed the status of the capital of the Jewish state (but had rejected an opposition amendment designed to make the resolution applicable to the Jordanian-held sector as well as to the Jewish-held New City of Jerusalem). In a parliamentary debate on the question the previous month, Israel's first Prime Minister, David Ben-Gurion, had stated that Israel regarded the November 1947 UN resolution in favour of the partition of Palestine and the internationalization of Jerusalem as no longer possessing any moral force, since the United Nations had failed to implement it.

For their part, the Western powers quickly sought to bring about a measure of stability in the post-armistice realities in Palestine. Under a tripartite declaration issued on May 25, 1950, Britain, France and the United States affirmed "their deep interest in and their desire to promote the establishment and maintenance of peace and stability in the area and their unalterable opposition to the use of force or threat of force between any of the states in that area", and pledged that "should they find that any of these states was preparing to violate frontiers or armistice lines" they would "immediately take action, both within and outside the United Nations, to prevent such violation". The same declaration also committed the three powers to preventing an arms race between the Arab states and Israel by laying down procedures under which the supply of arms to these countries would be restricted to those deemed to be required "to maintain a certain level of armed forces for the purposes of assuring their internal security and their legitimate self-defence and to permit them to play their part in the defence of the area as a whole". In the event, France saw no contradiction between this declaration and its arms supply agreement with Israel of 1952 (albeit secret at the time and principally a response to Egyptian support for the rebels then seeking to overthrow French rule in Algeria), while British attempts to construct an alliance with Iraq and Jordan in the early 1950s also involved the supply of arms.

Israel's interest in obtaining arms reflected the fact that from the territorial point of view the 1949 armistice agreements left the Jewish state with a serious security problem. In the north-east border area Israeli settlements were continually bombarded from positions on the Syrian Golan Heights; in the central coastal plain Israel was only nine miles wide at its narrowest point between the Jordanian West Bank and the sea; and in the south Palestinian *fedayeen* (guerrillas) based in the Egyptian-administered Gaza Strip mounted an increasing number of attacks on

Jewish targets across the armistice line. Israel responded to *fedayeen* attacks by carrying out retaliatory actions against guerrilla bases, one such Israeli raid on Gaza in February 1955 causing particularly strong Arab outrage and also provoking general international condemnation. Such raids convinced the Arabs in turn of their need for a modern weapons capability, this objective being a particular preoccupation of the new Egyptian regime of Abdel Gamal Nasser which had come to power in 1954 imbued with a novel mixture of pan-Arab nationalism and revolutionary socialism. In an historic development in September 1955 Nasser concluded a major arms deal with Czechoslovakia, which marked not only the start of increased Soviet influence in the Arab world but also the final breakdown of the Western powers' attempts to prevent an arms race in the Middle East.

Soon after the 1949 armistice Egypt had sought to impose an economic blockade on Israel by denying it the use of the Suez Canal—an action denounced as illegal by Israel but justified by Egypt on the grounds that a state of war still existed between the two countries—and from 1953 Egypt also began restricting Israeli sea-borne trade through the Straits of Tiran at the entrance to the Gulf of Aqaba. Stepped up in 1955, this Egyptian blockade of the southern Israeli port of Eilat combined with increasing Israeli disquiet over Egypt's promotion of *fedayeen* activities in the Gaza Strip contributed substantially to Israel's decision to launch an attack on Egypt in October 1956—in collusion (it later transpired) with Britain and France. For the two Western powers, the key motivation was Nasser's decision of July 1956—taken partly in retaliation for the UK-US decision to withdraw financial aid from the Aswan Dam project—to nationalize the (Anglo-French) Suez Canal Company, despite assurances given in the 1954 Anglo-Egyptian treaty under which British forces had been withdrawn from the Canal Zone. They therefore entered into an agreement with Israel—secret at the time—that an attack by the latter on Egyptian positions in Sinai would be followed by an Anglo-French occupation of the Canal Zone, to be justified in terms of the need to protect the waterway from the warring parties.

The sequence of events was as follows. On Oct. 29, 1956, the Israeli Army attacked Egyptian positions in the Gaza Strip and Sinai, with the declared purpose of destroying *fedayeen* bases. On the next day the British and French Governments issued 12-hour ultimatums to both Israel and Egypt, under which they demanded that the two sides should cease warlike actions and withdraw their troops from the immediate vicinity of the Suez Canal, and also requested Egypt to allow Anglo-French forces to be stationed temporarily on the canal to separate the belligerents and safeguard shipping. The rejection of the ultimatum by Egypt was followed by a British and French air offensive on Egyptian airfields and other military targets from Oct. 31 to Nov. 4 and then, on Nov. 5, by Anglo-French paratroop and commando landings in the Canal Zone. Meanwhile, Israeli forces overran the Gaza Strip and most of Sinai, including Sharm el Sheikh and the island of Tiran at the entrance to the Gulf of Aqaba.

The combined opposition of the United States and the Soviet Union brought a quick end to the 1956 Anglo-French-Israeli enterprise, principally because of the pressure which the US Government was able to exert on Britain. Sir Anthony Eden (UK Prime Minister) announced acceptance of a ceasefire on Nov. 6 and a general cessation of hostilities came into effect at midnight on Nov. 6-7, following which the Anglo-French forces were quickly withdrawn. They were replaced by a UN Emergency Force (UNEF) established by the UN General Assembly on Nov. 5, the first contingents of which arrived in Egypt on Nov. 15 and whose presence was agreed to by the Egyptian Government under certain conditions. In response to UN and US pressure Israel quickly evacuated most of its conquests in Sinai but kept its forces in the Gaza Strip and in the coastal strip from Eilat down to Sharm el Sheikh until March 1957. Its eventual withdrawal from these areas was carried out on the assumption that the UNEF units in Gaza would prevent *fedayeen* incursions into Israeli territory and on the basis of assurances from the leading maritime powers that they would support freedom of navigation in the Gulf of Aqaba.

The main beneficiary of the eclipse of Anglo-French influence in the Middle East caused by the Suez episode was the Soviet Union, which in the succeeding years consolidated its relations with the "progressive" Arab states such as Egypt, Syria and Iraq by means of arms supply and economic aid agreements. To counter this development, the United States became increasingly drawn into the power politics of the region, principally as a supporter of Israel but also as the dominant external power on the Gulf and the ally of the "conservative" Arab states such as Saudi Arabia. The basic Arab-Israeli conflict thus became interwoven with great-power rivalries and ambitions which increasingly threatened to transform Middle East instabilities into a wider conflict.

## Arab-Israeli Relations from 1957 to 1967 leading to the June 1967 War

With Israel restored to the borders established under the 1949 armistices, armed clashes between Arabs and Israelis continued to occur in the decade following the 1956 Suez war. There were a number of incidents on the Israel-Gaza border in May-June 1957, but by December of that year the area was comparatively peaceful, mainly because of the presence of UNEF. Israeli and Jordanian troops clashed in the Mount Scopus demilitarized zone of Jerusalem in August 1957 and May 1958, each side accusing the other of violation of the armistice agreement in the Jerusalem area. The main trouble area in this period, however, was the Israeli-Syrian border in the demilitarized zone south-east of the Sea of Galilee, which the Israelis claimed to be under their jurisdiction. The most serious incidents in this region took place in March 1962 and August 1963, although clashes were of frequent occurrence from 1957. In August 1963 Syria alleged that there were Israeli troop concentrations on the Syrian border, but an investigation by the UN Truce Supervision Organization (UNTSO) revealed no evidence of a military build-up.

In 1959 Egypt began a new blockade of Israeli trade through the Suez Canal, after having refrained, between 1956 and 1959, from interfering with the passage of Israeli goods when such cargoes were carried in vessels not flying the Israeli flag. During 1959 Egypt detained a number of ships of various nationalities carrying exports from Israel and impounded their cargoes. Egyptian sources justified their action on the ground that there was still a state of war between Israel and the Arab countries, and that Israel therefore had no right to ship goods through the Suez Canal.

A further cause of Arab-Israeli friction was the longstanding dispute over the waters of the River Jordan. A number of plans for an equitable division of the waters between Palestine and the riparian Arab states (Jordan, Syria, and Lebanon) were proposed between 1944 and 1955, the last of which was agreed at technical level by Israel and the Arab states under US auspices, but broke down at political level, largely because of Syrian opposition. Israel and Jordan subsequently went ahead with separate schemes, Israel pumping water from the Sea of Galilee to be carried by pipeline to the Negev in the south, and Jordan tapping the waters of the two tributaries, the Yarmuk and the Zarqa. Israel's action aroused the anger of the Arabs, whose heads of state, meeting in Cairo in January 1964, decided on a plan to reduce the flow of the northern tributaries of the Jordan, thus reducing the quantity of water Israel would be able to divert. It was some time before work could begin on this scheme, however, as Lebanon and Syria required assurances of their security from Israeli attack during implementation of the diversion projects.

The January 1964 Arab summit also adopted important resolutions endorsing the creation of Palestinian Arab representative bodies, on the basis of which the inaugural meeting of the Palestine National Council (PNC)—a Palestinian parliament-in-exile—was held in the Jordanian sector of Jerusalem in May-June 1964. This first session of the PNC took the decision to establish the Palestine Liberation Organization (PLO) as the armed wing of the Palestinian struggle and also adopted (on June 2) the Palestine National Charter (or "Covenant") as the basic statement of Palestinian Arab aims, which it remains today. Regarded by the Israelis as enshrining the Arab objective of destroying the Jewish state, the 33-article Charter states inter alia that "Palestine is the homeland of the Palestinian Arab people . . . [and] is an indivisible part of the Arab homeland" (Art. 1); that "Palestine, within the boundaries it had during the British mandate, is an indivisible territorial unit" (Art. 2); that "the Palestinian Arab people possess the legal right to their homeland and have the right to determine their destiny after achieving the liberation of their country in accordance with their wishes and entirely of their own accord and will" (Art. 3); that "the Palestinians are those Arab nationals who, until 1947, normally resided in Palestine regardless of whether they were evicted from it or have stayed there" and also all those born after that date of a Palestinian father "whether inside Palestine or outside it" (Art. 5); that "the Jews who had normally resided in Palestine until the beginning of the Zionist invasion will be considered Palestinians" (Art. 6).

The Charter also declares that "armed struggle is the only way to liberate Palestine" (Art. 9); that "the liberation of Palestine, from a spiritual point of view, will provide the Holy Land with an atmosphere of safety and tranquillity, which in turn will safeguard the country's religious sanctuaries and guarantee freedom of worship and of visit to all, without discrimination of race, colour, language or religion" (Art. 16); that "the partition of Palestine in 1947 and the establishment of the state of Israel are entirely illegal, regardless of the passage of time, because they were contrary to the will of the Palestinian people and to their natural right in their homeland, and inconsistent with the principles embodied in the Charter of the United Nations, particularly the right to self-determination" (Art. 19); that "the Balfour declaration, the mandate for Palestine and everything which has been based on them are deemed null and void" on the grounds that "claims of historical or religious ties of Jews with Palestine are incompatible with the facts of history and the true conception of what constitutes statehood" (Art. 20); that "the Palestinian Arab people . . . reject all solutions which are substitutes for the total liberation of Palestine and reject all proposals aiming at the liquidation of the Palestinian problem or its internationalization" (Art. 21); that "Zionism is a political movement originally associated with international imperialism and antagonistic to all action for liberation and to progressive movements in the world [and] is racist and fanatic in its nature, aggressive, expansionist and colonial in its aims and fascist in its methods" (Art. 22); and that "the Palestine Liberation Organization . . . is responsible for the Palestinian Arab people's movement in its struggle—to retrieve its homeland, liberate and return to it and exercise the right of self-determination in it—in all military, political and financial fields and also for whatever may be required by the Palestine case on the inter-Arab and international levels".

As the principal guerrilla arm of the PLO, the *Al Fatah* ("Conquest") group led by Yassir Arafat mounted numerous incursions into Israel, initially mainly from Jordan and increasingly during 1965 from Syrian territory. An intensification of such attacks in October and November 1966 gave rise to a serious political crisis which led directly to the third Arab-Israeli war. After a resolution calling on Syria to strengthen its measures for preventing guerrilla activities had been vetoed in the UN Security by the Soviet Union on Nov. 4, Israeli forces carried out a reprisal raid on a Jordanian village on Nov. 13, which was condemned by the Security Council on Nov. 25. In late November and early December 1966 violent rioting occurred in the principal towns of the Jordanian West Bank, where the population demanded arms to defend themselves against further Israeli attacks. By the end of 1966 both Israel and Jordan had taken military steps suggesting an anticipation of possible war, while from January 1967 tension between Israel and Syria increased sharply amid repeated armed clashes on the ground and in the air. During Israel's independence day celebrations on May 14, 1967, the Israeli Prime Minister, Levi Eshkol, warned that a serious confrontation with Syria was inevitable if Syrian-backed guerrilla activities continued.

The sequence of events immediately prior to the June 1967 war was as follows. *May 16*: The Egyptian Government declared a state of emergency throughout the country and announced that its forces were "in a complete state of preparedness for war". *May 17*: Syria and Jordan similarly announced that their forces were being mobilized. *May 18*: Egypt made an official request to the UN Secretary-General, U Thant, that UNEF forces should be withdrawn from Egyptian territory and the Gaza Strip (recalling that their presence was subject to Egyptian approval) and Iraq and Kuwait announced the mobilization of their forces. *May 19*: The UNEF was officially withdrawn, with U Thant explaining that "there seemed to me to be no alternative course of action which could be taken by the Secretary-General without putting into question the sovereign authority of the [Egyptian Government] within its own territory". *May 21*: Both Egypt and Israel announced the call-up of reservists, and the PLO announced that its forces had been placed under the military commands of Egypt, Syria and Iraq. *May 22*: It was announced in Cairo that President Nasser had accepted an offer of Iraqi army and air force units to assist Egypt in the event of an outbreak of hostilities. *May 23*: Nasser announced the closing of the Straits of Tiran to ships flying the Israeli flag and to any other vessel carrying strategic goods to Israel (including oil), this action being described by Eshkol as an act of aggression against Israel and as a violation of the freedom of navigation assurances given when Israel withdrew from Sharm el Sheikh in 1957. *May 24*: Egypt announced that the Gulf of Aqaba had been effectively sealed off, while contingents of Saudi Arabian troops were reported to have arrived in Jordan. *May 26*: Following a visit by Abba Eban (Israel's Foreign Minister) to Paris, London and Washington (May 24-25), Israel warned that it had the right to break the blockade of the Gulf of Aqaba if the United Nations or the maritime powers failed to act. *May 27*: U Thant reported to the UN Security Council that Egypt had assured him that it would "not initiate offensive action against Israel" but that Israeli shipping would not be allowed to pass through the Straits of Tiran. *May 28-29*: General mobilization was proclaimed in Sudan (May 28) and Algeria announced that military units were being sent to assist Egypt (May 29). *May 30*: King Hussein of Jordan visited Cairo and signed a defence pact with Egypt under which each country would consider an attack on either as an attack on both, while Abba Eban warned that if the Gulf blockade was not lifted soon Israel would "act alone if we must . . . but with others if we can". *May 31*: Iraqi troops and armoured units were reported to be moving into Jordan towards the Israeli border, while several Arab countries threatened to take action against the oil interests of Western states who aided Israel. *June 2-3*: More than 20 maritime nations were presented with a UK-US draft declaration affirming the right of free and innocent passage through the Gulf of Aqaba but containing no provision for any enforcement action. *June 4*: Nasser said that any such declaration would be regarded as a transgression of Egyptian sovereignty and "a preliminary to an act of war", while Iraq joined the Egypt-Jordan defence pact and Libya pledged troops to assist Egypt in the event of war. *June 5*: Early in the morning the Israeli

Air Force launched pre-emptive strikes against airfields in Egypt, Jordan. Syria and Iraq, destroying virtually all the air capability of these countries on the first day of what subsequently became known as the Six-Day War.

With the benefit of complete air supremacy, Israeli forces achieved a rapid and complete victory in the June 1967 war. By the time hostilities ended in a ceasefire on June 10 Israel had (i) captured the Gaza Strip and overrun the entire Sinai peninsula up to the Suez Canal, including Sharm el Sheikh; (ii) gained control of the Old City of Jerusalem and overrun all of Jordanian territory west of the Jordan; and (iii) captured the Golan Heights from Syria and penetrated some 12 miles into Syrian territory (this advance being achieved in the final stages of the fighting after both Israel and Syria had signified acceptance of a ceasefire). By the end of the war the Israeli armed forces were in occupation of an area more than three times greater than the territory of Israel at the outbreak of hostilities (see map 23 on page 188), the newly occupied territories extending to some 27,000 square miles (70,000 sq km) as compared with the 8,000 square miles (20,000 sq km) of the Jewish state within the 1949 armistice lines. Israeli soldiers killed in the fighting totalled 766 and Arab losses (never definitively announced) were thought to include about 10,000 Egyptian and 6,000 Jordanian dead.

An important feature of the 1967 war was a four-fold increase in the number of Palestinian Arabs under Jewish rule, from a pre-war total of some 300,000 to about 1,200,000 (as against a mid-1967 Jewish population of some 2,500,000). Although up to 200,000 Palestinians fled from the West Bank during the war, about 600,000 remained under the new Israeli adminstration, as did approximately 300,000 in the Gaza Strip. Virtually the entire population of the Syrian territory captured by Israel—about 60,000—fled eastwards during the fighting, leaving the Golan Heights practically uninhabited in the immediate post-war period.

## Arab Quest for Recovery of Occupied Territories leading to the 1973 Arab-Israeli War

Whereas Israel had been forced by US pressure to withdraw from the territory it had captured in the 1956 Sinai campaign, after the June 1967 war Israeli spokesmen immediately made it clear that there could be no return to the 1949 armistice lines. A final settlement of the Arab-Israeli conflict, it was stressed by Israel, was dependent on direct peace talks with the surrounding Arab states to establish definitive boundaries which took account of Israel's legitimate security interests. An eloquent exposition of the Israeli case was put during an emergency session of the UN General Assembly held from June 19 to July 21, 1967, by Foreign Minister Abba Eban, who rejected a Soviet demand that Israel should withdraw to the 1949 lines and argued as follows:

"What the Assembly should prescribe is not a formula for renewed hostilities but a series of principles for the construction of a new future in the Middle East. With the ceasefire established, our progress must not be backward to an armistice regime which has collapsed under the weight of years and the brunt of hostility. History summons us forward to permanent peace, and the peace that we envisage can only be elaborated in frank and lucid dialogue between Israel and each of the states which have participated in the attempt to overthrow her sovereignty and undermine her existence. We dare not be satisfied with intermediate arrangements which are neither war nor peace. Such patchwork ideas carry within themselves the seeds of future tragedy. Free from external pressures and interventions, imbued with a common love for a region which they are destined to share, the Arab and Jewish nations must now transcend their conflicts in dedication to a new Mediterranean future in concert with a renaissant Europe and an Africa and Asia which have emerged at last to their independent role on the stage of history. In free negotiation with each of our neighbours we shall offer durable and just solutions redounding to our mutual advantage and honour. The Arab states can no longer be permitted to recognize Israel's existence only for the purpose of plotting its elimination. They have come face to face with us in conflict. Let them now come face to face with us in peace. . . ."

In a speech to the *Knesset* on Oct. 30, 1967, Prime Minister Eshkol reiterated that Israel would not allow the situation which prevailed before June 5 to be restored and stated that in the face of the Arab position of non-recognition of Israel his Government would "maintain in full the situation as it was established in the ceasefire arrangements". In a further speech on Dec. 1 Eshkol enumerated five points on which Israel's policy was based: (i) permanent peace between Israel and her Arab neighbours; (ii) the achievement of peace by direct negotiations and conclusion of peace treaties between Israel and its neighbours; (iii) free passage for Israeli ships through the Suez Canal and the Straits of Tiran; (iv) agreed and secure borders between Israel and its neighbours; and (v) a settlement of the refugee problem "within a regional and international context" following the establishment of peace in the Middle East.

The Arab states, however, immediately adopted a policy of continued non-recognition of Israel and refusal to consider any form of peace negotiations. Speaking at the UN General Assembly session on June 26, 1967, King Hussein of Jordan accused Israel of having planned aggression against the Arab countries for many years and of initiating hostilities on June 5. Calling on the United Nations to condemn Israel and to enforce the return of Israeli troops to the pre-war lines, he warned that if this did not happen the Arab nation would rise again and that "the battle which began on June 5 will . . . become only a battle in what will be a long war". At a summit conference of Arab nations held in Khartoum in late August 1967 it was decided inter alia that "any necessary steps" would be taken towards consolidating Arab military strength and that the Arab states would enforce "the principles of non-recognition and non-negotiation" and would "make no peace with Israel, for the sake of the rights of the Palestinian people in their homeland".

Lengthy deliberations at the United Nations eventually resulted in the unanimous adoption by the Security Council on Nov. 22, 1967, of a resolution (242) proposed by Britain which emphasized "the inadmissibility of the acquisition of territory by war and the need to work for a just and lasting peace in which every state in the area can live in security". In its substantive passages this resolution affirmed that "the fulfilment of [UN] Charter principles requires the establishment of a just and lasting peace in the Middle East which should include the application of both the following principles: (i) withdrawal of Israeli armed forces from territories occupied in the recent conflict; (ii) termination of all claims or states of belligerency and respect for and acknowledgement of the sovereignty, territorial integrity and political independence of every state in the area and their right to live in peace within secure and recognized boundaries free from threats or acts of force". It further affirmed "the necessity (i) for guaranteeing freedom of navigation through international waterways in the area; (ii) for achieving a just settlement of the refugee problem; (iii) for guaranteeing the territorial inviolability and political independence of every state in the area through measures including the establishment of demilitarized zones".

Resolution 242 was accepted both by Israel and by the front-line Arab states except Syria, although on the basis of differing interpretations of the key phrase calling for an Israeli withdrawal "from territories occupied in the recent conflict". Israel cited the absence of the definite article before the word "territories" to mean that it was not bound to carry out a complete withdrawal, particularly since the resolution also referred to the right to "secure and recognized boundaries".

The Arab states, on the other hand, claimed that the resolution called for a complete Israeli withdrawal and cited the equally authentic French text, where the key phrase is rendered *"retrait des forces armées israéliennes des territoires occupés"*. It should be noted, incidentally, that such semantic arguments were of no interest to the PLO, which has always refused to accept Resolution 242 because it made no reference to the rights of the Palestinian people.

The outcome of the 1967 war and the terms of Resolution 242 set a new tone for the Arab-Israeli conflict, which thereafter revolved less around the fundamental Palestinian Arab challenge to the legitimacy of the state of Israel and more around the quest of Egypt, Syria and Jordan for the recovery of their lost territories. The Israelis made no move to annex their conquests, which were placed under military administration pending a negotiated peace settlement with the interested Arab governments under which definitive boundaries would be agreed. But they did very quickly (by legislation adopted in the *Knesset* on June 27, 1967) merge the Israeli New City of Jerusalem with the Old City and declare in July 1967 that Jerusalem was henceforth "one city indivisible, the capital of the state of Israel" —a step which was condemned not only by the Arabs but also by the UN General Assembly (on July 4 by 99 votes to none with 20 abstentions). The Israelis also began a controversial programme of establishing Jewish settlements in the occupied territories, which although limited in the early years and officially related to security requirements was strongly criticized by the international community, including the United States. In this situation the PLO and its various member organizations increasingly resorted to extreme methods, which included a growing number of attacks on Israeli targets outside Palestine, notably the El Al airline.

After six years of uneasy truce, the fourth Arab-Israeli war broke out on Oct. 6, 1973, when Egyptian and Syrian forces launched major offensives across the Suez Canal and on the Golan front respectively, choosing the Day of Atonement (*Yom Kippur*), the holiest day in the Jewish year, to do so and thereby apparently taking the Israeli armed forces by surprise. Although Jordan did not open a third military front against Israel, units of the Jordanian Army were sent to the Syrian front, as were strong Iraqi armoured contingents and relatively token Saudi Arabian and Kuwaiti units. On the Suez front Egypt received active military assistance from Morocco and Algeria and also from the Iraqi Air Force. The declared war aims of Egypt and Syria were to recover the Arab territories lost to Israel in 1967.

After some of the bitterest and most bloody fighting since World War II, marked by great tank battles and heavy losses of men and material on both sides, a binding ceasefire came into effect on Oct. 24 in response to two successive UN Security Council resolutions. By that time the Egyptian Army had established itself along much of the eastern bank of the Suez Canal north of Ismailia and held a narrow strip of Sinai varying from three to 10 miles in width in different sectors and amounting to some 500 square miles of territory. For their part, the Israeli forces, in addition to having contained an attempted Egyptian thrust deeper into Sinai, had consolidated a successful counter-offensive across the Suez Canal in the southern sector and controlled about 500 square miles of Egyptian territory west of the Great Bitter Lake and the town of Suez.

On the northern front the Syrians also achieved important initial successes, recapturing much of the Golan Heights lost in the 1967 war and advancing almost to the edge of Galilee plain. However, they were eventually checked and driven back in a powerful Israeli counter-offensive, so that when a ceasefire came into effect on Oct. 24 the Syrians had not only surrendered all their initial gains but had also lost an additional 300 square miles of territory to the Israelis, who had advanced to within 20 miles of Damascus.

Total Israeli casualties in the 1973 Arab-Israeli war included 2,400 soldiers killed. As in previous wars the casualties of the Arab side were never officially released.

## 1974 and 1975 Disengagement Agreements

The UN Security Council's first 1973 ceasefire resolution (338), which was adopted on Oct. 22 but not observed until a further resolution had been passed late the following day, was proposed jointly by the United States and the Soviet Union and received the support of 14 of the 15 Security Council member states, with China refraining from voting. In addition to calling for a ceasefire, it urged the parties concerned "to start immediately . . . the implementation of Resolution 242 [of November 1967] in all of its parts" and decided that immediate negotiations should be initiated "aimed at establishing a just and durable peace in the Middle East".

The co-operation of the two super-powers in securing the passage of Resolution 338 reflected their joint concern that the Middle East conflict might escalate into a broader confrontation, although the situation remained tense for several days. President Nixon disclosed on Oct. 26, 1973, that he had ordered a precautionary alert of US military forces throughout the world early the previous day after receiving information which had "led us to believe that the Soviet Union was planning to send a very substantial force" into the Middle East. In the event, the threat of a US-Soviet confrontation had been dissipated by the adoption during the night of Oct. 25-26 of a Security Council resolution providing for the creation of a UN peace-keeping force for the Middle East, the personnel of which would not be drawn from any of the five permanent members of the Security Council (i.e. the USA, the Soviet Union, Britain, France and China). On the basis of this resolution a new UN Emergency Force (UNEF) was deployed on the Suez front by early November 1973 and on Nov. 11 Egypt and Israel formally signed a ceasefire agreement at the "Kilometre 101" checkpoint on the Cairo-Suez road at the edge of the Israeli-occupied enclave west of the Suez Canal. This was the first major agreement between Israel and an Arab country since the signature of the 1949 armistice agreements.

A feature of the complex negotiations which led over the next two years to the conclusion of military disengagement agreements between Israel on the one hand and Egypt and Syria on the other was the key diplomatic role played by the United States and in particular by the US Secretary of State, Dr Henry Kissinger. Another important and related factor was the emergence from the 1973 war onwards of the "oil weapon" as a potent means by which the Arab states, taking advantage of their near-monopoly position as oil exporters, could exert pressure on Western states with a view to securing support for Arab conceptions of a just Middle East settlement, i.e. one which involved major concessions by Israel. At the time of the 1973 war use of this weapon took the form of an embargo on supplies to the United States and the Netherlands (because of their open support for Israel) and restrictions on supplies to other developed countries; subsequently it took the form of massive price increases which not only threw the economies of the industrialized states into recession but also had serious consequences for the existing international monetary system. Against this background (and with the ever-present threat of further total embargoes on Arab oil supplies), the quest for a resolution of the Arab-Israeli conflict took on added urgency for the industrialized countries, beyond their fundamental concern that Middle East instabilities represented a threat to world peace.

In December 1973 the United States and the Soviet Union made a joint effort to bring about meaningful Arab-Israeli negotiations by inviting Egypt, Jordan, Syria and Israel to a peace conference in Geneva on the basis of the UN Security

Council's call for a "just and durable peace"; however, Syria refused to attend (and the PLO was not invited) and the conference was adjourned inconclusively on Jan. 9, 1974. Thereafter, the Soviet Union was able to play little direct part in the overall Middle East negotiating process, particularly since President Sadat of Egypt had already reversed Nasser's policy of close alignment with the Soviet Union—a reversal culminating in his unilateral abrogation in March 1976 of the 1971 Egyptian-Soviet Treaty of Friendship and Co-operation.

With Egypt now accepting that the road to progress ran through Washington, Dr Kissinger was able to mount a direct diplomatic effort with the Middle East parties, the first fruit of which was the signature by Egypt and Israel on Jan. 18, 1974, of an initial military disengagement agreement. Under its terms Israel withdrew its forces from the areas west of the Suez Canal held since the October 1973 ceasefire and also pulled back several miles on the Sinai front east of the canal, where three roughly parallel zones were created, each about six miles wide. The first of these, immediately to the east of the canal, became an Egyptian limited-forces zone, the second a central buffer zone in which UNEF contingents were stationed and the third an Israeli limited-forces zone. For Egypt the general effect of the agreement was that it regained control of all Egyptian territory west of the canal and also the whole of the eastern bank; Israel, although withdrawing 12-13 miles east of the canal, was left in control of the rest of Sinai, including the strategically important Mitla and Giddi passes in Sinai and the Bir Gafgafa defence zone behind them, as well as Sharm el Sheikh commanding the Straits of Tiran.

Further intense "shuttle" diplomacy by Dr Kissinger resulted in the signature on May 31, 1974, of a similar military disengagement agreement by Syria and Israel covering the Golan front, where the two sides had continued to engage in regular hostilities notwithstanding the official existence of a ceasefire. The general effect of the agreement was that Israel withdrew from all the territory it had captured in the October 1973 war as well as from some areas occupied since the 1967 war, including the town of Quneitra. Limited-force zones were established on either side of a central buffer zone in which contingents of a newly-created UN Disengagement Observer Force (UNDOF) were stationed. The agreement also provided that Syrian civilians who had fled during the hostilities would be able to return to the areas vacated by Israel and Syrian administration restored. Since the May 1974 Syrian-Israeli disengagement agreement, no further changes have been negotiated as regards the territorial position on the Golan Heights.

As regards the Sinai front, however, a second Egyptian-Israeli disengagement agreement was signed on Sept. 4, 1975, again after protracted diplomatic efforts by Dr Kissinger. Under this agreement Israel withdrew its forces by a further 12 to 26 miles and the vacated area became the new UN buffer zone, with the old buffer zone being added to the existing Egyptian limited-forces zone. As part of this general withdrawal Israeli forces moved back to the eastern ends of the Mitla and Giddi passes and a new Israeli limited-forces zone was established adjacent to the vacated area on the eastern side. Israel also vacated the Abu Rudeis and Ras Sudar oilfields on the Gulf of Suez (by February 1976), together with a narrow coastal strip running northwards to Egyptian-controlled territory south of Suez (this strip being demilitarized and placed under joint UN-Egyptian administration).

Other features of the Egyptian-Israeli agreement were that each side undertook to refrain from the use or threat of force or military blockade, to observe the ceasefire scrupulously and to renew the UNEF mandate annually; that non-military cargoes moving to and from Israel in non-Israeli vessels would be allowed to pass through the Suez Canal; and that the United States would provide up to 200 civilian technicians to man electronic early-warning stations in the area of the Mitla and Giddi passes.

In conjunction with the second Egyptian-Israeli disengagement agreement, the United States made a number of important commitments to Israel, namely (i) to be "fully responsive" to Israel's defence, energy and economic needs; (ii) to hold consultations with Israel in the event of a "world power" (i.e. the Soviet Union) interfering militarily in the Middle East; (iii) to accept the Israeli view that a further Egyptian-Israeli agreement and any negotiations with Jordan should take place within the context of an overall Middle East peace settlement; (iv) to consult and "concert" policy with Israel on the timing and procedure of a reconvened Geneva peace conference; and (v) not to recognize or negotiate with the PLO under its present orientation.

Egypt was able to comply with the provision concerning Israel's right of passage through the Suez Canal because on June 5, 1974, President Sadat had reopened the waterway on the eighth anniversary of its forcible closure by Egypt at the start of the 1967 war. On Nov. 2, 1975, the Greek freighter *Olympus* made a north-south passage of the canal bound for the Israeli port of Eilat with a cargo of cement, which thus became the first Israeli cargo shipped through the canal with the official approval of the Egyptian Government since the establishment of the state of Israel in 1948.

For Egypt the 1974 and 1975 disengagement agreements were psychologically important because they confirmed and consolidated the limited territorial gains made in the 1973 war, in which the Egyptian armed forces had for the first time performed creditably against those of Israel. The attempted invasion of the new Jewish state in 1948 had ended in a debacle; in both the 1956 and the 1967 wars Nasser's forces had been comprehensively defeated; but in 1973 President Sadat became the "hero of the crossing" of the Suez Canal. Although many military analysts of the time took the view that if the fighting had continued Egypt would have been defeated for a fourth time, the ceasefire left Egyptian forces in control of the first stretch of territory wrested from Israel by military force since the creation of the latter in 1948. With Arab military honour thus restored—at least in Egyptian eyes—it became easier for Egypt to move towards its historic rapprochement with Israel.

### Egyptian-Israeli Rapprochement, the 1978 Camp David Agreements and the 1979 Egypt-Israel Peace Treaty

Completion of the implementation of the second Egyptian-Israeli disengagement agreement in February 1976 was followed by protracted international negotiations aimed at reconvening the Geneva peace conference as the appropriate forum for the negotiation of an overall Middle East settlement. However, these efforts repeatedly came up against the stumbling block of Israel's refusal to accept the PLO as a participant at a reconvened conference, whereas Egypt, Jordan and Syria insisted on some form of PLO participation in accordance with a decision taken by the October 1974 Arab League summit conference held in Rabat (Morocco) to recognize the PLO as the sole legitimate representative of the Palestinian people. Moreover, the Arab states continued to insist that a settlement must not only satisfy the legitimate rights of the Palestinians but also involve an Israeli withdrawal from all the territories conquered in 1967, including the former Jordanian sector of Jerusalem.

The prospects of further accommodation appeared to recede even further when the Israeli general election of May 1977 resulted in Menahem Begin becoming Prime Minister at the head of a Government dominated by his own right-wing nationalist *Likud* front. A major plank of the *Likud* programme was an assertion of inalienable Israeli sovereignty over all the land between the Mediterranean Sea and the Jordan river, in which context *Likud* opposed "any plan envisaging a renunciation of the smallest piece" of the West Bank on the grounds that any such renunciation "will lead inevitably to the creation of a Palestinian state which will be a threat to the security of the civil population, will place the existence of Israel in danger and will endanger any chance of peace". The *Likud* platform also called for unrestricted Jewish settlement throughout the historic "Land of Israel" (*Eretz Israel*), including the Arab-populated West Bank. It therefore marked a significant departure from the approach pursued by the hitherto dominant Israel Labour Party, which had been prepared to make territorial concessions on the West Bank as well as in Sinai and on the Golan Heights and had insisted that Jewish settlements in the occupied territories should only be authorized where security factors rendered them desirable. Yet it was to be Begin's Government, apparently much less prepared to compromise than its Labour-led predecessors, which took Israel into a reconciliation with Egypt involving large territorial concessions (albeit not affecting the new Israeli Government's conception of Jewish rights in the "Land of Israel").

In a speech to the Egyptian People's Assembly on Nov. 9, 1977, President Sadat urged other Arab states to unite in an all-out drive to reconvene the Geneva peace conference and declared that he was "ready to go to the *Knesset* itself" to unblock the peace-making process. Begin responded positively two days later, with the result that on Nov. 19-20, 1977, President Sadat undertook the first official visit ever made to Israel by an Arab leader and was received with the ceremonial appropriate to a head of state despite the existence of a technical state of war between the two countries. The centre-piece of the visit was an address by the Egyptian President to the *Knesset* in Jerusalem on Nov. 20 in which he explicitly accepted the existence of Israel as a Middle East state but reiterated his belief that a just and lasting peace depended on an Israeli withdrawal from all occupied Arab territory and on recognition of the rights of the Palestinians. The following month Menahem Begin became the first Israeli Prime Minister to be officially received in an Arab country when he had two days of talks with President Sadat in Ismailia on Dec. 25-26, 1977.

In most other Arab states the reaction to the radically new departure represented by the Sadat visit was one of hostility, which mounted as it became clear that Egypt was serious about achieving a rapprochement with Israel. Particularly vociferous in its condemnation was the PLO, which saw the new policy as a means by which Egypt would seek to recover its own lost territory in desertion not only of the agreed principles of Arab solidarity but also of the interests of the dispossessed Palestinian people.

The impetus towards a peace settlement created by Sadat's initiative was checked by a serious deterioration in the general Middle East situation from March 1978, when a major Palestinian guerrilla raid on Israel was immediately followed by a large-scale Israeli invasion of southern Lebanon designed to secure Israel's northern border against Palestinian incursions. However, the deployment of a UN peace-keeping force (UNIFIL) in southern Lebanon from late March and the subsequent withdrawal of Israeli forces by mid-June facilitated efforts by the United States to bring about a resumption of direct Egyptian-Israeli negotiations, culminating in talks between Sadat and Begin at Camp David (near Washington) in September 1978, with President Carter acting as intermediary. These talks resulted in the signature in Washington on Sept. 17 of two framework agreements, one on an overall Middle East settlement and the other specifically on the conclusion of a peace treaty between Egypt and Israel within three months.

The first of the Camp David agreements dealt in particular with the granting of what was termed "full autonomy" to the Palestinian Arab inhabitants of the West Bank and Gaza Strip, the following main stages being envisaged: (i) the inhabitants of the West Bank and Gaza would elect a "self-governing authority" whose powers would be defined in negotiations between Israel, Egypt and Jordan in which the delegations of Egypt and Jordan would be open to "Palestinians from the West Bank and Gaza and other Palestinians as mutually agreed"; (ii) the self-governing authority would replace the existing Israeli administration in these areas; (iii) a five-year transitional period would begin when the self-governing authority had been established and would be marked by the withdrawal of Israeli forces or their redeployment into "specified security locations"; (iv) not later than the third year of the transitional period negotiations would take place between Israel, Jordan, Egypt and the elected representatives of the West Bank and Gaza inhabitants "to determine the final status of the West Bank and Gaza" by the end of the transitional period. In an undertaking separate from the actual agreement President Sadat stated that Egypt was prepared to assume "the Arab role" in these negotiations on Palestinian autonomy "following consultations with Jordan and the representatives of the Palestinian people" (i.e. if these two parties refused to participate directly—as in fact turned out to be the case).

On the broader aspects of the Middle East conflict, the first framework agreement specified inter alia (i) that parallel negotiations would take place between Israel, Jordan and elected Palestinian representatives to conclude a peace treaty between Israel and Jordan by the end of the transitional period; (ii) that Egypt and Israel would seek to conclude within three months a full peace treaty on the basis of detailed specifications set out in the second Camp David framework agreement "while inviting the other parties to the conflict to proceed simultaneously to negotiate and conclude similar peace treaties with a view to achieving a comprehensive peace in the area"; and (iii) that peace treaties between Israel and each of its neighbours (i.e. Egypt, Jordan, Syria and Lebanon) should be based on principles establishing "relationships normal to states at peace with one another".

Contentious issues which remained unresolved under the Camp David agreements included the future of Jewish settlements in the Israeli-occupied territories and the status of east Jerusalem (it being reaffirmed by Begin in the latter connexion that the 1967 unification of the city as the "indivisible" capital of Israel was non-negotiable). These and other difficulties meant that the Dec. 17, 1978, target date for an Egyptian peace treaty could not be met (even though Sadat and Begin were jointly awarded the 1978 Nobel Peace Prize for their efforts at Camp David and earlier). However, further US mediation efforts culminating in some personal Middle East shuttle diplomacy by President Carter on March 8-13, 1979, resulted in President Sadat and Prime Minister Begin signing the first-ever Arab-Israel peace treaty in Washington on March 26.

The draft treaty and its associated documents had been approved by the *Knesset* on March 22 by 95 votes to 11 (with two abstentions, three deputies not participating in the vote and two absent) and the signed text was subsequently ratified by the Israeli Cabinet on April 1 (with one minister abstaining). In Egypt the draft treaty received unanimous approval from the Cabinet on March 15 and its definitive text was ratified by the People's Assembly on April 10 by 328 votes to 15 (with one abstention and 16 members absent) and also by the electorate as a whole in a national referendum on April 19 (by 99.5 per cent of the valid votes cast). Instruments of ratification were exchanged at the US surveillance post at Um-Khashiba in Sinai on April 25, 1979—at which point the 31-year-old state of war between Egypt and Israel was officially terminated.

The main provisions of the Egyptian-Israeli peace treaty and the various documents associated with it were as follows: (i) Israel would evacuate its military forces and civilians from the whole of the Sinai peninsula in a phased withdrawal over a three-year period, as part of which some two-thirds of Sinai, comprising the area west of a line from El Arish in the north to Ras Mohammed in the south, would be returned to Egypt in five subphases within nine months of the treaty being ratified (see map 24 on page 188); (ii) agreed security arrangements would be instituted involving the establishment of limited-force zones and the stationing of UN forces in key border areas, while the US Air Force would continue its surveillance flights over the area to verify compliance with the treaty's terms; (iii) after the completion of the Israeli withdrawal to the El Arish-Ras Mohammed line within nine months, normal diplomatic and other relations would be established between the two countries, including an exchange of ambassadors within 10 months of ratification; (iv) Israeli ships and cargoes would be granted the same right of passage in the Suez Canal and its approaches as the vessels of other countries; (v) both countries recognized the Straits of Tiran and the Gulf of Aqaba as international waterways; (vi) Egypt undertook to end its economic boycott of Israel and to sell oil from the Sinai oilfields to Israel on a non-discriminatory basis; (vi) within a month of the exchange of ratification instruments Egypt and Israel would begin negotiations with a view to implementing the provisions of the first Camp David framework agreement concerning the granting of "full autonomy" to the Palestinian Arab inhabitants of the West Bank and the Gaza Strip and the establishment of a "self-governing authority".

In letters addressed to Egypt and Israel the US Government confirmed that in the event of actual or threatened violation of the treaty the United States would, on request of one or both of the parties, consult with them and "take such other action as it may deem appropriate and helpful to achieve compliance with the treaty"; and that if the UN Security Council failed to establish and maintain the peace-keeping arrangements called for in the treaty the US President would be "prepared to take those steps necessary to ensure the establishment and maintenance of an acceptable alternative multinational force".

In an Israeli-US memorandum of understanding signed on March 26, 1979, the United States undertook to give strong support to Israel in certain circumstances, stating in particular: "The United States will provide support it deems appropriate for proper actions taken by Israel in response to . . . demonstrated violations of the treaty of peace. In particular, if a violation of the treaty of peace is deemed to threaten the security of Israel, including inter alia a blockade of Israel's use of international waterways, a violation of the provisions of the treaty of peace concerning limitation of forces or an armed attack against Israel, the United States will be prepared to consider, on an urgent basis, such measures as the strengthening of the US presence in the area, the providing of emergency supplies to Israel, and the exercise of maritime rights in order to put an end to the violation." The Egyptian Government stated subsequently, however, that it would not recognize the legality of this memorandum and considered it null and void. Among 16 reasons listed by Egypt for rejecting the memorandum were that it had never been mentioned to or negotiated with Egypt; that it could be "construed as an eventual alliance between the United States and Israel against Egypt"; and that it gave the United States "the right to impose a military presence in the region for reasons agreed between Israel and the United States".

In the Arab world the price paid by Egypt for its signature of the peace treaty with Israel was virtually total political and economic isolation. Acting on preliminary decisions taken following the signature of the Camp David agreements, the Foreign and Economy Ministers of all Arab League member states except Egypt, Oman and Sudan, meeting in Baghdad on March 27-31, 1979, imposed a wide-ranging political and economic boycott on Egypt, including an embargo on oil supplies. The measures agreed to by the conference included the withdrawal of all remaining Arab ambassadors from Cairo, the suspension of Egypt from Arab League membership as well as from a large number of joint Arab organizations and projects, and the transfer of the Arab League's headquarters from Cairo to

Tunis. Other international groupings which suspended Egypt's membership over the peace treaty with Israel included the Islamic Conference Organization, the Organization of African Unity, the Non-Aligned Movement and the Organization of Arab Petroleum Exporting Countries.

## Developments since 1979 Egyptian-Israeli Peace Treaty

Notwithstanding some last-minute uncertainty engendered by the assassination of President Sadat (on Oct. 6, 1981), the Israeli withdrawal from Sinai was carried out in accordance with the timetable laid down in the 1979 peace treaty. Completion of the fifth subphase on Jan. 26, 1980, took Israeli forces back to the El Arish-Ras Mohammed line, at which point the Egyptian-Israeli border was officially declared open. A month later, on Feb. 26, Israel and Egypt exchanged ambassadors —the Egyptian envoy taking up residence in Tel Aviv to signify Egypt's non-recognition of unified Jerusalem as the capital of Israel. Finally, on the third anniversary of the ratification of the 1979 treaty, Israel completed its withdrawal from the remainder of Sinai on April 25, 1982, after a core of hard-line Jewish settlers in the Yamit area of northern Sinai had been forcibly removed by the Israeli Army.

Concurrently with the final hand-over in Sinai, troops of an international peace-keeping force were deployed along the reinstated international border between Egypt and Israel. In accordance with the 1979 treaty, this force had been assembled at the instigation of the US Government outside the UN framework, it having become clear that the Soviet Union would veto any move in the Security Council to designate a UN force for the purpose. Countries which had declared their willingness to contribute troops to the Sinai force included (in addition to the United States itself) Britain, France, Italy, the Netherlands, Australia, Canada and New Zealand. As agreed by Egypt and Israel on April 26, 1982, the first duties of the new force included taking control of certain sections of the international frontier where precise demarcation remained in dispute, notably a stretch of about 750 metres at Taba (to the west of Eilat on the Gulf of Aqaba).

Against a backcloth of considerable unease within Israel over the Sinai withdrawal, Israeli ministers stressed that no further territorial concessions would be made to the Arabs. Indeed, in the period since the signature of the 1979 treaty Israel had taken several important steps to give internal legal substance to this attitude. On July 30, 1980, the *Knesset* had adopted legislation strengthening the status of Jerusalem as the "indivisible" capital of Israel, while on Dec. 14, 1981, the Golan Heights were effectively annexed under legislation which extended Israeli "law, jurisdiction and administration" to that area of former Syrian territory. Both of these moves were strongly condemned by the United Nations (which had repeatedly called upon Israel to refrain from altering the status of the occupied territories), as was the Begin Government's acceleration of Jewish settlement of the West Bank.

For its part, the Israeli Government repeatedly asserted its historic right to sovereignty over the "Land of Israel" and declared its aim of annexing the West Bank and the Gaza Strip at the end of the five-year transitional period laid down in the first Camp David framework agreement. At the time of the final Sinai withdrawal, however, this aim remained somewhat academic because the transitional period had not yet started and Israeli military administration remained in place. Despite constant efforts by the US Government to bring about progress in the Palestinian "autonomy" negotiations, Egypt and Israel remained deadlocked on the nature of the Palestinian "self-governing authority", the installation of which was to initiate the five-year transitional period. Various difficulties had prevented progress being made in these negotiations (not least the refusal to participate of two directly interested parties, namely the Palestinians themselves and Jordan), but the major underlying obstacle was the Israeli Government's insistence that "full autonomy" could imply no element of Palestinian sovereignty.

The April 1982 Sinai withdrawal therefore left Israel in control of virtually the whole of the territory of the former British Palestine mandate (which as explained above originally included the Golan Heights) and with an estimated Arab population of some 1,700,000 (including 500,000 in Israel proper) as against a Jewish population of about 3,400,000. While Israel continued to insist that Palestinian Arab political aspirations could be reconciled with its own territorial position, this view was clearly not shared by the Palestinians themselves, among whom increasingly violent opposition to Israeli rule was accompanied by widespread open support for the PLO. Against this background, the Arab-Israeli territorial conflict continued to have important external dimensions arising from Israel's unyielding occupation of territory captured from Syria and Jordan in 1967 and from its determination to eradicate the PLO guerrilla presence in Lebanon—this latter factor becoming the most critical aspect of the Arab-Israeli conflict after the Sinai withdrawal.

Although the international border between Israel and Lebanon has never itself been in dispute, the transplantation to Lebanon of the main bulk of Palestinian activists after their forcible expulsion from Jordan in September 1970 had led to increasing Israeli concern over the security of northern Galilee in the face of guerrilla attacks mounted from southern Lebanon. This concern had increased when Palestinian movements obtained substantial scope for autonomous action amid the collapse of central government authority which accompanied the 1975-76 civil war in Lebanon. Thereafter Israel had responded by making frequent direct attacks on Palestinian guerrilla bases in southern Lebanon and by promoting the establishment of a buffer zone under the control of anti-PLO Lebanese Christian forces immediately to the north of the border. At the same time Israel had repeatedly warned that it would not tolerate any move into southern Lebanon by the Syrian-dominated "Arab deterrent force" which had been stationed in Lebanon since the end of the civil war.

Nevertheless, from the Israeli point of view, the Lebanese border situation remained a serious security threat, with the result that in early June 1982—less than two months after the Sinai withdrawal—the Israel Defence Forces launched a fullscale invasion of Lebanon. The main aims of the latest invasion were widely seen as the elimination of the PLO as a military and political force and also the creation of conditions for a restoration of a sovereign and effective government of Lebanon by the Lebanese.

**A.J.D.**

# Bahrain-Iran

A longstanding dispute arising from an Iranian (Persian) claim to sovereignty over the island of Bahrain—which appeared to have been settled in December 1970 when the Government of the Shah of Iran had endorsed a UN Security Council resolution affirming the complete independence of the state of Bahrain—was revived in September 1979. The Iranian claim was strongly repudiated in Bahrain and also in Iraqi official circles. (For map of the Gulf region, see page 212.)

### History of the Dispute

The island of Bahrain was part of the Islamic empire between the seventh and 11th centuries and was thereafter ruled by various Arab dynasties until it was occupied by the Portuguese in 1522; it was under Persian domination from 1602 until 1783, this domination being interrupted by short periods of rule by Arab shaikhs and ended by the island's conquest by the rulers of Zubarah (Qatar), whose descendants have ruled Bahrain to the present day. Between 1861 and 1971 Bahrain was under British protection, with defence and external affairs being the responsibility of the United Kingdom.

An agreement concluded on Aug. 30, 1822, by the British Political Resident in the Gulf with the Persian authorities in Shiraz—which provided that Bahrain should be regarded as "subordinate to the [Persian] province of Fars" and that the British Government would supply Persia with war vessels to conquer Bahrain—was disowned as "unauthorized" by the British Governor of Bombay, who denounced the admission of the King of Persia's title to Bahrain as being without "the least proof". The agreement was also denounced by the Shah of Persia, who declared that it had been made "without his knowledge or injunction".

In 1844, however, the Persian Prime Minister submitted a claim to Bahrain in a note to the British Government, after the Ruler of Bahrain had been expelled by his nephew and had asked the British, the Persians and the Sultan of Muscat for help to enable him to regain Bahrain. When it became known that Persia was preparing military action in support of the expelled Shaikh, the British Government informed Persia that it would actively oppose any action against the lawful Government of Bahrain.

The Persian Prime Minister (Haji Meerza Aghassi), in a statement of March 15, 1844, listed the following arguments in favour of Persia's claim to Bahrain: (i) "The Persian Gulf from the commencement of the Shatt al-Arab to Muscat belongs to Persia and . . . all islands of that sea, without exception and without participation of any other government, belong entirely to Persia" (as was supported by the English usage of referring to the "Persian" Gulf); (ii) "Bahrain has always been under the authority of the Governor of Fars from 1300 AD"; (iii) "all European and Turkish books of geography as well as the books of travellers considered Bahrain as Persian"; and (iv) the 1822 agreement [see above] recognized Persia's ownership of Bahrain.

These arguments were refuted by the (British) East India Company, whose Secret Committee stated on July 31, 1845, inter alia (i) that the British Government had treated the Shaikhs of Bahrain as independent authorities since their occupation of the island in 1783; (ii) that Bahrain might have been a dependency of Fars while the Persians were in actual possession of the island but that to allege that the Persians had possessed it since 1300 AD was "contrary to the best evidence" that could be produced on the subject; and (iii) that the 1822 treaty had

209

no legal significance as it had been "expressly disavowed". The Committee there-fore concluded that Persia had no legitimate claim to sovereignty over Bahrain.

In subsequent years the British Government ignored Persia's claim to the island, but in a note dated April 29, 1869, the British Government conceded that it would inform the Persian Government beforehand "of any measures of coercion against himself which the conduct of the Shaikh of Bahrain may have rendered necessary" (the Shaikh having solicited military aid from Persia and Turkey and having attacked Qatar). The Persian Government considered this concession as involving British recognition of Persia's claim to Bahrain.

Persia did not raise the matter again until Nov. 22, 1927, when it protested to Britain against the conclusion of a treaty (on May 27, 1927) with Saudi Arabia, in which reference was made to the maintenance of "friendly and peaceful relations with the territories of Kuwait and Bahrain, who are in special treaty relations with [the British] Government". The Persian Government regarded this clause, "so far as it concerns Bahrain", as "an infringement of the territorial integrity of Persia". The British Foreign Secretary (Sir Austen Chamberlain), replying to the protest on Jan. 18, 1928, denied categorically that there were "any valid grounds upon which the claim of the Persian Government to the sovereignty over Bahrain is or can be based". This exchange was followed by further notes sent respectively on Aug. 2, 1928, and Feb. 18, 1929, when the British Government stated inter alia: "It would be necessary for Persia to prove that she is, or ever has been, the lawful owner of Bahrain, and that such rights as she may have acquired in former ages by conquest and the exercise of force outweigh those not only of the Portuguese but of the Arab inhabitants themselves."

Persia also protested unsuccessfully against the granting of oil concessions by the Shaikh of Bahrain (in a note to the British Government on July 23, 1930, and in another note, to the United States, on May 22, 1934).

In reply to a British statement of April 5, 1956, to the effect that Bahrain was an independent shaikhdom, the Persian Foreign Minister contended on April 8 that Bahrain was "an inseparable part of Persia"; that Persia would not recognize it as a British-protected shaikhdom; that during the 19th century Britain had several times recognized Persian sovereignty over the island; and that its ruling dynasty had on several occasions sworn fealty and paid taxes to Persia.

Following the passing of a bill by the Persian Parliament declaring Bahrain the 14th Persian province, the British position of not recognizing Persian sovereignty over Bahrain was reaffirmed on Nov. 27, 1957, by the then British Foreign Secretary (Ormsby Gore), who declared that the British Government would continue to fulfil its obligation to safeguard the independence of Bahrain, and that the Ruler of Bahrain had received an assurance to this effect.

Persia's claim was also rejected by the Arab League, which reaffirmed on Nov. 15, 1957, that Bahrain was "Arab territory". This was underlined by the fact that its population was overwhelmingly Arab, it being estimated in 1965 that the naturalized Iranian population of Bahrain was less than 7 per cent of the total Arab population. Nevertheless, the Shah of Iran restated his claim on Nov. 22, 1958, when he said at a press conference in Tehran: "We consider Bahrain an integral part of Persia." He added that he would gladly accept the allegiance of its Ruler "in the capacity of the first Iranian Governor-General of Bahrain".

## Developments leading to 1970 Settlement

In the late 1960s the Iranian attitude towards the Bahrain question became more conciliatory. On Jan. 5, 1969, the Shah declared that Bahrain's inhabitants (num-bering some 200,000 people) were welcome to decide their own fate, although Iran would not want the island to be made over to anyone else without Iranian consent.

At the request of both Iran and Britain, the United Nations Secretary-General (U Thant) agreed on March 28, 1970, to appoint a special representative to visit Bahrain in order to ascertain the wishes of its population in regard to its future status. This UN representative, Vittorio Winspeare Guicciardi (Italy), visited the island between March 30 and April 18, 1970, and in his report, issued on May 2, he declared: "My conclusions have convinced me that the overwhelming majority of the people of Bahrain wish to gain recognition of their identity in a fully independent and sovereign state free to decide for itself its relations with other states."

In this connexion the Ruler of Bahrain had on March 29, 1970, declared inter alia: "The question of Bahrain's relations with Iran is a matter which needs to be tackled at its very roots, not only because it concerns these two countries, but because it has a direct bearing upon the future stability of the whole area [after the withdrawal of Britain from the Gulf at the end of 1971]. . . . Our belief is that Bahrain is an Arab country [and] has its own independent personality and existence. We believe these to be facts which reflect the deepest feelings of the people of Bahrain, and that they should be acknowledged by all. We believe, too, that these facts are supported both in history and in the reality of the present situation; and that they allow of no doubt or of any contrary claim, which we never recognize nor admit in any way."

Meeting on May 11, 1970, at the request of Iran and the United Kingdom, the UN Security Council unanimously endorsed the report of the Secretary-General's special representative, and this endorsement was ratified by the Iranian *Majlis* (Lower House of Parliament) by 186 votes to four on May 14, and unanimously by Iran's Senate on May 18. This apparent settlement of the dispute was followed by visits to Tehran by the Prime Minister of Bahrain on May 24, 1975, and to Bahrain by the then Iranian Prime Minister (Abbas Hoveyda) on Nov. 29, 1975, when the latter stated that there were no difficulties in relations between Iran and Bahrain and that co-operation between them was being fostered by a joint ministerial commission.

## Revival of Iranian Claim

The 1970 settlement of the dispute was in line with the Shah's endeavours to improve Iran's relations with Arab countries, in which connexion he concluded a "treaty of reconciliation" with Iraq in 1975. With the advent to power of the Shah's successors and the establishment of the Islamic Republic of Iran in early 1979, the latter regime's relations with most Arab countries deteriorated, in particular those with Iraq, and the revival of Iran's claim to Bahrain underlined this development. The renewed Iranian claim to Iran was announced in September 1979 by Ayatollah Ruhani, a leading figure in the Iranian Islamic revolution; however, it was strongly rejected by the Bahrain Government on Sept. 22, 1979, and also denounced in Baghdad on Sept. 24 by *Al-Thawra*, the official organ of the ruling Baath party.

The Bahraini Ministry of the Interior announced on Dec. 13, 1981, that it had foiled an attempted coup by members of an Islamic Front for the Liberation of Bahrain said to have been trained in Iran. Of 73 persons charged in this connexion, inter alia with possession of arms supplied from Iran, three were on May 23, 1982, sentenced to death, 60 to 15 years in prison each and 10 to seven years each. The Iranian Government denied any implication in the alleged plot.

**H.W.D.**

# Bahrain-Qatar (Hawar Islands)

The question of the Hawar (Huwar) Islands, situated about 1½ miles (2.4 km) off the east coast of Qatar but under the sovereignty of Bahrain, has been the subject of exchanges between the two countries since 1967 and also of unsuccessful mediation efforts by Saudi Arabia. Following the adhesion of both countries to the Gulf Co-operation Council established in February 1981, efforts to resolve the dispute were pursued within that framework.

During a visit to Qatar by the Ruler of Bahrain in March 1967 (i.e. before the achievement of independence by the two countries in 1971) the Ruler of Qatar raised the question of the sovereignty over these islands. The subject was later discussed within the framework of an offshore boundary settlement between the two countries, with Qatar insisting on obtaining ownership of the islands before agreeing to a settlement satisfactory to Bahrain, but the latter did not agree to this demand.

In 1965 the islands and their surrounding waters had been included in a concession granted by Bahrain to the Continental Oil Company (Bahrain). Yusuf as-Shawari, Bahrain's Minister of Industry and Development, stated on March 1, 1980, that the islands were governed by a concession agreed between the Government of Bahrain and a group of US companies which were planning to drill a new experimental well in search of oil (following the failure of two earlier drilling attempts).

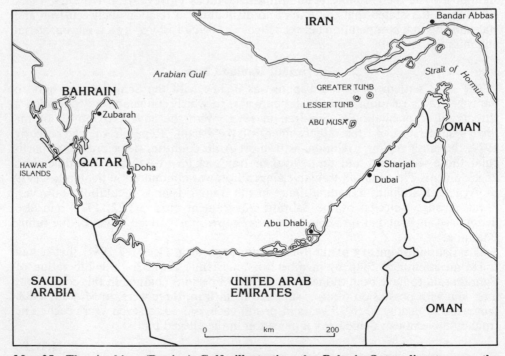

Map 25  The Arabian (Persian) Gulf, illustrating the Bahrain-Qatar dispute over the Hawar Islands and also showing Abu Musa and the Tunbs, which are disputed by Iran and the United Arab Emirates.

212

Shaikh Abdel Aziz bin Khalifa, the Qatar Minister of Finance and Petroleum, thereupon replied on March 4 that "all geographical, historial, legal and logical indications" categorically proved that "these islands constitute an indivisible part of Qatar, since they are situated within its territorial waters". The Minister added that Bahrain had nothing to support its claim of sovereignty over these islands except a British decision made in 1939, which Qatar considered "null and void" since it contradicted "the basic norms of international law governing such matters" and also "the established geographical, material and historical facts". The Minister also accused Yusuf as-Shawari of disregarding the fact that there was "an agreed mediation being conducted by a big sister state (i.e. Saudi Arabia) for solving the dispute", and he declared that Qatar was "keen" to safeguard its close fraternal relations with Bahrain and that he hoped that the two countries would settle the dispute "in a manner that would restore right in accordance with the principles of justice and law".

On March 7, 1980, diplomatic sources in Kuwait were quoted as saying that Saudi Arabia was again to mediate between Bahrain and Qatar in order to prevent the dispute from worsening and had asked officials in the two countries not to allow the media to complicate the situation.

The issue was complicated by a claim by the Shaikh of Bahrain relating to rights in Zubarah, on the northern coast of Qatar, on the grounds that it was his ancestral home and was inhabited by a tribe owing him allegiance. This is not regarded as a territorial claim but as one for jurisdiction over the subjects of a state in another territory; it has not been pursued in recent years, but in the view of the Shaikh of Bahrain it remains unsettled in the absence of any written agreement on the frontiers between the two states.

In February 1981 both Bahrain and Qatar—together with Kuwait, Oman, Saudi Arabia and the United Arab Emirates—became members of the newly-established Gulf Co-operation Council (GCC) of Arab states, one of the professed functions of which was to resolve territorial disputes between member-states. After the Qatar Government had protested in early March 1982 against the Bahrain Government's decision to name a new warship the *Hawar*, the GCC ministerial council, meeting in Riyadh on March 7-9, 1982, requested Saudi Arabia to continue its efforts to resolve the dispute. According to a statement issued at the conclusion of the meeting, both sides had agreed "to freeze the situation and not to cause an escalation of the dispute", to halt "information campaigns exchanged between the two countries" and to continue their fraternal relations on the basis of "a return to the status quo ante".

H.W.D.

# Iran-Iraq

A major source of strain in relations between Iran and Iraq has been the longstanding dispute over the Shatt al-Arab waterway, which runs into the Arabian (Persian) Gulf in the southern border area between the two countries. Whereas Iraq has traditionally claimed to have succeeded to the Ottoman empire's jurisdiction over the whole waterway and that therefore the border between the two countries in this area runs along the eastern (i.e. Iranian) bank, Iran has consistently maintained that such a delimitation is not only unjust but also contrary to the Thalweg line principle (whereby riverine frontiers are defined as following the median line in the deepest channel). Under early partial agreements, Iran succeeded in securing the application of the Thalweg principle to the vicinity of Mohammerah (Khorramshahr) in 1914 and to the waters off Abadan in 1937; moreover, in return for a cessation of Iranian support for Kurdish rebels in Iraqi Kurdistan, Iraq agreed in 1975 that the entire Shatt al-Arab should be delimited along the median line of the deepest channel. However, the Shia Moslem revolution in Iran in 1979 not only served to revive Arab Iraq's traditional suspicion of its non-Arab neighbour but also led to a reactivation of the Iraqi claim to the Shatt al-Arab. In September of the following year Iraq unilaterally abrogated the 1975 agreement, declared its sovereignty over the whole of the Shatt al-Arab and moved to assert its claim by force of arms.

The Shatt al-Arab ("Arab river")—given on some modern Iranian maps as the Arvand river—is formed by the confluence of the Euphrates and Tigris rivers and flows for some 160 miles (255 km) through a swampy delta before opening out into the Gulf. From the north the land boundary between Iran and Iraq reaches the waterway about 60 miles (100 km) from the coast and about 10 miles (16 km) upstream from the town of Khorramshahr. The area where the Shatt al-Arab flows into the sea has acquired major importance for both Iran and Iraq, in particular since the development of their respective oil industries. Iran has built its major oil refinery at Abadan (its principal oil terminal being on Kharg island in the Gulf), while Iraq's main terminal is at Fao at the southern end of the waterway and its main port at Basra upstream from Khorramshahr. This development of the Shatt al-Arab has served to accentuate what Iran regards as the anomaly of its ports being enclosed by territorial waters claimed by Iraq, whereas Iraq has attached increasing importance to the waterway as its main outlet to the sea and has also pointed out that Iran in any case possesses a substantial coastline further round the Gulf.

## Early Historical Background

The border between Iran (Persia) and the Turkish Ottoman empire was first defined in a treaty signed at Zuhab in 1639, although this document left the boundary line extremely vague in that the allocation of territory between the Zagros mountains to the east of the Shatt al-Arab and the Tigris to the west was based largely on tribal loyalties. Following the conclusion in 1724 of a Russo-Turkish agreement providing for the partition of Iran, the Turks invaded Iran and under the 1727 Treaty of Hamadan were ceded that country's western provinces. Although further hostilities in the 1740s resulted in a reaffirmation of the 1639 agreement in the Treaty of Kherden of 1746, the latter treaty was itself declared invalid under the first Treaty of Ezerum signed in 1823 after renewed warfare between the Turks and Iran in 1821-22.

Following the signature of the first Treaty of Ezerum in 1823 Britain and Russia exerted pressure on Turkey and Iran to achieve a resolution of their border difficulties, to which end a boundary commission was formed in 1843 comprising representatives of the four powers. As a result of the commission's work a second Treaty of Ezerum was signed in May 1847 which delimited a boundary in the Shatt al-Arab for the first time. Iran received the town and port of Mohammerah (Khorramshahr), the island of Abadan and its anchorage and the eastern bank of the river, but Turkey retained sovereignty over the waterway. (Mohammerah had been founded in 1812 by the Muhaisin tribe and had been claimed by both Iran and Turkey. The Shaikh of Mohammerah had maintained his independence, however, and controlled southern Arabistan, east of the Shatt al-Arab, where the Turks had also sought to enforce their suzerainty.) In the middle of the 19th century the Shatt al-Arab was only of minor importance to Iran as a trade channel, and the second Treaty of Ezerum in any case provided that "Persian vessels have the right to navigate freely without let or hindrance on the Shatt al-Arab from the mouth of the same to the point of contact of the frontiers of the two parties".

Under the 1847 treaty (which also settled certain other territorial issues between Iran and Turkey) the quadripartite boundary commission undertook to continue its work to delimit the entire frontier. However, the boundary line recommended by the commission in 1850 was rejected by both Iran and Turkey and further efforts to draw up a satisfactory border were halted by the Crimean War (1853-56). Several years after the war had ended Britain and Russia drafted separate maps of the Iran-Turkey border revealing a number of discrepancies, and in a joint map (known as the *Carte identique*) produced in 1869 stretches of the border were

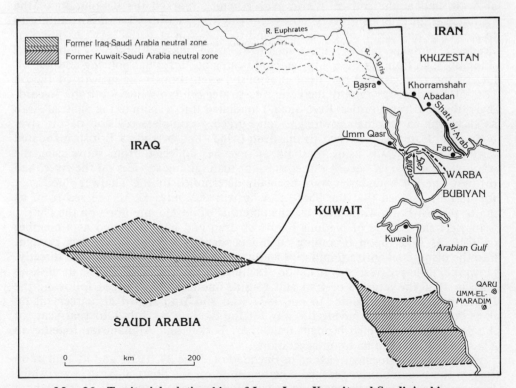

**Map 26   Territorial relationships of Iran, Iraq, Kuwait and Saudi Arabia.**

again left vague. Inhabitants of the southern border region were, however, understood to have reached an informal agreement under which the boundary was regarded as running down the centre of the Shatt al-Arab, with both sides controlling navigation.

### 20th-Century Developments prior to 1975 Agreement

In the early 20th century sovereignty over the Shatt al-Arab became an important issue for Iran with the growth of the port of Mohammerah and the discovery of oil at Masjed Sulaiman in 1908 (the latter necessitating the construction of an oil terminal). Iran was now particularly concerned that vessels carrying oil-drilling equipment and other cargo into new berths at Mohammerah had to anchor in Turkish waters and were obliged to pay Turkish import duties. In this situation Britain and Russia (which in 1907 had made a de facto division of Iran into Russian and British spheres of influence) again put pressure on Iran and Turkey to settle their differences and renewed efforts were made to work out a detailed delimitation of their boundary. In Constantinople on Nov. 17, 1913, a protocol was signed by representatives of the boundary commission which reaffirmed Turkish sovereignty over the Shatt al-Arab and again called for the boundary to be demarcated. In 1914, however, the commission reached a verbal agreement which recognized the changed importance of Mohammerah by moving the boundary opposite the port to the Thalweg line from about a mile below to a mile above the mouth of the Karun river, although the rest of the water remained under Turkish control. (The commission also demarcated the land boundary to the north where Iran, in return for Turkish concessions over the river boundary, ceded larger areas of territory to the Ottoman Government.)

From the late 19th century Britain had exercised effective control of the Shatt al-Arab, and at the end of World War I (which marked the dissolution of the Ottoman empire) British forces, now occupying Iraq, set up a Basra port authority to supervise navigation of the estuary and to maintain essential services (lighting, dredging, buoying, pilotage, etc.), such work being financed largely by commercial shipping. The Iranians were thus unable to carry out informal policing and patrolling of the river as they had done previously, even though the growth of the oil port of Abadan was rapidly increasing its strategic importance for Iran. Accordingly, the new Iranian ruler, Reza Shah, repudiated Iraq's claim to the Shatt al-Arab as successor to Ottoman sovereignty and urged a complete revision of the river boundary. Iran also protested (i) that Iraq (which had become a British mandated territory in 1920) was using the bulk of revenues collected from ships using the waterway for its own benefit rather than for maintaining services on the river, and (ii) that riverine boundaries were normally determined by the Thalweg line. Iraq, for its part, argued that the Shatt al-Arab was the only exit to the sea from its major port of Basra while Iran had the potential of developing ports on the Gulf.

In 1934 the League of Nations (of which Iraq had been accepted as a member on Oct. 3, 1932, upon becoming an independent, sovereign state) was brought into the dispute on an Iraqi initiative and urged Iran and Iraq to negotiate directly. However, little progress was made on reaching an agreement on the Shatt al-Arab until in 1936 the attitude of Iran and Iraq to one another changed following the Italian attack on Abyssinia. In mid-1937 Iran and Iraq signed an agreement on their border problems, paving the way for the signing, on July 8 of that year, of the Saadabad Pact which brought Iran, Iraq, Turkey and Afghanistan together in a treaty of friendship and non-aggression.

In the border agreement (signed in Baghdad on June 29, 1937, and in Tehran on July 5) the two countries reached a compromise on the Shatt al-Arab, over which Iran had become more amenable in view of its development of a new port (Bandar

Shahpur) on the Gulf. The agreement reaffirmed the boundary established by the four-party commission in 1913-14 but also applied the "Mohammerah principle" to Abadan, the border thus following the Thalweg line for some four miles (6.4 km) in the immediate vicinity of and downstream from the port. The treaty also provided for both countries to reach an agreement on matters concerning navigation, pilotage and collection of dues in the river, and furthermore laid down that ships using the river should fly the Iraqi flag except in the vicinity of Mohammerah and Abadan.

In the late 1950s improved technology enabled Iran to develop oil fields in the Gulf (a large oil terminal being built at Kharg island some 30 miles from the mainland), with the result that Iran became less dependent on Abadan (which had the disadvantage of having a shallow approach channel under Iraqi control). Nevertheless, Iran's other imports and exports still depended on Mohammerah and the Shatt al-Arab thus remained vital to Iran. In the mid-1960s the Shah of Iran (Mohammed Reza) reiterated his father's earlier accusations that ships using Iranian ports in the Shatt al-Arab contributed the preponderant part of revenues from the waterway, but that Iraq used none of these funds to benefit the river's facilities and moreover did not give a share to Iran as had been stipulated under the 1937 agreement. On April 19, 1969, Iran declared (i) that it no longer considered the 1937 treaty valid and (ii) that Iranian vessels would henceforth neither pay Iraqi tolls nor fly the Iraqi flag in the waterway. Iran alleged at the same time that the provisions of the 1937 treaty had been formulated to benefit British naval vessels using the Shatt al-Arab at that time, although this was no longer relevant, and again pointed out that international river boundaries normally followed the Thalweg line.

Iraq responded to Iran's abrogation of the 1937 treaty by declaring that the Shatt al-Arab was Iraqi territory and by threatening to take action against any Iranian vessels contravening the terms of the treaty. Despite these warnings no action was taken against an Iranian flagship which on April 22, 1969, sailed down the Shatt al-Arab to the Gulf with Iranian pilots and an Iranian escort and refused to pay dues to the Iraqi authorities. Iranian ships taking similar action were similarly unmolested, although in an apparent act of retaliation several thousand Iranians resident in Iraq were forcibly expelled.

### 1975 Reconciliation and Border Agreement

Strained relations between Iran and Iraq following Iran's abrogation of the 1937 treaty were exacerbated by (i) Iran's support for Kurdish rebels fighting against the Iraqi regime, and (ii) Iran's occupation in 1971 of three disputed islands in the Strait of Hormuz (Abu Musa and the Greater and Lesser Tunbs[1]), over which Iraq broke off diplomatic relations with Iran until 1973. Moreover, in the early 1970s there was a series of border incidents between the two countries. At a meeting of the UN Security Council in February 1974 both the Iranian and Iraqi Governments expressed their desire to settle their border dispute peacefully and through direct negotiations, although the main obstacle to a speedy resolution of the problem remained Iran's objections to the provisions of the 1937 agreement and Iraq's insistence that Iran fulfil its obligations.

The failure of Iran and Iraq to resolve their dispute through direct talks was of concern to other oil-exporting countries, certain of whom attempted to mediate. Eventually, in the course of a conference of the heads of state of members of the Organization of Petroleum Exporting Countries (OPEC) held in Algiers on March 4-6, 1975, Iran and Iraq, on the initiative of the Algerian President, reached an agree-

---

[1] For the dispute between Iran and the United Arab Emirates over these islands, see pages 219-22.

ment which they claimed "completely eliminated the conflict between the two brotherly countries". In a joint communiqué issued on the final day of the OPEC meeting Iran and Iraq agreed inter alia (i) to demarcate their land boundaries on the basis of the Protocol of Constantinople of 1913 and the detailed records (*procès-verbaux*) of the boundary commission of 1914 and (ii) to delimit the river frontier according to the Thalweg line. In return for Iraqi concessions on the Shatt al-Arab Iran ceased its support for Iraq's Kurdish guerrillas (whose rebellion collapsed).

During a meeting of their Foreign Ministers in Tehran on March 15-17, 1975, Iran and Iraq signed a protocol providing for the establishment of committees to (i) demarcate their land boundary; (ii) delimit the river boundary and (iii) prevent any violations of the border. Under a subsequent *procès-verbal* of May 20 the two sides agreed to draw up a final treaty on the boundary, and on June 13 the Governments of Iran and Iraq accordingly signed in Baghdad a Treaty Relating to the State Boundary and Good Neighbourliness. Under three protocols to this agreement the two sides (i) established that the border between the two countries in the disputed Shatt al-Arab waterway should be drawn according to the Thalweg line principle; (ii) delineated some 670 positions on the land border between the two countries on the basis of the Protocol of Constantinople of 1913; and (iii) provided for the establishment of border security arrangements to prevent the infiltration of undesirable elements in either direction.

With regard to the river frontier the relevant protocol provided for the boundary line to follow the Thalweg in the event of a "shift in the bed of the Shatt al-Arab or its mouth caused by natural phenomena" and also stipulated that a survey of the river was to be conducted jointly at least every 10 years.

### Iraqi Abrogation of 1975 Agreement and Outbreak of Iran-Iraq War in 1980

The Shia Moslem revolution in Iran of early 1979 led to a sharp deterioration in Iranian-Iraqi relations, as reflected in a number of border incidents and exchanges of hostile statements between the two states. On Sept. 17, 1980, President Sadam Hussein (who had become Iraqi head of state in mid-1979) unilaterally abrogated the agreement with Iran of June 1975 and thereupon claimed that Iraq's sovereignty over the Shatt al-Arab had been restored. On Sept. 21 Iraq launched a large-scale offensive against Iran and rapidly gained control of part of the province of Khuzestan on the eastern side of the Shatt al-Arab, capturing the town of Khorramshahr (formerly Mohammerah) and encircling Abadan. Oil installations in both countries suffered serious damage and ships in the Shatt al-Arab were blocked by the ferocity of the fighting.

Three days after the outbreak of the war Iraq (on Sept. 24) set conditions for a ceasefire, namely that Iran should (i) recognize Iraq's sovereignty over the border area; (ii) respect and recognize Iraq's sovereignty and "legitimate rights" in the Shatt al-Arab; and (iii) return to Arab ownership the three islands which it had occupied in the Strait of Hormuz. As the Iranian Government refused to fulfil these conditions fighting persisted and various Iraqi officials made certain other territorial demands, claiming in particular that Iraq had a "historic" and "nationalist" right to the Iranian province of Khuzestan (referred to as Arabistan by Iraq). This province, with vast oil reserves, was inhabited by some 2,000,000 Arabs who had already agitated for concessions from the new Islamic regime in Iran (and also previously from the Shah) and whom Iraq now promised to help form an independent state in Khuzestan if they so wished. In the face of Iran's total rejection of Iraq's demands, the latter country threatened to occupy more Iranian territory and also to forge closer ties with Iran's other minority groups, largely occupying border areas of the country.

Mediation efforts were undertaken by the United Nations, the Islamic Conference Organization and the non-aligned movement, but both Iran and Iraq remained
intractable, the latter insisting on Iranian territorial concessions and the former
refusing to accept a settlement outside the 1975 agreement. With regard to this
latter agreement, Iraq maintained that Iran had invalidated it by violating at least
two of its terms by (i) refusing to restore to Iraq the areas of Zein el-Kaous and
Seif-Saad (comprising some 400 square miles or 1,000 sq km) near Qasr-e-Shirin,
which had allegedly been "usurped" some 10 years earlier but which Iran claimed
it had returned in accordance with the agreement; and (ii) permitting a Kurdish
leader to return to Iran for the presumed purpose of rekindling the Kurdish rebellion.

The Iran-Iraq war continued sporadically throughout 1981, with the military
position changing little from that reached in the early stages of the fighting. Although
Iranian forces succeeded in September 1981 in lifting the Iraqi siege of Abadan, a
situation of military stalemate appeared to have been reached by early 1982, with
Iraq still in control of substantial stretches of the eastern bank of the Shatt al-Arab
waterway and also pockets of Iranian territory further north. However, from mid-
March 1982 the situation changed dramatically when the Iranians launched a major
counter-offensive in the southern war zone, driving the Iraqi forces back to the
border by mid-May and recapturing Khorramshahr on May 24. With its forces
having thus achieved what appeared to be a decisive military victory, the Iranian
Government stressed that it had no territorial ambitions against Iraq but insisted
that the latter should pay war reparations to Iran and that the Sadam Hussein
Government should be removed from power.

G.G.

# Iran-United Arab Emirates

A dispute has existed since the early 1970s between Iran and the United
Arab Emirates over the islands of Abu Musa, Greater Tunb and Lesser
Tunb, which are strategically situated at the entrance to the Persian (or
Arab) Gulf, opposite the Strait of Hormuz. The Tunb Islands are respectively known to the Arabs as Tunb as-Sughra and Tunb al-Kubra, and to
the Iranians as Tanb-e Bozorg and Bani Tanb. (For position of the three
islands, see map on page 214.)

On Nov. 30, 1971—two days before the proclamation of the United Arab Emirates
(UAE) as a new state, consisting of the Emirates of Abu Dhabi, Dubai, Sharjah,
Ras al-Khaimah, Fujairah, Ajman and Umm al-Quwain—Iranian troops occupied
the three islands of Abu Musa, Greater Tunb and Lesser Tunb. Abu Musa was
occupied by Iran under an agreement reached by the Government of Iran and the
Ruler of Sharjah, who had held sovereignty over the island, whereas the other two
islands were occupied by force after an attempt at negotiating their peaceful transfer
from the Ruler of Ras al-Khaimah, under whose jurisdiction they fell, had failed.

The agreement on Abu Musa, announced on Nov. 29, 1971, contained the following provisions: (i) Iranian troops would be stationed on part of Abu Musa, and in
this area the Iranian flag would be flown and Iran would exercise full jurisdiction;
(ii) Sharjah would retain jurisdiction over the rest of the island, including the existing Sharjah police post on it; (iii) both Iran and Sharjah recognized a 12-mile
territorial waters limit around the island, and both agreed to the existing con-

cessionaire—the (US) Buttes Gas and Oil Company—continuing oil exploration both on the island and offshore; (iv) revenues accruing from oil exploration would be shared equally between Iran and Sharjah; (v) Iran would give Sharjah £1,500,000 a year in aid until Sharjah's annual revenue from oil deposits reached £3,000,000; and (vi) Iranian and Sharjah nationals would have equal fishing rights in the island's territorial waters.

Notwithstanding this agreement, the UAE Council of Ministers stated on Dec. 2, 1971, that the UAE "repudiates the principle of the use of force, rejects Iran's recent occupation of a part of the cherished Arab homeland and advocates the need to respect legitimate rights and discuss any differences that may occur among states through internationally agreed methods".

## Conflicting Arab, Iranian and British Views

Iran's action against the three islands was condemned by all Arab states as an act of aggression against Arab territories, and at the request of Algeria, Iraq, Libya and the People's Democratic Republic of Yemen (South Yemen) the United Nations Security Council met on Dec. 9, 1971, to discuss the situation.

The representative of Iraq claimed during the debate that the islands had been "under Arab jurisdiction for centuries", and he rejected as "invalid" three reasons given by Iran for its action—alleged historical rights, filling a presumed "power vacuum" in the area, and finally the strategic value to Iran of the islands. He also criticized Britain for not honouring its obligation to defend the islands although Britain's special treaty relations with the Arab rulers who held sovereignty over the islands had "not terminated at the time of Iran's occupation of the islands". The representative of South Yemen stated that Iran had never "presented any convincing evidence of its claim to the islands" and had refused to negotiate the matter with the UAE but had chosen to use force.

On the other hand, the representative of Iran, invited to take part in the debate, declared that the Iranian title to the islands was long-standing and substantial, that both maps, hundreds of years old and modern, and a highly authoritative encyclopaedia treated the territories as belonging to Iran; that in line with its policy of settling disputes by peaceful means Iran had tried to settle the problem through negotiation; but that these efforts had failed and Iran had been left with no alternative but to exercise its sovereign right.

The British representative explained that his Government was satisfied with the agreement reached on Abu Musa between the Ruler of Sharjah and Iran, and that it had declared that it could not protect the Tunb Islands if agreement on their future was not reached before Britain's withdrawal from them (by Dec. 1, 1971). The UN Security Council subsequently decided to defer consideration of the question "in order to allow sufficient time for third-party efforts to work".

Iran's intention to occupy the islands had been stated by the Shah of Iran, who had been reported on Feb. 16, 1971, to have stressed that he would act "by force if necessary" if no peaceful agreements for the islands' transfer was reached before Britain's withdrawal from the Gulf before the end of 1971. The intention was subsequently reaffirmed by Iranian ministers, and on Nov. 10, 1971, Abbas Khalatbari, then Iran's Foreign Minister, was quoted as saying that Iran's sovereignty over the islands was "not negotiable" and that Iran had rejected Arab suggestions that they should be leased to Iran when Britain left the area.

Arguments used by Iran were (i) that the islands had been owned by Iran before they were occupied by Britain 150 years earlier "on the assumption that they were essential to combat piracy" in the Gulf; (ii) that Britain had "in pursuit of its imperial interests" considered the islands as belonging to the Arab Shaikhs of the Trucial States and had transferred them to the de facto administration of Sharjah and Ras al-Khaimah when Iran was "politically weak"; and (iii) that the islands had been shown in Iranian colours on a map which had been issued by the British Intelligence Section of the Ministry of Defence in 1886 and a copy of which had been presented to the Shah in 1888.

In the British view, however, Iran had no title to the islands which, Britain argued, had reverted to the administration of the Trucial coast of Qawasim by the early part of the second half of the 19th century, and the Rulers of Sharjah and Ras al-Khaimah had disclosed documentary evidence based on official British records, supporting their respective "prescriptive title" to the islands since 1872. On instructions from the Ruler of Sharjah on the question of Abu Musa, a firm of British counsels completed (in July 1971) a report based on the examination of "thousands of documents and hundreds of maps and charts" and concluding that Abu Musa had "from the earliest recorded date belonged to the Rulers of Sharjah". The report rebutted in particular the British map of 1886 [see above], stating that the colouring showing Abu Musa as Iranian was "in error" and had not had the consent of the Trucial Rulers.

The Iranian landing on Abu Musa was also criticized by the Arab League, which questioned the validity of the agreement between Iran and Sharjah on the grounds that the latter's Ruler had signed it under duress, i.e. under Iranian pressure and threat to take over the island by force if no solution satisfactory to Iran was reached. In this context it should be noted that Article 52 of the Convention on the Law of Treaties of May 23, 1969, states: "A treaty is void if its conclusion has been produced by the threat of use of force in violation of the principles of international law embodied in the Charter of the United Nations." It is, however, also important to note that the agreement had been concluded with the British Foreign Secretary acting as the channel of communication between Iran and Sharjah.

The Government of Iraq broke off its diplomatic relations with Iran and with Britain on Nov. 30, 1971 (i.e. after Iran's occupation of the islands), and described Iran's action as a "flagrant aggression in collusion with Britain", Iran also warned Britain that it had "the obligation to preserve the Arab character of the islands". The Arab League, in reports published on Dec. 2, 1971, similarly declared that Britain's failure to act was contrary to its treaty obligations towards the Trucial Rulers. The British Foreign Office, however, argued that it was impossible to stop the Iranian action just one day before the treaty relations were terminated on Dec. 1, 1971—an attitude which was criticized as "hypocrisy" in *The Times* on Dec. 2 on the grounds that a treaty was "as valid on the last day as on the first".

## Reaffirmation of Arab Claim to the Islands by Iraq

The question of sovereignty over the islands was again raised on Oct. 31, 1979, when the Iraqi ambassador in Beirut (Lebanon) issued a declaration containing far-reaching political demands to be fulfilled by the Government of the Islamic Republic of Iran—among them a demand for the evacuation of the three islands by Iran. All these demands were, however, rejected by Iran on Nov. 1 of that year.

On April 6, 1980, the Iraqi Foreign Minister was reported to have called, in a message to the UN Secretary-General, for the immediate withdrawal of Iranian troops from the islands and to have accused Iran of pursuing "an aggressive and expansionist policy in the Gulf region". The Iranian Foreign Minister, however, stated on the same day that Iran's differences with Iraq went beyond the disputed islands and that the Iraqi Government was "under the control of Zionists and imperialists" while "pretending that it wants to preserve Arab interests in the region". Following the outbreak of full-scale war between Iraq and Iran, the Iraqi Government on Sept. 24, 1980, reiterated its call for the return to Arab sovereignty of the three Gulf islands.

The UAE Government, in a message to the United Nations reported on Dec. 11, 1980, stated that while it desired to maintain good-neighbourly relations and co-operation to maintain security and stability in the Gulf area, it insisted on the restoration of its full sovereignty over the three islands and declared that it was ready to negotiate with the Iranian Government to reach a solution which would fully recognize the UAE's sovereignty over the islands in accordance with the UN Charter and principles. At the same time the UAE's representative at the United Nations asked for the distribution of this message as an official document of the UN General Assembly.

In a statement published on March 28, 1982, Shaikh Saqr bin Muhammed Al-Qasimi, the ruler of Ras al-Khaimah and a member of the UAE Supreme Council, said that his country would not compromise or change its position on the issue of the three islands, adding: "The three islands are an Arab right about which there can be no discussion. Iran's rulers know this better than others; however, no contact on this issue has been made between them and us."

**H.W.D.**

# Iraq-Kuwait

On June 25, 1961—just six days after Kuwait had gained independence—the Iraqi Prime Minister, Gen. Kassem, laid claim to all of Kuwait, arguing that the latter had been an "integral part" of Basra province under Ottoman rule and that Iraq had succeeded to Turkish territorial sovereignty over Basra with the dissolution of the Ottoman empire after World War I. Gen. Kassem was unsuccessful in winning international recognition for the validity of his claim to Kuwait (one of the world's leading petroleum producers) and in 1963, after his overthrow and the accession of President Aref, Iraq relinquished its claim and recognized Kuwait as a sovereign state. However, the otherwise good relations between these neighbouring countries over the following 10 years were marred by a long-standing dispute centring principally on Iraq's interest in two islands owned by Kuwait, namely Warba and Bubiyan. Iraqi possession of these islands, situated just south of the Iraq-Kuwait border in the north-east Arabian (Persian) Gulf, would give that country greatly improved access to the Gulf. In 1973 Iraqi troops moved towards this part of the frontier and occupied a border post, from which they were, however, rapidly forced to withdraw in the face of general Arab opposition. Iraq and Kuwait then began a series of negotiations—at times with external mediation—with a view to settling the border question but, despite frequently optimistic reports, agreement on the demarcation of their common border had not been reached by the end of 1981, the Iraqi Government having in mid-1981 revived its claim to Warba and Bubiyan. (For map showing the disputed islands, see page 215.)

### Historical Background

In the 19th century Kuwait had been administered as part of the Ottoman province of Basra, although the Turks had never occupied or gained full sovereignty over it. In 1896 Shaikh Mubarak the Great seized power in Kuwait after murdering his pro-Turkish half brother, Shaikh Mohammed, and asserted Kuwait's independence from the Ottoman empire, saying that his people owed no allegiance to the Turks. To this end Shaikh Mubarak sought protection from Britain and in 1899, without the authority of the Ottoman Sultan, an agreement was signed under which Britain undertook to give Kuwait protection in return for control over its foreign affairs. Under an Anglo-Turkish convention of July 29, 1913, Britain secured Turkish recognition of Kuwait's autonomy within an area formed by a 40-mile (64-km) radius around the town of Kuwait—but the outbreak of World War I in 1914 prevented ratification of this agreement. On Nov. 3, 1914, Shaikh Mubarak was promised British recognition as an "independent government under British protection" in return for his co-operation in the liberation of Basra from Ottoman rule. Kuwait retained this status until June 19, 1961, when an exchange of notes was signed between Britain and Kuwait which terminated the 1899 agreement between the two countries and provided for British recognition of Kuwait as a sovereign and independent state (although a military assistance agreement remained in force).

Iraq had formerly comprised the three Mesopotamian provinces (*vilayet*) of Baghdad, Mosul and Basra and was administered by the Ottoman empire through appointed governors (pashas) answerable to the Sultan-Caliph in Constantinople. After the dissolution of the Ottoman empire in 1918 it was agreed that Mesopotamia should form a self-governing state and on Oct. 20, 1920, Britain accepted a League of Nations mandate for Iraq until it was ready for independence. Under the Treaty of Lausanne of July 24, 1923, Turkey renounced all the territory it had previously possessed outside the borders of present-day Turkey, this renunciation applying also to Kuwait as a part of the former Ottoman province of Basra. After Britain had on Jan. 28, 1932, given up its mandate over Iraq, on Oct. 3 of that year Iraq became an independent sovereign state and was admitted to the League of Nations.

The border between Iraq and Kuwait had first been defined in an exchange of letters, dated April 4 and April 19, 1923, between Shaikh Ahmad al Sabah of Kuwait and Maj.-Gen. Sir Percy Cox, then British high commissioner for Iraq. In a subsequent exchange of letters, dated July 21 and Aug. 10, 1932, Shaikh Ahmad and the then Iraqi Prime Minister, Nuri al Said, reaffirmed the "existing frontier between Iraq and Kuwait" on the basis of the 1923 letters as follows: "From the intersection of the Wadi al-Audja with the Batin and thence northwards along the Batin to a point just south of the latitude of Safwan; thence eastwards passing south of Safwan Wells, Jebel Sanam and Umm Qasr leaving them to Iraq and so on to the junction of the Khor Zobeir with the Khor Abdulla. The islands of Warba, Bubiyan, Maskan (or Mashjan), Failakah, Auhah, Kubbạr, Qaru and Umm el-Maradim appertain to Kuwait." However, this early border demarcation was later regarded as invalid by Iraq on the grounds that Iraq had not been an independent state on the date of Nuri al Said's letter of July 21, 1932.

## The Iraqi Claim to Kuwait

On June 25, 1961, Gen. Kassem made a claim of Iraqi sovereignty over Kuwait, which he described as an "integral part of Iraq". Gen. Kassem's claim was based on the Iraqi argument that (i) Kuwait had been part of Basra province in the Ottoman empire, and (ii) that Britain and other powers had recognized Ottoman sovereignty over Kuwait both before and after the signature of the 1899 agreement under which Kuwait became a British protectorate. In addition, Gen. Kassem said that he had issued a decree appointing the Shaikh of Kuwait as *Qaim Maqaam* (prefect) of Kuwait.

Elaborating on Gen. Kassem's assertions, the Iraqi Foreign Ministry in a statement issued on June 26, 1961, said that it recognized neither the "secret agreement" of 1899, as it had been concluded without the authority of the Ottoman Sultan, nor the agreement of 1961, as it aimed "under the new cloak of national independence . . . to maintain imperialist influence and to keep Kuwait separate from Iraq". The statement added that formerly the Ottoman Sultan had appointed the Shaikh of Kuwait "by a decree conferring on him the title of *Qaim Maqaam* and making him representative of the Governor of Basra in Kuwait", and that the Shaikhs of Kuwait had thus "continued to derive their administrative powers from the Ottoman Sultan until 1914".

Kuwait rejected the Iraqi arguments, asserting that it had never been subjected to Turkish sovereignty, that Kuwait had been governed "without direct Turkish interference" by the same al Sabah dynasty since 1756 and that the title of *Qaim Maqaam* was never used in Kuwait and "never influenced the course of life or the independence of Kuwait from the Turkish empire". (It should be noted in this context, however, that historians of the area have generally taken the view that Shaikh Mubarak—in 1896—was the first Kuwaiti leader to refuse this title.)

In response to a Kuwaiti request for military assistance, prompted by rumours that Iraq was moving troops southwards in the Basra area (which Iraq denied), forces from Britain and also Saudi Arabia arrived in Kuwait by early July 1961, and Kuwait's own forces were mobilized. Efforts by the UN Security Council in early July to defuse the crisis were unsuccessful and mediation was taken over by the Arab League (which on July 20 admitted Kuwait as a member despite Iraqi opposition). On Aug. 12 the Arab League countries, Iraq alone dissenting, signed an agreement with Kuwait under which British forces were to be replaced by a force from the League itself and under which they also pledged (i) to preserve Kuwait's integrity and independence under her present regime; (ii) to regard any aggression against the shaikhdom as aggression against the League's members; and (iii) in the event of any such aggression, to render Kuwait immediate assistance and, if necessary, repel it with armed force. Notwithstanding this agreement Iraq reiterated its claim to Kuwait and withdrew its representatives from all countries which had recognized that country.

## Developments following Iraqi Recognition of Kuwait in 1963

The overthrow of Gen. Kassem on Feb. 3, 1963, led to an easing of the friction between Iraq and Kuwait. Under President Aref, the new Iraqi regime on Oct. 4, 1963 (in the course of a visit to Baghdad by an invited Kuwaiti delegation), entered into an agreement with Kuwait under which Iraq inter alia "recognized the independence and complete sovereignty of the state of Kuwait with its boundaries as specified in the letter of the Prime Minister of Iraq dated 21.7.1932 and which was accepted by the ruler of Kuwait in his letter dated 10.8.1932". In addition, the two countries agreed to work towards improving relations and establishing co-operation at all levels and to this end decided to establish immediately diplomatic relations at ambassadorial level.

Nevertheless, it became apparent that Iraqi recognition of Kuwait did not involve acceptance of the latter's frontiers, and in succeeding years longstanding Iraqi claims to certain parts of Kuwait's border territory were revived. Iraq's interest lay particularly in improving its access to the Gulf through the acquisition of the islands of Warba and Bubiyan, the importance of which had increased considerably in view of Iraq's development of the north Rumaila oilfield and the expansion of its port of Umm Qasr. In March 1973, with a view to forcing the issue, Iraqi forces occupied a border post in the disputed area but were forced to withdraw when Iraq was confronted with Arab disapproval of its action. Subsequently, talks between Iraq and Kuwait on the border issue were stepped up, with other Arab countries offering their assistance in mediation, and in May 1975 Iraqi officials announced that they had made concrete proposals to settle the dispute. These involved essentially the leasing by Kuwait to Iraq of half of Bubiyan for 99 years and the ceding of Kuwaiti sovereignty over Warba in return for Iraqi recognition of Kuwait's land borders. The following month Saudi Arabian sources, quoting Kuwaiti news reports, said that the two countries had finally established the basis for an agreement on the territorial issues in dispute.

However, on July 12, 1975, negotiations reached an impasse when the Kuwaiti National Assembly, while expressing support for the efforts latterly made to come to an agreement with Iraq, stressed "Kuwait's sovereignty over all its territory within the borders which have been approved in accordance with international and bilateral agreements between Kuwait and its neighbours". On Dec. 13, 1976, Kuwait's acting Minister of Information, Shaikh Jabir al-Ali, stressed that Warba and Bubiyan belonged to Kuwait as defined in the 1932 exchange of letters and the 1963 agreement between Iraq and Kuwait; he also complained that in addition to the "previous Iraqi military presence in Kuwait territory" south of the Umm Qasr area there were now "regular crossings by Iraqi forces all along the border between the two countries at varying depths".

Talks on the delimitation of the Iraq-Kuwait border made little progress over the following years, despite the formation in 1978 of a joint committee headed by the Interior Ministers of the two countries to work towards resolving outstanding issues. The outbreak of war between Iraq and Iran in September 1980 led to a revival of the Iraqi claim to Warba and Bubiyan in July 1981, when President Hussein of Iraq repeated the Iraqi proposals of 1975 and in particular the demand that Kuwait should grant Iraq a 99-year lease of half of Bubiyan. However, the Kuwait Government continued to assert its sovereignty over both islands, and in December 1981 a Kuwaiti spokesman said that no agreed date existed for a resumption of talks between the two sides.

G.G.

# Iraq-Saudi Arabia

Following the collapse of Ottoman power in Arabia during World War I, the emergence of what were to become the independent states of Iraq and Saudi Arabia was accompanied by bitter territorial rivalry between the two centres of power, exacerbated by the general absence of defined borders in the vast desert territories of the region. Under the aegis of Britain as the dominant post-Ottoman external power, the boundary between present-day Iraq and Saudi Arabia was first defined under agreements signed in 1922, which also created a neutral zone in the contentious eastern border area between the two sides. Although the status quo established by the 1922 agreements prevailed over the next 60 years, the question of the delimitation of the neutral zone remained a potential source of dispute between the two states, especially after the 1958 revolution in Iraq and that country's gravitation to the radical Arab camp opposed to the conservative line of the Saudi leadership. However, the new constellation of interests created by the 1979 revolution in Iran and the outbreak of the Iran-Iraq war the following year led Iraq and Saudi Arabia to sign an agreement in December 1981 defining their common border and also providing for the division of the neutral zone between the two countries. (For map showing the Iraq-Saudi neutral zone, see page 215.)

## Historical Background

By the early 19th century much of Arabia was under the control of the powerful Wahhabi army associated with the al-Saud family (ancestors of the present-day ruling family in Saudi Arabia), which had risen to power in the sultanate of Najd centred on Riyadh in central Arabia. Following a period of suppression by Ottoman forces in 1811-18 the Wahhabi movement enjoyed a revival in the 1820s but suffered a further decline in the latter part of the 19th century coincidentally with the rising power of the al-Rashid family of Hail in the Jabal Shammar area of northern Najd. In 1891 the al-Rashids inflicted a crushing defeat on the rival al-Sauds, occupying Riyadh and forcing the head of the al-Saud family, Abd ar-Rahman, to flee to Kuwait with his young son, Abd al-Aziz (Ibn Saud). By 1902 Ibn Saud had recaptured Riyadh and prior to the outbreak of World War I he had consolidated his authority in Najd and Hasa further south. Under the 1915 Treaty of Qatif, moreover, Britain recognized the independence and territorial integrity of Najd and acknowledged Ibn Saud as ruler of both Najd and Hasa, granting him a monthly subsidy.

After World War I territorial problems and tribal rivalries re-emerged and Ibn Saud sought to take control of Hail, in particular since Faisal, the son of the King of Hejaz (Sharif Hussain), had become King of Iraq. In 1921-22 Ibn Saud, his tribesmen now organized in Akhwan brotherhoods, defeated the al-Rashids in Jabal Shammar and spread his sphere of control up to the borders of Transjordan and Iraq, surrounding the kingdom of Hejaz, where the al-Hashimi tribe had latterly become serious rivals to the al-Sauds. Ibn Saud now posed a threat not only to Hejaz but also to Iraq (for which country Britain had accepted a mandate in 1920) and also Kuwait, a British protectorate.

British interest in eliminating the potential for conflict in Arabia gave rise to the signing of the Treaty of Mohammerah (Khorramshahr) on May 5, 1922, between Ibn Saud and the British high commissioner for Iraq, Maj.-Gen. Sir Percy Cox.

This treaty did not define a boundary between Iraq and Najd (Ibn Saud having objected to the "attempt to curb, by an imaginary line in the open desert, the movement of tribes who are accustomed to roam widely in search of pasturage and water"), but agreement was reached on the assignment of the Muntafiq, Dhafir and Amarat tribes to Iraq and the Shammar Najd tribe to Najd. Both sides undertook to prevent mutual aggression by the tribes, whose traditional wells and lands were allocated relative to the respective host government. It was further agreed that in order to "determine the location of these lands and wells and to fix a boundary line in accordance with this principle, a committee shall be formed of two persons with local knowledge from each government and presided over by a British official selected by the high commissioner".

Later in 1922 Ibn Saud finally agreed to the delimitation of the border between Najd and Iraq on condition that wells and watering places near the frontier would not be used for military purposes and that Najd tribes would not be refused access to watering places on the Iraqi side of the border. The agreement between Ibn Saud and King Faisal was incorporated into two protocols to the Uqair Convention of Dec. 2, 1922, which in addition to defining the boundary also established a neutral zone in which Iraq and Najd would enjoy equal rights. This diamond-shaped zone began at the extremity of Kuwait's western frontier at the junction of the Wadi al-Audja and the Wadi al-Batin, its northern border with Iraq running for some 119 miles (190 km) and its southern border with Saudi Arabia some 125 miles (200 km); at its widest north-south point, the zone measured about 40 miles (65 km) and had a total area of some 2,500 square miles (6,500 sq km).

Article I of the first protocol set out the precise boundaries of the neutral zone, which "will remain neutral and common to the two Governments of Iraq and Najd who will enjoy equal rights to it for all purposes". Article II stated: "Whereas many of the wells fall within the Iraq boundaries and the Najd side is deprived of them the Iraq Government pledges itself not to interfere with those Najd tribes living in the vicinity of the border should it be necessary for them to resort to the neighbouring Iraq wells for water, provided that these wells are nearer to them than those within the Najd boundaries." Article III stated: "The two Governments mutually agree not to use the watering places and wells situated in the vicinity of the border for any military purpose, such as building forts on them, and not to concentrate troops in their vicinity." Moreover, under the second protocol both sides agreed that if "any tribe or section of a tribe which is outside the boundaries of, and not subject to either government, desires its allegiance to one of them, they will not prevent it from doing so".

### Further Agreements between Ibn Saud and King Faisal

The conclusion of the agreements of 1922 did not put an end to the deep-seated rivalry between Ibn Saud and King Faisal or to tribal conflicts. In 1924-25 Ibn Saud succeeded in annexing Hejaz, which had previously been ruled by King Faisal's father, Sharif Hussain, while Najd's expansionist policies also threatened Transjordan, ruled by Faisal's brother, Abdullah. On Jan. 8, 1926, Ibn Saud was proclaimed King of Hejaz—Soviet recognition of his new position being accorded a month later and that of Britain on May 20, 1927, under the Treaty of Jeddah.

Following their conquest of Hejaz the Akhwan forces made a series of raids on Iraqi tribes inside Iraqi territory and also during their customary migration into Kuwait and Najd, and Iraq's use of aircraft to ward off such attacks was strongly opposed by Ibn Saud. However, in 1929 the latter was himself threatened by rebellious Najd tribes, with the result that he took steps to reach an understanding with King Faisal. In February 1930 the two leaders met on board a ship at the mouth of the Shatt al-Arab waterway and as a result of their discussions a Treaty of Friendship and Good Neighbourliness was signed the following year. Under this treaty both parties undertook to take steps to prevent tribal raiding and agreed at the same time that tribes of either country were to be permitted free movement within the territory of the other for pasturage or for purchasing provisions; a permanent frontier committee was established to oversee these matters.

There were no further serious incidents of raiding after the 1931 treaty and generally friendly relations prevailed between the two powers, assisted by the growth of the oil industry in both countries and consequent economic advances and by the gradual extension of administrative control throughout their respective territories. In 1932 the dual kingdom of Hejaz and Najd became the kingdom of Saudi Arabia and in the same year Iraq was admitted to the League of Nations as an independent state. Four years later the two countries concluded a Treaty of Arab Brotherhood and Alliance.

## Recent Developments leading to 1981 Border Agreement

An agreement concerning the administration of the neutral zone was signed between Iraq and Saudi Arabia in May 1938 but there were no further important developments relating to the zone for many years. In July 1975 it was reported in Saudi Arabia that the two countries had agreed to divide the zone equally by a line drawn as straight as possible which would necessitate modifying the existing border, but the agreement apparently remained unratified. However, the potential threat to the stability of the Gulf area posed by the Shia Moslem revolution in Iran in 1979 and the outbreak of war between Iran and Iraq in September 1980 impelled Saudi Arabia and Iraq to seek closer relations and in particular to achieve a definitive settlement of their common border and the neutral zone question.

Talks on these matters reached a positive outcome on Dec. 26, 1981, when the Saudi Interior Minister, Prince Nayef ibn Abdul Aziz, signed an agreement in Baghdad with his Iraqi counterpart, Sa'adoun Shaker, which the former subsequently described as a treaty ("because the previous agreement was the Mohammerah Treaty with the Uqair protocols"). According to Prince Nayef, the new agreement "defined and fixed" the border between Iraq and Saudi Arabia and also provided for the "division of the neutral zone", with the result that the frontier between the two states had been "stabilized".

G.G.

# Kuwait-Saudi Arabia

The Uqair Convention, signed on Dec. 2, 1922, between Kuwait, then a British protectorate, and the sultanate of Najd (which together with the kingdom of Hejaz formed the kingdom of Saudi Arabia in 1932), defined and delimited the boundary between the two powers and provided for the establishment of a neutral coastal zone immediately to the south of Kuwait over which both sides would have joint sovereignty pending a final settlement. Although in the 1960s Kuwait and Saudi Arabia reached agreement on the partitioning of the zone (and a new international land boundary came into effect), the area's huge oil reserves constitute a possible source of future territorial dispute between the two countries. Moreover, the agreements signed in the 1960s apply only to the land boundaries of the zone: difficulties still exist relating to offshore boundaries and also to the sovereignty of the Gulf islands of Qaru and Umm el-Maradim. (For map showing territorial relationship of Kuwait and Saudi Arabia, see page 215.)

The neutral zone consisted of some 2,500 square miles (6,500 sq km) of desert with a coastline about 40 miles (64 km) long on the Persian (Arabian) Gulf. Little interest was shown in reaching a final agreement on the area until the discovery of oil in southern Kuwait in the late 1930s. The changed importance of the zone and the consequent influx of workers and oil company personnel increased the problems involved in jointly administering the area; accordingly, following lengthy negotiations, Kuwait and Saudi Arabia agreed in principle in 1960 to divide the territory equally. In 1965 the two countries signed an agreement on the partitioning of the zone, the new international land boundary coming into effect following the exchange of instruments of ratification in 1966 and the signing of a subsequent demarcation accord at the end of 1967. By 1970 Kuwait and Saudi Arabia had, as agreed, completed the allocation of properties and facilities in the zone.

## Historical Background

During the centuries of Ottoman rule over Arabia, the present-day border region of Kuwait and Saudi Arabia was virtually uninhabited desert, although as a historic route for tribes moving northwards to the more fertile areas of the Tigris and Euphrates rivers it was the scene of frequent tribal rivalry. Prominent among the tribes in the 19th century was the Wahhabi movement, which attacked northwards from Najd and which, following a defeat at the hands of Ottoman forces, later revived as the powerful Ikhwan force. In the early 1900s this tribe gave its support to Abd al-Aziz (Ibn Saud) of the al-Saud family in Najd in his long dispute over border territories with Shaikh Salim of Kuwait (who was ruler in 1917-21).

Under an Anglo-Turkish convention of July 1913 Kuwaiti autonomy had been recognized up to a 40-mile (64-km) radius of the town of Kuwait; but this agreement was never ratified, and the final eclipse of Ottoman authority during World War I gave rise to a fluid situation in which Ibn Saud's forces engaged in armed hostilities with Shaikh Salim. Following a particularly serious raid by Ibn Saud on the Kuwaiti oasis area of Jahra in October 1920, Maj.-Gen. Sir Percy Cox, then British high commissioner in Iraq (which became a British mandate in 1920), decided that issues concerning tribal loyalties and rights would have to be resolved before permanent and peaceful boundaries could be established in Arabia.

Upon the death of Shaikh Salim in 1921 and the accession of his nephew,

Shaikh Ahmad (who ruled until 1950), Ibn Saud declared that he had no further dispute with Kuwait and that there was thus no need to determine a boundary. The British nonetheless proceeded with their efforts to define lasting borders in the area and, after lengthy deliberations between the parties concerned, a conference at Al Uqair reached boundary agreements on Dec. 2, 1922, under which neutral zones were established between Kuwait and Najd on the one hand and between Iraq and Najd on the other. (The latter agreement, which incorporated provisions of the earlier Treaty of Mohammerah of May 1922, is dealt with on pages 226-27.)

The Uqair Convention defined the territory of the neutral zone between Najd and Kuwait as follows: "The portion of territory bounded on the north by this line [i.e. the 'indisputable southern frontier of Kuwait'] and which is bounded on the west by a low mountainous ridge called Ash Shaq and on the east by the sea and on the south by a line passing from west to east from Ash Shaq to Ayn al-Abd and thence to the coast north of Ras al Mish'ab—in this territory the Government of Najd and Kuwait will share equal rights until through the good offices of the Government of Great Britain a further agreement is made between Najd and Kuwait concerning it."

Of the two principal parties to the Uqair Convention, Najd subsequently became part of the larger kingdom of Saudi Arabia established by Ibn Saud in 1932, while Kuwait continued as a British protectorate until achieving full independence in 1961.

### Agreement to partition the Neutral Zone

The granting of joint sovereignty to both parties in the neutral zone meant that they were able to exploit any natural resources there on an equal basis. After the discovery of oil in Kuwait's southern Burgan fields in 1938, attention was given to oil exploration in the neutral zone itself and towards the end of the following decade Kuwait and Saudi Arabia granted exploration rights in the territory to two private companies which later exploited the oil under a joint agreement. In 1948 Kuwait signed a contract with the American Oil Company (Aminoil) and the following year Saudi Arabia reached a similar agreement with the Pacific Western Oil Company (later renamed Getty Oil Company), both these agreements applying to the land area of the neutral zone. Moreover, in 1957-58 both Kuwait and Saudi Arabia granted the Japanese Oil Company separate concessions for offshore territories.

In view of the administrative problems caused by the construction of oil installations and the increased number of workers in the zone, Saudi Arabia and Kuwait began discussions in the late 1950s on the legal status of the zone and its offshore area. By the end of 1960 both parties had agreed (i) that the land area of the neutral territory should, in principle, be divided into two geographical parts, one to be annexed by Kuwait and the other by Saudi Arabia and (ii) that each country should form a committee of experts to draft boundary lines for the partitioned zone. Although talks were hampered over the following year in view of Kuwaiti protests that Saudi Arabia was exerting an unfair amount of control over the zone, further deliberations finally led to an exchange of notes between the two countries on Aug. 5, 1963. In this exchange Saudi Arabia and Kuwait reaffirmed their agreement in principle to divide the zone and, on the basis of a Kuwait proposal, decided furthermore that each separate part of the divided zone would be administered by one Government (Kuwait having rejected an earlier suggestion by Saudi Arabia that a system of joint administration be introduced on a condominium basis).

Following the initialling of a further bilateral agreement on March 8, 1964,

Kuwait and Saudi Arabia on July 7, 1965, signed an agreement at al-Hadda (Saudi Arabia) to divide the neutral zone geographically with the proviso that the "equal rights of the two parties shall be preserved in full in the whole partitioned zone as this had originally been decided by the Convention made at Al Uqair . . . and shall be safeguarded by the provisions of international responsibility". Under Article I of the agreement the boundary line between the two sections of the zone was to be "the line which divides them equally into two parts and which begins from a point at the mid-eastern shore on the low-tide line and ends at the western boundary line of the zone"; the part to the north of the dividing line would be annexed to Kuwait and the area lying to the south to Saudi Arabia (Art. II). Both Kuwait and Saudi Arabia would "exercise the rights of administration, legislation and defence" over their own part of the zone "in the same manner exercised in his territory of origin, while observing other provisions of the agreement, and without prejudice to the rights of the contracting parties to natural resources in the whole of the partitioned zone" (Art. III). Saudi Arabia and Kuwait undertook to respect the rights of the other to the "shared natural resources" which exist, or might exist, in its own annexed part (Art. IV).

With regard to territorial waters adjoining both parts of the zone, each country would have the same rights as it had over the land areas of the zone annexed to them, while "for the purpose of exploiting natural resources" in the partitioned zone, it was agreed that "not more than six marine miles shall be annexed to the principal land of that partitioned zone" (Art. VII). The northern boundary of the submerged zone adjoining the partitioned territory would be "delineated as if the zone has not been partitioned and without regard to the provisions of this agreement", and if both sides agreed they would "exercise their equal rights" in this submerged zone beyond the six-mile limit by means of "shared exploitation" (Art. VIII).

The agreement did not alter or affect the existing oil concessions in the zone (Art. IX), and "without prejudice to the concessionary oil agreements" each country guaranteed freedom of work to citizens of the other in its own annexed part "and the right to practice any profession or occupation on equal levels with its citizens, concerning oil resources granted in the present concessions or in what may supersede them in future" (Art. XV). With a view to safeguarding the continued efforts of both parties in exploiting natural resources in the zone it was agreed that a joint permanent committee would be established composed of an equal number of representatives from both sides, among them the two ministers responsible for natural resources (Art. XVII), who would jointly decide on matters concerning the amendment or granting of new oil concessions in the zone (Art. XX).

Instruments of ratification of the July 1965 agreement were exchanged in Jeddah (Saudi Arabia) on July 25, 1966. A demarcation agreement on the dividing line through the zone was signed on Dec. 17, 1967, instruments of ratification being exchanged on Dec. 18, 1969.

Talks between Kuwait and Saudi Arabia in the 1960s on the onshore and offshore boundaries of the neutral zone had also covered the islands of Qaru and Umm el-Maradim, situated respectively some 23 miles (37 km) and 16 miles (26 km) off the coast of the northern part of the zone. On the basis of an exchange of letters between Iraq and Kuwait in 1923 and 1932 both these islands belonged to Kuwait, but Saudi Arabia had contested their sovereignty. In 1961 Kuwait had offered to share with Saudi Arabia any oil proceeds which might accrue from the islands in return for Saudi Arabia's acknowledgement of Kuwait's sovereignty over them. Saudi Arabia declined this offer, however, preferring to delay a decision on the islands until the boundaries of the neutral zone had been settled. At the present time, the islands remain under Kuwaiti control, but Saudi Arabia has never formally abandoned its claim to sovereignty over them.

G.G.

# Other Arabian Peninsula Border Relationships

Saudi Arabia's southern and eastern borders—i.e. with the present states of the Yemen Arab Republic (North Yemen), the People's Democratic Republic of Yemen (South Yemen), Oman, the United Arab Emirates and Qatar—have not been finally determined by definitive agreements, nor have those of certain of the smaller Arabian peninsula states one with another. Generally speaking none of these situations appears to constitute an actual dispute at the present time, and indeed various agreements have been entered into in recent years to resolve outstanding border issues. Nevertheless, some of the relevant territorial relationships should be recorded for the potential which they may contain for future dissension between the states concerned.

### Saudi Arabia and the Yemens

The largely undemarcated border between Saudi Arabia and North Yemen was reported to have been the scene of armed confrontations in early 1980, in which five North Yemeni soldiers were said to have been killed. Western press reports suggested that the clashes were related to the Saudis' construction of a new road in the Boa district and may also have reflected their desire to exert pressure against North Yemen's proposed merger with South Yemen [see below] and gravitation towards closer relations with the Soviet Union.

As regards Saudi Arabia's relations with South Yemen, the former had opposed the latter following its creation in 1967 and had made frequent attempts to disrupt it either by encouraging northern tribes to make raids or by giving refuge and support to South Yemeni exiles opposed to the Marxist regime in Aden. However, although the Saudi-South Yemen border is also undemarcated, no actual territorial claims appear to have been made by either side, and since mid-1980 the two countries have expressed a mutual desire for improved relations.

### Saudi Arabia and the United Arab Emirates

A longstanding dispute between Saudi Arabia and Abu Dhabi (one of the United Arab Emirates) over the oil-rich Buraimi oasis was settled by an agreement signed by the respective heads of state in Jeddah in August 1974. Although no details were published, it was believed that under this agreement Saudi Arabia ceded six of the nine villages of the oasis to the United Arab Emirates in exchange for a triangular strip of land on Abu Dhabi's eastern border and also for a land corridor to the Gulf coast. (Saudi Arabia had ceded the three other Buraimi villages to Oman in 1971.)

### North and South Yemen

Although it appears that the border between these two countries is not fully demarcated, the two sides do not consider their common frontier to be in dispute. During the 1970s border clashes were reported from time to time involving both countries' armed forces as well as North Yemeni rebels backed by South Yemen. However, from March 1979 the two sides initiated serious negotiations with a view to eventual unification; despite Saudi Arabia's opposition to the proposed merger, agreement was reached in late 1981 on the creation of a "Yemen Council" and other joint bodies which were to prepare for the establishment of a unified state to be known as the Yemeni Republic.

### Oman and the United Arab Emirates

A territorial dispute between Oman and the United Arab Emirates surfaced in December 1977 when the former laid claim to a northern portion of Ras al-Khaimah (the most northerly of the seven emirates) where offshore oil deposits had been found. However, it was announced in Abu Dhabi on Sept. 18, 1979, that full agreement had been reached on the border dispute between the two countries and that in the Omani view "all principles and bases pertaining to the ending of all border problems had been adopted within a framework of full understanding in the interest of the area and in the joint interest of the two countries". Subsequently, the UAE Government announced on April 7, 1981, that the two sides had "agreed on specific bases for the redemarcation of the border" between Oman and Ras al-Khaimah; this agreement, said the statement, would "finally resolve the issues which have recently been raised" and would preserve "the historic ties between the two fraternal countries".

### Oman and South Yemen

Relations between Oman and South Yemen have been seriously strained in recent years by the support given by the latter to the military activities of the Popular Front for the Liberation of Oman (PFLO) in the Dhofar region of Oman, to which South Yemen has itself laid claim from time to time. The dispute has been an additional source of strain in relations between South Yemen and Saudi Arabia, the latter having repeatedly pressed the former to cease supporting the PFLO rebels. Efforts by Kuwait to mediate in the Oman-South Yemen dispute collapsed in mid-1980 after the Omani Government had agreed to make military facilities available to the United States.

**H.W.D.**

# 4. ASIA AND THE FAR EAST

## Introduction

Current territorial disputes between Asian countries fall into several different categories, reflecting the huge geographical extent of the region and its considerable political complexities. As detailed in the following section, there exist longstanding geopolitical rivalries between major Asian powers (e.g. between China and the Soviet Union) as well as traditional territorial tensions arising from ethnic factors. There are also disputes which have their origins in the ambiguities of colonial boundary-drawing or in dissatisfaction with territorial arrangements inherited from the colonial powers. Other unresolved issues exist where the post-war advance of communism has resulted in the territorial division of countries and yet others centre on conflicting claims to various islands, mainly in south-east Asian waters, over which sovereignty has not yet been established to universal agreement.

Over the last two decades several longstanding disputes over residual colonial territories in the Asian region have been resolved in one way or another. Thus for example the dispute between Indonesia and the Netherlands over West Irian (Dutch New Guinea), which developed into open military hostilities in early 1962, was settled by an agreement signed in August 1962 under which the territory became part of Indonesia in 1963 and was finally resolved in 1969 when the local Papuan population expressed their wish to remain in Indonesia. Moreover, in 1974 the new Portuguese Government recognized Indian sovereignty over the former enclaves of Goa, Daman, Diu, Dadra and Nagar Haveli, which had been occupied by Indian troops in December 1961 and incorporated into India the following year. On the other hand, neither Portugal nor a majority of the international community has recognized Indonesia's forcible incorporation of Portuguese East Timor into its territory in 1975-76, since when the demand has persistently been made that the people of the territory should have the right to self-determination.

Mention should be made of the two remaining colonial outposts on the Asian continent, namely the British colony of Hong Kong and the nearby Portuguese colony of Macao. Although the colonial status of neither territory is currently under challenge from the Chinese Government (for which reason the two situations are not definable as territorial disputes), the longer term position is a matter of some uncertainty in both cases, given that Communist China could at any time change its attitude. In the case of Hong Kong, the 99-year lease obtained by Britain in 1898 on the New Territories—the substantial mainland area adjacent to Hong Kong island and Kowloon peninsula (themselves ceded to Britain in 1842 and 1860 respectively)—expires in 1997 and any Chinese refusal to renew it would clearly render the position of the colony untenable. In the case of Macao, where a Portuguese trading presence dating from the 16th century was regularized by treaty in 1887, Portugal currently regards the colony as Chinese territory under Portuguese administration.

One factor which has an important bearing on the incidence of territorial dispute between Asian countries is the absence of an all-embracing regional organization through which such disputes might be resolved by diplomatic means. Although the sub-regional Association of South-East Asian Nations (linking Indonesia, Malaysia, the Philippines, Singapore and Thailand) has played a local role in this respect, Asia does not have its own equivalent of the Organization of African Unity or the Organization of American States, with their channels for peaceful settlement of disputes between member states. The United Nations Organization itself has on occasion successfully filled this void, but in other instances disputes have been aggravated by the lack of any regional forum to which interested parties can refer their claims.

# Afghanistan-Pakistan

An unresolved dispute exists between Afghanistan and Pakistan over areas on the eastern side of their common border inhabited by Pathan (or Pushtu or Pakhtoon) tribes, whose members are partly settled and partly nomads (i.e. seasonal migrants and also raiders or refugees crossing the border). The dispute has come into the open through Afghanistan's refusal to accept the internationally recognized border between the two countries and Afghan demands for integration of all Pathans either in Afghanistan or in an autonomous or perhaps independent Pakhtoonistan. In some instances Afghan claims have included the transfer to Afghanistan of the Pakistani province of Baluchistan (which would give Afghanistan access to the Indian Ocean).

The Pathan tribes are broadly of the same culture—Sunni Moslem in religion, Pushtu or Pakhtoon in speech—but they are politically divided into the settled tribes of the administered districts of Pakistan's North-West Frontier Province (NWFP), those of tribal agencies in that province and those of Afghanistan.

The border between the two countries was delimited, by means of a map, under an agreement between Afghanistan and British India in 1893 after the so-called Second Afghan War (of 1878-80) and became known as the Durand line. Both sides recognized the area between this line and British India as "free tribal territory"; although under British sovereignty, the inhabitants of this territory were not British subjects and retained their tribal autonomy. The agreement was confirmed by further treaties concluded in 1905, 1921 and 1930, and its effect was to divide the Pathans in such a way that some 2,400,000 remained in British territory.

## The Afghan Claim

It was the partition of India in 1947, when a weak Pakistan replaced the British Empire as a sovereign neighbour of Afghanistan, which induced the latter to declare its claim. Arguments adduced by Afghanistan for its claim were legal, historical and ethnic.

It was asserted in Afghanistan that the 1893 agreement was not legally binding because Afghanistan had signed it under duress; that in any case the tribal territories between Afghanistan and the administered areas of the British sphere formed independent territories; and that Pakistan could not inherit the rights of an "extinguished person" (i.e. the British in India).[1] It was also argued that historically Afghanistan had controlled much of India, and certainly the area of what was currently western Pakistan.[2] Finally it was pointed out that the Pathans in Afghanistan and Pakistan formed a single ethnic unit which should be united in one state.

On the other hand, it has been argued that the eastern Pathans had enjoyed close economic and political ties with the major states of the Indus Valley and had de-

---

[1] See Sir W. K. Fraser-Tytler, *Afghanistan*, London, 1953.

[2] In fact, following its formation in 1747 the state of Afghanistan had at its maximum extent as the Durrani Empire controlled (in 1797) an area reaching eastwards to Delhi and Lahore; the latter was ceded to the Mughal Empire in 1798 and Peshawar was lost in 1923 (see Taussig, "Afghanistan's Big Step", in *The Eastern World*, October 1961).

veloped linguistic differences with the western Pathans.[1] Moreover, in its widest extent the area claimed for Pakhtoonistan, stretching from the Pamir to the Arabic Sea and bounded in the west by Afghanistan and Iran and in the east by the Indus River, included large areas where there were few Pathans—such as Chitral, Gilgit, Baltistan and Baluchistan.

### Pathan Aspirations before the Achievement of Independence by Pakistan

In 1946 a British proposal that under the constitution of an independent India the North-West Frontier Province should, for the purpose of drafting provincial constitutions, be grouped with the Punjab, met with strong objections from NWFP political leaders. Khan Abdul Ghaffar Khan (a member of the Indian Congress working committee and leader of the autonomist Redshirt movement) said on Dec. 6, 1946, that the question of whether or not the province should join any group should be left to the free will of the province itself. Dr Khan Saheb, the Premier of the NWFP, said on Dec. 20: "The Frontier people do not bother themselves about sections or groups. They will have their independence and nobody can force them to join anybody else." Nawabzada Allah Nawaz Khan, the Speaker of the NWFP Legislative Assembly, stated on Dec. 16: "The Pathans and the Punjabis are two major nations by any definition or test of nationality, and the very thought of grouping the NWFP with the Punjab is revolting to the Pathan mind. We Frontier Pathans are a nation of 3,000,000, with our own distinctive culture, civilization, language, literature, names and nomenclature, legal codes, customs and calendar, history and traditions, aptitudes and ambitions. By all canons of international law a Pathan is quite a separate entity from a Punjabi."

On the other hand, Mohammed Ali Jinnah, the leader of the Moslem League, declared on April 30, 1947: "The question of a division of India, as proposed by the Moslem League, is based on the fundamental fact that there are two nations—Hindus and Moslems. We want a national state in our homelands which are predominantly Moslem and comprise six units—the Punjab, the NWFP, Sind, Baluchistan, Bengal and Assam."

Under a British plan announced on June 3, 1947, for the immediate transfer of British power to India, it was laid down that a referendum was to be held in the NWFP to choose between joining the Pakistan or the Hindustan Constituent Assembly. Khan Abdul Ghaffar Khan, however, urged that the electorate of the NWFP should be given the opportunity of voting for an independent state in the province under the name of Pathanistan. Both the Indian Congress and the Moslem League nevertheless accepted the British plan and its proposal to confine the vote in the NWFP to a straight decision on the issue of union with Pakistan or otherwise. Khan Ghaffar Khan reiterated his demand on June 24 (while admitting that Jinnah was opposed to the idea of a separate Pathan state) and declared on June 25 that the Redshirt movement would boycott the referendum.

On July 3, 1947, it was announced in London and New Delhi that the Government of Afghanistan had presented notes to the British and Indian Governments concerning the future of the tribal areas of the NWFP and drawing attention to an alleged desire of the tribesmen in these areas to dissociate themselves from India. The Afghan notes were said to have asked that the inhabitants of the NWFP and also of Baluchistan should have the right to decide whether their future should lie with Afghanistan or India or be based on complete independence. However, the British Governor of the NWFP (Sir George Cunningham) subsequently toured the tribal territories and heard all the *jirgas* (tribal assemblies) of the leading tribes stating that they were part of Pakistan and wished to retain the same relations with Pakistan as they had had with the British.

---

[1] See Sir O. Caroe, "Pathans at the Crossroads", in *The Eastern World*, No. 15, 1961.

The referendum, held from July 6 onwards (after many Hindus and Sikhs had left the NWFP during June), resulted, as announced on July 20, in 289,244 votes for union with Pakistan and only 2,874 for union with India (in a 50.99 per cent poll).

## The 1949-50 Afghan Campaign for an Independent Pakhtoonistan

In March 1949 the Kabul press and radio launched a campaign against Pakistan, demanding that the area between the Durand line and the Indus, comprising the NWFP and the tribal territory, should be recognized as an independent Pakhtoonistan and given the right of self-determination.

Afghan spokesmen claimed that the 1893 agreement establishing the Durand line had been "brought about by economic force" because the tribesmen drew from the British, and continued to draw from Pakistan, subsidies amounting to over £3,750,000 a year. They also claimed that the referendum by which the NWFP had entered Pakistan was unsatisfactory because it did not offer the Pathans (whom the Afghans considered as racially akin to themselves) the alternative of joining Afghanistan (where there were an estimated 3,000,000 Pathans out of a total population of 11,000,000, while there were 2,500,000 Pathans in the tribal territory and 3,000,000 in the NWFP).

A statement made by Khwaja Nazimuddin, then Governor-General of Pakistan, to the effect that the tribal territory formed an integral part of Pakistan, was strongly criticized by the Afghan Government in a communiqué issued on March 24, 1949, describing that statement as contrary to pledges allegedly given by Jinnah in 1948. Moreover, addressing a demonstration in Kabul on April 27, Shah Mahmud Khan, then Prime Minister of Afghanistan, said that his Government would "rescue our brother Afghans" from alleged atrocities by Pakistani forces, if possible by negotiation but if not "by other means". In Pakistan, however, Sir Muhammad Zafrulla Khan (then Foreign Minister) stated on July 11, 1949, that neither the Durand line agreement nor any subsequent treaty relating to the frontier was open

**Map 27    Territorial relationship of Afghanistan and Pakistan, also showing Kashmir.**

to question but that Pakistan would welcome discussions with Afghanistan on matters of economic co-operation.

The newly-established Government of Pakistan assured the Wazir and Mahsud tribal *jirgas* in the NWFP that it desired to eliminate all suspicion among Moslems and to abandon the military control of their areas established by the British India Government. The *jirgas* thereupon made pledges of full loyalty to Pakistan, and between Dec. 6 and 27, 1947, all Pakistan troops were withdrawn from Waziristan (in the NWFP), important frontier posts were abandoned and control of the areas reverted to civil armed forces recruited from the local tribesmen.

Nevertheless, there remained in the NWFP autonomist movements led by Khan Abdul Ghaffar Khan and the Fakir of Ipi, a rebellious tribal leader in Waziristan. On March 8, 1948, the former issued a manifesto announcing the formation of a Pakistan People's Party aspiring to autonomy for "cultural and linguistic units" in Pakistan and to the establishment of a "union of free socialist republics" in Pakistan. However, on June 15 he was arrested on suspicion of complicity with the Fakir of Ipi in the planning of disturbances, and on June 16 he was sentenced to three years' rigorous imprisonment. There followed arrests of some of his followers (including Dr Khan Saheb) and also of adherents of the Fakir of Ipi between June 28 and July 6, 1948, and the Redshirt organization was banned on Sept. 16.

During June 1949 Afghan territory was, apparently inadvertently, bombed by a Pakistani aircraft which was said to have been fired upon by followers of the Fakir of Ipi and by Afghans. At the same time Afghanistan accused Pakistan of having assisted Agha Amin Jan (half-brother of ex-King Amanullah of Afghanistan, who had abdicated in January 1929) in an unsuccessful attempt to seize the throne of Afghanistan (after he had for some months been living among the Mahsud tribe of Waziristan), but this was strongly denied by Pakistan, which claimed that the authorities of the tribal territories had dispersed Amin Jan's forces and had informed the Afghan Government of his activities. Pakistan in turn alleged that Afghan officials had welcomed the Fakir of Ipi when he had entered Afghanistan in June and were planning to proclaim him King of "Pathanistan".

In Britain the Secretary for Commonwealth Relations (then Philip Noel-Baker) said in the House of Commons on June 30, 1949, that Pakistan was in international law the inheritor of the rights and duties of the former Government of India and of the UK Government in the territories on the North-West Frontier, and that the Durand line was the international frontier. He added that the British Government had been in continuous consultation with Pakistan, was convinced that there was no outstanding question between Pakistan and Afghanistan that could not be settled by peaceful means, and was confident that there could be no question of armed aggression by Afghanistan.

The Afghan ambassador in London, however, stated on Aug. 4, 1949, that his Government could not accept the British view that Pakistan had inherited the rights and duties of the former Government of India in the tribal areas and that, if negotiations with Pakistan for a settlement failed, Afghanistan would appeal to the United Nations.

As part of an intensified Afghan campaign against Pakistan from December 1949, the Afghan ambassador to India alleged on Dec. 20 that the Government of Pakistan was refusing to "apply the UN Charter to an oppressed nation" and expressed regret that attempts which had been made by the Afghan Government to settle the matter with the Governments of Pakistan and Britain had achieved no result. He said in particular that the arrangements whereby the "Pakhtoons" (Pathans) had "found themselves debited to Pakistan's account as a mute transferable commodity" had aroused resentment among "the whole Pakhtoon nation" and that only the influence of the Afghan Government had restrained them from taking up arms. He further alleged that the flag of "Pakhtoonistan" had been hoisted throughout the tribal territory; that "national assemblies" had been set up in Tirah and the Khyber; and that the Pakistan Government had sent troops against the tribesmen, causing "immense loss of life", had bombed the Waziristan areas from the air, had enforced an economic blockade of the tribal territory and had imprisoned popular leaders from all over the NWFP and Baluchistan.

A number of border incidents which occurred in 1950 included, according to a Pakistan Government statement of Oct. 4 of that year, an invasion of Pakistan on Sept. 30 by "a large body of Afghan tribesmen and regular troops" commanded by a brigadier of the Afghan Army, who were driven back on Oct. 5 by Pakistani troops supported by aircraft. The Afghan Government, however, denied that any Afghan troops had been involved in the clashes and claimed that the detachment concerned had consisted entirely of tribesmen from the Pakistani side of the border who supported the "Pakhtoonistan" movement.

### Period of Dormancy following 1951 NWFP Elections

In elections held in the NWFP between Nov. 26 and Dec. 12, 1951 (the first to be held on an adult franchise, including that of women), the banned pro-Pakhtoonistan Redshirt movement nominated a number of candidates standing as independents; however, after the election all elected independent Moslems applied for Moslem League membership (as a result of which the Moslem League eventually held 80 of the 85 seats in the NWFP Legislative Assembly). The provincial Minister of Education observed that the result had "buried the myth of Pathanistan for all time" and that the fact that the Moslem League had captured all seven seats in the Charsadda sub-division (a former stronghold of the Redshirts) was significant of the scant "respect" which Pathans had for those hostile to Pakistan or to the existing Government. During the next few years the Pakhtoonistan issue remained dormant.

On Jan. 5, 1954, it was announced that Khan Abdul Ghaffar Khan, the former Redshirt leader who, after serving his three-year sentence, had been detained under security regulations, would be released. At the same time 45 other detainees were released unconditionally under a general amnesty, with their confiscated property being restored to them, and restrictions imposed on Dr Khan Saheb were lifted.

Afghanistan's Foreign Minister (then Sardar Mohammed Naim) asserted in a press statement during a visit to Karachi on Nov. 7, 1954, that the basic differences between Pakistan and Afghanistan did not involve any territorial adjustment, but he also said that the people of "Pushtoonistan" should be given opportunities to express themselves on "their status and their way of living". He emphasized that the two countries' national interests were similar and that there were good possibilities of close economic co-operation.

### Revival of the Dispute after the Integration of West Pakistan in One Administrative Unit

On Nov. 25, 1954, the NWFP Legislative Assembly unanimously approved a government proposal for the integration of West Pakistan into a single administrative unit. A subsequent proposal by the Government of Pakistan to incorporate the tribal territory of the NWFP in the unified Province of West Pakistan was met by protests (on March 29, 1955) by Sardar Mohammed Daud Khan, who had become Prime Minister and Minister of the Interior of Afghanistan on Sept. 7, 1953, and who was known to be a strong advocate of Afghan support for the tribal elements in the NWFP. On March 30 a formal Afghan note was presented in Karachi, protesting against the proposed merger of territory of "occupied and free Pakhtoonistan" in the new province—but the protest was rejected by the Pakistan Government on the ground that the unification of West Pakistan was a purely internal matter.

There followed large-scale demonstrations, leading to riots, before the Pakistan embassy in Kabul and also at Pakistan consulates elsewhere in Afghanistan. These incidents led to counter-demonstrations in Pakistan and to mutual recriminations, and on May 4 to the proclamation of a state of emergency in Afghanistan and a call-up of men between 25 and 32 years of age who had performed military service. The Pakistan Minister for States and Frontier Regions (Maj.-Gen. Iskander Mirza) said after a tour of the North-West Frontier areas on May 11: "We regard the Afghan Government's claim to sponsor the 'Pakhtoonistan' stunt as an interference in Pakistan's internal affairs, and we shall fight for the maintenance of the Durand line as our national boundary with Afghanistan. There can be no compromise on this issue."

Eventually the Afghan Government agreed on Sept. 9, 1955, to make amends for insults to the Pakistani flag during the Kabul riots earlier in the year, and both Governments undertook not to conduct propaganda calculated to arouse hatred and to incite violence against each other. A proposed meeting between the Prime Ministers of the two countries was, however, put off by the Afghan Government after it had been advised on Oct. 12, 1955, that Pakistan would not accede to Afghanistan's request for a postponement of the One-Unit Act setting up a unitary West Pakistan.

On Oct. 13 the Afghan Government, in a further note to the Government of Pakistan, expressed its concern at the incorporation of "Pushtunistan" in the new province of West Pakistan and asserted that this was against the wishes of the Pathans (Pushtus), but it still proposed a high-level meeting to settle "all outstanding differences". This proposal was rejected by Pakistan, which reiterated that all territories lying to the east of the Durand line were an integral part of Pakistan and completely outside the jurisdiction of the Afghan Government. Nevertheless, the Pakistan Government still expressed its willingness to have a meeting of ministers provided that matters purely of Pakistan's own concern were excluded from the discussions. The Afghan minister in Karachi and the Pakistan ambassador in Kabul were recalled in October 1955, as a result of which diplomatic relations between the two countries were in fact suspended.

After the Soviet Union had indicated that it supported Afghanistan in this dispute, the Council of the South-East Asia Treaty Organization (SEATO)—consisting of the Foreign Ministers of the organization's then eight member countries (Australia, France, New Zealand, Pakistan, the Philippines, Thailand, the United Kingdom and the United States)—declared on March 8, 1956, inter alia: "In so far as those [Soviet] statements referred to 'Pushtunistan', the members of the Council severally declared that their Governments recognized that the sovereignty of Pakistan extends up to the Durand line, the international boundary between Pakistan and Afghanistan."

A marked improvement in relations between the two countries from August 1956 (when the then President of Pakistan, Gen. Mirza, paid a state visit to Afghanistan) culminated in an agreement on June 10, 1957 (during a visit to Kabul by Hussein Shaheed Suhrawardy, then Prime Minister of Pakistan), to restore full diplomatic relations between the two countries, to co-operate in international affairs, to resolve their differences through friendly negotiations and to consolidate the existing basis for permanent friendship. However, the contentious Pathan issue came to the fore again after the proclamation of martial law and the abrogation of the Constitution of 1956 in Pakistan in October 1958.

Under martial law the leaders of the left-wing National Awami Party (NAP) were arrested, among them Khan Abdul Ghaffar Khan (who, after all remaining restrictions on his movements had been lifted in July 1955, had reportedly opposed the one-unit plan for West Pakistan and proposed a referendum to be held on this issue) and Abdus Samad Khan Achakzai (known as "the Baluchi Gandhi") as leaders of the movement for an autonomous Pathan province of "Pakhtoonistan" inside West Pakistan.

### Further Deterioration in Afghan-Pakistani Relations from 1960 - Soviet Support for Afghanistan's Position

From 1960 onwards relations between Afghanistan and Pakistan deteriorated rapidly, partly because of strong Soviet support for Afghanistan on the "Pakhtoonistan" issue. In a joint communiqué issued in Kabul at the end of a visit by Nikita Khrushchev, then Prime Minister of the Soviet Union, it was stated inter alia on March 4, 1960, that the two sides had "exchanged views on the destiny of the Pushtu people and expressed their agreement that the application of the principle of self-determination on the basis of the UN Charter for settling this issue would be a reasonable way of easing tension and ensuring peace in the Middle East". On his return to Moscow the Soviet Prime Minister asserted on March 5 that "historically" Pakhtoonistan had "always been part of Afghanistan".

In response to this development the Pakistan Foreign Minister (then Manzoor Qadir) said on March 6 that it was "regrettable that the Soviet Union deemed it fit to interfere in this country's internal affairs", and on March 7 he challenged the Afghan Government to hold a referendum in order to discover whether the Pathans of Afghanistan wished to join Pakistan. He said that he had made this proposal to the Afghan Foreign Minister (then Sardar Mohammed Naim) during talks in Rawalpindi in January 1960, but that the latter had replied that he had "not come to negotiate". Manzoor Qadir explained his proposal as follows: "It is reasonable to assume that Pakhtoons (Pathans), whether they live in Pakistan or in Afghanistan, want to be together and under the same flag. That flag can be the flag of either Pakistan or Afghanistan. . . . Since a referendum has already been held among the Pakhtoons of Pakistan [in 1947], who by an overwhelming majority decided to be in Pakistan, it is only logical that we should now ask the Pakhtoons in Afghanistan what their wishes are. In all probability their verdict will be in favour of Pakistan. In the unlikely event of Pakhtoons in Afghanistan choosing freely not to join Pakistan, any further steps to be taken can be considered."

The Pakistani suggestion of a referendum was, however, rejected by the Afghan Foreign Minister, and the Afghan Government subsequently refused to renew visas for Pakistanis living in Afghanistan. The Pakistan Foreign Minister stated on Aug. 4, 1960, that Pakistan had sent a number of notes protesting against alleged maltreatment of Pakistanis in Afghanistan, and in September 1960 and March 1961 mutual accusations were made about fighting in the border area.

On the latter occasion (i.e. in March 1961) it was alleged in Afghanistan that Pakistani forces were carrying out repressive measures against the Pathans, while *Pravda* (the official organ of the Soviet Communist Party) asserted on April 3 that eight Pakistani divisions supported by tanks and aircraft were active in the Pathan areas, bombing villages and causing substantial casualties; the paper reaffirmed Soviet support for the Afghan demand for Pathan self-determination and declared: "The situation emerging in the direct proximity of our frontier is not a matter of indifference to us." The Government of Pakistan admitted on April 6 that bombing operations had taken place in the Bajaur area early in March when, it claimed, a house had been used as headquarters and an ammunition dump by an Afghan agent for the distribution of arms, ammunition and money among the tribesmen of Bajaur.

Further fighting in the Bajaur area was reported in May 1961, when the Pakistan Minister for States and Frontier Regions stated that Afghan forces had attacked Pakistani border posts and had infiltrated the Bajaur area but had been repulsed, and that 20 Afghan agents had been arrested and had confessed that they had been commissioned by the Afghan Government to start terrorist activities in Pakistan. President Ayub Khan of Pakistan said on May 21 that, whereas in the past there had been raids by irregulars from Afghanistan, the Afghan Government had now for the first time used army troops in a border incident, and on May 23 he said that Afghanistan had recently received large quantities of Soviet arms; that the border situation was becoming serious as the great powers were showing interest; and that the people of the areas concerned did not want the setting-up of any "Pakhtoonistan"; but he admitted that trouble was being fomented among "the disgruntled and the poor".

### Temporary Severance of Diplomatic and Trade Relations ended by Tehran Agreement of 1963

Further concentrations of Afghan troops along the Durand line were reported by Pakistan military sources in June 1961, and in September of that year diplomatic and trade relations between the two countries were broken off, and the common border was closed (although as an exceptional measure the frontier was temporarily reopened on Jan. 29, 1962, to allow for the delivery of goods destined for Afghanistan under US aid schemes). The closure of the border also resulted in the exclusion from Pakistan of large numbers of Pathan tribal nomads (*powindahs,* who were Afghan nationals) who had normally crossed the border for winter employment in Pakistan.

Various mediation efforts failed to result in the reopening of the border until, after a change of Government in Afghanistan, agreement was reached in Tehran (Iran) on May 23, 1963, when the Governments of Afghanistan and Pakistan agreed (i) to restore diplomatic, consular and trade relations with each other; (ii) to see to it that the duties and conduct of their representatives would be in accordance with the recognized principles of international law, usage and practice, and would be confined to the discharge of their official functions; and (iii) to endeavour to create an atmosphere of goodwill, friendship and mutual trust.

However, the leader of the Afghan delegation (Sayyid Qasim Rashtiya, the Afghan Minister of Information and Broadcasting) was said to have stated in Tehran on May 29 that Afghanistan had never recognized the Durand line as his country's international boundary with Pakistan and that "Pakhtoonistan" continued to be the main issue dividing the two countries. Zulfiqar Ali Bhutto, then Pakistan's Prime Minister, however, said on the same day that "Pakhtoonistan" was "a closed issue" and that his Government would continue to refuse Afghan nomads access to Pakistan.

The Tehran agreement was implemented on July 20, 1963, when the border between Afghanistan and Pakistan was reopened.

The "Pakhtoonistan" issue was again raised in Afghanistan on Sept. 19, 1964, when the *Loe Jirga* (Grand Assembly of Afghanistan, a body which had been summoned only five times during 40 years to consider major questions of policy and which had in 1955 supported the Afghan Government's commitment to "Pakhtoonistan") approved, after adopting a new Constitution, a government-sponsored resolution referring to "the religious, national and historical duty" of the Afghans to support the rights of the Pathan people of Pakistan to self-determination and stating that Afghanistan was "waiting for the day when the issue of Pakhtoonistan will be settled on the basis of the true aspirations of the people and leaders of Pakhtoonistan".

### Constitutional Changes in Pakistan, 1970-73

In Pakistan new constitutional proposals published on March 29, 1970, and a presidential order issued in April of that year provided that the one-unit structure in West Pakistan was to be dissolved and the four former provinces restored—among them the NWFP and Baluchistan (including Las Bela).

After the Supreme Court of Pakistan had, on April 20, 1972, declared illegal the proclamation of martial law (on March 25, 1969), martial law was ended and Zulfiqar Ali Bhutto (who had become President of Pakistan on Dec. 20, 1971) was sworn in as President under the new Constitution on April 21, 1972. New provincial governments were thereupon formed, those of the NWFP (under Maulana Mufti Mahmood) and in Baluchistan (under Sardar Ataullah Mengal) being both based on coalitions of the (pro-Soviet) NAP and the *Jamiat-i-Ulema-i-Pakistan* (of left-wing mullahs).

In the new Constitution adopted by the Pakistan National Assembly on April 9, 1973, the territory of the Islamic Republic of Pakistan was defined as consisting of Baluchistan, the NWFP, the Punjab, Sind, the federally-administered tribal areas and such states or territories as were or might be included in Pakistan, whether by accession or otherwise.

### Revival of the Pakhtoonistan Issue by the Republican Regime in Afghanistan

Afghanistan's claim to the areas of Pakistan inhabited by Pathans was revived by the republican regime which came to power in Afghanistan on July 17, 1973, under Lt.-Gen. Sardar Mohammed Daud Khan, who had, as Prime Minister in 1953-63, expressed his support for the cause of "Pakhtoonistan". After a public rally in support of Afghanistan's claim had been held in Kabul on July 21, President Bhutto declared on July 26 that his country would scrupulously adhere to the good relations which it had enjoyed with Afghanistan, but he added that Pakistan was "quite capable" of defending itself against possible Afghan claims to the NWFP.

In an interview published in *Le Monde* on Feb. 3-4, 1974, President Daud said: "We support in every way the right of our brothers in Pakhtoonistan to self-determination." He added: "When bombs are falling on our brothers, when they are being murdered, if they ask for our aid we shall not remain indifferent." Although expressing the hope that the problem would be solved "in a friendly and peaceful way", he claimed that the NWFP and Baluchistan had "always formed an integral part of Afghanistan", from which they had been separated by "unequal and unjust treaties".

### Earlier Developments in the Pakistani Province of Baluchistan

In the Pakistani Province of Baluchistan it appeared that the overwhelming majority of the population had endorsed the province's adherence to Pakistan, but from 1963 onwards there was widespread unrest and armed opposition to the Federal Government, which sent in troops to restore order. At a *jirga* held on June 29, 1947, all the tribal chiefs of what was then British Baluchistan had decided by a unanimous vote to join Pakistan (although Kalat, the largest Indian state in Baluchistan, was not represented at the *jirga*, which was attended only by representatives of the British part of the territory).

On April 12, 1952, the Government of Pakistan announced that, on the basis of a recommendation by a committee on constitutional and administrative reforms in Baluchistan, the rulers of the Baluchistan states of Kalat, Las Bela, Makran and Kharan had agreed to integrate their territories in a single Union with a common executive, legislative and judiciary. On June 16, 1954, the Pakistan Government decided to merge the resultant Baluchistan States Union with the rest of Baluchistan under one central administration. Moreover, the *Shahi Jirga* of Baluchistan approved, on Nov. 29, 1954, the government proposal for the integration of West Pakistan in a single administrative unit [see above], and an agreement was signed on Jan. 3, 1955, by the rulers of the states forming the Baluchistan States Union for the merger of all these states in a unified West Pakistan.

In provincial elections held on Dec. 17, 1970, one seat in the Provincial Assembly was gained by a Pakhtoonkwa National Awami Party (PNAP), which had been formed by Abdus Samad Khan Achakzai (who had been a close associate of Mahatma Gandhi in the Indian independence movement, had opposed the formation of Pakistan, had after partition been imprisoned for many years for advocating the creation of an independent Pakhtoonistan, had later joined the NAP but had broken with it to form his own party, and had then been regarded as a supporter of Zulfiqar Ali Bhutto). The PNAP leader was assassinated in Quetta (the capital of Baluchistan) on Dec. 3, 1973, however, and his death was followed by riots which were subdued with the aid of troops.

The existence of a Baluchistan Liberation Front (BLF) had been reported in February 1973. It was said to have an office in Iraq and a clandestine radio operating from that country, and to be supplied with finance and guerrilla training for separatist activities in Baluchistan. On Feb. 10, 1973, the Pakistani authorities seized some 300 submachine-guns, 60,000 rounds of ammunition, 40 incendiary grenades and other military equipment at the Iraq embassy in Islamabad, but it was not clear whether these arms were intended for the BLF or for a similar movement in the south-east of Iran. The Government of Iraq subsequently emphasized its respect for Pakistan's sovereignty and territorial integrity.

In connexion with this arms find at the Iraq embassy, Sardar Akbar Bugti (leader of the Bugti tribe) alleged on Feb. 10, 1973, that NAP leaders had plotted the secession of Baluchistan with the help of foreign weapons. (Sardar Bugti had himself led a tribal rising in 1963, had been condemned to death and later pardoned by President Ayub Khan, had become the treasurer of the NAP but had resigned from it after the appointment of Ghaus Bakhsh Bizenjo as Governor of Baluchistan as the nominee of the NAP on April 29, 1972.) Although G. B. Bizenjo had on Feb. 13 categorically denied that the arms were meant for use in Baluchistan and had demanded a judicial inquiry, he was dismissed as governor by President Bhutto on Feb. 15 and replaced by Sardar Bugti, while the Government of Sardar Ataullah Mengal was also dismissed for failing to check "large-scale disturbances" and President's rule was imposed in Baluchistan.

Khan Abdul Wali Khan, the president of the NAP, and G. B. Bizenjo alleged on Feb. 20, 1973, that Sardar Bugti had, while abroad, sought foreign assistance (in Moscow, Baghdad, Kabul and London) for a plan for an independent Baluchistan, and they suggested that he was connected with the arms seized at the Iraq embassy.

A new provincial Government, of which Jam Ghulam Qadir of the Qayyum Moslem League was sworn in as Chief Minister on April 27, 1973, was opposed as illegal by Sardar Mengal, who declared on the same day that he and his followers in the NAP would "defeat it in the Assembly or if necessary in the streets". There followed widespread unrest and G. B. Bizenjo said on Aug. 13 that unless the Government's military intervention were ended quickly the situation in Baluchistan would become uncontrollable and sections of the NAP might be tempted to seek aid from abroad. He was thereupon arrested on Aug. 15, together with Sardar Mengal as well as the president of the Baluchistan NAP and the commander of the party's militia.

Sardar Bugti tendered his resignation as governor on Oct. 13, 1973, because he disagreed with the Federal Government's handling of affairs in Baluchistan. (He was said to have advised the Prime Minister to restore the NAP Government and to withdraw the troops from Baluchistan.) He was on Jan. 3, 1974, replaced as governor by the Khan of Kalat (the overlord of the Baluchi sardars or tribal chieftains). On April 14 Bhutto announced that military operations in Baluchistan would cease from May 15 and that an amnesty would be granted to all persons detained in the province except those accused of serious criminal offences. Guerrilla warfare nevertheless continued and opposition leaders alleged in the National Assembly on June 24 that 800 people had been killed by Air Force bombing a week earlier (but this was denied by the Federal Minister of Law).

## Mutual Accusations made in 1974

The Government of Pakistan repeatedly accused the Afghan Government of supporting the uprising in Baluchistan and of being responsible for bomb explosions in other provinces and alleged that the NAP connived with the Kabul regime. On June 19, 1974, it was asserted by Bhutto (who had ceased to be President and had become Prime Minister again on Aug. 13, 1973) that a professional assassin had been hired in Afghanistan to kill him in February 1973, and that a former general secretary of the NAP (Ajmal Khattak), who had lived in exile in Kabul since March 1973, had been involved in the plot. On Aug. 12 Radio Pakistan referred to another attempt by three Afghan guerrillas to kill Bhutto during a recent tour of Baluchistan.

On Oct. 1, 1974, the Pakistan Prime Minister stated in a note to the UN Secretary-General (Dr Kurt Waldheim) that he possessed "irrefutable evidence that the present Afghan Government is systematically organizing, aiding and abetting the commission of acts of sabotage and terrorism through hired elements within our territory". The Afghan Deputy Foreign Minister (Waheed Abdullah) thereupon declared in the UN General Assembly on Oct. 7 that "the use of force, oppression and imprisonment of those who demand their human rights" in Pakistan would "adversely affect the maintenance of peace and stability in our region", and he proposed that Pakistan and Afghanistan should negotiate a peaceful solution of the Pathan and Baluchi questions.

At the end of an official visit to Moscow by Bhutto in October 1974, it was stated in a joint communiqué that the two sides had "expressed the hope that differences between Pakistan and Afghanistan will be settled by peaceful means through negotiations on the basis of the principles of peaceful coexistence". There followed a brief period of improvement in relations between the two countries.

However, after two Pakistani military posts had been temporarily overrun by Pathan tribesmen near the Khyber Pass and hundreds of refugees from Baluchistan had fled to Afghanistan, Bhutto sent a second note to the UN Secretary-General which as published on Jan. 24, 1975, again accused Afghanistan of "actively encouraging and assisting subversive activities and acts of terrorism and sabotage within Pakistan".

## Pakistan Government Measures to curb Unrest in the North-West Frontier Province

On Feb. 8, 1975, Hayat Mohammad Khan Sherpao, Home Minister of the NWFP (and previously a member of the Federal Government), was killed by a bomb at Peshawar. Over 60 leading members of the NAP were thereupon arrested in the NWFP, the Punjab and Sind; the NAP was banned on Feb. 10 and its property and funds were confiscated; and over 300 more party members were arrested during the next three days. On Feb. 10 the National Assembly granted the Government full powers, in particular to extend the state of emergency beyond six months without parliamentary approval. The NWFP Government was dissolved on Feb. 17 and the province was for three months placed under the rule of the governor because "a neighbouring foreign power is actively involved in disturbing normal life in the province and there can be no doubt that this is a situation which is beyond the power of the provincial Government to control". Numerous bomb explosions took place in Peshawar during the next two months, and a new NWFP

Government (under a Chief Minister from the ruling Pakistan People's Party) was sworn in on May 3, 1975.

The ban on the NAP was on Oct. 30, 1975, upheld by the Pakistan Supreme Court, which ruled that the party had never reconciled itself to the existence and ideology of Pakistan; had attempted to bring about the secession of the NWFP and Baluchistan through insurrection, terrorism and sabotage; had, in order to destroy the idea of a single Moslem nation, promoted the concept that the Punjabis, Pathans, Baluchis and Sindhis constituted separate nations, each of which had the right of self-determination; and had attempted to propagate hatred of the Punjab in the other provinces.

Abdul Wali Khan and 30 other NAP officials were on April 21, 1975, charged with sabotage and causing bomb explosions. Isfayandar Wali (the son of the party's president) and two other men were on Aug. 2 sentenced to 10 years' rigorous imprisonment after having allegedly confessed to causing the explosion which killed H.M. Khan Sherpao, while Isfayandar Wali was sentenced to a further seven years under the Defence of Pakistan rules.

## Renewed Tension between Afghanistan and Pakistan, 1975-76

President Daud of Afghanistan renewed his Government's campaign against Pakistan on March 2, 1975, when he declared in a letter to the UN Secretary-General: "Afghanistan has, since the time the British divided our land by force of arms and annexed part of our territory to their empire, supported the lawful rights of these people [i.e. the Pathans and the Baluchis] and will continue to do so until they are fully restored." He protested against the dissolution of the NAP and the detention of its leaders in Pakistan; suggested that a UN fact-finding mission should investigate the situation in Baluchistan; and appealed for UN aid to refugees who had entered Afghanistan from Baluchistan and the NWFP.

On the other hand, for the Pakistan Government Prime Minister Bhutto stated in a letter to the UN Secretary-General published on April 12, 1975, that President Daud's letter betrayed "Afghanistan's expansionist design", and he reiterated that the frontier of Afghanistan had been delimited almost 100 years earlier by agreement between the Afghan and British Indian Governments, and that the areas inhabited by Pathan and Baluchi tribes on the Pakistani side of the frontier constituted integral parts of Pakistan's national territory. He denied that there had been an influx of refugees from Pakistan into Afghanistan and declared: "The Afghan agents provocateurs and a handful of sympathizers who, because of their commission or instigation of unlawful acts, have become unwelcome among the tribal people of Baluchistan have made their way into Afghanistan as fugitives from justice." Some of the so-called refugees, he stated, wished to return but had been forcibly detained in Afghanistan, and thousands of Afghans who traditionally migrated to Pakistan in the winter months were refusing to return to Afghanistan because of the "terror and oppression" which awaited them. He described President Daud's suggestion for a UN fact-finding mission as "a clear attempt to secure UN cover for [Afghanistan's] interference in Pakistan's internal affairs" and he asserted that Afghanistan's "provocative and aggressive posture, accompanied by continuous exhortations from Radio Kabul to its agents to commit acts of murder, sabotage and destruction in Pakistan" had been responsible for the assassination of H.M. Khan Sherpao. The Pakistan Prime Minister nevertheless repeated that Pakistan remained ready to enter into a dialogue with Afghanistan and was committed to a peaceful settlement of the differences between them in conformity with the principles of respect for territorial integrity and sovereignty, and non-interference in each other's domestic affairs.

The Pakistan Minister of State for Defence and Foreign Affairs (Aziz Ahmed) protested in a separate letter to the UN Secretary-General against steps taken by the latter to ascertain what could be done to help Pakistani refugees in Afghanistan and alleged that as a result of the "reign of terror" in Afghanistan over 170,000 refugees had entered Pakistan.

President Daud, in a further letter to the UN Secretary-General on Oct. 10, denied that Afghanistan entertained expansionist designs against Pakistan; stated that many of the Baluchis entering Afghanistan were women, children and elderly men; and repeated his request for a UN fact-finding mission as "the only way by which the international community could be informed correctly about the truth of the matter and about the real identity of the Baluchi refugees". In an interview with an Indian newspaper (*Blitz*) on March 8, 1975, the Afghan President had stated that Pakistan was directly involved in espionage, arms smuggling and other incidents inside Afghanistan and was strengthening its fortifications on the frontier.

With reference to an incident in the Panjshir district of Afghanistan on July 22, 1975, Kabul radio alleged that "reactionary troublemakers" had engaged in robbery and subversion and had confessed after their arrest that they had been armed and incited by the Pakistan Government. Pakistan radio, on the other hand, asserted that a revolt by some 700 tribesmen had been crushed by the Afghan Army, with over 600 people being killed.

There followed, during the next six months, further Pakistan radio allegations about revolts, riots, acts of sabotage and "barbaric repression" by the police in Afghanistan.

### 1975 Renewal of Afghan-Soviet Treaty - Contacts between Afghan and Pakistani Leaders

Following the renewal for a further 10 years of a 1931 Soviet-Afghan treaty on neutrality and mutual non-aggression (which had been extended for a further 10 years in 1965) during a state visit to Kabul by President Podgorny of the Soviet Union on Dec. 9-10, 1975, the tension between Afghanistan and Pakistan abated during 1976. In a joint communiqué issued at the end of the Soviet President's visit it was stated that the two sides were "firmly convinced that the outstanding problems that exist in the South Asian sub-continent should be resolved through talks without any interference from outside" and "expressed the hope that political discord between Afghanistan and Pakistan will be settled by peaceful means by way of talks".

At the invitation of President Daud, Prime Minister Bhutto visited Kabul on June 7-11, 1976, when the two leaders "exchanged views with the aim of solving their political and other differences on the basis of the five principles of peaceful coexistence" and agreed to refrain for the time being from hostile press and radio propaganda against each other. Moreover, a visit to Pakistan by President Daud took place on Aug. 20-24, 1976, as part of "a continuing dialogue" to find an honourable solution to the political and other differences between the two countries. Nevertheless a "Pakhtoonistan national day" was celebrated in Afghanistan on Aug. 31, with members of the Cabinet taking part in the ceremonies.

### Continued Unrest in Baluchistan

Although large numbers of rebels surrendered to government forces during the first half of 1975, guerrilla activities continued in Baluchistan in that year. The Chief Minister (Jam Ghulam Qadir) stated on March 4, 1975, that 44 people arrested had confessed that they had been given training in guerrilla warfare by Afghan army officers, and on May 19 it was officially announced that a store of light machine-guns with Afghan markings had been discovered, together with an instruction manual issued by the Afghan War Ministry—but Kabul radio described the announcement as "a blatant lie".

ASIA AND THE FAR EAST

On Dec. 31, 1975, the Federal Government suspended the Baluchistan Administration and Provincial Assembly and placed the province under governor's rule, inter alia because the provincial Government had "failed to make good use of the sizeable allocations made by the Federal Government for the development of Baluchistan".

On April 8, 1976, the Pakistan Prime Minister announced that the sardari system in Baluchistan and the NWFP had been abolished with immediate effect. Under this system the sardars (tribal chieftains) had held great power in the two provinces, had controlled private armies, administered justice, and collected taxes and other dues, including one-sixth of their tribesmen's crops. On April 10 the Prime Minister said that the former sardars must release all prisoners in their private jails, failing which the jail buildings would be demolished.

In the Iranian province of Baluchistan and Sistan (contiguous with the Baluchistan province in Pakistan), where about 550,000 Baluchis constitute the majority of the population and are predominantly Sunni Moslems (whereas the majority of Iranians are Shia Moslems), there exists a Baluchi movement campaigning for autonomy within Iran, economic assistance and cultural equality with the (Shi'ite) Sistans of the province, but this movement has not advocated union with Baluchis outside Iran.

### Clemency Measures taken by the Government of Gen. Zia ul-Haq

A change in the situation inside Pakistan took place with the assumption of power by Gen. Mohammed Zia ul-Haq on July 5, 1977, after protest demonstrations, strikes and riots had followed general elections held on March 7, 1977, and had led to the death of about 350 people. The change of regime involved the dissolution of the National Assembly and of all Provincial Assemblies, and it was followed by clemency measures affecting political opponents of the former Government of Zulfiqar Ali Bhutto.

On Aug. 15, 1977, it was announced that Gen. Zia ul-Haq had appealed to the Marri tribesmen who had fled Baluchistan in 1973-74 to return to their homes, promising that no action would be taken against them and they would be rehabilitated. Sardar Mengal, the former Chief Minister of Baluchistan (who had been on trial with other former NAP leaders), was released on bail on Aug. 19. On Dec. 9 Abdul Wali Khan and 15 other men, all facing trial on conspiracy charges, were also released on bail, and on Jan. 1, 1978, Gen. Zia announced that the charges against them had been withdrawn and that the special court set up to try them had been dissolved as the charges were "99 per cent politically motivated"—but that the ban on the NAP would remain in force. He claimed at the same time that 11,109 political prisoners had been released since July 1977 and that there were no political prisoners left in Pakistan except "a few" arrested under martial law. It was officially announced in Quetta on March 21 that over 900 people detained during the rebellion in Baluchistan had been released.

### The Issue of Afghan Moslem Rebel Refugees in Pakistan

The (Communist) Revolutionary Council which took power in Afghanistan in April 1978 appeared to maintain the previous Afghan Governments' attitude on the issue of "Pakhtoonistan", but a new factor affecting relations between Afghanistan and Pakistan was the massive influx of Afghan Moslem rebels who fled Afghanistan, more especially after the Soviet intervention in that country which began in December 1979.

On July 27, 1978, the Deputy Prime Minister and Minister of Foreign Affairs of Afghanistan (then Hafizullah Amin) expressed the hope that "the only political difference between Afghanistan and Pakistan regarding self-determination for the Pushtu [or Pathán] and Baluchi people" would be "solved through cordial and

249

realistic talks''. The Government of Pakistan stated in response on July 30: ''The national destiny of the Pushtu and Baluchi population of Pakistan as of the rest of the people was determined by them freely and jointly when they decided to establish the sovereign state of Pakistan. The Afghan statement, by calling into question Pakistan's territorial integrity, constituted a serious violation of the principles of the UN Charter, of peaceful co-existence and of the non-aligned movement.''

During 1978-79 various Moslem organizations waging guerrilla war against the pro-Soviet Afghan Government set up headquarters in Peshawar (NWFP). The number of Afghan Moslem refugees in Pakistan reached about 30,000 by Jan. 16, 1979, but rose to over 1,000,000 in 1980. The Pakistan Government stated officially on Jan. 31, 1979, that it had accepted the Afghan refugees on purely humanitarian grounds; that it did not allow them to train as guerrillas near Peshawar; and that its policy towards Afghanistan was one of ''good-neighbourliness and respect for the principles of non-interference in its internal affairs''. According to an estimate made on June 22, 1981, by the UN High Commissioner for Refugees the number of Afghan refugees in Pakistan had by then reached more than 2,000,000.

The Moscow *Pravda,* however, stated on March 19, 1979, that ''Afghan reactionaries'' were ''relying on support from certain circles in Pakistan, China and some Western countries'' and continued: ''Everything indicates that it was not without the knowledge of the official Pakistan authorities that the activities of the rebels developed.'' On June 1, 1979, it was stated in *Pravda*: ''The attacks on the sovereignty of the young democratic republic [of Afghanistan], the intrusion of armed gangs on its territory from Pakistan and the attempts to create a crisis in the region cannot leave the USSR indifferent.'' In response to such assertions, the Pakistan Government repeatedly denied that it was backing the rebel Moslems in Afghanistan and that its Army was planning to conduct raids into that country.

In Baluchistan more than 100,000 Pushtu refugees from Afghanistan were on Sept. 1, 1980, reported to have set up camps near Pishan (with more than 700,000 head of livestock brought in by them competing with the Baluchis' sheep for scarce grazing land).

Proposals for a peace settlement, made by the Afghan Government on May 14, 1980, called for ''a guaranteed ending of incursions into Afghanistan by bandit detachments from the territories of the neighbouring states, in the first place Pakistan''. The proposals were, however, rejected by Pakistan on June 11 on the ground that they did ''not offer an acceptable basis for a settlement of the crisis''.

H.W.D.

# Bangladesh-India

A dispute developed between India and Bangladesh in 1979 over a new island in the Bay of Bengal, which is called New Moore Island by India and South Talpatty Island by Bangladesh and which both Governments claim as part of their national territory. (For territorial relationship of Bangladesh and India, see map on page 252.)

The island lies in the estuary of the River Hariabhanga, the mid-stream of the main channel of which forms the border between Bangladesh and India, and of the Raimangal, an internal river of Bangladesh. Indian official statements maintain that it is 5.2 km from the Indian coast and 7.2 km from the nearest point in Bangladesh, and that the main channel of the Hariabhanga flows to the east of it, whereas Bangladesh claims that the main channel flows to the west. Its area varies between 12 sq km at low tide and 2 sq km at high tide.

The island, which is believed to have been formed after a cyclone and tidal wave in 1970, was discovered in the following year by India, which laid claim to it, named it New Moore Island and notified the British Admiralty of its location. The Bangladesh Government first laid claim to it at the end of 1978, and subsequently maintained that during a visit to Dacca in April 1979 Morarji Desai (then the Indian Prime Minister) had agreed to a joint survey to determine its location and ownership. A joint statement issued on Aug. 18, 1980, after a visit to Dacca by the Indian External Affairs Minister, P. V. Narasimha Rao, merely said that "the two sides agreed that after study of the additional information exchanged between the two Governments further discussion would take place with a view to settling it peacefully at an early date", no reference being made to a joint survey.

In May 1981, after an Indian naval survey ship had anchored off the island and landed personnel, Bangladesh gunboats entered the area, whereupon an Indian frigate came to the survey ship's assistance. In a subsequent exchange of notes each Government accused the other of acting in a provocative manner and of sending warships into its territorial waters. Bangladesh again proposed a joint survey in a note of May 18, but India rejected the proposal two days later.

C.H.

# China-India

The Sino-Indian frontier, which is some 2,500 miles (4,000 km) long, falls into three sections: (i) the eastern section, about 700 miles long, where Tibet borders on Arunachal Pradesh (formerly the North-East Frontier Agency); (ii) the central section, where Tibet borders on the independent kingdom of Bhutan, Sikkim (since 1975 a state of the Indian Union), the kingdom of Nepal and the Indian states of Uttar Pradesh and Himachal Pradesh; and (iii) the western section (including the Ladakh frontier), where Kashmir borders on Tibet and Xinjiang (Sinkiang) to the east and Xinjiang to the north. Since 1959 the eastern and western sections of the frontier have been the subject of major territorial disputes between India and China.

## The Eastern Section

The frontier problem in the eastern section arises from the mountainous terrain and the limited control formerly exercised by the British over the tribal peoples living in the foothills of the Himalayas and by the Chinese over Tibet. Chinese suzerainty over Tibet was nominally established in 1720, but in practice Tibet continued to be ruled by the priestly caste headed by the Dalai Lama. After the annexation of Assam by the British in 1838 British control was gradually extended into the tribal areas, which were placed under the jurisdiction either of political agents

**Map 28    The disputed Chinese-Indian border.**

or of the deputy commissioners of the adjoining districts of Assam. To regulate the entry of lowlanders into the tribal areas an "Inner Line" running along the foot of the hills was defined in 1873; this was purely an administrative device, however, the international boundary remaining undefined. During the same period Nepal, Sikkim and Bhutan increasingly fell within the British rather than the Chinese sphere of influence.

Following violations of the Sikkim border by the Tibetans, a British expeditionary force invaded Tibet in 1903-04, and in 1906 an Anglo-Chinese convention recognized Chinese suzerainty over Tibet. Chinese troops invaded the country in 1910, deposed the Dalai Lama, who fled to India, and proclaimed Chinese sovereignty (as opposed to suzerainty) over Tibet. After the Chinese revolution of 1911, however, the Chinese garrison in Tibet mutinied, and in the following year the Dalai Lama returned and declared Tibet independent.

To achieve a settlement of the controversy over Tibet's status a conference was held at Simla in 1913-14, at which Britain, China and Tibet were represented. Sir Henry McMahon, the head of the British delegation, submitted two documents to the conference, an agreement whereby Tibet would be divided into an outer zone under Chinese suzerainty and Tibetan rule and an inner zone under direct Chinese control, and a border agreement whereby the frontier between Tibet and India would follow the watershed of the Himalayas north of the tribal territories.

Both agreements and the attached map were initialled by the Chinese and Tibetan delegates, but were repudiated by the Chinese Government, which refused to ratify them. McMahon thereupon negotiated a secret agreement with the Tibetan delegation recognizing the "McMahon Line" as the frontier, but this was never ratified by the Tibetan Government, which did not accept the proposed borderline. In his report to London on the Simla conference the Viceroy of India stated that "a consideration of the eastern or Indian-Chinese portion of the north-east frontier did not form part of the functions of the conference", and that McMahon's proposals should be regarded as "personal and not at present carrying the endorsement of the Government of India".

After 1938 the British authorities adopted a forward policy in this area, and British control over the tribal territories was extended up to the McMahon Line. It was then discovered that in some areas south of the line the population were already paying taxes to the Tibetan Government. The McMahon Line appeared as the frontier on official Survey of India maps for the first time in 1939, although it was still shown as undemarcated until 1954. After India became independent in 1947 the new Government brought the tribal areas of the North-East Frontier Agency under the direct administrative control of the Governor of Assam, and in 1972 they became a union territory separate from Assam under the name of Arunachal Pradesh.

Although successive Chinese Governments continued to assert their claim to sovereignty over Tibet, internal strife and the war with Japan prevented them from enforcing it until after the Communist victory in the civil war. In 1950 Chinese troops occupied Tibet, and in the following year an agreement was signed whereby the Dalai Lama accepted Chinese suzerainty and China guaranteed Tibet's internal autonomy. This change in Tibet's status did not immediately affect relations between India and China, which remained friendly. Under an agreement signed in 1954 the two countries agreed to base their relations on the five principles of respect for each other's territorial integrity and sovereignty, non-aggression, non-interference in each other's internal affairs, equality and mutual benefit, and peaceful coexistence, whilst India renounced all extra-territorial rights in Tibet in return for concessions for Indians visiting trade centres and places of pilgrimage.

When his attention was drawn in 1950 to Chinese maps showing Tibet's southern boundary as extending to the Brahmaputra River in Assam, Jawaharlal Nehru, then the Indian Prime Minister, declared that the McMahon Line "is our frontier, and we will not allow anyone to cross it". The reference in the 1954 agreement to mutual respect for territorial integrity was interpreted in India as an implicit guarantee that China would accept the existing frontier. During a visit to India in 1956 Zhou Enlai (then the Chinese Premier) told Nehru that although the Chinese Government thought the McMahon Line unfair, because it was an accomplished fact and because of their friendly relations with India they were of the opinion that they should recognize it, but that they must consult the Tibetan authorities first. Chinese maps continued to show a frontier far south of the McMahon Line, however, and a number of minor border incidents occurred in the next three years, none of which involved any clashes between Chinese and India troops.

Relations seriously deteriorated after the Tibetan uprising of March 1959 and the flight of the Dalai Lama to India, which gave rise to Chinese allegations of Indian interference in Chinese affairs. In August 1959 a Chinese force occupied the Indian frontier post of Longju after expelling the small garrison. In a letter to Nehru published on Sept. 8 of that year Zhou Enlai stated that "the Chinese Government absolutely does not recognize the so-called McMahon Line", and maintained that Indian troops had unlawfully occupied Longju, which he claimed was in Chinese territory. The Indian Government declared in a note of Sept. 10 that it "stands firmly" on the McMahon Line, though it was prepared to "discuss the exact alignment of the line at places where it departs from the geographical features marking the international boundary". Two days later Nehru told the Indian Parliament that the Government was prepared to consider minor rectifications of "a mile here or a mile there", but not "to hand over the Himalayas". A map depicting China's territorial claims, compiled from official Chinese maps, which was published by the Indian External Affairs Ministry showed that China claimed about 32,000 square miles (83,000 sq km) of territory south of the McMahon Line, including three of the four political divisions of the North-East Frontier Agency (Kameng, Subansiri and Siang) and part of the fourth (Lohit).

Talks between Nehru and Zhou Enlai in Delhi in April 1960 and three series of talks between Indian and Chinese officials produced no result. The eastern section of the border remained quiet for three years after the Longju incident, but on Sept. 20 and Oct. 10, 1962, two clashes occurred in the area of the trijunction of the Bhutanese, Indian and Tibetan borders, with some loss of life on both sides. In a subsequent exchange of notes each side claimed to have acted in self-defence and accused the other of crossing the McMahon Line.

On Oct. 20, 1962, the Chinese army launched an offensive at the western end of the McMahon Line, which was followed by a similar offensive at the eastern end. During the next month the Chinese troops advanced over 100 miles south of the McMahon Line at the western end and 25 to 30 miles south at the eastern end, threatening the plains of Assam. On Nov. 21, however, the Chinese Government announced that its troops would observe a ceasefire and would withdraw to positions 20 kilometres (12 miles) north of the McMahon Line, and that it would set up checkpoints on its side of the line of actual control existing on Nov. 7, 1959. The Chinese subsequently withdrew, but established checkpoints at Dhola and Longju, at the western end and in the central sector of the McMahon Line respectively.

No progress has since been made towards the settlement of the dispute. Occasional border incidents have occurred, in the most serious of which four Indian soldiers were killed in October 1975. In the first Chinese statement on the subject for many years, Deng Xiaoping (a Deputy Premier) suggested to an Indian journalist on June 21, 1980, that "both countries should make concessions, China in the eastern sector and India in the western sector, so as to solve the Sino-Indian boundary question in a package plan". The Indian External Affairs Minister, P. V. Narasimha Rao, commented on July 2 that this suggestion was "somewhat more precise" than earlier Chinese proposals, and that India would respond to the move.

## The Central Section

Only minor disagreements have arisen concerning the status of a number of mountain passes and other relatively small areas in this sector, and no serious border incidents have occurred. When in 1954 an agreement on trade and travel between India and Tibet was being negotiated the Chinese draft stated that the Chinese Government agreed to open six mountain passes. This wording was challenged by the Indian delegation, which maintained that the passes were Indian. In its final form the agreement referred to them as border passes open to nationals of both countries.

A Chinese note of Dec. 26, 1959, stated that "according to Indian maps . . . the boundary line in the middle sector is relatively close to the delineation on the Chinese maps, but still a number of areas which have always belonged to China are included in India". The note based the Chinese claims to these areas on the fact that their population was of Tibetan origin. In reply, an Indian note of Feb. 12, 1960, recalled that Zhou Enlai had said in 1957 that the Sino-Burmese boundary line "is often found dividing into two parts a nationality living in compact communities on the borders" and had continued: "This is the result of historical development . . . When we solve the question of the undefined boundary line between China and Burma, we must realize beforehand that it will be hard to avoid separating the nationalities concerned."

## The Ladakh Frontier

Ladakh, formerly an independent state, came under the suzerainty of the Moghul Emperors in 1664. When the Tibetans invaded Ladakh in 1681-83 the Ladakhis defeated them with Moghul assistance, and a peace treaty signed in 1684 stated that "the boundaries fixed in the beginning . . . shall still be maintained". After the decline of the Moghul Empire Ladakh was conquered in 1834 by the Raja of Jammu, who in 1846 received the title of Maharaja of Jammu and Kashmir. A new war with Tibet in 1841-42 was concluded by a peace treaty signed by representatives of the Raja of Jammu, the Dalai Lama and the Chinese Emperor. Under this agreement Tibet recognized the Raja as the political overlord of Ladakh, although the Ladakhi Buddhists continued to regard the Dalai Lama as their spiritual overlord, and each side undertook to respect "the old-established frontiers". The accession of Jammu and Kashmir to the Indian Union in 1947 and the Chinese occupation of Tibet in 1950 brought the Governments in New Delhi and Peking into direct contact in this area.

The border area was described by Nehru in 1959 as "a barren and uninhabited region, 17,000 feet high and without a vestige of grass", and by Sir H. A. F. Rumbold (a former senior India Office official) in 1977 as a "frozen, uninhabitable wilderness". Neither the treaty of 1684 nor that of 1842 defined where the boundary was, and the region was not even surveyed until 1864. The British authorities in India proposed on a number of occasions down to 1899 that the boundary should be delimited, but received no response from the Chinese Government. Although the northern and eastern frontier of Jammu and Kashmir thus remained undefined, official British maps down to 1946 consistently showed it as following approximately the crest of the Karakoram Mountains. Suggestions which were put forward in 1897 that the boundary should be extended eastward to the crest of the Kuenlun range were rejected by the general staff, on the ground that the new frontier would be difficult to defend and strategically useless. In July 1954, however, the Indian Government published a new official map which for the first time showed the crest of the Kuenlun range as the frontier and included within Indian territory the whole of the Aksai Chin (an area of about 14,000 square miles, or 36,000 sq km), although since 1950 this area had been under Chinese control.

Strategically the Aksai Chin is of great importance to China, as it forms the link between Tibet and Xinjiang (Sinkiang), and in 1956-57 the Chinese built a road across it connecting the two regions. As India asserted its claim to sovereignty over the area only by sending occasional patrols, the Indian Government remained unaware of the road's existence until its attention was drawn to a Chinese press report. Two reconnaissance parties were sent in 1958 to investigate, one of which was captured by Chinese troops, whilst the other confirmed that the road ran through territory claimed by India. In response to Indian representations the Chinese Government released the arrested men, but maintained that the road ran only through Chinese territory.

In a letter of March 22, 1959, to Zhou Enlai, Nehru based India's claim to the Aksai Chin on the treaty of 1842. In his reply, published on Sept. 8, Zhou Enlai pointed out that "this treaty only mentioned in general terms that Ladakh and Tibet would each abide by their borders, and did not contain any specific provisions regarding the location of this section of the boundary", and continued: "This section of the boundary has never been delimited. Between China and Ladakh there does, however, exist a customary line derived from historical traditions, and Chinese maps have always drawn the boundary between China and Ladakh in accordance with this line."

A clash between an Indian police patrol and Chinese troops, in which nine of the former were killed, occurred on Oct. 21, 1959, in the Chang Chenmo valley, west of the Lanak La Pass, which lies on the borderline claimed by India. In a subsequent exchange of notes each Government alleged that the incident had taken place on its own territory and had been caused by an intrusion by the other's forces. According to an Indian External Affairs Ministry statement of Nov. 27, 1962, Chinese troops occupied 6,000 square miles (15,500 sq km) of territory in the disputed area during 1959-62, establishing checkposts and constructing roads connecting them with their bases.

Three encounters between Chinese and Indian troops occurred in July 1962 in the Galwan River valley, near Pangong Lake and in the Chip Chap valley, the only casualties being two Indian soldiers wounded in the last incident. On Oct. 20, 1962, the Chinese army opened an offensive in the Aksai Chin at the same time as that on the McMahon Line. Fighting took place in three areas: immediately south of the Karakoram Pass, around Pangong Lake, 100 miles to the south-east, and around Damchok, in the extreme south-east of the disputed territory. During the fighting the Chinese occupied all the Indian outposts east of the boundary claimed by China, but made no attempt to occupy an Indian post two miles west of this line, which had been evacuated by its garrison. As on the eastern front, China declared a cease-fire on Nov. 21, and announced that its troops would withdraw to positions 20 kilometres behind the line of actual control existing on Nov. 7, 1959. Since 1962 the situation in the Aksai Chin has generally remained peaceful, apart from an incident in September 1965 (when India was at war with Pakistan) in which three Indian policemen were killed.

## Demarcation of China-Pakistan Border

Pakistan and China announced on May 3, 1962, that they had agreed to demarcate their common border, i.e. the border of Xinjiang and the area of Kashmir under Pakistani control. An Indian note to Pakistan of May 10 of that year contended that Pakistan and China had no common boundary, as Kashmir formed "an integral part of the Indian Union"; that India would not be bound by the results of any bilateral discussions between Pakistan and China; and that the border of Kashmir west of the Karakoram Pass followed well-known natural features and did not require fresh delimitation. An agreement delimiting the boundary was signed in Peking on March 2, 1963. A Pakistani Foreign Ministry spokesman stated that out of 3,400 square miles (8,800 sq km) in dispute Pakistan had obtained 1,350 square miles under the agreement, including 750 square miles which were actually in Chinese possession, and China had obtained 2,050 square miles. Pakistan also abandoned her claim to over 13,000 square miles of Xinjiang territory, which had previously been shown as part of Kashmir on Pakistani but not on Indian maps.

After the delimitation of the border China and Pakistan co-operated in the construction of two all-weather highways linking the Pakistani-controlled area of Kashmir with Xinjiang, one of which, running through the Mintaka Pass, was opened in 1968, whilst the other (the Karakoram Highway), running through the Khunjerab Pass, was opened in 1978. Strong protests against both projects were lodged by India.

## Opening of Sino-Indian Negotiations on Border Dispute

After an improvement in Sino-Indian relations in 1981, preliminary negotiations between the two sides on the border question opened in Peking in December 1981 and were continued in a further round of talks in New Delhi in May 1982. However, no agreement was reached in these first two rounds on the basis for substantive negotiations, the quest for which was to continue in further bilateral meetings. It was understood that the Chinese side was seeking to establish the negotiations on the basis that China would retain the disputed territory in the western sector in return for giving up its claims in the eastern sector, whereas the Indian side was insisting on a sector-by-sector approach.

A clear indication of China's attitude in the resumed negotiations came in an article published by the Peking *Shijie Zhishi* in early 1982 and broadcast by Peking radio on March 31. After reiterating the reasons for China's rejection of the ''illegal'' McMahon Line, the article continued: ''The root of the Sino-Indian border issue lies in imperialism and colonialism in pre-independence India. However, the problems between China and India since that country gained independence are different from those between China and the imperialists of the past, since they are problems between two newly independent countries. In handling this problem we should first fix our vision on the common interests of uniting to oppose imperialism.

''Since the border problem is something left over from history, it is necessary both to consider the historical background and also bear in mind the current actual situation in dealing with it. Neither China nor India should impose demands on each other; instead, based on the five principles of peaceful co-existence, they should seek an all-round solution, fair and reasonable for both parties, by holding peaceful and friendly negotiations in the spirit of mutual understanding and accommodation. The status quo on the border should be maintained, pending solution of the problem. It is precisely in this spirit that the Chinese Government, although not recognizing the 'McMahon Line', does not cross this line, for the sake of striving for a negotiated solution. At the same time, we also oppose various past Indian moves in changing the status quo on the border.''

**C.H.**

# China-Japan-Taiwan (Senkaku Islands)

The uninhabited Senkaku Islands, known to the Chinese as the Tiaoyu and other Islands, situated about 200 miles (320 km) west of Okinawa (in the Ryukyu Islands) and about 100 miles (160 km) north-east of Taiwan, became the subject of a dispute between Communist China, Taiwan and Japan following the signing of the Peace Treaty between the Western Allies and Japan in San Francisco in 1951.

Under the 1951 treaty the Senkaku Islands were included in the Ryukyu Islands, which, in terms of a treaty between the United States and Japan of June 17, 1971, reverted to Japan on May 14, 1972. On the other hand, the People's Republic of China had declared on Dec. 30, 1971, that the Senkaku Islands appertained to the island of Taiwan and had, like the latter, been "an inalienable part of Chinese territory since ancient times"; moreover, the Government of the "Republic of China", i.e. Taiwan, had claimed them on June 11, 1971.

In February 1972 the Taiwan Government announced the incorporation of the islands in Taiwan, whereupon the Japanese Government protested on Feb. 17 and later issued a document stating that under the 1895 Treaty of Shimonoseki the islands had been incorporated in Japanese territory, together with Taiwan itself and the Pescadores Islands, after it had been established that the rule of the Chinese Empire did not extend to them.

During negotiations in February 1975 on a possible treaty of peace and friendship between China and Japan (which was eventually signed on Aug. 12, 1978) it was believed in Japan that China would shelve the issue of these islands. This was corroborated by the Chinese Government's attitude to an incident which occurred in April 1978, when a fleet of Chinese fishing vessels began to operate in the terri-

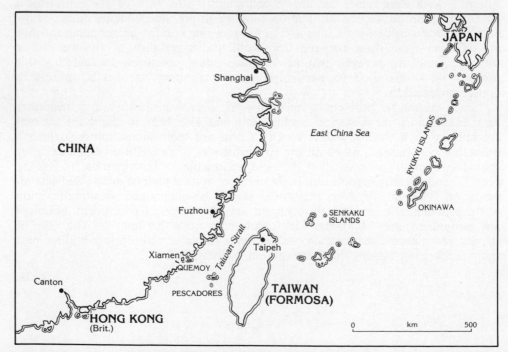

**Map 29   The location of the Senkaku Islands.**

torial waters of the Senkaku Islands, which the fishermen claimed to be in Chinese waters. Following Japanese representations to the Chinese Government a Chinese Deputy Premier stated on April 15 that the incident was not intentional but "an accidental affair", and on the following day the Chinese vessels withdrew from the vicinity of the islands. Liao Cheng-chi, then a vice-chairman of the Standing Committee of the National People's Congress of China, said on April 27 that the Government would make all-out efforts to avoid any conflicts over the Senkaku Islands.

After the signing of the treaty between China and Japan it was stated by a spokesman of Japan's ruling Liberal-Democratic Party on Aug. 13, 1978, that China had practically recognized Japan's control over the islands, and that Deng Xiaoping, then a Chinese Deputy Premier, had emphasized that no further incidents would take place in the area.

H.W.D.

# China-Soviet Union

The Sino-Soviet frontier falls into two sections, divided by the buffer state of Outer Mongolia: (i) the Far Eastern sector, which divides Manchuria from Eastern Siberia, and (ii) the Central Asian sector, which divides the Xinjiang Uygur Autonomous Region (Sinkiang) from the Soviet Republics of Khazakhstan, Kirghizia and Tajikistan. The boundaries in both sections, which were laid down by treaties between the Chinese Emperors and the Russian Tsars signed in 1858, 1860, 1864 and 1881, have been a subject of controversy between China and the Soviet Union since 1963.

### Origin of the Far Eastern Boundary

In the Far East the wastelands north of the River Amur and east of the River Ussuri were sparsely populated in the 17th century by hunting and fishing tribes, which paid tribute to the Manchu kings. After the Manchu conquest of China in 1644-62 they came under the suzerainty of the Chinese Empire, but they were never settled or effectively controlled by either the Manchus or the Chinese. Meanwhile Russian colonization of Siberia, which had begun in the late 16th century, had been pushed rapidly eastward, and in 1644 a Russian military expedition reached the mouth of the Amur. Further expeditions followed, and in 1665 a Russian outpost was established on the Amur. Russian encroachment met with armed resistance from the Manchus, and after nearly 40 years of sporadic fighting the Treaty of Nerchinsk, signed in 1689, fixed the boundary between the Russian and Chinese Empires north of the Amur along the line of the Stanovoi Mountains.

Russian troops and colonists again occupied the territory north of the Amur in the mid-19th century, when China was weakened by the Opium War of 1839-42 with Britain, the Taiping Rebellion of 1850-64 and the Second Opium War of 1858-60 with Britain and France. The Chinese commander on the Amur was forced in 1858 to sign the Treaty of Aigun, which gave Russia sovereignty over 185,000 square miles (480,000 sq km) of territory north of the Amur and placed 130,000 square miles between the Ussuri (the Amur's principal tributary) and the Pacific under joint Sino-Russian sovereignty pending a future decision on the matter. This agreement was confirmed later in the same year by the Treaty of Tianjin (Tientsin), and in subsequent negotiations in 1860 the Tsar demanded the area east of the Ussuri (the Maritime Territory) as his reward for remaining neutral in the Second Opium War and using his good offices to negotiate a peace settlement. The Chinese granted his claim by the Treaty of Peking, which also defined the Sino-Russian border in Central Asia. In their newly-acquired territories the Russians founded the city of Khabarovsk on the Amur in 1858, and the port and naval base of Vladivostok in the Maritime Territory in 1860.

## Origin of the Central Asian Boundary

Although earlier dynasties had temporarily imposed their suzerainty upon Xinjiang ("New Frontier"), Chinese supremacy was not finally established there until the late 17th century. The population consisted of Kazakhs, Tajiks, Kirghiz, Uighurs and Uzbeks, Turkish in race and Moslem in religion, and there was little Chinese settlement, apart from the military garrisons (who were encouraged to settle there with their families) and political exiles. The garrisons consisted of "permanent pickets" close to the towns and "movable pickets" set up in the frontier areas to prevent the nomadic population from driving their flocks and herds into Chinese territory. Although Chinese rule was exercised indirectly through local chieftains, it was bitterly resented by the native population, and armed uprisings occurred in 1825-26, 1827, 1830 and 1857.

From about 1840 onwards the Russians gradually extended their control of Central Asia into the Kazakh and Kirghiz steppes, which were nominally under Chinese suzerainty. The Treaty of Peking in 1860 fixed the boundary between the Chinese and Russian Empires as "following the mountains, great rivers and the present line of Chinese permanent pickets", and provided for a joint survey of the areas in dispute from the foothills of the Altai in the north to the Pamirs in the south. The survey was protracted for four years, as the Russians contended that under the treaty the boundary should follow the hills where the Chinese maintained permanent pickets, whilst the Chinese also claimed the territory farther west occupied by their movable pickets. The Treaty of Chuguchak (or Tarbagatai), signed in 1864, accepted the

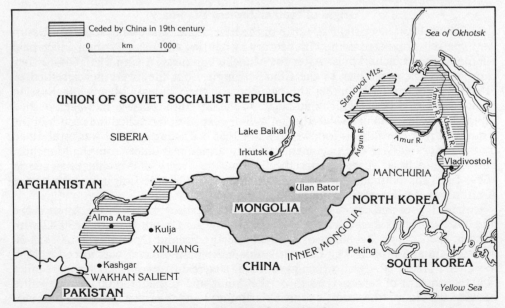

**Map 30   The Sino-Soviet border.**

Russian claim to 350,000 square miles (900,000 sq km) of territory which had not been under effective Chinese control, but in which Chinese movable pickets had operated.

In the same year the whole of Xinjiang revolted against Chinese rule and established its independence under the leadership of a local chieftain, Yakub Beg. To prevent the revolt from spreading into his own Central Asian territories the Tsar sent troops in 1871 which occupied the Ili River Valley as far as the town of Kulja. Although the Chinese reconquered Xinjiang with Russian assistance in 1877, the Russians continued to occupy Kulja and the Upper Ili Valley until 1881, when by the Treaty of St Petersburg or of Ili they agreed to evacuate the area.

### The Russian Revolution and the "Unequal Treaties"

After the overthrow of the Chinese Empire in 1911 the new republican regime headed by Dr Sun Yat-sen demanded the abrogation of all "unequal treaties" and the restoration of China's "traditional" frontiers, the term "unequal treaties" being applied to all agreements by which in the 19th and early 20th centuries China had been compelled to surrender territory or to grant extra-territorial rights to the Western powers, Russia and Japan. This concept met with considerable sympathy from the Bolsheviks after their seizure of power in 1917. By the Karakhan Declaration of July 25, 1919, the Soviet Government stated that it "declares null and void all the treaties concluded with China by the former Governments of Russia, renounces all seizure of Chinese territory and all Russian concessions in China, and restores to China, without any compensation and for ever, all that has been predatorily seized from her by the Tsar's Government and the Russian bourgeoisie".

The declaration specifically mentioned as annulled treaties dealing with spheres of influence in China, with rights of extra-territoriality and consular jurisdiction, concessions on Chinese territory, and the Russian share of the indemnities imposed on China after the suppression of the Boxer Rising of 1900. It did not mention the treaties of Aigun, Peking and Chuguchak, however, and on territorial questions it stated: "The Soviet Government has renounced the conquests made by the Tsarist Government which deprived China of Manchuria and other areas. Let the people living in those areas themselves decide within the frontiers of which state they may wish to dwell, and what form of government they wish to establish in their own countries. . . ."

An agreement between China and the Soviet Union signed on May 31, 1924, provided that at a future conference they were to "annul all conventions, treaties, agreements, protocols, contracts, etc., concluded between the Government of China and the Tsarist Government and to replace them with new treaties, agreements, etc., on the basis of equality, reciprocity and justice, . . . to re-demarcate their national boundaries . . . and pending such re-demarcation to maintain the present boundaries". Talks were held in 1926 to discuss the re-demarcation of the border and the conclusion of a new treaty, but no agreement was reached.

Thereafter the border question remained in abeyance, as China was preoccupied for over 20 years with the civil war between the Kuomintang and the Communists, the Japanese invasion and the renewed civil war which followed the defeat of the Japanese. It was still regarded as unsettled by the Chinese, however, and maps of Central Asia published by the Kuomintang Government laid claim to large areas of territory under Soviet control.

During this period of confusion Xinjiang remained virtually independent of central government control, and the Soviet Union was able to bring Xinjiang within its sphere of influence by supplying military aid to the provincial governors, who controlled both its internal and its external policies. A governor who adopted an anti-Soviet policy was expelled in 1944 by a Soviet-inspired Moslem uprising, and an

"East Turkestan Republic" was established in the Ili Valley with its capital at Kulja, in the region occupied by the Russians in 1871-81.

## Communist China and the Soviet Union, 1949-60

For over 10 years after the victory of the Chinese Communists in 1949 relations between China and the Soviet Union remained apparently friendly. The East Turkestan Republic was reintegrated into China. The Common Programme summarizing the new Government's policies said that it would examine all treaties and agreements with foreign powers concluded by the Kuomintang Government and either recognize, abrogate, revise or renegotiate them, but did not mention treaties concluded by earlier Chinese Governments. Chairman Mao Zedong, the new head of state, said on Dec. 16, 1949, that "the Soviet Union was the first to denounce unequal treaties and concluded with China new equal agreements", suggesting that China did not regard the boundary treaties as "unequal". The 30-year treaty of friendship, alliance and mutual assistance between China and the Soviet Union signed in 1950 contained no reference to boundary questions, apart from an undertaking by each side to respect the other's territorial integrity. As late as April 28, 1960, Zhou Enlai, the Chinese Prime Minister, described the differences on border questions between China and the Soviet Union as "insignificant divergencies on the maps" which could "easily be peacefully resolved".

There were nevertheless indications that China did not regard the boundary question as settled. Up to 1953 official Chinese maps showed the boundary between Xinjiang and Soviet Tajikistan in the Pamirs Plateau several hundred miles to the west of its present position, and later maps marked the frontier in this area as "undefined". A map in *A Short History of Modern China*, published in Peking in 1954, included among "Chinese territories taken by imperialism" the Far Eastern territories ceded in 1858 and 1860 and parts of Soviet Kazakhstan, Kirghizia and Tajikistan as far west as Lake Balkhash, as well as Nepal, Sikkim, Bhutan, Assam, Burma, Malaya, Thailand, Kampuchea, Vietnam, Laos, Korea and Sakhalin, and showed Outer Mongolia as an integral part of China.

## Deterioration of Sino-Soviet Relations, 1960-63

The boundary question again came to the fore as relations between China and the Soviet Union deteriorated from 1960 onwards. Later statements from both Soviet and Chinese sources revealed that border incidents began in July of that year, although at the time no publicity was given to such incidents by either side, and a Soviet statement alleged that the Chinese had violated the Soviet border over 5,000 times during 1960.

Defending Soviet policy during the Cuban missile crisis of October 1962, which had been criticized by China, Nikita Khrushchev (then the Soviet Prime Minister and Communist Party leader) in a speech of Dec. 12 contrasted the expulsion of the Portuguese from Goa by India with the Chinese Government's omission to take similar action against Macao and Hong Kong. In reply, the Peking *People's Daily* mentioned on March 8, 1963, nine treaties which former Chinese Governments had been forced to sign, including the Treaties of Aigun, Tianjin, Peking and Ili, and inquired: "In raising questions of this kind do you intend to raise all the questions of unequal treaties and invite a general settlement?" This comment—the first in which China had referred to the possibility of a revision of the frontiers—was interpreted as a suggestion that China reserved the right to demand the return of the territories ceded under the treaties named at some future date.

Chinese and Soviet statements issued in September 1964 indicated that a tense situation existed on the Xinjiang border. The *People's Daily* alleged on Sept. 6 that Soviet agencies and personnel had carried out "large-scale subversive activities in the Ili region of Xinjiang and incited and coerced several tens of thousands of Chinese citizens into going to the Soviet Union''. This statement appeared to confirm reports from Moscow that riots had occurred in Xinjiang among the Moslem Kazakhs, Uighurs and other nationalities, who resented mass Chinese settlement in the region and attempts to suppress their religion and languages, and that between the middle of 1962 and September 1963 about 50,000 Kazakhs and other tribesmen had fled into the Soviet Union.

A Soviet statement issued on Sept. 21, 1964, declared that "since 1960 Chinese servicemen and civilians have been systematically violating the Soviet border. . . . Attempts are also being made to 'develop' some parts of Soviet territory without permission.'' After quoting a document alleged to have been issued by the Chinese administration in Manchuria, instructing fishermen to ignore orders by Soviet border guards to keep off disputed islands in the Amur and the Ussuri, the statement continued: "The Soviet Government has invited the Chinese Government a number of times to hold consultations on the question of ascertaining separate sections of the border line, to exclude any possibility of misunderstanding. The Chinese side, however, evades such consultations while continuing to violate the border. This cannot but make us wary, especially in view of the fact that Chinese propaganda is making definite hints at the 'unjust demarcation' of some sections of the Soviet-Chinese border allegedly made in the past. However, the artificial creation of any territorial problems in our times, especially between socialist countries, would be tantamount to embarking on a very dangerous path. . . .''

### Boundary Negotiations, 1964

Boundary negotiations began in Peking on Feb. 25, 1964, but were suspended in the following May without any progress having been achieved. According to Soviet sources, the Soviet delegation put forward proposals for the "clarification" of certain sections of the border, but the Chinese delegation laid claim to over 1,500,000 sq km (580,000 square miles) of Soviet territory, while stating that China would not press her claims for the present. According to the Chinese version, the Chinese delegation, while regarding the Treaties of Aigun and Peking as "unequal treaties", offered to take them as a basis for determining the entire alignment of the boundary, subject to "necessary readjustments" at individual places on the boundary by both sides, but the Soviet delegation refused to accept these proposals. Although it was agreed in principle to resume the talks in Moscow at a later date, no further negotiations took place until 1969.

The controversy was revived by an interview given by Chairman Mao on July 10, 1964, to a group of Japanese Socialists, at which he said: "China has not yet asked the Soviet Union for an account about Vladivostok, Khabarovsk, Kamchatka and other towns and regions east of Lake Baikal, which became Russian territory about 100 years ago." (Kamchatka was colonized by the Russians in the early 18th century, and never formed part of the Chinese Empire.) *Pravda* printed the interview on Sept. 2, together with a long editorial which accused China of "an openly expansionist programme with far-reaching pretensions", citing the *Short History of Modern China* published in 1954 as evidence, and gave warning that "any attempt to recarve the map of the world" could lead to "the most dangerous consequences".

In an interview with a Japanese delegation on Sept. 15, 1964, Khrushchev pointed out that the Chinese Emperors had acquired Inner Mongolia, Manchuria, Tibet and Xinjiang, with their non-Chinese populations, by conquest, and suggested that if "Mao Zedong wishes to settle political questions not on a political but on an ethnographical basis" China should grant her non-Chinese people the right of self-determination.

## Border Tensions, 1966-67

In a letter sent to the other Communist parties of Eastern Europe early in 1966 the Soviet party accused China of provoking border conflicts, which, it stated, had increased in recent months, and of spreading allegations that "the Soviet Union unlawfully holds Chinese territory in the Far East". In reply the Chinese Foreign Minister, Marshal Chen Yi, accused the Soviet Union on May 20 of provoking over 5,000 incidents between 1960 and the end of 1965, and of concentrating troops on the Chinese frontier. He also alleged that the Soviet Union had rejected a Chinese proposal to settle frontier disputes on the basis of the treaties concluded between China and the Tsars, and had "insisted on going beyond these unjust treaties".

The tension on the borders greatly increased with the beginning of the Cultural Revolution in China in the summer of 1966. It was reported from Moscow on Oct. 2, 1966, that an estimated 2,000,000 Chinese had taken part in mass demonstrations on the Soviet frontier, especially in the Far Eastern sector, in support of China's territorial claims, and that Chinese troops had opened fire several times on Soviet ships plying on the Amur. The situation became particularly tense in January and February 1967, when for over a fortnight the Soviet embassy in Peking was besieged by howling mobs. Peking Radio asserted on Feb. 2 that a plot by the "Soviet revisionists and US and Japanese imperialists" to attack China through Manchuria had been smashed, and on Feb. 11 all Chinese frontier troops were placed on the alert. Western sources estimated the number of troops on the frontier at this time at nearly 40 Soviet divisions, many of which had recently been transferred there from Eastern Europe, and between 50 and 60 Chinese divisions, or more than 600,000 men. The tension relaxed after Feb. 12, 1967, when the siege of the Soviet embassy was lifted, and on Feb. 21 it was reported from Moscow that except for frontier guards all Chinese troops had been withdrawn about 100 miles from the Soviet and Mongolian borders.

## The Fighting on Damansky Island

Many minor border incidents were believed to have taken place in the later months of 1967 and in 1968, but neither side gave them any publicity at the time. According to later Chinese and Soviet statements, fighting took place on several occasions around a small uninhabited island in the Ussuri, known to the Russians as Damansky Island and to the Chinese as Chenpao Island, lying about 110 miles south of Khabarovsk and 250 miles north of Vladivostok.

The status of the island under the Treaties of Aigun and Peking is disputed. The Soviet Union maintained that a map approved by both Governments in 1861 showed the Chinese bank of the Ussuri as the boundary line in this area. The Chinese Foreign Ministry, on the other hand, contended that the map had been drawn unilaterally by the Russian authorities; that the island was situated on the Chinese side of the central line of the river's main channel, which under international law formed the boundary line; and that it had formed part of the bank on the Chinese side until eroded by the river, had always been under Chinese jurisdiction and had been admitted to be Chinese by the Soviet delegation at the 1964 boundary negotiations. The problem was complicated by the fact that after the breaking up of the ice in spring the Ussuri regularly floods its banks and frequently shifts its channel.

Armed clashes between Soviet and Chinese frontier guards, of which the two sides gave contradictory accounts, occurred on the island in March 1969, causing considerable loss of life. According to the Soviet version, about 300 Chinese soldiers crossed the frozen river to the island during the night of March 1-2, opened fire in the morning on Soviet frontier guards, and were expelled only after a two-hour battle in which the Soviet troops lost 31 killed. Chinese official statements, however, declared that a large Soviet force had opened fire on Chinese frontier guards on normal patrol duty, killing and wounding many of them.

Fighting on a much larger scale broke out on March 15, 1969, and continued for several hours, causing heavy casualties; Soviet press reports mentioned by name 12 officers and NCOs, including a colonel, who had been killed, suggesting that a full regiment of frontier guards and reserves had been engaged on the Soviet side. Sporadic incidents continued on the islands in the Ussuri and the Amur throughout the spring and summer, and caused a few casualties on each side.

### Proposals for New Negotiations

A Soviet note of March 29, 1969, after reaffirming the Soviet claim to Damansky Island, urged the Chinese Government "to refrain from any actions on the frontier that may cause complications and to solve any differences that may arise in a calm atmosphere", and proposed that the consultations started in 1964 should be resumed as soon as possible. At the suggestion of the Soviet chairman of the joint Sino-Soviet commission on navigation on the Far Eastern frontier rivers, the commission met in Khabarovsk from June 18 to Aug. 8, 1969, when an agreement was reached on measures for ensuring normal conditions for shipping on the Amur and Ussuri. The situation subsequently remained peaceful on this section of the frontier.

A long Chinese statement issued on May 24, 1969, after summarizing the Chinese case on the Damansky Island question, declared that "there exists a boundary question between China and the Soviet Union not only because Tsarist Russia annexed more than 1,500,000 sq km (580,000 square miles) of Chinese territory by the unequal treaties it imposed on China but also because it crossed in many places the boundary line stipulated by the unequal treaties and further occupied vast expanses of Chinese territory", and continued: "In the sector of the Wusuli (Ussuri) and Heilung (Amur) rivers the Soviet Government, in violation of the Treaty of Aigun, the Treaty of Peking and the established principles of international law, has gone so far as to draw the boundary line almost entirely along the Chinese bank, and in some places even on China's inland rivers and islands, marking as Soviet territory over 600 of the 700 and more Chinese islands on the Chinese side of the central line of the main channel, which cover an area of more than 1,000 sq km."

After contending that the treaties relating to the present Sino-Soviet boundary were all "unequal treaties", that they should all be annulled and that the boundary question remained an outstanding issue, the statement concluded: "Taking into consideration the fact that it was Tsarist Russian imperialism which compelled China to sign these treaties . . . and that large numbers of Soviet working people have lived on the land over a long period of time, the Chinese Government, out of the desire to safeguard the revolutionary friendship between the Chinese and Soviet peoples, is still ready to take these unequal treaties as the basis for determining the entire alignment of the boundary line between the two countries and for settling all existing questions relating to the boundary. Any side which occupies the territory of the other side in violation of the treaties must, in principle, return it wholly and unconditionally to the other side, and this brooks no ambiguity. . . . The Chinese Government maintains that what should be done is to hold negotiations for the overall settlement of the Sino-Soviet boundary question and the conclusion of a new equal treaty to replace the old unequal ones. . . ."

The Soviet Government's reply, issued on June 13, 1969, commented on the question of "unequal treaties": "Neither the appeal of 1919 nor the agreement between the Soviet Union and the Chinese Republic of 1924 contained, or could contain, indications that the treaties laying down the present Soviet-Chinese borders were regarded as unequal or secret. Naturally there was no question of annulling or revising them. Until recently the leaders of the People's Republic of China had themselves stressed that the Soviet State had abolished unequal treaties with China.'' Its proposals for future negotiations were as follows: ''The Soviet Union proposes that the unanimity of the two sides on the undisputed stretches of the frontier be recorded; that an understanding be reached on individual disputed stretches of the frontier through mutual consultations on the basis of treaty documents; that the two sides should proceed on the basis of the treaties in force, observing the principle of mutual concessions and the economic interests of the local population when delimiting the frontier line on stretches which have undergone natural changes; and that the agreement reached should be recorded by the two sides signing appropriate documents.'' In conclusion, it suggested that the consultations broken off in 1964 should be resumed in Moscow within the next two or three months.

### Agreement between Alexei Kosygin and Zhou Enlai

Meanwhile a series of incidents on the Central Asian border, for which each side held the other responsible, had begun in April 1969 and continued throughout the next three months, culminating in fighting on Aug. 13 which resulted in casualties on both sides. Tension reached such a height that on Aug. 23 the Chinese Communist Party issued a statement declaring that war might break out at any time. The situation was transformed, however, by the death on Sept. 3, 1969, of President Ho Chi Minh of North Vietnam and by the publication of his political testament, in which he appealed for ''the restoration of unity among the fraternal parties''. After attending his funeral the Soviet Prime Minister, Alexei Kosygin, flew to Peking on Sept. 11, where he met Zhou Enlai. As a result of this meeting the two sides agreed to reopen border talks.

The exact terms of the agreement reached between them subsequently became a subject of controversy. According to Soviet sources, it was agreed to take measures to avoid armed conflicts on the border, to settle border questions through negotiations, and to take steps to normalize relations between them, such as the restoration of diplomatic relations at ambassadorial level and the expansion of trade. According to the Chinese version, the two Prime Ministers compared Soviet and Chinese maps, established which parts of the frontier were in dispute, and agreed to withdraw their armed forces from these areas and to conclude an agreement on the preservation of the status quo on the border.

A Chinese statement of Oct. 7, 1969, announcing that it had been agreed to hold talks on the border question said: ''The responsibility for the development of the Sino-Soviet boundary question to such an acute state does not all rest with the Chinese side. The Chinese Government has never demanded the return of the territory Tsarist Russia had annexed by means of the unequal treaties. On the contrary, it is the Soviet Government that has persisted in occupying still more Chinese territory in violation of the stipulations of these treaties and, moreover, peremptorily demanded that the Chinese Government recognize such occupation as legal. Precisely because of the Soviet Government's persistence in its expansionist stand, many disputed areas have been created along the Sino-Soviet border, and this has become the root cause of tension on the border. . . .''

### Further Boundary Negotiations, 1969-78

Negotiations on the border opened at Deputy Foreign Minister level in Peking on Oct. 20, 1969, and continued with a number of breaks until the autumn of 1978. No progress was made, as the Soviet delegation rejected the Chinese demand for the withdrawal of troops from disputed areas, on the ground that the border line shown on Chinese maps did not coincide with that defined by the treaty documents. The Soviet delegation proposed in 1971 and again in 1973 that the two countries should sign a non-aggression pact; this was rejected as unnecessary by the Chinese side, which pointed out that the treaty of 1950 still remained in force, and demanded that the Soviet side should carry out the alleged agreement to withdraw its forces from the disputed areas.

In support of their claim that disputed areas existed, Chinese officials in Xinjiang told Western journalists that 20 areas along the Xinjiang border, varying in size from 390 to 11,600 square miles (1,000 to 30,000 sq km), were in dispute, and that Soviet troops had gradually occupied 185 square miles of Chinese territory during 1960-69 and another 1,080 square miles between 1972 and July 1977. The areas in question are largely desert, and are uninhabited or sparsely inhabited.

In the Far Eastern sector of the border territorial disputes concerned mainly islands in the Ussuri and the Amur. Agreement on one disputed point was reached at a session of the Sino-Soviet joint commission for navigation on the frontier rivers in 1977. The Treaty of Peking defines the boundary as following the Amur to its junction with the Ussuri and then turning south along the Ussuri. At the junction of the two rivers there is a triangular island with an area of 128 square miles, which is bounded by the Amur to the north, a narrow watercourse to the south-west and a broader one to the south-east. The ownership of the island is disputed, as the Soviet Union holds that the confluence lies west of the island and that the two watercourses are arms of the Amur, whereas the Chinese maintain that the confluence is east of the island, at Khabarovsk, and that the watercourses are arms of the Ussuri. The agreement, which did not deal with the question of ownership of the island, provided that Chinese shipping might use the eastern watercourse when the water in the other was too low for navigation.

Three comparatively minor frontier incidents occurred during 1978-80. In the first, Soviet border guards crossed to the Chinese bank of the Ussuri on May 9, 1978; according to the official Soviet apology, they had mistaken the Chinese bank for a Soviet island while pursuing an armed criminal by night, and withdrew on realizing their mistake. In the second, a Chinese was shot dead and another wounded and taken prisoner by Soviet frontier troops on the Xinjiang border on July 16, 1979; the two Governments disagreed on whether the incident occurred on Soviet or Chinese territory and whether the two Chinese were soldiers or civilians. In the third, a Chinese and a Soviet citizen were killed in a clash on the Argun River, which forms the border between Siberia and western Manchuria, on Oct. 5, 1980; the two Governments issued contradictory accounts of the incident, which disagreed on which side had opened fire.

### Inconclusive 1979 Talks in Moscow and Subsequent Developments

In accordance with the terms of the Sino-Soviet treaty of alliance of 1950, China gave notice on April 3, 1979, of its intention not to extend the treaty when it expired a year later, but proposed that negotiations should be held for the solution of outstanding issues and the improvement of relations between the two countries. After an exchange of notes and five preliminary meetings, talks formally opened in Moscow on Oct. 17, 1979, and continued until Nov. 30. According to unofficial reports, the Chinese delegation repeated its demand for the withdrawal of troops from disputed areas, and also called for the reduction of the strength of the Soviet troops on the frontier and their withdrawal from Outer Mongolia. Following the Soviet intervention in Afghanistan, the Chinese Government stated on Jan. 19, 1980, that it would be "inappropriate" to hold the second round of talks at present.

Further proposals for a settlement of the border question were put forward in an article by Li Huichuan, deputy leader of the Chinese delegation to the 1979 Moscow talks, which appeared in *The People's Daily* on June 17, 1981. The article was published on the day that Alexander Haig, the US Secretary of State, left Peking after talks at which no agreement was reached on the question of US sales of weapons to Taiwan, and was widely regarded as a warning to the United States that China might seek to improve her relations with the Soviet Union. A few days later Li Xiannian (a Vice-Chairman of the Communist Party) told a West German delegation that China wanted to resume negotiations on the normalization of relations, but that the talks must deal with the withdrawal of Soviet troops from the Chinese border and from Afghanistan.

In his article, Li Huichuan stated that the Sino-Soviet border had been determined by a series of "unequal treaties imposed on China by Tsarist Russian imperialism", under which Russia had annexed over 1,500,000 square kilometres of Chinese territory (about 580,000 square miles), an area three times the size of France, and that after the Russian Revolution the Soviet Government in 1920 had declared these treaties null and void. A Sino-Soviet agreement of 1924 had provided that the border would be redemarcated and that meanwhile the status quo would be maintained, but no agreement had been reached at talks held in 1926, with the result that "the Sino-Soviet border issue remains unsettled to this day". The Chinese Government, he continued, was prepared to take the existing treaties, "unequal" though they were, as the basis for determining the border line. Articles in the Soviet press, however, maintained that the present border had not only been delimited by the treaties, but had been "formed historically" and was "actually guarded" by Soviet troops, and the Soviet Government demanded that the "historically formed" and "actually defended" boundary line, which went far beyond that delimited by the treaties, should be taken as the basis for solving all boundary questions. In conclusion, Li Huichuan laid down the following conditions for a settlement: (i) the "unequal" nature of the treaties should be recognized; (ii) the boundary question should be settled through peaceful negotiations on the basis of the treaties; (iii) any territory occupied by either side in violation of the treaties must be returned, although adjustments might be made in these areas in the interests of the local inhabitants; (iv) a new treaty should be signed and the boundary line surveyed and demarcated; and (v) pending the reaching of a settlement the status quo should be maintained, armed conflicts should be avoided, the two countries' forces should withdraw from or refrain from entering all disputed areas (i.e. those at which the boundary line was drawn in a different way on the maps exchanged during the boundary negotiations in 1964), and an agreement on the maintenance of the status quo should be signed.

In a note of Sept. 25, 1981, the Soviet Government proposed that border negotiations should be resumed in Moscow. A Chinese official spokesman said on Dec. 29 that China had recently replied to the proposal, emphasizing that as previous negotiations had been unsuccessful adequate preparations should be made before they could be resumed. Subsequently, Sergei Tikhvinsky, deputy leader of the Soviet delegation to the Moscow talks, was reported to have arrived in Peking on Jan. 14, 1982, for 10 days of secret talks with Chinese Foreign Ministry officials. The Soviet Government again proposed on Feb. 1, 1982, that the border talks should be resumed, although a Foreign Ministry spokesman said on Feb. 23 that the Soviet Union did not intend to discuss "territorial questions". However, the Soviet approaches apparently met with a cold reception, as demonstrated when Wang Bingnan, president of the Chinese Association for Friendship with Foreign Countries, said on Feb. 23 that relations could not be improved unless the Soviet Union renounced its "policy of hegemonism and expansionism" and withdrew its troops from Afghanistan.

### Chinese Condemnation of 1981 Soviet-Afghan Border Treaty

Meanwhile, a new source of friction in Sino-Soviet relations had arisen in June 1981, when the Soviet Union signed a border treaty with Afghanistan which recognized as Soviet territory an area to the north-east of Afghanistan to which China laid claim. The signature of the treaty, on June 16, coincided with Soviet military occupation of the strategically important Wakhan salient (the narrow strip of Afghan territory running eastwards to the Chinese border between Soviet territory to the north and Pakistan to the south) and gave rise to suspicions in China and the West that the treaty provided for Soviet annexation of the salient.

Although no exact details of the treaty were published either by the Soviet Union or Afghanistan, official comments from both sides indicated that it provided only for the legal delimitation and affirmation of the existing boundary between the two countries. Nevertheless, the Chinese Foreign Ministry on July 22 declared the treaty "illegal and invalid", arguing that the Soviet Union had no right to conclude a border treaty with a third country involving this line, since the territory immediately to the north had been in dispute between Peking and Moscow for some 90 years. At the same time China stressed that it had no outstanding territorial disputes with Afghanistan itself, with which it had signed an agreement in November 1963 regulating the 43-mile (70-km) Chinese-Afghan border at the eastern end of the Wakhan salient.

China's case against the Soviet Union rested on an 1884 protocol "concerning the Chinese-Russian border in the region of Kashgar" (officially described by China as the "Sino-Russian Kashgar boundary treaty"). This agreement, which had been reached after a long period of Russian penetration into central Asia, had specified that from the Uz-Bel mountain pass in the Pamirs "the Russian boundary turns to the south-west and the Chinese boundary runs due south". According to Chinese accounts, the Russians had nevertheless in the 1890s proceeded to occupy some 20,000 square kilometres of Chinese territory by armed force and had subsequently attempted to legitimize this encroachment by describing a Chinese-Soviet exchange of notes in 1894 as a border treaty regulating the issue. According to China, however, the 1894 exchange of notes showed that the two sides had agreed to differ over the sovereignty of the area in question and had decided to maintain the status quo pending a permanent settlement.

The Soviet news agency Tass responded to the Chinese assertions on Aug. 11, 1981, by stating that the new Soviet-Afghan border treaty was a bilateral matter involving no third countries and by accusing China of "falsifying history" in order to invent a dispute over a question which had been finally settled in 1894. There was "no other line" than that determined in 1894, continued Tass, as demonstrated by the fact that the border in question was shown on Chinese maps exactly as on Soviet maps. This claim was in turn rejected by China on Aug. 31 as a "deliberate misrepresentation" in that the Chinese Government had consistently made known its view that the frontier in the Pamirs was not finally delineated and that a dispute existed which had yet to be settled.

**C.H.**

# China-Taiwan

Taiwan, officially the Republic of China, lies 150-200 kilometres off the south-east Chinese mainland coast and together with certain small islands controlled by the Republic has a total land area of 36,000 sq km and a population of some 18,000,000. Since December 1949 Taiwan has been the seat of the Kuomintang Government which fled from mainland China following the Communists' civil war victory, and both regimes have since claimed to be the only legitimate Government of all China. (For territorial relationship of China and Taiwan, see map on page 258.)

### Early and Post-War History

The island of Taiwan (also known as Formosa) was occupied in 1624 by the Dutch, who encouraged immigration from China in order to develop its agricultural resources. Supporters of the Ming dynasty, which had been overthrown by the Manchu invaders in 1644, expelled the Dutch in 1661 and used the island as a base for operations against the mainland until 1683, when it was conquered by the Manchus and incorporated into the Chinese Empire. Immigration continued throughout the 18th century, and by 1800 the Chinese population far outnumbered the aborigines.

After the Sino-Japanese War of 1894-95 Japan annexed Taiwan and the Pescadores (also known as the Penghu Islands), a group of 48 small islands 30 miles (48 km) west of Taiwan, which had been under Chinese rule since 1281. The 1943 Cairo Declaration issued by Britain, the United States and China laid down that the territories taken from China by Japan should be restored to Chinese sovereignty after the defeat of Japan, and in 1945 the Chinese Government took over the administration of Taiwan and the Pescadores pending the conclusion of a peace treaty. Although this change was initially welcomed in Taiwan, the corruption of the new administration led to a serious revolt in 1947.

On the mainland the civil war between the ruling Kuomintang and the Communists culminated in the proclamation of the People's Republic of China in Peking on Oct. 1, 1949, and the Kuomintang Government fled on Dec. 8 from Chengdu, to which it had transferred its capital, to Taiwan, where it established its new capital at Taipeh. It was followed by over 1,500,000 refugees, including about 750,000 members of the armed forces. Since then two regimes have both claimed to be the only legitimate Chinese Government—the People's Republic of China, controlling the mainland and 99.7 per cent of Chinese territory, and the Republic of China, controlling Taiwan and a number of offshore islands. Although Hainan, the largest of these, was occupied by the Communists in April 1950, the Kuomintang retained control of (i) the Pescadores; (ii) Quemoy, an island 12 miles (19 km) across, lying about four miles off the mainland port of Xiamen (Amoy), and three smaller islands nearby; (iii) Matsu, off Fuzhou (Foochow); (iv) the Nanchi Islands, about 130 miles (210 km) north of Taiwan; and (v) the Tachen Islands, off the coast of Zhejiang (Chekiang) province, about 200 miles (320 km) north of Taiwan. The Taiwan Government also maintained a garrison on Itu Aba, one of the Spratly Islands, in the South China Sea. Gen. Chiang Kai-shek, who had headed the Kuomintang Government of China since the late 1920s, became President of Taiwan and retained this post until his death in April 1975.

The People's Republic of China was immediately recognized by the Communist countries, and by January 1950 had also been recognized by 11 other European and Asian countries, including Britain. The process of international recognition, however, was delayed by the outbreak of the Korean War and China's interven-

270

tion in it. Resolutions in favour of the admission of the People's Republic to the United Nations were submitted annually to the General Assembly from 1950 onwards, but were regularly defeated up to 1969. In consequence China continued to be represented in the United Nations by the Taiwan Government, which held the status of a permanent member of the Security Council, with the right to veto any decision.

Japan renounced all claims to Taiwan and the Pescadores by the peace treaty signed at San Francisco in 1951, but the treaty did not define to which Chinese Government they belonged, and was denounced by both the Chinese Governments, neither of which had been invited to the San Francisco conference. In 1952, however, Japan signed a separate peace treaty with the Taiwan Government, which recognized all residents of Taiwan and the Pescadores who were of Chinese nationality as "nationals of the Republic of China".

The Kuomintang Government announced in June 1949 a blockade of all that part of the Chinese coast and territorial waters then under Communist control, which after its withdrawal to Taiwan it extended to the whole coast of mainland China. The blockade led to a number of attacks by Kuomintang warships and aircraft on British and US shipping. On June 27, 1950, two days after the outbreak of the Korean War, President Truman announced that he had ordered the US 7th Fleet to prevent any attack on Taiwan; that he was calling upon the Taiwan Government to cease all air and sea operations against the mainland; and that "the 7th Fleet will see that this is done". His successor, President Eisenhower, however, announced on Feb. 2, 1953, in his first State of the Union message to Congress, that he had issued instructions that "the 7th Fleet shall no longer be employed to shield Communist China".

Zhou Enlai, then Prime Minister of the People's Republic, stated on Aug. 11, 1954, that the "liberation" of Taiwan was an affair that concerned the Chinese people only, and that any attempt by foreign powers to resist it would constitute an infringement of China's sovereignty. John Foster Dulles, then the US Secretary of State, declared on Aug. 24 that the 7th Fleet would protect Taiwan against any attack from the mainland, as well as other islands the defence of which was intimately connected with that of Taiwan. In defiance of this warning, the Chinese Army began a heavy bombardment of Quemoy on Sept. 3, 1954, to which Kuomintang warships and aircraft replied by attacking military targets on the mainland. A mutual security treaty between the United States and the Taiwan Government was signed on Dec. 1, 1954, under which the United States undertook to defend Taiwan, the Pescadores and "such other territories as may be determined by mutual agreement" against any armed attack. The Taiwan Government gave an undertaking on Dec. 10 that it would not attack the mainland without prior consultation with the United States.

The small island of Yikiangshan, situated eight miles (13 km) north of the Tachen Islands, was captured by Communist forces on Jan. 18, 1955, and after heavy air attacks the Kuomintang forces evacuated the Tachen and Nanchi Islands in February. At President Eisenhower's request, a resolution authorizing him to employ the armed forces to protect Taiwan and the Pescadores, as well as "such related positions and territories of that area now in friendly hands" as he judged to be appropriate, was adopted by the House of Representatives on Jan. 25 and by the Senate three days later.

The bombardment of the Quemoy group of islands was resumed after a long interval on Aug. 23, 1958. A declaration issued on Sept. 4 of that year extended the limit of China's territorial waters from three to 12 nautical miles, and stated that no foreign warships or aircraft might enter Chinese territorial waters and the airspace above them without permission from Peking. Although the effect of the declaration was to bring the Quemoys and Matsu within the new 12-mile limit, US warships were used from Sept. 7 to escort supply convoys to Quemoy. The Chinese Government suspended the bombardment on Oct. 6, and announced that supplies might be sent to Quemoy on condition that there was no US escort, but resumed the shelling on Oct. 20 on the ground that this condition had not been observed. From Oct. 25, however, shelling was confined to odd dates, to allow supplies to be brought in on alternate days.

Sporadic shelling continued over the next 20 years, although during the latter part of this period the shells largely contained propaganda leaflets. Communist leaders continued to announce their determination to "liberate" Taiwan and Kuomintang leaders their determination to "liberate" the mainland, but neither side made any serious attempt to carry out its threats. Occasional clashes occurred, however, including periodic raids on the coast by Kuomintang commandos and a naval engagement in the Taiwan Strait in 1965 in which each side claimed to have inflicted serious damage on the other.

The People's Republic gradually emerged from its isolation, despite its strained relations with the Soviet bloc after 1960 and the damage to its international reputation caused by attacks on foreign embassies during the Cultural Revolution. During the later 1950s and the 1960s it was recognized by an increasing number of countries, including Egypt in 1956, France in 1964 and Italy in 1970. The 1970 session of the General Assembly voted in favour of the admission of the People's Republic to the United Nations by 51 votes to 49, with 25 abstentions, but the resolution remained inoperative, as the Assembly had previously passed a resolution declaring the Chinese representation issue an "important question" requiring a two-thirds majority for its adoption.

## Impact of US Recognition of Communist China

The dramatic improvement in relations between the People's Republic and the United States from 1971 onwards transformed relations between the People's Republic and Taiwan and between both and the outside world. After it had been announced on July 15, 1971, that President Nixon had accepted an invitation to visit the People's Republic, William Rogers (then Secretary of State) said on Aug. 2 that the United States would support the admission of the People's Republic to the United Nations, while opposing "any action to expel the Republic of China or otherwise deprive it of representation in the United Nations". The General Assembly, however, rejected on Oct. 25, 1971, a US "important question" resolution, and adopted an Albanian resolution recognizing the representatives of the People's Republic as "the only lawful representatives of China to the United Nations" by 76 votes to 35, with 17 abstentions. The People's Republic in consequence replaced the Republic of China (Taiwan) in the General Assembly and the Security Council.

President Nixon paid an official visit to China on Feb. 21-27, 1972, at the conclusion of which he and Zhou Enlai issued a long communiqué in Shanghai. On the Taiwan question this stated: "The Chinese side reaffirmed its position: the Taiwan question is the crucial question obstructing the normalization of relations between China and the United States; the Government of the People's Republic of China is the sole legal Government of China; Taiwan is a province of China which has long been returned to the motherland; the liberation of Taiwan is China's internal affair in which no other country has the right to interfere; and all US forces and military installations must be withdrawn from Taiwan. The Chinese Government firmly opposes any activities which aim at the creation of 'one China, one Taiwan', 'one China, two Governments', 'two Chinas' and 'independent Taiwan', or advocate that 'the status of Taiwan remains to be determined'. The US side declared: The United States acknowledges that all Chinese on either side of the Taiwan Strait maintain that there is but one China and that Taiwan is a part of China. The US Government does not challenge that position. It reaffirms its interest in a peaceful settlement of the Taiwan question by the Chinese themselves. With this prospect in mind, it affirms the ultimate objective of the withdrawal of all US forces and military installations from Taiwan. In the meantime, it will progressively reduce its forces and military installations on Taiwan as the tension in the area diminishes. . . .''

President Nixon's visit was followed by the recognition of the People's Republic by several major states, including Japan, West Germany, Australia, New Zealand and Spain. During a visit to Peking in September 1972 the then Japanese Prime Minister, Kakuei Tanaka, signed a joint statement with Zhou Enlai recognizing the Government of the People's Republic as the sole legal Government of China, and stating that the Japanese Government ''fully understands and respects'' the Chinese Government's stand that ''Taiwan is an inalienable part of the territory of the People's Republic of China''. By July 1974 the People's Republic was recognized by 95 countries, and Taiwan by only 33.

The United States and the People's Republic agreed in 1973 to establish liaison offices in each other's capitals. The movement towards normalization of relations, which developed slowly during the next four years, made rapid progress in 1978, and coincided with a marked softening in the Chinese Government's attitude towards Taiwan. In a speech to the National People's Congress on Feb. 26, 1978, Hua Guofeng, then the Prime Minister, declared that ''the Chinese People's Liberation Army must make all the preparations necessary for the liberation of Taiwan'', but also stated that ''it has been our consistent policy that 'all patriots belong to one big family', 'whether they come over early or late' ''. A senior Chinese official assured a visiting US Congressman in July 1978 that Peking did not rule out a negotiated settlement with the Taiwan regime, as the Communist Party and the Kuomintang had worked together in 1924-27 and again during the war with Japan. Deng Xiaoping, then the senior Deputy Premier, told *The New York Times* on Nov. 29 that China would seek a negotiated settlement which took into account the fact that Taiwan's political system differed from that of the mainland, although it would not enter into any pledge to abstain from the use of force, as such a pledge would make the Taiwan authorities refuse to negotiate.

It was announced on Dec. 15, 1978, that the People's Republic and the United States had agreed to recognize each other and to establish diplomatic relations from Jan. 1, 1979. The joint communiqué said: ''The USA recognizes the Government of the People's Republic of China as the sole legal Government of China. Within this context, the people of the USA will maintain cultural, commercial and other unofficial relations with the people of Taiwan. . . . The Government of the USA acknowledges the Chinese position that there is but one China and Taiwan is part of China. . . .''

The two Governments at the same time issued statements defining their respective positions on the Taiwan question. The US statement, after announcing that the mutual defence treaty of 1954 would be terminated and that the remaining US military personnel would be withdrawn from Taiwan within four months, emphasized that ''the USA continues to have an interest in the peaceful resolution of the Taiwan issue, and expects that the Taiwan issue will be settled peacefully by the Chinese themselves''. The Chinese statement said: ''The question of Taiwan was the crucial issue obstructing the normalization of relations between China and the USA. It has now been resolved between the two countries in the spirit of the Shanghai communiqué. . . . As for the way of bringing Taiwan back to the embrace of the motherland and reunifying the country, it is entirely China's internal affair. . . .'' President Chiang Ching-kuo of Taiwan commented on Dec. 16: ''Under whatever circumstances, the Republic of China will neither negotiate with

273

the Chinese Communist regime nor compromise with communism, and she will never give up her sacred tasks of recovering the mainland and delivering the compatriots there."

The shelling of Quemoy and Matsu was officially terminated on Jan. 1, 1979, when the Standing Committee of the National People's Congress proposed that the military confrontation between the People's Republic and Taiwan should be "ended through discussion". President Chiang, however, declared on the same day that "our anti-Communist struggle will never cease until the Chinese Communist regime has been destroyed".

The American Institute in Taiwan was incorporated on Jan. 16, 1979, to enable the US and Taiwanese peoples to maintain commercial, cultural and other relations without official government representation or diplomatic relations, and on Feb. 15 the Taiwan Government announced the establishment of the Taiwan Co-ordination Council for North American Affairs to act as a liaison office in Washington. An agreement between the two organizations signed on Oct. 2, 1980, provided that they and their staffs would enjoy full diplomatic privileges and immunities. The People's Republic protested against the agreement in a note to Washington of Oct. 15.

Although no progress towards reunification was made during 1979-80, the leaders of the People's Republic continued to refer to the question in conciliatory terms, and ceased to speak of the "liberation" of Taiwan. In contrast to his speech of Feb. 26, 1978, Hua Guofeng merely said when addressing the National People's Congress on Sept. 7, 1980, that "we shall work energetically for the return of Taiwan to the motherland, fulfilling our lofty aim of unifying our homeland at an early date".

## 1981 Chinese Proposals for Reunification

In a major new development in late 1981, Marshal Ye Jianying (Chairman of the Standing Committee of the Chinese National People's Congress—a post equivalent to head of state) put forward detailed proposals for the peaceful reunification of China and Taiwan. Although the Chinese Government had previously suggested that within a reunited China Taiwan might retain full autonomy as well as its own armed forces and economic system, Marshal Ye's proposal was the first in which the Chinese Communist Party had officially offered to share power with the Kuomintang.

Marshal Ye's nine-point plan, which he put forward in an interview with the New China News Agency on Sept. 30, 1981, was formulated as follows: "(i) In order to bring an end to the unfortunate separation of the Chinese nation as early as possible, we propose that talks be held between the Communist Party of China and the Kuomintang of China on a reciprocal basis so that the two parties will co-operate for the third time to accomplish the great cause of national reunification. The two sides may first send people to meet for an exhaustive exchange of views. (ii) It is the urgent desire of the people of all nationalities on both sides of the straits to communicate with each other, reunite with their families and relatives, develop trade and increase mutual understanding. We propose that the two sides make arrangements to facilitate the exchange of mails, trade, air and shipping services, family reunions and visits by relatives and tourists, as well as academic, cultural and sports exchanges, and reach an agreement thereon. (iii) After the country is reunified, Taiwan can enjoy a high degree of autonomy as a special administrative region, and can retain its armed forces. The central Government will not interfere with local affairs on Taiwan. (iv) Taiwan's current socio-economic system will remain unchanged, as will its way of life and its economic and cultural relations with foreign countries. There will be no encroachment on the proprietary rights and lawful right of inheritance over private property, houses, land and enterprises, or on foreign investments. (v) People in authority and representative personages of various circles in Taiwan may take up posts of leadership in national political bodies and participate in running the state. (vi) When Taiwan's local finance is in difficulty, the central Government may subsidize it as is fit for the circumstances. (vii) For people of all nationalities and public figures of various circles in Taiwan who wish to come and settle on the mainland, it is guaranteed that proper arrangements may be made for them, that there will be no discrimination against them, and that they will have freedom of entry and exit. (viii) Industrialists and businessmen in Taiwan are welcome to invest and engage in various economic undertakings on the mainland, and their legal rights, interests and profits are guaranteed. (ix) The reunification of the motherland is the responsibility of all Chinese. We sincerely welcome people of all nationalities, public figures of all circles and all mass organizations in Taiwan to make proposals and suggestions regarding affairs of state through various channels and in various ways.''

Responding to Marshal Ye's proposals, Sun Yun-suan (Taiwan's Prime Minister) said in the Legislative Yuan (Parliament) on Oct. 2: "The nine-point overture of the Chinese Communists . . . has not gone to the heart of the problem, which is whether China should adopt a free and democratic system or a totalitarian and dictatorial one. . . . We implement benevolent rule, whereas the Chinese Communists enforce a tyrannical one, so there is no room for compromise." President Chiang Ching-kuo declared at a meeting of the central standing committee of the Kuomintang on Oct. 7: "We shall never negotiate with the Chinese Communists. . . . I want to tell our compatriots on the Chinese mainland that we are resolved to remove the yoke that the Communists have imposed upon them. . . .''

Despite these rebuffs, Chinese spokesmen continued to elaborate on Marshal Ye's proposals. Peng Deqing, the Minister of Communications, said on Oct. 3 that his ministry was ready to establish regular passenger and cargo services with Taiwan by sea and air at any time. Zheng Tuobin, Minister of Foreign Trade, on Oct. 7 suggested measures for the expansion of trade between China and Taiwan whereby each would supply the other's needs; China, for example, could supply Taiwan with coal, oil and herbal medicines at preferential prices. Chang Yanqing, vice-president of the Bank of China, proposed on Oct. 10 that exchange transactions and settlement of accounts should be conducted through bank representatives in Hong Kong until direct transactions could be established, and stated that the bank was ready to open savings accounts for Chinese in Taiwan and to guarantee freedom to deposit and withdraw money.

Hu Yaobang, who had succeeded Hua Guofeng as Chairman of the Communist Party in June 1981, repeated the proposal for co-operation between the Kuomintang and the Communist Party on Oct. 9, in a speech to commemorate the 70th anniversary of the revolution of 1911, which overthrew the Ching dynasty and established the Chinese Republic. Chairman Hu said that the three great tasks confronting China were to modernize agriculture, industry, national defence, and science and technology, to defend world peace, and "to ensure Taiwan's return to the motherland". "The question of Taiwan is entirely China's internal affair," he continued. "It should be settled by the leaders and people on both sides of the strait. The Kuomintang and the Communist Party co-operated twice in history, to complete the northern expedition [in 1926-27] and conduct the war against Japanese aggression. This gave a strong impetus to our nation's progress. Why can we not have a third period of co-operation between the Kuomintang and the Communist Party to build a unified state? It is true that neither of the previous co-operations lasted long, but fairminded people all admit that the two unfortunate splits were not caused by the Communist Party. We do not wish to settle old accounts here. Let bygones be bygones! Let the past lessons help us to co-operate better in the future!''

He continued: ''There is nothing in our present proposal which is unfair or should cause anxiety to the Taiwan side. If the Taiwan side is still worried about something, it may raise questions for study and settlement in the course of negotiations. It is understandable for a certain distrust to exist as a result of long-term separation. But if we do not come into contact and talk things over, how can we remove the barriers and build up mutual trust?'' In conclusion, he suggested that the late President Chiang Kai-shek's remains should be brought back to China for burial in his family cemetery, which had been kept in good repair, and invited President Chiang Ching-kuo, Sun Yun-suan and other Kuomintang leaders to visit the mainland, even if they did not wish to enter into talks for the time being. A Taiwan Government spokesman described this invitation on the same day as ''another joke''.

**C.H.**

# China-Vietnam

Major disputes between Vietnam and China have developed since 1975 over four territorial and boundary questions: (i) their common frontier, (ii) territorial waters in the Gulf of Tonkin, (iii) the Paracel Islands and (iv) the Spratly Islands. The dispute over the Spratly Islands, which are claimed by Taiwan and the Philippines as well as by Vietnam and China, is dealt with elsewhere [see pp. 329-31].

### The Frontier Dispute

The Sino-Vietnamese frontier, 1,200 kilometres long, was defined by a convention between the French Government, which then exercised a protectorate over Tonkin, and the Chinese Empire signed in Peking in 1887. This was slightly modified by a second convention signed in 1895, stones being erected to mark the frontier. Under the conventions the frontier was not clearly delineated at certain points, where the population living on either side traditionally crossed it freely.

A Vietnamese memorandum of March 15, 1979, claimed that as France had wished to sign a trade agreement with China it had conceded some Vietnamese territory to China under the 1887 convention, and that before the Chinese Communists came to power in 1949 previous Chinese Governments had ''seized more than 60 places on Vietnamese territory''. A commentary issued by the New China News Agency (NCNA) on May 13, 1979, on the other hand, maintained that the 1887 convention had been an ''unequal treaty'', and that the Imperial Government had ''surrendered to France''.

Vietnam was partitioned in 1954 into a Communist state in the north, with its capital at Hanoi, and a pro-Western state in the south, with Saigon as its capital. Until the reunification of the country in 1975 North Vietnam was preoccupied with its relations with its southern neighbour, and in the undeclared war which developed between them it was largely dependent on China for military aid. In these circumstances North Vietnam was in no position to press its territorial claims against China.

In November 1957 the Vietnamese Workers' (Communist) Party proposed that the two countries should maintain the status quo and should settle any border disputes through negotiations, this proposal being accepted by the Chinese Communist Party in April 1958. Vietnamese statements issued in 1979, however, alleged that after 1954 the Chinese Government had taken advantage of the situation to carry out a large number of encroachments by sending Chinese to settle on Vietnamese territory, moving the border stones, building roads on Vietnamese territory, altering the border line on maps printed in China for the Vietnamese Government, and sending troops to occupy border areas. In particular, it was alleged that during repairs to the international railway line between China and Vietnam in 1955 the Chinese had deliberately moved the junction point more than 300 metres into Vietnamese territory.

Clashes on the border began in 1974. Although no details were published by either side at the time, later Vietnamese statements alleged that the Chinese had been responsible for 179 border incidents and encroachments on Vietnamese territory in that year, whilst Chinese statements accused North Vietnam of making 121 "provocative attacks on the Chinese border" in 1974. The Chinese Government proposed on March 18, 1975, that negotiations should take place on the border question, but the North Vietnamese Government, while agreeing in principle, suggested on April 12 that they should be postponed, as it was preoccupied with the war in South Vietnam, then approaching its end. According to Chinese sources, the Chinese Government repeated its proposal in 1976 and again early in 1977, on both occasions without result.

During a visit to Peking by Pham Van Dong (the Vietnamese Prime Minister), Li Xiannian, a Chinese Deputy Premier, handed him a memorandum on June 10, 1977, in which he said that although "no big dispute" over the border had arisen before 1974, since that year Vietnam had "continually provoked disputes", and that some shooting incidents had occurred. Admitting that "some of these incidents

**Map 31   The China-Vietnam border.**

277

were caused by violations of our policies by our local personnel", he gave an assurance that measures would be taken to prevent them from crossing the border, and again proposed that negotiations be held, to which Pham Van Dong agreed.

Negotiations between the two countries' Deputy Foreign Ministers opened in Peking on Oct. 7, 1977. According to Chinese reports, the Chinese side put forward the following proposals for a settlement: (i) the two sides should recheck the alignment of the entire boundary and settle all disputes on the basis of the Sino-French conventions; (ii) areas under either side's jurisdiction which lay beyond the boundary line should be returned to the other side unconditionally; (iii) the two sides should settle any differences on the alignment of the boundary through friendly consultations; and (iv) they should then conclude a new boundary treaty, delimit the boundary and erect new boundary markers.

The Vietnamese side submitted on Jan. 12, 1978, a draft agreement as a basis for discussion, the fundamental principles of which were similar to the Chinese proposals. The Chinese in turn put forward on Jan. 24 an enlarged version of their previous proposals, which provided inter alia that "readjustments" to the border might be made in a small number of cases where the two sides agreed. The Vietnamese asked on May 10 for clarifications on this point and a number of others. According to a later Vietnamese Foreign Ministry statement, the Chinese refused to discuss these questions and insisted on discussing only their own proposals of Jan. 24, thus causing a deadlock.

The negotiations were broken off in the summer of 1978 without any agreement having been reached. The Vietnamese memorandum of March 15, 1979, said that they had failed because the Chinese "did not respond to any proposal of the Vietnamese side", whilst the NCNA commentary of May 13, 1979, said that the Vietnamese had "suspended the negotiations under the pretext that its representatives were 'too busy' to negotiate".

Relations between China and Vietnam rapidly deteriorated during 1978 as a result of Chinese support for Kampuchea in its border war with Vietnam, the mass exodus of the Chinese community from Vietnam from April onwards, the admission of Vietnam to the Soviet-led Council for Mutual Economic Assistance (Comecon) in June 1978, the ending of Chinese economic aid to Vietnam in July, and the conclusion of a treaty of friendship and co-operation between Vietnam and the Soviet Union in November. According to diplomatic sources in Hanoi, serious fighting occurred on the border in April 1978, and from September onwards both Vietnam and China frequently reported incidents on the border, a number of which were said to have led to fatal casualties. Eight protests were lodged by Vietnam in the last four months of the year, and six by China.

The situation reached crisis point after Vietnamese troops invaded Kampuchea on Dec. 25, 1978, drove the Chinese-supported Government from the capital, Phnom-Penh, and installed a Vietnamese-sponsored Government on Jan. 8, 1979. Clashes on the Sino-Vietnamese border increased both in number and in scale during January and the first half of February 1979; the Vietnamese Foreign Ministry said on Feb. 14 that whereas there had been 583 Chinese armed encroachments on Vietnamese territory in 1978, since the beginning of 1979 there had already been 230, in which over 40 people had been killed, hundreds wounded and over 20 abducted to China.

Chinese troops invaded Vietnam along the entire length of the frontier on Feb. 17, 1979, and after a fortnight of heavy fighting entered Lang Son, 11 miles (18 km) south of the border. On March 1 China proposed that the two Governments should open negotiations, but Vietnam refused to negotiate until the Chinese had withdrawn to "the other side of the historic borderline". The Chinese Government accordingly announced on March 5 that its troops were withdrawing, and on

March 16 that their withdrawal had been completed. The Vietnamese Government, however, alleged on March 27 that Chinese troops were still occupying 10 points on Vietnamese territory.

Negotiations opened in Hanoi on April 18, when the Vietnamese side proposed that both sides should establish a demilitarized zone by withdrawing their armed forces to a distance of three to five kilometres from the line of actual control prior to Feb. 17, 1979, and that border problems should be settled on the basis of respect for the borderline laid down in the conventions of 1887 and 1895. The Chinese side put forward as a basis for a settlement an eight-point statement of principles covering the whole field of Sino-Vietnamese relations which included a proposal that, pending a settlement of border disputes on the basis of the Sino-French conventions, each side should strictly maintain the status quo as it existed in 1957-58, The talks were adjourned on May 18, resumed in Peking on June 28, and continued until Dec. 19, 1979, without any progress having been made. As all Vietnamese proposals for another session were rejected by the Chinese, the head of the Vietnamese delegation left for Hanoi on Feb. 8, 1980, and on March 6 China proposed that the second round of talks should be concluded and a third round held in Hanoi in the second half of the year. Several Vietnamese proposals for the resumption of the talks were subsequently rejected by China.

Throughout 1979, 1980 and the first half of 1981 the two sides continued to accuse each other of causing border incidents. A Vietnamese statement of Dec. 29, 1980, for example, alleged that during that year the Chinese forces had carried out over 2,500 armed provocations, made repeated raids deep into Vietnamese territory, regularly shelled centres of population, occupied many hilltop positions along the border, and killed or wounded hundreds of Vietnamese border guards and civilians. Similar allegations were repeatedly brought by China against Vietnam.

## The Gulf of Tonkin Dispute

The Gulf of Tonkin (known to the Vietnamese as the Bac Bo Gulf and to the Chinese as Beibu Wan) lies between Vietnam to the west, the Chinese mainland to the north, and the Luichow Peninsula and the island of Hainan (both Chinese) to the east, and at its greatest extent is 170 nautical miles wide. It has two outlets to the South China Sea, that to the south, which is 125 nautical miles wide at its narrowest point, and another to the east through the Hainan Strait.

The Franco-Chinese convention of 1887 stated that islands in the Gulf lying to the east of longitude 105 degrees 43 minutes east of the Paris meridian (or 108 degrees 03 minutes 13 seconds east of the Greenwich meridian) belonged to China, and islands to the west of this meridian belonged to Vietnam. The Vietnamese maintain that this meridian marks the boundary between the two countries' territorial waters across the entire gulf. The Chinese, however, contend that both the wording of the convention and the attached map make plain that this article refers only to the offshore islands and does not lay down a sea boundary line.

A statement of the Chinese case published in the Peking *Guangming Daily* on Dec. 2, 1980, put forward the following additional arguments: (i) If the line were extended southward to take in the entire Gulf it would be more than 130 nautical miles east of the Vietnamese coast and only about 30 miles west of Hainan, and would give Vietnam two-thirds of the area of the Gulf. (ii) No expert on international law had ever mentioned that the Gulf belonged to Vietnam and China. (iii) Under international law the sea area within a territorial bay was regarded as inland waters (through which ships could pass only with a special permit), but since 1887 neither France nor Vietnam had ever treated foreign ships sailing across the Gulf as ships passing through inland waters. (iv) A French decree on the fishery area in Indo-China laid down that territorial waters extended 20 kilometres from the shore, and made no special provision for the Gulf of Tonkin. (v) Vietnam announced in 1964 that its territorial waters extended 12 nautical miles from the shore, and this was accepted in the latest fishery agreement between China and Vietnam.

The North Vietnamese Foreign Ministry informed the Chinese Government on Dec. 26, 1973, of North Vietnam's intention to prospect for oil in the Gulf of Tonkin, and proposed that, as the sea boundary had not been delimited, negotiations should be held on the subject. The Chinese Foreign Ministry accepted this proposal on Jan. 18, 1974, but stipulated that prospecting should not take place in the area between the 18th and 20th parallels and the 107th and 108th meridians, and that third countries should not be involved in the exploration and exploitation of the Gulf. When negotiations opened in Peking on Aug. 15, 1974, the Vietnamese delegation maintained that the boundary had already been delineated in the 1887 convention, and proposed that it should be officially delineated. As the Chinese refused to accept this contention, the talks were suspended at the end of November without agreement being reached.

At the negotiations on the land and sea boundaries which began on Oct. 7, 1977, the Chinese refused to discuss the land border unless the Vietnamese gave up their claim that a sea boundary already existed. As a compromise, the Vietnamese suggested that the land border should first be discussed and that each side should maintain its own views on the Gulf of Tonkin, which would be discussed later. As no agreement was reached on the land border, the question of the sea boundary also remained unsettled. A Vietnamese Foreign Ministry statement of Dec. 13, 1979, protested against reports that China had signed contracts with foreign firms to explore for oil in the Gulf of Tonkin as a breach of the convention of 1887.

## The Paracel Islands

The Paracel Islands, known to the Chinese as the Xisha (Western Sands) Islands and to the Vietnamese as Hoang Sa, consist of about 130 barren and waterless islands, none larger than a square mile (1.6 sq km) in area, lying about 165 miles (265 km) south-east of the Chinese island of Hainan and 225 miles (360 km) east of the Vietnamese coast. They are divided into two main groups, the Crescent group to the west and the Amphitrite group to the east. The Western name "Paracels" is derived from the Portuguese word for reef.

A Chinese Foreign Ministry document of Jan. 30, 1980, claimed that the islands were discovered by Chinese mariners and were described in Chinese geographical works of the third century AD; that the Chinese Emperor exercised jurisdiction over them in the 11th century; and that they were shown as Chinese territory in official maps of the 18th and early 19th centuries. A Chinese fleet which visited the islands in 1909 set up stone tablets and hoisted the Chinese flag, and two years later they were placed under the administration of Hainan island. The document therefore claimed that "consecutive jurisdiction was exercised over them by successive Chinese governments for more than a thousand years".

A Vietnamese White Book of Sept. 28, 1979, on the other hand, maintained that "the Vietnamese feudal state was the first in history to occupy, claim ownership of, exercise sovereignty over and exploit" the islands, and in support of this claim quoted Vietnamese geographical works of the 17th and 18th centuries. The Emperor of Annam ordered the occupation of the islands in 1816, and his successor in 1836 commanded a survey of them to be carried out and markers to be erected.

The French Government, which then exercised sovereignty over Cochin China and a protectorate over Annam and Tonkin, claimed in a note to China in 1931 that the Empire of Annam had a prior title to the islands, and in 1938 the Emperor Bao Dai annexed them to the territory of Thua Thien province. In the following year, however, they were occupied by the Japanese. Japan renounced her claim to them by the peace treaty signed in San Francisco in 1951, but the treaty did not state to whom they belonged. A Chinese official statement commenting on the draft treaty claimed that they had "always been China's territory". At the San Francisco conference, the Vietnamese delegate formally affirmed Vietnam's claim to the islands, whilst in the absence of China, which was not represented, the Soviet delegate described them as China's "inalienable territory".

After Vietnam was divided in 1954 into two states, the South Vietnamese Government continued to assert its claim to the Paracels, whereas the North Vietnamese Government temporarily accepted China's claim to them. According to the Chinese Foreign Ministry document cited above, North Vietnamese official statements in 1958 and 1965 referred to the islands as Chinese territory, and they were shown and referred to as such in maps and textbooks issued by the North Vietnamese Government down to 1974. Both China and South Vietnam exercised control over some of the islands during the period from 1954 to 1974; Woody Island, the main island in the Amphitrite group, was occupied by the Chinese, whilst South Vietnam maintained a small garrison on Pattle Island, the largest of the Crescent group, to man a radio and meteorological station.

After the South Vietnamese Government had announced its intention of carrying out surveys for oil off its coast opposite the Paracels, the Chinese Foreign Ministry issued a statement on Jan. 11, 1974, affirming its claim to the islands, this claim being rejected by South Vietnam on the following day. South Vietnamese warships which were sent to the islands withdrew after an engagement with Chinese warships on Jan. 19, and on the following day Chinese troops occupied the three islands still under South Vietnamese control. A North Vietnamese spokesman commented in a non-committal statement on Jan. 21 that "disputes handed down by history, often very complex ones", should be settled through negotiations. Both the United States and the Soviet Union adopted a strictly neutral attitude towards the dispute, and a request by the South Vietnamese Government for a meeting of the UN Security Council failed to secure the necessary support for placing the question on the Council's agenda.

Following the overthrow of the Saigon regime in 1975 and the reunification of Vietnam in the following year, the Hanoi Government openly laid claim to the Paracels. The Vietnamese White Book of 1979 stated that the question had been discussed between the Vietnamese and Chinese Governments in September 1975, and that the latter had admitted that a dispute existed. An official Vietnamese map issued in 1976 showed the Paracels as Vietnamese territory. A government statement of May 20, 1977, said that Vietnamese territorial waters were 12 miles wide and that its exclusive economic zone extended to 200 nautical miles from the coast, and referred to "the islands and archipelagoes belonging to Vietnamese territory and situated outside the territorial waters mentioned" without specifying the islands and archipelagoes in question. In the memorandum which Li Xiannian handed to Pham Van Dong on June 10, 1977 [see above], he accused Vietnam of making the Paracels, "over which there was never any issue", a major subject of dispute. According to Chinese sources, Pham Van Dong replied that "in the war of resistance we of course had to place resistance to US imperialism above everything else", and that earlier Vietnamese statements on the subject must be understood "in the context of the historical circumstances of the time".

Both sides issued a series of statements in 1979 and 1980 reaffirming their claims to the Paracels. At the negotiations held in Hanoi in April and May 1979 the Chinese delegation demanded that Vietnam should recognize China's sovereignty over the islands, this demand being rejected by Vietnam. Following reports that China had signed contracts with foreign companies to prospect for oil around the Paracels, the Vietnamese Foreign Ministry gave warning on Dec. 13, 1979, that companies which conducted exploration in this area without Vietnam's consent "must bear all consequences of their wrongdoings".

A further Vietnamese White Paper on the Paracels and Spratlys, published by the Foreign Ministry in January 1982, concluded as follows: "On the basis of historical facts and international law it cannot be denied that the Hoang Sa and Truong Sa archipelagoes have long since and always been Vietnamese territory. The Vietnamese state took possession of these archipelagoes when they were not under the sovereignty of any nation, and it has been continuously and effectively exercising its sovereignty over them. The Chinese state in the past had never taken possession of these two archipelagoes which it calls 'Xisha' and 'Nansha' and had never exercised its sovereignty over them. China had not even raised any claim over these two archipelagoes until the early years of the 20th century, but Peking is now fabricating facts and distorting history to back up its claims that 'Xisha' and 'Nansha' have since ancient times been Chinese territories.

"The real problem here is not the question of a dispute between Vietnam and China, but it is the Chinese aggression and occupation of the Hoang Sa archipelago, part of Vietnamese territory, and the Chinese claim of the Truong Sa archipelago as part of China. The Chinese authorities must return to Vietnam the Hoang Sa archipelago and renounce all claims to the Hoang Sa and Truong Sa archipelagoes—this is a matter of course, in conformity with international law. The ambition of the Peking authorities over the two Vietnamese archipelagoes of Hoang Sa and Truong Sa manifests all the more clearly their policy of big-nation expansionism and hegemony which is aimed at conquering Vietnam as well as Laos and Kampuchea, gradually controlling and eventually turning the East Sea into a Chinese lake and using the Indo-Chinese peninsula as a springboard for their expansion into South-East Asia.

"The act of aggression of the reactionary clique in the Peking ruling circles against the Hoang Sa archipelago and their scheme to annex the Truong Sa archipelago constitute not only an encroachment upon Vietnam's sovereignty and territorial integrity but also an immediate threat to the interests of the countries in the East Sea area, as well as to peace and stability in South-East Asia. The Vietnamese people are determined to defend the territorial integrity of their country and their sovereignty over the two archipelagoes of Hoang Sa and Truong Sa against all expansionist design of the reactionary clique in the Peking ruling circles. This just struggle enjoying the sympathy and support of the world's peace-loving and progressive forces, fighting against imperialism and Peking's expansionism and hegemonism, will certainly end in total victory."

C.H.

# India-Pakistan

The dispute between India and Pakistan over the state of Jammu and Kashmir arose from the circumstances in which British India was partitioned in 1947. The accession of the princely states to either India or Pakistan took place smoothly, except in three states in which the religion of the ruler differed from that of the majority of his subjects. After the Moslem ruler of the overwhelmingly Hindu state of Junagadh had announced its accession to Pakistan, with which his territory was nowhere contiguous, the state was occupied by Indian troops and was incorporated into India after a plebiscite, despite Pakistani protests. The Moslem Nizam of Hyderabad, which was entirely surrounded by Indian territory, announced that he wished to maintain its independence, but when order threatened to break down Indian troops moved in and the Nizam agreed to accede to India. The third state was Jammu and Kashmir, generally referred to as Kashmir. (For map showing division of Kashmir, see page 238.)

## Kashmir before 1947

The state was founded by Gulab Singh, a Hindu military adventurer who in return for his services was created Raja of Jammu by the Sikh ruler Ranjit Singh in 1822, and who conquered Ladakh in 1834. After the defeat of the Sikhs by the British in 1846, Gulab Singh undertook to pay the indemnity of 75,000 rupees demanded by the British from the Sikhs, on condition that he was given Kashmir, then under Sikh rule. This arrangement was confirmed by the Treaty of Amritsar, Gulab Singh being recognized by the British as Maharaja of Jammu and Kashmir.

Jammu and Kashmir has an area of about 85,000 square miles (220,000 sq km), and borders on India to the south, Pakistan to the west, Afghanistan to the north-west and China to the north and east. According to a census conducted in 1941, it then had a population of 4,021,616, of whom 77.1 per cent were Moslems, 20.1 per cent Hindus, and 2.08 per cent Sikhs, Buddhists and others. The Valley of Kashmir is overwhelmingly Moslem; Hindus constitute the great majority of the population of Jammu, in the south, and also form a considerable part of the population of Srinagar, the capital of the state; the Sikhs are also found mainly in Jammu and Srinagar; and the Buddhists are confined to Ladakh, in the north. Economically Kashmir is linked with Pakistan by its river system, as its three main rivers, the Indus, the Chenab and the Jhelum, all flow into Pakistan, which is largely dependent on them for its irrigation.

Strong opposition to the autocratic rule of the Maharaja, Sir Hari Singh, developed before the Second World War under the leadership of Sheikh Mohammed Abdullah, who in 1930 founded the Moslem Conference to agitate for reforms. He broke away from it in 1938, however, to form the Kashmir National Conference, a non-communal organization which maintained close links with the Indian National Congress. He launched an agitation demanding constitutional government in 1945, and was subsequently imprisoned.

## The Accession of Kashmir to India

When India and Pakistan became independent on Aug. 15, 1947, it was generally assumed that Kashmir, as a contiguous state with a predominantly Moslem population, would accede to Pakistan. The Maharaja, however, hesitated whether to accede to Pakistan or to India or to seek to maintain Kashmir's independence, and accordingly proposed to both India and Pakistan that both should enter into a standstill agreement with Kashmir. The Indian Government asked for further discussions;

283

Pakistan accepted the proposal, but as a means of pressure began an economic blockade of Kashmir, rail and road traffic being discontinued and supplies of food and petrol cut off. Early in October 1947 an armed revolt of the Moslem peasantry in Poonch province, south-west of Srinagar, was joined by many deserters from the Kashmir state forces and by thousands of tribesmen from Pakistan armed with modern weapons supplied by the Pakistan Army, and on Oct. 27 the invaders captured Baramula, only 30 miles north-west of Srinagar.

In a letter to Lord Mountbatten, then Governor-General of India, the Maharaja stated: "With the conditions obtaining at present in my state, and the emergency of the situation, I have no option but to ask for help from the Indian Dominion. Naturally they cannot send the help asked for by me without my state acceding to India. I have accordingly decided to do so, and attach the Instrument of Accession." In his reply accepting Kashmir's accession Lord Mountbatten wrote: "In consistence with their policy that, in the case of any state where the issue of accession has been the subject of dispute, the question should be decided in accordance with the wishes of the people of the state, it is the Government's wish that, as soon as law and order have been restored in Kashmir and her soil cleared of the invader, the question of the state's accession should be settled by reference to the people."

The accession of Kashmir to India was officially announced on Oct. 27, 1947. At the same time Indian troops were flown to the Srinagar front to reinforce the Maharaja's forces, and by the end of the month the invaders, who had advanced to within 18 miles (29 km) of the state capital, had been driven back several miles. Sheikh Abdullah, who had recently been released from prison, was sworn in as Prime Minister on Oct. 31. The rebels meanwhile set up their own "Provisional Government of Azad (Free) Kashmir", headed by Sardar Mohammad Ibrahim, president of the Moslem Conference.

On Oct. 28, 1947, Jawaharlal Nehru, then Indian Prime Minister, invited the Prime Minister of Pakistan, Liaquat Ali Khan, to meet him in Delhi to discuss the Kashmir question, and proposed that Pakistan should co-operate in preventing the raiders from entering Kashmir. He also gave an assurance that India had no desire to intervene in Kashmir's affairs once the state had been cleared of the raiders, and regarded the question of accession as one solely for the decision of the Kashmiri people. The Pakistan Government, however, declared on Oct. 30 that "the accession of Kashmir to India is based on fraud and violence, and as such cannot be recognized". Nehru repeated in a broadcast on Nov. 2 that "we are prepared, when peace, law and order have been established, to have a referendum held under international auspices like the United Nations".

### Indian Complaint to the United Nations

On Dec. 22, 1947, the Indian Government requested Pakistan to deny to the invading tribesmen all use of its territory for operations against Kashmir, all military and other supplies, and all other aid that might prolong the struggle. As no reply was received, the Indian Government made a formal complaint to the UN Security Council on Dec. 30, stating that the invaders, who included Pakistani nationals, were using Pakistani territory as a base for operations, drew much of their military equipment, transport and supplies from Pakistan, and were being trained and guided by Pakistani officers. Nehru stated on Jan. 2, 1948, that in addition to the 50,000 raiders already in Kashmir, another 100,000 were being trained and equipped in Pakistan by the Pakistan Army.

After both sides had put their case before the Security Council, it was agreed on Jan. 20, 1948, that a commission of three members should visit India and Pakistan to investigate the facts and report to the Security Council. Differences arose, however, over two issues. Whereas Pakistan demanded the immediate establishment of an "impartial" administration in Kashmir and the withdrawal of the Indian forces under the commission's supervision, India insisted that Sheikh Abdullah's Government should hold a plebiscite under the commission's aegis, and that the Indian forces must stay to ensure external and internal security so long as Kashmir remained acceded to India. The Security Council accordingly adopted on April 21, 1948, a resolution containing the following proposals for the settlement of the dispute:

(1) The commission, whose membership would be increased to five, would place itself at the two Governments' disposal to facilitate measures for the restoration of peace and the holding of a plebiscite.

(2) Pakistan would withdraw all her nationals who had entered Kashmir to take part in the fighting, prevent such persons from entering Kashmir and refuse them all aid.

(3) When the commission was satisfied that the tribesmen were withdrawing and an effective ceasefire was in force, India would reduce her forces in Kashmir to the minimum required for the maintenance of order.

(4) The plebiscite would be conducted by a Plebiscite Administration headed by a Plebiscite Administrator appointed by the UN Secretary-General. During the plebiscite the Kashmir state forces and police would be under the supervision of the Plebiscite Administration.

(5) To ensure that the plebiscite was completely impartial, the Kashmir Government would be enlarged to include representatives of the major political groups in the state, and the Indian Government would undertake to ensure freedom of speech, assembly and movement, the release of all political prisoners, and guarantees against intimidation and victimization.

Both India and Pakistan informed the Security Council that although they were prepared to lend the commission all assistance in their power, they could not commit themselves to accept all the resolution's recommendations. India objected to the proposals for the withdrawal of Indian troops, the control of the state forces by the Plebiscite Administration and the inclusion of members of other parties in the state Government, while Pakistan demanded the withdrawal of all Indian troops and maintained that a Government headed by Sheikh Abdullah would be unlikely to permit a free plebiscite.

## The Ceasefire in Kashmir

The Indian troops meanwhile had cleared the Kashmir Valley of the invaders in November 1947, but in the following month the tribesmen opened a new front in south-west Kashmir, where heavy fighting continued until March 1948. Regular Pakistani troops entered Kashmir early in May to reinforce the tribesmen, and took a major part in a new offensive in north-west and north Kashmir which began in August 1948.

The UN Kashmir Commission, consisting of representatives of Argentina, Belgium, Colombia, Czechoslovakia and the United States, visited India and Pakistan in July, and put forward the following proposals on Aug. 13, 1948:

(1) India and Pakistan would simultaneously issue a ceasefire order, would not augment the military potential of the forces under their control, and would create and maintain an atmosphere favourable to the promotion of further negotiations. The commission would appoint military observers to supervise the observance of the ceasefire.

(2) The Pakistani troops, whose presence constituted "a material change in the situation", the tribesmen and "Pakistani nationals not normally resident therein who have entered the state for the purpose of fighting" would be withdrawn. Pending a final solution, the territory evacuated by Pakistani troops would be administered by the local authority under the commission's surveillance. When the tribesmen

285

had withdrawn and the Pakistani troops were being withdrawn, the Indian Government would begin to withdraw the bulk of its forces in stages to be agreed with the commission. India would maintain within the lines existing at the ceasefire those troops which the commission considered necessary for the maintenance of order.

(3) India and Pakistan would enter into consultations with the commission to determine fair and equitable conditions whereby free expression of the will of the people would be ensured.

India accepted the proposals, but Pakistan maintained that only the Azad Kashmir Government could issue ceasefire orders. It also demanded that the Azad Kashmir Government should continue to administer the territories under its control, that the Azad Kashmir forces should remain intact and that all Indian troops should be withdrawn. As a result the fighting continued until, following further mediation efforts by the UN Commission, a ceasefire was agreed upon on Dec. 31, 1948, and came into force on the following day. Agreement was reached on July 26, 1949, on the ceasefire line, which ran from Manawar on the Pakistan frontier north to Keran, and thence east to the glacier area. Under the agreement troops would remain at least 500 yards from the ceasefire line (to be supervised by a UN observer team), and neither side would introduce fresh troops into Kashmir.

## UN Commission's Resolution on Plebiscite

A resolution on the holding of a plebiscite was adopted by the UN Commission on Jan. 5, 1949, and accepted by India and Pakistan, its provisions being as follows:

(1) The accession of Kashmir would be decided through a free and impartial plebiscite, which would be held when the commission found that the ceasefire and truce arrangements set forth in Parts 1 and 2 of the resolution of Aug. 13, 1948, had been carried out and arrangements for a plebiscite completed.

(2) The UN Secretary-General would nominate a Plebiscite Administrator, who would be formally appointed by the Kashmir Government.

(3) After Parts 1 and 2 of the resolution of Aug. 13, 1948, had been implemented and the commission was satisfied that peaceful conditions had been restored, the commission and the Plebiscite Administrator would determine in consultation with India the final disposal of the Indian and state armed forces, and in consultation with the local authorities the final disposal of other armed forces.

(4) All Kashmir citizens who had left the state on account of the disturbances would be free to return.

(5) All persons who had entered Kashmir since 1947 for other than lawful purposes would be required to leave.

(6) All authorities in Kashmir would undertake to ensure that there was no intimidation or bribery of voters in the plebiscite, that no restrictions were placed on legitimate political activity, that all political prisoners were released and that minorities were afforded adequate protection.

By agreement with the Governments of India and Pakistan, Fleet-Admiral Chester Nimitz, the US naval commander in the Pacific during World War II, was appointed Plebiscite Administrator on March 21, 1949.

As no agreement had been reached on the implementation of the truce, the UN Commission proposed on Aug. 9, 1949, that a joint meeting at ministerial level should discuss the withdrawal of the Pakistani forces, the tribesmen and the bulk of the Indian forces. The Indian Government in reply suggested the inclusion of three other items in the agenda: clarification of the phrase "local authority" in the resolution of Aug. 13, 1948, disbanding and disarming of the Azad Kashmir forces, and the administration and defence of the mountainous and sparsely populated regions of northern Kashmir. As the Pakistan Government objected to these items, the meeting did not take place. A proposal by the commission that Admiral Nimitz should arbitrate on the differences between them was accepted by Pakistan but rejected by India, on the ground that the disbanding and disarming of the Azad Kashmir forces was "no more a matter for arbitration than the complete withdrawal of Pakistani forces".

## Failure of Mediation Attempts

In a report of Dec. 12, 1949, the commission recommended the appointment of a single person to endeavour to bring India and Pakistan together on all unresolved issues. A resolution adopted by the Security Council on March 14, 1950, provided for the dissolution of the commission and the appointment of a mediator, who would supervise a jointly-agreed programme of demilitarization and decide when it had gone far enough to enable a plebiscite to be held. Sir Owen Dixon, an Australian high court judge, was appointed mediator on April 12, 1950.

During talks with both Governments in the spring and summer he proposed that a plebiscite should be held only in those areas where the people's desires were uncertain, notably in the Valley of Kashmir, and that those areas where the inhabitants' desires were known should be partitioned between India and Pakistan. This proposal was accepted by India but rejected by Pakistan. A suggestion for a partition of Kashmir without a plebiscite proved impracticable, as it became evident that both parties would in that event insist upon having the Valley of Kashmir.

Following the failure of Sir Owen Dixon's mission, the Security Council adopted a resolution on March 30, 1951, providing for the appointment of a UN Representative for India and Pakistan, who would effect the demilitarization of Kashmir on the basis of the UN Commission's resolution. Dr Frank P. Graham, president of North Carolina University, was appointed to the post of UN Representative on April 30. After prolonged negotiations with the Indian and Pakistan Governments, he reported to the Security Council on March 31, 1953, that substantial differences still existed on the number of the armed forces which should remain on either side of the ceasefire line, and suggested that India and Pakistan should negotiate directly instead of through a UN mediator as hitherto. Subsequent negotiations and correspondence between Nehru and Mohammed Ali, then Prime Minister of Pakistan, produced no result, and in a final letter of Sept. 21, 1954, the latter declared that as there was no scope left for further direct negotiations the issue should revert to the Security Council.

## Constitutional Developments in Kashmir

The question had meanwhile been complicated by constitutional developments in Indian Kashmir. Like all the princely states, Kashmir had acceded to India with regard to defence, communications and foreign policy only, but whereas the other states had since integrated themselves fully with the Indian Union, Article 370 of the Indian Constitution, adopted in 1949, limited the Union Parliament's power to legislate for Kashmir to those three subjects and such other matters as the President might by order specify, with the concurrence of the state Government.

Despite Pakistani protests, a Kashmir Constituent Assembly was elected on Oct. 15, 1951, and National Conference candidates were returned unopposed in all but two of the constituencies, in which they defeated independent candidates. An agreement between the Indian and Kashmir Governments concluded in July 1952 provided that the Head of the State would be elected by the State Legislature; that the Indian national flag would have the same position in Kashmir as in other parts of India, but the Kashmir state flag would be retained; and that although citizenship would be common, the existing law preventing non-residents from acquiring immovable property in Kashmir would remain. Hereditary monarchy was subsequently abolished, and Yuvraj Karan Singh, the son of the former Maharaja, who had been acting as regent since his father left Kashmir in 1949, was elected *Sadr-i-Riyasat* (Head of State) by the Constituent Assembly.

The degree to which Kashmir should be integrated with India gave rise to violent controversy inside the state, and the *Praja Parishad*, a Hindu communalist organization, launched an agitation in Jammu demanding the complete accession of Kashmir to India. This was strongly opposed by Sheikh Abdullah (the Prime Minister), who emphasized in his public statements that Kashmir must enjoy complete internal autonomy. After a split in the Cabinet, in which he was opposed by three of his four ministers, he was dismissed by Yuvraj Karan Singh on Aug. 8, 1953, and was arrested later the same day.

The Constituent Assembly finally ratified Kashmir's accession to India on Feb. 15, 1954, and the Indian President issued an order on May 14 greatly extending the application of the Indian Constitution to Kashmir. The Indian Government was empowered to legislate for Kashmir on the majority of the subjects included in the Union List (i.e. the list of subjects on which only the Central Government might legislate), but the Concurrent List of subjects on which both the Central and the State Governments might legislate would not apply to Kashmir, these subjects being reserved for the State Government.

### Indian Protests against Pakistani Military Alliances

Mohammed Ali announced on Feb. 22, 1954, that Pakistan had asked the United States for military aid, and on Feb. 25 President Eisenhower stated that the United States would comply with this request. In a letter to the Indian Prime Minister, President Eisenhower gave an assurance that this decision was not directed against India, and offered similar assistance to the Indian Government, which declined the offer. Nehru said in the Indian Parliament on March 1 that the Kashmir issue "has to be considered from an entirely different point of view, when across the border large additional forces are being placed at the disposal of Pakistan", and called for the withdrawal of the American observers attached to the UN team on either side of the ceasefire line, as they could "no longer be treated by us as neutrals". The American observers were subsequently withdrawn. Admiral Nimitz had previously resigned on Sept. 4, 1953, after Nehru had suggested that the Plebiscite Administrator should be chosen from one of the smaller countries.

In a letter of March 5, 1954, to Mohammed Ali, Nehru said that the granting of US military aid to Pakistan had changed "the whole context of the Kashmir issue", and continued: "If two countries have actually been conducting military operations against each other in the past, and are in a state of truce, military aid given to either of them is an act unfriendly to the other. . . . What was said at a previous stage about the quantum of forces has little relevance. We can take no risks now, as we were prepared to take previously, and we must retain full liberty to keep such forces and military equipment in Kashmir as we may consider necessary in view of this new threat to us." Although in reply Mohammed Ali denied that Pakistan intended to seek a military solution in Kashmir, Nehru continued to uphold his view that US military aid to Pakistan had radically altered the situation.

Indian suspicions were increased by Pakistan's entry into a network of military alliances. On May 19, 1954, a Mutual Defence Assistance Agreement between Pakistan and the United States was signed. At the Manila conference, in which India had refused to take part, Pakistan on Sept. 8, 1954, became a founder member of the South-East Asia Treaty Organization (SEATO), together with the United States, the United Kingdom, France, Australia, New Zealand, the Philippines and Thailand. On July 1, 1955, Pakistan joined the Baghdad Pact alliance, of which the United Kingdom, Turkey and Iraq were already members, and which was subsequently joined by Iran.

A communiqué issued by the SEATO Council on March 8, 1956, called for "an early settlement of the Kashmir question through the United Nations or by direct negotiations". In a speech on March 20 Nehru commented: "How the question of Kashmir could come within the scope of the SEATO Council is not clear to us. Its reference to Kashmir could only mean that that military alliance is backing Pakistan in its disputes with India. . . ." Despite this protest, the Council of the Baghdad Pact on April 19 issued a similar call for "an early settlement" of the Kashmir dispute.

### Indian Rejection of Plebiscite Plan

The Indian Home Minister, G. B. Pant, said on July 9, 1955, that the conditions for a settlement in Kashmir had been transformed by changes in the situation, including the military alliance between Pakistan and the United States and the "definite decision" taken by the Kashmir Constituent Assembly. In reply to Pakistani protests against this statement, Nehru pointed out on Aug. 22 that at the time of the accession of Kashmir India had made a unilateral declaration that the people of the state would be consulted, no mention being made of a plebiscite. Two years later the UN Commission had adopted a resolution (which had been accepted first by India and later by Pakistan) recommending the holding of a plebiscite, provided that certain conditions were fulfilled. There had since been many discussions on the fulfilment of these conditions which had not led to any settlement, and meanwhile there had been developments which would "be taken into consideration".

Following the SEATO Council's pronouncement on Kashmir, Nehru said in the Indian Parliament on March 29, 1956, that the holding of a plebiscite could not be considered until Pakistan had withdrawn all her forces, which still remained in Kashmir eight years after the Security Council had categorically demanded their withdrawal. US military aid to Pakistan had created "not only a new military situation but a new political situation", and that situation had become progressively worse because of the conclusion of the SEATO and Baghdad pacts, which "tend to encircle us". Asked at a press conference on April 2 whether he was no longer in favour of a plebiscite, he said that that inference was "largely correct". He announced on April 13 that he had suggested to the Pakistan Government the holding of discussions to settle the question by a demarcation of the border on the basis of the ceasefire line. Chaudhri Mohammad Ali, who had succeeded Mohammed Ali as Prime Minister of Pakistan in 1955, dismissed this proposal on the following day as "preposterous".

The Constituent Assembly adopted on Nov. 17, 1956, a constitution declaring that Kashmir was "an integral part of the Union of India", and that its territories comprised "all territories which on Aug. 15, 1947, were under the sovereignty or suzerainty of the ruler of the state" (i.e. including Azad Kashmir). All sovereignty rested with the state, which had executive and legislative powers in all matters "except those in which [the Indian] Parliament has power to make laws for the state under the provisions of the Constitution of India".

In response H. S. Suhrawardy (Chaudhri Mohammad Ali's successor as Prime Minister of Pakistan) declared on Nov. 17, 1956, that Pakistan would never recognize "the right of this or any other such body to represent and legislate on behalf of the people of Jammu and Kashmir", and that by an international agreement, which could not be repudiated by one party to suit its own ends, the question of accession would remain open until it was decided by a free and impartial plebiscite.

### Unsuccessful Negotiations, 1957-63

At Pakistan's request, the UN Security Council resumed consideration of the Kashmir question on Jan. 16, 1957. The Pakistani Foreign Minister, F. K. Noon, maintained that the accession to India by the "puppet Constituent Assembly" was "wholly devoid of any legal effect", as the Assembly did not represent Azad Kashmir, its members had been returned unopposed because the population had boycotted the elections, and it had not voted in favour of accession until after Sheikh Abdullah had been imprisoned. He therefore proposed that all Indian and Pakistani forces should be withdrawn from Kashmir, the local forces disbanded and a UN force introduced in preparation for a plebiscite.

The Indian representative, Krishna Menon, maintained in reply that the only problem confronting the Security Council was the Indian complaint about Pakistani aggression. Denying that India was under any legal commitment to hold a plebiscite, he said that the conditions for a truce agreement laid down in the resolution of Aug. 13, 1948, had not been fulfilled by Pakistan, which had not withdrawn its troops, and the Indian Government therefore did not consider itself bound by the resolution.

The Security Council adopted on Jan. 24, 1957, a resolution reaffirming the principle that the final disposition of Kashmir would be made through a plebiscite conducted under UN auspices, and declaring that any action taken by the Constituent Assembly would not constitute a disposition of the state in accordance with this principle. At the Council's request the Swedish representative, Gunnar Jarring, visited India and Pakistan in March and April for discussions with the two Governments. The Indian Government maintained that as Part 1 of the resolution of Aug. 13, 1948, had not been implemented by Pakistan it was premature to discuss the implementation of Parts 2 and 3 or of the resolution of Jan. 5, 1949. The Pakistan Government, on the other hand, maintained that it had fully implemented Part 1 of the 1948 resolution, and that the time had come to proceed to the implementation of Part 2.

After considering Jarring's report, the Security Council adopted on Dec. 2 a resolution directing Dr Graham to visit India and Pakistan and to make recommendations to the two Governments for furthering implementation of the UN Commission's resolutions. Dr Graham accordingly submitted the following plan to them on Feb. 15, 1958: (i) The two Governments would undertake to refrain from statements and actions which would aggravate the situation. (ii) They would reaffirm that they would respect the ceasefire line. (iii) Following the withdrawal of the Pakistan Army from Kashmir, a UN force would be stationed on the Pakistan side of the Kashmir border. (iv) The UN representative would hold discussions with the two Governments on the possibility of a plebiscite. (v) A conference of the two Prime Ministers on these questions would be held at the earliest practicable date. These recommendations were accepted in principle by Pakistan, but were rejected by India on the grounds that they bypassed the question of Pakistan's failure to implement the resolution of Aug. 13, 1948, and would "place the aggressor and the aggressed on the same footing".

No major developments in the dispute took place until Jan. 11, 1962, when Pakistan asked for a meeting of the Security Council on the question. When the Council met on April 27 (the meeting having been postponed because of the Indian general elections), Sir Muhammad Zafrulla Khan offered on behalf of Pakistan to submit the question to arbitration or to the International Court of Justice, and rejected the Indian claim that a plebiscite was no longer needed as the people of Kashmir had expressed their will in the elections to the Srinagar Assembly. In reply Krishna Menon contended that whatever Lord Mountbatten had written or Nehru had said did not necessarily mean a plebiscite, and pointed out that whereas Pakistan had had no elections in 15 years, there had been three elections in Kashmir since partition (to the Constituent Assembly in 1951 and to the Legislative Assembly in 1957 and 1962). He maintained that the only basis for a plebiscite was the resolution of Jan. 5, 1949, and that the conditions for a plebiscite no longer existed. An Irish resolution reminding the two parties of the principles contained in the commission's resolutions and urging them to enter into negotiations with a view to a settlement was vetoed by the Soviet delegate.

As a result of an Anglo-American initiative, a series of talks were held at ministerial level between Dec. 27, 1962, and May 16, 1963, in preparation for direct talks between Nehru and President Ayub Khan of Pakistan. After India had refused to consider a plebiscite, the two delegations discussed proposals for the partition of Kashmir, but no agreement was reached, as neither side was prepared to abandon its claim to the Kashmir Valley. India offered to transfer to Pakistan about 3,000 square miles (7,750 sq km) west and north of the Valley, in addition to those parts of Kashmir already held by Pakistan, totalling about 34,000 square miles (88,000 sq km) out of a total area of 85,000 square miles (220,000 sq km); Pakistan, on the other hand, was prepared to cede to India only about 3,000 square miles in the extreme south of Jammu. In consequence the proposal for talks between Nehru and President Ayub automatically lapsed.

The integration of Kashmir with India was carried a stage farther in 1964, when the provisions of the Indian Constitution enabling President's rule to be proclaimed if the constitutional machinery broke down and empowering the Indian Parliament to legislate for a state where President's rule was in force were extended to Kashmir by presidential order. An amendment to the Kashmir Constitution adopted by the State Assembly in March 1965 provided that, as in the other Indian states, the *Sadr-i-Riyasat* should be known as the Governor, that instead of being elected by the Assembly he should be appointed by the President of India, and that the Prime Minister should be known as the Chief Minister.

### The War of 1965 and the 1966 Tashkent Declaration

A major crisis was precipitated when on Aug. 5, 1965, armed infiltrators from Azad Kashmir began entering Indian Kashmir in an unsuccessful attempt to foment a revolt. In order to prevent further raiders from crossing the ceasefire line, Indian troops occupied a number of points on the Pakistani side of the line from Aug. 16 onwards. The Pakistan Army launched an offensive into Jammu on Sept. 1, whereupon the Indian Army invaded Pakistan in three sectors during Sept. 6-8, 1965. Fighting continued until Sept. 23, when a ceasefire came into force at the demand of the Security Council.

At the Soviet Government's invitation, Lal Bahadur Shastri (who had succeeded Nehru as Prime Minister on the latter's death in 1964) met President Ayub Khan in Tashkent (Uzbekistan) for talks on Jan. 4-10, 1966. In a joint declaration they affirmed their intention to settle their disputes by peaceful means, and stated that they had discussed the Kashmir question against this background. They also agreed that all armed personnel of the two countries should be withdrawn to the positions which they had held before Aug. 5, 1965, and that the two sides would continue meetings "at the highest and other levels on matters of direct concern to both countries".

In accordance with the Tashkent Declaration, talks took place in Rawalpindi on March 1-2, 1966, between Swaran Singh and Zulfiqar Ali Bhutto, the Indian and Pakistani Foreign Ministers respectively. Diplomatic exchanges on the possibility of holding further talks continued throughout the spring and summer, but led to no result, as Pakistan maintained that the most important issue to be discussed was that of Kashmir, whereas the Indian Government continued to uphold its view that Kashmir was an integral part of India.

### The War of 1971 and the Simla Agreement

During the Indo-Pakistan war of Dec. 3-17, 1971, caused by the civil war in East

Pakistan (now Bangladesh), both sides crossed the ceasefire line in Kashmir. Pakistani troops occupied 52 square miles (135 sq km) east of the line in the Chhamb sector, west of Jammu, whilst the Indian forces occupied 480 square miles (1,240 sq km) west and north of the line in the Poonch, Tithwal and Kargil sectors.

At talks in Simla between Indira Gandhi, who had become Indian Prime Minister in 1966, and President (as he then was) Bhutto of Pakistan, it was agreed on July 3, 1972, that "the line of control resulting from the ceasefire of Dec. 17, 1971, shall be respected by both sides without prejudice to the recognized position of either side", and that talks should continue on arrangements for the establishment of a durable peace, including a final settlement of the Kashmir question. Mrs Gandhi said on July 12 that although India continued to regard the Pakistani-held areas of Kashmir as Indian territory, it was prepared to consider any proposal for converting the ceasefire line into a permanent border.

After the Simla talks the Indian Government sent a memorandum to the United Nations requesting the withdrawal of the UN observers, on the ground that the former ceasefire line no longer existed. Pakistan asked that they should be retained, however, as the line was still intact except in a few pockets and the issue had not been withdrawn from the United Nations.

## Constitutional Status of Indian Kashmir

The constitutional status of Indian Kashmir was defined as follows by an agreement concluded in 1974 between the Indian Government and Sheikh Abdullah, who was subsequently reinstated as Chief Minister:

(1) Relations between Kashmir and the Indian Union would continue to be governed by Article 370 of the Indian Constitution.

(2) The residuary powers of legislation would remain with the state of Kashmir, although the Union Parliament would continue to have powers to make laws relating to the prevention of activities directed towards the secession of a part of Indian territory from the Union.

(3) Where any provision of the Indian Constitution had been applied to Kashmir with adaptations and modifications, these might be altered or replaced by presidential order, but the provisions already applied without modification were unalterable.

(4) The State Government might review laws made by Parliament or extended to the state after 1953 on any matter on the Concurrent List, and might decide which of them needed amendment or repeal. The State Government would be consulted on the application to Kashmir of laws made by Parliament in future on matters on the Concurrent List.

(5) The President's assent would be necessary for any amendment to the Kashmir Constitution passed by the State Legislature relating to the appointment and powers of the Governor, elections and the composition of the Legislative Council (the Upper House of the State Legislature).

## Constitutional Status of Azad Kashmir

The constitutional status of Azad Kashmir is anomalous, as Pakistan in theory still regards the whole state as disputed territory. The Pakistani Constitution of 1956 said that if the people of Kashmir decided to accede to Pakistan the relationship between Kashmir and Pakistan would be determined by the people of the state, and this wording was imitated in the subsequent Constitutions of 1962 and 1973. Azad Kashmir in consequence has never been represented in the Pakistan National Assembly, although until 1974 the Pakistan Cabinet regularly included a Minister for Kashmir Affairs.

Until 1961 the President of Azad Kashmir was elected by the Moslem Conference, but in that year a system of indirect election similar to that then in force in Pakistan was introduced, whereby the President and a State Council of eight members were elected by 1,200 elected members of "basic democracies" in Azad Kashmir and 1,200 elected representatives of Kashmiris settled in Pakistan. This system was abolished by the Azad Kashmir Government Act of 1964, which provided that the President of Azad Kashmir should be appointed by the Pakistani Ministry of Kashmir Affairs and should be responsible to its Joint Secretary. In 1968 it was announced that the President would be elected by the State Council, which was enlarged by the addition of four nominated members, from among its own members.

Following an agitation in Azad Kashmir against "Pakistani domination", a Constitution was introduced in 1970 whereby the President and a 25-member Legislative Assembly were elected by adult franchise. This was replaced in 1974 by a new Constitution, which established an Azad Kashmir Council consisting of the Prime Minister of Pakistan as chairman, five Pakistani ministers or members of Parliament nominated by him, and seven members elected by the Azad Kashmir Assembly. The Council would lay down policy and exercise full legislative and executive powers to deal with matters not reserved exclusively for the Pakistan Government or the Azad Kashmir Assembly, the Pakistani Ministry of Kashmir Affairs being abolished. The President of Azad Kashmir would be elected by popular vote, and the Prime Minister by the Assembly. After the coup in Pakistan led by Gen. Mohammad Zia ul-Haq in 1977 the Azad Kashmir Assembly was dissolved, like the National and Provincial Assemblies in Pakistan, and in 1978 Gen. Zia, who had assumed the presidency of Pakistan, dismissed the President of Azad Kashmir, replacing him with his own nominee.

## Recent Developments in Indo-Pakistan Relations, 1980-82

The Soviet intervention in Afghanistan at the end of 1979 led to a temporary improvement in relations between India and Pakistan notwithstanding each side's suspicion that arms acquisitions by the other indicated an attempt to obtain military superiority. After talks in Islamabad in April 1980 between Swaran Singh (by now ex-Foreign Minister of India) and Agha Shahi (who later became Foreign Minister of Pakistan), the latter stated publicly that he had given assurances that "acquisition of arms by Pakistan would be purely for self-defence in view of the new situation [i.e. in Afghanistan] that has arisen", while the former said that both sides should have no difficulty in discussing the Kashmir issue in accordance with the Simla agreement. Moreover, President Zia met Mrs Gandhi for talks in Salisbury in April 1980 during Zimbabwe's independence celebrations and the Indian Prime Minister said afterwards that she had withdrawn her objections to Pakistan receiving military aid.

However, relations between the two countries again deteriorated during the summer of 1980, principally because both sides took major steps to strengthen their armed forces but also because of continuing tensions over the Kashmir issue. A statement issued by the Indian External Affairs Ministry on July 4, 1980, deplored the fact that President Zia had raised the Kashmir question at recent Islamic Conference meetings and described this action as "inconsistent with the spirit of the Simla agreement". Nevertheless, President Zia again raised the matter in an address to the UN General Assembly on Oct. 1, 1980, when he said that the process of normalizing Indo-Pakistan relations "can and will be further accelerated with a peaceful settlement of the question" and referred to the UN's inability to "redeem its promise to the people of Jammu and Kashmir to enable them to decide their future in accordance with its relevant resolutions".

Although the Indian and Pakistan Foreign Ministers agreed during talks in June 1981 that each country had the right to acquire arms for its own security, Indian unease increased in November 1981 when a US decision to sell advanced F-16 warplanes to Pakistan received confirmation. At the same time clashes between Indian and Pakistani troops on the Kashmir ceasefire line were reported to have reached their highest frequency for several years. Against this background President Zia made a public suggestion in late September that India and Pakistan should enter into negotiations on a mutual non-aggression pact, this proposal being formally communicated to the Indian Government on Nov. 11. Although India initially reacted with considerable scepticism, the two sides eventually began talks on the proposal in January 1982 and a further round was held the following month. Some progress was understood to have been made in the first round, but the second session was in effect broken off by India in protest against a statement made by a Pakistani diplomat to a recent meeting of the UN human rights' commission in Geneva in which he had compared the Indian part of Kashmir to Palestine as a region "under foreign military occupation".

C.H.

# Indonesia-Portugal (East Timor)

The island of Timor to the north-west of Australia was for several centuries divided between Dutch and Portuguese colonial rule, in the western and eastern halves of the island respectively. After West Timor had joined with other parts of the Dutch East Indies to become the Republic of Indonesia in 1949, East Timor continued under Portuguese rule until the mid-1970s but was then incorporated into Indonesia in August 1976 following Indonesian military intervention. Whereas the territory is now regarded by Indonesia as its 27th province (called Loro Sae), the Portuguese Government and a majority of UN member states have refused to recognize Indonesia's claim to sovereignty over East Timor and have asserted that its people have the right to self-determination of their status.

## Background to the Dispute

The territory of East Timor was one of the remnants of the South-East Asian part of the Portuguese empire, most of which was taken over by the Dutch in the 17th century and became the Dutch East Indies; whereas the latter (including West Timor) became independent as the Republic of Indonesia in 1949, East Timor remained under Portuguese rule throughout this period. During the colonial era East Timor was largely under the influence of Roman Catholic priests who gave it a Portuguese character and converted to Catholicism about 40 per cent of the local population and thus made it distinct from the Moslem population of Indonesian West Timor. To the Portuguese East Timor was of value mainly because of the export of sandalwood, most of it to China, but it was never properly developed. In 1974 the territory had no made-up roads outside Dìli (the capital); per capita income was about $40 per annum; the illiteracy rate was over 90 per cent (out of a total population officially stated to number 653,211 persons); and there was only one secondary school.

In the wake of the April 1974 revolution in Portugal, which led to the decolonization of Portuguese overseas territories, the population of East Timor was divided over its political future—the options being separate independence, integration with Indonesia or continued links with Portugal—and by 1975 the two main factions were involved in civil war. When it appeared that the territory was going to be ruled by a left-wing liberation movement (the Revolutionary Front for Independence, or Fretilin), East Timor was in December 1975 seized by Indonesian forces (officially described as volunteers), who supported the pro-Indonesian parties in East Timor. The latter set up a provisional Government, which asked for East Timor's incorporation in Indonesia, and this subsequently took place in August 1976.

Fretilin, which had set up a rival Government of the "Democratic Republic of East Timor", was supported, and the Indonesian action condemned, by a majority of United Nations member states, mainly on the grounds that the population of East Timor had not been consulted on its political future. While guerrilla warfare by Fretilin forces continued on a diminishing scale, the Indonesian authorities began to develop their new province by building roads, restoring the country's infrastructure devastated by the civil war and setting up schools where tuition was in the Indonesian language.

The de facto incorporation of East Timor in Indonesia was gradually accepted by a growing number of powers (though not by a majority of UN member states), and those which recognized it de jure included Australia and New Zealand. Under international law as interpreted by the United Nations, Portugal is still regarded as responsible for East Timor and its eventual decolonization, whereas Indonesia claims to have completed the decolonization process in the territory. The Governments of the United States and of Australia in particular have made it clear that they do not wish to embarrass the Government of Indonesia, a non-communist state in a region where it is desired to exclude communist influence.

**Map 32   East Timor.**

## Emergence of Political Parties in Portuguese Timor

After the Portuguese revolution of April 1974, the new Government of Portugal first discussed the future of Portuguese Timor with Indonesian leaders on Oct. 17, 1974, when Dr Antônio de Almeida Santos, then Portuguese Minister for Inter-Territorial Co-ordination, visited Jakarta and said that he did not consider total independence of the territory to be a realistic solution because a majority of its people wished to maintain ties with Portugal. He added that the best way to decolonize Timor would be by a referendum to be held in May 1975, and that a constituent assembly should be elected before that date.

The future of the territory was also discussed in Java early in September 1974 by President Suharto of Indonesia and Gough Whitlam, the then (Labor) Prime Minister of Australia, who were reported to have agreed that annexation by Indonesia would be the best solution for Timor. The Australian Government was said to hold the view that an independent Timor would not be able to survive as a state and would be "a potential threat to the region". Both sides agreed to respect the wishes of the Timorese people and not to interfere. A member of the Portuguese Supreme Revolutionary Council, however, declared at the end of May 1975 that the plan to hold a referendum in East Timor had been discarded.

Political parties formed in Portuguese Timor after the Portuguese revolution included (i) the Democratic Union of Timor (*União Democrática de Timor*, UDT), which stood for continued, though looser, connexions with Portugal; (ii) the Timorese Democratic People's Union (Apodeti), which advocated the union of the territory (as an autonomous province) with Indonesia on historical, geographical and ethnic grounds; and (iii) the Timorese Social Democratic Association (ASDT), which stood for full independence of the territory, possibly after a five-year transitional period, on the grounds that 90 per cent of the population were uneducated and without political consciousness and an immediate referendum would therefore give a distorted picture and open the way to corruption and manipulation. The ASDT was eventually superseded by Fretilin, which called for immediate independence and which was widely regarded as pro-communist.

At the end of a conference held in Macao between the Portuguese Government, the UDT and Apodeti on June 26-28, 1975, it was affirmed that the people of East Timor had "the right to self-determination with all its consequences, including independence" on "the principle according to which it lies with the people of Timor, and with them alone, to define the political future of the territory". Portuguese sovereignty was to continue until October 1978 unless otherwise agreed by the Portuguese Government and the proposed Timorese People's Assembly. In the meantime there was to be a Portuguese-controlled Government under a high commissioner and five assistant secretaries (for some of whose posts the Timorese parties would be allowed to submit names of candidates, and of whom three would be Portuguese and the other two probably Timorese). A constitutional law published in Lisbon on July 13, 1975, provided for elections to be held in October 1976 to the People's Assembly, which would draft political and administrative statutes for the territory.

## Outbreak of Civil War and Loss of Control by Portugal

The emergence of Fretilin as an anti-Indonesian revolutionary movement aroused a hostile reaction in Indonesia (whose Government had stated on Feb. 25, 1975, that it had no territorial ambition and was not planning an invasion of East Timor). In mid-1975 the UDT and Indonesian officials had several meetings in Jakarta and Kupang (the capital of Indonesian West Timor), after which the UDT president, Francisco Xavier Lopes da Cruz, declared that his party would soon take action against Fretilin (which had attacked UDT members in outlying areas), and on

Aug. 6 he declared: "We are realists. If we want to be independent we must follow the Indonesian political line; otherwise it is independence for a week or a month."

On Aug. 11, 1975, the UDT staged a coup and gained control of important sectors of Díli. On the following day the UDT demanded immediate independence from Portugal and the imprisonment of all Fretilin members, in response to which the President of Portugal stated in Lisbon on the same day that these demands were unacceptable and claimed that the Governor of Portuguese Timor was still in full control. The action of the UDT led to the outbreak of full-scale civil war between the forces of Fretilin on the one hand and on the other those of the UDT, fighting as an Anti-Communist Movement (MAC) and supported by Apodeti and two smaller groups—the Kota and *Trabalhista* (Labour) parties.

On Aug. 21 the Portuguese authorities admitted that they had lost control of the territory. Several hundred Portuguese were evacuated to Australia, where they reported that atrocities had been committed by both sides in the civil war. On Aug. 27 the Governor and members of his administration were evacuated to Atauro, an island 30 miles (48 km) north of Díli. By Sept. 1, 1975, Fretilin had taken control of Díli and on Sept. 8 it claimed to have gained complete control of East Timor; it also stated that it was ready for peace talks; that it had dropped its original demand for immediate independence from Portugal; and that it wished to move gradually towards self-government, with the installation of a provisional government early in 1976, the election of a constituent assembly and independence within a few years.

The Indonesian Defence Ministry stated on Sept. 7, 1975, that Indonesian pre-emptive strikes against Fretilin positions might be considered if these were advanced any closer to the Indonesian border; on Sept. 9 it added that it refused to accept any Portuguese move to hand the territory over to a Fretilin Government; and on Sept. 13 Dr Adam Malik, the Indonesian Foreign Minister, declared that his country had the right to intervene in East Timor if the war being waged there endangered Indonesian territory, but at the same time he appealed to all factions to cease fighting. Although Fretilin claimed on Oct. 11 that it was in full control of Portuguese Timor and had established a transitional administration, the Indonesian Government stated on Oct. 14 that pro-Indonesian forces were holding large sections of the territory and would by the end of October be in control of all of it. It was estimated in Jakarta that since the outbreak of the fighting between 40,000 and 50,000 inhabitants had fled from East Timor and that Díli's population had decreased from 25,000 to about 5,000.

In a memorandum of understanding signed in Rome on Nov. 3, 1975, after a meeting between the Indonesian and Portuguese Foreign Ministers, it was agreed that Portugal represented the legitimate authority in Portuguese Timor and was fundamentally responsible for its decolonization; that there should as soon as possible be a meeting between the Portuguese authorities and all the territory's political parties to bring the fighting to an end; and that Portugal would make "all efforts towards a speedy and orderly implementation of the act of self-determination by the people of Portuguese Timor". Fretilin, however, was on Nov. 6 reported to have refused to recognize the results of the Rome meeting, and on Nov. 14 it asserted that a full Indonesian invasion was imminent (while in Australia it was claimed that it had already begun).

On Nov. 28, 1975, Fretilin declared the territory independent as the Democratic Republic of East Timor, of which Francisco Xavier do Amaral (the Fretilin president) was sworn in as President on Nov. 29, and a Government was formed on Dec. 1 under Nicolau dos Reis Lobato as Prime Minister. Fretilin claimed that some 50 Afro-Asian countries had pledged support for an independent East Timor, and on Dec. 1 the new republic was recognized by Mozambique. The four pro-

Indonesian parties, on the other hand, declared on Nov. 29 that, as Fretilin's action had "removed the last remains of Portuguese sovereignty in Timor", East Timor was now part of Indonesian territory. The Lisbon Government for its part rejected the declarations of both Fretilin and the pro-Indonesian parties, and on Nov. 30 it formally requested United Nations help in settling the East Timor problem.

## Indonesian Occupation of East Timor

On Dec. 7, 1975, some 1,000 paratroopers from Indonesia, supported by a naval bombardment, entered East Timor and seized Díli, from which they expelled Fretilin's troops. In Jakarta it was announced that Díli had been "liberated by the people's resistance, spearheaded by Apodeti, the UDT and the Kota and *Trabalhista* parties" and that these resistance forces were "supported by Indonesian volunteers". The Portuguese Government on the same day broke off all diplomatic relations with Indonesia (which the latter had in 1964 reduced to consular level because of Portugal's colonial policies) and announced that it would resort to the United Nations with the aim of securing the cessation of "Indonesia's military intervention" as well as a peaceful negotiated solution to the conflict and the decolonization process.

Dr Malik, then Indonesian Foreign Minister, on the other hand said on Dec. 8 that he considered Portuguese sovereignty in Timor to have ended with Fretilin's declaration of independence on Nov. 28; that Díli was being ruled by a coalition of the four pro-Indonesian parties; that Fretilin's resistance had ended; and that Indonesian troops would remain in East Timor only until its people had decided their own future.

The Indonesian Minister of Information said in a statement issued on Dec. 8 that "the presence of Indonesian volunteers in Portuguese Timor" was founded on a number of considerations, among them "the inability of Portugal to control the situation so that the Rome memorandum could not, as a practical matter, be implemented"; a request for help made by the four pro-Indonesian parties; the Indonesian Government's "moral responsibility to guarantee the proper, orderly and peaceful decolonization of Portuguese Timor in accordance with the aspirations and desires of all the people in the territory"; the Indonesian Government's inability to "permit the situation in East Timor to go on indefinitely and to endanger national security and the stability of the South-East Asian region"; and the need "to take steps to end these continuing developments and safeguard national territorial integrity, to defend the sovereignty of the state and to protect the Indonesian people from disturbances, attacks, invasion, plunder and other provocative acts by Fretilin".

Indonesian and pro-Indonesian forces subsequently consolidated their hold on East Timor, and on Dec. 17 a provisional Government was formed with Arnaldo dos Reis Araujo (of Apodeti) as Chief Executive Officer. Four days earlier, the Portuguese enclave of Ocussi Ambeno (on the north coast of Indonesian West Timor) had been officially incorporated in Indonesia; moreover, following the evacuation of the Portuguese governor and his administration from the island of Atauro early in December, the island was occupied by pro-Indonesian forces on Dec. 28, when the Indonesian flag was hoisted on it. The Portuguese presence in East Timor was thus finally ended. Meanwhile, the fighting continued, with Indonesian radio claiming in January 1976 that pro-Indonesian forces controlled two-thirds of East Timor and Fretilin claiming control over 80 per cent of the territory. Francisco Xavier Lopes da Cruz, Vice-Chairman of the provisional Government, said in mid-February that up to 60,000 people had lost their lives in East Timor since August 1975.

## Incorporation of East Timor in Indonesia

The Indonesian Foreign Ministry announced on March 21, 1976, that the provisional Government of East Timor had decided to establish a Parliament to approve the merger of the territory with Indonesia and that the United Nations had been informed accordingly. Two months later a petition to integrate East Timor into Indonesia was approved on May 31 by the newly-formed Parliament of East Timor—a People's Representative Council of 28 members. Of 25 countries invited to send observers to the Council's session, only India, Iran, Malaysia, New Zealand, Nigeria, Saudi Arabia and Thailand did so, while countries which boycotted the session included Australia, Japan, Papua New Guinea, the Philippines, Singapore and the United States.

After the Council's petition had been officially handed over to President Suharto of Indonesia in Jakarta on June 7, 1976, East Timor was symbolically transferred to an Indonesian fact-finding mission on June 24. The United Nations had been invited to take part in this mission but had declined to do so on the grounds that no UN observers had supervised the election of the Council's members who had drawn up the petition. On June 29 the Indonesian Government announced its official acceptance of the merger; a bill legalizing East Timor's annexation was passed by the Indonesian Parliament on July 17; and on Aug. 17 East Timor was proclaimed Indonesia's 27th province under the name of Loro Sae, with Arnaldo dos Reis Araujo as its first Governor and Francisco Xavier Lopes da Cruz as his deputy.

Guerrilla warfare continued during subsequent years to be conducted by groups of followers of Fretilin and also of the UDT, but many of Fretilin's leaders surrendered or were captured or killed by Indonesian forces, while others represented Fretilin's cause outside East Timor. Following an amnesty offered by President Suharto on Aug. 16, 1977, to all Fretilin supporters who surrendered by the end of that year, large numbers of them were said to have given themselves up, the total being about 60,000, according to Indonesian claims made in mid-1978. Among those who surrendered was Francisco Xavier do Amaral (whom Fretilin had, on Sept. 13, 1977, removed from his posts of president of the organization and President of the Democratic Republic of East Timor, replacing him by Nicolau dos Reis Lobato, who was, however, killed in battle on Jan. 1, 1979). On May 22, 1979, it was reported that President Suharto had appointed the former Fretilin president as deputy governor of the province.

## United Nations Condemnation of Indonesia's Action

The UN Trusteeship Committee passed, on Dec. 11, 1975, by 69 votes (including Australia, China and the Soviet Union) to 11 (Dahomey, India, Indonesia, Iran, Japan, Malaysia, Mauritania, Morocco, the Philippines, Saudi Arabia and Thailand), with 38 abstentions (including the member countries of the European Community, New Zealand, Singapore and the United States) a resolution calling on Indonesia to withdraw from Portuguese Timor immediately and to desist from "further violations of the territorial integrity" of Portuguese Timor. Dr Malik, however, stated on the same day that his country did not feel bound by the resolution and that Indonesia had no troops in the territory except volunteers.

The UN General Assembly, on Dec. 12, 1975, passed, by 72 votes to 10 with 43 abstentions, a resolution calling on Indonesia to withdraw from East Timor and to enable the latter's people to decide their own future, and condemned the "military intervention of the armed forces of Indonesia". The UN Security Council, meeting at Portugal's request, on Dec. 22 unanimously called on Indonesia to withdraw its forces from East Timor without delay and requested Portugal to co-operate with the United Nations to enable East Timor's people to exercise their right of self-determination. This resolution was also rejected by Indonesia the next day.

Dr Malik said after a visit to Díli on Jan. 9-10, 1976, that his Government regarded East Timor as de facto part of Indonesia, but that he had suggested to the provisional Government that a consultation of East Timor's people should take place in a year's time. On Jan. 13, however, he stated that the provisional Government had invited the Indonesian Government to proclaim its sovereignty over East Timor; that they had discarded the idea of consultation; and that they now wanted a law declaring the territory to be part of Indonesia.

Following talks involving Dr Waldheim (the UN Secretary-General) and representatives of Indonesia, Portugal, Australia and Fretilin, a UN special envoy (Vittorio Winspeare Guicciardi, a UN Under-Secretary-General) visited Lisbon and Jakarta in mid-January and arrived in East Timor on Jan. 18, when Arnaldo dos Reis Araujo was reported to have told him that East Timor had already declared itself part of Indonesia and that a consultation of the people was "superfluous". A proposed visit by the UN special envoy to Fretilin bases in East Timor was called off by Fretilin on Feb. 5 because of Indonesian bombardments and the advance of pro-Indonesian forces.

The UN Security Council, which had debated the situation in East Timor for two weeks, adopted, on April 22, 1976, a resolution sponsored by Guyana and Tanzania and calling on Indonesia to withdraw all its forces from East Timor without delay and requesting the UN Secretary-General to charge his special envoy with pursuing his mission of fact-finding and consultation with the parties concerned. The resolution was approved by 12 votes to none with two abstentions (Japan and the United States) and without Benin (formerly Dahomey) taking part in the vote.

In subsequent years the cause of the right of the people of East Timor to self-determination continued to be defended in the movement of non-aligned countries and at successive sessions of the UN General Assembly. Thus the fifth conference of heads of state and government of non-aligned countries, held in Colombo on Aug. 16-19, 1976, included in its political declaration, as demanded by Mozambique, a reaffirmation of the right of self-determination for the people of East Timor. Moreover, a further call for "self-determination for the people of East Timor" was included in the political declaration adopted by consensus on Sept. 9, 1979, by the sixth conference of the heads of state and government of non-aligned countries held in Havana. This was done despite the fact that a special envoy of President Castro of Cuba had stated in Jakarta on April 11, 1979, that the issue of East Timor would not be included in the conference agenda.

### Later Australian, New Zealand and Portuguese Attitudes to East Timor Issue

The Australian Government's attitude to the conflict developed gradually from criticism of Indonesia's action to acceptance of the incorporation of East Timor in Indonesia as an accomplished fact. In a report released on June 16, 1977, two Australian Foreign Ministry officials accepted the incorporation of East Timor in Indonesia as an "irreversible fact". They found that the towns of the territory and their environs were completely controlled by the provincial authorities; that small areas in the hills were controlled by Fretilin forces; and that the rest of the population was scattered throughout a no man's land. In their view there was no evidence that Fretilin could mount major operations, but guerrilla harassment could probably be expected for some years.

In an earlier report published on Feb. 21, 1977, James Dunn (a former Australian consul in East Timor and head of the foreign affairs division of the Australian Parliament's research service) estimated that up to 100,000 Timorese had been massacred by Indonesian troops after the 1975 invasion and that those killed had included about 7,000 Chinese (about half East Timor's Chinese population). The Indonesian Government objected on March 1 to Dunn's "hostile activities", and Andrew Peacock (Australia's Foreign Minister) stated in Parliament on March 16 that the Dunn report had no official status.

On Jan. 20, 1978, the Foreign Minister of Australia announced that the Government had recognized the incorporation of East Timor into Indonesia, although it remained critical of the means by which this integration had been achieved. On Dec. 15 of that year he said that Australia had decided to recognize formally the Indonesian takeover of East Timor, but added: "The acceptance of this situation does not alter the opposition which the Government has consistently expressed regarding the manner of the incorporation." Anthony Street, the newly-appointed Australian Foreign Minister, said during a visit to Jakarta on Nov. 14, 1980, that as far as Australia and Indonesia were concerned the East Timor problem had been settled.

The New Zealand ambassador to Indonesia stated on July 20, 1978, that his Government supported President Suharto in refusing to tolerate outside interference in East Timor's integration in Indonesia, and that New Zealand would reinforce its support for the integration by participating in the development of Indonesia's newest province.

Portugal's continuing insistence on the East Timor people's right to self-determination was demonstrated when the Portuguese Prime Minister on Sept. 5, 1979, received six leaders of a new National Movement for the Liberation of and Independence of Timor-Díli, which had been formed with the intention of bringing together the UDT, Fretilin and all other Timorese forces in a united effort to achieve the territory's independence under a Christian regime. Moreover, on Sept. 13, 1980, the Portuguese Government (of the centre-right Democratic Alliance) issued a statement announcing that it would seek direct talks with Indonesian officials on independence for East Timor but reaffirming that Portugal remained "faithful to its obligations and responsibilities towards Timor"; asserting that the Timorese people had the right to self-determination, the statement added that recognition by Portugal of "the situation created in East Timor" would not be involved in the talks. The Indonesian Government rejected the Portuguese proposal on Sept. 21.

Although the Portuguese Government continued, during 1981, to claim sovereignty over East Timor, it was disclosed in a report—which was not released in Lisbon until Oct. 16, 1981—that in June 1975 there had been secret talks in Hong Kong between Indonesian and Portuguese officials and that the latter had advised the Indonesians that the Portuguese (left-wing) leaders at the time (President Francisco da Costa Gomes, Prime Minister Vasco Gonçalves and members of the Revolutionary Council) would accept East Timor's incorporation in Indonesia.

### Continued Unsettled Situation in East Timor

The Indonesian Foreign Minister (Dr Mochtar Kasumaatmadja) said in London on Oct. 15, 1979, that since 1975 about 60,000 people had died as a result of the civil war and starvation, but added that 200,000 people were benefiting from relief operations and that another 62,000 would be covered by a new Red Cross programme. In November 1979 the population of East Timor was officially stated to total 522,433 people (which meant a decline, since 1974, by more than 130,000, of whom about 5,000 had left for Australia and an estimated 25,000 for West Timor).

In June 1981 the East Timor People's Representative Council sent to President Suharto of Indonesia a report in which, although "undying gratitude" was expressed for East Timor's incorporation in Indonesia, it was stated that the conduct of Indonesian officials and troops was that of "conquerors towards a conquered

301

people'' and that numerous acts of murder, torture and other violence had been committed. According to a letter sent in November 1981 by the head of the Roman Catholic Church in East Timor to the chairman of the Australian Catholic Relief, Indonesian forces had in military operations in July-September 1981 killed many people, including women and children. On Feb. 23, 1982, the Catholic Institute for International Relations stated in London that Indonesian control was ''still not unchallenged'' in East Timor and that the Indonesian Army was carrying out large-scale operations in the eastern part of the territory.

H.W.D.

# Japan-Soviet Union

Since 1945 relations between Japan and the Soviet Union have been over-shadowed by a territorial dispute over a number of islands off the north-east coast of Japan which were occupied by the Soviet Union in the closing stages of World War II. The islands in question are the Habomai group together with Shikotan, Kunashiri and Etorofu, all of which are regarded by Japan as integral parts of its national territory. Although the two countries normalized their diplomatic relations in 1956, the unresolved dispute over the northern islands has been the main stumbling-block to the conclusion of a formal peace treaty between Japan and the Soviet Union; indeed, with the passage of time the dispute has become more intractable. Whereas the Soviet Union appeared to be willing in the mid-1950s to return the Habomai islands and Shikotan to Japan provided the latter signed a peace treaty which recognized Soviet sovereignty over Kunashiri and Etorofu, in recent years the Soviet Union has insisted that the territorial issue between the two countries is now closed.

## The Disputed Islands

The islands in dispute between Japan and the Soviet Union are the Habomai group (i.e. Suisho, Shibotsu, Yuri Akiyiri and Taraku) as well as Shikotan, Kunashiri and Etorofu—all situated off the north-east coast of Hokkaido, the northern-most of Japan's four main islands. The disputed islands comprise a total land area of 4,996 square kilometres, of which Etorofu accounts for 3,139 sq km, Kunashiri 1,500 sq km, Shikotan 255 sq km, and the Habomais 102 sq km. In terms of distance, Suisho island in the Habomais is only five kilometres from the nearest point of Nemuro peninsula on the north-east tip of Hokkaido.

Etorofu and Kunashiri are generally regarded as the two most southern islands of the Kurile chain of 20 main islands running south from the Kamchatka penin-sula to the east of Sakhalin island; but whereas Soviet sovereignty over the 18 Kurile islands stretching from Uruppu island northwards is not in dispute, Japan has consistently maintained that Etoforu and Kunashiri are distinct from the northern Kurile islands and that together with the Habomai group and Shikotan they are historically part of Japan in that until 1945 Russian influence had at no time extended south of Uruppu island. Japan also claims that as regards flora and fauna all the disputed islands are Japanese in botanical character and have a mild climate, whereas the islands from Uruppu to the north are subarctic. For its part, the Soviet Union has contested Japanese versions of the history of the disputed islands in the context of early Russian-Japanese relations and has in any case consistently maintained that its sovereignty over them was clearly established under agreements between the allied powers concluded towards the end of World War II. It also officially describes the disputed islands as the southern Kuriles.

The disputed islands occupy an important strategic position in that the seas around them provide the Soviet Navy with ice-free deep-water access from the Sea of Okhotsk to the Pacific Ocean, while the islands themselves contain several deep-water, ice-free natural harbours as well as large tracts of open land suitable for military bases. Moreover, the waters around the islands are a rich fisheries area traditionally exploited by Japanese fishermen.

### Historical Background

Japanese and Russian accounts of the early history of the disputed islands differ as to which side was the first to become the dominant influence in the area in question. They also express conflicting views as to the validity and significance of certain treaties signed by Japan and Imperial Russia in the 19th and early 20th centuries. Japan maintains in particular that the Treaty of Commerce, Navigation and Delimitation (also known as the Shimoda treaty) signed with Russia in 1855—and also the 1875 Russo-Japanese treaty under which Japan conceded Russian sovereignty over Sakhalin in exchange for the Kurile islands—both confirmed Japanese sovereignty over the disputed islands. On the other hand, the Soviet Union contends that these treaties have no present-day significance, arguing that Russian territorial concessions to Japan in this period were exacted under duress and specifically that the Japanese aggression against Russia in 1904 nullified all agreements between the two sides.

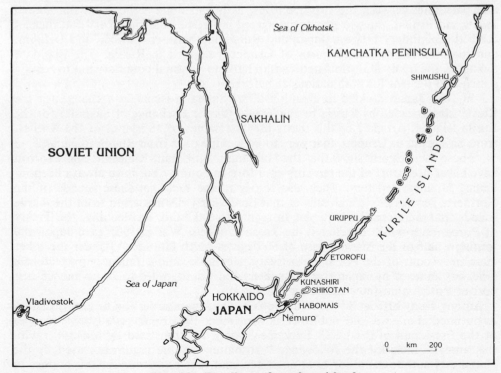

**Map 33  The disputed northern islands.**

A document entitled "Japan's Northern Territories" issued by the Japanese Foreign Ministry in 1977 gave the following account of early Russo-Japanese territorial relations: "The Japanese were aware of Sakhalin and the Kurile islands long before the Russians ever knew of their existence. It was Japan which actually developed these northern regions. But the Japanese had to withdraw from these areas later because of the inroads made by the Russians. Towards the end of the 16th century Russia advanced eastward over the Ural mountains and through Siberia. At the beginning of the 18th century she ruled the Kamchatka peninsula and had discovered Alaska. By that time the Russians were in the northern part of the Kuriles and had come into contact with the Japanese there.

"In 1792 the Soviet envoy, Adam Kirilovich Laksman, came to Nemuro in Hokkaido. He was followed by Nikolai Petrovich Rezanov, who came to Nagasaki in 1804 to try to open trade with Japan. The Shogunate [the hereditary military government which ruled Japan from 1192 to 1867], however, refused to respond, by citing Japan's traditional policy of isolationism. In response to these advances made by Russia, the Shogunate conducted surveys of the northern areas by sending Juzo Kondo and Rinzo Mamiya, among others, to the Kuriles and Sakhalin. In governing these islands, the Shogunate endeavoured to build up defences for these regions by establishing guard stations on Etorofu and other islands to the south in order to prevent incursions by foreign explorers or settlers.

"Meanwhile, Russia moved into the Kuriles not only by sending in survey expeditions but also by attempting to colonize the islands through a Russo-American company. Russian influence, however, at no time reached southward beyond Uruppu island because, as mentioned above, the Shogunate had established guard stations on Etorofu and other southern islands to prevent just such incursions. In view of these facts, when the Shogunate concluded the Treaty of Commerce, Navigation and Delimitation with Russia in 1855, realizing a new interchange of goods and personnel between the two countries, as it had done earlier with the United States and Britain, the two signatories agreed in Article II of the treaty that thenceforth the boundary between Japan and Russia lay between Etorofu and Uruppu, and that the Kurile islands north of Uruppu belonged to Russia. The island of Sakhalin, the treaty also stipulated, was to have no national boundary but to remain a mixed settlement for both nations as before.

"In 1875 Japan decided to abandon all of Sakhalin island in exchange for the Kurile islands ceded by Russia by the Treaty for the Exchange of Sakhalin for the Kurile Islands. Article 2 of this treaty lists the names of 18 islands of the Kuriles, from Shimushu to Uruppu, that were to be handed over from Russia to Japan.

"These facts clearly show that the Habomais, Shikotan, Kunashiri and Etorofu have never been part of the territory of a foreign country but have always been inherent Japanese territory. They also testify to the fact that these islands of the Northern Territories were already at that time clearly distinguished from the Kurile islands that were ceded by Russia. In regard to Sakhalin, incidentally, the Treaty of Portsmouth which concluded the Russo-Japanese War in 1905 gave Japan the southern half of the island, south of 50 degrees north latitude." [Under the other main provisions of the Portsmouth treaty, Korea became a Japanese protectorate (and was annexed by Japan five years later) and Russia ceded to Japan the ice-free port of Port Arthur (now Lushun in China).]

Among many official Soviet refutations of the Japanese version of earlier history as outlined above was one published in September 1981 by *Izvestia* (the newspaper of the Presidium of the USSR Supreme Soviet). As translated by Moscow radio, this analysis included the following: "Absolutely all the arguments used by the [Japanese] authorities today hold no water, and first and foremost this applies to the assertion that the Kuriles are traditionally Japanese territory. Let us recall in this connexion that right up to the mid-19th century the so-called northern territories that Tokyo claims now were not part of Japan proper. What is more, even Hokkaido island, the northern part of present-day Japan, was not part of the country. Only a small peninsula in the southern part of Hokkaido was colonized by the Japanese principality of Matsumae. True, in 1798, the Japanese Government proclaimed Hokkaido its territory, but was unable to actually rule it. In 1821 Hokkaido had to be returned to Matsumae principality. Only in 1834 did Japan again proclaim the island its territory, but even then the act was purely nominal. When in 1862 two Americans . . . arrived in the south of Hokkaido, they noted that for the Japanese the island was an absolutely enigmatic land.

"So it is not hard to understand, bearing all this in mind, what the claims to the Kuriles are worth, for these islands were peacefully developed by Russia long before even Hokkaido, an island that lies south of the Kuriles, became part of Japan. Claims are being made in Japan that the Russians, by signing in 1855 the Shimoda treaty, recognized Japan's legitimate rights to part of the islands of the Kurile chain. But that is a clear-cut distortion of the historic truth. The Shimoda treaty did not give Japan any legitimate rights and could not recognize such because it was not intended as something clearing up the issue of legitimate rights. The treaty was signed by the Russian diplomat Putyatin in Japan, then actually as a hostage, forced by the naval guns of England and France, countries with whom Russia was then in a state of war [i.e. in the Crimean War of 1853-56].

"Later on the Russian Government reminded Japan that Putyatin had signed the treaty in violation of the instructions given him, and if the document was left in force that was solely because of Russia's sincere desire to live in peace and friendship with Japan. In other words, the treaty did not establish the legitimacy of the Japanese rights but signified ceding to Japan a territory that had, by that time, been developed by the Russians and was part of Russia. The subsequent events in the Far East showed that Russia's hopes for peaceful relations with Japan were vain hopes. Japan took the road of aggression against Asian countries and regarded Russia only as an enemy. Eventually, in 1904, Japan attacked Russia, so Russia's territorial concessions were annulled. That they were a mistake was proved by history."

### Circumstances of Soviet Occupation of Disputed Islands in 1945

Over the next four decades the territories ceded to Japan under the 1905 and other treaties remained part of the Japanese empire, which in the 1930s embarked upon a course of massive territorial expansion by military conquest. As regards its relations with the Communist Government which came to power in Moscow in 1917, Japan signed the Anti-Comintern Pact with Germany in November 1936 (Italy joining a year later) and following the outbreak of fullscale war between Japan and China in 1937 Japanese forces on several occasions clashed with Soviet troops on the Soviet-Mongolian border, notably in the Nomonhan region in mid-1939. However, as Hitler launched his invasion of the Soviet Union in April 1941 the Tokyo and Moscow Governments signed a neutrality pact which was to survive until the very last days of World War II. Not until five days before the unconditional Japanese surrender on Aug. 14, 1945, did the Soviet Union enter the war against Japan, and by the end of the month Soviet forces had occupied Sakhalin and the Kurile islands right down to the northern coast of Hokkaido (meeting no resistance from the now surrendered Japanese).

The Soviet Union's declaration of war on Japan was made on the evening of Aug. 8, 1945 (48 hours after the atomic bomb attack on Hiroshima), and came into effect the following day. The war declaration referred to a "request by the Japanese Government to the Soviet Government to mediate in the war in Far East" but rejected this proposal in view of Japan's refusal to capitulate unconditionally. It therefore associated the Soviet Union with the proclamation issued at Potsdam the previous month by the United States and Britain (and approved by the Republic of China) calling upon the Japanese to surrender and reaffirming the stipulations regarding Japanese-held territories contained in the earlier Cairo declaration issued by the United States, Britain and China following a summit conference in the Egyptian capital on Nov. 22-26, 1943. It is these documents, together with the agreements reached between the United States, Britain and the Soviet Union at Yalta in February 1945, which are at the centre of the continuing dispute between Japan and the Soviet Union over the northern islands.

The November 1943 Cairo conference brought together President Roosevelt of the United States, Winston Churchill (the British Prime Minister) and Gen. Chiang Kai-shek of China. Their joint declaration recorded that they had "agreed upon future military operations against Japan" and had resolved "to bring unrelenting pressure against their brutal enemies by sea, land and air". It continued: "The three great allies are fighting this war to restrain and punish the aggression of Japan. They covet no gain for themselves and have no thought of territorial expansion. It is their purpose that Japan shall be stripped of all the islands in the Pacific which she has seized or occupied since the beginning of World War I in 1914, and that all the territories that Japan has stolen from the Chinese, such as Manchuria, Formosa and the Pescadores, shall be restored to the Republic of China. Japan will also be expelled from all other territories which she has taken by violence or greed. The aforesaid three Great Powers, mindful of the enslavement of the people of Korea, are determined that in due course Korea shall become free and independent."

At the Yalta conference of Feb. 4-11, 1945, Roosevelt, Churchill and Stalin agreed in a protocol which remained secret at the time but which was eventually published in Washington, London and Moscow on Feb. 11, 1946, that "in two or three months after Germany has surrendered and the war in Europe has terminated the Soviet Union shall enter into the war against Japan on the side of the allies". Among the specified conditions for this action were (i) that "the status quo in Outer Mongolia shall be preserved" [i.e. its independence would be recognized]; (ii) that "the former rights of Russia violated by the treacherous attack of Japan in 1904 shall be restored", under which heading it was stipulated that "the southern part of Sakhalin, as well as the islands adjacent to it, shall be returned to the Soviet Union"; and (iii) that "the Kurile islands shall be handed over to the Soviet Union". The protocol also recorded that the three leaders "have agreed that these claims of the Soviet Union shall be unquestionably fulfilled after Japan has been defeated".

During the US-UK-Soviet Potsdam conference of July 17-Aug. 2, 1945, the United States and Britain on July 26 issued a proclamation to the Japanese people calling for surrender to avoid the total destruction of Japan. Article 8 of this proclamation (which was approved by radio by Gen. Chiang Kai-shek) specified: "The terms of the Cairo declaration shall be carried out and Japanese sovereignty shall be limited to the islands of Honshu, Hokkaido, Kyushu, Shikoku, and such minor islands as we determine."

In the Soviet view the above agreements between the war-time allies, and particularly the Yalta secret protocol, restored the "historical status quo" in the Far East and confirmed Soviet sovereignty over all the northern islands occupied by Soviet forces at the end of World War II. The sentiments underlying this attitude received forceful articulation from Stalin himself when he broadcast to the Soviet people on Sept. 2, 1945, to announce the Japanese surrender and the Soviet occupation of Sakhalin and the Kuriles. In this broadcast the Soviet leader said: "The Japanese invaders inflicted damage not only on our allies—China, the USA and

Great Britain—but also most serious damage on our country. Therefore we have a special account of our own to settle with Japan. In February 1904, while negotiations between Japan and Russia were still in progress, Japan took advantage of the weakness of the Tsarist Government and treacherously, without declaring war, attacked our country and assaulted a Russian squadron at Port Arthur in order to disable Russian warships and thus to place her own navy in a position of advantage. Characteristically, 37 years later, Japan repeated exactly the same treacherous device against the USA at Pearl Harbour.''

Stalin continued: ''Russia suffered defeat in the war with Japan, and Japan took advantage of Tsarist Russia's defeat to wrest southern Sakhalin from Russia, to strengthen her hold over the Kurile islands, and in this way to close for our country in the east all outlets to the ocean. But the defeat of 1904 left painful memories in the minds of our people. Our people trusted, waiting for the day to come when Japan would be routed and the stain wiped out. For 40 years we, men of the older generation, have waited for this day. And now it has come. Japan has acknowledged her defeat and signed the act of unconditional surrender. This means that southern Sakhalin and the Kurile islands will pass to the Soviet Union, and from now on will not serve as a means for isolating the Soviet Union from the ocean and as a base for Japanese attack on our Far East, but as a means of direct communication for the USSR with the ocean and a base for the defence of our country against Japanese aggression.''

On the other hand, Japan has consistently maintained that none of the allied agreements towards the end of World War II specifically mentioned the Habomais, Shikotan, Kunashiri and Etorofu and that therefore they were never intended to confirm Soviet sovereignty over these islands. As regards the 1943 Cairo declaration, Japan argues (in its Foreign Ministry document of 1977) that since the Kuriles were ceded to Japan by Russia by ''peaceful negotiations'' surrounding the 1875 treaty, these islands ''can in no way be considered as territories which Japan took 'by violence and greed'''. Moreover, Japan argues, ''it is clear that the northern territories, which are distinct from the Kurile islands and are inherent territories of Japan, were not included in the areas thus designated''.

As regards the Yalta agreement, the Japanese Foreign Ministry document again stresses that ''the names of the islands to be included in the term 'Kurile islands' were not specified'', and continues: ''From a legal point of view the Yalta agreement was only a declaration of common objectives made by the leaders of Great Britain, the United States and the Soviet Union. On this point, the United States Government, one of the participants in this agreement, said in an aide-mémoire to Japan dated Sept. 7, 1956 [see below], that it 'regards the so-called Yalta agreement as simply a statement of common purposes by the then heads of the participating powers and not as a final determination by those powers or of any legal effect in transferring territories'. Furthermore, Japan is not a party to the Yalta agreement nor is there any mention of the Yalta agreement in the Potsdam declaration which Japan accepted. Therefore, Japan is not legally bound by it. Likewise, the Soviet Union cannot claim any rights against Japan on the basis of this agreement, which is not binding upon Japan.''

On the Potsdam proclamation, the same document makes the following observations: ''The final disposition of territories as a result of war is to be made by a peace treaty, and in that sense the stipulations of the Potsdam declaration cannot have any legal effect, as distinguished from that of a peace treaty, with regard to the final disposition of territories. Besides, the declaration merely states 'such minor islands as we determine' and does not specify the names of any islands. Nor can it be interpreted as the expression of a principle which runs counter to the principle of no territorial expansion as contained in the Cairo declaration. As clearly stated in Article 8, the Potsdam declaration is the successor to the Cairo declaration, and Japan accepted it as such at the time of surrender. Further, Soviet participation in the Potsdam declaration can be taken as proof that it admitted the principle of no territorial expansion contained in the Cairo declaration.''

A further document of this period which has been cited in the dispute is the memorandum issued on Jan. 29, 1946, by the Supreme Allied Commander in Japan, Gen. Douglas MacArthur, under the title ''Governmental and administrative separation of certain outlying areas from Japan''. This memorandum (SCAPIN No. 677) stipulated that ''for the purposes of this directive Japan is defined to include the four main islands of Japan and the approximately 1,000 smaller adjacent islands . . . and excluding inter alia the Kurile (Chishima) islands, the Habomai island group and Shikotan island''. It also stated that ''nothing in this directive shall be construed as an indication of allied policy relating to the ultimate determination of the minor islands referred to in Article 8 of the Potsdam declaration''.

The MacArthur memorandum thus excluded not only Kunashiri and Etorofu (as covered by the term ''Kurile islands'') but also the more southerly Habomais and Shikotan from the territorial scope of the allied military administration; for this reason it has been cited by the Soviet Union as further evidence of the intention of the war-time allies that the islands should become Soviet territory. Japan, on the other hand, argues that the memorandum was ''an expedient measure to facilitate the administrative functions of the occupation'' and had ''nothing to do with the final determination of the territorial issue'', as shown by its reference to Article 8 of the Potsdam declaration.

### 1951 San Francisco Peace Treaty and Related Developments

At the conclusion of a conference held in San Francisco in September 1951, a peace treaty with Japan was signed on Sept. 8, 1951, by 48 of the 51 wartime allies or associated states represented; the three countries which participated but did not sign were the Soviet Union, Czechoslovakia and Poland (while Burma, India and Yugoslavia did not attend and neither Communist nor Nationalist China was invited to participate). The treaty, which came into force on April 28, 1952, committed Japan inter alia to recognizing the independence of Korea and renouncing all claims to (i) Korea, Formosa (Taiwan) and the Pescadores, (ii) the Kurile islands and ''that portion of Sakhalin and the islands adjacent to it over which Japan acquired sovereignty as a consequence of the Treaty of Portsmouth of Sept. 5, 1905'', (iii) the Pacific islands formerly mandated to Japan by the League of Nations, (iv) any territory in Antarctica, and (v) the Spratly and Paracel islands. Under the treaty Japan also agreed to place under UN trusteeship, with the United States as the sole administering authority, the Ryukyu islands south of 29° N (including Okinawa), the Bonin islands, the Volcano islands, Marcus island and some smaller islands.

During the lengthy drafting negotiations associated with the San Francisco treaty, the Soviet Union had repeatedly objected to the procedure being followed and also to certain of the terms generally agreed by the non-communist countries involved. In particular, it had demanded that the treaty should be drawn up by the four major wartime allies (i.e. Britain, China, the USA and the USSR) rather than by the 12-nation Far Eastern Commission, as favoured by the United States and Britain. Soviet spokesmen also, before and after the treaty's signature, criticized its provisions as containing insufficient safeguards against a revival of Japanese militarism and as a US device to convert Japan into a military bridgehead in the Far East.

At the same time, these broad divergences were accompanied by the surfacing of disputation over the particular question of the northern islands. Already, in a speech delivered in Los Angeles on March 31, 1951, John Foster Dulles (then President Truman's foreign affairs adviser) had noted that "South Sakhalin and the Kurile islands were allotted to Russia at Yalta" but had added: "Any peace treaty validation of Russia's title should, we suggest, be dependent on Russia's becoming a party to that treaty." At the San Francisco conference itself, as it transpired that the Soviet Union would not sign the treaty with Japan, Dulles made it clear that the only definition of peace terms binding on Japan and the allies were those contained in the Potsdam declaration and that private understandings among some of the allied powers were not binding upon either Japan or the allies.

In Japan itself the territorial question had become an important issue in the debate over the proposed peace treaty terms. Against a background of demands from opposition deputies in the Diet that the northern islands (as well as the Ryukyu and Bonin islands) should be returned to Japan under the peace treaty, the Government submitted materials to the United States intended to show that the Habomais and Shikotan were part of Hokkaido and that Kunashiri and Etorofu had never belonged to a foreign country. Moreover, at the peace conference the Japanese Prime Minister, Shigeru Yoshida, called the attention of the participants to Japan's view that the Soviet-held northern islands were integral parts of Japan proper.

As regards the actual terms of the peace treaty, the Japanese Government has consistently pointed out that Japan's renunciation of South Sakhalin and the Kuriles was not accompanied by any stipulation that they should belong to another country and that "unilateral measures" by the Soviet Union to absorb these territories "have no legal effect in transferring title". It has also stressed that in any case the geographical limits of the term "Kurile islands" were again not clearly defined and that therefore "it is quite natural for Japan to consider that the Habomais, Shikotan, Kunashiri and Etorofu are not included in the term".

Following the entry into force of the San Francisco peace treaty on April 28, 1952, the Allied Council for Japan (consisting of representatives of the United States, the British Commonwealth, the Soviet Union and China) was dissolved and the Japanese Government informed the Soviet mission in Tokyo that it no longer had any *raison d'être*. On June 20 the head of the Soviet mission was recalled to Moscow, and since there had been no formal termination of the state of war between Japan and Soviet Union it followed that there could be no diplomatic relations between the two countries.

On the same day as the signing of the San Francisco peace treaty, Japan and the United States entered into a bilateral defence pact under which the Japanese Government agreed to the indefinite retention of US forces "in and about Japan" so as to deter any armed aggression against the latter country. Eight years later this pact was replaced by a treaty of mutual co-operation and security (signed on Jan. 19, 1960, and in force from June 23, 1960) under which Japan was no longer treated as the weaker partner but was placed on an equal footing with the United States. The new treaty was clarified by an exchange of notes, in one of which the treaty area was defined as the territory under Japanese rule at any time therefrom, while the parties also agreed to consult together in the event of an armed attack or threat of attack against the islands over which Japan claimed residual sovereignty.

## Unsuccessful Japanese-Soviet Peace Treaty Negotiations and 1956 Joint Declaration

In view of the Soviet Union's non-signature of the 1951 peace treaty with Japan, the two sides subsequently entered into discussions on the conclusion of a separate peace treaty, on which formal negotiations eventually opened in London on June 1, 1955. Over the following 14 months the issue of the northern islands became central to these negotiations, and although both sides made concessions on their initial positions it eventually caused the breakdown of the talks in August 1956. On the other hand, agreement was reached on the termination of the state of war between Japan and the Soviet Union and the resumption of diplomatic relations, as set out in a joint declaration signed by the two sides in October 1956.

The opening Soviet conditions put forward in the first round of talks in June-September 1955 included the territorial stipulation that Japan should relinquish all claims to South Sakhalin, the Kurile islands, the Habomais and Shikotan, whereas the Japanese side initially demanded the return of these same territories. When the second round of negotiations began in January 1956 (also in London) the Soviet Union indicated its willingness to return the Habomais and Shikotan to Japanese sovereignty but continued to uphold its claim to South Sakhalin and the Kuriles on the grounds (i) that Japan had renounced all right, claim and title to these territories under the San Francisco peace treaty; and (ii) that the allies had agreed to their cession to the USSR at the Yalta conference. Japan on the other hand maintained (i) that the San Francisco treaty did not determine the ultimate ownership of South Sakhalin and the Kuriles; (ii) that Etorofu and Kunashiri were an integral part of Japanese territory over which Japanese sovereignty had been recognised by the San Francisco treaty, which had not defined the term "Kuriles"; and (iii) that the Soviet Union could not claim title to these territories by virtue of a treaty which it had not signed. The Japanese Government therefore proposed that the southern Kuriles should be returned to Japan and that the future of South Sakhalin should be decided by a conference of the signatories of the San Francisco treaty and the Soviet Union.

The London talks were suspended on March 20, 1956, but negotiations resumed in Moscow on July 31, when the Japanese side immediately announced that Japan had renounced its claim to South Sakhalin and the northern Kuriles but could not relinquish Etorofu and Kunashiri. At the second round of talks on Aug. 3 the Soviet side reaffirmed its view that Etorofu and Kunashiri formed part of the Kuriles, the future of which had been decided at Yalta and San Francisco, to which Japan responded that it could not be bound by the Yalta agreement, to which it was not a party, and that under the Potsdam and Cairo declarations the Soviet Union had renounced territorial aggrandisement as a war aim. With both sides adhering to their positions, the talks remained deadlocked and were eventually suspended on Aug. 13, 1956, on which date the Japanese Foreign Minister expressed the view at a Moscow press conference that it was advisable for Japan to conclude a peace treaty even on the Soviet terms. But an emergency meeting of the Japanese Cabinet on the same day sent him instructions not to sign the treaty at that stage.

Amid considerable criticism of the proposed terms of the treaty within Japan, the Japanese Prime Minister, Ichiro Hatoyama, sent a personal message to his Soviet counterpart, Nikolai Bulganin, in which he proposed that the territorial question should be temporarily shelved and that negotiations should be resumed on the basis of a five-point plan covering the ending of the state of war between the two countries, the exchange of ambassadors, the repatriation of Japanese war criminals held in the Soviet Union, the conclusion of a 10-year fisheries agreement and Soviet support for the admission of Japan to membership of the United Nations. After talks between Hatoyama and Bulganin in Moscow, a formal agreement was reached on Sept. 29, 1956, "to continue negotiations, even after Japanese-Soviet relations are normalized, in order to conclude a peace treaty, including the territorial issue, and to establish complete peace relations".

On the basis of these preliminaries, the Japanese and Soviet Prime Ministers proceeded to the signature in the Kremlin on Oct. 19, 1956, of a joint declaration providing for the termination of the state of war between the two countries and

310

the re-establishment of diplomatic relations and also regulating other aspects of their bilateral relations. This declaration, Paragraph 9 of which referred to the territorial issue, was worded as follows:

"(1) The state of war between the USSR and Japan ends on the day the present declaration comes into force, and peace and good-neighbourly relations are established between them.

"(2) Diplomatic and consular relations between the USSR and Japan are re-established, and the two states will exchange ambassadors without delay. The question of the opening of consulates in the Soviet Union and Japan will be settled through diplomatic channels.

"(3) The USSR and Japan confirm that they will be guided by the principles of the UN Charter in their mutual relations, and in particular by the following principles in Article 2 of the Charter: (*a*) to settle their international disputes by peaceful means in such a manner as not to endanger international peace, security, and justice; (*b*) to refrain in their international relations from using the threat of force, or its use, against the territorial integrity or political independence of any state, or from acting in any other manner incompatible with the aims of the United Nations; (*c*) the USSR and Japan confirm that, in accordance with Article 51 of the UN Charter, each of the states enjoys the inalienable right of individual or collective defence; (*d*) the USSR and Japan mutually undertake not to interfere directly or indirectly in each other's internal affairs, whether out of economic, political, or ideological motives.

"(4) The Soviet Union will support Japan's application for membership of the United Nations.

"(5) All Japanese citizens sentenced in the Soviet Union will be freed and repatriated as soon as the joint declaration enters into force. As regards those Japanese whose fate is unknown, the USSR, at Japan's request, will continue to attempt to investigate their fate.

"(6) The Soviet Union waives all claims to reparations against Japan. The USSR and Japan mutually waive all claims for war damages on behalf of the state, its organizations and citizens, against the other state, its organizations and citizens, which may have arisen since Aug. 9, 1945.

"(7) The Soviet Union and Japan agree to start negotiations as soon as possible for the purpose of concluding treaties or agreements with a view to placing their trade, shipping and other business relations on a stable and friendly basis.

"(8) The Convention on Fishing in the Open Seas of the North-West Pacific, and the agreement between the Soviet Union and Japan on mutual co-operation in sea-rescue operations signed in Moscow on May 14, 1956, enter into force simultaneously with the present joint declaration. Taking into consideration the interest of both the Soviet Union and Japan in the preservation and rational utilization of natural fishing resources and other marine biological resources, the two countries will take measures, in a spirit of co-operation, to preserve and develop the fishing resources and to regulate and limit catches in the open sea.

"(9) The USSR and Japan agree to continue, after the re-establishment of diplomatic relations between them, negotiations on the conclusion of a peace treaty. In this connexion, the USSR, meeting the wishes of Japan and taking into account the interests of the Japanese state, agrees to hand over to Japan the Habomai and Shikotan islands, with the reservation that the actual transfer of these islands to Japan is to take place after the conclusion of a peace treaty between the Soviet Union and Japan.

"(10) The present joint declaration is subject to ratification and comes into force when instruments or ratification are exchanged. Exchange of instruments of ratification will take place as soon as possible in Tokyo."

In recent years the Japanese Government has consistently cited Paragraph 9 of the 1956 joint declaration to refute the Soviet contention that there is no territorial issue between the two countries. It argues that the negotiations referred to were clearly intended to concern the territorial question, since the major problems normally covered by a peace treaty had been resolved by the joint declaration, and specifically the problem of Kunashiri and Etorofu, since it had already been agreed that the Habomais and Shikotan would revert to Japan on the conclusion of a peace treaty.

Shortly before the signature of the joint declaration a significant development occurred when the United States defined its view on the Japan-Soviet peace treaty negotiations and in particular on the territorial question. An aide-mémoire issued by the US State Department on Sept. 7, 1956, contained the following passages: "The United States regards the so-called Yalta agreement as simply a statement of common purposes by the then heads of the participating powers, and not as a final determination by those powers or of any legal effect in transferring territories. The San Francisco peace treaty (which conferred no rights upon the Soviet Union because it refused to sign) did not determine the sovereignty of the territories renounced by Japan, leaving that question, as was stated by the US delegate at San Francisco, to 'international solvents other than this treaty'. It is the considered opinion of the United States that, by virtue of the San Francisco peace treaty, Japan does not have the right to transfer sovereignty over the territories renounced by it therein. In the opinion of the USA, the signatories of the San Francisco treaty would not be bound to accept any action of this character, and they would presumably reserve all their rights thereunder. The USA has reached the conclusion, after careful examination of the historical facts, that the islands of Etorofu and Kunashiri (along with the Habomai islands and Shikotan, which are part of Hokkaido) have always been part of Japan proper, and should in justice be acknowledged as under Japanese sovereignty. The USA would regard Soviet agreement to this effect as a positive contribution to the reduction of tension in the Far East."

The October 1956 Japanese-Soviet joint declaration and related conventions came into force on Dec. 12, 1956, when instruments of ratification were exchanged between the two Governments in Tokyo. During the debate on the agreements in the Japanese Lower House the previous month 58 deputies of the ruling Liberal-Democratic Party absented themselves from the proceedings in protest against the omission of any specific provision in the joint declaration for continued negotiations on Japan's claim to Etorofu and Kunashiri.

Consequent upon the formal ending of the state of war between Japan and the Soviet Union and the restoration of full diplomatic relations between the two countries, a Japanese application for membership of the United Nations was unanimously approved by the Security Council on Dec. 12 and by the General Assembly on Dec. 18, 1956.

## Developments in 20 Years following 1956 Joint Declaration

Within a few years of the signing of 1956 joint declaration, the conclusion in January 1960 of the new Japan-US mutual co-operation and security treaty referred to above brought about a hardening of the Soviet stance on the northern islands, any territorial concession on which it now specifically linked with a withdrawal of all foreign (i.e. US) troops from Japanese territory as well as the conclusion of a formal peace treaty. In a memorandum of Jan. 27, 1960, protesting against the new Japan-US treaty, the Soviet Government stated that it "perpetuates the actual occupation of Japan, places her territory at the disposal of a foreign power . . . and its provisions inevitably lead to the military, economic and political subordination of Japan". In this "new situation" and in view of the fact that the treaty was "directed against the Soviet Union and also against the Chinese People's Republic", the Soviet Government could not "allow itself to contribute to an extension of the territory used by foreign armed forces" by handing over the Habomai islands and Shikotan, which would be transferred to Japan "only on condition that all foreign troops are withdrawn from the territory of Japan and a peace treaty is concluded between the USSR and Japan".

The Japanese Government responded on Jan. 28 by accusing the Soviet Union of "interference in Japan's domestic affairs" and of wishing to impose an additional condition on the Soviet undertaking of 1956, thereby revealing "the Soviet attitude of contempt for international pledges". A week later, on Feb. 5, the Japanese Government formally rejected the Soviet demand for the withdrawal of foreign troops.

During the latter half of 1961 the US-Japan security treaty and the territorial question formed the subject of correspondence between the Soviet and Japanese Prime Ministers. The exchange opened with a message from Nikita Khrushchev to Nasanosuke Ikeda (delivered by the Soviet First Deputy Prime Minister, Anastas Mikoyan, during a visit to Tokyo in August 1961) in which the Soviet leader appealed to Japan to close "foreign military bases" and end its alliance with the United States, since these two factors did "not help in deepening mutual trust and normalizing relations between Japan and the Soviet Union". In his reply Prime Minister Ikeda rejected Khrushchev's assertions and called on the Soviet Union to restore good relations by settling territorial differences between the two countries and signing a peace treaty. Replying on Sept. 25, Khrushchev categorically refuted Japanese territorial claims, asserting specifically that the status of Kunashiri and Etorofu had been permanently settled "through various international agreements".

In a further letter to Khrushchev on Nov. 15, 1961, the Japanese Prime Minister described the Soviet leader's arguments as "contrary to fact and lacking adequate grounds", adding that Japan could "not remain indifferent" to the fact that the Soviet Government was sending more and more Soviet citizens to Kunashiri and Etorofu, whose final status could only be settled in a peace treaty. After saying that the international agreements cited by Khrushchev were "presumably" the Yalta agreement and the 1951 San Francisco peace treaty, Ikeda maintained that the Yalta accord did not determine legally to whom the Kurile islands should belong, even though it contained a statement of common purpose towards them; moreover, Japan had not been a party to the Yalta agreement, while the Potsdam declaration, which Japan had accepted, contained no reference to Yalta. In these circumstances, he continued, Japan was not bound legally or politically by the Yalta decisions, which the Soviet Government could therefore not invoke in this question. While accepting that under the San Francisco peace treaty Japan had renounced all rights to South Sakhalin and the main Kurile group, Ikeda pointed out that the treaty had not laid down the final ownership of these territories and that since the Soviet Union had refused to sign the treaty it could not cite its provisions to support the Soviet case. He also reiterated that Japan had never renounced its claims to Kunashiri and Etorofu, having always contended that the Japanese renunciation had applied only to the 18 islands of the main Kurile group, and that the two southernmost islands formed part of Japan proper.

In his reply to Ikeda, which was published on Dec. 12, 1961, Khrushchev again rejected the Japanese arguments. He declared that the Soviet Union would not transfer to Japan its rights over South Sakhalin and the Kuriles, maintaining that they had been acquired under the Yalta agreement, and asserted that Japan was attempting to evade obligations undertaken in international agreements after its unconditional surrender in August 1945.

Over the following decade there were no significant diplomatic developments relating to the basic Japanese-Soviet territorial dispute, but economic relations between the two countries flourished to the extent that the Soviet Union became one of Japan's main trading and economic co-operation partners. In July 1966 Andrei Gromyko became the first Soviet Foreign Minister to pay an official visit to Japan and a joint communiqué issued on the occasion announced that a bilateral consular convention had been signed and that the two countries had agreed to hold regular consultations "both on questions of bilateral Soviet-Japanese relations and on international problems in the solution of which both countries are interested". Without specifically referring to the territorial issue, the communiqué also said that both sides had agreed that it was "possible further to develop relations between Japan and the USSR in all spheres in the spirit of the Soviet-Japanese declaration of 1956" and that the "development of friendly and good-neighbourly relations between Japan and the Soviet Union will greatly contribute to the safeguarding of peace and security in Asia and to the cause of world peace".

Gromyko paid a further visit to Tokyo in January 1972 during which he had extensive talks with his Japanese counterpart, Takeo Fukuda, and also with the Japanese Prime Minister, Eisaku Sato. The principal result of the talks, as recorded in an official communiqué, was a decision to hold further Soviet-Japanese talks later in the year with a view to the conclusion of a peace treaty. Although the communiqué made no specific reference to the question, it was understood that the Japanese side had again raised the question of the northern islands in relation to a possible peace treaty. When the specified talks took place in Moscow at the level of Foreign Ministers in October 1972, they ended inconclusively amid continued deadlock on the territorial issue. Meanwhile, Japan had on June 26, 1968, secured the reversion of the Bonin and Volcano island groups together with certain smaller islands (under an agreement signed with the United States on April 5, 1968), while on June 17, 1971, a further Japan-US agreement provided for the return to Japanese jurisdiction of the Ryukyu islands (including Okinawa)—the latter agreement being subsequently implemented on May 15, 1972.

In March 1973 the new Japanese Prime Minister, Kakuei Tanaka, sent a letter to the General Secretary of the Soviet Communist Party, Leonid Brezhnev, stressing that the conclusion of a peace treaty was indispensable for the establishment of good-neighbourly relations with the Soviet Union and proposing that further discussion on a peace treaty should be held within the year. After the Soviet leader had responded favourably, Tanaka paid a four-day visit to Moscow on Oct. 7-10, 1973—the first Japanese Prime Minister to do so since Hatoyama's visit in 1956. In a joint communiqué issued after Tanaka's talks with Brezhnev and other Soviet leaders there was again no specific reference to the territorial question, the document containing the following passage: "The two sides recognized that to conclude a peace treaty by resolving the yet unresolved problems remaining since World War II would contribute to the establishment of truly good-neighbourly relations between the two countries and conducted negotiations on matters concerning the content of such a peace treaty. The two sides agreed to continue negotiations for the conclusion of a peace treaty between the two countries at an appropriate time during 1974."

According to the Japanese version of the Tanaka visit to Moscow in October 1973, the question of the northern islands formed the main topic in four meetings between the Japanese Prime Minister and Brezhnev, during which the former twice secured the concurrence of the latter that the territorial issue constituted one of the unsettled post-war issues between the two countries. In the Japanese view, therefore, the talks produced a confirmation that the territorial question, as an unsettled post-war issue, should form the subject of negotiations between the two countries for ultimate resolution in the context of a Japan-Soviet peace treaty.

The next round of talks did not in fact take place until January 1975, when Kiichi

Miyazawa (Japanese Foreign Minister) visited Moscow to urge the Soviet Government to resume formal negotiations on a peace treaty. On this occasion Gromyko proposed that the two countries should postpone the conclusion of a peace treaty and sign instead a treaty of good-neighbourliness and co-operation, but this suggestion was rejected as inappropriate by Miyazawa. In response to Gromyko's request that Japan should take a "realistic attitude", the Japanese Foreign Minister insisted that if the Soviet Union wished genuinely to establish friendly relations with Japan a truly realistic attitude would be to resolve the territorial issue under a peace treaty. A communiqué issued after Miyazawa's visit repeated the formulation used in the October 1973 text, making no reference to the territorial question as such, but the Japanese Foreign Minister stated that Japan would continue to press its claim.

The new Soviet proposal was repeated in a personal letter from Brezhnev to the Japanese Prime Minister, Takeo Miki, which as delivered on Feb. 13, 1975, suggested that the two sides could conclude a friendship treaty "while continuing negotiations for a peace treaty". This proposal was immediately rejected by the Japanese Government, however, on the grounds that a peace treaty was the first requirement and also that the prior conclusion of a friendship treaty would represent a virtual shelving of the northern islands question. An important factor in these new exchanges was the improvement in Sino-Japanese relations which had been underway since the early 1970s and the negotiations then in progress between Japan and China on a bilateral treaty of peace and friendship. The Soviet Government repeatedly warned Japan that it would regard the conclusion of such a treaty as an unfriendly act and directed particular criticism at the proposed inclusion of an "anti-hegemony" clause as propounded by China (whose use of this term was generally seen as referring in particular to the Soviet Union). When the China-Japan peace and friendship treaty was eventually signed in Peking on Aug. 17, 1978—containing in Article 2 a specification that neither side "should seek hegemony in the Asia-Pacific region or in any other region" and that each "is opposed to efforts by any other country or group of countries to establish such hegemony"—the Soviet Government delivered a formal protest to the Japanese Government and official Soviet sources claimed that Japan had yielded to Peking's "diktat" by deciding to sign the treaty on China's terms.

Meanwhile, Andrei Gromyko had paid a further visit to Tokyo in January 1976 during which he was reported to have indicated the Soviet Union's willingness to return the Habomais and Shikotan to Japan if the latter agreed to sign a treaty of good-neighbourliness and co-operation with the Soviet Union. However, it was understood that the Japanese Government had again rejected this proposal and emphasized Japan's insistence on the return of all the islands in dispute. At the end of the Gromyko visit the Japanese Foreign Minister said that he had made no progress in discussions on the territorial issue, asserting that the Soviet Union appeared to be "obsessed" with the proposed Sino-Japanese treaty and disclosing that Gromyko had not accepted his explanation that the controversial "anti-hegemony" clause in such a treaty would not be directed against the Soviet Union but rather had universal application.

### Tensions in Japanese-Soviet Relations, 1976-80

Japanese accounts of the territorial question suggest that from about 1975 the Soviet Union began to take a harder line, in particular by maintaining that the Japanese claim for the return of the northern islands was a "baseless and unwarranted demand made by a small segment of people" and that it was "instigated directly from outside". Such assertions were consistently rejected through diplomatic channels by the Japanese Government, which in 1976 also protested when the Soviet Union imposed a requirement that Japanese citizens wishing to visit the graves of relatives on the northern islands should have valid Japanese passports and Soviet visas. Tensions also developed in Japanese-Soviet relations in late 1976 when a Soviet pilot landed a supersonic MiG-25 warplane in Hokkaido in Sept. 7 and was subsequently granted political asylum in the United States; despite Soviet demands for its immediate return, the aircraft was retained for examination by Japanese and US military experts and not returned until mid-November, causing the Soviet Union to take a number of diplomatic and other measures which were interpreted as indicating its displeasure.

Moreover, in December 1976 the territorial issue became directly entangled with questions of fishery rights when on Dec. 10 the Soviet Union proclaimed a 200-mile fishing zone around its coasts and announced that fishing operations could be undertaken by foreigners in this zone only on the basis of agreements or other forms of understanding reached with the Soviet Government. The Japanese Government responded on Jan. 26, 1977, by extending Japan's territorial waters limit from three to 12 nautical miles (with the exclusion of the three international straits of the region), specifying that the new 12-mile limit would encompass the disputed northern islands. On Feb. 24 the Soviet Government announced that it would enforce the 200-mile fishing zone from March 1 and made it clear that the zone would incorporate the waters around the northern islands—this being described by the Japanese Government on Feb. 25 as "an unfriendly and regrettable act" and as unacceptable to Japan. However, during talks in Moscow on Feb. 28 between the Japanese Agriculture Minister and the Soviet Fisheries Minister it was agreed that for the time being the Soviet Union would "not apply coercive measures" against Japanese fishing vessels within the zone.

Later in 1977, on May 27, an interim Soviet-Japanese fisheries agreement was signed in Moscow providing for Japanese fishing operations during the rest of the year in seven limited areas within the Soviet 200-mile zone. Moreover, after Japan had itself implemented a 200-mile fishing zone from July 1, 1977, it signed a further interim agreement with the Soviet Union on Aug. 4 granting reciprocal rights to Soviet fishermen within the Japanese zone (this agreement containing a stipulation that nothing in it would impair the positions of either side on any outstanding bilateral or multilateral problem). Negotiations conducted in Moscow between Sept. 29 and Oct. 20, 1977, resulted in the extension for a further year—until the end of 1978—of the two interim Japanese-Soviet fisheries agreements; but as a result of Japan's decision to proceed with the signature of a peace and friendship treaty with China in August 1978 [see above], the Soviet Government announced an indefinite postponement of negotiations on a longer-term fisheries agreement with Japan. From the Japanese point of view, this breakdown of co-operation with the Soviet Union over fishing rights was significant not only because of the traditional importance of Japanese fishing operations in waters now within the Soviet economic zone but also because of the relationship between the fisheries with the territorial issue—the failure to resolve the latter being an important underlying factor in tensions over the former. According to official Japanese figures issued in 1977, more than 1,500 Japanese fishing vessels had been seized by the Soviet authorities over the three post-war decades and nearly 13,000 Japanese fishermen had undergone the experience of detention.

During the disputation over fisheries the Japanese and Soviet Governments continued diplomatic contacts on the basic peace treaty question, but according to Japanese accounts of these further exchanges the Soviet side from late 1976 took the line that no territorial dispute existed between the two countries. After talks between Sunao Sonoda (Japanese Foreign Minister) and Soviet leaders in Moscow in February 1978 had ended without a communiqué being issued, Sonoda reported on his return to Tokyo that the Soviet side had again denied the existence of a territorial problem and claimed that this was a "unilateral negation" of the undertaking given in the 1973 Tanaka-Brezhnev communiqué. Later in the month the Soviet newspaper *New Times* asserted that a peace treaty could be based "only on a recognition by both sides of the realities that have emerged as a result of World War II".

On Feb. 11, 1978, the Soviet ambassador to Japan, Dmitry Polyansky, presented the Japanese Government with a draft treaty of good-neighbourly relations and co-operation between the two countries, but this was immediately rejected by the Japanese Prime Minister (Takeo Fukuda) principally on the grounds that it failed to mention the territorial issue and that such a treaty could not precede a formal peace treaty. This attitude came under strong attack in the official Soviet media, notably in *Pravda*, which on March 3 carried an article claiming that the Japanese Government was "closing its eyes to reality" and arousing "revanchist illusions" among the Japanese people.

Throughout the period 1979-80 the Japanese Government repeatedly drew attention to what it claimed was a significant build-up of Soviet forces on the northern islands, including the stationing of some 2,000 troops on Shikotan (which had not been militarized since 1960). By May 1980 Soviet military strength in the northern islands was estimated by Japan at some 13,000 troops, compared with about 1,000 in 1976, and Japan also claimed that direct command communications had been established between Kunashiri, Etorofu and Vladivostok (the base of the Soviet Pacific fleet). On Oct. 6, 1979, the Japanese Government announced its intention to begin aerial reconnaissance over Shikotan as part of its periodic inspections of the northern islands, this step being condemned as "wild interference" by the Soviet Union.

In a newspaper interview published on March 7, 1980, Dmitry Polyansky said that the Soviet Union would under no circumstances reopen the territorial question. His remarks coincided with the adoption of a resolution by the Japanese House of Representatives calling for an early return of the northern islands and the withdrawal of all Soviet military facilities from them. The resolution, the third of its kind since 1973, called for efforts to consolidate peaceful and friendly relations with the Soviet Union and for the conclusion of a peace treaty. In response to the Soviet claim that the territorial question was now closed, the Japanese Foreign Minister stressed that this was a unilateral decision with which Japan could not agree since in Japan's view the matter had been left as an unresolved issue in the 1956 joint declaration and later communiqués.

On May 7 Polyansky defended the Soviet military build-up in the region on the grounds that it "should not be considered in isolation from the military and political situation in that area" and that the Soviet Union could not neglect such factors as the anti-Soviet co-operation of Japan and the United States, the strengthening of US-Chinese relations and the instability of the Korean peninsula and Indo-China. On Aug. 19 a Moscow radio broadcast claimed that Japan's "illegal and groundless" claim to the northern islands was largely responsible for what it described as the "stagnant" state of Soviet-Japanese relations, while on Sept. 2 the Soviet news agency Novosti marked the 35th anniversary of Japan's formal surrender at the end of World War II by publishing a strongly-worded article accusing Japan and the United States of falsifying the history of that period and also referring to Japan's "dangerous alliance with American and Chinese hegemonists on the basis of nationalism and anti-Sovietism".

Further aggravation of Japanese-Soviet relations occurred in late 1980 when a Japanese salvage company began operations to lift the contents of a former Tsarist naval vessel (*Admiral Nakhimov*) which had sunk off the Japanese coast in 1905 with a cargo of gold, platinum and other precious metals whose current value was variously estimated at between $3,800 million and $40,000 million. The vessel had been seized by the Japanese during the Russo-Japanese war and had subsequently been sunk outside the former three-mile Japanese territorial waters limit but inside the 12-mile limit introduced in 1977. On Oct. 3, 1980, the Soviet Union claimed proprietary rights over the ship, to which the Japanese Government responded (on Oct. 10) that no precedent existed for the return of a ship submerged for so long and (on Oct. 20) that the vessel was rightfully the property of the Japanese Government. This in turn brought an angry reaction from the salvage company, which claimed the ship as its own property and which caused some annoyance in Japanese Government circles by directly offering the vessel to the Soviet Union in exchange for the return to Japan of the northern islands (the official Japanese view being that only governments could negotiate on the territorial issue).

## Recent Developments

In January 1981 the Japanese Government announced that Feb. 7 had been designated as "Day of the Northern Territories" and would henceforth be the occasion of a national demonstration of protest over the Soviet Union's refusal to recognize the Japanese claim and also over its militarization of the islands. At the same time Japan requested the other countries which had signed the 1951 San Francisco peace treaty not to mark the disputed northern islands as Soviet territory on maps published by them.

Addressing a rally in Tokyo on Feb. 7, 1981, the Japanese Prime Minister, Zenko Suzuki, said that it was "to be deeply regretted, for the sake of promoting peaceful and friendly relations", that the islands had not yet been returned to Japan, and he reiterated the Japanese view that a peace treaty with the Soviet Union could be concluded only on the basis of their return. Following the Japanese Government's announcement, the Soviet Foreign Ministry had on Jan. 20 called in the Japanese ambassador in Moscow to protest at the designation of Feb. 7 and had warned him that Japan was thereby undermining the positive achievements of Soviet-Japanese relations. Moreover, a statement from the Soviet news agency Tass on this occasion repeated the Soviet view that no outstanding territorial issue existed with Japan and asserted that Japan was "working to stir up artificially the non-existent territorial issue".

Further forceful expression of the Soviet position was given in an article by the Tokyo correspondent of *Izvestia* published in mid-June 1981 as follows: "The 'territorial problem', which is an invention from beginning to end, is in fact an open infringement of the sovereignty and territorial integrity of the Soviet Union which has been raised to the status of state policy. In the whipping up of barefaced hostility towards a neighbouring state which has always supported good-neighbourliness, peace and equality in mutual relations, it is impossible not to see the revival of a completely different 'tradition'. This tradition was decisively stopped in 1945: by putting their signature to the act of unconditional surrender the then leaders of Japan promised in the name of the Emperor, the Government and their ancestors to fulfil the conditions of the Potsdam declaration.

"The shameless campaign of encroachment on Soviet territory which is being carried out at present shows that these obligations are being thrown aside by Tokyo. In fact, not one of the 'arguments' used by the present authorities and their propaganda apparatus to whip up nationalist hysteria around non-existent problems holds water. Least persuasive of all is the assertion that the Kurile islands are supposedly 'age-old Japanese territory'. The USSR's primordial rights to the Kurile islands were acknowledged by its allies long before the defeat of Japanese militarism in World War II. Japan's pledges irrevocably stem from the act signed by its authorized representatives on unconditional surrender in which the validity of the Potsdam declaration, and before it of the Crimea [i.e. Yalta] conference, were recognized. If

Tokyo after the event is claiming the role of an unexpectedly far-sighted interpreter of the Yalta decisions, then such attempts can only be interpreted as a desire to revise the results of World War II and to take a kind of propaganda revenge for the defeat of Japanese militarism in 1945.

"In its encroachments on Soviet territories, Japanese ruling circles often receive support from the USA. There are many examples of this, but only one conclusion can be drawn: Washington's repudiation of the war-time understandings on a post-war settlement goes back to the 'cold war' era, when the Truman administration began to throw overboard the legacy of Roosevelt and its own pledges of the first post-war years. However, Tokyo's vain attempts to recarve the map of the Far East in alliance with Washington and Peking are senseless. No matter how hard the enthusiasts of revanchism and their interested benefactors try to turn back the wheel of history, their efforts are doomed to failure."

Despite this and other indications of Soviet displeasure with the approach of the Japanese Government, Zenko Suzuki and members of his Cabinet embarked on what was officially described as a "tour of inspection" of the northern islands on Sept. 9, 1981, visiting the Nemuro peninsula on the north-eastern tip of Hokkaido and flying by helicopter along the Japanese coast. This action was described as "absurd" and "provocative" by official Soviet sources, which again accused Japanese ruling circles of fanning anti-Sovietism over a non-existent territorial question.

The official Soviet view that no territorial dispute existed with Japan was reiterated by the Soviet Prime Minister, Nikolai Tikhonov, in an interview with Japanese journalists given in Moscow and issued by Tass on Feb. 13, 1982. In answer to a question on the state of Soviet-Japanese relations and the prospects for a peace treaty, Tikhonov said inter alia: "The Soviet Union has been and remains in favour of placing Soviet-Japanese relations on the firm basis of a treaty. It is not our fault that a peace treaty has not been concluded to this day. You know well the reason for its absence. It is the unrealistic stand of the Japanese side. We have declared many times, including at the highest level, that there is no such subject in our relations as the allegedly unsettled 'territorial issue'. Meanwhile, the Japanese side is making attempts to interpret unilaterally in a distorted way certain provisions of the Soviet-Japanese statement of Oct. 10, 1973. That statement . . . registered agreement to continue talks on the conclusion of a peace treaty. To assert that the Soviet Union has admitted the existence of the invented 'territorial issue' means deliberately distorting our stand and misleading the Japanese public. These actions of the Japanese side do nothing to bring closer the prospects of reaching agreement on a peace treaty."

A.J.D.

# North Korea-South Korea

The present boundary between the Democratic People's Republic of Korea (North Korea) and the Republic of Korea (South Korea) is a provisional line established under the 1953 armistice which brought to an end three years of armed conflict between the Communist North and the US-backed South. Since then both North and South Korea have continued to claim legitimate jurisdiction over all Korea, and periodic initiatives towards the reunification of the country have made no substantive progress.

During World War II an agreement was reached between the Allies to the effect that there was to be, after the defeat of Japan, an independent Korea—a nominally independent Korea having existed until the defeat of Russia by Japan in 1904-05, whereafter Korea had become a Japanese protectorate and had been annexed by Japan in 1910. Under this agreement there was to be a temporary period of Allied control with the Soviet Union being in charge of the zone north of the 38° N parallel and the United States of the zone to the south of it, and a mixed US-Soviet commission was to set up a provisional Korean Government representing all "democratic" parties and mass organizations. However, in the northern zone a provisional Communist Government was set up in February 1946 under the authority of the Soviet occupation forces, and following unsuccessful negotiations concerning a possible unified government in 1946-47 a provisional Legislative Assembly was set up in the South, dominated by a Representative Democratic Council, a right-wing nationalist coalition led by Dr Syngman Rhee. Upon an initiative by the United States in 1947, the UN General Assembly resolved, against Soviet objections, that elections should be held under UN supervision throughout Korea, but the UN Supervision Commission subsequently appointed was refused permission to enter North Korea in 1948. Separate elections were therefore held (under UN supervision) in the South only in May 1948, and the independent Republic of Korea was established in August of that year.

Soviet forces were withdrawn from North Korea in December 1948 and US forces from South Korea in mid-1949. In June 1950 Soviet-equipped North Korean

**Map 34   The division of Korea.**

320

forces crossed the 38° N line in an attempt to conquer the South and almost succeeded in doing so, although US naval and air support was given to South Korea's forces. An appeal by the UN Security Council for the withdrawal of North Korea's forces was ignored, and the Security Council thereupon recommended, in the absence of the Soviet Union (which boycotted the Council's session), that UN member states should assist South Korea. As a result, 16 UN member states sent contingents to form a UN Command under (the US) Gen. Douglas MacArthur. The UN and South Korean forces, repelling those of North Korea, crossed the 38th parallel in September 1950. The People's Republic of China had earlier issued a warning that it would cross its boundary with North Korea (i.e. the Yalu river) if UN forces moved into North Korea. After Gen. MacArthur had, despite this warning, ordered a "final" offensive against the North, China entered the war in October 1950 and drove the UN forces back into the South.

The war continued until 1953, when an armistice was concluded and a provisional boundary was agreed along a demilitarized zone, mainly to the north of the 38th parallel, and to be supervised by UN forces. This armistice line has remained the effective boundary between North and South Korea.

## Unsuccessful Negotiations on Reunification

Proposals for talks on a possible reunification of North and South Korea were made by North Korea on April 12, 1971, but were rejected by South Korea on the grounds that they contained demands which were "utterly impossible to satisfy and quite unreasonable". However, on July 4, 1972, it was announced that agreement had been reached that "peaceful unification of the fatherland" should be achieved "as early as possible", that mutual hostile propaganda and armed provocation should cease and that a North-South co-ordinating committee should be set up. Representatives of the two sides first met at Panmunjom (the seat of the joint military armistice commission) on Oct. 12, 1972, and in November of that year they agreed to establish the proposed North-South co-ordinating committee, which held its first meeting on Nov. 30-Dec. 1, 1972. Further talks were, however, suspended in August 1973.

On Jan. 18, 1974, President Park Chung Hee of South Korea proposed the conclusion of a non-aggression pact between the two Governments. At the same time he rejected earlier North Korean proposals for the withdrawal of foreign troops from all of Korea (in effect of the 40,000 US troops still remaining in South Korea), the reduction of each side's armed forces to 100,000 men, a ban on the introduction of foreign military equipment and the abolition of the armistice agreement. His proposal concerning a non-aggression pact was rejected by North Korea on Jan. 26, 1974.

There followed, during 1974-75, a number of naval incidents in which gunboats and fishing vessels of both sides were sunk, and it was also found that North Korean forces had dug tunnels beneath the demilitarized zone. In an incident in the joint security zone around Panmunjom two US officers were killed in fighting with North Korean soldiers on Aug. 5, 1976. Under an agreement reached on Sept. 6 of that year the joint security area was divided into two parts by the military demarcation line, and guards were required to remain on their own side of the line.

On Jan. 12, 1977, President Park again proposed the conclusion of a non-aggression pact and added that he could see no objection to the withdrawal of the US troops once such a pact had been concluded. His proposal was rejected by North Korea on Jan. 25, when North Korea demanded the unconditional withdrawal of the US forces. On Jan. 1, 1979, President Park called for a resumption of talks between North and South Korea, and three meetings were subsequently held between representatives of the two sides in February and March 1979 but revealed fundamental differences over the level at which talks should be held. A joint US-South Korean proposal for tripartite talks was rejected by North Korea on July 10, 1979.

On Jan. 12, 1980, the North Korean Government, for the first time, acknowledged the South Korean Government (which it had previously regarded as a "US puppet"), and a new effort to revive talks between the two sides was begun in March 1980. While a number of meetings of representatives of both sides took place at Panmunjon, relations between North and South Korea deteriorated sharply as a result of a number of incidents involving the infiltration of North Korean agents into the South and the sinking of naval vessels, and leading to the placing on alert of the armies of both North and South Korea by June 25. Early in September 1980 the North Korean Army began to transmit broadcasts calling on the South Korean forces to overthrow President Chun Doo Hwan (who had succeeded President Park after the latter's assassination on Oct. 26, 1979).

On Aug. 11, 1980, it had been reported that North Korea had declared itself ready for peace talks with the United States (which had always refused to negotiate with North Korea without South Korean participation) without prior withdrawal of US troops. On Sept. 14 President Kim Il Sung of North Korea stated that, if the USA agreed to sign a peace treaty with North Korea, the latter would repudiate its military alliance with China and the Soviet Union and would not go on to a "war footing" to seek reunification with the South. On President Chun Doo Hwan the North Korean President made a bitter attack on Sept. 25, saying that North Korea was "not prepared to hold talks" with him because he had "no intention" of unifying Korea. South Korea nevertheless again asked for a renewal of the unification talks on Oct. 7.

President Kim Il Sung declared on Oct. 10, 1980, that the situation in Korea was so strained that there was "a constant danger of war breaking out at any moment" and that this danger could be removed only if the 1953 armistice agreement were replaced by a peace treaty with the United States. He proposed that the North and the South should be reunited as a confederal state in which each side would exercise regional autonomy and would retain its own ideology and social system without trying to impose them on the other. A Supreme National Confederal Assembly should be formed, in which the North and the South should have an equal number of representatives, and should appoint a Confederal Standing Committee, which would decide on political affairs, defence, foreign affairs and other questions of common concern. Economic co-operation and exchanges between North and South should be established on the basis of recognizing their different economic systems. The northern and southern armies should be combined into a single national army.

These North Korean proposals were officially denounced by the South Korean Government on Oct. 15 on the grounds that they contained conditions "preposterous and tantamount to self-destruction" of South Korea. In a New Year broadcast published on Jan. 12, 1981, the South Korean President invited President Kim Il Sung to visit the South Korean capital "without any condition attached and free of any burden", and he added that he was prepared to visit North Korea if invited; he also said that it was South Korea's paramount task to reunify the homeland into an independent and democratic state. In North Korea, however, the invitation was rejected out of hand on Jan. 19 on the grounds that President Chun Doo Hwan was "not a man worthy for us to do anything with".

### North Korean Territorial Claims

At a meeting of the joint military armistice commission on Dec. 1, 1973, the North Korean delegation put forward a claim to the territorial waters around five small islands (Paengyong, Daechong, Sochong, Yonpyong and U) situated six to 10 miles off the North Korean coast, to the west of Panmunjom, which the 1953 armistice agreement had placed under the military control of the UN Command. This claim was not accepted by the other delegations to the committee.

On June 21, 1977, the North Korean Government adopted a decree, to come into effect on Aug. 1 of that year, on the extension of the North Korean economic zone to 200 miles from the coast in the Sea of Japan and to the half-way line between North Korea and China in the Yellow Sea, and the exclusion of all foreign vessels from fishing and other economic activities in that zone without previous permission. On Aug. 1, 1977, the North Korean Supreme Command announced that North Korea's military boundary extended up to 50 miles from the coast in the Yellow Sea and up to 200 miles in the Sea of Japan, that foreign military vessels and aircraft were prohibited within this boundary, and that foreign civil shipping and aircraft might operate in it only by prior agreement. These decisions were recognized neither by South Korea nor by Japan.

H.W.D.

# Malaysia-Philippines (Sabah)

A territorial claim to Sabah—known as British North Borneo until September 1963 and constituting the north-eastern part of the island of Borneo, and bordering on Indonesian territory—was first enunciated by the Government of the Republic of the Philippines in 1961, largely on historical grounds, when plans were being formulated by Britain and Malaya for the formation of a Federation of Malaysia, which was eventually to embrace Malaya, Singapore, Sarawak and Sabah. The Philippine claim was rejected by both Britain and Malaya, and later by Malaysia, but it was pursued by the Philippines, with the result that for three years diplomatic relations between Malaysia and the Philippines were suspended. However, the formation of the Association of South-East Asian Nations (ASEAN) in 1967 led to an improvement in relations between the two countries, and 10 years later the Philippine President announced that as a contribution to the unity of the organization his Government would cease prosecuting its claim to Sabah.

### Philippine Declarations regarding Sabah and British Response, 1961-63

Following the approval by the Governments of Britain and Malaya (as announced in a joint statement issued on Nov. 23, 1961) of a plan for the formation of a Federation of Malaysia, a press campaign was launched in the Philippines against the proposed incorporation of British North Borneo in the projected Federation. The arguments put forward in support of the Philippine claim to Sabah, and the legal position as seen by the British side, reflected contrasting interpretations of the historical background to the dispute, as given in the following outline (itself based on an account published at the time in *The Times* of London).

In 1877 and 1878 the Sultans of Brunei and Sulu agreed to transfer their rights in North Borneo to a British syndicate formed by Alfred Dent (later Sir) and Baron Gustavus de Overbeck. The concession was taken over in 1881 by the British North

Borneo Company, which was incorporated by Royal Charter in that year, and remained so until 1946, when North Borneo became a British colony after having been a British protectorate since 1883. The 1878 deed provided that the Sultan of Sulu, on behalf of himself and his heirs and successors, "granted and ceded" to Dent and Baron de Overbeck, "for ever and in perpetuity, all rights and powers . . . over all the territories and lands tributary [to the Sultan] on the mainland of Borneo . . . with all islands within three marine leagues of the coast". In return, the Sultan and his heirs and successors were guaranteed an annual payment of $5,000 (Malayan). In 1903 the Sultan signed a confirmatory deed stating that "all the islands that are near the territory" [of North Borneo] had been ceded "to the Government of British North Borneo" and specifically enumerating the islands affected, because their names had not been individually mentioned in the 1878 agreement. At the same time the annual payment to the Sultan was increased by a further $300 (Malayan).

The Philippines based its claim to North Borneo on the contention that the whole transaction was illegal *ab initio*, since the Sultan of Sulu had no right to dispose of the territory; alternatively, it was argued that if the Sultan had such a right, he intended to lease the territory and not sell it outright. In the latter respect argument centred on the translation of the Malay word *padak*, a vaguer term than the official translation "grant and cede" (although the original deed also included the phrase "for ever and in perpetuity"). As regards the legality or otherwise of the cession, the Philippine contention was that Spain, and not the Sultan, was sovereign in the area of North Borneo and the Sulu archipelago. Treaties concluded between Spain and the Sultan of Sulu in 1836, 1851 and 1864 were, however, not recognized by Britain on the ground that Spain was unable to control the Sultan, and in 1885 Spain

**Map 35  Territorial relationship of Malaysia and Philippines, showing the Spratly Islands.**

signed a treaty with Britain and Imperial Germany renouncing in Britain's favour sovereignty over the territories "on the continent of Borneo formerly belonging to the Sultan of Sulu". In return, Britain recognized Spanish sovereignty over the Sulu archipelago, a group of islands midway between Mindanao (the southernmost of the Philippine islands) and North Borneo. As North Borneo was then under the control of the British North Borneo Company, the 1885 treaty in effect legalized the position then existing.

Following the Spanish-American War of 1898 the United States replaced Spain as the sovereign power in the Philippines, and by an Anglo-American convention of 1930 the US Government recognized that North Borneo was under British protection. This convention was expressly cited in 1946 when President Truman proclaimed the independence of the Philippine Republic. Supporters of the Philippine claim contended, however, that the Philippine Republic could not be bound by undertakings previously entered into with a colonial power.

On the death of the then Sultan of Sulu, the Government of the Philippines (then under US sovereignty) declared that it would not recognize the Sultanate's authority over the Sulu archipelago, the Philippines thereby assuming power in place of the Sultan and his heirs and successors. Thus the Sulu archipelago was under Philippine sovereignty when the independent Philippine Republic came into existence in 1946.

In a resolution adopted unanimously by the Philippine House of Representatives on April 30, 1962, it was declared: "The claim of the Philippine Republic upon a certain portion of the island of Borneo and adjacent islands is valid." The House accordingly requested President Diosdado Macapagal of the Philippines to "take the necessary steps consistent with international law and procedure" for the recovery of the territory. Accordingly, on June 22, 1962, the Philippine Government sent a note to the British Government, asking for talks on the question of North Borneo and expressing the hope that disputes between the two countries would be settled peacefully and in an atmosphere of goodwill. The British Government agreed, in a note sent to the Philippines on Aug. 7, 1962, that such talks should be held but reiterated that in its view the status of North Borneo was not in dispute.

Earlier, President Macapagal had proposed, on July 27, 1962, the formation of an independent Greater Malaya, comprising the Philippines, Malaya, Singapore, North Borneo, Sarawak and Brunei, and superseding "the British-sponsored Federation of Malaysia". Declaring that "Asians should not accept a European project as a substitute for an Asian project, planned and carried out by Asians themselves in the true and enduring interests of the Asian world", he said that "the great arc of islands consisting of the Philippine archipelago, North Borneo, Singapore and the Malayan peninsula would form a formidable geographical, cultural, economic and political unity that would be a powerful force for freedom, progress and peace".

In a statement issued on Jan. 28, 1963, the Philippine President described North Borneo as essential to Philippine national security in the light of the continuing communist danger in South-East Asia. At the same time he emphasized that his Government, while claiming British North Borneo, also recognized the principle of self-determination, and he therefore urged that the people of North Borneo should be allowed to declare—perhaps in a referendum under United Nations auspices— whether they wished to be independent, part of the Philippines, or "placed under another state".

At the end of talks which were held in London on Jan. 28-Feb. 1, 1963, between Emmanuel Pelaez, then Philippine Vice-President and Minister of Foreign Affairs, and Lord Home, then British Foreign Secretary, it was stated inter alia that the Philippine delegation had made a detailed statement of their Government's claim to North Borneo, whilst the British government had explained why this claim "could not be accepted"; that it had been agreed to exchange copies of documents relating to the legal position; and that the British Government hoped that after the establishment of the Federation of Malaysia it would be possible for Britain and the Philippines to reach agreement.

### North Borneo Majority Decisions in Favour of Incorporation in the Federation of Malaysia

The North Borneo Legislative Assembly unanimously approved the entry of the territory into the proposed Federation on Sept. 12, 1962. In elections held to local councils (on the basis of adult suffrage) in North Borneo in December 1962 a total of 95 out of the 110 seats were won by supporters of the proposed Federation. The newly-elected council members subsequently took part in the indirect (three-tier) elections of a new Legislative Council. During 1963 it was established, both by the British Government and by the United Nations, that a majority of the inhabitants of North Borneo approved the proposed incorporation of the territory in the Federation of Malaysia.

A Commission of Inquiry, appointed by the British Government on Jan. 17, 1962, under the chairmanship of Lord Cobbold (a former Governor of the Bank of England) to ascertain the views of the people of Sarawak and North Borneo on the proposed Federation, stated in its unanimously adopted report (published on Aug. 31, 1963) inter alia that about one-third of the population of the two territories strongly favoured early realization of the Federation, that another third also favoured it, although under various safeguards and conditions, and that the last third included a "hard core, vocal and politically active", which would oppose Malaysia on any terms unless it was preceded by independence and self-government; this "hard core" was estimated to amount to "near 20 per cent in Sarawak and somewhat less in North Borneo".

A UN mission sent to Sarawak and North Borneo to establish whether the 1962 elections had been properly conducted and reflected the wishes of the population regarding Malaysia found (in its report published on Sept. 14, 1963) that in properly conducted elections a majority of the voters had shown their desire to join the Federation. The mission had been joined by observers from Indonesia and the Philippines, and on arrival in North Borneo it had been greeted by a mass demonstration in favour of Malaysia and opposed to rule by Indonesia.

### Period of "Confrontation" between Malaysia and the Philippines, 1963-66

The Federation of Malaysia came into being on Sept. 16, 1963, when North Borneo officially took the name of Sabah. The newly-established Federation was, however, not recognized by Indonesia (which entered upon a period of "confrontation" with Malaysia), while the Government of the Philippines downgraded its embassy in Kuala Lumpur (the Malaysian capital) to the status of a consulate. Tunku Abdul Rahman, the Malaysian Prime Minister, thereupon announced on Sept. 17 that (in addition to the severance of diplomatic relations with Indonesia) all of Malaysia's diplomatic staff had been withdrawn from Manila on the ground that the Philippine decision to reduce the status of its embassy was "not acceptable".

Although diplomatic relations between Malaysia and the Philippines subsequently remained suspended, there was some improvement in relations between the two countries as a result of a meeting in Pnom-Penh (Cambodia) on Feb. 10-12, 1964, by Tunku Abdul Rahman and President Macapagal, who stated afterwards that they had "cleared the air" in their dispute; that they had agreed to consider the mutual establishment of consulates as a step towards the resumption of normal diplomatic relations; and that the two Governments would consider the "best way"

326

to settle the Philippine claim to Sabah, including the possible reference of the question to the International Court of Justice. Consular relations between the two countries were thereafter restored on May 8, 1964. Following an agreement concluded on June 1, 1966, on the ending of the three-year "confrontation" between Malaysia and Indonesia, full diplomatic relations were officially resumed between Malaysia and the Philippines on June 3, 1966.

## Renewed Suspension of Diplomatic Relations following Revival of Philippine Claim in 1968

The Philippine claim to Sabah was revived in 1968, when it was discussed by Malaysian and Philippine officials meeting in Bangkok (Thailand) from June 17 to July 16. At this meeting Leon Maria Guerrero, the Philippine chief delegate, upholding his country's claim to the territory, demanded that the dispute should be referred to the International Court of Justice, whereas Tan Sri Ghazali bin Shafie, the Malaysian chief delegate (and later Foreign Minister) rejected the Philippine claim as neither legally nor politically valid. As no agreement was reached the Malaysian delegation left the talks on July 16. The Philippine Government thereupon withdrew its ambassador from Kuala Lumpur in protest against "Malaysia's intransigence" and its "abrupt rejection of the Philippine claim" to Sabah.

On Aug. 26, 1968, the Philippine House of Representatives passed a bill including Sabah within the national boundaries of the Philippine Republic, and this bill was signed by President Ferdinand Marcos on Sept. 18 of that year. On the same day Tunku Abdul Rahman, at the end of a Malaysian cabinet meeting, denounced the bill as "a violation of Malaysia's sovereignty and territorial integrity" and "a highly provocative act tantamount to aggression". On the following day Malaysia suspended its diplomatic relations with the Philippines and abrogated an anti-smuggling agreement between the two countries, under which some Philippine customs officers had been stationed in Sabah.

Narciso Ramos, then Philippine Secretary for Foreign Affairs, on Oct. 15, 1968, reiterated his country's demand that the Sabah question should be referred to the International Court of Justice and added that his Government would accept the Court's judgment, although until the question was settled the Philippine Government would not recognize the authority of the Malaysian Government to represent the people and territory of Sabah. This refusal to recognize Malaysia's right to speak for Sabah was restated by the Philippine Government on Oct. 16. Tunku Abdul Rahman thereupon announced on Oct. 23 that diplomatic status had been removed from the remaining staff at the Philippine embassy in Kuala Lumpur, and on Nov. 19 it was announced in Manila that the Philippine Government had decided to withdraw its entire diplomatic staff from the Malaysian capital.

## Resumption of Diplomatic Relations in 1969 and Philippine Renunciation of the Claim in 1977

Following the formation of the Association of South-East Asian Nations (ASEAN) in August 1967, with both Malaysia and the Philippines being members of this organization, it was announced at a meeting of ASEAN member countries' Foreign Ministers in Malaysia on Dec. 16, 1969, that the two sides had agreed to resume their diplomatic relations. The Sabah question was not raised again by the Philippines during the following years, and at the second meeting of the heads of state and government of the ASEAN member countries, held in Kuala Lumpur, President Marcos declared on Aug. 4, 1977, that, as a contribution to the unity of the ASEAN, the Republic of the Philippines intended to renounce its claim to Sabah.

As a result, the President and Datuk Hussein bin Onn, the Prime Minister of Malaysia, agreed to establish joint border patrols between Sabah and the Philippines in order to prevent piracy, smuggling and drug traffic, while Malaysia also undertook to prevent Malaysian extremist Moslems from smuggling weapons to Moslem separatists in the southern Philippines. As a result of continued warfare between Philippine armed forces and the Moro National Liberation Front in the southern islands of the Philippines, over 90,000 Moslems were said to have reached Sabah by the end of 1978.

H.W.D.

# Malaysian Continental Shelf

On an official map of the Malaysian continental shelf published in December 1979 in Kuala Lumpur, the capital of Malaysia, a number of islands and areas were shown as parts of Malaysia whereas they were either claimed, or stated to be in dispute, by several other states in south and east Asia. (For map of the region, see page 324.)

**China.** Large areas in the South China Sea, off the coast of Borneo, were shown on the Malaysian map as part of Malaysia, whereas on a Chinese map published in 1975 these areas were claimed as Chinese territory. The Chinese Government, however, does not appear to have made any representations to Malaysia in regard to this discrepancy.

**Indonesia.** On Feb. 8, 1980, the Indonesian Government protested, in a note to Malaysia, against the inclusion in Malaysia (on the 1979 map) of the islands of Sipadan and Ligitan (situated south of Sabah, in the Sulawesi Sea), the ownership of which the Government of Indonesia regarded as being in dispute. On April 8, 1980, it was reported that officials from Malaysia and Indonesia would meet to discuss the issue.

Meetings between Indonesian and Malaysian representatives in Kuala Lumpur in February 1981 and in Jakarta in June-July 1981 considered alternatives drafts of a treaty intended to elaborate further the basic terms of a 1976 memorandum of understanding concerning (i) the recognition by Malaysia of the archipelagic state principles and Indonesian sovereignty over her territorial sea and archipelagic waters and (ii) the recognition by Indonesia of the right of Malaysia to continue to enjoy existing rights and all other legitimate interests which the latter had traditionally exercised in the Indonesian territorial sea and archipelagic waters lying between Peninsular Malaysia and Sabah/Sarawak. Following further discussions, a treaty incorporating the above undertakings was signed by the two countries in March 1982.

**Singapore.** On April 8, 1980, it was reported that Singapore had laid claim to the island of Pulau Batu Puteh (called Pedra Branca by Singapore) in the Strait of Singapore south-west of Johore. Having belonged to the Sultanate, the island was regarded as part of its territory by Malaysia, although Singapore had been allowed to station a lighthouse on it, with the lighthouse keeper being the island's sole inhabitant. Both governments were said to have agreed to bring their claims to the negotiating table.

**Thailand.** On April 10, 1980, it was reported that the Thai Government had submitted an aide-mémoire to the Malaysian embassy in Bangkok, pointing out that the 1979 Malaysian map failed to take into account an overlapping area of an estimated 3,200 square kilometres off the Kelantan coast (in the southern part of the Gulf of Thailand) which was to be exploited by a joint authority agreed upon by the two countries' Prime Ministers at a meeting held in Chiang Mai (northern Thailand) on Feb. 19-21, 1979. The Thai Deputy Foreign Minister described the dispute as "a minor issue" which could be resolved.

**Vietnam.** On April 9, 1980, it was disclosed in Kuala Lumpur that the Government of Vietnam was ready to discuss with Malaysia its territorial dispute arising out of the Malaysian map, in connexion with which Vietnam claimed in particular the coral reef of Pulau Kecil Amboyna, about 100 miles (160 km) north of Sabah. It had been reported on March 2, 1980, that Vietnam had stationed a garrison on this reef, and the Malaysian Foreign Minister had stated afterwards that there was no question of sending troops to remove Vietnam's garrison from the reef (which is situated to the south-east of the disputed Spratly Islands, claimed by Vietnam and partly also by China and the Philippines—see below).

Vietnam also laid claim to the triangular area off the Kelantan coast which was the subject of a 1979 agreement between Malaysia and Thailand [see above].

**H.W.D.**

# The Spratly Islands

The Spratly Islands (known to the Chinese as the Nansha Islands, to the Vietnamese as the Truong Sa and to the Philippines as Kalayaan) are a group of islets, coral reefs and sandbars in the South China Sea dispersed over 600 miles (965 km), which are claimed by the People's Republic of China, the Republic of China (Taiwan), Vietnam and the Philippines. (The dispute between the Chinese People's Republic and Vietnam over the nearby Paracel Islands is dealt with on pp. 280-82.)

The Spratly Islands lie nearly 300 miles (480 km) west of the Philippine island of Palawan, slightly over 300 miles east of Vietnam and about 650 miles south of Hainan, the nearest Chinese territory. All the islands are very small; the largest, Itu Aba (known to the Chinese as Taiping), has an area of only 90 acres (36 hectares). They occupy a position of strategic importance, however, as they command the sea passage from Japan to Singapore. Oil was discovered in 1976 at Reed Bank, midway between Palawan and the Spratlys, and has been developed by the Philippines since 1979.

The two Chinese Governments claim that the islands were discovered by Chinese navigators, were used by Chinese fishermen for centuries and came under Chinese administration in the 15th century, and that China's sovereignty over them was never disputed until the 1930s. They also claim that the Spratlys form a continuation of the Paracel Islands, which are claimed by both China and Vietnam. Vietnam maintains that the Spratlys became part of the Empire of Annam in the early 19th century, and that they had not previously been under the administration of any country. The Philippines bases its claim on proximity and administrative control,

329

but has laid no claim to Spratly Island itself, which lies over 200 miles (320 km) south-west of the main group of islands.

The French Government, which then ruled Vietnam, annexed the Spratlys in 1933, despite protests from China and also from Japan, which claimed to have been in continuous commercial occupation of them since 1917. The islands were occupied and annexed by Japan in 1939. Following the defeat of Japan in the Second World War, a naval expedition sent by the Chinese (Kuomintang) Government formally took possession of them in 1946, and left a garrison on Itu Aba. Japan renounced her claim by the peace treaty signed in San Francisco in 1951, but the treaty did not state to whom the islands belonged. The Vietnamese delegate to the San Francisco peace conference declared that Vietnam had recovered her sovereignty over them, but this claim was rejected by both Chinese Governments, neither of which was represented at the conference. After the division of Vietnam into two states in 1954 the South Vietnamese Government continued to uphold its claim to the islands.

In May 1956, after a private Philippine expedition had surveyed and occupied a number of the islands, the Philippine Government laid claim to them for the first time. This claim was disputed by China, Taiwan and South Vietnam, and a South Vietnamese garrison occupied Spratly Island in August 1956. After the Taiwan garrison on Itu Aba had fired on a Philippine fishing boat, the Philippine Government sent a note in July 1971 demanding their withdrawal. At a press conference on July 10, 1971, President Marcos of the Philippines maintained that after Japan renounced its sovereignty over the islands they had become a de facto trusteeship of the allied powers, and that this trusteeship precluded the setting up of garrisons on any of them without the allies' consent. He stated that the Philippines were in effective control of three of the larger islands, however, and according to news agency reports Philippine troops were landed on these islands.

The South Vietnamese Government issued a decree in September 1973 incorporating the Spratly Islands into Phuoc Tuy province. As contracts for offshore oil exploration and exploitation off Phuoc Tuy had previously been granted to four foreign companies, the decree made it legally possible for other contracts to be granted in the area off the Spratlys. A Chinese Foreign Ministry statement of Jan. 11, 1974, denounced the decree as "a wanton infringement of China's territorial integrity and sovereignty". After the expulsion of the South Vietnamese garrison from the Paracel Islands by the Chinese a few days later, South Vietnamese troops occupied three of the Spratly Islands.

During the civil war in Vietnam the North Vietnamese Government and the Communist South Vietnamese Provisional Revolutionary Government adopted a neutral attitude towards the dispute, in order to avoid friction with their Chinese allies, but in April 1975, shortly before the surrender of Saigon, Vietnamese Communist troops took possession of the islands previously occupied by South Vietnamese garrisons. When the Philippine Government announced in May 1976 that a consortium of Swedish and Philippine companies had contracted to explore for oil in the area, the Provisional Revolutionary Government, which had effectively ruled South Vietnam since the fall of Saigon, declared that "the Republic of South Vietnam again reaffirms its sovereignty over the Spratly archipelago and reserves the right to defend this sovereignty". Similar protests were issued by the Chinese and Taiwan Governments. The reunification of Vietnam in July 1976 brought the Hanoi Government into direct confrontation with China on the issue.

The Philippine Government set up a military command on Palawan in March 1976, and by March 1978 had established garrisons on seven of the islands. It reached an agreement with Vietnam in January 1978 to solve the dispute "in a spirit of conciliation and friendship", however, and concluded a similar agreement with China in the following March. At a press conference on Sept. 14, 1979, President

Marcos made it clear that the Philippines confined its claim to the seven islands under its occupation. These islands, he declared, were "unoccupied, unowned and unpossessed islands" which had not even been shown on maps before the Second World War, and the Philippines had therefore occupied them as "new territory or *res nullius*". In August 1980 the Vietnamese Foreign Ministry protested to the Philippines over what it described as the latter's "occupation" of the Comodor Reef in "the Vietnamese archipelago of Truong Sa".

The dispute was a major factor in the deterioration of relations between China and Vietnam after 1975. Whereas before that year North Vietnam had not openly disputed China's claim, an official Vietnamese map issued in 1976 showed the Spratly Islands as Vietnamese territory. A Chinese Foreign Ministry statement of Dec. 29, 1978, declared that the islands had "always been part of China's territory" and that claims to sovereignty over them by any foreign country were all illegal and null and void. The Vietnamese Foreign Ministry rejected these "arrogant allegations" on the following day, but added that it advocated a policy of settling all international disputes by peaceful methods. During talks between China and Vietnam held in Hanoi in April and May 1979 the Chinese delegation demanded that Vietnam should recognize and respect China's sovereignty over the islands, this demand being rejected by Vietnam. The Vietnamese Government reaffirmed its claim to sovereignty in a White Book issued on Sept. 28, 1979, to which the Chinese Foreign Ministry replied at length in a document published on Jan. 30, 1980.

C.H.

# 5. THE AMERICAS AND ANTARCTICA

## Introduction

Nearly every country in Latin and Central America has or has had claims to territory or waters of a neighbouring state. The majority of these claims date back to the colonial era and in particular to the many uncertainties attached to the boundaries of the independent nations which emerged in the 19th century, for the most part on the basis of old Spanish administrative divisions. Although the successor states subscribed to the principle of *uti possidetis juris* (under which they were presumed to possess sovereignty within the relevant Spanish administrative areas), the eventual development of remoter areas revealed that the old boundaries were often unclear or, in some cases, non-existent. In recent years, moreover, competing claims to newly-discovered or potential economic resources such as minerals or hydro-electricity have given an added dimension to many such territorial uncertainties.

Like other regional groupings, the Organization of American States (OAS) has aspired to provide a forum and mechanism for the peaceful resolution of border and territorial disputes between member states; the Organization also specifically excludes from membership applicant states which are involved in a territorial dispute with an existing member. Such constraints have had some effect in preventing armed conflict over territorial claims, of which there have been few instances in recent years between OAS member states. Nevertheless, a number of such disputes remain unresolved and constitute a serious source of actual or potential strain between various states of the region.

Important factors determining whether and when these situations develop into open confrontation include the domestic political circumstances of the government or governments involved and also the particular constellation of political forces in the area concerned. In the latter respect, for example, the current struggle in Central America between revolutionary movements and states on the one hand and traditionalist forces on the other has generally relegated territorial dispute to the background, although in at least one instance it has exacerbated territorial tensions between states in opposing camps.

It should also be noted that most Latin American states have a much longer independent history than many former colonial territories in other parts of the world. This has meant that in many cases territorial disputes originally deriving from colonial uncertainties have had time to acquire strong nationalist overtones, especially where Latin American countries have in the past gone to war over territorial issues. In this sense, some Latin American territorial disputes bear a close resemblance to those familiar from the pre-1945 history of Europe.

Nationalism is also a crucial factor in another category of disputes dealt with in the following section, namely those between Latin American states and external powers which retain dependencies or responsibilities in the region. Some longstanding issues of this type have been settled in recent years (e.g. the Panama-US dispute over the Panama Canal Zone); others remain extremely contentious (e.g. Guatemala's claim to the whole of the former British colony of Belize); and in April 1982 one such dispute—that between Argentina and the United Kingdom over the Falkland Islands—escalated into open military conflict. Furthermore, conflicting claims in Antarctica—frozen at the moment but basically unresolved—also involve the United Kingdom in territorial dispute with both Argentina and Chile.

# Argentina-Chile (Beagle Channel)

Since the 19th century the small islands of Picton, Lennox and Nueva, situated at the eastern entrance to the Beagle Channel (off Tierra del Fuego and north of Cape Horn), have been at the centre of a dispute between Argentina and Chile. A 1977 ruling by a court of arbitration awarding the islands to Chile was rejected by Argentina, as were papal proposals for a settlement presented to both Governments in December 1980. (For position of the disputed islands, see map on page 340.)

Although the islands have technically been under Chilean sovereignty since the last century, Argentina feared that its access to the Atlantic from its own naval base at Ushuaia, on the north bank of the Beagle Channel, as well as access to its Antarctic bases and to potential resources of oil, minerals, fish and krill in the South Atlantic and Antarctic region, might be impeded if Chile was allowed formal access to the Atlantic under the 1977 ruling. The dispute has been complicated by the fact that Argentina and Chile have overlapping claims in the Antarctic, and that both claim 200-mile sea limits (Chile since 1953 and Argentina since 1967).

A previous border dispute over the Palena region (a strip of territory in the Andes) had been settled on Dec. 14, 1966, by a British court of arbitration which awarded 70 per cent of the territory to Argentina and the remainder to Chile.

## History of the Dispute

When Argentina achieved independence from Spain in the early 19th century it assumed sovereignty over territory east of the Andes which had previously been administered by the Viceroyalty of La Plata. Chile's territory (west of the Andes) was controlled by the Viceroyalty of Peru until Chile declared independence in 1810, and even then the fierce Araucanian Indians prevented immigrants from settling in the far south until well into the 19th century. In the 1840s Chile established settlements on Brunswick Peninsula (at Puerto del Hambre and Punta Arenas) against Argentinian protests but no real dispute emerged at the time, and in 1855 the Argentine Confederation and Chile signed a treaty of friendship, commerce and navigation which provided that both sides recognized as their boundaries those which they had had on independence in 1810.

The dispute over ownership of the southern territory erupted in the 1870s, when guano deposits were found in the region and Chile regarded them as being on its own territory, this leading to clashes and incidents. To clarify the delimitation of their frontier (which stretched for nearly 3,000 miles or some 4,800 km) the two countries signed a treaty on July 23, 1881, in Buenos Aires. In the south, this assigned to Chile all islands west of Tierra del Fuego and south of the Beagle Channel down to Cape Horn, while Chile renounced claims to Patagonia, and the Magellan Strait remained neutral for shipping. Chile has since based its claim to the disputed islands on the 1881 treaty, which also laid down that Staten Island (off the eastern tip of Tierra del Fuego), the small neighbouring islands, and other islands which could be said to be in the Atlantic, east of Tierra del Fuego and off the east coast of Patagonia, would belong to Argentina.

Argentina, however, claimed that a so-called "two-ocean" principle was established in an 1893 supplement to the treaty, which stated (in Article 2) that Argentina could claim no territory on the Pacific side and Chile none on the Atlantic side, the division being a meridian passing through Cape Horn. Chile maintained that this principle applied only for the purposes of the formal exchange of territorial rights laid down in the 1881 treaty.

## The 1977 Arbitration Award

Under a treaty of May 28, 1902 (renewable every 10 years), the British Crown was made responsible for arbitrating in territorial disputes between Chile and Argentina (in connexion with disputes at that time over more northerly sectors of the border). When called upon in 1971 to intervene in the Beagle Channel affair, Britain in July of that year, after consultations with the two parties, referred the dispute to arbitration by five former judges of the International Court of Justice (ICJ).

In the meantime, Argentina announced in March 1972 that it did not intend to renew the 1902 treaty when it expired in September of that year; accordingly the Foreign Ministers of the two countries signed an agreement in Buenos Aires on April 5, 1972, to the effect that any dispute between them which could not be solved by direct negotiations should be referred directly to the ICJ. It was established that the signature of the new agreement would not affect the arbitration currently in progress and that the 1902 treaty would remain in force with respect to that arbitration until its conclusion.

The five judges (from Britain, France, Nigeria, Sweden and the United States) sat in Geneva under the chairmanship of the British judge, Sir Gerald Fitzmaurice, and studied 28 volumes of evidence and more than 400 maps submitted to them by the two parties. They also visited the area as guests of both Chile and Argentina. Finally, on Feb. 18, 1977, they delivered their findings to the British Government, which made them public on May 2, 1977, in the form of a declaration from Queen Elizabeth II ratifying the unanimous decision of the court of arbitration and recognizing the sovereignty of Chile over Picton, Lennox and Nueva and other islands in the area of the Beagle Channel.

The award included a hydrographic chart on which a red line established the boundary between the territorial and maritime jurisdictions of the two countries in the area, being set approximately at the middle of the Beagle Channel, from meridian 68°36′36.5″ to meridian 66°25′ longitude, to the north-west of Nueva Island. It established that all the islands, islets, reefs, banks and shoals situated north of the red line belonged to Argentina and those south of the line to Chile, citing as examples the Becasses islets (Argentina) and the Snipe islet (Chile), and that the Beagle Channel's southern arm, the Goree Channel, was not, as claimed by Argentina, part of the main channel. Furthermore, the ICJ's report on the tribunal's findings laid down that Chile's title (in terms of the 1881 treaty) to the southern islands would automatically also "involve jurisdiction over the appurtenant waters and continental shelf and adjacent submarine areas . . .'by the applicable rules of international law".

The Chilean Government immediately announced officially (on May 2) that it would "closely observe the conditions of the award". However, Argentina stated that it intended to review its own position on acceptance over the next nine months (i.e. before the award was due to enter into force on Feb. 2, 1978), and before the end of this period of deliberation it stated formally on Jan. 25, 1978, that it had "decided to declare null and void the decision of Her Britannic Majesty on the Beagle Channel question". Argentina cited among the reasons for its rejection (i) that the court had ruled on other islands whose status was not a matter within its jurisdiction, (ii) that there had been contradictions of reasoning, faulty legal interpretation, and geographical and historical errors, and (iii) that the arguments and proofs advanced by each party had not been fairly evaluated. It concluded that the Government "reasserts Argentina's sovereignty over all islands, maritime areas, continental shelves and seabed which belong to it beyond any doubt since they are located in the Atlantic Ocean, east of the Cape Horn meridian, in line with the spirit and letter of the 1881 and 1893 treaties and the 1902 treaty". It also announced that it would "implement all measures necessary to defend its rights in the area up to Cape Horn" but reiterated that it wished to seek a peaceful solution.

Chile stated in response on Jan. 26, 1978, that Argentina's unilateral rejection was contrary to international law and bilateral treaties, that the court's ruling thus remained mandatory and fully valid, and that it had submitted to Argentina a rejection of its declaration containing also a reaffirmation of Chilean rights. Chile in the meantime published a map delineating Chilean jurisdiction over waters in the South Atlantic based on the court's ruling and accompanied by a decree which extended Chilean claims outside the arbitration area and over waters in the south. This provoked a protest from Argentina, which in August 1977 placed a navigational beacon on the island of Barnevelt (over which Chile had traditionally had sovereignty) in symbolic opposition to Chilean penetration of the Atlantic and the effective extension of its sea limits and its claims over the Antarctic.

## Submission of Dispute to Vatican Mediation

The two countries in late 1977 began what appeared to be preparations for a military confrontation in the area (Argentina being in military terms the stronger). Warlike gestures over the next few months included the inspection of troops in border regions, army and naval manoeuvres in sensitive areas, and also the arrest by Argentina of many Chileans in January 1978 in the provinces of Chubut and Mendoza, bordering on Chilean territory. President Videla and President Pinochet met in Mendoza on Jan. 19, 1978, for several hours of talks on "matters of joint concern, especially with regard to the southern area", a communiqué stating that they had "laid the basis for reaching an agreement". A second meeting was postponed after Argentina formally rejected the court ruling, but the two Presidents met again in Puerto Montt (Chile) on Feb. 20 and signed an act as the first step towards creating "a harmonious atmosphere which may lead to a peaceful solution of our controversies and, subsequently, to determining our two nations' respective rights under the legal system".

Under the Act of Puerto Montt, a joint negotiating commission was set up and was allocated 180 days to carry out talks on resolving the dispute. The Act listed the main areas of disagreement, proposed a plan of work, and noted the interest of the two sides in the physical integration of the area and also the desire to defend their legal rights in the Antarctic, while ensuring that citizens of both countries, especially those living in the border areas, should regard each other as brothers.

During the 180-day period six rounds of negotiations took place, Chile withdrawing from the fifth. Preparations for a possible war also continued at the same time and Argentina enforced certain transit restrictions against Chile. On the expiry of the 180-day period on Nov. 2, 1978, the two countries announced that, while agreement had been reached on the joint economic development of the region and on the co-ordination of their Antarctic policy, they had not resolved the delimitation of their maritime zones. On the same day the Chilean Foreign Minister (Hernán Cubillos Sallato) noted in a communication to the Argentinian Government that "positive results" had been achieved regarding some of the points at issue but also noted the lack of agreement on "the final demarcation of the Chilean and Argentinian jurisdiction in the southern region" and on navigational rights in the Magellan Strait, and proposed that a "friendly government" should be asked to mediate in the dispute. Argentina agreed on Nov. 8, 1978, that the conflict should be submitted to arbitration, and on Dec. 11 the two countries' Foreign Ministers met in Buenos Aires to designate a mediator.

However, immediate agreement was not reached, and further military confrontations were already at this stage taking place in southern waters, while Argentina was carrying out blackout and civil defence exercises in various cities. Argentina protested to the UN Security Council on Dec. 21, 1978, that Chile had illegally deployed troops and artillery on the Beagle Channel islands, whereas Chile stated in response that Argentina had generated tension by committing numerous violations of air, sea and land areas which belonged to Chile and that it was trying to change the status of islands which had "long been under the peaceful and effective sovereignty of Chile".

On the same day tension was defused when both Argentina and Chile accepted an official offer from the Vatican to mediate in the conflict. Cardinal Antonio Samore, a former papal nuncio to various Latin American countries, accordingly held preliminary contacts with both sides before a declaration was signed in Montevideo on Jan. 8, 1979, whereby Argentina and Chile agreed (i) not to have recourse to force in their mutual relations, (ii) to return gradually to the military situation existing at the beginning of 1977 and (iii) to refrain from adopting any measures which might disturb "harmony in any sector". The Cardinal was formally appointed as mediator in April 1979 and negotiations opened in Rome in May of that year.

Throughout 1979 and 1980 Argentinian and Chilean delegations held meetings with Cardinal Samore, and on Dec. 12, 1980, proposals were presented at the Vatican to the Chilean and Argentinian Foreign Ministers, respectively René Rojas Galdames and Brig.-Gen. Carlos Washington Pastor. Details of the proposals were not officially disclosed but were reported to contain plans to make the area surrounding the disputed islands into a jointly-controlled zone of peace from which all military installations and weapons would be withdrawn, but for sovereignty over the three islands to be retained by Chile.

Argentinian sources also claimed that Chile would, under the proposals, have jurisdiction over 12 miles of territorial waters east of the islands but would share the development of resources in the outer six miles, while Argentina would have sovereignty over a contiguous fan-shaped zone stretching 200 miles into the Atlantic and would also share the exploitation of resources with Chile. Unconfirmed sources in Rome added that three smaller islands further south which had traditionally been Chilean (Barnevelt, Evout and Deceit) might be transferred to Argentinian sovereignty.

The Argentinian Government on March 25, 1981, communicated to the Vatican its effective rejection of the papal proposals, acceptance of which had been announced by Chile on Jan. 8 and confirmed officially on Feb. 13 by President Pinochet. A period of strained relations ensued following the arrest of two Argentinian officers by the Chilean authorities in April, as a result of which the border was closed on April 29; and although the situation improved in June (after an exchange of prisoners including the two officers and the reopening of the border on June 12) tension again increased sharply in September 1981 over the alleged intrusion of an Argentinian cruiser into disputed waters south of the islands of Deceit and Herschel.

The Argentinian Foreign Minister (now Oscar Camilión) travelled to Rome at the beginning of September 1981 to deliver alternative mediation proposals to Cardinal Samore, which reportedly included (i) plans for the Beagle Channel area to become a demilitarized zone under Argentinian jurisdiction (rather than the "sea of peace" said to have been proposed by the Pope) and (ii) plans for the establishment of cross-border development areas in southern Argentina (including the disputed area) and also in the northern border region.

### Argentina's Unilateral Abrogation of 1972 Arbitration Agreement

The Argentinian Foreign Ministry on Jan. 21, 1982, announced the unilateral termination of the 1972 treaty committing both sides to seeking ICJ arbitration in their dispute, on the grounds that it had proved ineffective and was no longer serving Argentina's national interests; the treaty had been due to expire in December 1982 but was renewable unless either side gave notice of abrogation in the preceding six months. Argentina reaffirmed its confidence in the papal mediation process as the sole appropriate channel for the achievement of a just and peaceful solution, expressed willingness to draw up a new treaty with Chile for resolving disputes, and also proposed that both sides should suspend purchases abroad of war matériel. Talks resumed between the Chilean and Argentinian delegations and Cardinal Samore in Rome on Feb. 1, 1982, after a 13-month break.

In a further naval incident on Feb. 19, 1982, an Argentinian naval patrol boat anchored off Deceit to provide support for boats taking part in an international yacht race, but was ordered to leave by a Chilean torpedo boat. Warning shots were said to have been fired by the Chilean boat before naval vessels of both countries converged on the area, while Chile said that two Argentinian combat aircraft had flown low over Chilean ships "in an act of open provocation".

**J.B.**

# Argentina-Paraguay

A dispute has existed since the 19th century over the exact position of the north-eastern part of the border between Argentina and Paraguay, which

**Map 36   The Pilcomayo waters dispute between Argentina and Paraguay.**

338

is theoretically constituted by the course of the Pilcomayo river (which has its source in Bolivia). The dispute has centred on the fact that the course of the river has from time to time changed by up to 1½ kilometres towards either side.

In 1974 Argentina and Paraguay signed an agreement to conduct studies on how the Pilcomayo's flood waters could best be exploited. Argentina subsequently carried out certain works designed to control the movement of the river and to lessen flood damage, but it claimed that this work had led to no change in the border. Early in November 1980 the Paraguayan Government alleged that Argentina was unilaterally using water from a portion of the Pilcomayo river shared with Paraguay. Elpidio Acevedo, Paraguay's Deputy Minister of Foreign Affairs, stated in Buenos Aires that his Government had proof that over the past two years Argentina had deliberately been altering the course of the river and that this action was contrary both to the principles of international law and to agreements entered into by the two Governments.

This allegation was rejected in a statement issued by the Argentinian Foreign Ministry on Nov. 9, 1980, declaring inter alia: "The portion [of the river] shared with Paraguay is changing course as a result of the very special geological formation of the area and the sediment carried by the river. As a result the waters have drained into Argentinian and Paraguayan territories at three different points. . . . The situation has been duly studied by the Argentinian and Paraguayan Governments and agreement has been reached to implement the appropriate measures to dam up the above-mentioned drainage so that the waters can return to their normal course as soon as possible. . . . Seeking an effective and equitable use of the waters of the Pilcomayo river, the Argentinian, Bolivian and Paraguayan Governments are conducting a joint study with the co-operation of the Organization of American States within a framework of a project for multiple use of the Pilcomayo."

In Argentina fears were expressed that the timing of the revival of the dispute by Paraguay might lead to delays in the construction of a proposed joint Argentinian-Paraguayan hydro-electric project at Yacyretá on the Paraná river, on which Argentina and Paraguay had signed an agreement on Aug. 30, 1979.

**H.W.D.**

# Argentina-United Kingdom (Falkland Islands)

Since the establishment in 1833 of British sovereignty over the Falkland Islands in the South Atlantic, Argentina has disputed Britain's ownership of these islands (which it calls Las Malvinas) and their dependencies, the South Georgia and South Sandwich Islands. Argentina claims sovereignty over the islands because of their proximity to its coastline and its occupation of the Falklands for several years in the early 19th century. The British claim is based largely on Britain's continuous occupation of the islands since 1833 and on the fact that the Falklanders themselves have expressed their wish to remain British. In claiming continued sovereignty over the islands Britain has quoted UN General Assembly Resolution 1515/XV (approved on Dec. 14, 1960) on the right of colonial territories to independence and self-determination, which states that the wishes of the inhabitants of such territories must be respected. In a move which brought Britain and Argentina to the brink of war, Argentinian forces on April 2, 1982, invaded and occupied the Falkland Islands, overwhelming the small contingent of Royal Marines stationed there and installing an Argentinian military governor; the island of South Georgia was also occupied (on April 3) against British resistance. Britain responded immediately by dispatching a powerful naval task force

**Map 37  The disputed Falkland (Malvinas) Islands and their dependencies, also showing the Beagle Channel islands disputed between Argentina and Chile.**

to the South Atlantic with the aim of providing a military option if diplomatic efforts to secure an Argentinian withdrawal failed.

## Geographical, Political and Historical Background

The Falklands themselves lie some 300 miles (480 km) to the east of Argentina almost opposite the mouth of the Magellan Strait. They have a land surface of 4,618 square miles (11,950 sq km) and a population of less than 2,000 (which is declining). The main islands are East Falkland and West Falkland. The South Georgia and South Sandwich Islands (making up the dependencies) lie considerably further to the south. South Georgia, an island of 1,450 square miles (3,750 sq km), is situated 800 miles (1,285 km) east-south-east of the Falklands group and houses a British scientific base. The South Sandwich Islands lie about 470 miles (750 km) south-east of South Georgia and were uninhabited until the occupation of Southern Thule island in December 1976 by about 50 Argentinian scientists. The other former dependencies (mainly the South Shetland and South Orkney Islands) now constitute part of the British Antarctic Territory, established on March 3, 1962 [see pages 386-88]. The Falkland Islands and Dependencies are administered by a Governor, a Legislative Council and an Executive Council. The Governor is also the High Commissioner for the British Antarctic Territory. A small detachment of British Royal Marines had been stationed in the islands since 1966, when a small group of right-wing Argentinian nationalists staged a symbolic invasion.

The then uninhabited Falkland Islands were discovered in 1592 by Captain Davis of the *Desire* and were given their name (after the Treasurer of the Navy, Viscount Falkland) by Captain Strong of the *Welfare*, who made the first recorded landing there in 1690. French settlers landed in 1764 and named the islands "Les Malouines" (after their home town of St Malo), from which the Argentinian name Malvinas is derived. The French settlers relinquished their rights to Spain in 1766, but a British settlement established in 1765-66 was recognized by Spain in 1771—although only after a Spanish move to expel the British had brought the two countries to the brink of war. The settlement was withdrawn in 1774 on grounds of economy, and Spain withdrew its own garrison in 1811, so that at the time of Argentine independence in 1816 (as the United Provinces of the River Plate) the islands were uninhabited. However, the British left a plaque declaring that the Falklands were the "sole right and property" of King George III.

The islands meanwhile became a base for the British and US sealing and whaling industries, and temporary settlements sprang up there. In 1820 the Buenos Aires Government sent a ship to the islands to proclaim its sovereignty as successor to the former colonial power, and Luis Vernet was declared governor of the Falklands in 1829 by the United Provinces; however, in 1831, after complaints from sealers about interference with their trading, an American warship expelled the Argentinians. The remaining Argentinians were expelled by a British warship in 1832, and British sovereignty was established early the following year.

The first recorded landing on South Georgia was made by Captain James Cook in 1775 (although it had been sighted at least twice during the previous 100 years), and the South Sandwich Islands were discovered during the same voyage. Argentina first made formal claim to South Georgia in 1927 and to the South Sandwich Islands in 1948.

In December 1947, after an Argentinian naval expedition had landed on the South Shetlands and South Orkneys and had established bases in British Antarctica, the British Government proposed the submission of its claim to sovereignty over the dependencies (which also involved Chile) to the International Court of Justice (ICJ); this was rejected by both Argentina and Chile, which expressed the conviction of their "indisputable rights" to the "South American Antarctic".

In 1955 Britain unilaterally submitted the dispute over the dependencies to the ICJ, pointing out that British claims to the territories had been formally confirmed and defined in Letters Patent issued in 1908 and 1917. However, the ICJ in 1956 decided not to hear Britain's application in view of Argentina's and Chile's refusal to submit to the Court's jurisdiction.

## Inconclusive Negotiations between Argentina and Britain

Negotiations between Britain and Argentina began in 1966 after the UN General Assembly had in December 1965 approved a resolution noting the existence of a dispute over the Falklands and inviting the two countries to enter into negotiations "with a view to finding a peaceful solution to the problem", bearing in mind the interests of the islanders.

After a period in which negotiations between Argentina and Britain had been mainly concerned with technicalities such as communications between the islands and the Argentinian mainland, the Argentinian Government in 1973 (on the return to power of Gen. Juan Perón) again brought up the question of sovereignty over the Falkland Islands. In a note to the UN Secretary-General (Dr Kurt Waldheim) on Nov. 5, 1973, Argentina called for an end to the "colonial situation", accused Britain of "paralysing" talks on sovereignty, and said that Britain's "anxiety to respect the right of self-determination of the inhabitants of the islands [under Resolution 1514/XV] would be more praiseworthy and legitimate" if the population had been consulted when the islands were annexed in the 19th century. The UN General Assembly subsequently in December 1973 adopted a resolution (3160/ XXVIII) calling on both countries to "arrive at a peaceful solution of the conflict of sovereignty between them" in order to "put an end to the colonial situation".

The following year, amid reports that the British Government was considering granting oil exploration rights off the Falkland Islands to a Canadian company, there were calls from certain political and press sectors in Argentina for an invasion of the islands and for the severance of trade and communications links. In January 1975 Argentina extended its control over air travel to the Falkland Islands (which was operated solely by the Argentinian Air Force from Argentina) by making it obligatory for all travellers to obtain clearance from the Argentinian Foreign Ministry, in contravention of a July 1971 communications agreement between Britain and Argentina which stated that only Argentinians travelling to the Falklands needed a special tourist card.

In October 1975 the Argentinian ambassador was recalled from London after Argentina objected to the dispatch of a British mission to the islands, headed by Lord Shackleton, to carry out an "economic and fiscal" survey at the request of the Falkland Islands Executive Council and to assess prospects and make recommendations on developments in "oil, minerals, fisheries and alginates" as well as to advise on capital expenditure needs over the next five years. Argentina warned that both sides had agreed in 1964 to "abstain from unilateral innovations in fundamental aspects of the question" and that the exploitation of natural resources would not be possible, as they belonged to Argentina.

When the Shackleton mission nevertheless arrived in Port Stanley (the Falklands capital) aboard the Royal Navy ice patrol ship *Endurance* in January 1976, travelling from an undisclosed Latin American country because the Argentinian Government had refused to let the team members use the normal air route via Buenos Aires, the Argentinian Foreign Ministry expressed the opinion that the UK ambassador to Buenos Aires should be withdrawn on the basis of (i) the presence of the mission in the Falklands, (ii) the refusal of the British Government to resume negotiations on the sovereignty issue, and (iii) a note from the UK Foreign and Commonwealth Secretary on Jan. 12, 1976, to the effect that the sovereignty dispute was "sterile" and calling for talks on economic co-operation. The ambassador accordingly left for London on Jan. 19.

During February 1976 another British ship engaged in scientific research in the South Atlantic (the *Shackleton*) was intercepted by an Argentinian destroyer which fired shots across its bows and tried to arrest the ship; however, the *Shackleton* on the orders of the Falklands Governor ignored the attempt and sailed directly to Port Stanley with the destroyer following closely. Argentina claimed in a letter to the UN Security Council on Feb. 11, 1976, that the ship was searching for oil when challenged, while Britain protested to the Security Council at the "provocative" action of Argentina and urged the latter to stop harassing peaceful vessels in contravention of international law. The *Shackleton* left Port Stanley to continue its research on Feb. 17 after talks had been held in New York between British and Argentinian Government representatives on ways of resuming negotiations and normalizing relations.

In accordance with a UN resolution (31/49) of Dec. 1, 1976—which urged Britain and Argentina to "expedite the negotiations concerning the dispute over sovereignty" in line with Resolutions 2065/XX and 3160/XXVIII and called on both parties to refrain from taking decisions which implied the introduction of unilateral modifications in the situation—a UK Foreign Office Minister of State, Edward Rowlands, visited Buenos Aires in February 1977 with a view to seeking formal talks. Prior to the actual visit Rowlands went to the Falklands "to hear from the islanders at first hand how they view their future". On his way back to Buenos Aires Rowlands said in a statement that his delegation would attempt to work out terms of reference with Argentina for subsequent formal negotiations on political relations and economic co-operation, and that such talks would have to take into account "the broad issues affecting the sovereignty of the islands, including sovereignty"; he claimed that Britain's intention to seek a basis for negotiation had the approval of the Falkland Islands Councils. At the same time the Argentinian Foreign Ministry issued a statement to the effect that the intention of Argentina in the forthcoming talks remained the recovery of the Falklands, and that discussions about the economy remained subordinate to this.

The talks took place on Feb. 22-23, 1977, a joint communiqué stating afterwards that they had been held "in a constructive spirit" and that the two delegations now needed to consult with their governments over certain points. It described the talks as considering "all aspects of the future of the Falkland Islands, the South Georgias and the South Sandwich Islands and Anglo-Argentinian co-operation in the South-West Atlantic area, and to explore the possibility of establishing terms of reference for subsequent negotiations".

Fresh rounds of talks were held in 1977 in Rome and New York, and after the latter round the two sides agreed to set up two working groups "on political relations, including sovereignty, and on economic co-operation". A third round was held in Lima in February 1978.

Full diplomatic relations were resumed between Britain (now under a Conservative Government) and Argentina in late 1979; the new Minister of State at the Foreign and Commonwealth Office, Nicolas Ridley, had talks in New York in April 1980 with Air-Commodore Carlos Cavandoli (the Argentinian Under-Secretary of State for Foreign Relations) and also with a representative of the Falklands Legislative Council, Adrian Monk. Later in that year (Nov. 22-29) Ridley visited the Falklands for talks with the islanders on how best to approach the dispute with Argentina over status; en route he also paid a courtesy call on Air-Commodore Cavandoli in Buenos Aires. While the visit was in progress the Falkland Islands Office in London said that one of several options being put to the islanders by the British minister was that of a transfer of sovereignty to Argentina coupled with a lease-back of the islands (this, according to the Office, being the option most favoured by Whitehall). Lord Carrington, the UK Foreign and Commonwealth Secretary, stressed on Nov. 26, however, that there was no question of Britain's acting against the wishes of the islanders.

### Escalation of Dispute into Military Conflict

In January 1981 the Falkland Islands Legislative Council passed a resolution stating that, although it was not pleased with any of the ideas presented by Nicolas Ridley regarding the sovereignty issue, it agreed that the British Government should continue talks with Argentina and that the Legislative Council should be represented; furthermore, the British delegation should try to reach an understanding to freeze the dispute for an indefinite period. An Argentinian Foreign Ministry spokesman replied that Argentina would negotiate only with Britain on the islands and that the resolution (a copy of which had been handed over by the British ambassador) was therefore of no concern to it.

Representatives of the islands' Legislative Council took part in the next three rounds of talks, which were held in New York in April 1980, February 1981 and February 1982, and a joint communiqué issued after the February 1982 talks— the first to take place under the new military Government of Gen. Leopoldo Galtieri, which had taken office on Dec. 22, 1981—said that they had been held in a "cordial and positive spirit" and that the two sides had reaffirmed their resolve to find a solution to the dispute. Nevertheless, the Argentinian Foreign Ministry issued a statement only two days later (on March 1) warning that, unless a speedy negotiated settlement was reached, Argentina would "put an end" to negotiations, "seek other means" of resolving the dispute, and feel free to choose "the procedure which best corresponds to its interests".

The conflict between Britain and Argentina escalated sharply soon afterwards, following the illegal landing on South Georgia on March 19 of a party of about 60 Argentinian scrap merchants with an apparently valid commercial contract to dismantle disused whaling installations. The British Antarctic Survey team on South Georgia ordered them to leave and to seek permission from the British authorities if they wished to continue their work, and most of the party subsequently departed on March 21, lowering the Argentinian flag which they had raised. However, the Galtieri Government, which claimed to have no prior knowledge of the landing, refused a British request that it should make arrangements for the removal of the remaining dozen men, to whom supplies were delivered by an Argentinian naval vessel on March 25. The British Ministry of Defence confirmed on March 24 that the *Endurance* was in the area and was ready to give assistance if required; the presence of Argentinian warships and naval vessels was reported in the area soon afterwards.

Despite a UN Security Council meeting on April 1 and last-minute diplomatic efforts, Argentinian troops invaded the Falklands on April 2, the Argentinian junta announcing the "recovery of the Malvinas, the Georgias and the South Sandwich Islands for the nation". The small detachments of British marines on the Falklands and South Georgia were overwhelmed, and the British governor, Rex Hunt, was deported and replaced by an Argentinian military governor, Maj.-Gen. Mario Benjamín Menéndez.

The UN Security Council on April 3 adopted by 10 votes to one (Panama) with four abstentions (China, Poland, Spain and the Soviet Union) a resolution (502) demanding the immediate cessation of hostilities and an immediate withdrawal of all Argentinian forces from the Falklands, and calling on the Argentinian and British Governments to seek a diplomatic solution and to respect fully the UN Charter.

The British Government reacted to the Argentinian invasion by dispatching a large naval task force to the South Atlantic, the main body of which had arrived in Falklands waters by late April. During the approximately three weeks taken by the British warships to complete the 8,000-mile journey to the South Atlantic, intensive diplomatic exchanges took place, with the US Government acting as Intermediary, in an effort to resolve the dispute by negotiation. However, the Argentinian Government refused to yield on its fundamental claim to sovereignty over the islands (which it garrisoned with some 10,000 troops), while Britain insisted on an Argentinian military withdrawal as the basic requirement for a peaceful resolution of the immediate crisis. After British forces had recaptured South Georgia on April 25, the Argentinian Foreign Minister stated that Argentina was "technically at war" with Britain, and thereafter a series of major clashes involving considerable loss of life occurred between the ships and aircraft of the opposing sides.

Further mediation attempts by the Peruvian Government and the UN Secretary-General failed to break the deadlock, with the result that on May 21 British troops landed in force on East Falkland to effect a military repossession of the islands. In subsequent heavy land fighting, the main body of the Argentinian forces was pushed back to Port Stanley (the capital), where an unconditional Argentinian surrender was eventually secured on June 14. The restoration of British administration quickly followed (the ousted British governor being returned to act jointly with a newly-appointed military commissioner) and the British Government made it clear that for the foreseeable future there could be no further negotiations with Argentina on the status of the islands. British casualties in the fighting included a total of 255 killed, while Argentinian fatalities were unofficially estimated to have been three or four times higher.

In Argentina the Falklands defeat resulted in the fall of the Galtieri Government and the assumption of the presidency by Gen. Reynaldo Bignone. The new Government indicated its acceptance that military hostilities with Britain had effectively ended but at the same time stressed that Argentina still maintained its claim to sovereignty over the islands.

J.B.

# Belize-Guatemala

The British Crown Colony of Belize (formerly British Honduras) became independent in September 1981, its achievement of independence having been hindered since 1945 by a Guatemalan claim to its territory dating back to 1859. Under the Guatemalan Constitution of 1945 Belize was regarded as the 23rd department of that country, and Guatemala thus claimed that the granting of self-determination to Belize would disrupt its own national unity and territorial integrity. While the British Government was prepared to grant full independence to the colony, Belize feared that in the event of a British withdrawal without adequate defence guarantees Guatemala would invade to implement its claim, and Anglo-Guatemalan talks over recent years produced no clear assurances from Guatemala on the future integrity of Belize. However, following an overwhelming vote at the United Nations in November 1980 in favour of the independence of Belize, the British Government decided to proceed with granting independence and convened a constitutional conference followed by tripartite negotiations in which the basis for Guatemalan acceptance of Belize's independence appeared to have been established. Although it later transpired that Guatemala had not substantially modified its position, Belize nevertheless proceeded to full independence as a constitutional monarchy on Sept. 21, 1981, with British troops continuing to be stationed there for an indefinite period.

Mexico also has a dormant claim to the northern half of Belize and had previously stated that it would reactivate this claim "in the event of any change in the colony's status which is not in accordance with the right of its inhabitants to self-determination".

## History of the Dispute

Extending over an area of 8,866 square miles (23,000 sq km), British Honduras was granted internal self-government in 1964 and changed its name to Belize on June 1, 1973. It had become a Crown Colony in 1871, having been a British colony since 1862 and under British sovereignty since 1798.

The first settlers were English timbercutters and their Black slaves in the mid-17th century. Under the 1670 Treaty of Madrid Spain conceded certain rights to the timbercutters who, over the previous 30 years, had established themselves on the uninhabited shores of the Belize river. The British Government did not, however, lay claim to the territory officially. Over the next 130 years the territory was subjected to repeated attacks by Spain, which claimed sovereignty over it. Finally, the Spanish fleet was defeated by a small Belizean boat fleet at the Battle of St George's Cay on Sept. 10, 1798, and British sovereignty over Belize was explicitly recognized by the Peace of Amiens in 1802.

When Mexico and Guatemala became independent in 1821 they both claimed sovereignty over Belize as successors to the Spanish Crown in the region. Their claims were rejected by Britain, however, in view of the fact that British settlers had by this time already established themselves as far south as the Sarstoon river (the present southern boundary). Mexico recognized British Honduras in 1826 and renounced claims to it in 1893 by treaty; the United States also recognized it in 1850 (together with British Guiana) as exceptions to the Monroe Doctrine. However, Guatemala continued to regard Belize as part of its territory.

In 1859 Britain tried to settle the territorial dispute between Guatemala and

British Honduras by means of a frontier convention, one of whose articles provided for the construction by the two countries of a means of communication between Guatemala and the Atlantic across Belize; this article was never implemented and has remained a bone of contention. A supplementary convention was signed in 1863 under which the British Government undertook to pay a substantial amount towards the cost of a road, although this never came to fruition despite the later renewal of the offer by Britain.

Guatemala on Sept. 24, 1945, conveyed to the British Government the text of a draft decree declaring the 1859 convention null and void and inserting into its own Constitution a clause laying claim to the whole of British Honduras as Guatemalan territory. Its claim was based on the contention that, as the 1859 convention on communications had never been implemented, the whole convention was null and void and that Guatemala therefore had a claim to the whole of British Honduras, or at least to the southern part. The claim was wholly rejected by Britain, which said that even had the convention lapsed this would be no reason why any part of the territory should belong to Guatemala, since Britain had been in possession for 150 years (i.e. since before the convention was signed or Guatemala became independent). In January 1946 Britain invited Guatemala to submit the dispute to

**Map 38   Present territorial relationship of Belize and Guatemala and also of El Salvador and Honduras.**

the International Court of Justice, and repeated the invitation on subsequent occasions, but Guatemala never took it up.

British Honduras achieved internal self-government on Jan. 1, 1964, following a constitutional conference in London on July 10-22, 1963, at which only British Honduras and Britain were represented. Guatemala (ruled at that time by Col. Enrique Peralta) broke off diplomatic relations with Britain on the last day of the conference, claiming that the British Government's decision to move towards the independence of British Honduras was "a unilateral action which is a flagrant violation of the inalienable and sovereign rights of Guatemala". Prior to this, President Ydigoras Fuentes of Guatemala had raised the issue of sovereignty again in December 1961 and talks on the issue had taken place in Puerto Rico in April 1962 at the instigation of Britain. Among matters agreed at the talks were the creation of mixed committees of representatives of Guatemala, Britain and British Honduras on mutual relations, and on economic and social development.

In July 1965 Britain and Guatemala requested the United States to mediate in their dispute. Accordingly, President Johnson appointed a New York lawyer, Bethuel M. Webster, who on April 18, 1968, delivered a report which proposed that Britain and Guatemala should conclude a treaty, to which Britain should try to secure the accession of British Honduras on the latter's independence. It was proposed that the treaty should contain the following conditions: (i) that British Honduras should attain independence by Dec. 31, 1970, with the probable name of Belize; (ii) that there should be unrestricted trade, travel and other contacts between Guatemala and British Honduras; and (iii) that a road should be constructed between the two countries.

George Price, the Prime Minister of British Honduras, declared on May 9, 1968, that his Government rejected Webster's proposals because they failed to recognize the colony's right to sovereignty. Britain thus responded on May 20 that since the British Honduras Government, with the endorsement of its House of Representatives, had asked Britain not to accede to such a treaty with Guatemala, and since the dispute with Guatemala could only be settled in accordance with the wish of the British Honduras people, it could not endorse the mediator's proposals.

## Developments in 1970s

In 1971 Guatemalan troop movements in the border area gave rise to fears of a Guatemalan invasion of British Honduras. Guatemala subsequently protested over a British military training exercise held there in February 1972 to coincide with British naval manoeuvres in the Caribbean, and the outcome was that Guatemala in March 1972 broke off informal talks on the Belize issue. At the end of the troop exercise Britain decided to increase the size of its permanent British garrison in Belize from one to two companies (i.e. to about 700 men), giving rise to another protest from Guatemala. The presence of an increased number of troops proved a stumbling block to further talks, which did not resume until February 1975. On their resumption, Britain rejected Guatemalan proposals envisaging the cession of the southern quarter of Belize (south of latitude 16° 30'), including an area thought to contain oil deposits, in return for the renunciation by Guatemala of its claim to the rest of the colony. The talks broke down in July 1975.

Reports of increased Guatemalan military activity in the border areas in October 1975 led Britain in November 1975 to send reinforcements to its garrison in Belize at George Price's request. By Nov. 8 its military strength in the colony had been increased to over 1,000 men, supported by six Hawker Harrier vertical takeoff aircraft and a frigate, which patrolled offshore with a detachment of Marines aboard. The UK Foreign and Commonwealth Secretary in the then Labour Government, James Callaghan, told the House of Commons in a statement on Nov. 6 that the British garrison in Belize had been strengthened because of the increased Guatemalan military activity on the border and because of "statements by Guatemalan ministers of their intention to incorporate Belize in Guatemala". He said that he had informed Guatemala in September that "if there were an invasion of a British colony which is seeking to become independent and whose independence is denied only by the Guatemalan claim, we would fulfil our responsibilities to that colony".

Despite Guatemalan opposition to the reinforcement of the British military presence in Belize, however, no further action was taken by Guatemala, and at the end of November 1975 Britain and Guatemala agreed to hold fresh talks, with Belizean participation, early the following year.

The UN General Assembly on Dec. 8, 1975, adopted a resolution on Belize (3432/XXX)—with Mexico abstaining and Guatemala not participating—which had already been adopted by the UN Trusteeship Committee on Nov. 21. This resolution (i) reaffirmed the "inalienable right of the people of Belize to self-determination and independence"; (ii) declared that the "inviolability and territorial integrity of Belize must be preserved"; (iii) called upon all states to respect the right of the people of Belize to self-determination, independence and territorial integrity and to facilitate the attainment by them of their goal of a secure independence"; (iv) called also upon Britain as the administering power, acting in close consultation with the Government of Belize, and on Guatemala, to "pursue urgently their negotiations for the earliest possible resolution of their differences of opinion concerning the future of Belize in order to remove such obstacles as have hitherto prevented the people of Belize from exercising freely and without fear their inalienable right to self-determination and independence"; and (v) declared that "any proposals for the resolution of these differences of opinion that may emerge from negotiations between the administering power and the Government of Guatemala must be in accordance with paragraphs (i) and (ii) above".

A similar resolution (31/50) was adopted by the General Assembly on Dec. 1, 1976, urging all states to refrain from any action threatening the territorial integrity of Belize, on which Mexico again abstained. Panama, which had previously supported Guatemala's claim, voted in favour of Resolution 31/50, causing Guatemala to sever diplomatic relations with Panama in May 1977.

Meanwhile, George Price's People's United Party (PUP), which was returned to power in Belize in the October 1974 general elections after calling for early independence, tried during 1975 to internationalize the sovereignty issue, winning the support of the non-aligned movement and being backed by various independent Caribbean states including Jamaica, Cuba, Guyana and Trinidad and Tobago. The Government also decided to seek UN support for its cause, and invited the opposition United Democratic Party (UDP) to join the PUP in formulating a case. The UDP accepted, after agreeing to a formula which affirmed its own commitment to Belize's right to self-determination while reserving its position on the timing of independence (to which it adopted a more gradualist approach).

Talks recommenced between the three parties in April 1976 (after delays due to the earthquake in Guatemala in February 1976) and more talks were held in June and September 1976, the latter (in Panama City) being followed in October by the first ever bilateral meeting between Belizean and Guatemalan officials (in Honduras). At this stage (the end of 1976) Guatemala was said to have agreed to certain economic co-operation proposals including the use of free-port facilities in Belize City, but it still refused to abandon its claim to that part of Belize south of latitude 16° 30′. No progress had been made on the fundamental issue of Belizean territorial integrity after independence.

In July 1977 the British military presence was again strengthened in Belize because of tension between the colony and Guatemala; the latter's troops were reported to be massing on the border, and Guatemalan leaders spoke of the possibility of an armed conflict with Britain. A Royal Navy frigate took up position off Belize, British forces were moved to within two miles of the border, and the Hawker Harrier detachment (which had been withdrawn just before the April 1976 talks) was again deployed in the colony. Despite the military tension, however, further tripartite talks were held in July 1977 in Washington.

While in Washington the British and Guatemalan delegates also had separate talks on the Belize issue with Cyrus Vance, the US Secretary of State in the Carter Administration—the previous US Administration (under President Ford) having implicitly supported continuation of the status quo with a view to maintaining the British presence as a buffer against Cuban influence. George Price said on July 8 that he would welcome a US endorsement of Belize's right to "complete independence" and he called for a US defence guarantee after independence if Britain continued to decline to undertake such a commitment.

In line with a commitment made in a joint communiqué after the Washington talks, a British Foreign Office minister (Edward Rowlands) visited Guatemala in July 1977 while the military alert was still in force along the border with Belize. At a press conference in Guatemala City on July 28 he said that he had personally assured President Laugerud that "the British Government is not an aggressor, will not be an aggressor and will not intimidate or apply intimidating pressure on the negotiations", which would be resumed on an unspecified date. President Laugerud, however, said in a speech at the end of July that no further negotiations could take place until the British reinforcements were withdrawn from Belize, where the British military presence constituted "a physical aggression against Guatemalan territory".

## Negotiations leading to Independence of Belize

Over the next two years (i.e. until the end of 1979) no substantial progress was made towards a settlement, although the parties concerned had numerous contacts and negotiations. The United States assumed an active role, and an increasing number of countries of the region came to support Belize's position.

Following talks in London in January 1978 involving Dr David Owen (then UK Foreign and Commonwealth Secretary), George Price and Edward Rowlands, Dr Owen told the House of Commons on Jan. 25 that "various proposals including the possibility of territorial adjustments" had recently been discussed between Britain and Guatemala. Price himself emphasized at a press conference later on Jan. 25 that no Belizean territory could be ceded. He revealed for the first time that during the past six months the British Government had been considering various proposals for the cession to Guatemala of an area of Belize's southern territory (including seabed) which had been progressively reduced in size over that period from about 2,000 square miles (5,200 sq km)—comprising land south of the Monkey River plus seabed—to about 1,500 square miles (land south of the Rio Grande plus seabed), and finally to about 1,000 square miles (land south of the Moho river plus seabed between the Moho river and Ranguana Cays, where oil prospecting was in progress); this latest proposal would give Guatemala sovereignty over a sea access route to its Caribbean port of Puerto Barrios. His own view was that the cession of land would create not solve problems and, since the latest London talks had failed to produce an acceptable basis for settlement, Belize would now seek security guarantees from Caribbean countries.

Accordingly, in February and March 1978 George Price had contacts with Bahamas, Barbados, Grenada, Guyana, Jamaica and Trinidad and Tobago, and told a press conference in March that certain countries had indicated their readiness to participate in "multilateral security arrangements which would defend the territorial integrity of an independent Belize"; his Government had, however, ruled out the possibility of asking for Cuban military aid in order to avoid problems with the USA.

Belize's intention at this stage appeared to be the stationing of a security force in Belize which would be strong enough to allow Belize to attain independence without having to negotiate a settlement with Guatemala first, but the Guatemalan Government indicated in mid-May 1978 (while a further round of Anglo-Guatemalan talks was in progress) that it was maintaining its demand for a territorial concession and was also demanding in the current talks the formation of a joint Guatemala-Belize military staff and joint consultations on Belize's external relations.

Subsequently, at a meeting in New York in June 1978 Dr Owen, Price and Dean Lindo (the UDP leader) drew up a "memorandum of understanding" whereby (i) Britain undertook to invite the Belizean Government and opposition to participate in all future talks with Guatemala, (ii) Britain agreed to submit any agreement reached at such talks to a national referendum in Belize and (iii) Price and Lindo agreed to "put the issue of the Anglo-Guatemalan dispute above party politics and treat the search for a solution as a national objective".

After Maj.-Gen. Fernando Romeo Lucás García became President of Guatemala on July 1, 1978, fresh talks involving representatives of the new Government opened in September in New York; in December, however, Guatemala rejected British settlement proposals whereby Belize would after independence have refrained from (i) introducing measures regarding its offshore jurisdiction in the Bay of Amatique which would block Guatemala's sea access to its Caribbean ports, and (ii) from entering into any pacts with third countries without Guatemalan agreement. Guatemala would for its part have been granted preferential customs treatment for trade through the port of Belize City, and Britain would have financed the construction of a new road from Guatemala through Belize to the Caribbean. The UN General Assembly on Dec. 13, 1978, adopted a resolution (33/36) urging a settlement to the dispute on the basis of Belize's "right to self-determination, independence and territorial integrity"; the resolution was supported by 128 states, this time including Costa Rica and Colombia (which had voted against a previous resolution on Nov. 27, 1977). In a further resolution (34/38) adopted on Nov. 21, 1979, referring to the inviolability and territorial integrity of Belize, Latin American countries voting for the first time in favour of Belize's right to self-determination included Brazil, Dominican Republic, Ecuador and Nicaragua.

Tripartite talks opened in May 1980 at which Britain was reported to have taken the line that, if a mutually acceptable agreement could not be reached, Britain would unilaterally move the territory towards independence. Guatemala's position in 1980 was considerably weaker than it had been hitherto. This was due to the deterioration of Guatemala's internal security situation, which led the United States and also Mexico to wish to seek a stable solution to the Belize issue in the interests of regional security. Washington was also anxious at this stage that Britain should continue to exercise its defence commitment to Belize after eventual independence.

On Nov. 11, 1980, the UN General Assembly adopted by 139 votes (including the United States) to none, with seven abstentions and with Guatemala absent, a resolution (35/20) to the effect that Belize should be granted independence by the end of 1981, calling upon Britain to convene a constitutional conference to prepare for Belizean independence; and urging Britain to "continue to ensure the security and territorial integrity of Belize". It also called on Guatemala and independent

Belize to "work out arrangements for post-independence co-operation on matters of mutual concern". The British Government accordingly announced on Dec. 2 that it intended to convene a constitutional conference in the near future.

At a round of talks involving Britain, Guatemala and a Belizean delegation in London beginning on March 5, 1981, all three delegations accepted 16 heads of agreement, whose text was formally signed on March 16 by ministerial representatives of the three countries as follows:

"The United Kingdom and Guatemala, in order to settle the controversy between them over the territory of Belize, have reached agreement on the following points:

"(1) The United Kingdom and Guatemala shall recognize the independent state of Belize as an integral part of Central America, and respect its sovereignty and territorial integrity in accordance with its existing and traditional frontiers, subject, in the case of Guatemala, to the completion of the treaty or treaties necessary to give effect to these heads of agreement.

"(2) Guatemala shall be accorded such territorial seas as shall ensure permanent and unimpeded access to the high seas, together with rights over the seabed thereunder.

"(3) Guatemala shall have the use and enjoyment of the Ranguana and Sapodilla [Zapotillo] cays, and rights in those areas of the sea adjacent to the cays, as may be agreed.

"(4) Guatemala shall be entitled to free port facilities in Belize City and Punta Gorda.

"(5) The road from Belize City to the Guatemalan frontier shall be improved; a road from Punta Gorda to the Guatemalan frontier shall be completed. Guatemala shall have freedom of transit on these roads.

"(6) Belize shall facilitate the construction of oil pipelines between Guatemala and Belize City, Dangriga and Punta Gorda.

"(7) In areas to be agreed an agreement shall be concluded between Belize and Guatemala for purposes concerned with the control of pollution, navigation and fishing.

"(8) There shall be areas of the seabed and the continental shelf to be agreed for the joint exploration and exploitation of minerals and hydrocarbons.

"(9) Belize and Guatemala shall agree upon certain developmental projects of mutual benefit.

"(10) Belize shall be entitled to any free port facilities in Guatemala to match similar facilities provided to Guatemala in Belize.

"(11) Belize and Guatemala shall sign a treaty of co-operation in matters of security of mutual concern, and neither shall permit its territory to be used to support subversion against the other.

"(12) Except as foreseen in these heads of agreement, nothing in these provisions shall prejudice any rights or interests of Belize or of the Belizean people.

"(13) The United Kingdom and Guatemala shall enter into agreements designed to re-establish full and normal relations between them.

"(14) The United Kingdom and Guatemala shall take the necessary action to sponsor the membership of Belize in the United Nations, the Organization of American States, Central American organizations and other international organizations.

"(15) A joint commission shall be established between Belize, Guatemala and the United Kingdom to work out details to give effect to the above provisions. It will prepare a treaty or treaties for signature by the signatories to these heads of agreement.

"(16) The controversy between the United Kingdom and Guatemala over the territory of Belize shall therefore be honourably and finally terminated."

George Price said in a nationwide broadcast on March 17 that "Belize has gained its overwhelming objectives while protecting the basic rights of the Belizean people and adhering fully to the UN resolutions that protect our sovereignty and territorial integrity". In Guatemala, the Government presented the heads of agreement as an honourable means of settling the dispute in the face of strong international pressure.

The Mexican Government was reported to be happy with the agreement and to have no intention of pressing its dormant claim, but the Honduran Government made an official protest to Britain over the status of the Sapodilla cays, to which it had a longstanding dormant claim. Honduras also claimed a right to participate in the proposed negotiations on the grounds that "the delimitation of sea areas could lead to situations of conflict to the detriment of Honduras's legitimate rights".

The British Government formally announced on March 20, 1981, that a constitutional conference would begin in London on April 6. However, the UDP continued to oppose the heads of agreement as a sell-out of Belizean interests, and mounted an anti-government campaign which developed into public disorders and led to the declaration of a state of emergency in Belize from April 2 to 24. In view of the emergency George Price did not attend the London constitutional conference, the Belize delegation being led by Carl Rogers, the deputy leader of the PUP. The UDP boycotted the conference.

Negotiations on a treaty to give formal effect to the heads of agreement were held in New York from May 20 to 28, 1981, by a tripartite commission of British, Guatemalan and Belizean Government representatives. A further round held in New York on July 6-10 became deadlocked after Guatemala reportedly insisted that its interpretation of the heads of agreement would allow the establishment of naval facilities on Ranguana and Sapodilla cays, this being rejected by Britain and Belize.

In the absence of agreement on a treaty, and following Belize-UK talks in London on July 19-23, 1981, it was announced on July 26 that independence would be granted to Belize notwithstanding on Sept. 21 and that British troops would continue to be stationed there for "an appropriate period" thereafter. Guatemala responded by restating its intention to "reserve its legal and historic rights" over Belize, although it made it clear that no attempt would be made to occupy Belizean territory by force after independence. On Sept. 7 Guatemala broke off all remaining diplomatic links with Britain, severed commercial ties, and closed its border with Belize.

Independence Day on Sept. 21 was declared a day of national mourning in Guatemala, and the ceremony in Belize was boycotted by the UDP. George Price became the first Prime Minister of independent Belize.

**J.B.**

# Bolivia-Chile
# (Lauca River Waters)

A dispute over the use of the waters of the River Lauca (which has its source in Chile and flows on to the Andean plateau of Bolivia), which had existed for several years, reached a critical point in 1962 after Bolivia had warned Chile on March 22 of that year that the diversion of water from the river by Chile would be regarded as an act of aggression, as such a diversion could not be undertaken without the agreement of both countries. (For the separate dispute between Bolivia, Chile and Peru over the question of Bolivian access to the sea, see pages 355-58.)

Despite the Bolivian warning, the Chilean President on April 14, 1962, ordered that the sluice gates of a new dam on the Lauca river should be opened to supply an irrigation scheme and a new hydro-electric project in Chile. Bolivia in turn contended that this action reduced the flow of the Lauca river waters into Bolivia and broke off its diplomatic relations with Chile on April 16.

The Bolivian Government also appealed to the Council of the Organization of American States (OAS) to find a solution to the dispute. The Council unanimously decided on May 24, 1962, to call on Bolivia and Chile to come to an agreement by making use of any of the peaceful means for settling disputes contained in the 1947 Inter-American Treaty for Reciprocal Assistance (the Treaty of Rio). Bolivia and Chile, however, failed to agree on such means, with Bolivia favouring mediation by five Latin American states and Chile wishing to call for arbitration by the International Court of Justice, on the grounds that the issue was a legal and not a political matter.

On Sept. 3, 1962, however, the Bolivian Government temporarily withdrew from participation in the activities of the OAS, stating that it had acted "in strict accordance with the terms of the [OAS] resolution of May 24", whereas the Chilean Government appeared not to intend to contribute to the reaching of an immediate solution because it was "the beneficiary of the present illegal situation". Bolivia also claimed that the humidity in the area had already been reduced, that the salinity of Lake Coipasa (into which the Lauca river flows) had been raised, that difficulties had been created in agriculture and cattle-raising in three provinces, and that Chile was also attempting to divert waters from the Caquena river (which like the Lauca rises in Chile and flows into Bolivia).

After the OAS had studied the question for over a year without reaching a solution, the Bolivian Government announced on June 12, 1963, that it would withdraw permanently from the OAS, which it called "an incompetent organ" as it had failed to solve the dispute. However, this decision was not carried out and a few months later Bolivia resumed its participation in the work of the OAS.

The first dialogue between Bolivia and Chile for 12 years was held by (the right-wing) Presidents Hugo Banzer Suárez of Bolivia and Augusto Pinochet Ugarte of Chile in Brasilia (in the presence of President Ernesto Geisel of Brazil) on March 16, 1974, and President Pinochet stated afterwards that Chile was ready to resolve the dispute. A Chilean proposal made in 1976 and providing for an exchange of territory whereby Bolivia would acquire a corridor to the sea also contained a clause under which Bolivia was to grant Chile the use of the Lauca river waters. Although President Banzer at first accepted these proposals as "a global basis for negotiation", they were generally rejected in Bolivia.

On March 17, 1978—by which date no progress had been made in negotiations concerning Bolivia's access to the sea—the Bolivian Government again broke off its diplomatic relations with Chile. During 1979 relations between the two countries deteriorated further, and no announcement has been made in recent years on any progress towards a solution of the Lauca river waters dispute.

H.W.D.

# Bolivia-Chile-Peru

Bolivia has been landlocked since losing its coastal territory in the Pacific War of 1879-84, when Chile seized the then Bolivian port of Antofagasta and the surrounding coastline. Peru, which joined the war in support of Bolivia, lost its own southern provinces of Tacna and Arica to Chile but retrieved Tacna in 1929 under the Treaty of Ancón. Bolivia's efforts to regain an outlet to the Pacific Ocean have since been hampered by a provision in the Treaty of Ancón to the effect that no Chilean territory formerly belonging to Peru could be surrendered to a third country without the consent of Peru. Bolivia also failed to win proper access to the Atlantic Ocean via the Paraguay river in the Chaco War of the early 1930s.

### History of the Dispute
The exact border between Chile and Bolivia was not defined when the two

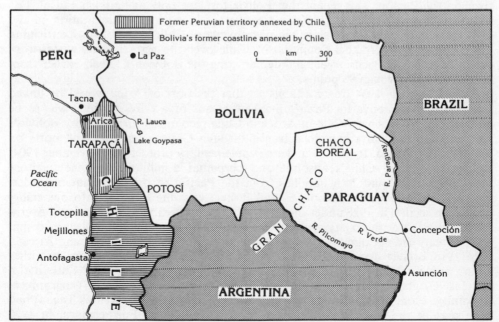

**Map 39** **The above map illustrates the dispute over Bolivian access to the sea, and also the separate dispute between Chile and Bolivia over the Lauca river waters.**

countries became independent from the (Spanish) Viceroyalty of Peru—this process being accomplished by Chile in 1810 and Bolivia (which was formerly encompassed by the Audiencia of Charcas) in 1824. In 1866 the two countries reached an agreement setting their boundary along the 24°S parallel of latitude to the south of Antofagasta (in the Atacama desert) but providing that the proceeds from nitrate and guano deposits extracted from a common zone between the 23rd and 25th parallels should be equally divided.

After Bolivia had broken an agreement signed with Chile at Sucre in 1874 by placing fresh taxes on Chilean firms already exploiting nitrates in the common zone, a Chilean expeditionary force in February 1879 took possession of Antofagasta and Mejillones (on the coast) and Caracoles (inland). Chile called on Peru to proclaim its neutrality in the conflict, and, when the latter refused, declared war on both Peru and Bolivia. Peru thereupon joined forces with Bolivia under a treaty concluded secretly in February 1873, but a joint Peruvian-Bolivian army was defeated at Tarapacá in November 1879 and the Peruvians retreated to Tacna, losing the whole of the Tarapacá nitrate area to Chile.

After this Bolivia played little further part in the Pacific war, although Peru fought on, with the result that Lima and Callao were occupied by Chilean troops in 1881. Chilean forces remained in Lima until 1883, when General Miguel Iglesias was elected President of Peru with Chilean backing and then proceeded to sign the Treaty of Ancón on Oct. 20, 1883. The treaty ceded to Chile in perpetuity and unconditionally the province of Tarapacá and provided that the provinces of Tacna and Arica would remain in Chilean possession and subject to Chilean administration for 10 years, at the end of which time a plebiscite would be held to decide whether the territories should remain in Chilean hands or revert to Peru.

The last Chilean forces withdrew from Lima in August 1884, and the same year (in April) a separate truce was signed between Chile and Bolivia, terminating the state of war between them and providing that, while the truce remained in force, Chile was to administer the territory from the 23rd parallel to the south of the Loa river on the Pacific. This meant that Bolivia lost not only its seaports but also its nitrate territory. In October 1904 a treaty was signed in implementation of the 1884 truce agreement, re-establishing peace between Chile and Bolivia, confirming the absolute and perpetual dominion of Chile over the former Bolivian territory occupied since the Pacific War, and demarcating the Bolivian-Chilean border from north to south through 96 points.

Article 3 of the 1904 treaty established that the port of Arica would be linked with the plateau above La Paz (Bolivia) by means of a railway which was to be built at Chile's expense, while in Article 6 Chile recognized in perpetuity Bolivia's free and full right of commercial transit through Chilean territory and ports on the Pacific seaboard. In return, under a supplementary protocol of November 1904, Bolivia recognized Chile's absolute and perpetual dominion over the territory between the 23rd and 24th parallels from the Pacific to the Argentinian border. By 1913 the railway was completed and Bolivia was due to come into ownership of its own section in 1928 under the terms of the 1904 treaty. The Peruvian Government protested at the bilateral treaty between Chile and Bolivia and warned that such a treaty did not diminish its own rights to the provinces of Tacna and Arica.

In 1918 Bolivia demanded an outlet to the sea by means of a port in either Tacna or Arica provinces, to which it asserted that neither Peru nor Chile had a conclusive right. It stated its preference for Arica on the grounds of geographical proximity, economic considerations and the fact that Arica (as well as Tacna) had been part of the Charcas Audiencia before independence. Furthermore, in 1920 Bolivia called on the League of Nations to obtain a revision of the 1904 treaty on the grounds that it had been imposed by force, that Chile was not carrying out some of its fundamental provisions, that a permanent threat of war existed in the current situation, and that it had no access to the sea. The League ruled, however, that a treaty could only be modified by the parties to it.

Meanwhile, on expiry of the 10-year period stipulated under the Treaty of Ancón, no attempt was made by Chile to stage a plebiscite in Tacna and Arica. By the early 1920s, when the USA was asked to intervene, the areas had already become Chileanized; when registration of voters was carried out in preparation for the holding of a plebiscite it was found that most Peruvians had failed to enrol, so that the plan to hold a plebiscite was abandoned. Peru and Chile in 1929 resumed diplomatic relations, which they had broken off some 20 years earlier, and on June 3, 1929, an agreement also known as the Treaty of Ancón was signed in Lima, returning the territory of Tacna to Peru and leaving Arica in Chilean hands. A complementary protocol of the same date stated that neither government could without the consent of the other cede to any third party any or all of the territory previously in dispute, or build new international railways across it.

Tacna was handed back to Peru at a ceremony on Aug. 28, 1929, and the following year Arica was incorporated by Chile into the province of Tarapacá, its northern boundary forming the frontier with Peru.

### The Chaco War

From the late 1870s Bolivia sought the settlement of an old claim to part of the vast and largely uninhabited Chaco territory, including an area between the Pilcomayo and Verde rivers which was awarded to Paraguay as against Argentina in November 1878. Aspiring partly to gain an outlet to the Atlantic, Bolivia based its claim on the assumption that the Audiencia of Charcas had always exercised jurisdiction as far east as the Paraguay river. A number of agreements on delimitation of territory in the Chaco were signed but not ratified between Bolivia and Paraguay over the next few years, including the Soler-Pinilla protocol of Jan. 12, 1907.

In 1928 the two sides attacked each other's outposts in the Chaco and, despite attempts at arbitration by other South American countries, fighting took place sporadically in 1930-31, breaking out in earnest in 1932. The Bolivian forces were greater in number and better equipped than the Paraguayans but many of them were Indians accustomed to high altitudes and they died in large numbers on the hot plains of the Chaco. Paraguay, on the other hand, was fighting on familiar ground; its forces under Col. José Félix Estigarribia advanced steadily and by the end of 1934 had captured thousands of square miles of territory beyond Bolivia's line of outposts. After 100,000 men had died, a truce entered into force in 1935 and peace talks were held in Buenos Aires. A final boundary was established in 1938, whereby most of the territory was ceded to Paraguay, and Bolivia was granted the right of rail access to the Paraguay river.

### Renewed Bolivian Claims to Sea Outlet

In 1962 Bolivia broke off diplomatic relations with Chile after the latter was accused of reducing the flow of the Lauca river waters into Bolivia [for which dispute, see pages 354-55], and relations were not resumed until 1975. In the 1970s with General Hugo Banzer in office in Bolivia and General Augusto Pinochet in power in Chile, the question of access to the sea was elevated to a major nationalistic issue in Bolivia, and in 1974 Bolivia and Chile initiated high-level contacts for the first time in 12 years.

In December 1975 Chile put forward a series of proposals aimed at resolving Bolivia's sea access problem. They required, however, that Bolivia should (i) relinquish an equal amount of her own territory (reportedly in a mineral-rich area of Potosí department in south-west Bolivia) in exchange for a corridor to the sea;

(ii) purchase from Chile the Chilean sector of the Arica-La Paz railway; (iii) allow Chile full use of the Lauca river waters; (iv) undertake to keep any land corridor demilitarized; and (v) pay compensation for the use of port facilities. President Banzer accepted the proposals as a basis for negotiation but they were generally ill-received in Bolivia.

Chile itself later declined to consider a set of Peruvian proposals put forward in November 1976 whereby Bolivia should be granted a corridor of land 8½ miles (13½ km) wide along the Chilean-Peruvian frontier, two miles north of the Arica-La Paz railway; an international zone should be set up under the joint control of Chile, Peru and Bolivia where the corridor reached the coast; and port facilities at Arica should be administered by all three countries. Peru also proposed that Bolivia should be allowed to establish a port under its sole sovereignty in the international zone, and that the sea area around the zone should be Bolivia's territorial waters.

Relations between Peru and Chile continued to be strained over the question of Bolivian access to the sea. Moreover, in March 1978 President Banzer of Bolivia again broke off relations with Chile on the grounds that it was not showing sufficient flexibility over the issue. The centenary of the outbreak of the Pacific War was commemorated emotionally in Bolivia in 1979.

**J.B.**

# Colombia-Nicaragua

The new Sandinista Government of Nicaragua on Feb. 4, 1980, unilaterally declared null and void a 1928 treaty under whose terms Colombian sovereignty had been confirmed over the Caribbean archipelago of San Andrés and Providencia, held by Colombia since the 19th century. San Andrés and Providencia, as well as the cays of Roncador, Quitasueño and Serrana whose sovereignty is also in dispute, are all situated within 200 miles (320 km) of Nicaraguan shores on the Nicaraguan Rise (an undersea bank between Nicaragua and Jamaica) in an area which is thought to contain hydrocarbon deposits; their distance from Colombia is considerably further, although they are somewhat nearer to Panama, which was a province of Colombia until 1903 and which has a dormant claim to the islands. San Andrés, Providencia, Roncador, Serrana and Quitasueño are currently administered as part of Colombian territory.

The new regime in Nicaragua (installed in July 1979 after the overthrow of President Anastasio Somoza) claims that the islands and cays are part of its 200-mile continental shelf, jurisdiction over which it asserted in December 1979. It bases the delimitation of its territory on the "natural boundaries" principle enshrined in the 1826 Declaration of Independence of the United Provinces of Central America and endorsed in 19th-century Nicaraguan constitutions. It also points out that, in the many bilateral treaties signed by Nicaragua with other countries in the 19th and early 20th centuries, no mention was ever made of a Colombian right to these islands until the Bárcenas Meneses-Esguerra treaty was signed in 1928 under US coercion.

358

Colombia bases its claim to the islands and cays on a royal order of 1803. According to this, the Spanish Crown delegated to the Viceroyalty of Santa Fé de Bogotà (of which present-day Colombia and also Panama were then a part) the defence of San Andrés and Providencia and the Mosquito (i.e. Atlantic) coast to prevent pirate incursions. Nicaragua, however, claims that the 1803 order was purely military and points out that under a further royal order of 1806 responsibility for the defence of the areas was restored to the Captaincy-General of Guatemala (under which Nicaragua was administered at the time); it states furthermore that only royal decrees and not royal orders were juridically applicable as regards border questions. Nicaragua also disputes Colombia's assertion that the cays have always been considered, geographically and juridically, as part of the San Andrés archipelago, and rejects a 1972 treaty signed in Bogotà on Sept. 8 between the USA and Colombia under which the former recognized Colombian sovereignty over the three cays (and which was ratified by the US Senate on July 31, 1981).

## History of Dispute

Nicaragua was a focus of interest for the colonial powers in the 19th century because of the possibility of constructing an interoceanic canal across its territory. In the 18th century Britain had established a protectorate on the Mosquito coast (including part of present-day Honduras), known as the Miskito "kingdom", and its presence in the area was not finally ended until 1894. The 1905 Altamirano-Harrison treaty between Britain and Nicaragua subsequently recognized full Nicaraguan sovereignty over the coast.

**Map 40** **The above map illustrates Nicaragua's territorial claims against Colombia, and also the latter country's dispute with Venezuela over delimitation of the Gulf of Venezuela.**

The United States tried unsuccessfully to annex Nicaragua to the southern slave states in the mid-19th century and intervened militarily there in 1912-25 and again in 1926-33. It first proposed to Nicaragua that a treaty should be concluded recognizing Colombian sovereignty over San Andrés and Providencia in 1925 (apparently as a recompense to Colombia for the loss of Panama, whose independence in 1903 the USA had supported), but it was not until the second term of office of President Adolfo Díaz of Nicaragua (1926-28) that the Bárcenas Meneses-Esguerra treaty was signed with Colombia on March 24, 1928. The treaty stated that Colombia recognized Nicaraguan sovereignty over the Mosquito coast in exchange for Nicaraguan recognition of Colombian sovereignty over San Andrés and Providencia (but expressly excepted Roncador, Quitasueño and Serrana). It was not ratified until March 6, 1930, however, when President Moncada of the Liberal Party was in power in Nicaragua.

Just after the signature of the treaty, the USA and Colombia on April 10, 1928, came to an agreement regulating the juridical status of Roncador, Quitasueño and Serrana—the USA having earlier taken over the cays (in 1919) under the "Guano law" whereby islands considered by the USA as *terrae nullius* became its property if guano was discovered there. The agreement (in the form of an exchange of notes) laid down that in view of the claims of both countries over the islands the status quo should be maintained, Colombia should continue to fish around the islands and the USA should maintain navigational aids in the area.

In support of its contention that Colombia had no well-founded claim to the Mosquito coast or the adjacent islands, Nicaragua has cited a number of treaties concluded between Nicaragua and other countries, or between other countries. These have included (i) the Molina-Gual treaty of 1825 between Colombia and the United Provinces of Central America, which pledged that both sides would "guarantee the integrity of each other's respective territories . . . on the same basis as they naturally occurred before the present war of independence"; and (ii) the Nicaraguan-Spanish treaty of 1850, which recognized the independence of Nicaragua and its adjacent islands, stating that Spain "renounced in perpetuity in the most formal and solemn manner for itself and its successors the sovereignty, rights and actions which correspond to it over the American territory situated between the Atlantic Ocean and the Pacific with its adjacent islands, formerly known under the denomination of the Province of Nicaragua and now a Republic of the same name".

Nicaragua has also claimed that its sovereignty over the Mosquito coast was recognized implicitly in the 1850 Clayton-Bulwer and 1852 Crampton-Webster treaties (both concluded between Britain and the USA), which stated that only the Central American states themselves could exercise sovereignty over Central American territory. Moreover, explicit Nicaraguan sovereignty over the Mosquito coast was recognized in the 1860 Treaty of Managua, concluded between Britain and Nicaragua while the British settlement still existed on the coast.

On the basis of an 1894 treaty between Nicaragua and Honduras which declared that both were sovereign masters of their countries, it was later established between the two states that they had full sovereignty over their Atlantic coasts and adjacent islands. As stated above, Britain also recognized Nicaraguan sovereignty over the Mosquito coast and hence over its adjacent islands in the 1905 Altamirano-Harrison treaty.

Nicaragua also points out that when the Bárcenas Meneses-Esguerra treaty was signed and ratified, the constitution in force was that of 1911, which stated in Article 1 that Nicaraguan territory included "the adjacent islands". Article 2 stated that, since sovereignty was "inalienable and imprescriptible and resides essentially with the people", treaties should not be concluded "which are opposed to national independence and integrity or which affect its sovereignty in any war", except

360

such as tended towards union with one or more of the Central American republics. The subsequent constitution of 1939 contained largely similar provisions, while the 1948 constitution also included Nicaragua's continental shelf and the stratosphere as under Nicaraguan jurisdiction.

### Current State of Dispute

In unilaterally abrogating the Bárcenas Meneses-Esguerra treaty in 1980 Nicaragua stressed that the measure was not intended as a sign of aggression against a neighbour nation whose people it had always respected, nor was it claiming a part of Colombia's continental shelf, but rather territory which was geographically, historically and juridically an integral part of Nicaragua. It said that the circumstances of Nicaragua's history since 1909 had prevented it from defending its rights to the continental shelf, the jurisdictional waters and the island territories, and that treaties disadvantageous to Nicaragua such as the Bárcenas Meneses-Esguerra treaty and the earlier Chamorro-Bryan agreement of 1914 (which was later abrogated) were signed under duress and therefore lacked legal validity.

In response to Nicaragua's moves the Colombian Government reinforced its military presence in and around San Andrés and recalled its ambassador for consultations. The two countries agreed to hold talks (pending which they maintained their original positions) and Colombia also referred its case to the UN Law of the Sea conference. In February 1982 Colombia reaffirmed its sovereignty over the disputed islands by "implementing" the 1972 treaty with the United States.

**J.B.**

# Colombia-Venezuela

The boundary between Colombia and Venezuela—originally based on that between the (1810) Spanish captaincies-general of Venezuela and Granada —was not properly determined until 1932, when the final implementation was achieved of an arbitration award made on March 24, 1922, by the Swiss Federal Council, to which the two countries had in 1916 decided to submit their long-standing dispute for arbitration. Notwithstanding this land border settlement the two countries have in recent years been at issue over the delimitation of their respective sovereignties in the Gulf of Venezuela and the area around the Los Monjes Islands to the north-east of the Goajirá Peninsula. (For a map of the region, see page 359.)

Under a treaty signed in Bogotá (the capital of Colombia) on April 24, 1894 (but not subsequently ratified), Colombia had ceded to Venezuela certain territories, including settlements on the east coast of the Goajirá Peninsula (i.e. the west coast of the Gulf of Venezuela). In a previous arbitration award of March 16, 1891, by the King of Spain, the whole of that peninsula had been awarded to Colombia.

In connexion with the discovery of oil resources in the area of the Gulf of Venezuela and Lake Maracaibo, a new dispute arose in the 1920s on the question of sovereignty over the waters and resources of the Gulf of Venezuela and the area around the islands of Los Monjes. The latter are situated to the north-east of the

Goajirá Peninsula and were occupied by Venezuela under the dictatorship of President Pérez Jiménez in 1953-58.

In December 1965 it was alleged in Venezuela that Colombia had granted certain US oil companies concessions for prospecting for oil in Venezuelan territory. The two Governments nevertheless agreed in that year to engage in talks on the "delimitation of marine and submarine areas" between their two countries. In 1968 the Venezuelan Foreign Minister defined his Government's position as follows: "The submarine areas of the Gulf of Venezuela south of the parallel through Castilletes and Punta Salinas [i.e. roughly 12° N] in their entirety form part of Venezuelan territory [and] are in no case the object of negotiations, and therefore we recognize no kind of concessions in this area." In Bogotá it was claimed in April 1973 that the islands of Los Monjes did not have their own continental shelf, and in the same month the talks were broken off by Colombia.

On July 20, 1975, President López Michelsen of Colombia declared that the Gulf of Venezuela was "a historic bay, a condominium of the two riparian states —Colombia and Venezuela". He also quoted a statement which he had made in August 1974, as follows: "Our right to the continental shelf and the waters which cover it is derived from the geographical fact that this bay is not exclusively surrounded by Venezuelan territory." His thesis was, however, utterly rejected in Venezuela.

On Jan. 28, 1976, it was reported that the Colombian Government would not submit its claim regarding the Los Monjes Islands area to the International Court of Justice but was ready to discuss it in direct talks with Venezuela on the delimitation of marine and submarine areas in the Caribbean Sea. At the same time, the Venezuelan Foreign Minister was reported to have stated that Venezuela's sovereignty over the Los Monjes Islands was unquestionable.

The Colombian Foreign Minister disclosed on Nov. 17, 1978, that talks were being held with Venezuela "in a spirit of cordiality and understanding" on the dispute over marine and submarine areas in what he called the Gulf of Maracaibo [i.e. of Venezuela] and added that Colombia rejected the appointment of a tribunal to arbitrate in the dispute. This idea was also rejected by the Venezuelan Foreign Minister during talks held in Bogotá on Dec. 11-13, 1978.

On March 14, 1979, President Luis Herrera Campíns of Venezuela was reported to have appointed a commission to travel to Colombia to resume negotiations on the demarcation in the Gulf of Venezuela. In response to a statement by the Colombian Council of State recognizing Venezuelan sovereignty over the Los Monjes Islands, the Venezuelan Foreign Ministry issued, on March 30, a statement welcoming this announcement as "a positive factor" in the talks but noting that the status of the islands had never been the subject of debate during marine and submarine demarcation talks between the two countries.

The talks were continued until it was announced in a broadcast in Bogotá on Oct. 21, 1980, that agreement had been reached on a draft treaty on the delimitation of marine areas, including "internal waters" and "exclusive economic zones". The draft treaty provided inter alia for the "innocent passage" of all merchant vessels using ports of the two countries and that of their warships and non-commercial state-owned vessels. It reaffirmed that the Los Monjes Islands were part of Venezuela but recognized limited Colombian rights in the Gulf. On the question of oil production the draft treaty laid down (in Article 4) that "if a hydrocarbons field extends to both sides of the boundary line established in this treaty each party will explore and exploit the deposit within its own marine areas and will receive one-half of the hydrocarbons extracted but will also be responsible for one-half of the corresponding cost" and that "those deposits that do not cross the boundary line will be developed unilaterally by the country in which they are found".

The draft treaty was strongly opposed by certain circles in both countries, but particularly in Venezuela (where there was widespread hostility towards Colombians, of whom several hundred thousand had entered Venezuela in search of work in recent years). Those opposing what they called "the ceding of Venezuelan waters to Colombia" included some members of the ruling Christian Social Party (COPEI), leading members of the opposition *Acción Democrática* (but not ex-President Carlos Andrés Pérez, who publicly supported the draft treaty), all left-wing parties and, above all, the armed forces.

President Herrera Campíns had stated after its publication that the treaty would not be signed unless a clear consensus existed on its terms. At the same time the Venezuelan Minister of Energy assured Colombia that Venezuela would not drill for oil in the disputed area until the issue was settled. Further talks between representatives of the two Governments on the boundary issue were suspended in November 1980, and it was only at a meeting of the two countries' Presidents in Venezuela on Oct. 2, 1981, that the possibility of renewed talks on the sea boundary dispute was mentioned, but there was no indication of the terms on which it might eventually be settled.

Regarding the two countries' common land border, the Colombian Foreign Minister announced on Jan. 29, 1982, that Colombia and Venezuela would begin to demarcate the border on Feb. 1. In Venezuela it was stated on Jan. 29 that the demarcation would take some nine months and that, as there was no problem of delineation, the purpose of the demarcation was merely to prevent confusion among the people living in the area and to comply with international agreements.

H.W.D.

# Cuba-United States

The US Guantánamo base in Cuba is the only US base in the world on communist territory. It was leased to the United States for a nominal rent in 1903 as a naval and coaling base by the newly formed Republic of Cuba, the United States being granted full jurisdiction and control over the territory containing the base in return for recognizing Cuban sovereignty over the area. The agreement on the lease was confirmed by a treaty of 1934. In 1960, following a deterioration in US-Cuban relations after Fidel Castro came to power, President Eisenhower issued a statement to the effect that the agreement could only be modified or abrogated with the consent of both parties, and that the USA had no intention of taking any such step. Diplomatic relations between the two countries were severed in January of the following year, and in 1964 the United States made the base self-sufficient after Cuba cut off fresh water supplies on Feb. 6 of that year. Cuba regards the base as being illegally occupied and has not cashed any of the rent payment cheques since 1960.

The Guantánamo base is located on the southern coast of the eastern tip of the island of Cuba, at the foot of the Sierra Maestra mountains, in an area of 117 square miles (300 sq km), one-third of which is taken up by Guantánamo Bay. The bay, the third largest in Cuba, is a deep, sheltered inlet in a strategic location, which was considered at the time of its acquisition as fundamental to the maintenance of US interests in the Caribbean, South America and Central America, as well as for control of the Panama Canal.

## Historical Background

Cuba was a Spanish colony from the 15th century until 1898, except for a brief period of British occupation in 1762-63. Cuban rebels struggled to achieve the island's independence in the latter half of the 19th century, and the latest of these independence revolts (in 1895) led to the intervention three years later of the United States, which had shown interest in the island from the beginning of the century. A brief war ensued, after which Spanish dominion over Cuba was transferred to the USA with the signature on Dec. 10, 1898, of the Treaty of Paris.

Before the United States declared war on Spain, a joint resolution was passed by the US Congress on April 1898, authorizing the USA to intervene. The resolution declared that "the United States hereby disclaims any disposition or intention to exercise sovereignty, jurisdiction or control over said island except for the pacification thereof, and asserts its determination, when that is accomplished, to leave the government and control of the island to its people". It also stated that "the people of the island of Cuba are, and of right ought to be, free and independent"; and that "it is the duty of the United States to demand, and the Government of the United States does hereby demand, that the Government of Spain at once relinquish its authority and government in the island of Cuba and withdraw its land and naval forces from Cuba and Cuban waters".

Cuba remained under US military jurisdiction from 1898 to 1902, when the Government of Cuba was handed over to the island's first President under the terms of the Platt Amendment (named after a Connecticut senator, Orville H. Platt, who presented it to the US Senate, although its text was drawn up by the

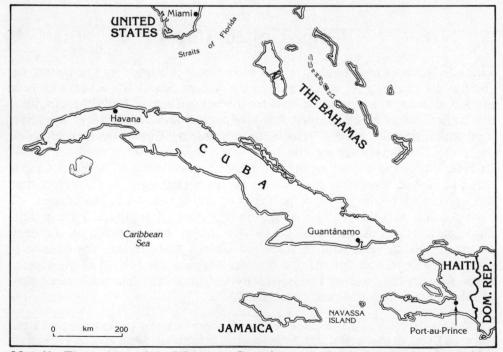

**Map 41  The position of the US base at Guantánamo in Cuba, also showing the position of Navassa Island (US), which is claimed by Haiti.**

Secretary of War, Elihu Root). The amendment authorized the US President to relinquish the government and control of the island of Cuba to its people "as soon as a government shall have been established in said island under a constitution which, either as a part thereof or in an ordinance appended thereto, shall define the future relations of the United States with Cuba".

The amendment also stated, however, "that the Government of Cuba consents that the United States may exercise the right to intervene for the preservation of Cuban independence, the maintenance of a government adequate for the protection of life, property and individual liberty, and for discharging the obligations with respect to Cuba imposed by the Treaty of Paris on the United States, now to be assumed and undertaken by the Government of Cuba".

Furthermore, Article VII stated that "to enable the United States to maintain the independence of Cuba, and to protect the people thereof, as well as for its own defence, the Government of Cuba will sell or lease to the United States the lands necessary for coaling or naval stations at certain specified points to be agreed upon with the President of the United States".

The Platt Amendment was approved by the Cuban constitutional convention by a narrow majority on June 12, 1901, notwithstanding the earlier failure of the Cuban side to have certain qualifications attached to it and in the face of the US threat to continue to occupy the island if it was rejected. The amendment was attached to the new 1901 constitution, but Cuba has regarded it ever since as contradicting the 1898 joint resolution, which committed the USA to respect for Cuban independence.

In line with Article VIII of the Platt Amendment, which said that the provisions of Article VII would be embodied in a treaty with the USA, a Permanent Treaty was signed on May 22, 1903, between Cuba and the United States, providing for the perpetual lease of lands for coaling and naval stations. It became operative through an agreement signed by Cuba on Feb. 16, 1903, and by the USA on Feb. 23 of that year, which stated that Cuba and the USA were desirous to "execute fully Article VII of the Platt Amendment" and that they had thus reached agreement as follows:

"*Article I*. The Republic of Cuba hereby leases to the United States, for the time required for the purposes of coaling and naval stations, the following described areas of land and water situated in the island of Cuba: (i) in Guantánamo . . . and (ii) in north-western Cuba in Bahía Honda. . . . *Article II*. The grant of the foregoing article shall include the right to use and occupy the waters adjacent to said areas of land and water, and to improve and deepen the entrances thereto and the anchorages therein, and generally to do any and all things necessary to fit the premises for use as coaling or naval stations only, and for no other purpose. Vessels engaged in the Cuban trade shall have free passage through the waters included within this grant. *Article III*. While on the one hand the United States recognizes the continuance of the ultimate sovereignty of the Republic of Cuba over the above described areas of land and water, on the other hand the Republic of Cuba consents that during the period of the occupation by the United States of said areas under the terms of this agreement the USA shall exercise complete jurisdiction and control over and within said areas with the right to acquire (under conditions to be hereafter agreed upon by the two governments) for the public purposes of the United States any land or other property therein by purchase or by exercise of eminent domain with full compensation to the owners thereof."

On Dec. 10, 1903, the USA took possession of the land and sea areas leased for the establishment of the base at Guantánamo at a price of $2,000 a year in US gold throughout the period it occupied and used the areas.

On May 29, 1934, Cuba and the USA signed a Treaty on Relations which abrogated the 1903 treaty and the Platt Amendment, although Article II of the new treaty provided the following: "Until the two contracting parties agree to the modification or abrogation of the stipulations of the agreement in regard to the lease to the USA of lands for coaling and naval stations signed . . . in 1903 . . . the stipulations of that agreement with regard to the naval station of Guantánamo shall continue in effect. . . . So long as the USA shall not abandon the said naval station of Guantánamo or the two governments shall not agree to a modification of its present limits, the station shall continue to have the territorial area that it now has, with the limits that it has on the date of the signature of the present treaty".

## Developments since 1960

Since the advent of Fidel Castro to power in 1959, the sharp deterioration in relations between Cuba and the USA has elevated the US presence at Guantánamo to a major subject of contention. At the UN General Assembly on Sept. 26, 1960, Dr Castro described the US presence on the island as "the most tragic case in the entire history of the bases now scattered over the world" and the base as being "forcibly placed in what is undeniably our territory, a good distance from the coasts of the United States, against Cuba and against the people, imposed by force and constituting a threat to and concern for our people". In a speech on July 26, 1962, the Cuban leader said that the naval base was "a dagger stuck in the heart of Cuba" and a piece of land which Cuba would not reclaim by force but would never renounce.

President Eisenhower, however, stated on Nov. 1, 1960: "Our rights in Guantánamo are based on international agreements with Cuba and include the exercise by the United States of complete jurisdiction and control over the area. These agreements with Cuba can be modified or abrogated only by agreement between the two parties. . . . Our Government has no intention of agreeing to the modification or abrogation of these agreements and will take whatever steps may be appropriate to defend the base. The people of the United States, and all of the peoples of the world, can be assured that the United States' presence in Guantánamo and the use of the base pose no threat whatever to the sovereignty of Cuba, to the peace and security of its people, or to the independence of any of the American countries. Because of its importance to the defence of the entire hemisphere, particularly in the light of the intimate relations which now exist between the present Government of Cuba and the Sino-Soviet bloc, it is essential that our position in Guantánamo be clearly understood."

The US Government broke off relations with Cuba on Jan. 3, 1961, after Cuba demanded a substantial reduction in the number of US personnel at the US embassy in Havana. Other major crises erupted (i) in April 1961, when a small force of anti-Castro exiles allegedly backed by the USA landed in the Bay of Pigs in an abortive attempt to overthrow the regime; and (ii) in October 1962, when the presence of Soviet missile bases was discovered in Cuba. Dr Castro in February 1961 said that relations between the USA and Cuba could only be normalized if a number of conditions were met by the former, one of these being the withdrawal of the USA from the Guantánamo base.

Cuba has based its demand for the withdrawal of the USA from Guantánamo not only on historical considerations but also on UN General Assembly resolutions, notably (i) Resolution 2105/XX of Dec. 20, 1965, which calls on colonial powers to dismantle military bases in the colonial territories and to refrain from setting up new ones, and (ii) Resolution 2344/XXII of Dec. 19, 1967, which calls on the UN Disarmament Committee to renew its study of the means of eliminating foreign military bases in the Asian, African and Latin American countries in line with

Resolution 2105/XX. The Cuban position has also been supported in resolutions approved at conferences of the Non-Aligned Movement.

In 1976 Cuba adopted by referendum a new constitution, Article X of which states: "The Republic of Cuba rejects and considers illegal and null and void all treaties, pacts and concessions which were signed in conditions of inequality or which disregard or diminish its sovereignty over any part of the national territory."

**J.B.**

# Ecuador-Peru

For 150 years a large area of the Amazon Basin in what is now the north Peruvian department of Loreto has been claimed by Ecuador. The dispute over the area evolved after various territorial reorganizations under Spanish colonial rule left Ecuador, on its independence, without access to either the Amazon river or the region's other major waterway, the Marañon, and thus without direct access to the Atlantic. After hostilities had again erupted over the issue in 1941, the two sides signed an internationally agreed protocol in Rio de Janeiro the following year which delineated the border, allocating the whole of the disputed territory to Peru. This protocol was unilaterally declared null and void in 1960 by the Ecuadorean Government of the day, and since then successive governments have reaffirmed Ecuador's rights over the Amazon Basin, while official Ecuadorean maps show the territory as being within Ecuador's frontiers. Peru, however, has regarded the border problem as being regulated by the Rio protocol and is not prepared to consider sacrificing more territory after losing large areas to Chile and Brazil in the 19th century. In 1981 the dispute flared up again with a five-day war between the two countries.

The area currently in dispute covers 125,000 square miles (325,000 sq km) and includes the Amazon and Marañon rivers. It contains Iquitos, a fast-developing city on the west bank of the Amazon, and also Peru's main jungle oil-producing region (in territory between the Tigre and Corrientes rivers in the north).

Peru has an area of 496,224 square miles (1,285,000 sq km) and a population of 17,400,000 people; its armed forces are among the strongest and best-equipped in Latin America (numbering some 100,000 men) and the country produces about 10,000,000 tonnes of oil annually. Ecuador has an area of 270,000 square miles (700,000 sq km), a population of 7,900,000 and armed forces numbering only about 40,000 men. Nearly half its territory falls within the area of application of the Amazon Co-operation Treaty (on the harmonious development of the Amazon Basin)—the largest proportion in relation to surface area of any of the treaty's signatories, which also include Brazil and Peru; however, its route to the Atlantic is of necessity via Pacific ports and the Panama Canal. Ecuador claims to have discovered the Amazon, maintaining that the expedition led by Francisco de Orellano set out from Quito in 1542 (although this is also disputed by Peru). Ecuador equals Peru in producing about 10,000,000 tonnes of oil annually and is a member of the Organization of Petroleum Exporting Countries (OPEC).

## History of the Dispute

The main area of contention between Ecuador and Peru was the province of Maynas, although parts of Tumbes and Jaén provinces were also at issue. Under Spanish rule Maynas was part of the area ruled as the Audiencia of Quito by the Viceroyalty of Peru, whose southern border (according to a Spanish Royal Decree of 1740) ran along the Marañon and Amazon from Tumbes, on the Pacific coast, to the borders of the Portuguese territories (Brazil). The Audiencia of Quito was in 1739 attached as an integral territory to the Viceroyalty of Nueva Granada (also known as Santa Fé de Bogotà).

In further administrative changes under a Spanish Royal Decree of 1802, the Government and Commandancy-General of Maynas were separated from Nueva Granada and reattached to the Viceroyalty of Peru, together with the government of Quijos province. In the 1802 decree (wherein Peru also incorporated Tumbes, Jaén, and the Maynas Commandancy-General into its own Constitution), the frontiers of the Commandancy-General of Maynas were described as extending along the Marañon to the frontiers of the Portuguese colonies and also along all the other rivers which entered the Marañon on its northern and southern banks, and other smaller streams, up to where those rivers ceased to be navigable because of falls or insurmountable rapids.

Peru thus contended that at the time of its own independence in 1821 Maynas was administered by the Viceroyalty of Peru, and it points out that Ecuador did not exist as such at the time (being until 1830 part of the Gran Colombia federation into which the Viceroyalty of Nueva Granada was converted on its liberation from the Spanish). Ecuador, on the other hand, maintained that the 1802 decree separated only certain military and ecclesiastical aspects of Maynas province from the administration of Nueva Granada, and that Maynas was thus still part of the Viceroyalty of Nueva Granada at that time, and not under Peruvian jurisdiction. Ecuador has since based its claim to the disputed area largely on (i) an 1829 peace

**Map 42  Ecuador's territorial claim against Peru.**

and border treaty, signed between Peru and Gran Colombia, and (ii) an 1830 protocol to this treaty, whose existence is disputed by Peru.

The 1829 Treaty of Guayaquil was concluded in an effort to settle the territorial conflict which had erupted into a crisis in 1828 after Peru reasserted a claim to Jaén province and also to the whole of Maynas by convening elections there in 1826. Gran Colombia opposed the Peruvian claim to Jaén at this stage on the grounds that Jaén had requested to be reincorporated into the Gran Colombia federation in 1824 despite having earlier become independent; as for Maynas, Peru had previously restricted itself to convening elections in the southern part of that province.

On expiry of an ultimatum to Peru to relinquish Jaén and southern Maynas, Gran Colombia declared war on Peru in July 1828, and in September of that year Peru blockaded Gran Colombia's ports. The Peruvian Navy captured Guayaquil in 1829 and the Army occupied the Colombian province of Loja, but was defeated. The immediate conflict ended with a Colombian victory over Peru at Tarqui in February 1829 and a preliminary peace agreement was concluded. Following a change of government in Peru in June 1829, a truce was signed at Piura in July and talks took place, resulting in the signature of the Guayaquil treaty on Sept. 22, 1829, which stated that both parties recognized as their territorial limits "those of the old viceroyalties". Peru regards this treaty as null and void because it was concluded with Gran Colombia and says that, even had it been valid, it would have been superseded by a later treaty of alliance and friendship, signed with Ecuador in 1832 in Lima, which stated that the existing boundaries should be recognized until a boundary convention was negotiated.

On Aug. 11, 1830—just before Ecuador emerged as a separate state—Gran Colombia and Peru signed the Mosquero-Pedemonte protocol, supplementary to the Treaty of Guayaquil, establishing guidelines for the delimitation of their borders. It stated that the Marañon, the Macará and the Tumbes rivers were to be the definitive borders and recognized the full sovereignty of Gran Colombia over all territory on the left bank of the Marañon, and that of Peru over all territory on the right bank. Peru claims that the original of this protocol has never been exhibited by Ecuador.

Efforts to negotiate a boundary treaty in the early 1840s failed, and in November 1853 Ecuador passed a law establishing its right to free navigation on rivers such as the Chinchipe, Santiago, Morona, Pastaza, Tigre, Curaray, Naucana, Napo and Putomayo, and other Amazon tributaries. This provoked a protest from Peru that the rivers came within the limits established by the 1802 decree and were therefore part of Peru. In 1857 Peru broke off relations with Ecuador after Ecuador decided to pay off certain debts to British creditors in the form of land, including parts of Quijos and Canelos provinces over which Peru claimed sovereignty. Preparations for war were made by Peru and Ecuador over this issue, and a blockade of Ecuador's ports was decreed in 1858 by President Castilla of Peru and was not lifted until August 1859. Peru subsequently claimed that these hostilities were another reason for the invalidation of the Guayaquil treaty, but Ecuador denied that a proper war had taken place and asserted that the treaty remained in force.

In 1860 the Mapasingue Convention was signed, annulling Ecuador's transfer of land to British creditors and establishing as a provisional basis for the delimitation of territory the 1802 decree and also the legal principle of *uti possidetis juris* (whereby new states of the post-colonial era accepted the same boundaries which they had enjoyed under colonial rule). It was, however, rejected by the Peruvian Congress and by the newly-established constitutional Government of Ecuador, and the latter country has since claimed that the Treaty of Guayaquil remained the basis for delimitation.

In 1887 the two sides signed the Espinosa-Bonifaz Treaty, which established that they wished to solve amicably any border questions and that any such issues should be submitted to the King of Spain for arbitration. On the basis of this treaty, therefore, arbitration began in 1904, but when Ecuador in 1910 learned the apparently adverse outcome of the findings (which were not officially published) it decided not to accept them. Negotiations recommenced in 1936 to seek a settlement of the border issue on the basis of a status quo established in advance as well as a de facto line regarding territorial positions; however, these negotiations proved fruitless and were adjourned after two years.

## The 1941 War and the Rio Protocol

On July 5, 1941, despite efforts by Argentina, Brazil, and the United States to forestall a conflict, hostilities broke out between Peru and Ecuador, the immediate cause being the stationing of garrisons in disputed border areas. Incidents continued sporadically until September and Peru gained the upper hand, after which the mediatory nations established a demilitarized zone (under the Talara Agreement of Oct. 2, 1941) and, in a memorandum of Oct. 4, called upon the two sides to withdraw their troops not less than 10 miles (16 km) behind the 1936 status quo line as a prior condition to negotiating a settlement.

The Protocol of Rio de Janeiro was concluded on Jan. 29, 1942, between Peru and Ecuador with the participation of the mediatory nations after negotiations which began on Jan. 13. It was ratified by the Congresses of both Peru and Ecuador on Feb. 26, 1942, and it established the border between the two countries as internationally recognized today.

Its main provisions were as follows:

"*Article 1*. The Governments of Peru and Ecuador solemnly affirm their determined intention to maintain between the two peoples relations of peace and friendship, understanding and goodwill and to abstain each in respect of the other from any act capable of disrupting these relations.

"*Article 2*. The Government of Peru will within 15 days withdraw its military forces to the line described in Article 8 of this protocol.

"*Article 3*. The United States, Argentina, Brazil and Chile will co-operate by means of military observers in order to adjust to the circumstances the evacuation and withdrawal of troops under the terms of the previous article.

"*Article 4*. The military forces of the two countries will remain in their positions until the definitive demarcation of the frontier line. Until then, Ecuador shall have civil jurisdiction only in the zones which Peru shall evacuate, which remain in the same state as was the demilitarized zone of the Act of Talara.

"*Article 5*. The negotiation of the USA, Argentina, Brazil and Chile shall continue until the frontiers between Ecuador and Peru have been definitively demarcated, and this protocol and its execution shall remain under the guarantee of [these] four countries.

"*Article 6*. Ecuador shall enjoy the same concessions for navigation on the Amazon and its northern tributaries as Brazil and Colombia, beyond those which are agreed in a treaty on commerce and navigation designed to facilitate navigation on these rivers.

"*Article 7*. Any doubt or disagreement which may arise over the execution of this protocol shall be resolved by the parties with the collaboration of the representatives of the USA, Argentina, Brazil and Chile within the shortest possible time."

*Article 8* established the border line with reference to named points.

"*Article 9*. It is understood that the line described above shall be accepted by Ecuador and Peru for the establishment by technicians in that field of the frontier between the two countries. The parties shall nevertheless, in proceeding with their plan of the terrain, be able to grant each other reciprocal concessions which they consider proper in order to adjust to the geographical reality. Such rectifications shall be carried out with the collaboration of representatives of the USA, Argentina, Brazil and Chile."

Considerable problems of demarcation ensued in various sectors, notably in the zone between the Zamora and Santiago rivers in the Condor mountains where a new river, the Cenepa, was discovered. President Galo Plaza Lasso said in a message to the Ecuadorean Congress in August 1951 that this discovery should give Ecuador the right to additional territory, which under the Rio protocol had been divided simply by the watershed between the Zamora and Santiago rivers; he also said that his Government could not accept "a frontier in this sector which does not recognize the inalienable Amazonian right of Ecuador and does not allocate it a proper and sovereign right to the Marañon river". Demarcation of the frontier then stopped, leaving a 50-mile stretch of the border uncharted. However, it was not until 1960 that the protocol was declared null and void by President José Velasco Ibarra of Ecuador, although the guarantor powers ruled on Dec. 7, 1960, that this repudiation was not valid. Among the reasons given for repudiating the protocol, Ecuador states that territorial rights cannot be acquired by force (according to the 1933 Montevideo Convention on the Rights and Duties of States) and that it was pressured into signing the protocol against its true wishes.

## The 1981 Hostilities

During the 20 years up to 1980 there were no major developments in the border dispute, although Ecuador continued to assert rights to the Amazon Basin. The Ecuadorean Foreign Minister, Alfonso Barrera, spoke on Oct. 28, 1980, of the need for an alternative to the congested Panama Canal and said that Ecuador was in favour of "finding an outlet to the Atlantic via the Amazon river". His predecessor, Alfredo Pareja Diezcanseco, had stated on May 21, 1980, that "a territorial conflict does exist between Ecuador and Peru" which Ecuador wished to settle in accordance with international law; however, Fernando Belaúnde Terry (at the time President-elect of Peru) said that he did not agree with "the thesis that Peru has territorial conflicts with Ecuador".

On Jan. 28, 1981—the eve of the 39th anniversary of the signature of the Rio protocol—fighting erupted in the Condor mountains between Ecuadorean and Peruvian troops. The fighting centred around three military border posts—Paquisha, Mayayco and Machinaza—which Peru said had been illegally occupied by Ecuadorean forces earlier in the month (one of them being seven miles inside Peru, in the Coimana river valley). After five days of hostilities, during which time the Organization of American States convened in emergency session and both countries imposed states of emergency, a ceasefire came into force on Feb. 1, by when it appeared that Peru had driven the Ecuadorean forces back from the border posts. A commission composed of the military attachés of the USA, Argentina, Brazil and Chile (who helped negotiate the ceasefire) was charged with supervising the border area.

**J.B.**

# El Salvador-Honduras

A treaty demarcating two-thirds of the 343-kilometre common frontier between El Salvador and Honduras was signed in 1980 as a major step towards ending a border dispute dating back to the 19th century, when both countries attained independence as separate nations. As well as terminating the effective state of war which had existed between them since they engaged in brief hostilities in July 1969, the treaty contained an undertaking to reach agreement within five years on the remaining disputed stretch of border including the border pockets (*bolsones territoriales*) which formed part of the demilitarized zone set up in 1970. (For map of the region, see page 347.)

### Efforts to resolve Border Issue in 19th Century

Both El Salvador and Honduras belonged to a federation of Central American states until this was dissolved in 1838. According to Honduras's first political constitution, decreed on Dec. 11, 1825, the country's territorial area corresponded to that covered under Spanish rule by the "Bishopric of Honduras", while El Salvador's first two constitutions (1824 and 1841) specified that its own territorial area corresponded to certain Spanish administrative areas and established its frontiers broadly as the River Paz (in the west), the inlet of Conchagua (in the east), the province of Chiquimula (in the north) and the Pacific Ocean to the south.

A number of local border disputes had already emerged by 1884, on April 10 of which year the two sides signed a border convention in San Miguel (El Salvador). In the light of available data on territorial claims between them, this convention fixed land and sea limits from the Gulf of Fonseca (in the Pacific) to the Guatemalan frontier. However, Honduras regarded this convention as prejudicing the rights of Hondurans because it had not taken into account the claims of certain localities on the frontier, and thus the Honduran Congress on Feb. 7, 1885, abrogated the convention—although Honduras agreed the following month to take all the necessary measures to arrive at a permanent solution to the border problem. Accordingly, representatives of the two governments met on Sept. 28, 1886, in Tegucigalpa (Honduras) and decided to set up commissions to determine the delimitation of the border by mutual agreement, it being agreed (i) that both governments would respect the outcome; (ii) that if no agreement was reached the dispute would be submitted to a friendly nation for arbitration; and (iii) that, while the new border line was being drawn, the 1884 line, regarded as the status quo, would be respected.

The two commissions set to work in late 1888 but could only reach agreement on the section of the frontier "constituted by the Goascorán river, from its mouth in La Unión bay (Gulf of Fonseca) upriver to where it flows into the Guajiniquil river", this section being declared "undisputed and indisputable". The commissions were then dissolved without further agreement being reached, and although the two governments agreed in San José de Costa Rica on Jan. 3, 1889, to put the dispute to the President of Costa Rica for arbitration, no such step was taken.

On Jan. 19, 1895, the Bonilla-Velasco border convention was signed in San Salvador, under the terms of which representatives of the two countries met on Nov. 13, 1897, to work out the delimitation of the frontier between Opatoro and Santa Ana (Honduras) and Lislique and Poloros (El Salvador). The treaty bore little fruit, however, since it was ratified by neither country, and there were few further developments during the period of the treaty's subsequent extension up to 1916. Moreover, no significant progress towards solving the border issue was made over the next 50 years.

## The 1969 Football War and its Aftermath

Although the immediate cause of the 1969 war was football violence following World Cup qualifying matches between the two countries' national teams, the major underlying cause was a deep-rooted conflict over Salvadorean immigration to and settlement in Honduras. From the 1920s onwards thousands of Salvadoreans left their densely-populated country and took over pieces of land in Honduras for cultivation; although a bilateral migration agreement was signed in 1965 giving them the opportunity to regularize their position in Honduras, the latter country estimated that less than 1 per cent of the migrants took advantage of this facility.

In January 1969 the Honduran Government applied an agrarian reform which meant that thousands of Salvadoreans were expelled from the land on which they had lived. With 300,000 facing deportation, and with the homeward exodus of Salvadoreans gathering force and placing increasing strains on the Salvadorean economy, the latter country's military Government in June 1969 broke off diplomatic relations with Honduras following the football incidents, and full-scale fighting began on July 14 after a series of border incidents in the preceding two weeks. The Salvadorean armed forces occupied an area of Honduran territory and bombarded towns and border areas before hostilities ceased on July 18 under a truce negotiated by the Organization of American States (OAS).

The OAS on Oct. 27, 1969, passed seven resolutions regarding bilateral relations between El Salvador and Honduras, covering (i) peace and treaties, (ii) free transit, (iii) diplomatic and consular relations, (iv) border questions, (v) the Central American Common Market, (vi) claims and differences and (vii) human and family rights. These were to form the basis of the general peace treaty signed in October 1980. In the meantime, however, a bilateral working group with a Uruguayan moderator was set up to work towards solving their differences, and met throughout 1970 and 1971.

On June 4, 1970, a "Plan for the Establishment of a Zone of Security with a View to Pacification" was signed in San José de Costa Rica, creating a three-kilometre-wide demilitarized zone on each side of the traditional border, and measures were adopted to put this into effect not only on land but also at sea and in the airspace above the demilitarized zone. OAS military observers were designated to supervise the execution of the plan, and Guatemala, Nicaragua and Costa Rica became its guarantors. However, although the plan was designed to allow the inhabitants of both countries to return to the frontier area in safety, its content was stated to have no bearing on any border claim.

Contacts between representatives of the two countries continued over the next few years and work progressed towards the elaboration of a treaty on the basis of the seven OAS resolutions. In July 1976 there were fresh military incidents on the border which led to meetings between the Foreign Ministers of the guarantor nations of the San José plan, and subsequently to the signature on Aug. 9, 1976, of the Act and Protocol of Managua, which placed OAS military observers on the frontier itself. The protocol specified the areas where incidents had frequently occurred as Dolores, Sabanetas, Sazalapa and Las Pilas (in Honduras) and Sazalapa and Monteca (in El Salvador).

## The 1980 Peace Treaty

Following four years of negotiation under the mediation of Dr José Luis Bustamante y Rivero (a former President of Peru and also of the International Court of Justice in The Hague), a general peace treaty was signed in Lima (Peru) on Oct. 30, 1980, by the Salvadorean and Honduran Foreign Ministers, respectively Fidel Chávez Mena and Col. César Elvir Sierra. Instruments of ratification were subsequently exchanged on Dec. 10, 1980, at a ceremony in Tegucigalpa.

Section IV of the treaty, covering border questions, described the delimitation of the 225 kilometres of border over which there was no controversy (Art. 16) and stated that the border was "invariable in perpetuity". The demarcation of this section of the border, the delimitation of that in the disputed areas, and the determination of the juridical situation with regard to islands and maritime areas were referred to a mixed border commission set up on May 1, 1980, which was to complete its task within five years (Arts. 18-19).

To delimit the border in the disputed areas (among which were parts of the Chalatenango and La Unión provinces of El Salvador and the Goascorán river delta), the mixed commission was authorized to use as a basis documents issued by the Spanish Crown or by any other Spanish secular or ecclesiastical authority during the colonial epoch which dealt with jurisdictional areas or territorial limits; other evidence would be taken into account of a legal, historical or human nature, or of a kind recognized under international law (Art. 26). Each new delimitation required the approval of both governments in the form of additional protocols to the treaty (Art. 27), and if there was a disagreement within the border commission itself the case would be referred to both governments for a pronouncement to be made within 60 days (Art. 28). It was further established that if no agreement was reached on the areas in dispute within the five years laid down, the case would be submitted to the International Court of Justice (Art. 31).

Until the frontier had been fully delimited, the two parties undertook not to alter the status quo which existed in the disputed areas prior to July 14, 1969, and to re-establish the status quo in so far as it had been modified, in order to guarantee peace in the areas in question (Art. 37). During the five-year period of work of the border commission neither side could unilaterally have recourse to other peaceful means of solving the conflict or place it before international bodies (Art. 38), with the proviso that if both sides agreed it could be submitted to the International Court of Justice within the five years (Art. 39).

The other major provisions of the treaty were that both sides agreed to maintain "firm and lasting peace, solid fraternity and permanent constructive co-operation" (Art. 2); that they would allow free transit across their territory of each other's goods and nationals (Arts. 7-9); that they would restore diplomatic relations fully without further formalities (Arts. 10-14); that they would contribute to the restructuring of the Central American Common Market (Arts. 40-41); that they would not claim compensation for damages incurred in or just before July 1969 (Art. 42); and that they would respect the rights of each other's nationals and allow them to reside freely in their countries (Arts. 44-45).

The border between El Salvador and Honduras was reopened on Dec. 11, 1980.

**J.B.**

# France-Suriname

Suriname (until 1975 a Dutch overseas dependency) and the French overseas department of Guiana are currently in dispute over the sovereignty of a triangular area of land totalling some 5,000 square kilometres and lying between two upper tributaries of the River Maroni (Marowijne). The dispute resembles that between Suriname and Guyana [see pages 378-81] in that it centres on uncertainties over the course of a river which both countries agree in principle to be their joint boundary, but which is still in its upper reaches somewhat inaccessible and under-developed in terms of natural resources. The area in question is thickly forested, mountainous and has many fast-flowing rivers which originate in the Tumac-Humac range forming the border with Brazil in the south. At present the economic importance of the area in dispute is uncertain, though explorations for bauxite and for gold are believed to have been undertaken by the French. Early disputes over the course of the lower reaches of the river have been settled at various times, but the outstanding disagreement over its upper course, and hence over the sovereignty of the land concerned, seems unlikely to be settled in the near future despite the renewal of efforts to this end during the 1970s.

France and the Netherlands, as colonial powers controlling the area, first reached an agreement in 1688 specifying that the Maroni river should form the boundary

**Map 43   Suriname's territorial disputes with France (French Guiana) and Guyana, also showing Venezuela's claim to the Essequibo region of Guyana.**

375

between their respective colonies. At this stage, however, neither country attached great importance to the largely uncharted interior of the territory, preferring to concentrate on the more easily accessible lands in the coastal regions and on the Maroni estuary, which is navigable for a distance of some 25 miles (40 km). The lower 100 miles (160 km) of the Maroni have since then always been agreed to form the boundary between the two colonies; differences arose, however, in the early 19th century as to whether the boundary further inland should follow the Tapanahoni river (originating in the south-west in what is now Suriname) or the Awa (or Lawa) river (flowing from the south), these two rivers being of comparable length although the Awa is wider at the confluence.

Dutch colonists had by this time begun the exploration and settlement of the area between the Tapanahoni and the Awa, although there was also a limited French presence in the area. The boundary question remained very vague for many years, but acquired a new currency in 1815 when France and Portugal concluded a basic agreement on a dispute over the sovereignty of part of northern Brazil (colonized at that time by Portugal but claimed by France). In establishing the French Guiana/Brazilian border under Article 107 of the 1815 Congress of Vienna settlement, Portugal allowed French Guiana all of the territory to the west of the River Oyapock, which still forms the department's south-eastern border with Brazil. It was agreed at the Congress of Vienna that Article 107 was to be implemented by a subsequent convention; this convention, signed by France and Portugal on Aug. 28, 1817, also defined French Guiana's western boundary as following the Maroni and Tapanahoni rivers, but this arrangement was reached without the consultation of the Netherlands, which protested at the decision.

On Nov. 9, 1836, the colonial governors of Cayenne and Suriname reached a formal agreement which declared that the western boundary of French Guiana was to be the right bank of the Maroni river from its source. The failure of this agreement to define the source as either the Tapanahoni or the Awa gave it little credibility, however, and in 1849 the Dutch Government declared that it had not settled the boundary question. The governors of the two colonies therefore set up a mixed commission in 1861 to decide on the main course of the river, but it reported that it had been unable to decide on a main course and that the name Maroni could not legitimately be applied to any part of the river above the confluence of the Tapanahoni and the Awa. Discussions on the matter continued thereafter but eventually lapsed in 1876.

Renewed efforts to resolve the dispute led on Nov. 29, 1888, to the signature in Paris of an undertaking to put the dispute before an independent arbitrator. Tsar Alexander III of Russia was eventually selected, but he accepted the invitation only on condition that he should be free, if he wished, to define a middle course between the two rivers as the boundary, rather than merely choosing one or the other.

Although the Netherlands initially objected to this condition, agreement was finally reached on April 28, 1890, and the arbitration body, sitting on May 13-25, 1891, found (i) that the Dutch had maintained military outposts on the Awa since about 1700; (ii) that the French Government had on occasions recognized Dutch jurisdiction over negroes in the disputed area; (iii) that both parties had agreed that the Maroni river from its source should be their joint boundary; (iv) that the 1861 commission had preferred the Awa as the upper course of the Maroni; and (v) that the Awa should therefore be considered the upper course and boundary between the two colonies, all land west of the Awa being Dutch territory. In August 1891 a meeting of governors agreed that exploration permits already issued by the French Government in respect of the area west of the Awa should be considered valid for a period of 40 years.

The rapid development of the Awa region soon led to further uncertainties as to which of the Awa's tributaries, the Itany (Litani) (flowing from the south-west) or the Marouini (Marowijni) (flowing from the south-east), ought to be considered its main course; it is this dispute which is still current. At the same time a number of disagreements arose over the use of the Maroni estuary, and consequently a conference was called at the Hague on April 25-May 13, 1905, to discuss these problems. It reported (i) that the boundary should follow the Maroni, the Awa and the Itany rivers, and (ii) that the Thalweg principle (defining the border as following the deepest channel) should apply to the estuary.

A further agreement signed by France and the Netherlands in Paris on Sept. 30, 1915, replaced the Thalweg decision (disputed by the Netherlands) with another which declared essentially that the navigation limits in the estuary should be defined by the median line of the stream at ordinary water level, and that the sovereignty of each island in the estuary should be determined according to whether the greater part of its area lay on the Suriname or the French Guiana side. It was also agreed that all minerals obtained from the river should be shared equally between the two colonies and that any important project capable of changing the course of the stream or of affecting shipping should be subject to the approval of both sides.

Despite the 1905 recommendations, however, the area between the Marouini and the Itany continued to be claimed by the Netherlands, and discussions since then have achieved no positive results on the issue. Suriname took over the claim to the disputed territory when it achieved its independence from the Netherlands in 1975, and negotiations conducted in November 1975 and February 1977 resulted in the formulation of a treaty between France and Suriname whereby the latter would recognize French sovereignty over most of the area still in dispute in return for French development aid totalling some 500,000,000 francs for the joint development of any resources in the area. The treaty was initialled on Aug. 15, 1977, but despite further meetings in August 1978 it had not been signed or ratified by early 1981, and there were at that time no indications of any intention on the part of Suriname to proceed with it.

**M.W.**

# Guyana-Suriname

Relations between Guyana (formerly British Guiana) and Suriname (formerly Dutch Guiana) have been periodically strained by a still unresolved dispute dating from the late 19th century over the sovereignty of a triangular area of land lying within the territory currently administered by Guyana. The area in dispute, comprising some 6,000 square miles (15,000 sq km), is situated between two tributaries of the Corentyne river and is bordered on the third and southern side by the watershed which marks the boundary shared by Guyana and Suriname with Brazil. Numerous attempts to reach a peaceful bilateral settlement of the issue have taken place since 1966, but a 1970 agreement on the mutual demilitarization of the disputed land has apparently not yet been implemented. (For map illustrating this dispute, see page 375.)

The origins of the dispute lay largely in the extreme inaccessibility of the terrain in the foothills of the Guiana Highlands, and in consequent confusion over the true course of certain tributaries of the Corentyne river. Whereas a boundary agreement signed between two Dutch colonial governors in 1800 had referred only to the main course of the Corentyne, subsequent investigations established in 1871 that its longest course was not, as hitherto believed, along the Cutari and Curuni rivers running down from central southern Suriname, but rather along the so-called New river, which rises in Guyana well to the west of the Cutari/Curuni, joining the lower reaches of the Corentyne between the 3rd and 4th parallels. Guyana adheres to the original (i.e. Cutari/Curuni) interpretation of the main course, while Suriname maintains that the New river (which it has unilaterally designated the Upper Corentyne) represents its true western boundary, and claims the New River Triangle as its sovereign territory.

At present the disputed area has little economic significance, since no significant mineral deposits have yet been located (bauxite mining being the major source of export revenue for both countries); however, the many freely flowing rivers in the area offer considerable scope for hydro-electric development, and balata (a form of ersatz rubber) is extracted from trees in the area below the high southern savannah.

## Early Agreements and Explorations

The first recorded disputes between Suriname and Berbice (now the easternmost county of Guyana) over the ownership of land west of the Corentyne took place in the late 18th century in the form of a domestic conflict (in that both Suriname and Berbice had been Dutch possessions since the mid-17th century). The land then at issue was coastal territory largely comprising fertile cotton plantations, and the metropolitan Government in Amsterdam ruled in 1794 that the territory of Berbice extended as far as the west bank of the Corentyne river.

By 1799 both Berbice and Suriname had been acquired by the British, but the Dutch governors of the two colonies (A. I. van Imbyse van Battenburg and J. F. Frederici respectively) were retained in office. The two men sought agreement on the confirmation of the west bank as the eastern boundary of Berbice, and a proclamation to this effect was published by the Governor and Councils of Berbice on Feb. 7, 1800. Guyana has since claimed that although bilaterally agreed the proclamation did not in itself constitute a boundary agreement; for its part Suriname has maintained that the agreement was subsequently confirmed by the 1815 Peace of Paris and claims also, contrary to Guyana's assertions, that the

Peace of Paris made a definite ruling on the sovereignty of the river itself, giving the entire width of the river up to but not including the west bank, as well as all islands, to Suriname.

Meanwhile, the Dutch had regained control of both colonies in 1802, although the following year the British recaptured Berbice and in 1831 the colonies of Berbice, Essequibo and British Demerara were united to form British Guiana.

In 1841 the United Kingdom Government commissioned Robert Schomburgk, an explorer, to investigate the boundaries of British Guiana; the Suriname authorities were invited to send a Commissioner with him on his exploration of the (hitherto uncharted) Corentyne but explained that they had no authority from the Netherlands to do so. Schomburgk reported on his return that the Curuni and Cutari rivers were the main tributaries of the Corentyne, and mapped these rivers as constituting the boundary between Suriname and British Guiana; this interpretation formed the basis of all British and most Dutch maps for the remainder of the century, despite the discovery made in 1871 by a British geologist, Barrington Brown, that the New river was in fact larger than the Curuni/Cutari. Barrington Brown expressed the view that the Curuni/Cutari might in fact be only a tributary, but, like Schomburgk, he mapped it as the source of the Corentyne.

Dutch claims to the New river as the source of the Corentyne arose at the time of the 1899 arbitral tribunal investigating British Guiana's border with Venezuela. The British Government reacted by describing the Cutari as "a definite and always easily ascertainable boundary . . . [which] should not be upset by geographical discoveries made long subsequent to the original adoption of the boundary and by theories so uncertain as those which are held to determine the true source of a river".

## Dutch Moves towards Settlement of the Border Dispute

The controversy over the New river subsided somewhat over the next 30 years as the Netherlands Government adopted a more conciliatory attitude to the dispute. A prominent Dutch geographer, Dr Yzerman, told the Dutch Royal Geographical Society in 1924 of his opinion that the Cutari river basin was considerably larger than that of the New river, and his arguments were in 1925 and 1926 repeatedly cited by Dutch Government ministers in rejecting Dutch claims to the disputed land on the grounds that no adequate information justifying such claims was available.

In 1926 the British Government concluded a treaty with Brazil for the demarcation of the latter's common border with British Guiana. The treaty avoided exact reference to the area in dispute between Suriname and British Guiana by means of the following formulation: "The British Guiana/Brazil frontier shall lie along the watershed between the Amazon basin and the basins of the Essequibo and Corentyne rivers as far as the point of junction or convergence of the frontier of the two countries with Dutch Guiana. . . ."

The Dutch Government suggested to the United Kingdom in 1929 that a treaty should be formulated establishing the Suriname/British Guiana border, and on Aug. 4, 1930, offered to settle on the definition of the border as "the left bank of the Corentyne and the Cutari up to its source, which rivers are Netherland territory". This firm Dutch claim to the whole width of the Corentyne and Curuni/Cutari contrasted with the de facto situation in that, in the absence of a universally accepted border treaty, the actual boundary had normally been treated by both countries as following the middle of the river. Nonetheless, Britain declared its willingness to negotiate on this basis, and a final draft of a border treaty was formulated; however, it was never signed because of the outbreak of World War II in 1939. More successful was the fixing in 1936 of a tri-junction point (as provided for in the treaty with Brazil mentioned above), which was established in accordance with the Netherlands' suggestion that a boundary line should be drawn from the source of the Cutari, leading over a particular named rock, and that the trijunction point should be the intersection of such a line with the Brazilian watershed. A definitive map was drawn up and was signed by Brazil, the United Kingdom and the Netherlands.

### Revival of Dutch and Surinamese Claims to the New River Triangle

After World War II the Dutch attitude hardened considerably, and in 1962 the Netherlands presented a revised draft border definition which discarded the Curuni/Cutari line and revived the claim to the New River Triangle. British Guiana was offered the sovereignty of the Corentyne and New rivers up to mid-stream, and Suriname designated the New river as the Upper Corentyne, a step currently described by Guyana as having no significance in international law. The United Kingdom rejected the Dutch proposals and Suriname, anticipating Guyana's achievement of independence (which finally took place in May 1966), called on the British Government in April 1966 to place on record that the boundary of Suriname and Guyana was in dispute.

Representatives of Guyana and Suriname met in London in June 1966 to discuss the dispute, but subsequently presented widely varying accounts of the meeting. Suriname described it as one between "good friends and neighbours" (May 1968), but the then Guyanese Minister of State for Foreign Affairs, S. S. Ramphal QC, reported in February 1968 that there had been a "free and frank exchange of views during which Guyana asserted its rights to the New river area and sought to demonstrate how utterly indefensible was the Suriname contention that the boundary could be otherwise than on the Cutari".

The situation deteriorated markedly in December 1967, when Guyana expelled from the disputed area a group of Surinamese who were thought to be involved in surveys for a new Surinamese hydro-electric dam. (Suriname has since received the support of the World Bank for a hydro-electric project situated outside the disputed area but dependent on water whose origin is in dispute.) Suriname described the expulsion as an inadmissible use of force, and prolonged diplomatic exchanges followed during which Suriname was alleged to have threatened the expulsion of all 2,000 Guyanese workers from its territory. S. S. Ramphal replied on Feb. 2, 1968, that Guyana would not surrender its sovereignty over the New River Triangle, but offered to re-open negotiations with Suriname, and in 1970 new discussions took place, leading to a commitment (as yet believed to be unfulfilled) to demilitarize the area.

A further incident was reported in August 1969, when Guyana alleged that armed Surinamese workers had been driven from the New River Triangle while attempting to set up a landing strip and military camp. Suriname dismissed the report, claiming instead that Guyanese troops had landed at the Tigri aerodrome in Suriname and occupied it, and adding later that Guyanese forces had illegally occupied a frontier post in the disputed area.

Suriname maintained its claim to the New River Triangle after its acquisition of independence from the Netherlands in November 1975, and a series of minor incidents continued to trouble relations between the two countries despite renewed efforts to reach agreement. In September 1977 the Guyanese authorities confiscated four trawlers, one of which was part-owned by the Suriname Government, alleging that they had been fishing in an exclusive 200-mile fisheries zone proclaimed by Guyana without payment of the appropriate fee. Suriname retaliated on Jan. 1, 1978, by withdrawing fishing licences from about 100 Guyanese who had traditionally worked the Corentyne river, and was said to have used gunboats to harass loggers on the river. Talks were opened in February 1978 in Paramaribo, the capital of Suriname, leading in mid-1978 to the settlement of the fisheries dispute and to the return of the Surinamese trawler.

Linden Forbes Sampson Burnham, Prime Minister (later President) of Guyana, and Henck Arron, then Prime Minister of Suriname, held talks in Barbados in April 1979, during which the two countries signed a fishing agreement and agreed to reopen negotiations on the border dispute. The Arron Government was subsequently overthrown on Feb. 25, 1980, by a military coup in Suriname, but the "National Military Council" which then took over the running of the country was understood to have continued Suriname's contacts with Guyana through a civilian government installed on March 15, 1980.

M.W.

# Guyana-Venezuela

During the 19th century Venezuela and Guyana (then British Guiana) claimed overlapping areas of territory covering about 50,000 square miles (130,000 sq km), consisting mainly of dense tropical rain forest which had discouraged early colonization and development. Despite an 1899 ruling by a court of arbitration which awarded much of the disputed territory to British Guiana, Venezuela in the 1960s reasserted its claim to Guyana's present territory west of the Essequibo river. In 1970 Venezuela and Guyana signed a protocol declaring a 12-year moratorium on the border issue, which has nevertheless remained a source of friction between the two countries. (For map illustrating this dispute, see page 375.)

Guyana, which has an area of 83,000 square miles (215,000 sq km) in its present boundaries, was ceded to Britain by the Dutch in 1814; it obtained internal self-government in 1961, became fully independent on May 26, 1966, and has been a co-operative republic within the Commonwealth since 1970. Venezuela, with a present land area of 352,000 square miles (910,000 sq km), declared itself an independent republic in 1811 after three centuries of Spanish rule and separated from the Gran Colombia federation in 1830.

### Historical Background to Dispute

The British claim prior to 1899 was to the drainage basin of the Cuyuni river (in the eastern part of what is now Bolívar state, Venezuela) up to within a few miles of the Orinoco and Caroni rivers. The Venezuelan claim was, and remains, to all territory west of the Essequibo river (i.e. about two-thirds of present-day Guyana).

The major issue at the centre of the claim was the degree of control exercised by the Dutch in the area west of the Essequibo prior to British rule, which Guyana claimed was extensive. It said that the Dutch settlement of Kykoveral (established in 1616) had controlled the Essequibo; that the Dutch had controlled trade as well as the indigenous population by means of trading posts established on the upper Essequibo as well as on the Pomeroon, Barima and Cuyuni rivers; and that the provinces of Essequibo and Berbice had been recognized as Dutch possessions under the 1648 Treaty of Munster which ended the Spanish-Dutch wars.

Venezuela said in support of its own claim that the Essequibo formed the most natural eastern frontier for Venezuela and pointed to the geographical unity of the land between the Orinoco and the Essequibo. It claimed that Spain had first discovered, explored and settled the British Guiana region and had exercised political control over it, and it produced evidence of the activity of Spanish missions in the area (which Guyana disputed).

The boundaries of British Guiana were established in the mid-19th century on the basis of explorations carried out by Robert Schomburgk, a surveyor and botanist engaged by the British Government for that purpose. Starting in 1841 Schomburgk surveyed most of the colony's territory in the disputed and other areas, preparing as he went maps on which he marked the boundary line he had established. According to the Schomburgk Line, the boundary between British Guiana and Venezuela began at the mouth of the Amacuro river, followed it to its source in the Imataca mountains, ran along the crest of the ridge to the sources of the Acarabisi creek, then to the junction of the Cuyuni river with the Venamo (Wenamu), and finally to the Venamo's source in Mount Roraima.

Further surveys were later carried out by two British geologists, James Sawkins and Barrington Brown, from 1867 to 1871. They travelled over the present North-West District of Guyana, as well as the Demarara and Essequibo rivers, the Rupununi and Mahu savannas, and the Takatu and Kwitaro rivers. Brown alone explored the whole of the southern district, discovering the Kaieteur Fall in 1870, and the two men surveyed the Corentyne, Berbice and Mazaruni rivers together before leaving the colony in 1871.

In the early 1880s the boundary issue was raised after the British Government discovered that the Venezuelan Government had made two grants of land in the Amacuro region within the Schomburgk Line. The whole area granted (including part of Venezuela proper, islands at the mouth of the Orinoco, the whole of the coastal district between the Orinoco and Pomeroon, and the area between all that section and the Essequibo) was destined to be part of a new federal territory. Britain immediately took steps to reassert British claims and in 1866 declared the boundaries of British Guiana officially, also issuing a map showing the Schomburgk Line.

After Britain had proclaimed the borders of its colony it took further steps to pre-empt Venezuelan claims to the Barima and Amacuro areas, where British people had already settled, by proclaiming the region the North-West District of British Guiana. Gold was discovered there in the 1890s, much of the activity centring on the Barima and Arakaka.

After an incident in 1895 in which two inspectors of the British Guiana police were seized by Venezuelan police from a station on a tributary of the Cuyuni river, President Grover Cleveland of the USA (who was supporting Venezuela in its territorial claim) warned Britain that any unilateral action by Britain would constitute an infringement of the Monroe Doctrine (under which the USA regarded any attempt by European powers to reassert or extend their influence in the Americas as dangerous to its peace and security), and he demanded that the dispute should be submitted to arbitration. After a period of strained relations between Britain and the United States, Britain agreed, and an arbitration treaty was signed in 1897 with Venezuela, both countries agreeing to accept the tribunal's award as a "full, perfect and final settlement". The tribunal which was appointed consisted of two Americans, two British members and a Russian president.

The ruling of the court of arbitration, announced in 1899, awarded to British Guiana most of the territory within the Schomburgk Line and to Venezuela a valuable portion at the mouth of Orinoco river. British Guiana lost some land in the North-West District and much of the Cuyuni Basin, the loss amounting to about 5,000 square miles (13,000 sq km). A mixed border commission appointed by the two governments met and demarcated the border, an agreement recording the demarcation line being signed in 1905.

In the meantime the King of Italy had also been asked to arbitrate on British Guiana's border dispute with Brazil. His pronouncement in 1901 again followed the Schomburgk Line, although British Guiana lost some territory.

## Reopening of the Border Issue

In 1951 Venezuela questioned the validity of the 1899 ruling and demanded the reopening of the border issue on the basis of the posthumous publication of a memorandum by Sevro Mallet-Prevost, an American counsel, which alleged that the award had been an illegal compromise and that international political pressures had been used to obtain it. This was denied by the British Government, but Venezuela raised the issue at the 17th session of the UN General Assembly in 1962, stating that it could no longer accept the arbitral award and that Venezuela wished to put it on record before British Guiana became independent that Venezuela did not accept that the border issue was settled. Accordingly, Britain agreed to engage in talks with Venezuela and British Guiana to re-examine all the documentary evidence on the border question, but stressed that this did not constitute an offer to engage in substantive talks about a revision of the frontier.

The talks led to the signature on Feb. 17, 1966, of the Geneva Agreement between Britain and Venezuela which established procedures for the settlement of their dispute. Article 1 provided for the setting up of a mixed commission to seek satisfactory solutions for the practical settlement of the controversy; Article 2 provided that within two months of the entry into force of the agreement each country would appoint two representatives to the commission; Article 3 required the commission to present six-monthly reports on progress; and Article 4 said that if full agreement had not been reached within four years from the date of the agreement, any outstanding questions would be referred to the respective governments, which would then "without delay choose one of the means of peaceful settlement provided in Article 33 of the UN Charter". Article 5 provided that no new or enlarged claim might be asserted while the agreement was in force, except within the mixed commission.

The work of the mixed commission was repeatedly interrupted by border incidents. In October 1966 Forbes Burnham, then Prime Minister of Guyana, said that about 100 Venezuelans had entered the Guyanese section of Ankoko island (on the Venamo river) and had begun mining operations; and in July 1968 Venezuela published a decree declaring territorial rights over waters beyond Guyana's three-mile limit, for a further nine miles—i.e. affecting waters to the west of the mouth of the Essequibo. This decree was immediately declared null and void by the Guyana Parliament, while the British Government informed the Venezuelan ambassador in London of its concern over the decree. Finally, in February 1970 Guyana protested to Venezuela over "military attacks against Guyanese territory", whereupon Venezuela denied that its troops had opened fire near the disputed Ankoko island and said that Guyanese units had provoked the incidents.

After receiving in June 1970 the final report of the mixed commission, which had failed to settle the dispute, the Governments of Britain, Guyana and Venezuela on June 18, 1970, signed the Protocol of Port of Spain. This protocol, which was supplementary to the Geneva Agreement (Article 4 of which was suspended while the protocol was in force), placed a 12-year moratorium on the territorial dispute.

Article 1 stated that "so long as this protocol remains in force and subject to the following provisions, the Government of Guyana and the Government of Venezuela shall explore all possibilities of better understanding between them and their peoples and in particular shall undertake periodical reviews, through normal diplomatic channels, of their relations with a view to promoting their improvement and with the aim of producing a constructive advancement of the same".

Article 2 stated that as long as the protocol remained in force "no claim whatever arising out of the contention referred to in Article 1 of the Geneva Agreement shall be asserted by Venezuela to territorial sovereignty in the territories of Guyana or by Guyana to territorial sovereignty in the territories of Venezuela". Article 5 stated that the protocol would remain in force for an initial period of 12 years which would be renewable thereafter for successive 12-year periods.

In October 1978 President Carlos Andrés Pérez became the first Venezuelan head of state to visit Guyana; he and Forbes Burnham afterwards indicated only that they had established "an intelligent understanding on the border dispute". However, after an official visit to Venezuela early in April 1981 Forbes Burnham (who had been installed as the first executive President of Guyana in January 1981) said that his country would "not cede an inch" of the Essequibo region to Venezuela, whereas President Luis Herrera Campins of Venezuela reiterated his country's claim to the region and denied reports of a proposed six-year extension of the 12-year moratorium under the Protocol of Port of Spain, due to expire in June 1982.

On June 2 the Venezuelan President disclosed that he had told President Burnham that the Venezuelan Government was committed to "keeping alive the historic claim to the Essequibo territory"; that there was, for the time being, no possibility of continuing to implement the Port of Spain protocol; and that Venezuela had "to continue to study the Geneva Agreement [of 1966] for a way to reach a satisfactory solution which would permit a practical settlement of the issue". He claimed that the Geneva Agreement was not only "the law of the Republic" (of Venezuela) but had also been signed by the Governments of Great Britain, Guyana and Venezuela, who were "committed to comply with it". Venezuela notified Britain on Dec. 11, 1981, that it would not extend the Port of Spain moratorium when it expired.

In January 1981 the Government of Cuba officially expressed its support for Guyana's territorial integrity. This was strongly resented in Venezuela, whereupon the Cuban Communist Party's organ *Granma* on May 9, 1981, denounced what it called "anti-Cuban manoeuvres of Luis Herrera Campins's Government in connexion with the border dispute between Venezuela and Guyana".

**J.B.**

384

# Haiti-United States (Navassa Island)

A longstanding dispute exists between Haiti and the United States over the sovereignty of Navassa Island, a small uninhabited outcrop of rock situated in the Jamaica Channel about 32 miles (50 km) west of Haiti. The US claim to the island under a 19th-century Guano Act has been periodically contested by Haiti, although the issue has never been formally submitted to arbitration. Dormant for many years, the dispute resurfaced in mid-1981 when the island was symbolically (and briefly) "occupied" by a group of Haitian nationals with official backing. (For location of Navassa Island, see map on page 364.)

Navassa Island, with an area of about two square miles (5 sq km), is claimed by the United States under the "Guano Island C Act" of the 1860s, one of a series proclaiming sovereignty over uninhabited islands in the Caribbean and Pacific with a view to exploiting their deposits of guano (seabird droppings), a valuable source of nitrogen fertilizer. During World War II the United States built a lighthouse on the island, while in the 1950s Haiti built a church there for use by passing fishermen (although the island is difficult to land on by boat).

On July 18, 1981, a group of six Haitian radio hams (i.e. amateur enthusiasts) landed on Navassa by helicopter with the intention of transmitting from the island under its rarely-used call prefix (as had been achieved two years previously by a group of US hams). Although the permission of the US Coastguard was normally required to land on the island, the Haitian hams declined to seek such approval on the grounds that Navassa belonged to Haiti, depicting their action as a symbolic occupation of the island. Official government approval of the landing was indicated by the fact that President Duvalier made three helicopters available to the group, who were accompanied by a camera crew from the Haitian national television station. At the same time the Haitian Communications Authority allocated a Haitian radio call prefix to the island, hitherto identified by an American prefix.

On landing on the island, the Haitian party was greeted by a detachment of six US Marines, who took down the names and addresses of the hams before returning by helicopter to a nearby US Navy vessel. The camera crew then recorded a ceremonial raising of the Haitian flag on the island.

A.J.D.

# Antarctica

The question of territorial claims in the Antarctic south of 60° latitude was frozen for 30 years—until 1991—under a treaty which was signed by 12 countries in 1959 and which entered into force in 1961. Seven of the signatories have claims to territory in the Antarctic (Argentina, Australia, Britain, Chile, France, New Zealand, Norway) and the claims of three of these—Argentina, Britain and Chile—overlap. Argentina and Chile have both proclaimed 200-mile limits off their sections of Antarctica.

The Antarctic mainland covers 5,350,000 square miles (13,900,000 sq km) and its ice mass represents about three-quarters of the world's store of fresh water. The area is believed to contain oil, gas, hydrocarbons, iron, coal and other minerals (in quantities not yet ascertained), as well as substantial resources of fish and krill (a protein-rich crustacean which is most dense around the Antarctic Convergence). The main harvesters of krill in the area are the USSR, Japan, Chile, Norway, Poland, South Korea, East and West Germany and Taiwan.

A number of islands within the Antarctic Convergence are claimed by more than one country. The South Shetlands are claimed by Argentina, Britain and Chile, while the South Sandwich Islands, the South Orkneys, South Georgia Island and Shag Rocks are disputed by Argentina and Britain. The South Shetlands and South Orkneys form part of the British Antarctic Territory, established on March 3, 1962; this territory includes that part of Antarctica lying between 20° W and 80° W longitude stretching south of 60° S to the South Pole, plus the islands, and covers a total

**Map 44   Existing territorial claims in Antarctica.**

386

land and sea area of about 3,000,000 square miles (7,750,000 sq km) including the Weddell Sea.

Chile claims the same right of sovereignty over its sector of the Antarctic as over mainland Chile and has incorporated the sector into its internal regional administration. Part of the Chilean sector is also claimed by Ecuador because of the position of the Galapagos Islands. The following countries have established scientific research bases in Antarctica since 1944: Argentina, Australia, Britain, Chile, France, Japan, New Zealand, Poland, South Africa, Soviet Union and the United States.

The United States and the Soviet Union both stressed in 1959 that, although they had no specific territorial claims to parts of the Antarctic, they did not relinquish the right to make such claims nor did they necessarily recognize the claims of other powers.

## The Treaty of the Antarctic

The treaty was signed on Dec. 1, 1959, at the conclusion of a conference on peaceful international scientific co-operation in the Antarctic, which had first been proposed by President Eisenhower in 1958 for International Geophysical Year. It entered into force on June 23, 1961, after its ratification by all 12 original signatories, namely Argentina, Australia, Belgium, Britain, Chile, France, Japan, New Zealand, Norway, South Africa, Soviet Union and United States. Other countries which later acceded were Brazil, Czechoslovakia, Denmark, East Germany, West Germany, Netherlands, Poland and Romania. (Poland had become a consultative member, with the right of veto at consultative meetings, in accordance with Article IX of the treaty which said that any country which had acceded was entitled to participate in meetings during such time as it "demonstrates its interest in Antarctica by conducting substantial scientific research there, such as the establishment of a scientific station or the dispatch of a scientific expedition".)

Apart from freezing all territorial claims for its 30-year duration, the treaty set the region aside for peaceful scientific research, made all installations liable to inspection by any other signatory, banned all military activities and proclaimed the region nuclear-free. The Preamble to the treaty stated that the signatory governments recognized "that it is in the interest of all mankind that Antarctica shall continue forever to be used exclusively for peaceful purposes and shall not become the scene or object of international discord".

Article I provides (i) that Antarctica shall be used for peaceful purposes only and that any measure of a military nature, such as the establishment of military bases and fortifications, the carrying out of military manoeuvres, as well as the testing of any type of weapons, shall be prohibited; and (ii) that the treaty shall not prevent the use of military personnel or equipment for scientific research or for any other peaceful purpose. Article II specifies that freedom of scientific investigation in Antarctica and co-operation toward that end, as applied during the International Geophysical Year, shall continue, subject to the provisions of the treaty.

Article IV contains the following provisions: (i) nothing contained in the treaty shall be interpreted as (*a*) a renunciation by any contracting party of previously asserted rights of or claims to territorial sovereignty in Antarctica, (*b*) a renunciation or diminution by any contracting party of any basis of claim to territorial sovereignty in Antarctica which it may have, whether as a result of its activities or those of its nationals in Antarctica, or otherwise, (*c*) prejudicing the position of any contracting party as regards its recognition or non-recognition of any other state's right of, or claim or basis of claim to, territorial sovereignty in Antarctica; (ii) no acts or activities taking place while the treaty is in force shall constitute a basis for asserting, supporting or denying a claim to territorial sovereignty in Antarctica, or create any rights of sovereignty in Antarctica, and no new claim, or enlargement of an existing claim, to territorial sovereignty in Antarctica shall be asserted while the treaty is in force.

Article V provides (i) that any nuclear explosions in Antarctica and the disposal there of radioactive waste material shall be prohibited; and (ii) that in the event of the conclusion of international agreements concerning the use of nuclear energy, including nuclear explosions and the disposal of radioactive waste material, to which all of the contracting parties whose representatives are entitled to participate in future consultative meetings are parties, the rules established under such agreements shall apply in Antarctica. Article VI specifies that the provisions of the treaty shall apply to the area south of 60° S latitude, including all ice shelves, but nothing in the treaty shall prejudice or in any way affect the rights, or the exercise of the rights, of any state under international law with regard to the high seas within that area.

Article VII establishes that each contracting party has the right to designate observers to carry out inspection with complete freedom of access to all areas of Antarctica. Aerial observation can be carried out at any time and notice has to be given of all expeditions to and within Antarctica, all stations occupied by a country's nationals, and any military personnel or equipment intended to be introduced into it subject to Article I of the treaty. Article XI provides that any dispute which cannot be settled by consultation among the signatories themselves should be submitted to the International Court of Justice.

Argentina and Chile stated that while agreeing to the freezing of territorial claims for 30 years under the terms of the treaty, they did not thereby relinquish claims to the territory included within British Antarctica.

A series of consultative meetings were held at intervals over the next 20 years, mainly to discuss the protection of the Antarctic environment and other eco-systems dependent on it. The problem of regulating the exploration and exploitation of minerals after 1991, when the signatories would be freed from restraints under the treaty, was also a major source of concern and potential conflict.

**J.B.**

# Selected Bibliography

Al-Baharna, Husain M.—*The Arabian Gulf States: Their Legal and Political Status and Their International Problems* (2nd revised edition, Beirut 1975).

Bernstein, Itamar—*Delimitation of International Boundaries: A Study of Modern Practice and Devices from the Viewpoint of International Law* (Tel Aviv 1974).

Blum, Y. Z.—*Secure Boundaries and Middle East Peace in the Light of International Law and Practice* (Jerusalem 1971).

Brownlie, Ian—*African Boundaries: A Legal and Diplomatic Encyclopaedia* (London & Los Angeles 1979).

Burrell, R. M.—*The Persian Gulf* (New York 1972).

Cukwurah, A. O.—*The Settlement of Boundary Disputes in International Law* (Manchester 1967).

Dodd, C. H., & Sales, M. E.—*Israel and the Arab World* (London 1970).

East, W. G., & Moodie, A. E. (eds.)—*The Changing World: Studies in Political Geography* (London 1956).

East, W. G., & Prescott, J. R. V.—*Our Fragmented World: An Introduction to Political Geography* (London 1975).

East, W. G., Spate, O. H. K., & Fisher, C. A. (eds.)—*The Changing Map of Asia* (5th edition, London 1971).

Gilbert, Martin—*The Arab-Israeli Conflict: Its History in Maps* (London 1974).

Gross, Feliks—*World Politics and Tension Areas* (New York 1966).

Horrell, Muriel—*The African Homelands of South Africa* (Johannesburg 1973).

Hoskins, Catherine—*Case Studies in African Diplomacy 2: The Ethiopia-Somalia-Kenya Dispute, 1960-67* (Dar es Salaam 1969).

*International Boundary Studies*—series published by the Geographer of the US Department of State, Washington DC.

Ireland, Gordon—*Boundaries, Possessions and Conflicts in South America* (Cambridge, Mass. 1938).

Kelly, J. B.—*Eastern Arabian Frontiers* (New York 1964).

Luard, D. E. T. (ed.)—*The International Regulation of Frontier Disputes* (London 1970).

McEwen, A. C.—*International Boundaries of East Africa* (Oxford 1971).

Marchant, Alexander—*Boundaries of the Latin American Republics: An Annotated List of Documents, 1493-1943* (Department of State, Washington 1944).

Prescott, J. R. V.—*The Geography of Frontiers and Boundaries* (London 1965).

Prescott, J. R. V.—*Boundaries and Frontiers* (London 1978).

Prescott, J. R. V.—*Map of Mainland Asia by Treaty* (Melbourne 1975).

Sharma, Surya P.—*International Boundary Disputes and International Law* (Bombay 1976).

Stuyt, A. M.—*Survey of International Arbitrations, 1794-1970* (Leiden 1972).

Touval, Saadia—*The Boundary Politics of Independent Africa* (Cambridge, Mass. 1972).

Widstrand, Carl Gösta (ed.)—*African Boundary Problems* (Uppsala 1969).

# Subject Index

# Names Index